1001 TRAILER CONSTRUCTION DETAILS

1001 TRADITIONAL CONSTRUCTION DETAILS

STEPHEN A. MOUZON
with David L. Mouzon

McGRAW-HILL
NEW YORK CHICAGO SAN FRANCISCO LISBON LONDON
MADRID MEXICO CITY MILAN NEW DELHI SAN JUAN
SEOUL SINGAPORE SYDNEY TORONTO

McGraw-Hill

*A Division of The **McGraw·Hill** Companies*

Copyright

2 3 4 5 6 7 8 9 0 DOC/DOC 0 7 6 5 4 3 2

ISBN 0-07-138202-X

Printed and bound by R. R. Donnelley & Sons Company.

Design

Stephen A. Mouzon

Bibliographical Note

This book includes a compilation of 1001 of the details in McGraw-Hill's *Architectural Elements: Traditional Construction Details* CD-ROM published in 2000.

Acknowledgments

This project would not have been possible without the love, faith and tireless effort of David Mouzon, Wanda Mouzon and Sally Mouzon, nor without the foresight and perseverance of Wendy Lochner.

Sales Information

McGraw-Hill books are available at special quantity discounts to use as premiums and sales promotions, or for use in corporate training programs. For more information, please write to the Director of Special Sales, Professional Publishing, McGraw-Hill, Two Penn Plaza, New York, NY 10121-2298. Or contact your local bookstore.

CONTENTS

Part I. Detail Design Principles 1
Detail Layout 2
Lineweights 4
Profile Lines 6
Dimensions 8
Text 10
Incorporation into Drawings 12

Part II. Details 15
Bath Details 17
Cabinet Details 27
Door Details 259
Envelope Details 449
Finishes Details 571
Graphics Details 581
HVAC, Plumbing & Electrical Details 607
Miscellaneous Details 631
Porch Details 647
Railing Details 663
Sitework Details 687
Trim Details 759
Vertical Circulation Details 829
Window Details 843

1001 TRADITIONAL CONSTRUCTION DETAILS

PART I
Detail Design Principles

Many architects assume that a beautiful working drawing is a waste of time, since only the contractor will use it. We feel very strongly that a thoughtfully laid out approach to detailing actually saves time, and certainly results in drawings that meet the equally important goals of clarity and beauty. This system of detailing has been rigorously developed over 15 years around Renaissance principles of layout & design. One of the results is a collection of computer-drawn details that can stand shoulder-to-shoulder graphically with libraries drawn on the board a century ago. The remainder of this first section deals with the principles employed in the creation of these details.

The foundation of any drawing is the layout. The layout should be clear, simply proportioned & repeatable. It is absolutely essential to rigorously adhere to a consistent layout system if an entire sheet of details is to be beautiful. The appearance of the sheet is only half of the benefit, however, of a consistent system. Drawings that consistently put the same information in the same location will be easier to read and less likely to be misunderstood by the contractor.

The next prerequisite for clarity and beauty in architectural drawings is a consistent system of lineweights. Unfortunately, knowledge of any system of lineweights is a rarity in today's world of CAD drawings. A common-sense system built around the hierarchy of importance of building elements is easy both to learn and to implement.

Some elements in a drawing are of such importance that they require additional emphasis through the use of extra-heavy lines. We refer to these lines as profile lines since they usually follow the profile of important elements. Good draftspersons from the hand-drawn era would even go to such lengths as to offset the profile lines to the exterior of the object being profiled. This method is unheard-of today, but contributes to much clearer drawings.

Nearly every detail includes some type of dimension to set out the size or spacing of construction elements. Dimensions should be located in rigorously consistent locations so as to be easily located by the contractor and to contribute to the overall harmony of the finished sheet.

Text is also present in essentially every detail to describe the objects shown. Complicated systems of keynotes were once developed to avoid copious amounts of hand-lettering (and drafting salaries), but these systems were never easy to remember or use. There is no reason, in a world where typing is many times faster than hand-lettering, to use obscure systems to describe what is being drawn.

1

DETAIL LAYOUT

The foundation of any drawing is the layout. A consistent layout serves both the goal of clarity and the goal of beauty by making the location of information consistent and easy to find, and by putting every detail on a sheet in harmony with the appearance of the others.

These details adhere to Renaissance and Classical systems of layout and proportion. The proportions are very elemental. The detail box itself is a 5" x 5" square. This allows 24 details to be laid out on a D-size sheet (6 wide, 4 high). These details use 1/4" for large spaces & 1/8" for small spaces. The distance between one detail and the next is therefore 1/4", whereas the distance between the scale box and the detail box is 1/8" (see next page for illustration).

Details are divided into two equal halves. The left half is reserved for text and interior, or less detailed portions of the drawing if necessary. The right half is reserved for the detailed section of the drawing and the dimensions. This leaves dimensions on the outer side of the detail which is typically more contoured and text on the inside, where leaders can cross portions of the drawing elements without causing undue confusion. This approach also prevents direct conflict between dimensions & text.

The element being drawn should generally center vertically within the detail box, and should run to the perimeter of the box on all sides. There are some cases where the object is strongly weighted to either the top or the bottom. Crown mould details and baseboard details are two classic examples. In these cases, a sheet of details looks much more consistent if the drawing elements are justified in the direction they are weighted. In other words, the crown mould should slide to the top of the detail box whereas the baseboard should slide to the bottom of the detail box. This will align the floor lines on all baseboard details and the ceiling lines on all crown details, creating a harmonious appearance on sheets with several of either type.

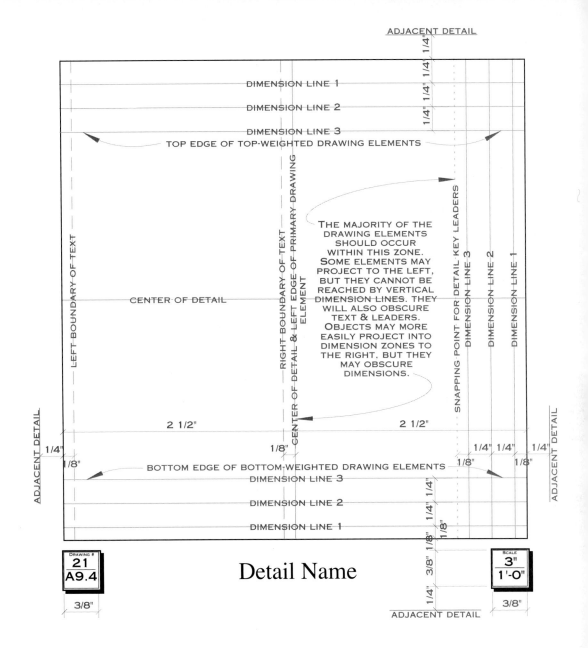

ADJACENT DETAIL

DIMENSION LINE 1

DIMENSION LINE 2

DIMENSION LINE 3

TOP EDGE OF TOP-WEIGHTED DRAWING ELEMENTS

THE MAJORITY OF THE DRAWING ELEMENTS SHOULD OCCUR WITHIN THIS ZONE. SOME ELEMENTS MAY PROJECT TO THE LEFT, BUT THEY CANNOT BE REACHED BY VERTICAL DIMENSION LINES. THEY WILL ALSO OBSCURE TEXT & LEADERS. OBJECTS MAY MORE EASILY PROJECT INTO DIMENSION ZONES TO THE RIGHT, BUT THEY MAY OBSCURE DIMENSIONS.

LEFT BOUNDARY OF TEXT

CENTER OF DETAIL

RIGHT BOUNDARY OF TEXT

CENTER OF DETAIL & LEFT EDGE OF PRIMARY DRAWING ELEMENT

SNAPPING POINT FOR DETAIL KEY LEADERS

DIMENSION LINE 3

DIMENSION LINE 2

DIMENSION LINE 1

2 1/2"

2 1/2"

1/8"

1/4" 1/4" 1/4"

BOTTOM EDGE OF BOTTOM-WEIGHTED DRAWING ELEMENTS

DIMENSION LINE 3

DIMENSION LINE 2

DIMENSION LINE 1

1/8"

1/8"

ADJACENT DETAIL

1/4"

1/8"

ADJACENT DETAIL

DRAWING #
21
A9.4

3/8"

Detail Name

SCALE
3"
1'-0"

3/8"

ADJACENT DETAIL

3

LINEWEIGHTS

A consistent system of lineweights is an absolute prerequisite for clear and beautiful architectural drawings. These details are built around a simple hierarchical lineweight system based on the "squint principle". The "squint principle" states that as you squint at a drawing, the least essential elements should disappear first and the most essential elements should disappear just before your eyes entirely close.

Items such as dimension and text leaders are absolutely inessential to the drawing elements and should therefore be the thinnest lines. Centerlines and other layout-related lines fall into the same category. Certain lines on elevations such as breaks in surfaces that don't involve displacement of one surface from another disappear very quickly when squinting at the actual building and should also use the thinnest lineweight. These details use .045 mm lines for these items. These lines could reasonably be called hairlines since they are very close to the thickness of a human hair. Thinner lines may be possible with some plotters, but essentially disappear to any but the sharpest eyes when viewed from a reasonable distance. .045 mm lines have been demonstrated to be legible to average eyes.

The primary lineweight of the drawing should be relatively thin in order to keep the drawing from getting muddy and unclear, but should be noticeably thicker than hairlines. These details use .13 mm lines for the primary lineweight.

The author once used .18 mm lines for a number of functions, but found them to be indiscernible from .13 mm lines on most plotters.

Any lines thicker than .13 mm are considered profile lines and are used to enhance certain parts of drawings. Section-type details are profiled where the solids meet the air. Larger air gets larger lines. This means that the edge of a solid open to an air space at least 4' wide is profiled with the thickest profile line, which is .50 mm. The edge of a solid open to an air space between 1' & 4' wide is profiled with a .35 mm line, whereas the edge of a solid open to an air space between 1" & 1' wide is profiled with a .25 mm profile line, which is the thinnest profile line used. Air spaces less than 1" wide generally are not profiled because they are essentially solid.

Elevation-type details are profiled in a similar manner based on displaced planes. Planes that are displaced by about 30' or more are profiled with a .50 mm line. Planes that are displaced by between 6' and 30' are profiled with a .35 mm line. Planes that are displaced by between 1' and 6' are profiled with a .25 mm line. Planes displaced less than 1' are generally not profiled.

Some may recognize the lineweight system as being the Koh-I-Noor Rapidiograph system. There are several systems available, but this one is based on a logarithmic progression in line sizes which makes the most sense in terms of readability of the drawing.

.045 mm (hairline) ————————————————

.13 mm (primary drawing line) ————————————————

.25 mm (thin profile line) ————————————————

.35 mm (medium profile line) ————————————————

.5 mm (thick profile line) ————————————————

.7 mm (elevation ground line) ————————————————

1.0 mm (special-purpose profiles) ————————————————

Lineweights

PROFILE LINES

Profile lines deserve their own section in the discussion on lineweights. Good drafters a century ago understood them well and used them to great advantage. One of the secrets of skilled hand-drafters was the placement of the profile lines. They laid out drawings with thin drawing lines at the edge of the object being delineated. Once the content of the drawing was essentially complete, they went back over the drawing with profile lines. The secret was the fact that the profile lines were not drawn precisely on top of the thin drawing lines, but were offset to the outside of the object. In other words, the inner surface of the thin drawing line aligned with the inner surface of the thick profile line, throwing all of the extra thickness of the profile line to the outside of the object. This created a very subtle halo effect around the object that much more elegantly popped out the object in question.

Some may read this description and ask if it really matters that much. Studies have shown that the difference on both plans and elevations is nominal since those drawings are of a smaller scale and are of a somewhat more diagrammatic nature. Profile lines on any elevation details are drawn directly over the drawing line.

The difference on wall sections and details, however, is much more marked because of the more pictoral nature of these large-scale drawings. Heavy profile lines that eat into the volume of an object actually distort the shape of the object slightly whereas offset profile lines preserve the original shape.

This effect is achieved in a manner that sounds complicated but quickly becomes second nature to the accomplished drafter. The goal is to align the inner surfaces of the drawing line and the profile line. Some may ask why the drawing line should be maintained at all, but it is crucially important to keep the drawing line in CAD files since it is the point that dimensions are snapped to, not the offset profile line. Dimensioning is generally done with the Profile Lines Layer turned off.

Aligning the inner surface is most easily accomplished in most CAD software by copying the appropriate Drawing Layer lines to the Profile Lines Layer and then offsetting them the appropriate amount. Keep in mind that the offset is based on the distance between the centers of the lines in order to align the inner edges. Finding the distance between the centers is fairly simple. If the scale of the drawing is 3/4" = 1'-0", then the scale factor is 1:16. The distance between the centers of the two lines at full scale is half the difference of their diameters, so if the profile line is .50 mm and the drawing line is .13 mm, then the offset should be (.50 mm - .13 mm) / 2. In order to adjust to the scale of the drawing, this formula must be multiplied by the scale factor, which in this example is 16. The formula then becomes (.50 mm - .13 mm) x 16 / 2, or .37 mm x 8. The quick way to think of it is the difference in lineweights multiplied by half the scale factor. Beginning drafters often despair when hearing this formula, but the difference in the drawings is well worth the time the system takes to learn.

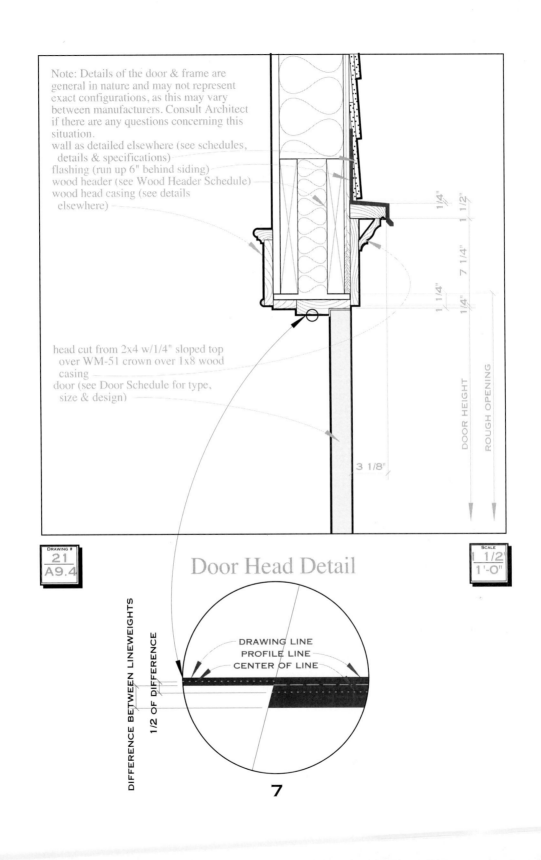

Note: Details of the door & frame are general in nature and may not represent exact configurations, as this may vary between manufacturers. Consult Architect if there are any questions concerning this situation.

wall as detailed elsewhere (see schedules, details & specifications)
flashing (run up 6" behind siding)
wood header (see Wood Header Schedule)
wood head casing (see details elsewhere)

head cut from 2x4 w/1/4" sloped top over WM-51 crown over 1x8 wood casing
door (see Door Schedule for type, size & design)

1/4"
1 1/2"
7 1/4"
1 1/4"
1/4"

DOOR HEIGHT
ROUGH OPENING

3 1/8"

DRAWING #		SCALE	
21		1 1/2"	
A9.4		1'-0"	

Door Head Detail

DIFFERENCE BETWEEN LINEWEIGHTS
1/2 OF DIFFERENCE

DRAWING LINE
PROFILE LINE
CENTER OF LINE

7

DIMENSIONS

Dimensions should be located in rigorously consistent locations throughout an entire set of working drawings so as to be easily located by the contractor and to contribute to the overall harmony of the finished sheet. These details use a typical dimension line spacing of 1/4", which provides ample space for the dimensions without wasting space. Use of a reasonable font size at this spacing allows superscript & subscript text when the dimensions are too small to fit side by side on the dimension line (see 1/4" subscript dimension at top of detail).

These dimensions use Copperplate 31AB text, which is very visually clear. The font size is 7 point. This seems small, but Copperplate is a bold font, so it is very readable.

The first choice for dimension line location is to the right and bottom of the drawing elements as shown on this detail. Dimensions may be pulled to the top of the detail if necessary, but may never in any case be pulled to the left, since this would conflict with the text.

Most CAD details use too great a spacing on both witness line overstrike at the dimension line and witness line cutback at the drawing element. These details use a dimension of 1/16" in both cases. Some CAD details overstrike the dimension string itself, but this can be very visually confusing. All dimension strings should terminate exactly at the witness line.

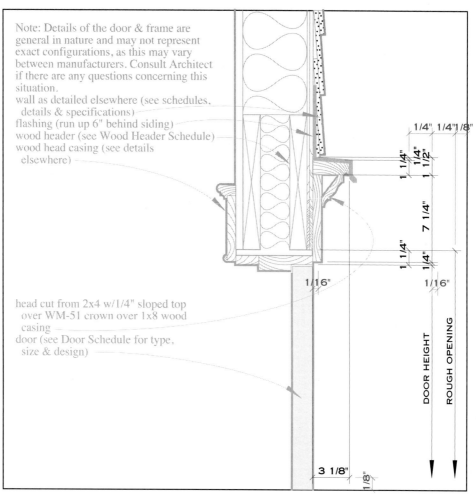

Note: Details of the door & frame are general in nature and may not represent exact configurations, as this may vary between manufacturers. Consult Architect if there are any questions concerning this situation.

wall as detailed elsewhere (see schedules, details & specifications)

flashing (run up 6" behind siding)

wood header (see Wood Header Schedule)

wood head casing (see details elsewhere)

head cut from 2x4 w/1/4" sloped top over WM-51 crown over 1x8 wood casing

door (see Door Schedule for type, size & design)

1/4" 1/4" 1/8"

1 1/4"
1/4"
1/2"
1"

7 1/4"

1 1/4"
1/4"

1/16"   1/16"

DOOR HEIGHT

ROUGH OPENING

3 1/8"   1/8"

DRAWING #
21
A9.4

Door Head Detail

SCALE
1 1/2"
1'-0"

9

TEXT

All notes on these details are in simple text format. Complicated systems of keynotes were once developed to avoid copious amounts of hand-lettering (and drafting salaries), but these systems were never easy for the drafter to remember or for the contractor to use. There is no reason, in a world where typing is many times faster than hand-lettering, to use obscure systems to describe what is being drawn.

Text is organized to the left of the drawing elements to avoid conflict with dimensions. Many CAD packages encourage the use of "leader text" which basically is a single note with a leader line attached, or some variation thereof. The problem with this system is that it invariably leads to a jumble of individual notes all over the drawing with no apparent organization. Aligning all of the notes becomes very laborious and is generally never done. The end result is a very sloppy appearance.

These details were all drawn with a single text block containing all notes on the drawing. This naturally justifies all of the text, which is much cleaner.

Multiple leader lines unfortunately cannot be attached to a single text block in most CAD packages. Leader lines on these details were individually drawn after the text was placed. This may seem somewhat time-consuming, but it is a much quicker method than trying to deal with many individual leader text notes.

Many architects use various "architect script" fonts such as Tekton for notes on drawings & details. Their primary justification, other than nostalgia, is that if last-minute changes need to be made in a drawing, they can be made by hand without having to re-plot the drawing.

The first problem with use of these fonts is that if handwritten notes are allowed to become a part of the drawing then the drawing ceases to become a CAD file and all future modifications to the drawing must be done on that sheet of paper rather than on the computer file. The inadvisability of this approach should be obvious. It requires a dual system of drawing production because an office must furnish hand-drafting facilities as a result. The single sheet of paper becomes fragile & precious, rather than being yet another printout of a backed-up computer file. There are many more reasons, although these two should suffice.

The second reason for not using "architect script" fonts is that they simply are not as legible. Study after study has shown that simple serif book fonts are the most legible Western-language fonts in existence. The vast majority of books and newspapers use simple serif book fonts for this reason. Studies have also shown that text in ALL CAPS is more difficult to read. Most "architect script" fonts are all caps fonts. There is no reason that a CAD drawing should have to masquerade as a hand-drawn drawing. The objective of these details was not to look like a hand-drawn drawing, but to actually be better than details drawn by hand. The text used for notes on all of these details is Times (9 point).

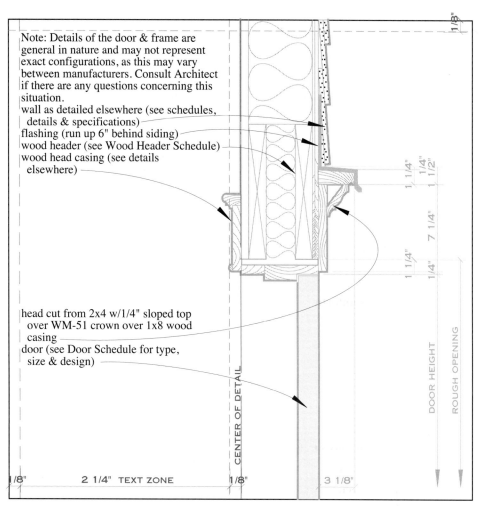

Note: Details of the door & frame are general in nature and may not represent exact configurations, as this may vary between manufacturers. Consult Architect if there are any questions concerning this situation.

wall as detailed elsewhere (see schedules, details & specifications)

flashing (run up 6" behind siding)

wood header (see Wood Header Schedule)

wood head casing (see details elsewhere)

head cut from 2x4 w/1/4" sloped top over WM-51 crown over 1x8 wood casing

door (see Door Schedule for type, size & design)

1/8"

2 1/4" TEXT ZONE

1/8"

3 1/8"

CENTER OF DETAIL

1 1/4"
1/4"
1 1/2"

1 1/4"
7 1/4"

1 1/4"
1/4"

DOOR HEIGHT

ROUGH OPENING

1/8"

DRAWING #
21
A9.4

Door Head Detail

SCALE
1 1/2"
1'-0"

11

INCORPORATION INTO DRAWINGS

The importance of individual high-quality details is incontrovertible, but the method by which they are incorporated into a set of drawings is almost equally important. The two most important issues are the physical layout and the numbering system.

These details are all designed to fit on a 4 high x 6 wide grid on a D-size sheet. If 1/4" is allowed between the sides of the details and 3/4" is allowed between the tops & bottoms (allowing space for the detail number, scale & title) then ample room remains on the sheet for a title block on the right and a binding strip on the left.

Strict adherance to the grid is crucial to a clear an appealing sheet. Drawings that simply cannot fit within a single grid can be expanded either in width or height to accommodate the drawing elements.

Details can be mixed with other drawings or with notes, schedules or other information. These other elements need not have boundaries around them. It is helpful if schedules and notes are formatted to the standard 5" width. Notes or schedules that cannot fit within this size should be formatted to a 10-1/4" width which fills 2 zones plus the space between them.

No detail will do anyone any good if the contractor cannot find it. The most effective drawing numbering involves assigning each zone a number as shown on the opposite page. A detail takes the number of its zone, no matter how many details are on the sheet. Details can be added later and the numbers will never have to be changed. This assures that keynotes never have to be changed unless the detail is physically moved to another zone. A detail which spans multiple zones takes the number of the lower left zone which it includes.

It can be useful to distinguish between major drawings & minor drawings. Major drawings are general in nature, such as plans or elevations of any sort. Major drawings should probably use a different system of numbering; it is suggested to use an A, B, C... series to number major drawings and a 1, 2, 3... series to number details and sections.

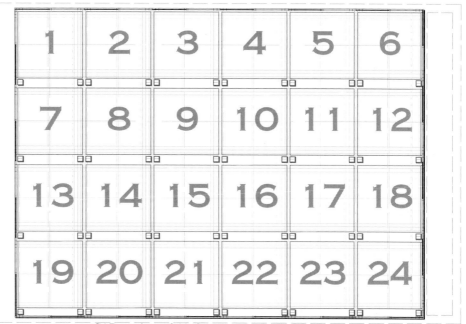

CAD versions of this format are available from the author.
Sheet numbers for multiple-zone drawings are shown below.

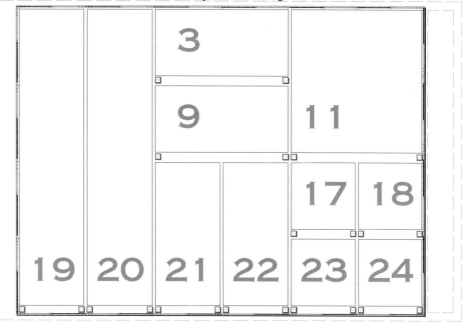

13

PART II
Details

The details that follow are full-scale reproductions of the details in McGraw-Hill's Architectural Elements: Traditional Construction Details CD-ROM. The CD-ROM contains 1,300 details, whereas this book contains 1,001. Only uncommon or obscure details were omitted from the book, leaving those which reflected a more consistent range of detailing content. The text on each page just above the page number represent the detail names in the CD-ROM. The omitted details account for the breaks in sequence in the detail names in the book.

These details explode a number of myths about architectural detailing. Architecture is often categorized as "traditional" or "modern", with the assumption that true traditional architecture must be constructed using ancient means. These details are built strictly around the proportions & configurations of traditional architecture, but the means of construction are thoroughly modern.

Some question this approach to detailing, but history has shown that traditional architecture has always adapted to emerging construction techniques. These details simply carry on that tradition.

BATH DETAILS

Details in this section are meant to include only plumbing fixture, accessory & partition details that cannot reasonably be included in the Cabinet Details or in other sections. Most ADA-specific plumbing details appear here. The contents of this section are as follows:

ADA Bath Details 18
Bath Elevations 19

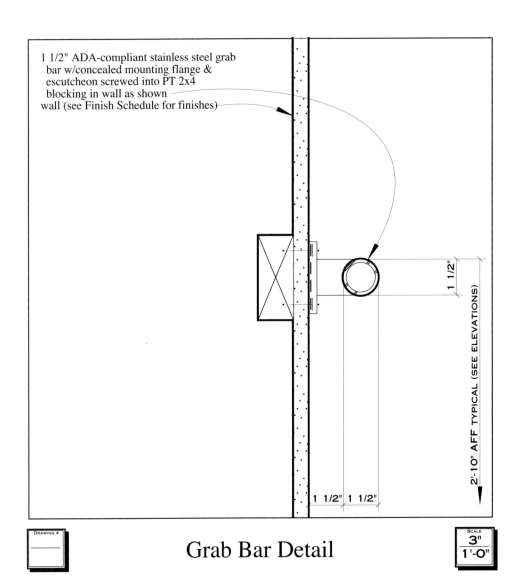

1 1/2" ADA-compliant stainless steel grab
  bar w/concealed mounting flange &
  escutcheon screwed into PT 2x4
  blocking in wall as shown
wall (see Finish Schedule for finishes)

1 1/2"

2'-10" AFF TYPICAL (SEE ELEVATIONS)

1 1/2" 1 1/2"

DRAWING #			SCALE

Grab Bar Detail

SCALE
3"
1'-O"

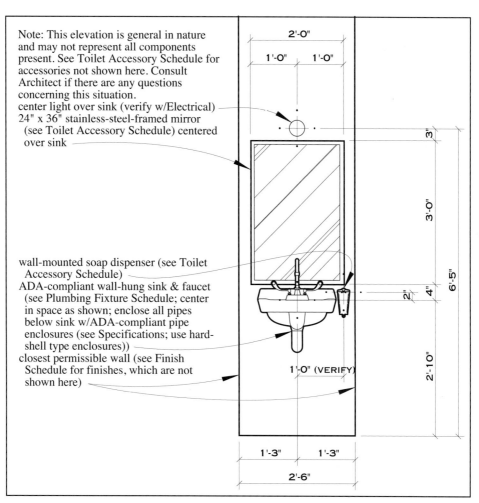

Note: This elevation is general in nature and may not represent all components present. See Toilet Accessory Schedule for accessories not shown here. Consult Architect if there are any questions concerning this situation.

center light over sink (verify w/Electrical)

24" x 36" stainless-steel-framed mirror (see Toilet Accessory Schedule) centered over sink

wall-mounted soap dispenser (see Toilet Accessory Schedule)

ADA-compliant wall-hung sink & faucet (see Plumbing Fixture Schedule; center in space as shown; enclose all pipes below sink w/ADA-compliant pipe enclosures (see Specifications; use hard-shell type enclosures))

closest permissible wall (see Finish Schedule for finishes, which are not shown here)

2'-0"

1'-0" 1'-0"

3"

3'-0"

6'-5"

2"

4"

2'-10"

1'-0" (VERIFY)

1'-3" 1'-3"

2'-6"

Wall-Hung Sink Elevation

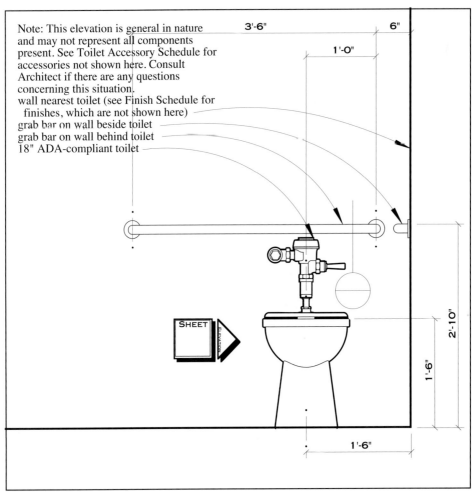

Note: This elevation is general in nature
and may not represent all components
present. See Toilet Accessory Schedule for
accessories not shown here. Consult
Architect if there are any questions
concerning this situation.
wall nearest toilet (see Finish Schedule for
  finishes, which are not shown here)
grab bar on wall beside toilet
grab bar on wall behind toilet
18" ADA-compliant toilet

3'-6"   6"

1'-0"

2'-10"

1'-6"

1'-6"

SHEET

ELEVATION

Front Handicap Toilet Elevation

DRAWING #

SCALE
3/4"
1'-0"

BE002
20

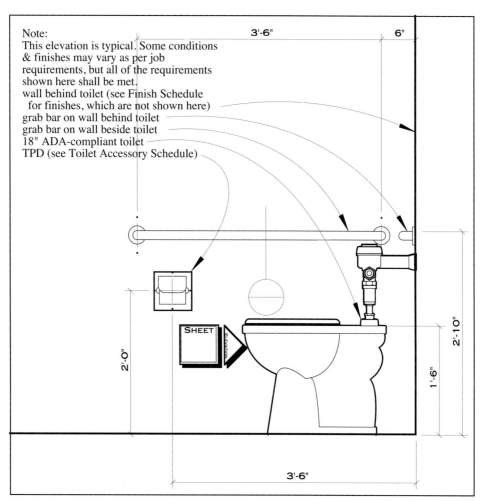

Note:
This elevation is typical. Some conditions
& finishes may vary as per job
requirements, but all of the requirements
shown here shall be met.
wall behind toilet (see Finish Schedule
  for finishes, which are not shown here)
grab bar on wall behind toilet
grab bar on wall beside toilet
18" ADA-compliant toilet
TPD (see Toilet Accessory Schedule)

3'-6"   6"

2'-10"

1'-6"

2'-0"

SHEET
ELEVATION

3'-6"

DRAWING #

Side Handicap Toilet Elevation

SCALE
3/4"
1'-0"

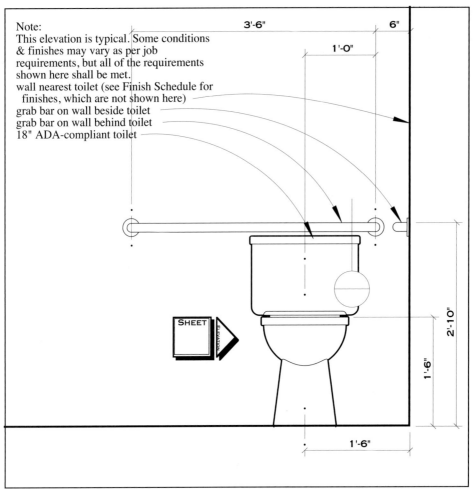

Note:
This elevation is typical. Some conditions
& finishes may vary as per job
requirements, but all of the requirements
shown here shall be met.
wall nearest toilet (see Finish Schedule for
  finishes, which are not shown here)
grab bar on wall beside toilet
grab bar on wall behind toilet
18" ADA-compliant toilet

3'-6"
6"
1'-0"
2'-10"
1'-6"
1'-6"

Front Handicap Toilet Elevation

DRAWING #

SCALE
3/4"
1'-0"

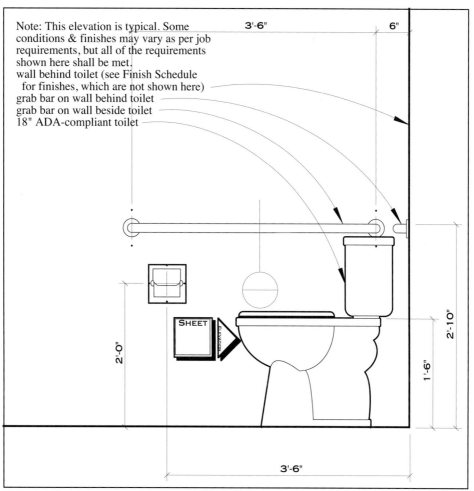

Note: This elevation is typical. Some
conditions & finishes may vary as per job
requirements, but all of the requirements
shown here shall be met.
wall behind toilet (see Finish Schedule
  for finishes, which are not shown here)
grab bar on wall behind toilet
grab bar on wall beside toilet
18" ADA-compliant toilet

3'-6"   6"

2'-0"

2'-10"

1'-6"

SHEET
ELEVATION

3'-6"

DRAWING #

Side Handicap Toilet Elevation

SCALE
3/4"
1'-0"

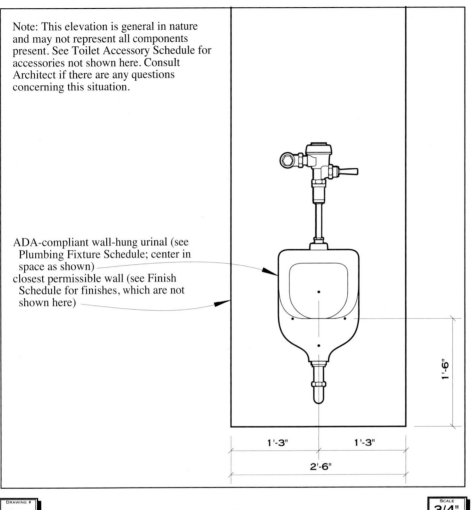

Note: This elevation is general in nature and may not represent all components present. See Toilet Accessory Schedule for accessories not shown here. Consult Architect if there are any questions concerning this situation.

ADA-compliant wall-hung urinal (see Plumbing Fixture Schedule; center in space as shown)
closest permissible wall (see Finish Schedule for finishes, which are not shown here)

1'-6"

1'-3"   1'-3"

2'-6"

DRAWING #

SCALE
3/4"
1'-0"

Urinal Elevation

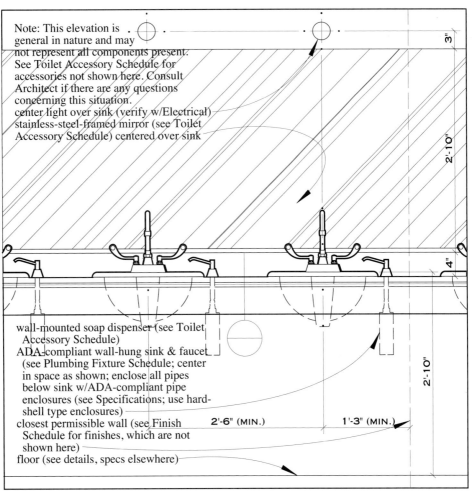

Note: This elevation is
general in nature and may
not represent all components present.
See Toilet Accessory Schedule for
accessories not shown here. Consult
Architect if there are any questions
concerning this situation.
center light over sink (verify w/Electrical)
stainless-steel-framed mirror (see Toilet
Accessory Schedule) centered over sink

3"

2'-10"

4"

wall-mounted soap dispenser (see Toilet
Accessory Schedule)
ADA-compliant wall-hung sink & faucet
(see Plumbing Fixture Schedule; center
in space as shown; enclose all pipes
below sink w/ADA-compliant pipe
enclosures (see Specifications; use hard-
shell type enclosures)
closest permissible wall (see Finish   2'-6" (MIN.)   1'-3" (MIN.)
Schedule for finishes, which are not
shown here)
floor (see details, specs elsewhere)

2'-10"

DRAWING #		SCALE

Sink Elevation

$$\frac{3/4"}{1'-0"}$$

CABINET DETAILS

Details in this section include both details and 3/4" = 1'-0" sections through cabinets of all major types, including wall cabinets, base cabinets, vanities & shelving units. The contents of this section are as follows:

Cabinet Details:

Counter Details 28
Flat Paneled Cabinet Door Details 41
Flush Plastic Laminate Cabinet Door Details 82
Flush Wood Cabinet Door Details 90
Glazed Cabinet Door Details 104
Raised Paneled Cabinet Door Details 143
Counter Nosing Details 172
Flat Paneled Cabinet Drawer Details 184
Flush Plastic Laminate Cabinet Drawer Details 190
Flush Wood Cabinet Drawer Details. 196
Hidden Cabinet Drawer Front Details 202
Paneled Cabinet Drawer Details w/No Glides (Old Style). 209
Paneled Cabinet Drawer Details 218
Cabinet Shelf Details. 227
Base Cabinet Pull-Out Type Details 230

Cabinet Sections:

Base Cabinet Sections 243
Vanity Sections 250
Wall Cabinet Sections 253

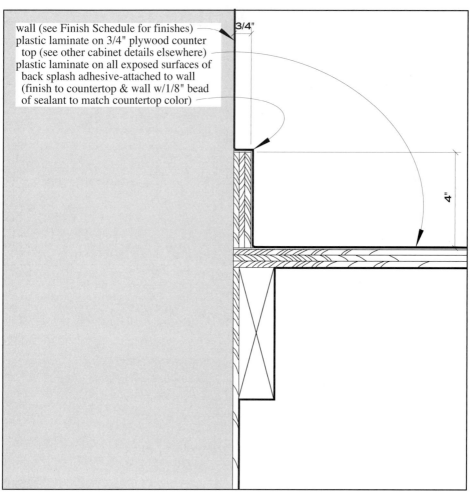

wall (see Finish Schedule for finishes)
plastic laminate on 3/4" plywood counter
 top (see other cabinet details elsewhere)
plastic laminate on all exposed surfaces of
 back splash adhesive-attached to wall
 (finish to countertop & wall w/1/8" bead
 of sealant to match countertop color)

3/4"

4"

DRAWING #

Plastic Laminate Backsplash Detail

SCALE
$\frac{3"}{1'-0"}$

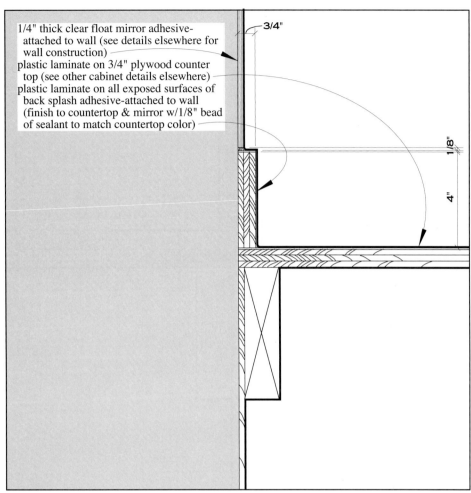

1/4" thick clear float mirror adhesive-attached to wall (see details elsewhere for wall construction)

plastic laminate on 3/4" plywood counter top (see other cabinet details elsewhere)

plastic laminate on all exposed surfaces of back splash adhesive-attached to wall (finish to countertop & mirror w/1/8" bead of sealant to match countertop color)

3/4"

1/8"

4"

Plastic Laminate Backsplash Detail

DRAWING #

SCALE
$\dfrac{3"}{1'\text{-}0"}$

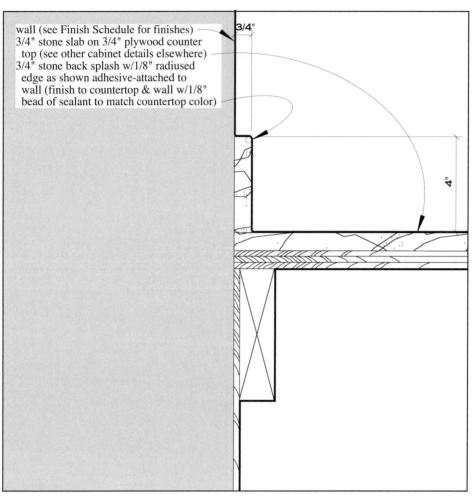

wall (see Finish Schedule for finishes)
3/4" stone slab on 3/4" plywood counter
 top (see other cabinet details elsewhere)
3/4" stone back splash w/1/8" radiused
 edge as shown adhesive-attached to
 wall (finish to countertop & wall w/1/8"
 bead of sealant to match countertop color)

3/4"

4"

Stone Backsplash Detail

DRAWING #

SCALE
3"
1'-0"

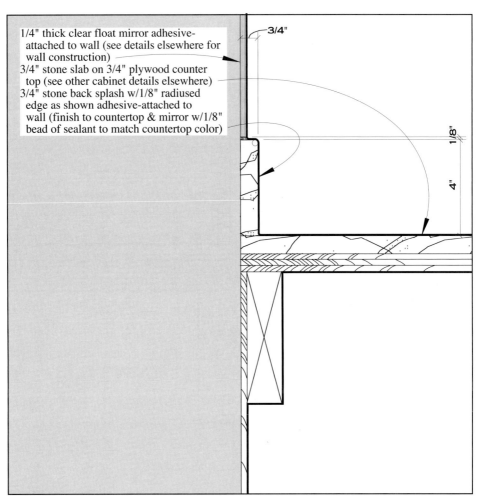

1/4" thick clear float mirror adhesive-attached to wall (see details elsewhere for wall construction)

3/4" stone slab on 3/4" plywood counter top (see other cabinet details elsewhere)

3/4" stone back splash w/1/8" radiused edge as shown adhesive-attached to wall (finish to countertop & mirror w/1/8" bead of sealant to match countertop color)

3/4"

1/8"

4"

Stone Backsplash Detail w/Mirror

SCALE
3"
1'-0"

DRAWING #

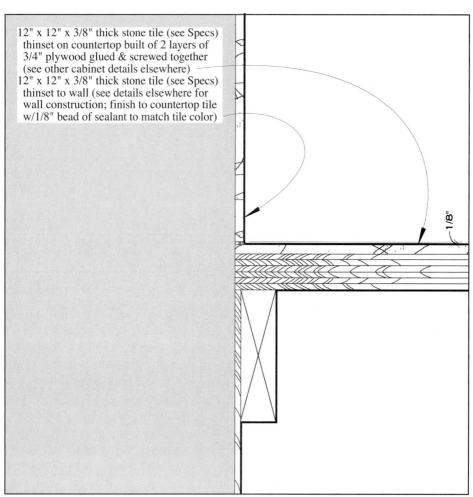

12" x 12" x 3/8" thick stone tile (see Specs) thinset on countertop built of 2 layers of 3/4" plywood glued & screwed together (see other cabinet details elsewhere)

12" x 12" x 3/8" thick stone tile (see Specs) thinset to wall (see details elsewhere for wall construction; finish to countertop tile w/1/8" bead of sealant to match tile color)

1/8"

DRAWING #

Stone Tile Backsplash Detail

SCALE
3"
1'-0"

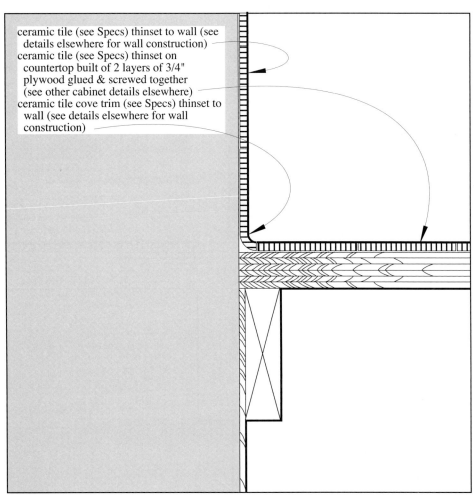

ceramic tile (see Specs) thinset to wall (see details elsewhere for wall construction)

ceramic tile (see Specs) thinset on countertop built of 2 layers of 3/4" plywood glued & screwed together (see other cabinet details elsewhere)

ceramic tile cove trim (see Specs) thinset to wall (see details elsewhere for wall construction)

Ceramic Tile Backsplash Detail

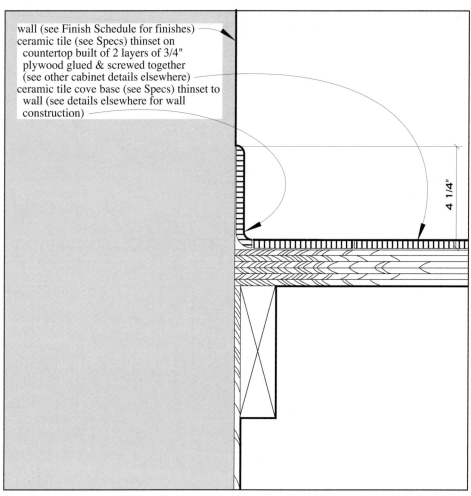

wall (see Finish Schedule for finishes)
ceramic tile (see Specs) thinset on
countertop built of 2 layers of 3/4"
plywood glued & screwed together
(see other cabinet details elsewhere)
ceramic tile cove base (see Specs) thinset to
wall (see details elsewhere for wall
construction)

4 1/4"

DRAWING #

Ceramic Tile Backsplash Detail

SCALE
3"
1'-0"

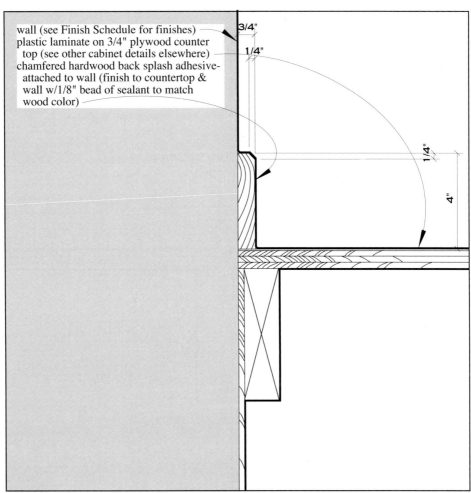

wall (see Finish Schedule for finishes)
plastic laminate on 3/4" plywood counter
top (see other cabinet details elsewhere)
chamfered hardwood back splash adhesive-
attached to wall (finish to countertop &
wall w/1/8" bead of sealant to match
wood color)

3/4"

1/4"

1/4"

4"

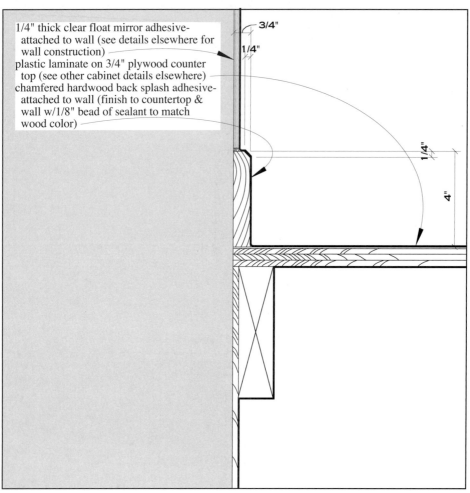

1/4" thick clear float mirror adhesive-
attached to wall (see details elsewhere for
wall construction)
plastic laminate on 3/4" plywood counter
top (see other cabinet details elsewhere)
chamfered hardwood back splash adhesive-
attached to wall (finish to countertop &
wall w/1/8" bead of sealant to match
wood color)

3/4"

1/4"

1/4"

4"

DRAWING #

Chamfered Wood Backsplash w/Mirror

SCALE
3"
1'-0"

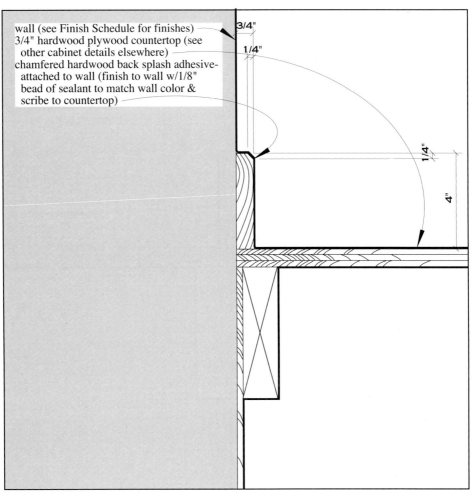

wall (see Finish Schedule for finishes)
3/4" hardwood plywood countertop (see
   other cabinet details elsewhere)
chamfered hardwood back splash adhesive-
   attached to wall (finish to wall w/1/8"
   bead of sealant to match wall color &
   scribe to countertop)

3/4"

1/4"

1/4"

4"

DRAWING #

Chamfered Wood Backsplash Detail

SCALE
3"
1'-0"

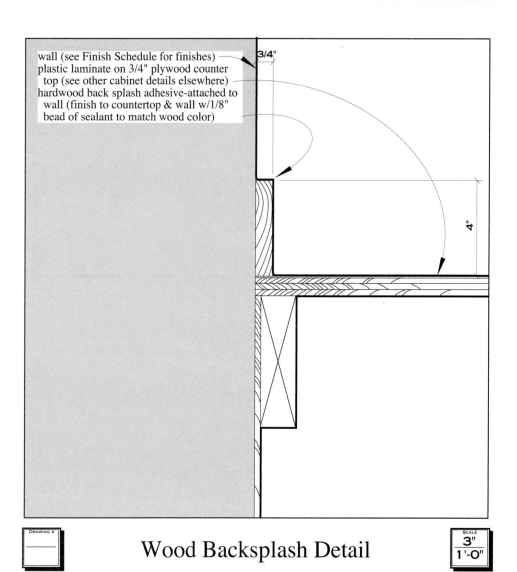

wall (see Finish Schedule for finishes)
plastic laminate on 3/4" plywood counter
 top (see other cabinet details elsewhere)
hardwood back splash adhesive-attached to
 wall (finish to countertop & wall w/1/8"
 bead of sealant to match wood color)

3/4"

4"

Wood Backsplash Detail

DRAWING #

SCALE
3"
1'-O"

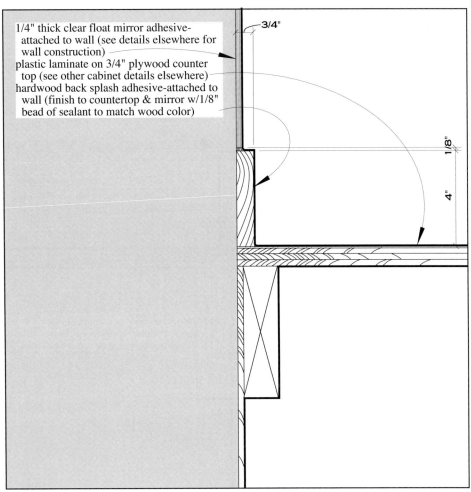

1/4" thick clear float mirror adhesive-attached to wall (see details elsewhere for wall construction)

plastic laminate on 3/4" plywood counter top (see other cabinet details elsewhere)

hardwood back splash adhesive-attached to wall (finish to countertop & mirror w/1/8" bead of sealant to match wood color)

3/4"

1/8"

4"

DRAWING #

Wood Backsplash Detail w/Mirror

SCALE
3"
1'-0"

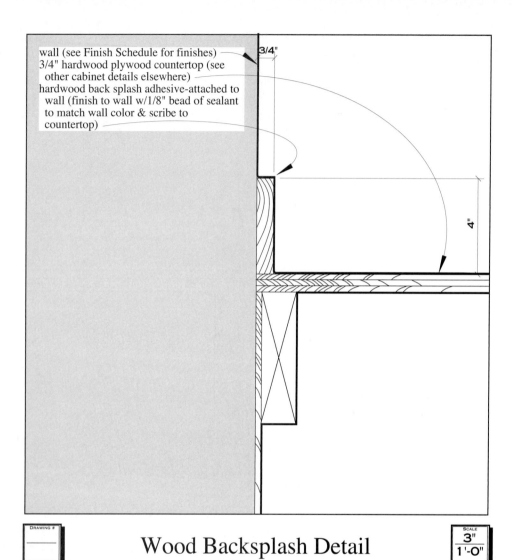

wall (see Finish Schedule for finishes)
3/4" hardwood plywood countertop (see other cabinet details elsewhere)
hardwood back splash adhesive-attached to wall (finish to wall w/1/8" bead of sealant to match wall color & scribe to countertop)

3/4"

4"

Wood Backsplash Detail

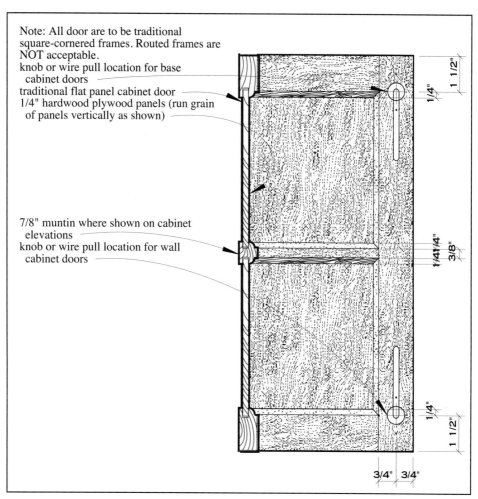

Note: All door are to be traditional square-cornered frames. Routed frames are NOT acceptable.

knob or wire pull location for base cabinet doors

traditional flat panel cabinet door

1/4" hardwood plywood panels (run grain of panels vertically as shown)

7/8" muntin where shown on cabinet elevations

knob or wire pull location for wall cabinet doors

1 1/2"

1/4"

1/4"

3/8"

1/4"

1/4"

1 1/2"

3/4"   3/4"

Flat Panel Door Section/Elevation

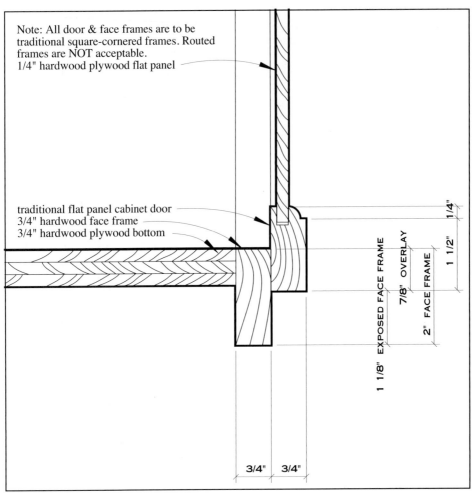

Note: All door & face frames are to be traditional square-cornered frames. Routed frames are NOT acceptable.
1/4" hardwood plywood flat panel

traditional flat panel cabinet door
3/4" hardwood face frame
3/4" hardwood plywood bottom

1/4"

1 1/2"

7/8" OVERLAY

2" FACE FRAME

1 1/8" EXPOSED FACE FRAME

3/4"   3/4"

Flush Overlay Door Bottom Detail

DRAWING #

SCALE
HALF
SIZE

CDDF1002
42

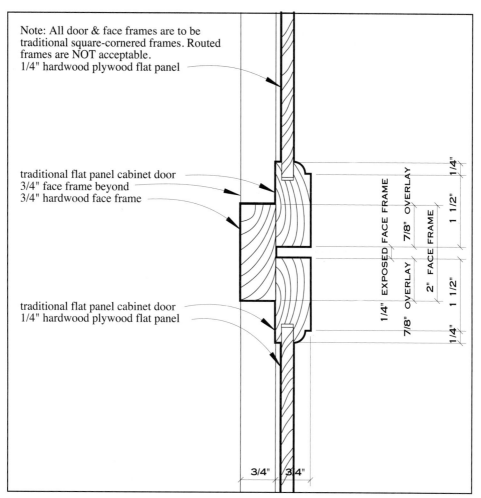

Note: All door & face frames are to be
traditional square-cornered frames. Routed
frames are NOT acceptable.
1/4" hardwood plywood flat panel

traditional flat panel cabinet door
3/4" face frame beyond
3/4" hardwood face frame

traditional flat panel cabinet door
1/4" hardwood plywood flat panel

1/4" EXPOSED FACE FRAME
7/8" OVERLAY
1 1/2"
1/4"
2" FACE FRAME
7/8" OVERLAY
1 1/2"
1/4"

3/4"   3/4"

Flush Overlay Meeting Door Detail

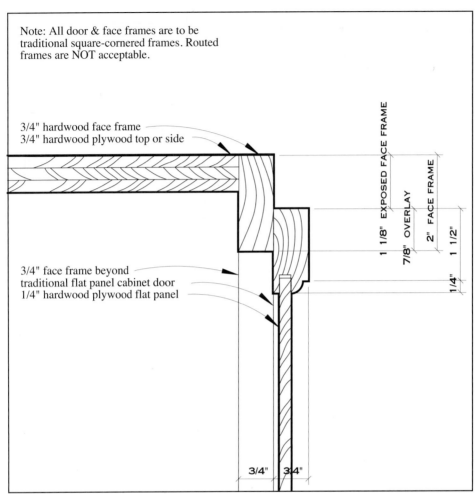

Note: All door & face frames are to be
traditional square-cornered frames. Routed
frames are NOT acceptable.

3/4" hardwood face frame
3/4" hardwood plywood top or side

3/4" face frame beyond
traditional flat panel cabinet door
1/4" hardwood plywood flat panel

1 1/8" EXPOSED FACE FRAME

7/8" OVERLAY

2" FACE FRAME

1 1/2"

1/4"

3/4"   3/4"

DRAWING #

Flush Overlay Door Top or Side Detail

SCALE
HALF
SIZE

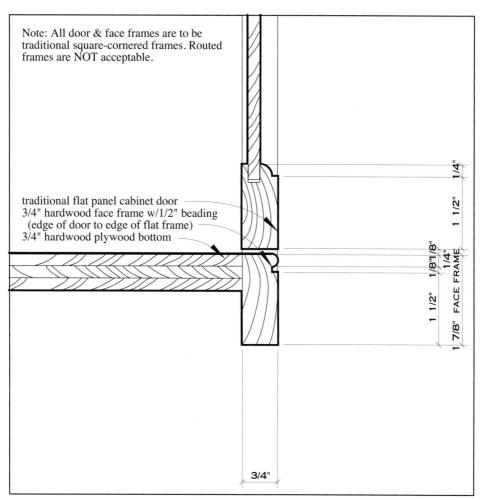

Note: All door & face frames are to be
traditional square-cornered frames. Routed
frames are NOT acceptable.

traditional flat panel cabinet door
3/4" hardwood face frame w/1/2" beading
  (edge of door to edge of flat frame)
3/4" hardwood plywood bottom

1/4"

1 1/2"

1/8"

1/8"

1/4"

1 1/2"

1 7/8" FACE FRAME

3/4"

Inset Door Bottom Detail

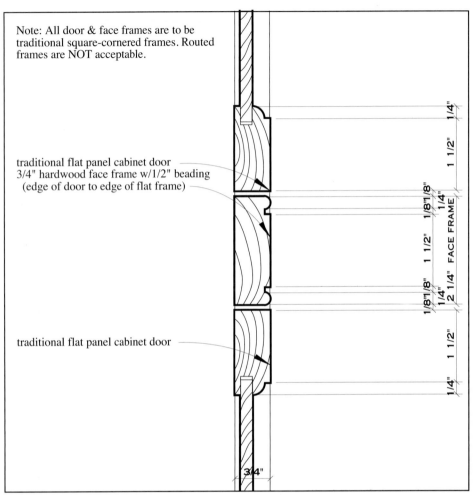

Note: All door & face frames are to be traditional square-cornered frames. Routed frames are NOT acceptable.

traditional flat panel cabinet door 3/4" hardwood face frame w/1/2" beading (edge of door to edge of flat frame)

traditional flat panel cabinet door

1/4"

1 1/2"

1/8" 1/8"

1/4"

1 1/2" FACE FRAME

1/8" 1/8"

1/4"

2 1/4"

1 1/2"

1/4"

3/4"

Inset Meeting Door Detail

DRAWING #

SCALE
HALF
SIZE

CDDF1006
46

Note: All door & face frames are to be
traditional square-cornered frames. Routed
frames are NOT acceptable.

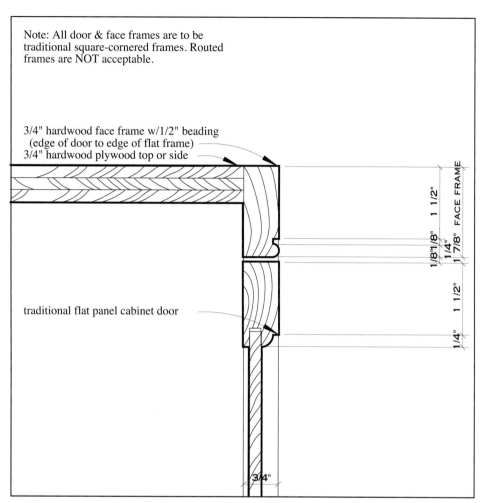

3/4" hardwood face frame w/1/2" beading
 (edge of door to edge of flat frame)
3/4" hardwood plywood top or side

traditional flat panel cabinet door

FACE FRAME

1 1/2"

1/8" 1/8"
    1/4"
       1 7/8"

1 1/2"

1/4"

3/4"

DRAWING #

Inset Door Top or Side Detail

SCALE

**HALF
SIZE**

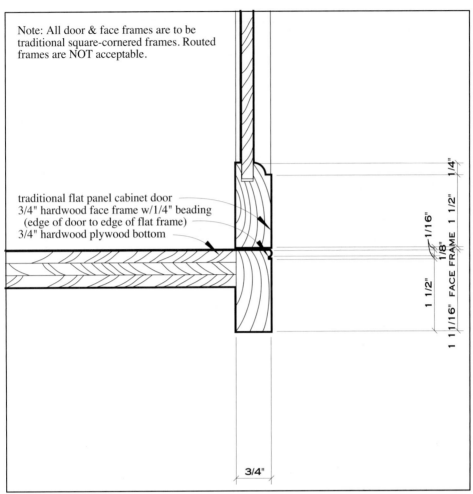

Note: All door & face frames are to be
traditional square-cornered frames. Routed
frames are NOT acceptable.

traditional flat panel cabinet door
3/4" hardwood face frame w/1/4" beading
  (edge of door to edge of flat frame)
3/4" hardwood plywood bottom

1/4"

1 1/2" FACE FRAME 1 1/2"

1/16"

1/8"

1 1/2"

1 11/16" FACE FRAME

3/4"

Inset Door Bottom Detail

DRAWING #

SCALE
HALF
SIZE

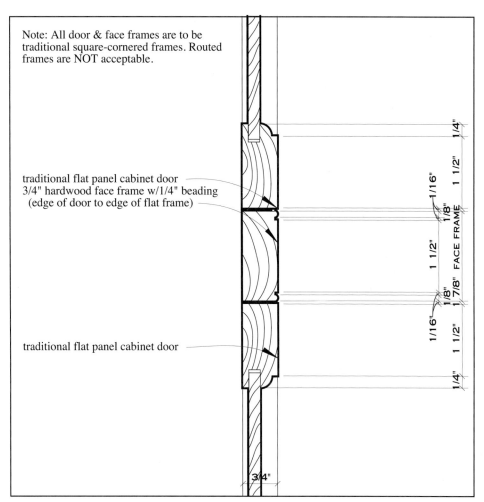

Note: All door & face frames are to be traditional square-cornered frames. Routed frames are NOT acceptable.

traditional flat panel cabinet door
3/4" hardwood face frame w/1/4" beading
 (edge of door to edge of flat frame)

traditional flat panel cabinet door

1/4"

1 1/2"

1/16"

1/8"

1 1/2"

FACE FRAME

1 7/8"

1/8"

1/16"

1 1/2"

1/4"

3/4"

Inset Meeting Door Detail

DRAWING #

SCALE
HALF
SIZE

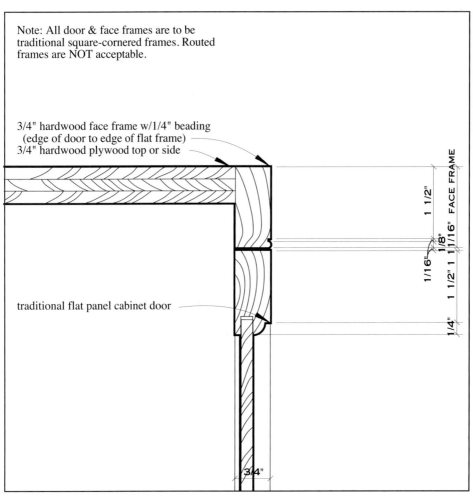

Note: All door & face frames are to be
traditional square-cornered frames. Routed
frames are NOT acceptable.

3/4" hardwood face frame w/1/4" beading
  (edge of door to edge of flat frame)
3/4" hardwood plywood top or side

traditional flat panel cabinet door

1 1/2"

FACE FRAME

1/16" 1/8" 1 11/16"

1 1/2" 1 1/2"

1/4"

3/4"

Inset Door Top or Side Detail

DRAWING #

SCALE
HALF
SIZE

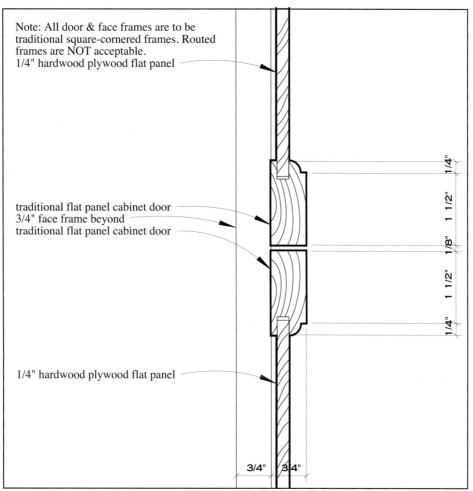

Note: All door & face frames are to be
traditional square-cornered frames. Routed
frames are NOT acceptable.
1/4" hardwood plywood flat panel

traditional flat panel cabinet door
3/4" face frame beyond
traditional flat panel cabinet door

1/4" hardwood plywood flat panel

1/4"
1 1/2"
1/8"
1 1/2"
1/4"

3/4"   3/4"

Meeting Door Detail Without Frame

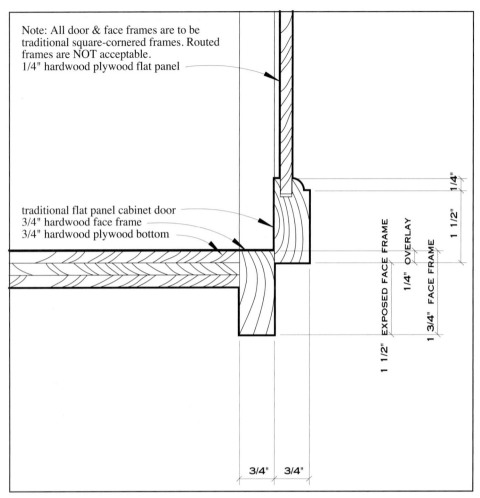

Note: All door & face frames are to be traditional square-cornered frames. Routed frames are NOT acceptable.
1/4" hardwood plywood flat panel

traditional flat panel cabinet door
3/4" hardwood face frame
3/4" hardwood plywood bottom

1/4"

1 1/2"

1 1/2" EXPOSED FACE FRAME

1/4" OVERLAY

1 3/4" FACE FRAME

3/4"   3/4"

DRAWING #

Reveal Overlay Door Bottom Detail

SCALE
HALF SIZE

CDDF1012
52

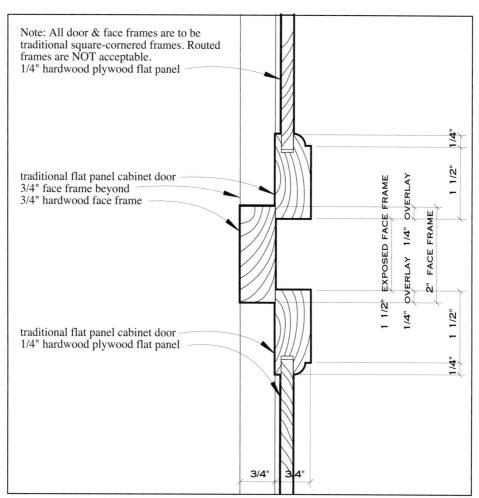

Note: All door & face frames are to be
traditional square-cornered frames. Routed
frames are NOT acceptable.
1/4" hardwood plywood flat panel

traditional flat panel cabinet door
3/4" face frame beyond
3/4" hardwood face frame

traditional flat panel cabinet door
1/4" hardwood plywood flat panel

1/4"

1 1/2"

1 1/2" EXPOSED FACE FRAME

1/4" OVERLAY

1/4" OVERLAY

2" FACE FRAME

1 1/2" OVERLAY

1 1/2"

1/4"

3/4"   3/4"

Reveal Overlay Meeting Door Detail

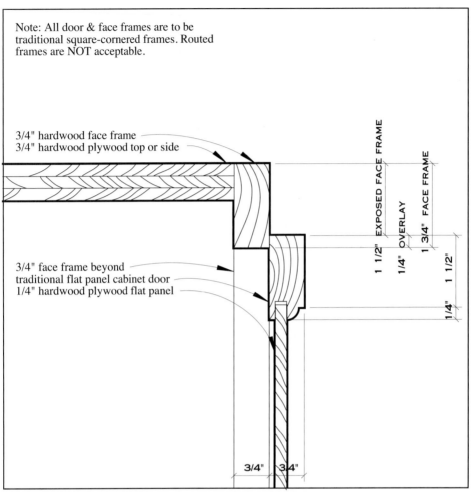

Note: All door & face frames are to be
traditional square-cornered frames. Routed
frames are NOT acceptable.

3/4" hardwood face frame
3/4" hardwood plywood top or side

3/4" face frame beyond
traditional flat panel cabinet door
1/4" hardwood plywood flat panel

1 1/2" EXPOSED FACE FRAME
1/4" OVERLAY
1 3/4" FACE FRAME
1 1/2"
1/4"

3/4" 3/4"

Reveal Overlay Door Top or Side Detail

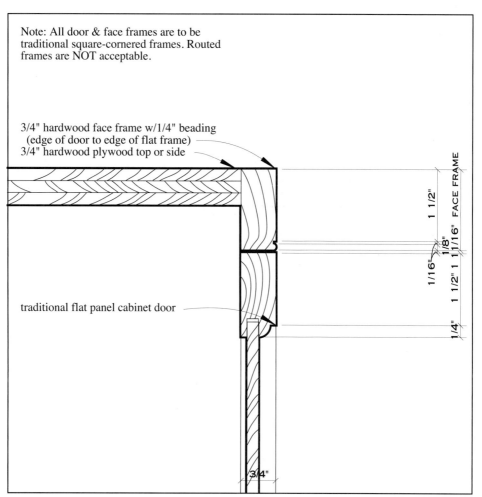

Note: All door & face frames are to be
traditional square-cornered frames. Routed
frames are NOT acceptable.

3/4" hardwood face frame w/1/4" beading
 (edge of door to edge of flat frame)
3/4" hardwood plywood top or side

traditional flat panel cabinet door

1 1/2"   FACE FRAME

1 1/16"   1 1/2"

1/8"

1/16"

1/4"

3/4"

DRAWING #

Inset Door Top or Side Detail

SCALE
HALF
SIZE

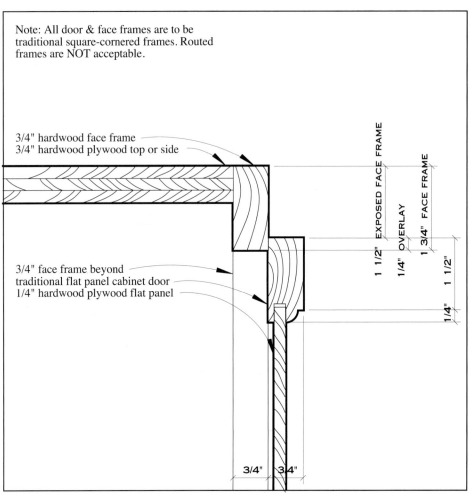

Note: All door & face frames are to be traditional square-cornered frames. Routed frames are NOT acceptable.

3/4" hardwood face frame
3/4" hardwood plywood top or side

3/4" face frame beyond
traditional flat panel cabinet door
1/4" hardwood plywood flat panel

1 1/2" EXPOSED FACE FRAME

1/4" OVERLAY

1 3/4" FACE FRAME

1 1/2"

1/4"

3/4" 3/4"

Reveal Overlay Door Top or Side Detail

DRAWING #

SCALE
HALF
SIZE

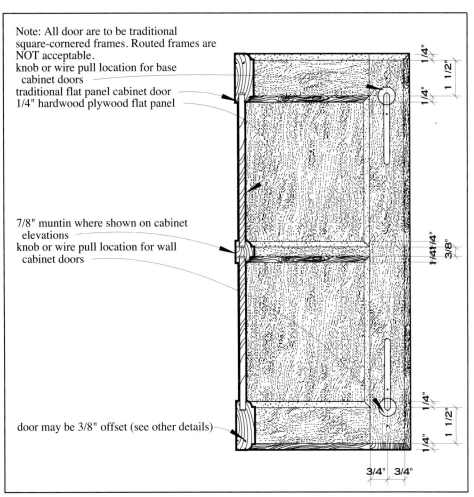

Note: All door are to be traditional square-cornered frames. Routed frames are NOT acceptable.

knob or wire pull location for base cabinet doors

traditional flat panel cabinet door

1/4" hardwood plywood flat panel

7/8" muntin where shown on cabinet elevations

knob or wire pull location for wall cabinet doors

door may be 3/8" offset (see other details)

1/4"

1 1/2"

1/4"

1/4"

3/8"

1/4"

1/4"

1 1/2"

1/4"

3/4" 3/4"

DRAWING #

Flat Panel Door Section/Elevation

SCALE

3"
―――
1'-0"

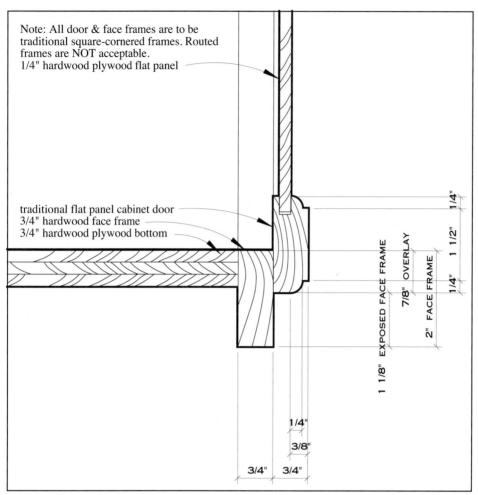

Note: All door & face frames are to be traditional square-cornered frames. Routed frames are NOT acceptable.
1/4" hardwood plywood flat panel

traditional flat panel cabinet door
3/4" hardwood face frame
3/4" hardwood plywood bottom

1/4"

1 1/2"

1/4"

7/8" OVERLAY

2" FACE FRAME

1 1/8" EXPOSED FACE FRAME

1/4"

3/8"

3/4"   3/4"

Flush Overlay Door Bottom Detail

SCALE
HALF
SIZE

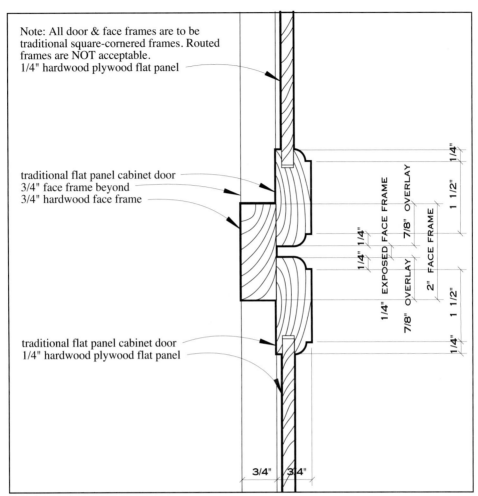

Note: All door & face frames are to be traditional square-cornered frames. Routed frames are NOT acceptable.
1/4" hardwood plywood flat panel

traditional flat panel cabinet door
3/4" face frame beyond
3/4" hardwood face frame

traditional flat panel cabinet door
1/4" hardwood plywood flat panel

1/4"

1 1/2"

1/4"

7/8" OVERLAY

1/4" EXPOSED FACE FRAME

2" FACE FRAME

1/4"

7/8" OVERLAY

1 1/2"

1/4"

3/4" 3/4"

Flush Overlay Meeting Door Detail

Note: All door & face frames are to be
traditional square-cornered frames. Routed
frames are NOT acceptable.

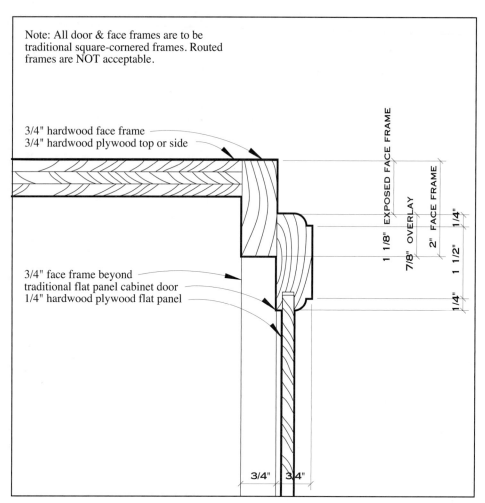

3/4" hardwood face frame
3/4" hardwood plywood top or side

3/4" face frame beyond
traditional flat panel cabinet door
1/4" hardwood plywood flat panel

1 1/8" EXPOSED FACE FRAME

7/8" OVERLAY

2" FACE FRAME

1 1/2"

1/4"

1/4"

3/4"   3/4"

Flush Overlay Door Top or Side Detail

SCALE
HALF
SIZE

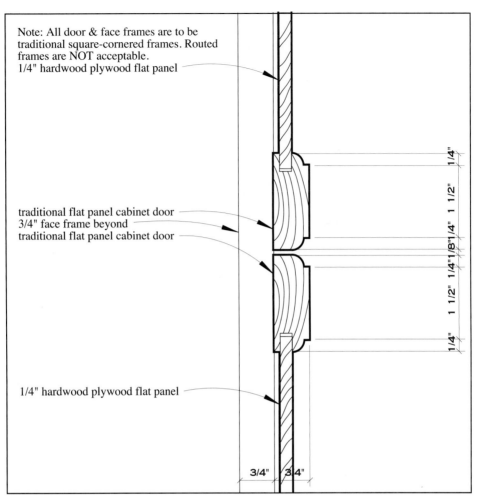

Note: All door & face frames are to be traditional square-cornered frames. Routed frames are NOT acceptable.
1/4" hardwood plywood flat panel

traditional flat panel cabinet door
3/4" face frame beyond
traditional flat panel cabinet door

1/4" hardwood plywood flat panel

1/4"

1 1/2"

1/4"1/8"1/4"

1 1/2"

1/4"

3/4" 3/4"

DRAWING #

Meeting Door Detail Without Frame

SCALE
HALF SIZE

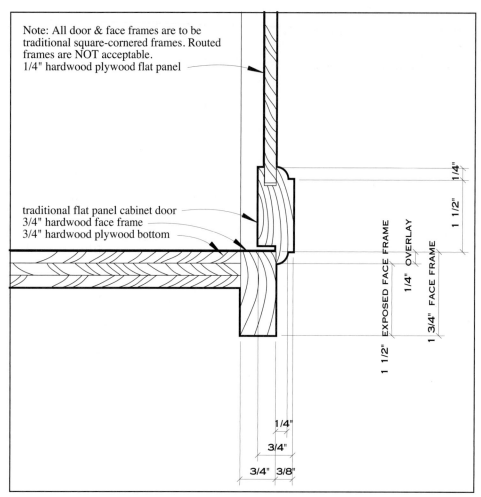

Note: All door & face frames are to be
traditional square-cornered frames. Routed
frames are NOT acceptable.
1/4" hardwood plywood flat panel

traditional flat panel cabinet door
3/4" hardwood face frame
3/4" hardwood plywood bottom

1/4"

1 1/2"

EXPOSED FACE FRAME

1/4" OVERLAY

1 3/4" FACE FRAME

1 1/2"

1/4"

3/4"

3/4" 3/8"

3/8" Offset Door Bottom Detail

DRAWING #

SCALE
HALF
SIZE

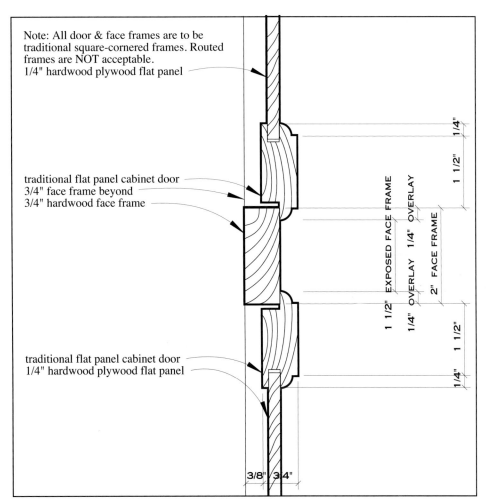

Note: All door & face frames are to be traditional square-cornered frames. Routed frames are NOT acceptable.
1/4" hardwood plywood flat panel

traditional flat panel cabinet door
3/4" face frame beyond
3/4" hardwood face frame

traditional flat panel cabinet door
1/4" hardwood plywood flat panel

1/4"

1 1/2"

1 1/2" EXPOSED FACE FRAME

1/4" OVERLAY

1/4" OVERLAY

2" FACE FRAME

1 1/2"

1/4"

3/8" 3/4"

DRAWING #

3/8" Offset Meeting Door Detail

SCALE
HALF
SIZE

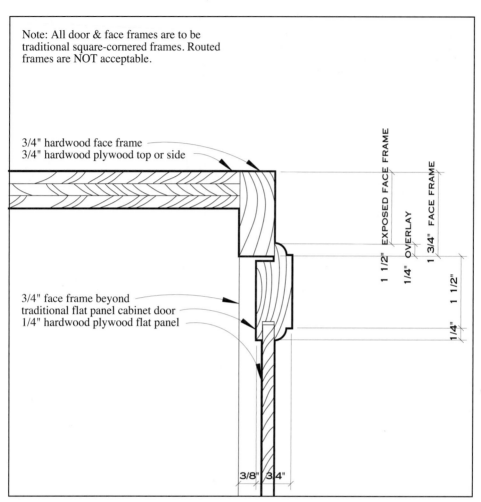

Note: All door & face frames are to be
traditional square-cornered frames. Routed
frames are NOT acceptable.

3/4" hardwood face frame
3/4" hardwood plywood top or side

3/4" face frame beyond
traditional flat panel cabinet door
1/4" hardwood plywood flat panel

1 1/2" EXPOSED FACE FRAME

1/4" OVERLAY

1 3/4" FACE FRAME

1 1/2"

1/4"

3/8" 3/4"

DRAWING #

3/8" Offset Door Top or Side Detail

SCALE
HALF
SIZE

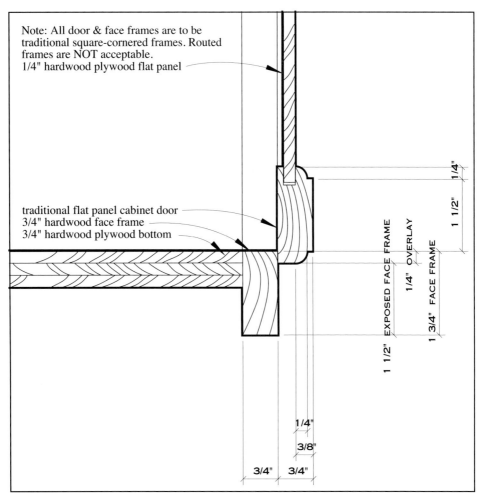

Note: All door & face frames are to be
traditional square-cornered frames. Routed
frames are NOT acceptable.
1/4" hardwood plywood flat panel

traditional flat panel cabinet door
3/4" hardwood face frame
3/4" hardwood plywood bottom

1/4"

1 1/2"

1/4" EXPOSED FACE FRAME

1/4" OVERLAY

1 3/4" FACE FRAME

1 1/2" EXPOSED FACE FRAME

1/4"

3/8"

3/4"   3/4"

Reveal Overlay Door Bottom Detail

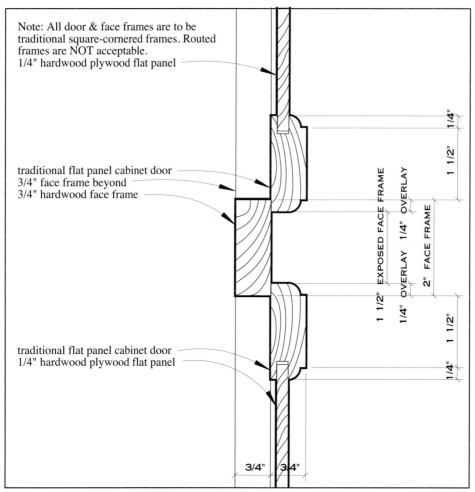

Note: All door & face frames are to be traditional square-cornered frames. Routed frames are NOT acceptable.
1/4" hardwood plywood flat panel

traditional flat panel cabinet door
3/4" face frame beyond
3/4" hardwood face frame

traditional flat panel cabinet door
1/4" hardwood plywood flat panel

1/4"

1 1/2"

1 1/2" EXPOSED FACE FRAME

1/4" OVERLAY

2" FACE FRAME

1/4" OVERLAY

1 1/2"

1/4"

3/4"   3/4"

DRAWING #

Reveal Overlay Meeting Door Detail

SCALE
HALF
SIZE

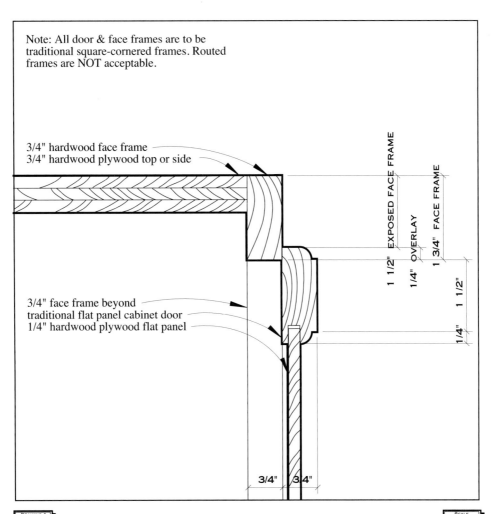

Note: All door & face frames are to be traditional square-cornered frames. Routed frames are NOT acceptable.

3/4" hardwood face frame
3/4" hardwood plywood top or side

3/4" face frame beyond
traditional flat panel cabinet door
1/4" hardwood plywood flat panel

1 1/2" EXPOSED FACE FRAME

1/4" OVERLAY

1 3/4" FACE FRAME

1 1/2"

1/4"

3/4" 3/4"

Reveal Overlay Door Top or Side Detail

DRAWING #

SCALE
HALF SIZE

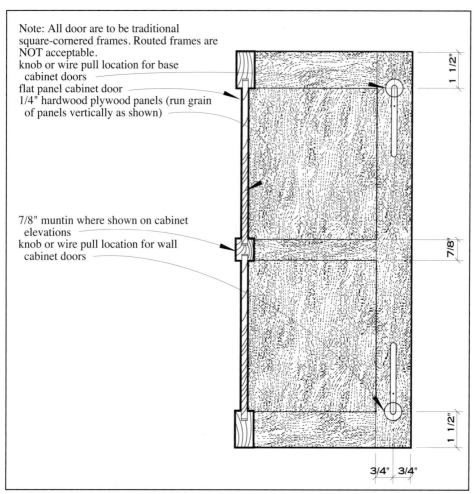

Note: All door are to be traditional
square-cornered frames. Routed frames are
NOT acceptable.
knob or wire pull location for base
   cabinet doors
flat panel cabinet door
1/4" hardwood plywood panels (run grain
   of panels vertically as shown)

7/8" muntin where shown on cabinet
   elevations
knob or wire pull location for wall
   cabinet doors

1 1/2"

7/8"

1 1/2"

3/4"   3/4"

DRAWING #

Flat Panel Door Section/Elevation

SCALE
3"
1'-0"

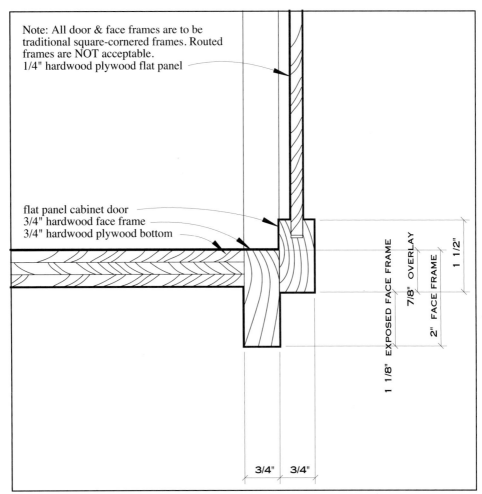

Note: All door & face frames are to be
traditional square-cornered frames. Routed
frames are NOT acceptable.
1/4" hardwood plywood flat panel

flat panel cabinet door
3/4" hardwood face frame
3/4" hardwood plywood bottom

1 1/8" EXPOSED FACE FRAME

7/8" OVERLAY

2" FACE FRAME

1 1/2"

3/4"   3/4"

DRAWING #

Flush Overlay Door Bottom Detail

SCALE
HALF
SIZE

CDDF3002
69

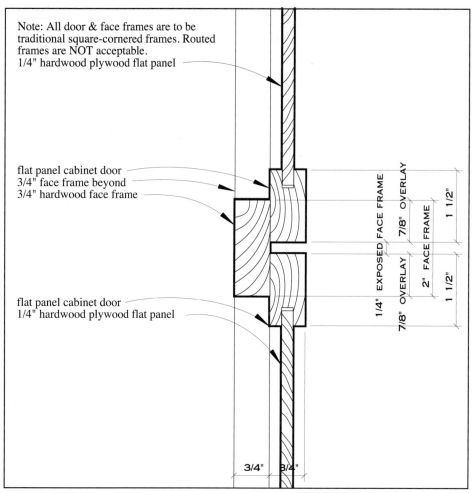

Note: All door & face frames are to be
traditional square-cornered frames. Routed
frames are NOT acceptable.
1/4" hardwood plywood flat panel

flat panel cabinet door
3/4" face frame beyond
3/4" hardwood face frame

flat panel cabinet door
1/4" hardwood plywood flat panel

1/4" EXPOSED FACE FRAME
7/8" OVERLAY
7/8" OVERLAY
2" FACE FRAME
1 1/2"
1 1/2"
7/8" OVERLAY

3/4"   3/4"

Flush Overlay Meeting Door Detail

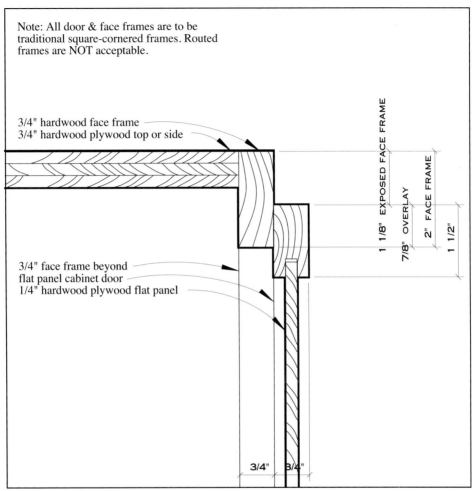

Note: All door & face frames are to be traditional square-cornered frames. Routed frames are NOT acceptable.

3/4" hardwood face frame
3/4" hardwood plywood top or side

1 1/8" EXPOSED FACE FRAME

7/8" OVERLAY

2" FACE FRAME

1 1/2"

3/4" face frame beyond
flat panel cabinet door
1/4" hardwood plywood flat panel

3/4" 3/4"

DRAWING #

Flush Overlay Door Top or Side Detail

SCALE
HALF
SIZE

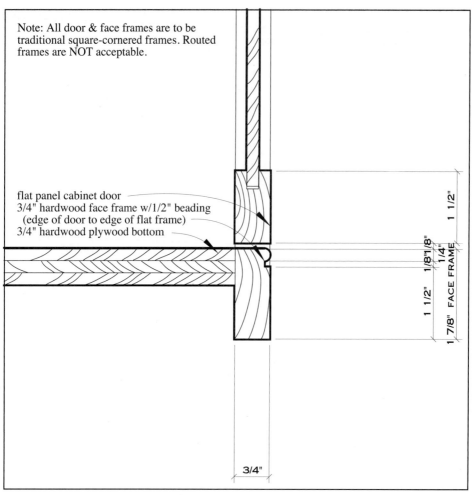

Note: All door & face frames are to be traditional square-cornered frames. Routed frames are NOT acceptable.

flat panel cabinet door
3/4" hardwood face frame w/1/2" beading
  (edge of door to edge of flat frame)
3/4" hardwood plywood bottom

1 1/2"

1/8"

1/4"

1/8"

1 1/2"

1 7/8" FACE FRAME

3/4"

Inset Door Bottom Detail

DRAWING #

SCALE
HALF
SIZE

Note: All door & face frames are to be
traditional square-cornered frames. Routed
frames are NOT acceptable.

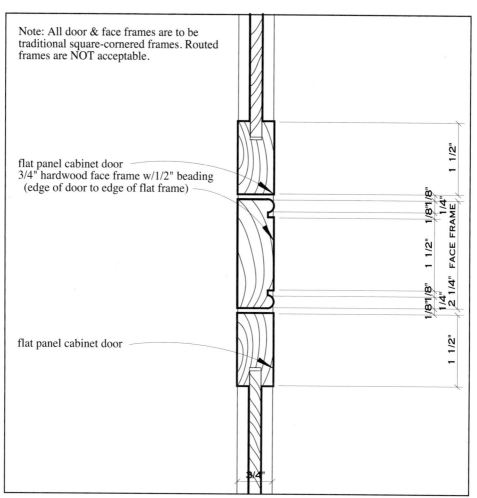

flat panel cabinet door
3/4" hardwood face frame w/1/2" beading
 (edge of door to edge of flat frame)

flat panel cabinet door

1 1/2"

1/8"|/8"
1/4"
2 1/4" FACE FRAME
1/8"|/8"
1/4"
1 1/2"

1 1/2"

3/4"

Inset Meeting Door Detail

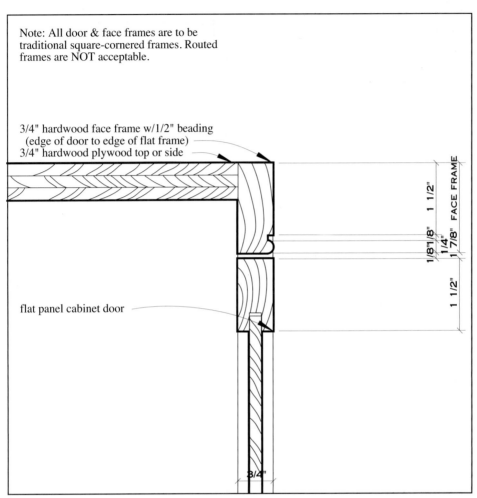

Note: All door & face frames are to be
traditional square-cornered frames. Routed
frames are NOT acceptable.

3/4" hardwood face frame w/1/2" beading
 (edge of door to edge of flat frame)
3/4" hardwood plywood top or side

flat panel cabinet door

1 1/2" 1 7/8" FACE FRAME

1/8" 1/4" 1 1/2"

3/4"

DRAWING #		SCALE

Inset Door Top or Side Detail

HALF SIZE

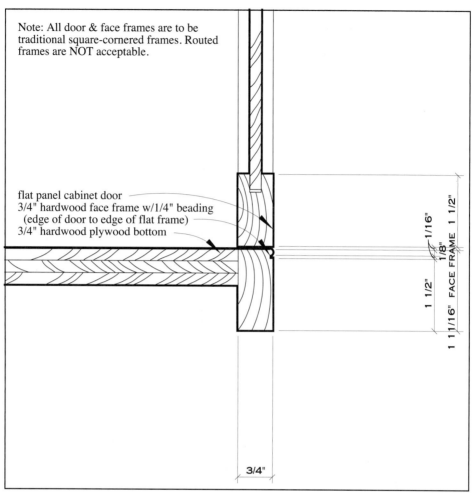

Note: All door & face frames are to be traditional square-cornered frames. Routed frames are NOT acceptable.

flat panel cabinet door
3/4" hardwood face frame w/1/4" beading
  (edge of door to edge of flat frame)
3/4" hardwood plywood bottom

1 1/16"
1/8"
1/16"
1 1/2"
1 11/16" FACE FRAME
1 1/2"

3/4"

Inset Door Bottom Detail

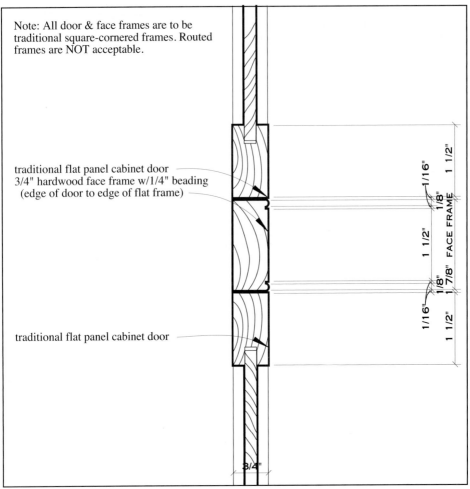

Note: All door & face frames are to be
traditional square-cornered frames. Routed
frames are NOT acceptable.

traditional flat panel cabinet door
3/4" hardwood face frame w/1/4" beading
 (edge of door to edge of flat frame)

traditional flat panel cabinet door

3/4"

1/16"
1 1/2"
1/8"
1 1/2" FACE FRAME

1 1/2"
1/8"
1 7/8"
1/16"
1 1/2"

Inset Meeting Door Detail

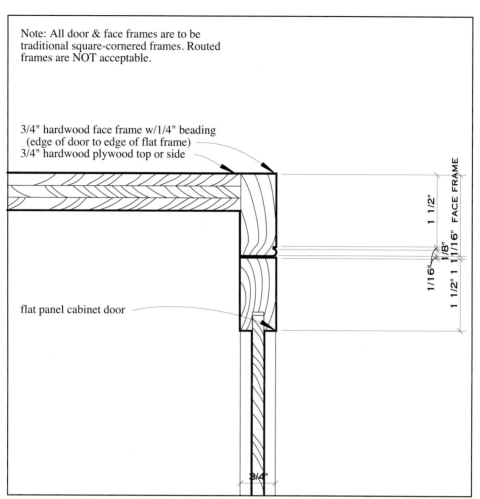

Note: All door & face frames are to be traditional square-cornered frames. Routed frames are NOT acceptable.

3/4" hardwood face frame w/1/4" beading (edge of door to edge of flat frame)
3/4" hardwood plywood top or side

flat panel cabinet door

1 1/2"

1 1/2" FACE FRAME

1/16"
1/8"
1 1/16"

1/16"
1 1/2"

3/4"

Inset Door Top or Side Detail

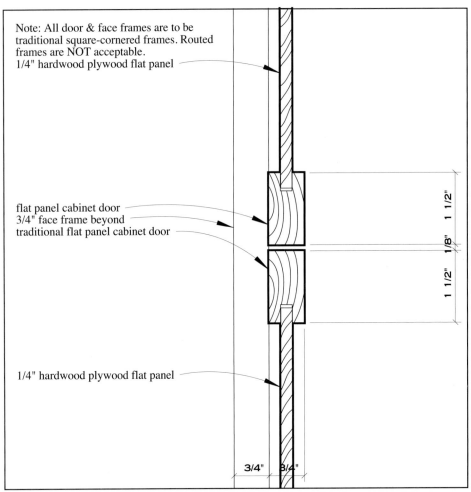

Note: All door & face frames are to be
traditional square-cornered frames. Routed
frames are NOT acceptable.
1/4" hardwood plywood flat panel

flat panel cabinet door
3/4" face frame beyond
traditional flat panel cabinet door

1/4" hardwood plywood flat panel

1 1/2"

1/8"

1 1/2"

3/4"   3/4"

DRAWING #

Meeting Door Detail Without Frame

SCALE
HALF
SIZE

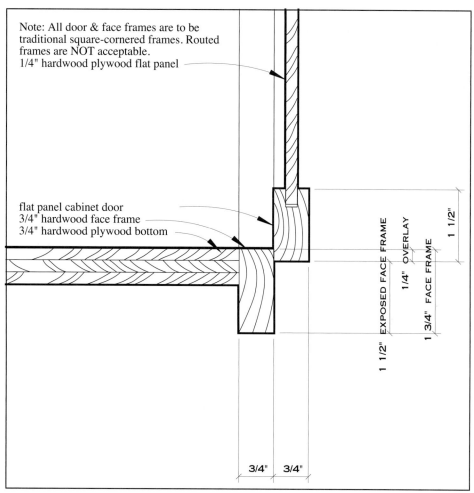

Note: All door & face frames are to be
traditional square-cornered frames. Routed
frames are NOT acceptable.
1/4" hardwood plywood flat panel

flat panel cabinet door
3/4" hardwood face frame
3/4" hardwood plywood bottom

1 1/2"

1 1/2" EXPOSED FACE FRAME

1/4" OVERLAY

1 3/4" FACE FRAME

3/4"   3/4"

DRAWING #

Reveal Overlay Door Bottom Detail

SCALE
HALF
SIZE

CDDF3012
79

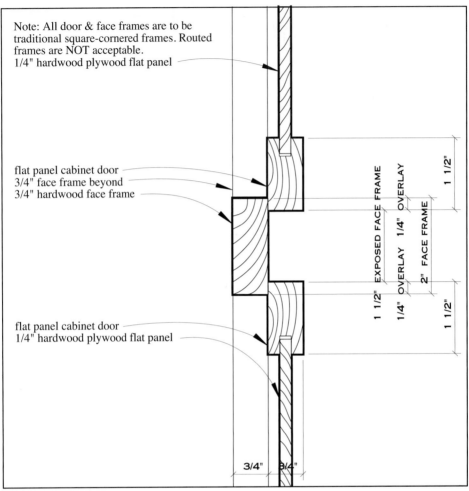

Note: All door & face frames are to be
traditional square-cornered frames. Routed
frames are NOT acceptable.
1/4" hardwood plywood flat panel

flat panel cabinet door
3/4" face frame beyond
3/4" hardwood face frame

flat panel cabinet door
1/4" hardwood plywood flat panel

1 1/2" EXPOSED FACE FRAME

1/4" OVERLAY

2" FACE FRAME

1 1/2"

1/4" OVERLAY

1 1/2"

3/4"   3/4"

Reveal Overlay Meeting Door Detail

CDDF3013
80

Note: All door & face frames are to be
traditional square-cornered frames. Routed
frames are NOT acceptable.

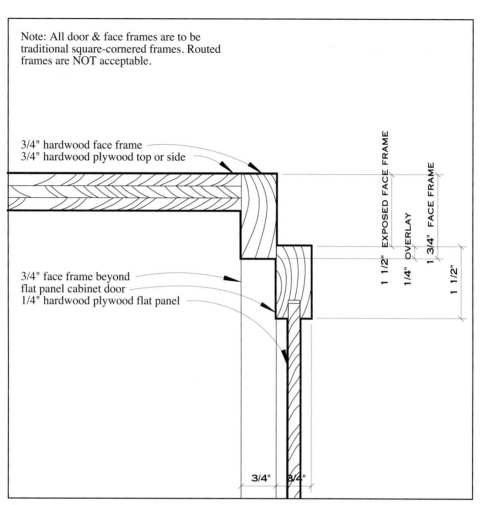

3/4" hardwood face frame
3/4" hardwood plywood top or side

3/4" face frame beyond
flat panel cabinet door
1/4" hardwood plywood flat panel

1 1/2" EXPOSED FACE FRAME

1/4" OVERLAY

1 3/4" FACE FRAME

1 1/2"

3/4"   3/4"

Reveal Overlay Door Top or Side Detail

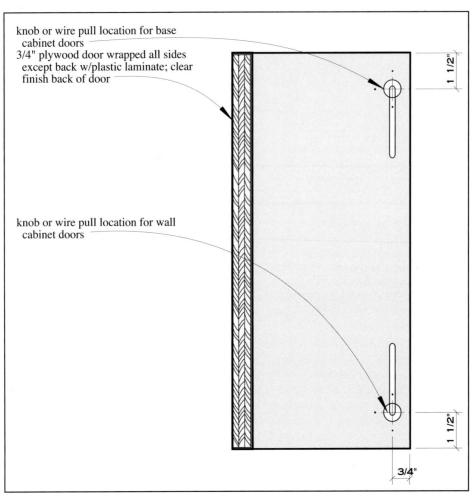

knob or wire pull location for base
    cabinet doors

3/4" plywood door wrapped all sides
    except back w/plastic laminate; clear
    finish back of door

knob or wire pull location for wall
    cabinet doors

1 1/2"

1 1/2"

3/4"

Flush PL Door Section/Elevation

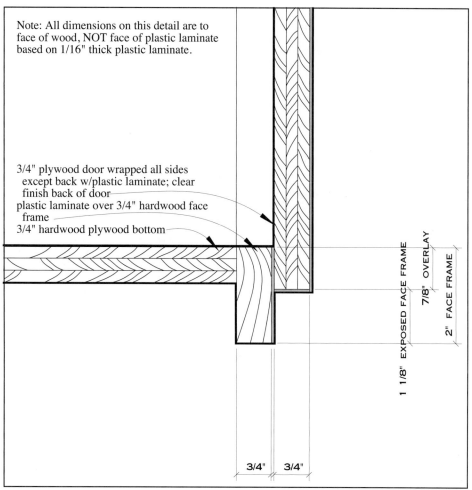

Note: All dimensions on this detail are to face of wood, NOT face of plastic laminate based on 1/16" thick plastic laminate.

3/4" plywood door wrapped all sides except back w/plastic laminate; clear finish back of door
plastic laminate over 3/4" hardwood face frame
3/4" hardwood plywood bottom

1 1/8" EXPOSED FACE FRAME

7/8" OVERLAY

2" FACE FRAME

3/4"   3/4"

DRAWING #

Flush Overlay Door Bottom Detail

SCALE
HALF SIZE

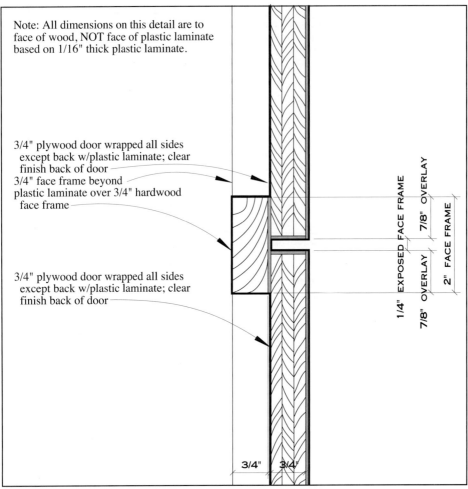

Note: All dimensions on this detail are to face of wood, NOT face of plastic laminate based on 1/16" thick plastic laminate.

3/4" plywood door wrapped all sides except back w/plastic laminate; clear finish back of door
3/4" face frame beyond plastic laminate over 3/4" hardwood face frame

3/4" plywood door wrapped all sides except back w/plastic laminate; clear finish back of door

1/4" EXPOSED FACE FRAME
7/8" OVERLAY
7/8" OVERLAY
7/8" OVERLAY
2" FACE FRAME

3/4"   3/4"

Flush Overlay Meeting Door Detail

SCALE
HALF
SIZE

CDDFP003
84

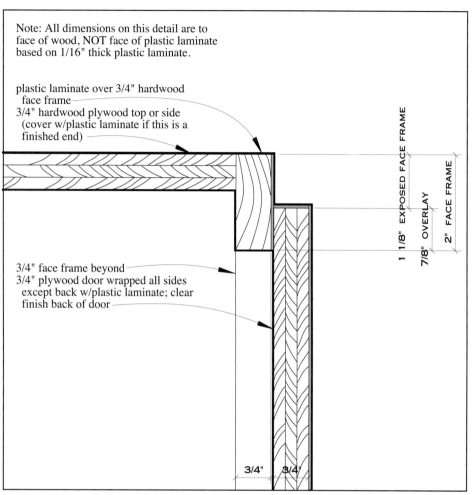

Note: All dimensions on this detail are to face of wood, NOT face of plastic laminate based on 1/16" thick plastic laminate.

plastic laminate over 3/4" hardwood face frame

3/4" hardwood plywood top or side (cover w/plastic laminate if this is a finished end)

3/4" face frame beyond

3/4" plywood door wrapped all sides except back w/plastic laminate; clear finish back of door

1 1/8" EXPOSED FACE FRAME

7/8" OVERLAY

2" FACE FRAME

3/4"   3/4"

DRAWING #

Flush Overlay Door Top or Side Detail

SCALE
HALF
SIZE

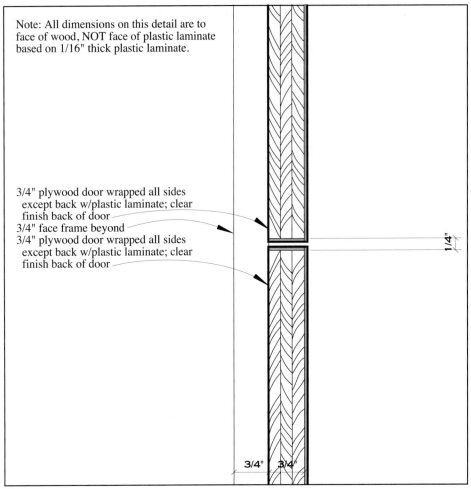

Note: All dimensions on this detail are to face of wood, NOT face of plastic laminate based on 1/16" thick plastic laminate.

3/4" plywood door wrapped all sides except back w/plastic laminate; clear finish back of door

3/4" face frame beyond

3/4" plywood door wrapped all sides except back w/plastic laminate; clear finish back of door

1/4"

3/4" 3/4"

DRAWING #

Meeting Door Detail Without Frame

SCALE
HALF
SIZE

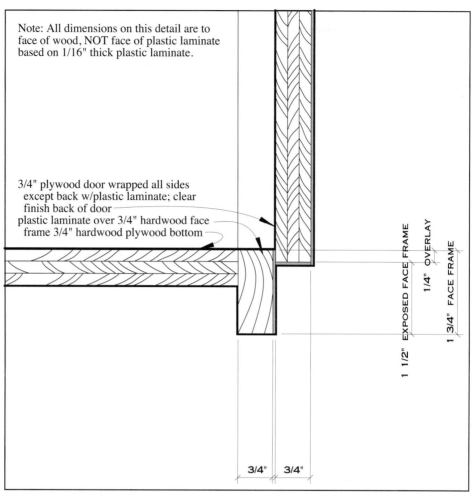

Note: All dimensions on this detail are to
face of wood, NOT face of plastic laminate
based on 1/16" thick plastic laminate.

3/4" plywood door wrapped all sides
  except back w/plastic laminate; clear
  finish back of door
plastic laminate over 3/4" hardwood face
  frame 3/4" hardwood plywood bottom

EXPOSED FACE FRAME 1 1/2"

1/4" OVERLAY

1 3/4" FACE FRAME

3/4"   3/4"

DRAWING #

Reveal Overlay Door Bottom Detail

SCALE
HALF
SIZE

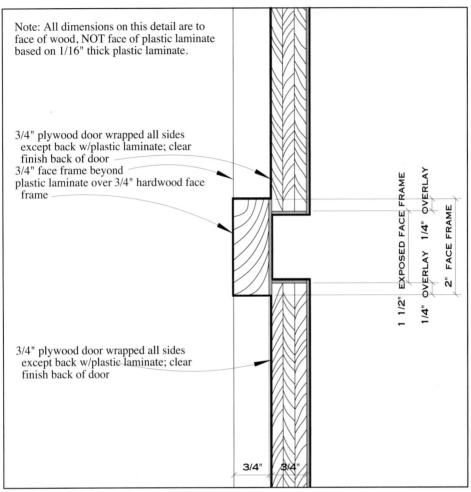

Note: All dimensions on this detail are to face of wood, NOT face of plastic laminate based on 1/16" thick plastic laminate.

3/4" plywood door wrapped all sides except back w/plastic laminate; clear finish back of door

3/4" face frame beyond

plastic laminate over 3/4" hardwood face frame

3/4" plywood door wrapped all sides except back w/plastic laminate; clear finish back of door

1 1/2" EXPOSED FACE FRAME
1/4" OVERLAY
1/4" OVERLAY
2" FACE FRAME

3/4"   3/4"

DRAWING #

Reveal Overlay Meeting Door Detail

SCALE
HALF
SIZE

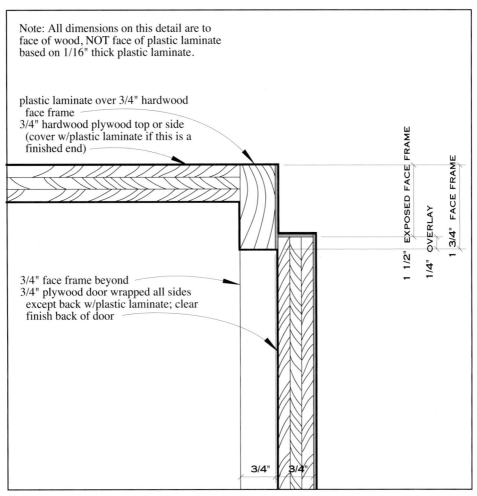

Note: All dimensions on this detail are to face of wood, NOT face of plastic laminate based on 1/16" thick plastic laminate.

plastic laminate over 3/4" hardwood face frame

3/4" hardwood plywood top or side (cover w/plastic laminate if this is a finished end)

3/4" face frame beyond

3/4" plywood door wrapped all sides except back w/plastic laminate; clear finish back of door

1 1/2" EXPOSED FACE FRAME

1/4" OVERLAY

1 3/4" FACE FRAME

3/4"   3/4"

DRAWING #

Reveal Overlay Door Top or Side Detail

SCALE
HALF SIZE

CDDFP008
89

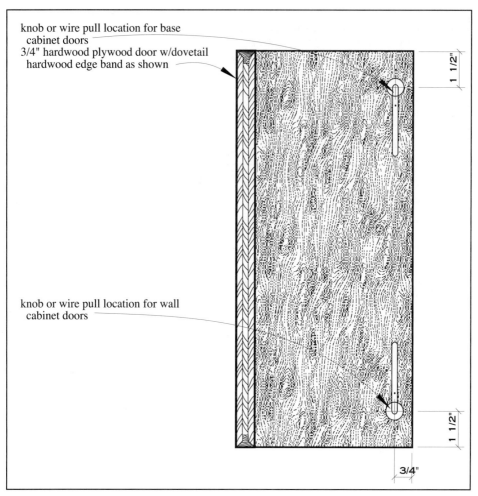

knob or wire pull location for base
  cabinet doors

3/4" hardwood plywood door w/dovetail
  hardwood edge band as shown

knob or wire pull location for wall
  cabinet doors

1 1/2"

1 1/2"

3/4"

Flush Door Section/Elevation

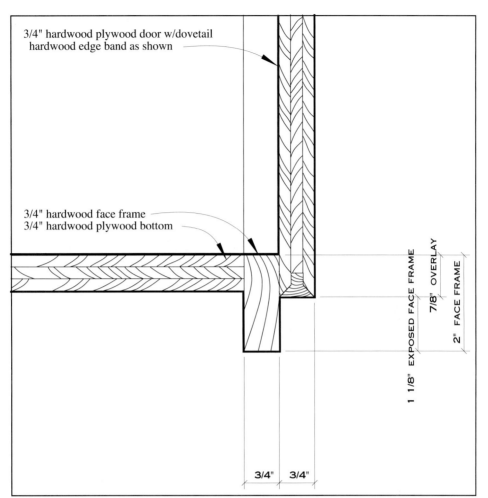

3/4" hardwood plywood door w/dovetail
hardwood edge band as shown

3/4" hardwood face frame
3/4" hardwood plywood bottom

1 1/8" EXPOSED FACE FRAME

7/8" OVERLAY

2" FACE FRAME

3/4"   3/4"

DRAWING #

Flush Door Bottom Detail

SCALE

HALF
SIZE

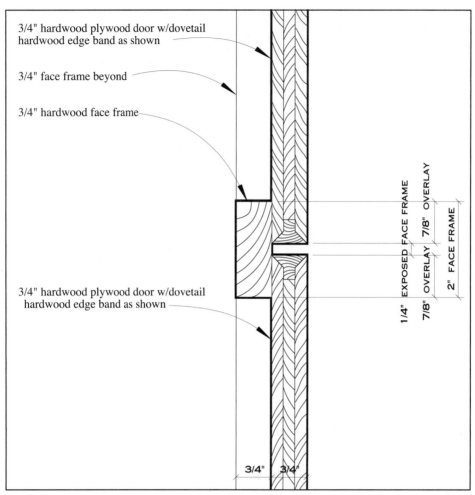

3/4" hardwood plywood door w/dovetail hardwood edge band as shown

3/4" face frame beyond

3/4" hardwood face frame

3/4" hardwood plywood door w/dovetail hardwood edge band as shown

1/4" EXPOSED FACE FRAME

7/8" OVERLAY

7/8" OVERLAY

2" FACE FRAME

3/4"   3/4"

DRAWING #

Flush Overlay Meeting Door Detail

SCALE
HALF SIZE

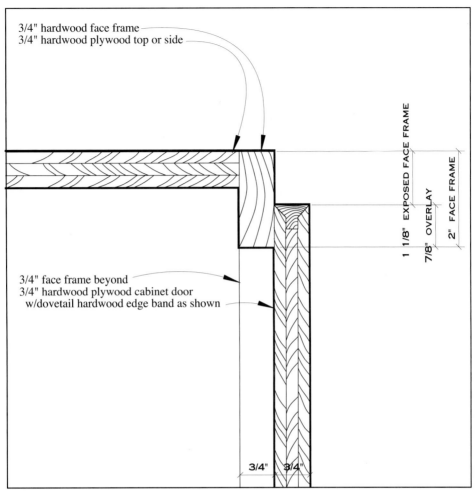

3/4" hardwood face frame
3/4" hardwood plywood top or side

1 1/8" EXPOSED FACE FRAME

7/8" OVERLAY

2" FACE FRAME

3/4" face frame beyond
3/4" hardwood plywood cabinet door
 w/dovetail hardwood edge band as shown

3/4" 3/4"

DRAWING #	Flush Overlay Door Top or Side Detail	SCALE HALF SIZE

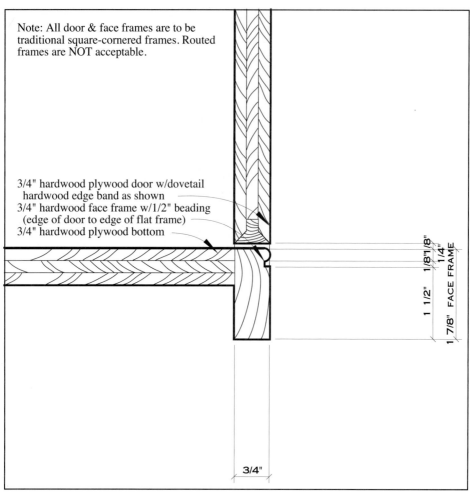

Note: All door & face frames are to be
traditional square-cornered frames. Routed
frames are NOT acceptable.

3/4" hardwood plywood door w/dovetail
  hardwood edge band as shown
3/4" hardwood face frame w/1/2" beading
  (edge of door to edge of flat frame)
3/4" hardwood plywood bottom

1/8" 1/8"
1/4"
1 1/2"
1 7/8" FACE FRAME

3/4"

Inset Door Bottom Detail

Note: All door & face frames are to be
traditional square-cornered frames. Routed
frames are NOT acceptable.

3/4" hardwood plywood door w/dovetail
  hardwood edge band as shown
3/4" hardwood face frame w/1/2" beading
  (edge of door to edge of flat frame)

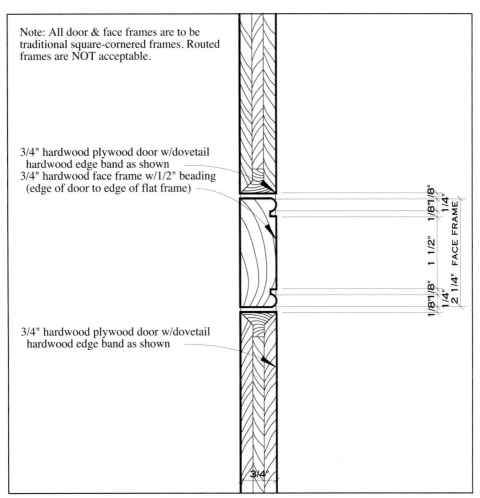

3/4" hardwood plywood door w/dovetail
  hardwood edge band as shown

Inset Meeting Door Detail

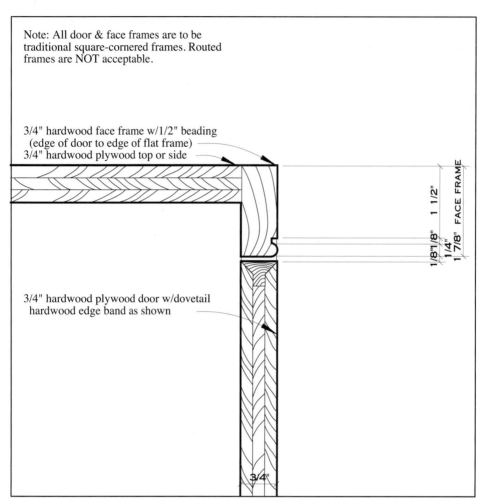

Note: All door & face frames are to be
traditional square-cornered frames. Routed
frames are NOT acceptable.

3/4" hardwood face frame w/1/2" beading
  (edge of door to edge of flat frame)
3/4" hardwood plywood top or side

FACE FRAME

1 1/2"

1/8" 1/8"
1/4"
1 7/8"

3/4" hardwood plywood door w/dovetail
  hardwood edge band as shown

3/4"

DRAWING #		SCALE

Inset Door Top or Side Detail

HALF SIZE

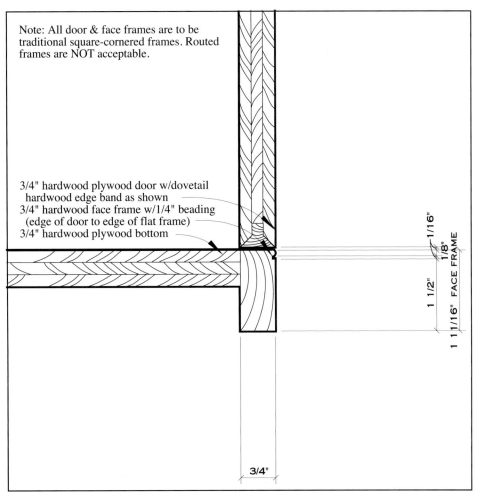

Note: All door & face frames are to be
traditional square-cornered frames. Routed
frames are NOT acceptable.

3/4" hardwood plywood door w/dovetail
  hardwood edge band as shown
3/4" hardwood face frame w/1/4" beading
  (edge of door to edge of flat frame)
3/4" hardwood plywood bottom

1/16"
1/8"
1 1/2"
1 11/16" FACE FRAME

3/4"

Inset Door Bottom Detail

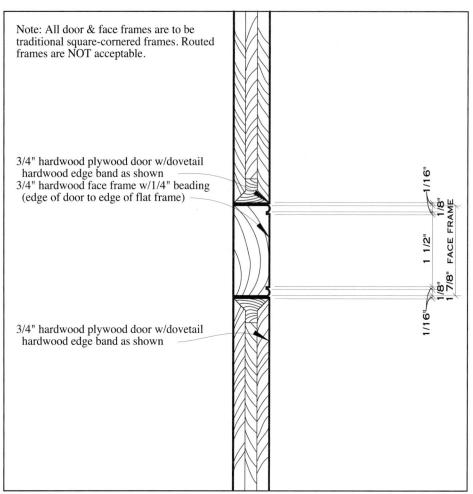

Note: All door & face frames are to be traditional square-cornered frames. Routed frames are NOT acceptable.

3/4" hardwood plywood door w/dovetail hardwood edge band as shown
3/4" hardwood face frame w/1/4" beading (edge of door to edge of flat frame)

3/4" hardwood plywood door w/dovetail hardwood edge band as shown

1/16"
1/8"
1 1/2" FACE FRAME
1 7/8"
1/8"
1/16"

DRAWING #

Inset Meeting Door Detail

SCALE
HALF SIZE

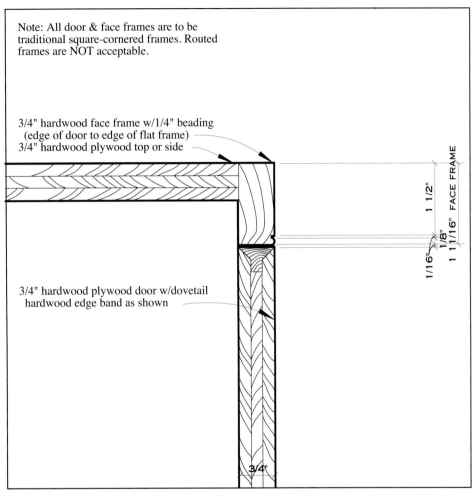

Note: All door & face frames are to be
traditional square-cornered frames. Routed
frames are NOT acceptable.

3/4" hardwood face frame w/1/4" beading
 (edge of door to edge of flat frame)
3/4" hardwood plywood top or side

3/4" hardwood plywood door w/dovetail
 hardwood edge band as shown

1 1/2"

1/16"

1/8"

1 1/16" FACE FRAME

1 1/16" FACE FRAME

3/4"

DRAWING #

Inset Door Top or Side Detail

SCALE
HALF
SIZE

CDDFW010
99

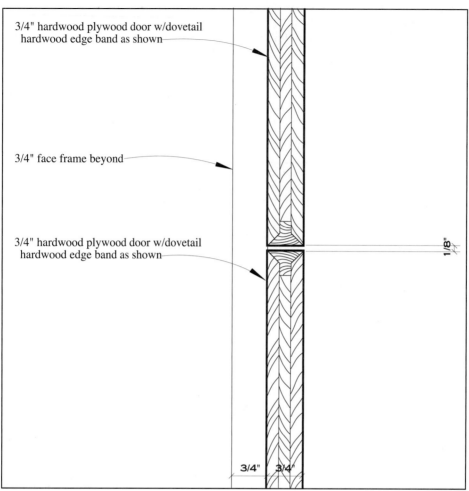

3/4" hardwood plywood door w/dovetail hardwood edge band as shown

3/4" face frame beyond

3/4" hardwood plywood door w/dovetail hardwood edge band as shown

1/8"

3/4" 3/4"

Meeting Door Detail Without Frame

DRAWING #

SCALE
HALF
SIZE

CDDFW011
100

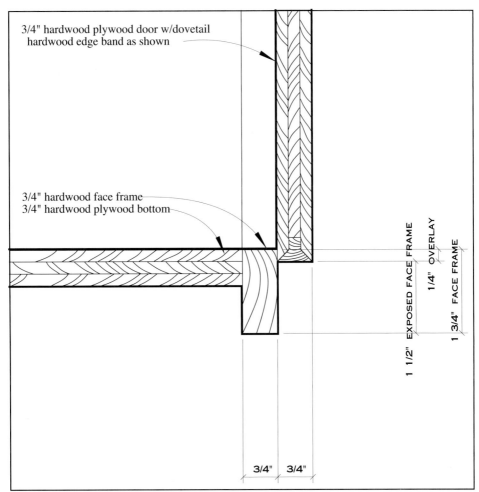

3/4" hardwood plywood door w/dovetail hardwood edge band as shown

3/4" hardwood face frame
3/4" hardwood plywood bottom

1 1/2" EXPOSED FACE FRAME

1/4" OVERLAY

1 3/4" FACE FRAME

3/4"   3/4"

Reveal Overlay Door Bottom Detail

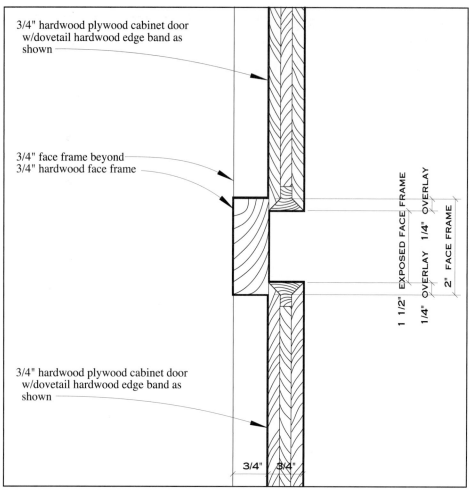

3/4" hardwood plywood cabinet door w/dovetail hardwood edge band as shown

3/4" face frame beyond
3/4" hardwood face frame

1 1/2" EXPOSED FACE FRAME

1/4" OVERLAY

1/4" OVERLAY

2" FACE FRAME

3/4" hardwood plywood cabinet door w/dovetail hardwood edge band as shown

3/4"   3/4"

Reveal Overlay Meeting Door Detail

SCALE
HALF
SIZE

CDDFW013
102

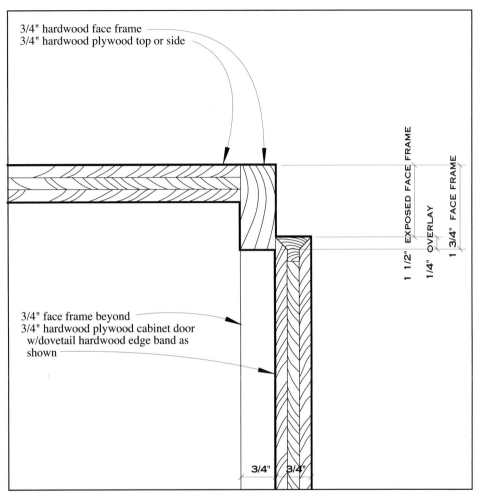

3/4" hardwood face frame
3/4" hardwood plywood top or side

3/4" face frame beyond
3/4" hardwood plywood cabinet door
  w/dovetail hardwood edge band as
  shown

1 1/2" EXPOSED FACE FRAME

1/4" OVERLAY

1 3/4" FACE FRAME

3/4"   3/4"

Reveal Overlay Door Top or Side Detail

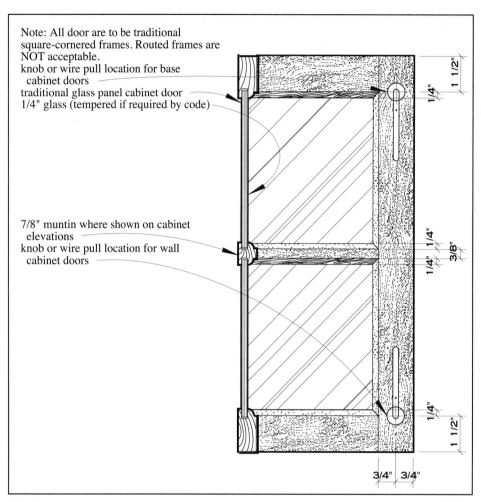

Note: All door are to be traditional square-cornered frames. Routed frames are NOT acceptable.

knob or wire pull location for base cabinet doors

traditional glass panel cabinet door

1/4" glass (tempered if required by code)

7/8" muntin where shown on cabinet elevations

knob or wire pull location for wall cabinet doors

1 1/2"
1/4"

1/4"
1/4"
3/8"

1/4"
1 1/2"

3/4" 3/4"

Glass Panel Door Section/Elevation

SCALE
3"
1'-0"

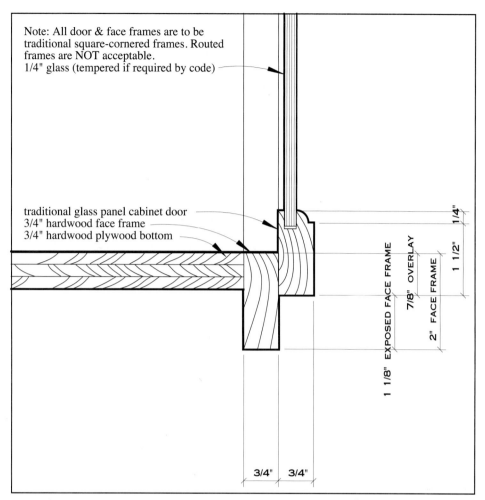

Note: All door & face frames are to be traditional square-cornered frames. Routed frames are NOT acceptable.
1/4" glass (tempered if required by code)

traditional glass panel cabinet door
3/4" hardwood face frame
3/4" hardwood plywood bottom

1/4"

1 1/2"

1 1/8" EXPOSED FACE FRAME

7/8" OVERLAY

2" FACE FRAME

3/4"   3/4"

Flush Overlay Glazed Door Bottom

DRAWING #

SCALE
HALF SIZE

CDDG1002
105

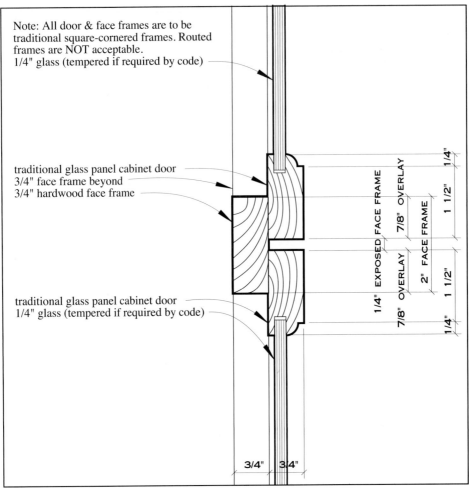

Note: All door & face frames are to be
traditional square-cornered frames. Routed
frames are NOT acceptable.
1/4" glass (tempered if required by code)

traditional glass panel cabinet door
3/4" face frame beyond
3/4" hardwood face frame

traditional glass panel cabinet door
1/4" glass (tempered if required by code)

1/4" EXPOSED FACE FRAME

7/8" OVERLAY

2" FACE FRAME

7/8" OVERLAY

1/4"

1 1/2"

1 1/2"

1/4"

1/4"

3/4"   3/4"

DRAWING #

Flush Overlay Meeting Glazed Doors

SCALE
HALF
SIZE

CDDG1003
106

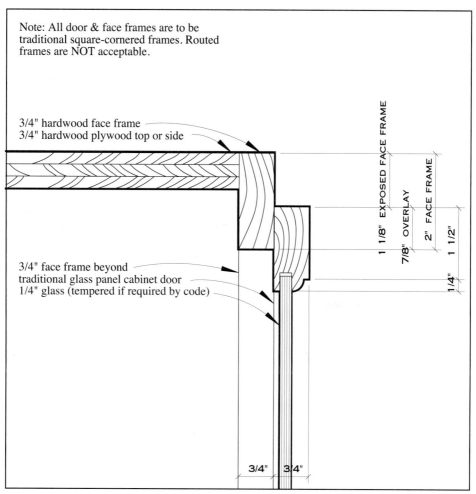

Note: All door & face frames are to be
traditional square-cornered frames. Routed
frames are NOT acceptable.

3/4" hardwood face frame
3/4" hardwood plywood top or side

3/4" face frame beyond
traditional glass panel cabinet door
1/4" glass (tempered if required by code)

1 1/8" EXPOSED FACE FRAME

7/8" OVERLAY

2" FACE FRAME

1 1/2"

1/4"

3/4"   3/4"

DRAWING #

Flush Overlay Glazed Door Top or Side

SCALE
**HALF
SIZE**

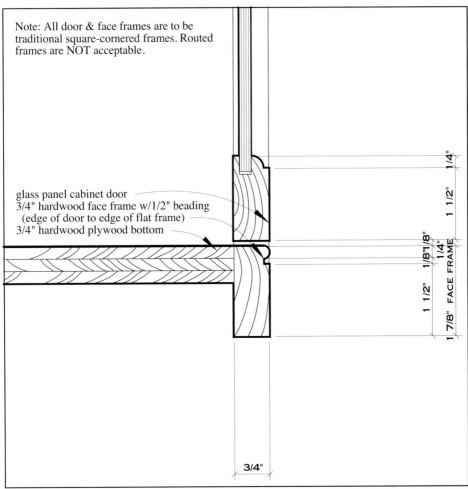

Note: All door & face frames are to be
traditional square-cornered frames. Routed
frames are NOT acceptable.

glass panel cabinet door
3/4" hardwood face frame w/1/2" beading
  (edge of door to edge of flat frame)
3/4" hardwood plywood bottom

1/4"

1 1/2"

1 1/2"

1/8" 1/8"

1/4"

1 7/8" FACE FRAME

3/4"

Inset Door Bottom Detail

DRAWING #

Note: All door & face frames are to be
traditional square-cornered frames. Routed
frames are NOT acceptable.

glass panel cabinet door
3/4" hardwood face frame w/1/2" beading
 (edge of door to edge of flat frame)

glass panel cabinet door

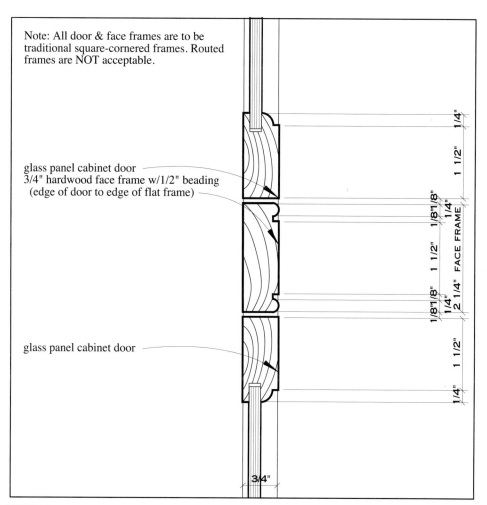

3/4"

Inset Door Meeting Door Detail

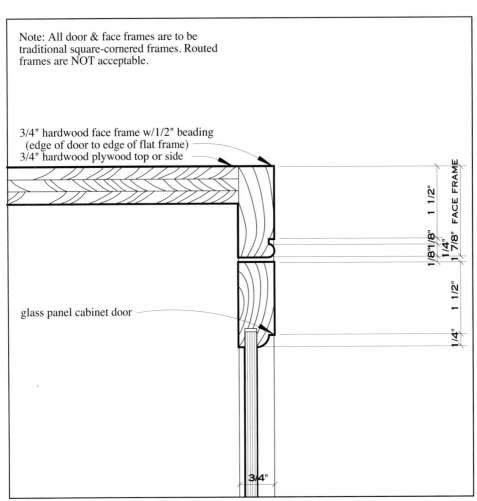

Note: All door & face frames are to be
traditional square-cornered frames. Routed
frames are NOT acceptable.

3/4" hardwood face frame w/1/2" beading
 (edge of door to edge of flat frame)
3/4" hardwood plywood top or side

1 1/2" — FACE FRAME

1/8" 1/4" 1 7/8"

glass panel cabinet door

1 1/2"

1/4"

3/4"

Inset Door Top or Side Detail

DRAWING #

SCALE
**HALF
SIZE**

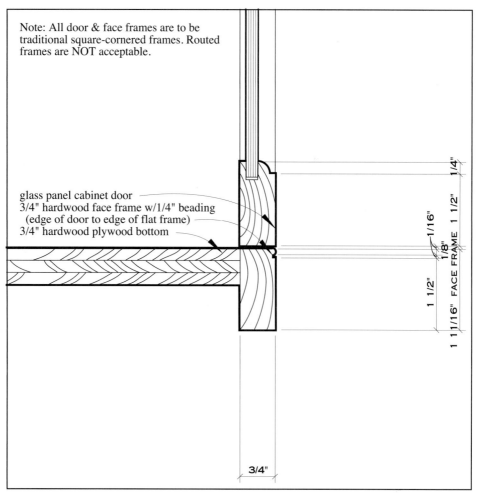

Note: All door & face frames are to be traditional square-cornered frames. Routed frames are NOT acceptable.

glass panel cabinet door
3/4" hardwood face frame w/1/4" beading
 (edge of door to edge of flat frame)
3/4" hardwood plywood bottom

1/4"

1/16"

1 1/2" FACE FRAME 1 1/2"

1/8"

1 1/2"

1 11/16" FACE FRAME

3/4"

DRAWING #

Inset Door Bottom Detail

SCALE
HALF SIZE

CDDG1008
111

Note: All door & face frames are to be
traditional square-cornered frames. Routed
frames are NOT acceptable.

glass panel cabinet door
3/4" hardwood face frame w/1/4" beading
  (edge of door to edge of flat frame)

glass panel cabinet door

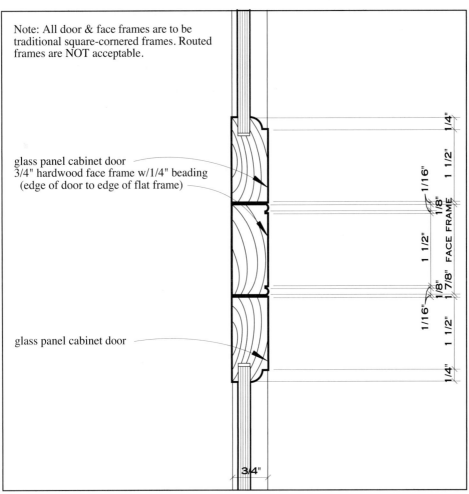

3/4"

Inset Door Meeting Door Detail

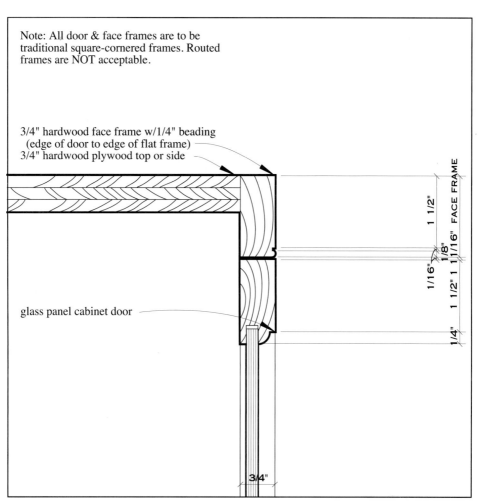

Note: All door & face frames are to be
traditional square-cornered frames. Routed
frames are NOT acceptable.

3/4" hardwood face frame w/1/4" beading
  (edge of door to edge of flat frame)
3/4" hardwood plywood top or side

glass panel cabinet door

1 1/2" FACE FRAME

1 1/2"

1/8"

1/16" 1 1/16"

1/16" 1 1/2"

1/4"

3/4"

DRAWING #

Inset Door Top or Side Detail

SCALE

HALF SIZE

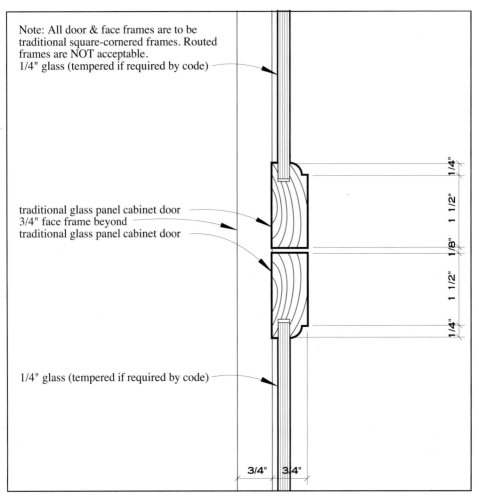

Note: All door & face frames are to be traditional square-cornered frames. Routed frames are NOT acceptable.
1/4" glass (tempered if required by code)

traditional glass panel cabinet door
3/4" face frame beyond
traditional glass panel cabinet door

1/4" glass (tempered if required by code)

1/4"

1 1/2"

1/8"

1 1/2"

1/4"

3/4"   3/4"

DRAWING #

Meeting Door Detail Without Frame

SCALE

HALF
SIZE

CDDG1011
114

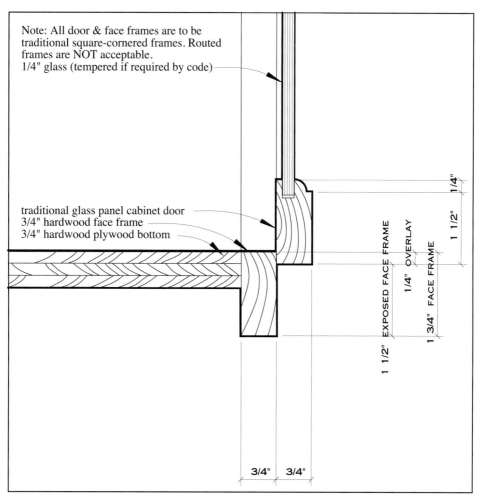

Note: All door & face frames are to be
traditional square-cornered frames. Routed
frames are NOT acceptable.
1/4" glass (tempered if required by code)

traditional glass panel cabinet door
3/4" hardwood face frame
3/4" hardwood plywood bottom

1/4"

1 1/2"

EXPOSED FACE FRAME

1/4" OVERLAY

1 3/4" FACE FRAME

1 1/2"

3/4"   3/4"

DRAWING #

Reveal Overlay Glazed Door Bottom

SCALE
HALF
SIZE

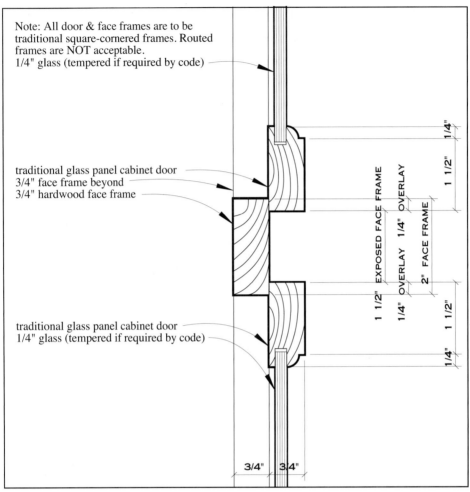

Note: All door & face frames are to be
traditional square-cornered frames. Routed
frames are NOT acceptable.
1/4" glass (tempered if required by code)

traditional glass panel cabinet door
3/4" face frame beyond
3/4" hardwood face frame

traditional glass panel cabinet door
1/4" glass (tempered if required by code)

1/4"

1 1/2"

1 1/2" EXPOSED FACE FRAME

1/4" OVERLAY 1/4" OVERLAY

2" FACE FRAME

1 1/2"

1/4"

3/4" | 3/4"

Reveal Overlay Meeting Glazed Doors

CDDG1013
116

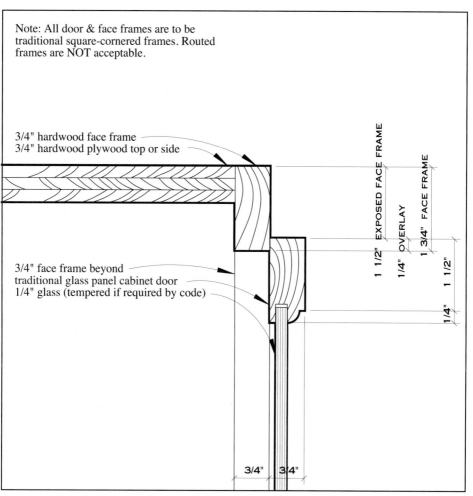

Note: All door & face frames are to be
traditional square-cornered frames. Routed
frames are NOT acceptable.

3/4" hardwood face frame
3/4" hardwood plywood top or side

3/4" face frame beyond
traditional glass panel cabinet door
1/4" glass (tempered if required by code)

1 1/2" EXPOSED FACE FRAME

1/4" OVERLAY

1 3/4" FACE FRAME

1 1/2"

1/4"

3/4"   3/4"

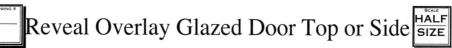

DRAWING #

Reveal Overlay Glazed Door Top or Side

SCALE
HALF
SIZE

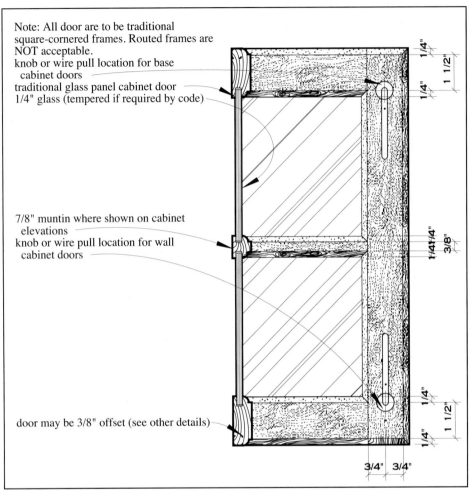

Note: All door are to be traditional
square-cornered frames. Routed frames are
NOT acceptable.
knob or wire pull location for base
  cabinet doors
traditional glass panel cabinet door
1/4" glass (tempered if required by code)

7/8" muntin where shown on cabinet
  elevations
knob or wire pull location for wall
  cabinet doors

door may be 3/8" offset (see other details)

1/4"
1 1/2"
1/4"
1/4"
1/4"
3/8"
1/4"
1 1/2"
1/4"
3/4"   3/4"

Glass Panel Door Section/Elevation

SCALE
$\frac{3"}{1'-0"}$

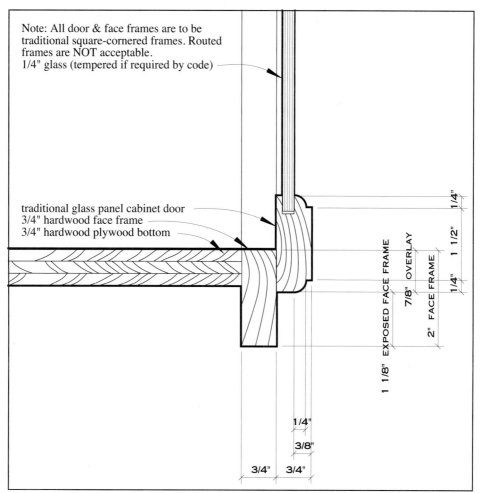

Note: All door & face frames are to be
traditional square-cornered frames. Routed
frames are NOT acceptable.
1/4" glass (tempered if required by code)

traditional glass panel cabinet door
3/4" hardwood face frame
3/4" hardwood plywood bottom

1/4"

1 1/2"

1/4"

7/8" OVERLAY

2" FACE FRAME

1 1/8" EXPOSED FACE FRAME

1/4"

3/8"

3/4"   3/4"

Flush Overlay Glazed Door Bottom

SCALE
HALF
SIZE

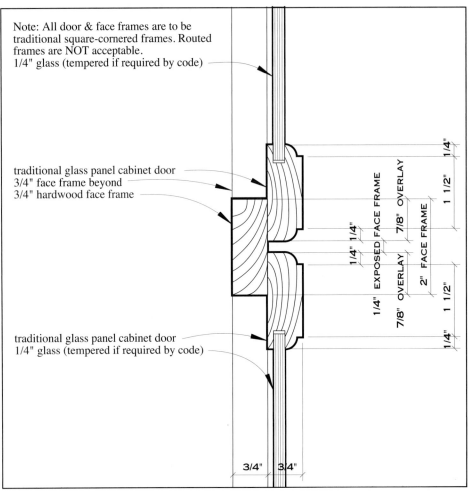

Note: All door & face frames are to be
traditional square-cornered frames. Routed
frames are NOT acceptable.
1/4" glass (tempered if required by code)

traditional glass panel cabinet door
3/4" face frame beyond
3/4" hardwood face frame

traditional glass panel cabinet door
1/4" glass (tempered if required by code)

1/4"

1 1/2"

7/8" OVERLAY

1/4" EXPOSED FACE FRAME

1/4" 1/4"

2" FACE FRAME

7/8" OVERLAY

1 1/2"

1/4"

3/4" 3/4"

DRAWING #

Flush Overlay Meeting Glazed Doors

SCALE
HALF
SIZE

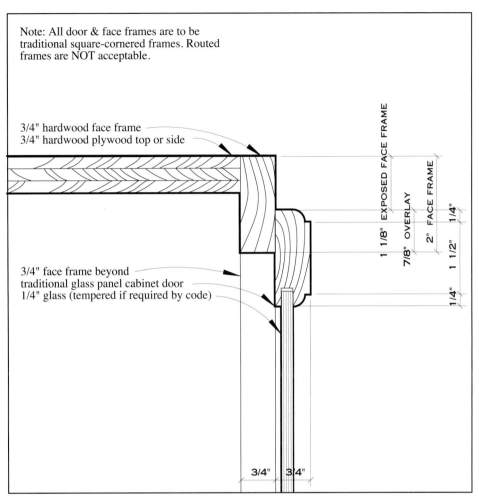

Note: All door & face frames are to be traditional square-cornered frames. Routed frames are NOT acceptable.

3/4" hardwood face frame
3/4" hardwood plywood top or side

1 1/8" EXPOSED FACE FRAME

7/8" OVERLAY

2" FACE FRAME

1/4"

1 1/2"

1/4"

3/4" face frame beyond
traditional glass panel cabinet door
1/4" glass (tempered if required by code)

3/4"   3/4"

 DRAWING #

Flush Overlay Glazed Door Top or Side

 SCALE HALF SIZE

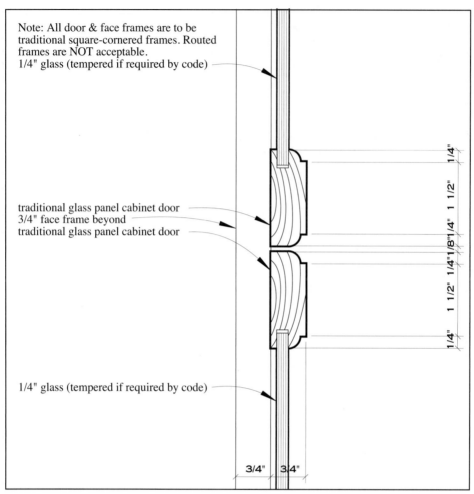

Note: All door & face frames are to be traditional square-cornered frames. Routed frames are NOT acceptable.
1/4" glass (tempered if required by code)

traditional glass panel cabinet door
3/4" face frame beyond
traditional glass panel cabinet door

1/4" glass (tempered if required by code)

1/4"
1 1/2"
1/4"
1/8"
1/4"
1 1/2"
1/4"

3/4"   3/4"

DRAWING #

Meeting Door Detail Without Frame

SCALE
HALF
SIZE

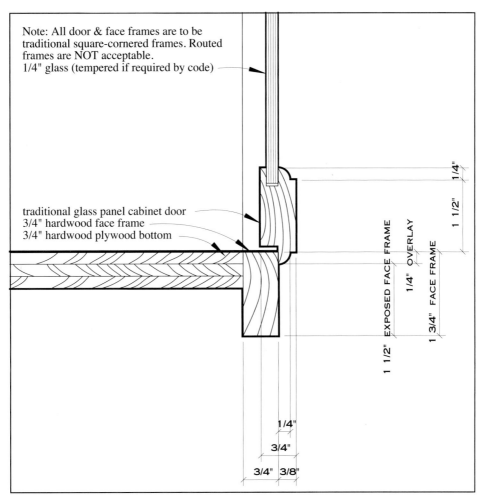

Note: All door & face frames are to be
traditional square-cornered frames. Routed
frames are NOT acceptable.
1/4" glass (tempered if required by code)

traditional glass panel cabinet door
3/4" hardwood face frame
3/4" hardwood plywood bottom

1/4"

1 1/2"

1 1/2" EXPOSED FACE FRAME

1/4" OVERLAY

1 3/4" FACE FRAME

1/4"

3/4"

3/4"   3/8"

3/8" Offset Glazed Door Bottom

SCALE
HALF
SIZE

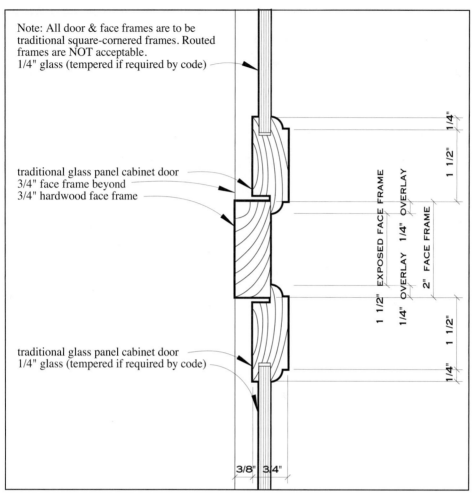

Note: All door & face frames are to be traditional square-cornered frames. Routed frames are NOT acceptable.
1/4" glass (tempered if required by code)

traditional glass panel cabinet door
3/4" face frame beyond
3/4" hardwood face frame

traditional glass panel cabinet door
1/4" glass (tempered if required by code)

1/4"
1 1/2"
1 1/2" EXPOSED FACE FRAME
1/4" OVERLAY   1/4" OVERLAY
2" FACE FRAME
1 1/2"
1/4"

3/8"   3/4"

DRAWING #

3/8" Offset Meeting Glazed Doors

SCALE
HALF
SIZE

Note: All door & face frames are to be
traditional square-cornered frames. Routed
frames are NOT acceptable.

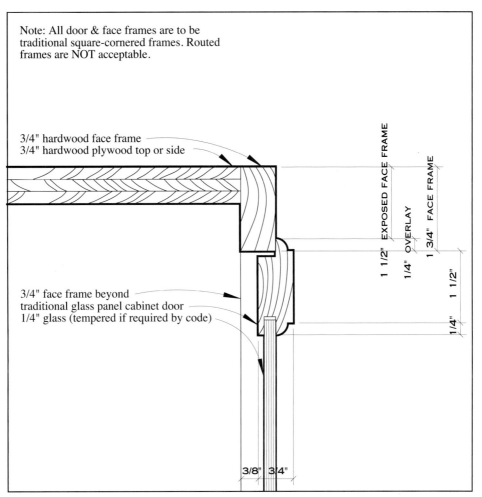

3/4" hardwood face frame
3/4" hardwood plywood top or side

3/4" face frame beyond
traditional glass panel cabinet door
1/4" glass (tempered if required by code)

EXPOSED FACE FRAME

1 1/2"

1/4" OVERLAY

1 3/4" FACE FRAME

1 1/2"

1/4"

3/8" 3/4"

 3/8" Offset Glazed Door Top or Side

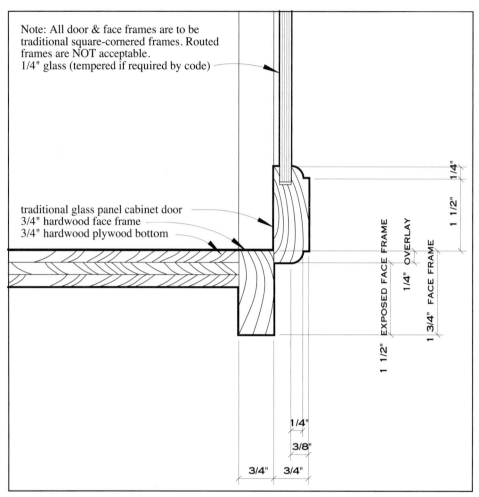

Note: All door & face frames are to be traditional square-cornered frames. Routed frames are NOT acceptable.
1/4" glass (tempered if required by code)

traditional glass panel cabinet door
3/4" hardwood face frame
3/4" hardwood plywood bottom

1/4"

1 1/2"

1 1/2" EXPOSED FACE FRAME

1/4" OVERLAY

1 3/4" FACE FRAME

1/4"

3/8"

3/4" 3/4"

DRAWING #

Reveal Overlay Glazed Door Bottom

SCALE
HALF SIZE

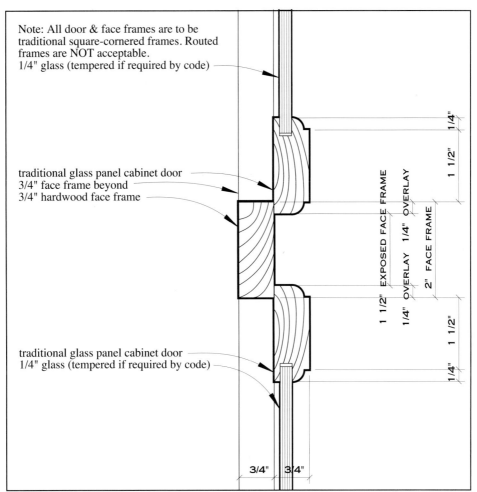

Note: All door & face frames are to be traditional square-cornered frames. Routed frames are NOT acceptable.
1/4" glass (tempered if required by code)

traditional glass panel cabinet door
3/4" face frame beyond
3/4" hardwood face frame

traditional glass panel cabinet door
1/4" glass (tempered if required by code)

1/4"

1 1/2"

1 1/2" EXPOSED FACE FRAME

1/4" OVERLAY

1/4" OVERLAY

2" FACE FRAME

1 1/2"

1/4"

3/4"   3/4"

Reveal Overlay Meeting Glazed Doors

DRAWING #

SCALE
HALF
SIZE

Note: All door & face frames are to be
traditional square-cornered frames. Routed
frames are NOT acceptable.

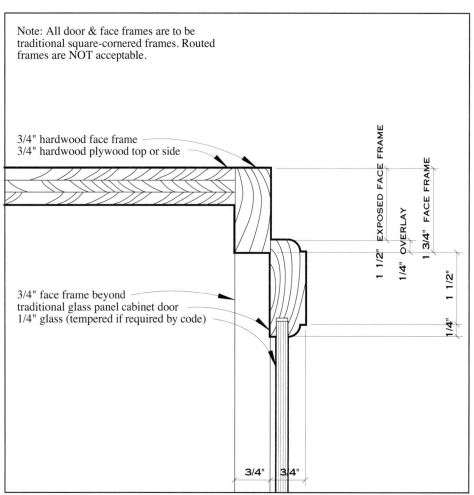

3/4" hardwood face frame
3/4" hardwood plywood top or side

1 1/2" EXPOSED FACE FRAME

1/4" OVERLAY

1 3/4" FACE FRAME

1 1/2"

1/4"

3/4" face frame beyond
traditional glass panel cabinet door
1/4" glass (tempered if required by code)

3/4"   3/4"

DRAWING #

Reveal Overlay Glazed Door Top or Side

SCALE
HALF
SIZE

Note: All door are to be traditional
square-cornered frames. Routed frames are
NOT acceptable.
knob or wire pull location for base
  cabinet doors
glass panel cabinet door
1/4" glass (tempered if required by code)

7/8" muntin where shown on cabinet
  elevations
knob or wire pull location for wall
  cabinet doors

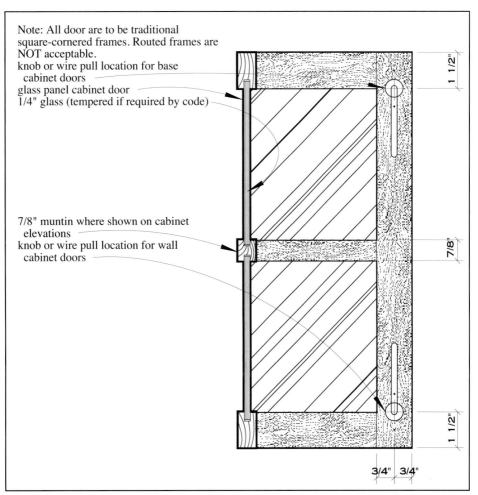

1 1/2"

7/8"

1 1/2"

3/4" 3/4"

Glass Panel Door Section/Elevation

DRAWING #

SCALE
$\dfrac{3"}{1'\text{-}0"}$

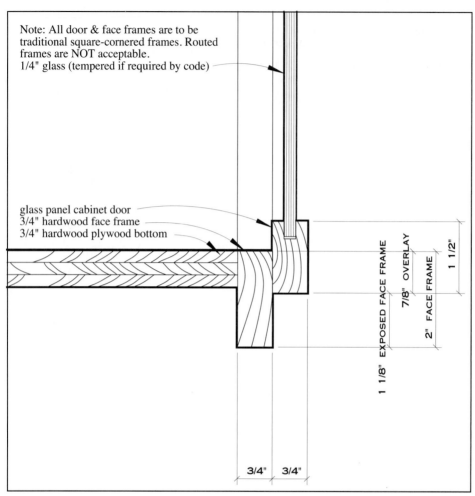

Note: All door & face frames are to be
traditional square-cornered frames. Routed
frames are NOT acceptable.
1/4" glass (tempered if required by code)

glass panel cabinet door
3/4" hardwood face frame
3/4" hardwood plywood bottom

1 1/8" EXPOSED FACE FRAME

7/8" OVERLAY

2" FACE FRAME

1 1/2"

3/4"   3/4"

DRAWING #

Flush Overlay Glazed Door Bottom

SCALE
HALF
SIZE

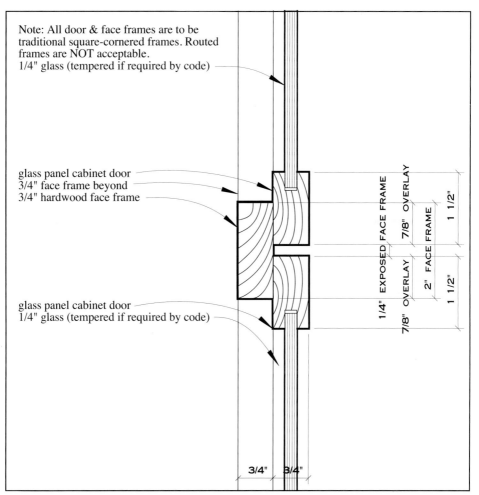

Note: All door & face frames are to be
traditional square-cornered frames. Routed
frames are NOT acceptable.
1/4" glass (tempered if required by code)

glass panel cabinet door
3/4" face frame beyond
3/4" hardwood face frame

glass panel cabinet door
1/4" glass (tempered if required by code)

1/4" EXPOSED FACE FRAME

7/8" OVERLAY

1 1/2"

7/8" FACE FRAME

2" FACE FRAME

1 1/2"

7/8" OVERLAY

3/4" 3/4"

DRAWING #

Flush Overlay Meeting Glazed Doors

SCALE
HALF
SIZE

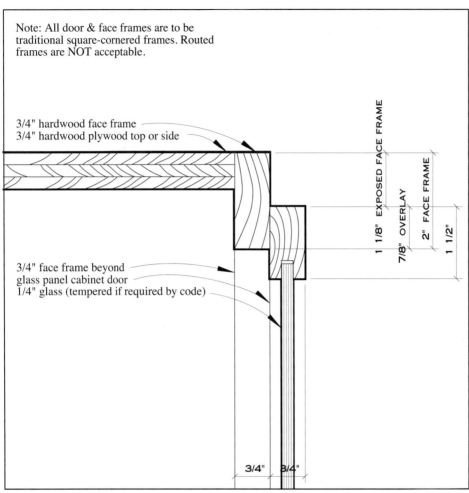

Note: All door & face frames are to be traditional square-cornered frames. Routed frames are NOT acceptable.

3/4" hardwood face frame
3/4" hardwood plywood top or side

1 1/8" EXPOSED FACE FRAME

7/8" OVERLAY

2" FACE FRAME

1 1/2"

3/4" face frame beyond
glass panel cabinet door
1/4" glass (tempered if required by code)

3/4"   3/4"

DRAWING #

Flush Overlay Glazed Door Top or Side

SCALE
HALF
SIZE

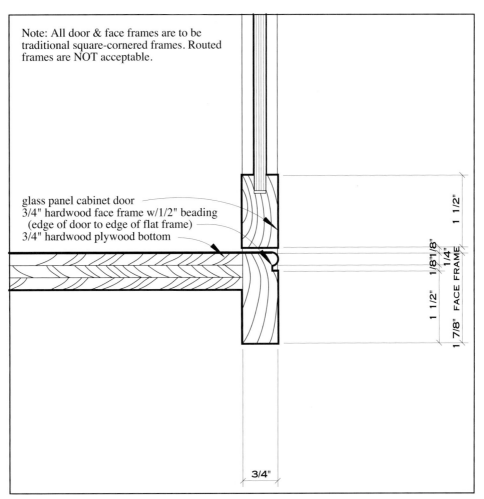

Note: All door & face frames are to be
traditional square-cornered frames. Routed
frames are NOT acceptable.

glass panel cabinet door
3/4" hardwood face frame w/1/2" beading
(edge of door to edge of flat frame)
3/4" hardwood plywood bottom

1 1/2"

1/8" 1/8"
1/4"
1 1/2"
1 7/8" FACE FRAME

3/4"

Inset Door Bottom Detail

Note: All door & face frames are to be
traditional square-cornered frames. Routed
frames are NOT acceptable.

glass panel cabinet door
3/4" hardwood face frame w/1/2" beading
 (edge of door to edge of flat frame)

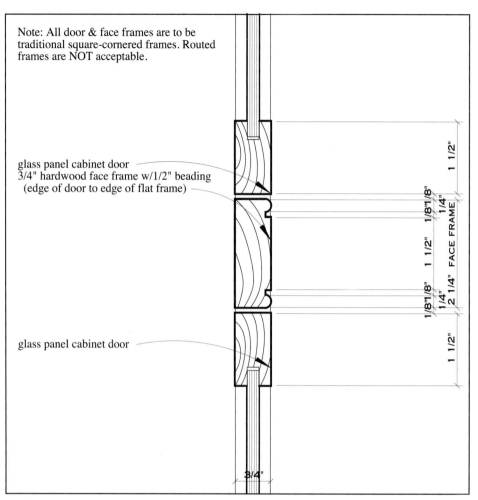

glass panel cabinet door

1 1/2"

1/8" 1/8"
1/4"

1 1/2" FACE FRAME

1/8" 1/8"
1/4"
2 1/4"

1 1/2"

3/4"

DRAWING #

Inset Door Meeting Door Detail

SCALE
HALF
SIZE

Note: All door & face frames are to be
traditional square-cornered frames. Routed
frames are NOT acceptable.

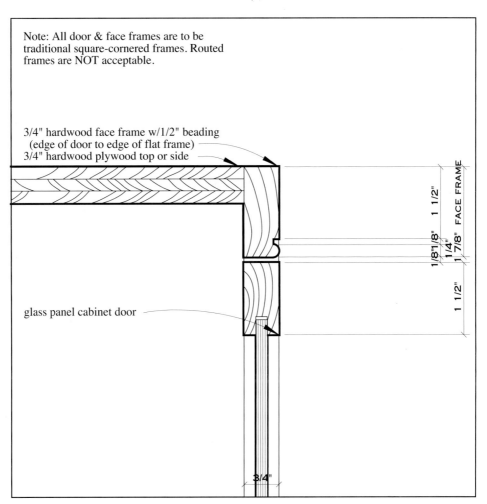

3/4" hardwood face frame w/1/2" beading
  (edge of door to edge of flat frame)
3/4" hardwood plywood top or side

glass panel cabinet door

1 1/2" FACE FRAME

1 1/2"

1/8"
1/4"
1 7/8"

3/4"

DRAWING #

Inset Door Top or Side Detail

SCALE
HALF
SIZE

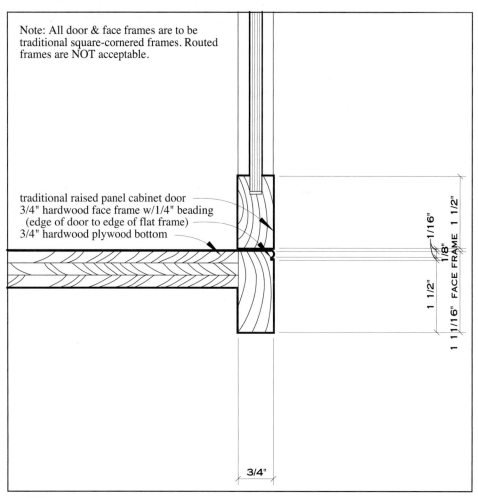

Note: All door & face frames are to be
traditional square-cornered frames. Routed
frames are NOT acceptable.

traditional raised panel cabinet door
3/4" hardwood face frame w/1/4" beading
 (edge of door to edge of flat frame)
3/4" hardwood plywood bottom

1/16"

1/8"

1 1/2"

1 1/2" FACE FRAME 1 1/2"

1 1/16" FACE FRAME

3/4"

Inset Door Bottom Detail

Note: All door & face frames are to be
traditional square-cornered frames. Routed
frames are NOT acceptable.

traditional raised panel cabinet door
3/4" hardwood face frame w/1/4" beading
(edge of door to edge of flat frame)

traditional raised panel cabinet door

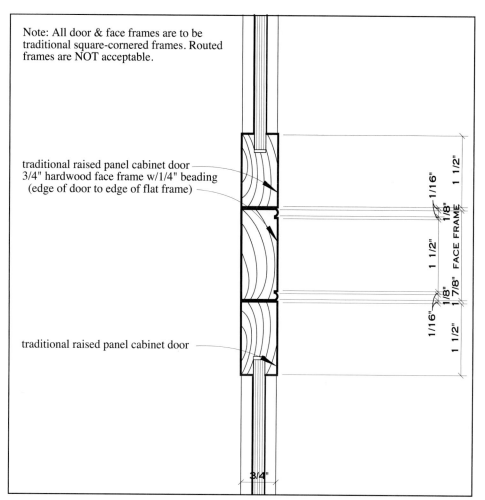

3/4"

DRAWING #

Inset Door Meeting Door Detail

SCALE
HALF
SIZE

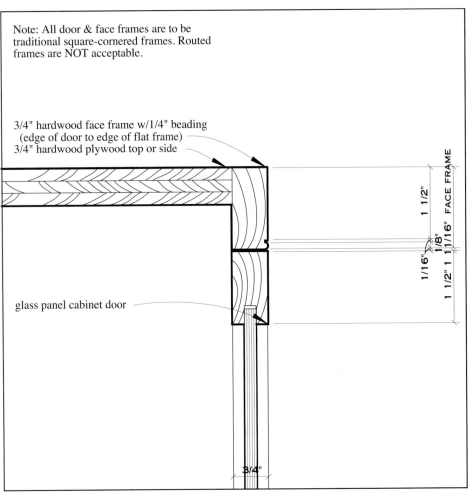

Note: All door & face frames are to be
traditional square-cornered frames. Routed
frames are NOT acceptable.

3/4" hardwood face frame w/1/4" beading
(edge of door to edge of flat frame)
3/4" hardwood plywood top or side

glass panel cabinet door

1 1/2"

1 1/16" FACE FRAME

1/16" 1/8"

1 1/2" 1 1/16"

3/4"

DRAWING #

Inset Door Top or Side Detail

SCALE
HALF
SIZE

CDDG3010
138

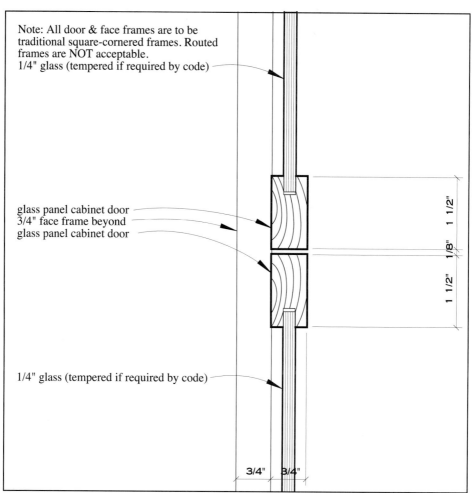

Note: All door & face frames are to be
traditional square-cornered frames. Routed
frames are NOT acceptable.
1/4" glass (tempered if required by code)

glass panel cabinet door
3/4" face frame beyond
glass panel cabinet door

1 1/2"

1/8"

1 1/2"

1/4" glass (tempered if required by code)

3/4"   3/4"

Meeting Door Detail Without Frame

SCALE
HALF
SIZE

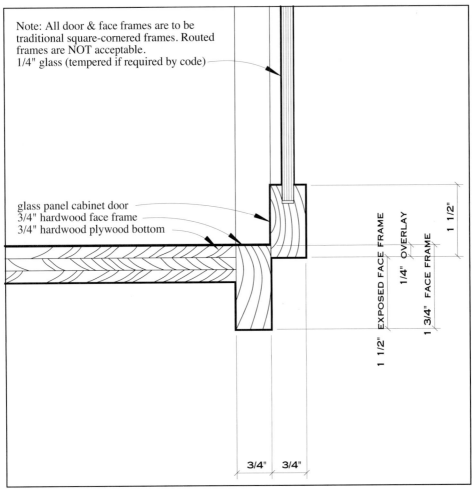

Note: All door & face frames are to be traditional square-cornered frames. Routed frames are NOT acceptable.
1/4" glass (tempered if required by code)

glass panel cabinet door
3/4" hardwood face frame
3/4" hardwood plywood bottom

1 1/2" EXPOSED FACE FRAME

1/4" OVERLAY

3/4" FACE FRAME

1 1/2"

1 3/4"

3/4" 3/4"

DRAWING #

Reveal Overlay Glazed Door Bottom

SCALE
HALF
SIZE

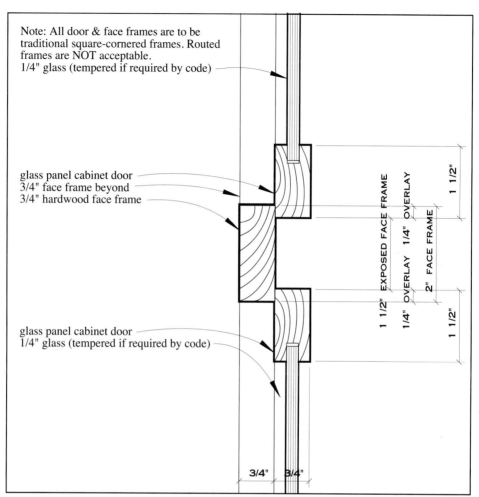

Note: All door & face frames are to be
traditional square-cornered frames. Routed
frames are NOT acceptable.
1/4" glass (tempered if required by code)

glass panel cabinet door
3/4" face frame beyond
3/4" hardwood face frame

glass panel cabinet door
1/4" glass (tempered if required by code)

1 1/2" EXPOSED FACE FRAME

1/4" OVERLAY

2" FACE FRAME

1/4" OVERLAY

1 1/2"

1 1/2"

 3/4" 3/4"

Reveal Overlay Meeting Glazed Doors

DRAWING #

SCALE
**HALF
SIZE**

CDDG3013
141

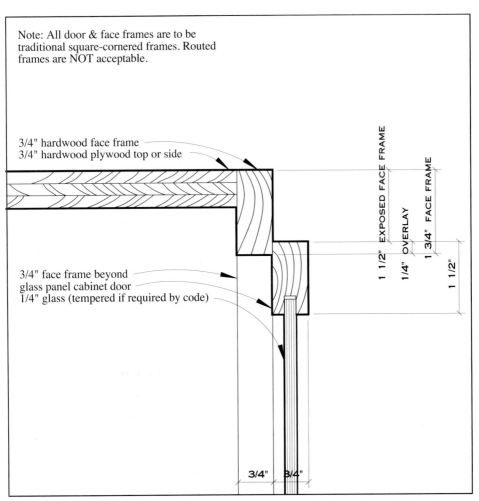

Note: All door & face frames are to be
traditional square-cornered frames. Routed
frames are NOT acceptable.

3/4" hardwood face frame
3/4" hardwood plywood top or side

3/4" face frame beyond
glass panel cabinet door
1/4" glass (tempered if required by code)

1 1/2" EXPOSED FACE FRAME

1/4" OVERLAY

1 3/4" FACE FRAME

1 1/2"

3/4"   3/4"

Reveal Overlay Glazed Door Top or Side

DRAWING #

SCALE
HALF
SIZE

Note: All door are to be traditional
square-cornered frames. Routed frames are
NOT acceptable.
knob or wire pull location for base
    cabinet doors
traditional raised panel cabinet door
knob or wire pull location for wall
    cabinet doors

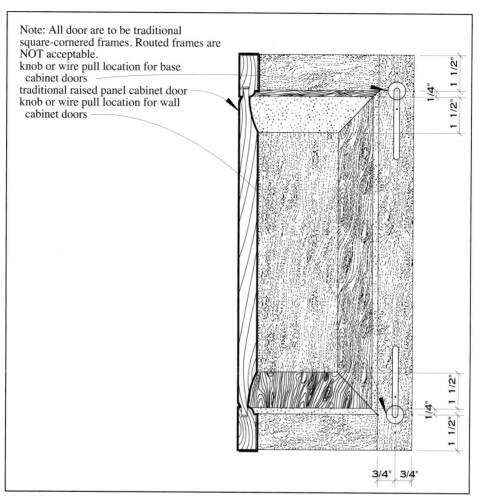

1 1/2"
1/4"
1 1/2"
1 1/2"

1/4"
1 1/2"
1 1/2"

3/4"   3/4"

Raised Panel Door Section/Elevation

SCALE
3"
1'-0"

DRAWING #

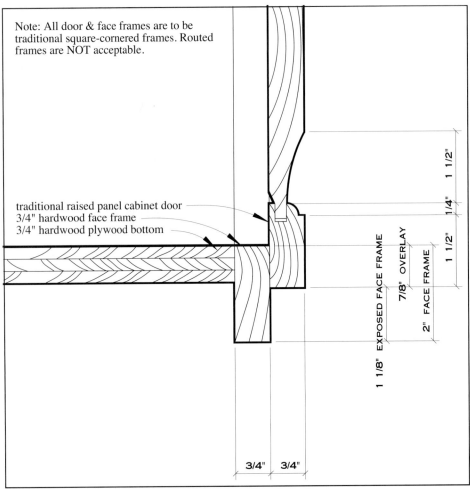

Note: All door & face frames are to be traditional square-cornered frames. Routed frames are NOT acceptable.

traditional raised panel cabinet door
3/4" hardwood face frame
3/4" hardwood plywood bottom

1 1/2"

1/4"

1 1/2"

1 1/8" EXPOSED FACE FRAME

7/8" OVERLAY

2" FACE FRAME

3/4"   3/4"

Flush Overlay Door Bottom Detail

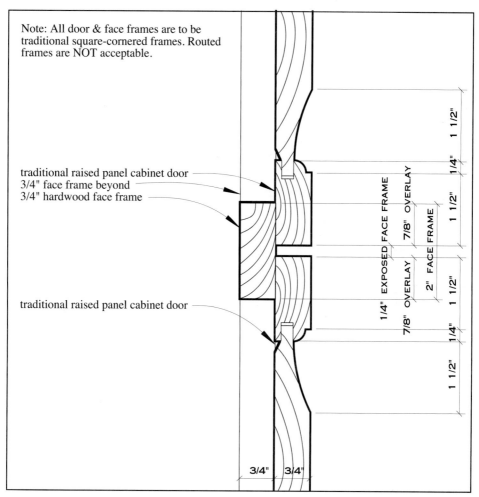

Note: All door & face frames are to be
traditional square-cornered frames. Routed
frames are NOT acceptable.

traditional raised panel cabinet door
3/4" face frame beyond
3/4" hardwood face frame

traditional raised panel cabinet door

1 1/2"

1/4"

1 1/2"

1 1/2"

1/4"

1 1/2"

1/4" EXPOSED FACE FRAME
7/8" OVERLAY

7/8" OVERLAY
1/4" EXPOSED FACE FRAME

2" FACE FRAME

3/4" 3/4"

DRAWING #

Flush Overlay Meeting Door Detail

SCALE
HALF
SIZE

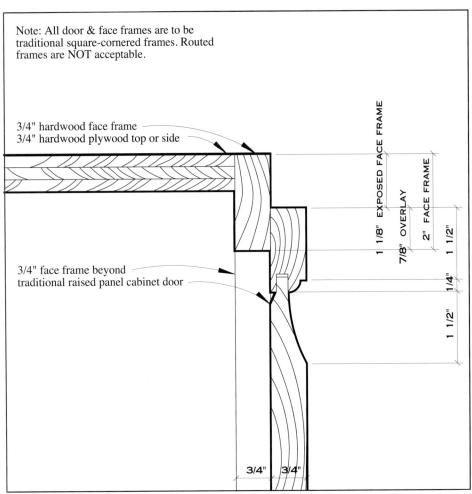

Note: All door & face frames are to be
traditional square-cornered frames. Routed
frames are NOT acceptable.

3/4" hardwood face frame
3/4" hardwood plywood top or side

3/4" face frame beyond
traditional raised panel cabinet door

1 1/8" EXPOSED FACE FRAME

7/8" OVERLAY

2" FACE FRAME

1 1/2"

1/4"

1 1/2"

3/4"   3/4"

DRAWING #

Flush Overlay Door Top or Side Detail

SCALE
**HALF
SIZE**

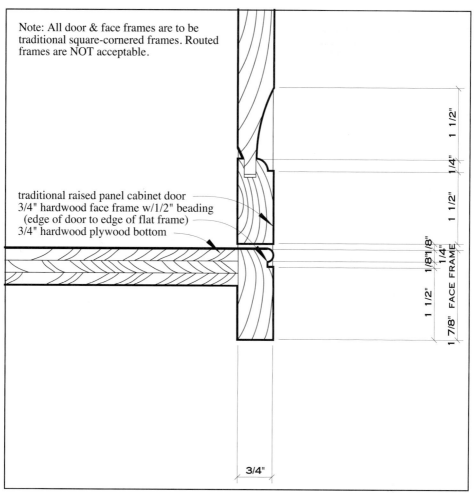

Note: All door & face frames are to be traditional square-cornered frames. Routed frames are NOT acceptable.

traditional raised panel cabinet door
3/4" hardwood face frame w/1/2" beading
(edge of door to edge of flat frame)
3/4" hardwood plywood bottom

1 1/2"

1/4"

1 1/2"

1/8"1/8"

1/4"

1 1/2"

1 7/8"

FACE FRAME

3/4"

DRAWING #

Inset Door Bottom Detail

SCALE
HALF
SIZE

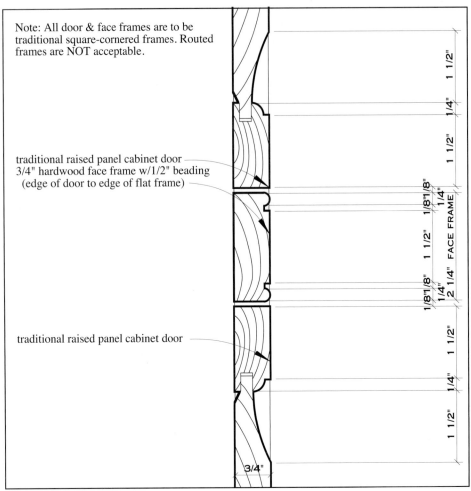

Note: All door & face frames are to be traditional square-cornered frames. Routed frames are NOT acceptable.

traditional raised panel cabinet door
3/4" hardwood face frame w/1/2" beading
(edge of door to edge of flat frame)

traditional raised panel cabinet door

1 1/2"

1/4"

1 1/2"

1/8" 1/8"
1/4"
1 1/2" FACE FRAME

1/8" 1/8"
1/4"
2 1/4"

1 1/2"

1/4"

1 1/2"

3/4"

DRAWING #

Inset Door Meeting Door Detail

SCALE
HALF
SIZE

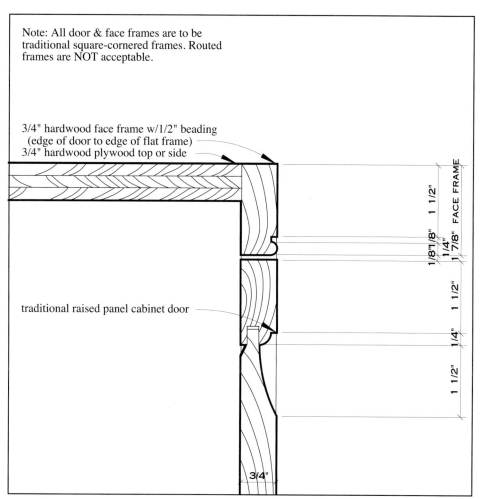

Note: All door & face frames are to be traditional square-cornered frames. Routed frames are NOT acceptable.

3/4" hardwood face frame w/1/2" beading
 (edge of door to edge of flat frame)
3/4" hardwood plywood top or side

traditional raised panel cabinet door

1 1/2"
1/8" 1/8" 1/4"
1 7/8" FACE FRAME
1 1/2"
1/4"
1 1/2"

3/4"

DRAWING #

Inset Door Top or Side Detail

SCALE
HALF
SIZE

CDDR1007
149

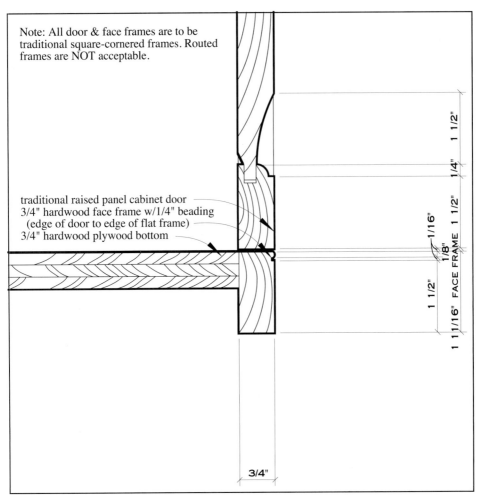

Note: All door & face frames are to be traditional square-cornered frames. Routed frames are NOT acceptable.

traditional raised panel cabinet door
3/4" hardwood face frame w/1/4" beading (edge of door to edge of flat frame)
3/4" hardwood plywood bottom

1 1/2"

1/4"

1 1/2"

1/16"

1/8"

FACE FRAME

1 1/2"

1 1/2"

1 11/16"

3/4"

Inset Door Bottom Detail

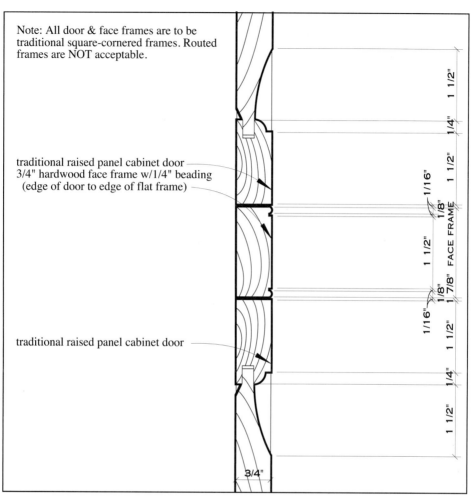

Note: All door & face frames are to be traditional square-cornered frames. Routed frames are NOT acceptable.

traditional raised panel cabinet door 3/4" hardwood face frame w/1/4" beading (edge of door to edge of flat frame)

traditional raised panel cabinet door

3/4"

1 1/2"

1/4"

1 1/2"

1/16"

1/8"

1 1/2"   FACE FRAME

1/8"

1 7/8"

1/16"

1 1/2"

1/4"

1 1/2"

DRAWING #

Inset Door Meeting Door Detail

SCALE
HALF
SIZE

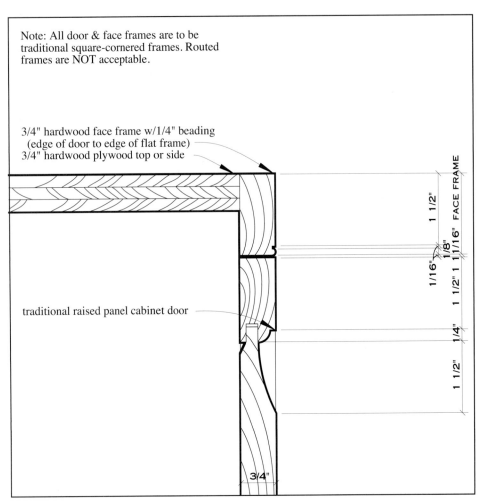

Note: All door & face frames are to be
traditional square-cornered frames. Routed
frames are NOT acceptable.

3/4" hardwood face frame w/1/4" beading
  (edge of door to edge of flat frame)
3/4" hardwood plywood top or side

1 1/2" FACE FRAME

1/16" 1/8" 1 11/16"

traditional raised panel cabinet door

1 1/2"

1/4"

1 1/2"

3/4"

DRAWING #

Inset Door Top or Side Detail

SCALE
HALF
SIZE

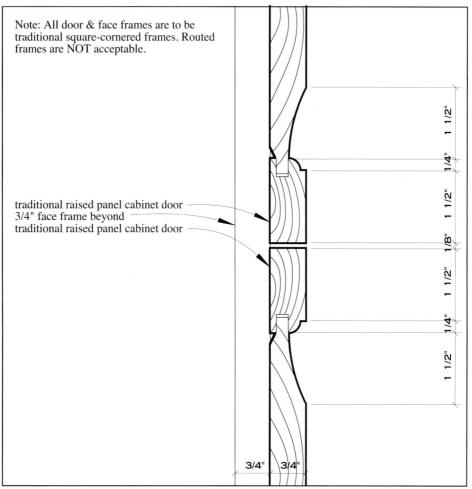

Note: All door & face frames are to be
traditional square-cornered frames. Routed
frames are NOT acceptable.

traditional raised panel cabinet door
3/4" face frame beyond
traditional raised panel cabinet door

1 1/2"

1/4"

1 1/2"

1/8"

1 1/2"

1/4"

1 1/2"

3/4"   3/4"

Meeting Door Detail Without Frame

SCALE
HALF
SIZE

CDDR1011
153

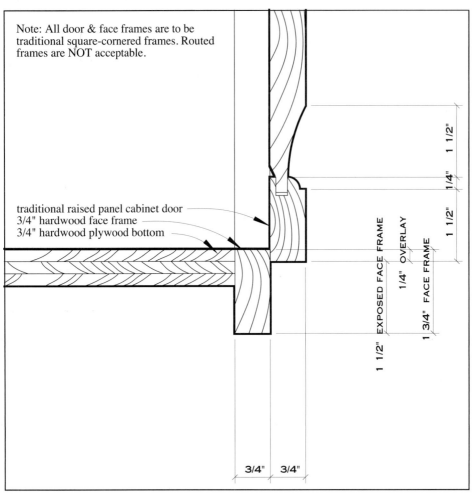

Note: All door & face frames are to be
traditional square-cornered frames. Routed
frames are NOT acceptable.

traditional raised panel cabinet door
3/4" hardwood face frame
3/4" hardwood plywood bottom

1 1/2"

1/4"

1 1/2"

1 1/2" EXPOSED FACE FRAME

1/4" OVERLAY

1 3/4" FACE FRAME

3/4"   3/4"

Reveal Overlay Door Bottom Detail

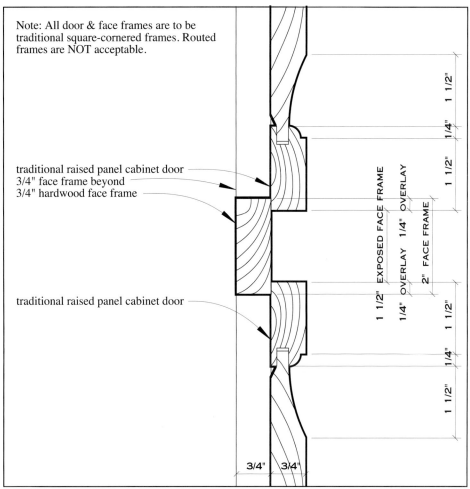

Note: All door & face frames are to be traditional square-cornered frames. Routed frames are NOT acceptable.

traditional raised panel cabinet door
3/4" face frame beyond
3/4" hardwood face frame

traditional raised panel cabinet door

1 1/2"
1/4"
1 1/2"
1 1/2" EXPOSED FACE FRAME
1/4" OVERLAY 1/4" OVERLAY
2" FACE FRAME
1 1/2"
1/4"
1 1/2"

3/4" 3/4"

Reveal Overlay Meeting Door Detail

SCALE
HALF
SIZE

DRAWING #

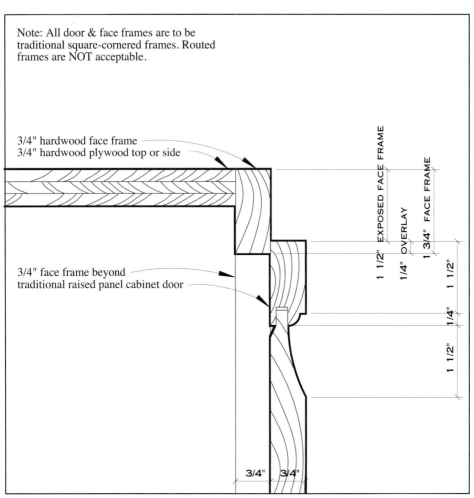

Note: All door & face frames are to be
traditional square-cornered frames. Routed
frames are NOT acceptable.

3/4" hardwood face frame
3/4" hardwood plywood top or side

3/4" face frame beyond
traditional raised panel cabinet door

1 1/2" EXPOSED FACE FRAME

1/4" OVERLAY

1 3/4" FACE FRAME

1 1/2"

1/4"

1 1/2"

3/4" 3/4"

Reveal Overlay Door Top or Side Detail

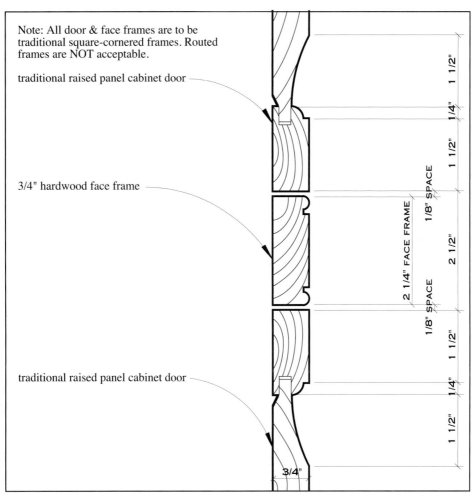

Note: All door & face frames are to be
traditional square-cornered frames. Routed
frames are NOT acceptable.

traditional raised panel cabinet door

3/4" hardwood face frame

traditional raised panel cabinet door

1 1/2"

1/4"

1 1/2"

1/8" SPACE

2 1/4" FACE FRAME

2 1/2"

1/8" SPACE

1 1/2"

1/4"

1 1/2"

3/4"

DRAWING #

Meeting Door Detail

SCALE
HALF
SIZE

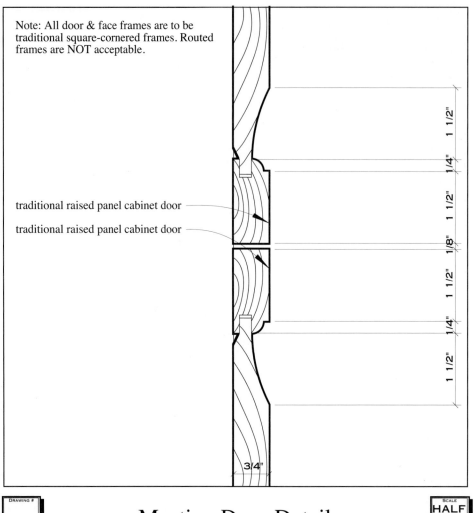

Note: All door & face frames are to be traditional square-cornered frames. Routed frames are NOT acceptable.

1 1/2"

1/4"

1 1/2"

1/8"

1 1/2"

1/4"

1 1/2"

traditional raised panel cabinet door

traditional raised panel cabinet door

3/4"

DRAWING #

Meeting Door Detail

SCALE
HALF
SIZE

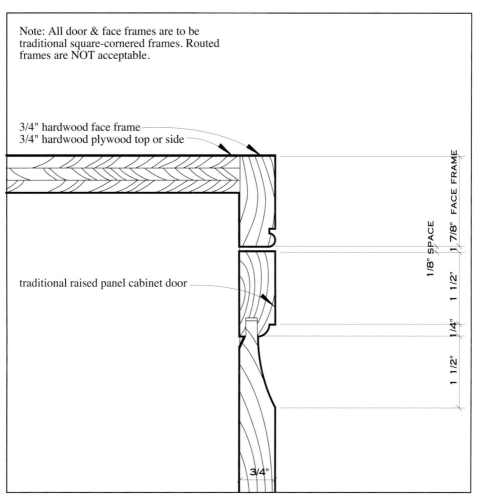

Note: All door & face frames are to be
traditional square-cornered frames. Routed
frames are NOT acceptable.

3/4" hardwood face frame
3/4" hardwood plywood top or side

traditional raised panel cabinet door

1/8" SPACE

1 7/8" FACE FRAME

1 1/2"

1/4"

1 1/2"

3/4"

Flush Door Top or Side Detail

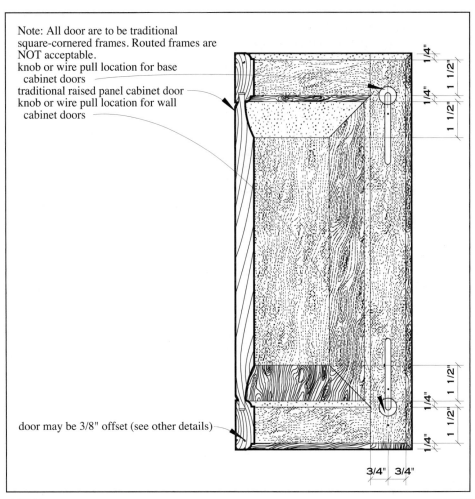

Note: All door are to be traditional square-cornered frames. Routed frames are NOT acceptable.
knob or wire pull location for base cabinet doors
traditional raised panel cabinet door
knob or wire pull location for wall cabinet doors

door may be 3/8" offset (see other details)

1/4"
1/4"
1 1/2"
1/4"
1 1/2"
1 1/2"

1 1/2"
1/4"
1 1/2"
1/4"

3/4"   3/4"

DRAWING #

Raised Panel Door Section/Elevation

SCALE
$\frac{3"}{1'-0"}$

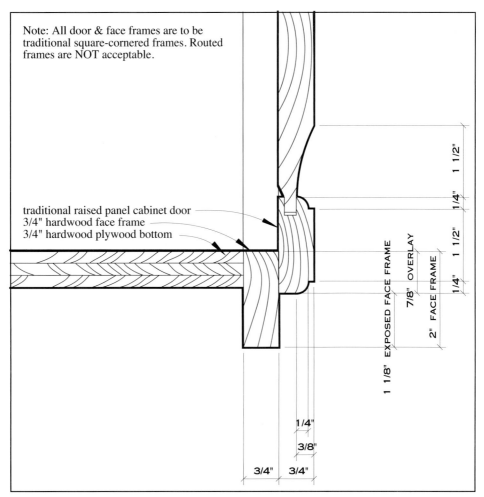

Note: All door & face frames are to be
traditional square-cornered frames. Routed
frames are NOT acceptable.

traditional raised panel cabinet door
3/4" hardwood face frame
3/4" hardwood plywood bottom

1 1/2"

1/4"

1 1/2"

1/4"

1 1/8" EXPOSED FACE FRAME

7/8" OVERLAY

2" FACE FRAME

1/4"

3/8"

3/4"   3/4"

Flush Overlay Door Bottom Detail

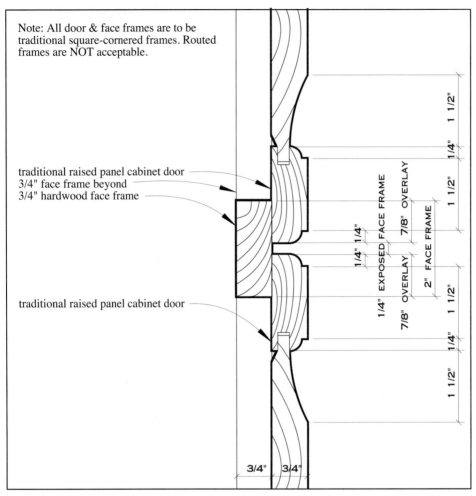

Note: All door & face frames are to be
traditional square-cornered frames. Routed
frames are NOT acceptable.

traditional raised panel cabinet door
3/4" face frame beyond
3/4" hardwood face frame

traditional raised panel cabinet door

1 1/2"

1/4"

1 1/2"

7/8" OVERLAY

1/4" EXPOSED FACE FRAME

2" FACE FRAME

1/4" 1/4"

7/8" OVERLAY

1 1/2"

1/4"

1 1/2"

 3/4" 3/4"

Flush Overlay Meeting Door Detail

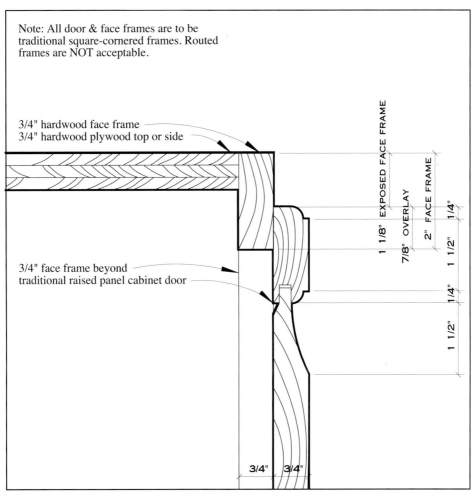

Note: All door & face frames are to be
traditional square-cornered frames. Routed
frames are NOT acceptable.

3/4" hardwood face frame
3/4" hardwood plywood top or side

3/4" face frame beyond
traditional raised panel cabinet door

1 1/8" EXPOSED FACE FRAME

7/8" OVERLAY

2" FACE FRAME

1/4"

1 1/2"

1/4"

1 1/2"

3/4"   3/4"

  Flush Overlay Door Top or Side Detail

DRAWING #

SCALE
HALF
SIZE

CDDR2004
163

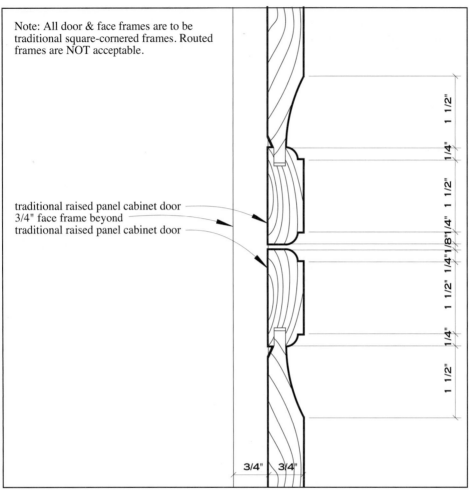

Note: All door & face frames are to be
traditional square-cornered frames. Routed
frames are NOT acceptable.

1 1/2"

1/4"

1 1/2"

1/4" 1/8" 1/4"

traditional raised panel cabinet door
3/4" face frame beyond
traditional raised panel cabinet door

1 1/2"

1/4"

1 1/2"

3/4"   3/4"

DRAWING #

Meeting Door Detail Without Frame

SCALE
HALF
SIZE

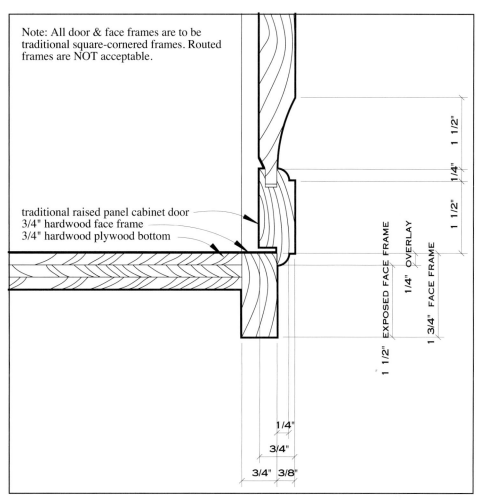

Note: All door & face frames are to be traditional square-cornered frames. Routed frames are NOT acceptable.

traditional raised panel cabinet door
3/4" hardwood face frame
3/4" hardwood plywood bottom

1 1/2"

1/4"

1 1/2"

1 1/2" EXPOSED FACE FRAME

1/4" OVERLAY

1 3/4" FACE FRAME

1/4"

3/4"

3/4" 3/8"

DRAWING #

3/8" Offset Door Bottom Detail

SCALE
HALF
SIZE

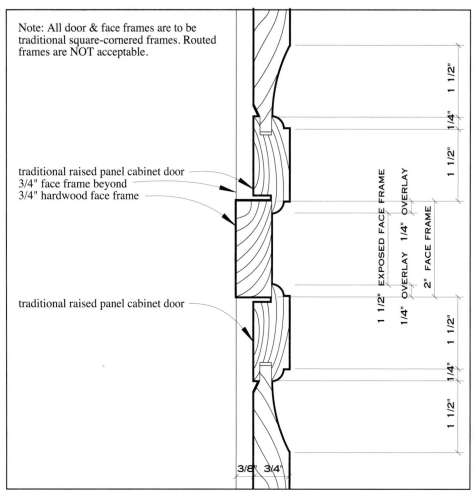

Note: All door & face frames are to be traditional square-cornered frames. Routed frames are NOT acceptable.

traditional raised panel cabinet door
3/4" face frame beyond
3/4" hardwood face frame

traditional raised panel cabinet door

1 1/2"

1/4"

1 1/2"

1 1/2" EXPOSED FACE FRAME

1/4" OVERLAY

1/4" OVERLAY

2" FACE FRAME

1 1/2"

1/4"

1 1/2"

3/8" 3/4"

3/8" Offset Meeting Door Detail

SCALE
HALF
SIZE

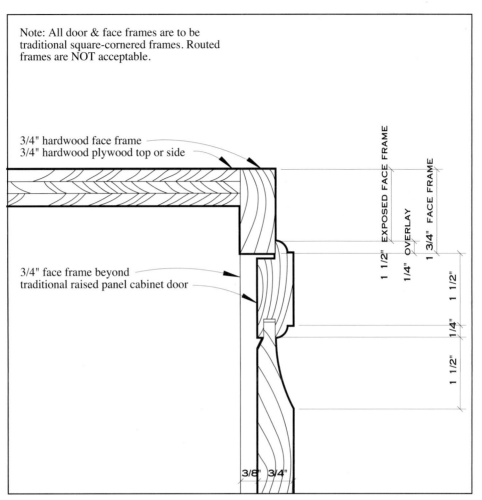

Note: All door & face frames are to be
traditional square-cornered frames. Routed
frames are NOT acceptable.

3/4" hardwood face frame
3/4" hardwood plywood top or side

3/4" face frame beyond
traditional raised panel cabinet door

1 1/2" EXPOSED FACE FRAME

1/4" OVERLAY

1 3/4" FACE FRAME

1 1/2"

1/4"

1 1/2"

3/8"   3/4"

3/8" Offset Door Top or Side Detail

SCALE
HALF
SIZE

DRAWING #

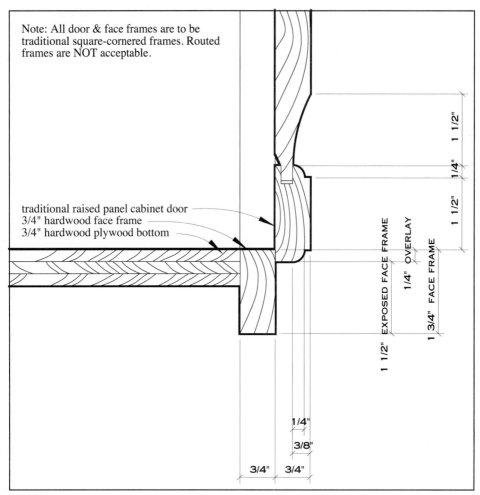

Note: All door & face frames are to be traditional square-cornered frames. Routed frames are NOT acceptable.

traditional raised panel cabinet door
3/4" hardwood face frame
3/4" hardwood plywood bottom

1 1/2"

1/4"

1 1/2"

EXPOSED FACE FRAME 1 1/2"

1/4" OVERLAY

3/4" FACE FRAME 1

1/4"

3/8"

3/4"   3/4"

DRAWING #

Reveal Overlay Door Bottom Detail

SCALE
HALF
SIZE

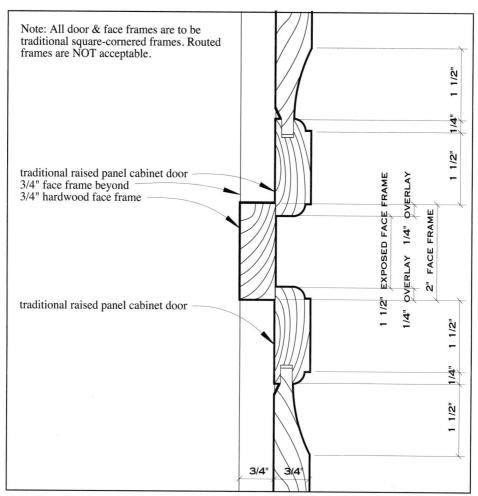

Note: All door & face frames are to be traditional square-cornered frames. Routed frames are NOT acceptable.

traditional raised panel cabinet door
3/4" face frame beyond
3/4" hardwood face frame

traditional raised panel cabinet door

1 1/2"

1/4"

1 1/2"

1 1/2" EXPOSED FACE FRAME

1/4" OVERLAY

1/4" OVERLAY

2" FACE FRAME

1 1/2"

1/4"

1 1/2"

3/4"   3/4"

DRAWING #

Reveal Overlay Meeting Door Detail

SCALE
HALF
SIZE

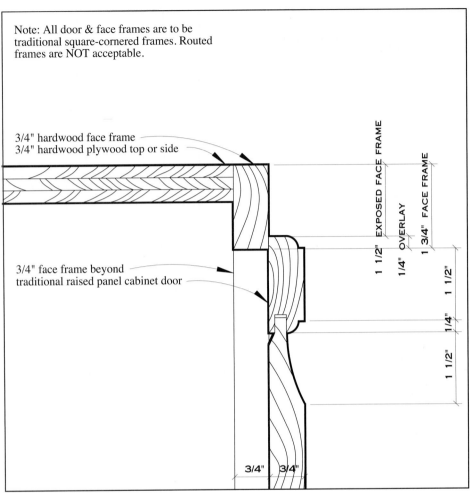

Note: All door & face frames are to be traditional square-cornered frames. Routed frames are NOT acceptable.

3/4" hardwood face frame
3/4" hardwood plywood top or side

3/4" face frame beyond
traditional raised panel cabinet door

EXPOSED FACE FRAME

1 1/2" EXPOSED FACE FRAME

1/4" OVERLAY

1 3/4" FACE FRAME

1 1/2"

1/4"

1 1/2"

3/4"   3/4"

Reveal Overlay Door Top or Side Detail

DRAWING #

SCALE
HALF
SIZE

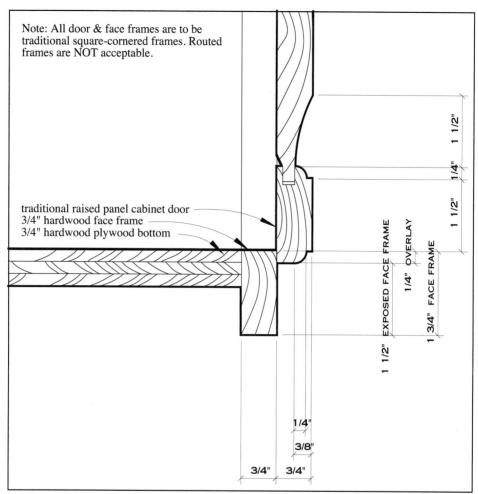

Note: All door & face frames are to be traditional square-cornered frames. Routed frames are NOT acceptable.

traditional raised panel cabinet door
3/4" hardwood face frame
3/4" hardwood plywood bottom

1 1/2"

1/4"

1 1/2"

1 1/2" EXPOSED FACE FRAME

1/4" OVERLAY

1 3/4" FACE FRAME

1/4"

3/8"

3/4"   3/4"

Reveal Overlay Door Bottom Detail

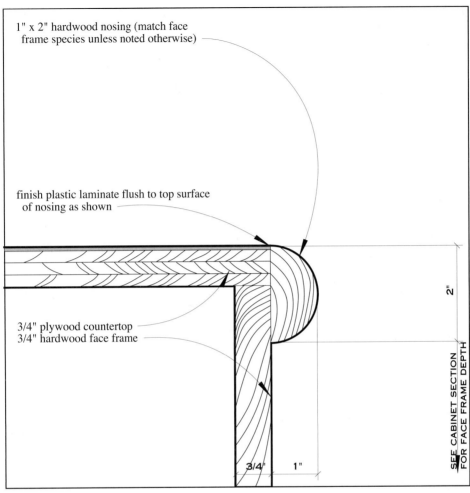

1" x 2" hardwood nosing (match face
  frame species unless noted otherwise)

finish plastic laminate flush to top surface
  of nosing as shown

3/4" plywood countertop
3/4" hardwood face frame

2"

SEE CABINET SECTION
FOR FACE FRAME DEPTH

3/4"   1"

DRAWING #	Hardwood Nosing w/PL Counter	SCALE HALF SIZE

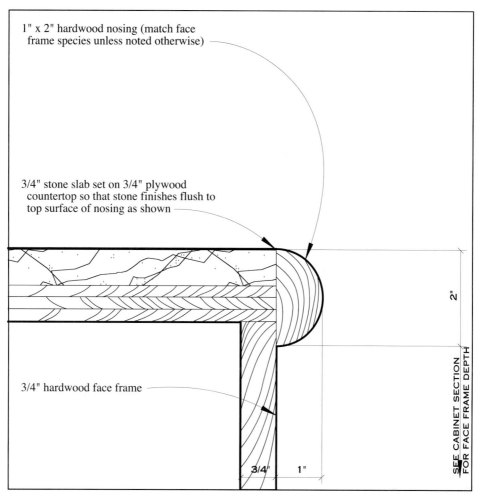

1" x 2" hardwood nosing (match face frame species unless noted otherwise)

3/4" stone slab set on 3/4" plywood countertop so that stone finishes flush to top surface of nosing as shown

3/4" hardwood face frame

2"

SEE CABINET SECTION
FOR FACE FRAME DEPTH

3/4" 1"

DRAWING #

Hardwood Nosing w/Stone Counter

SCALE
HALF
SIZE

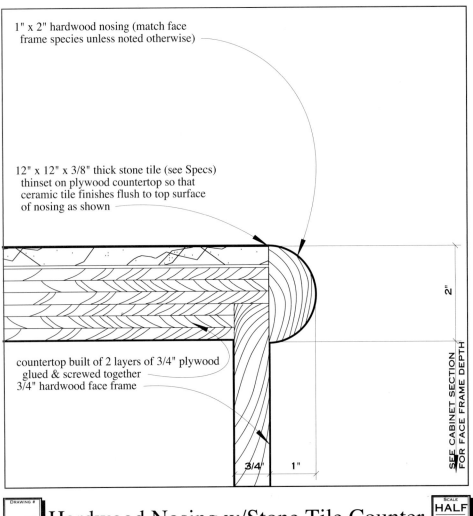

1" x 2" hardwood nosing (match face
frame species unless noted otherwise)

12" x 12" x 3/8" thick stone tile (see Specs)
thinset on plywood countertop so that
ceramic tile finishes flush to top surface
of nosing as shown

countertop built of 2 layers of 3/4" plywood
glued & screwed together
3/4" hardwood face frame

2"

SEE CABINET SECTION
FOR FACE FRAME DEPTH

3/4"   1"

Hardwood Nosing w/Stone Tile Counter

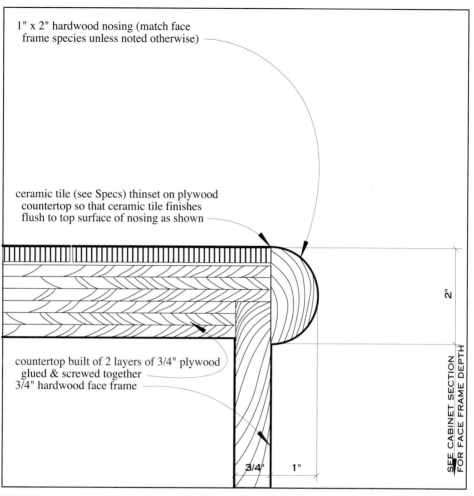

1" x 2" hardwood nosing (match face
frame species unless noted otherwise)

ceramic tile (see Specs) thinset on plywood
countertop so that ceramic tile finishes
flush to top surface of nosing as shown

countertop built of 2 layers of 3/4" plywood
glued & screwed together
3/4" hardwood face frame

2"

SEE CABINET SECTION
FOR FACE FRAME DEPTH

3/4" 1"

DRAWING #

Hardwood Nosing w/Tile Counter

SCALE
HALF
SIZE

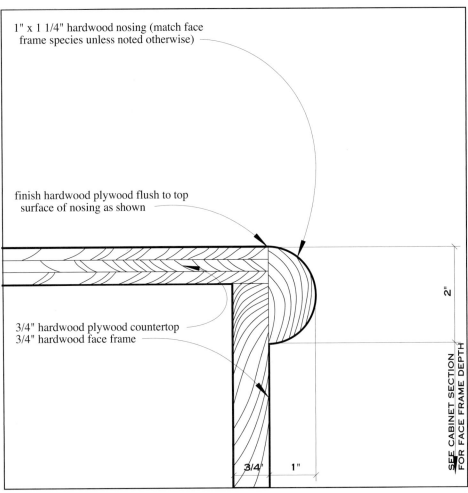

1" x 1 1/4" hardwood nosing (match face frame species unless noted otherwise)

finish hardwood plywood flush to top surface of nosing as shown

3/4" hardwood plywood countertop
3/4" hardwood face frame

2"

SEE CABINET SECTION FOR FACE FRAME DEPTH

3/4"   1"

DRAWING #

Hardwood Nosing w/Wood Counter

SCALE
HALF
SIZE

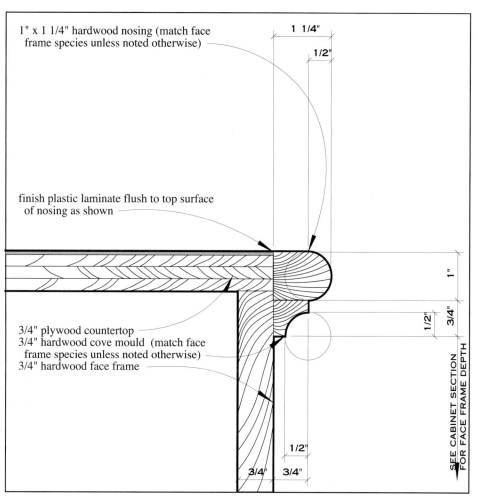

1" x 1 1/4" hardwood nosing (match face frame species unless noted otherwise)

1 1/4"

1/2"

finish plastic laminate flush to top surface of nosing as shown

3/4" plywood countertop
3/4" hardwood cove mould (match face frame species unless noted otherwise)
3/4" hardwood face frame

1"

1/2"

3/4"

SEE CABINET SECTION FOR FACE FRAME DEPTH

1/2"

3/4" 3/4"

DRAWING #

Hardwood Nosing w/PL Counter

SCALE
HALF
SIZE

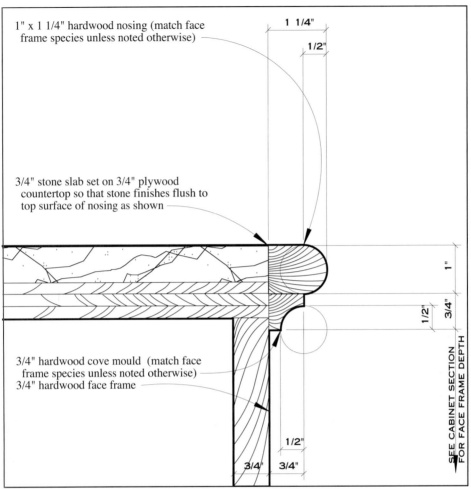

1" x 1 1/4" hardwood nosing (match face
frame species unless noted otherwise)

1 1/4"

1/2"

3/4" stone slab set on 3/4" plywood
countertop so that stone finishes flush to
top surface of nosing as shown

1"

1/2"

3/4"

3/4" hardwood cove mould (match face
frame species unless noted otherwise)
3/4" hardwood face frame

SEE CABINET SECTION
FOR FACE FRAME DEPTH

1/2"

3/4"   3/4"

DRAWING #

Hardwood Nosing w/Stone Counter

SCALE
HALF
SIZE

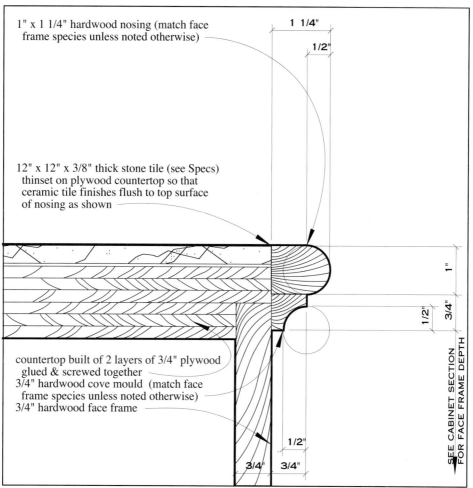

1" x 1 1/4" hardwood nosing (match face frame species unless noted otherwise)

1 1/4"

1/2"

12" x 12" x 3/8" thick stone tile (see Specs) thinset on plywood countertop so that ceramic tile finishes flush to top surface of nosing as shown

1"

1/2"

3/4"

countertop built of 2 layers of 3/4" plywood glued & screwed together
3/4" hardwood cove mould (match face frame species unless noted otherwise)
3/4" hardwood face frame

SEE CABINET SECTION FOR FACE FRAME DEPTH

1/2"

3/4"   3/4"

Hardwood Nosing w/Stone Tile Counter

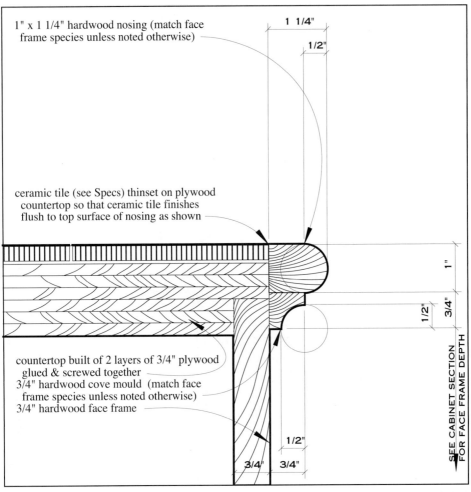

1" x 1 1/4" hardwood nosing (match face frame species unless noted otherwise)

1 1/4"

1/2"

ceramic tile (see Specs) thinset on plywood countertop so that ceramic tile finishes flush to top surface of nosing as shown

1"

3/4"

1/2"

countertop built of 2 layers of 3/4" plywood glued & screwed together
3/4" hardwood cove mould (match face frame species unless noted otherwise)
3/4" hardwood face frame

SEE CABINET SECTION FOR FACE FRAME DEPTH

1/2"

3/4"   3/4"

DRAWING #

Hardwood Nosing w/Tile Counter

SCALE
HALF
SIZE

CDN019
180

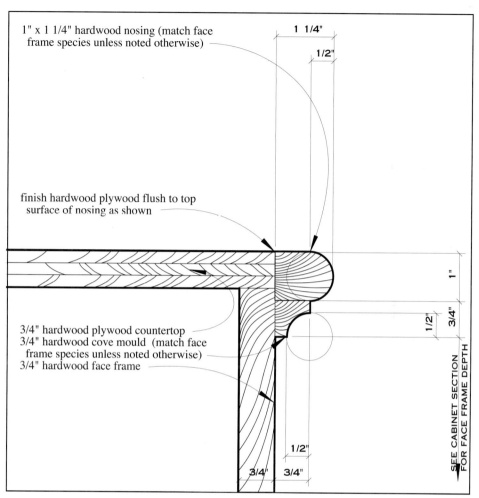

1" x 1 1/4" hardwood nosing (match face frame species unless noted otherwise)

finish hardwood plywood flush to top surface of nosing as shown

3/4" hardwood plywood countertop
3/4" hardwood cove mould (match face frame species unless noted otherwise)
3/4" hardwood face frame

1 1/4"

1/2"

1"

1/2"

3/4"

1/2"

3/4"   3/4"

SEE CABINET SECTION FOR FACE FRAME DEPTH

Hardwood Nosing w/Wood Counter

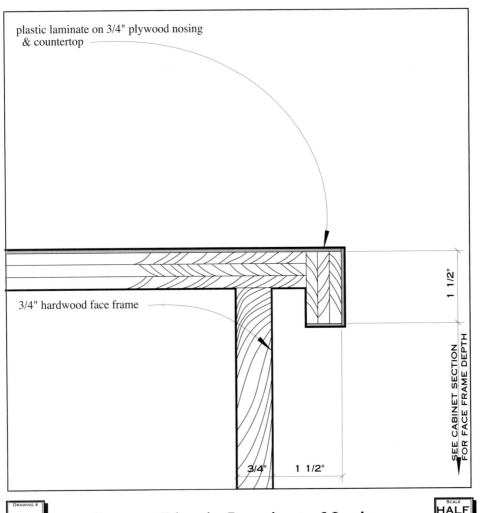

plastic laminate on 3/4" plywood nosing
& countertop

3/4" hardwood face frame

1 1/2"

SEE CABINET SECTION
FOR FACE FRAME DEPTH

3/4"   1 1/2"

Square Plastic Laminate Nosing

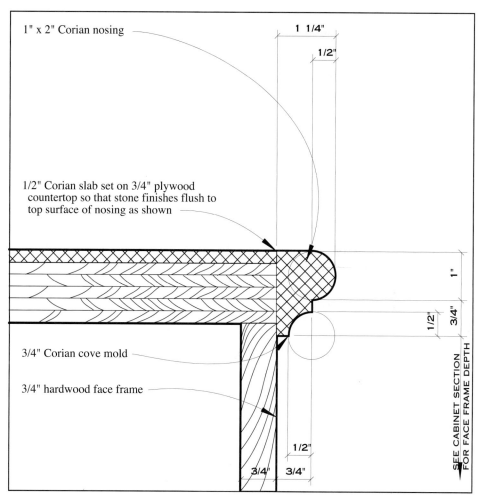

1" x 2" Corian nosing

1 1/4"

1/2"

1/2" Corian slab set on 3/4" plywood
countertop so that stone finishes flush to
top surface of nosing as shown

1"

3/4"

1/2"

3/4" Corian cove mold

3/4" hardwood face frame

SEE CABINET SECTION
FOR FACE FRAME DEPTH

1/2"

3/4" 3/4"

DRAWING #

Corian Nosing w/Corian Counter

SCALE
HALF
SIZE

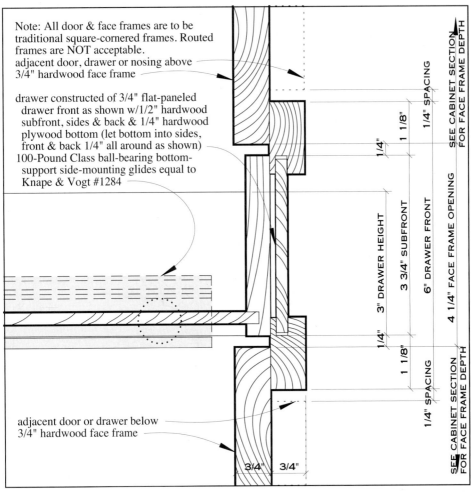

Note: All door & face frames are to be
traditional square-cornered frames. Routed
frames are NOT acceptable.
adjacent door, drawer or nosing above
3/4" hardwood face frame

drawer constructed of 3/4" flat-paneled
drawer front as shown w/1/2" hardwood
subfront, sides & back & 1/4" hardwood
plywood bottom (let bottom into sides,
front & back 1/4" all around as shown)
100-Pound Class ball-bearing bottom-
support side-mounting glides equal to
Knape & Vogt #1284

adjacent door or drawer below
3/4" hardwood face frame

SEE CABINET SECTION
FOR FACE FRAME DEPTH

1/4" SPACING

1 1/8"

1/4"

3" DRAWER HEIGHT

3 3/4" SUBFRONT

6" DRAWER FRONT

4 1/4" FACE FRAME OPENING

1/4"

1 1/8"

1/4" SPACING

SEE CABINET SECTION
FOR FACE FRAME DEPTH

3/4"   3/4"

Flush Overlay Cabinet Drawer Detail

DRAWING #

SCALE
HALF
SIZE

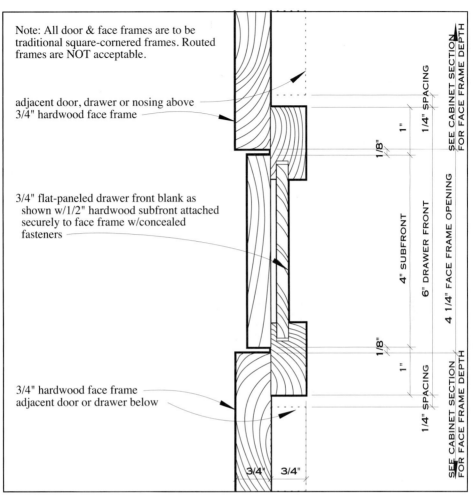

Note: All door & face frames are to be traditional square-cornered frames. Routed frames are NOT acceptable.

adjacent door, drawer or nosing above 3/4" hardwood face frame

3/4" flat-paneled drawer front blank as shown w/1/2" hardwood subfront attached securely to face frame w/concealed fasteners

3/4" hardwood face frame adjacent door or drawer below

SEE CABINET SECTION FOR FACE FRAME DEPTH

1/4" SPACING

1"

1/8"

4" SUBFRONT

6" DRAWER FRONT

4 1/4" FACE FRAME OPENING

1/8"

1"

1/4" SPACING

SEE CABINET SECTION FOR FACE FRAME DEPTH

3/4"   3/4"

 DRAWING #

Flush Overlay Cabinet Drawer Blank

 SCALE **HALF SIZE**

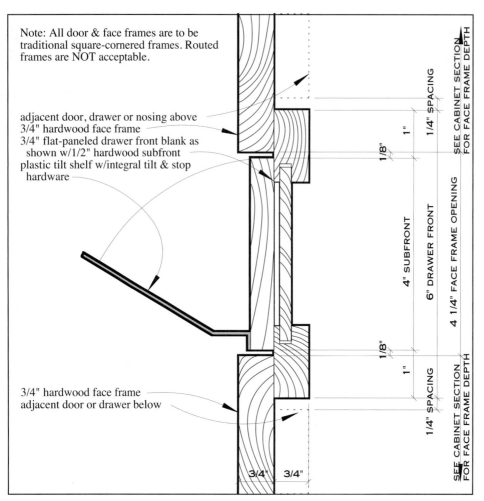

Note: All door & face frames are to be
traditional square-cornered frames. Routed
frames are NOT acceptable.

adjacent door, drawer or nosing above
3/4" hardwood face frame
3/4" flat-paneled drawer front blank as
 shown w/1/2" hardwood subfront
plastic tilt shelf w/integral tilt & stop
 hardware

3/4" hardwood face frame
adjacent door or drawer below

1/4" SPACING

1"

1/8"

SEE CABINET SECTION
FOR FACE FRAME DEPTH

4" SUBFRONT

6" DRAWER FRONT

4 1/4" FACE FRAME OPENING

1/8"

1"

1/4" SPACING

SEE CABINET SECTION
FOR FACE FRAME DEPTH

3/4" 3/4"

Flush Overlay Cabinet Tilt Drawer

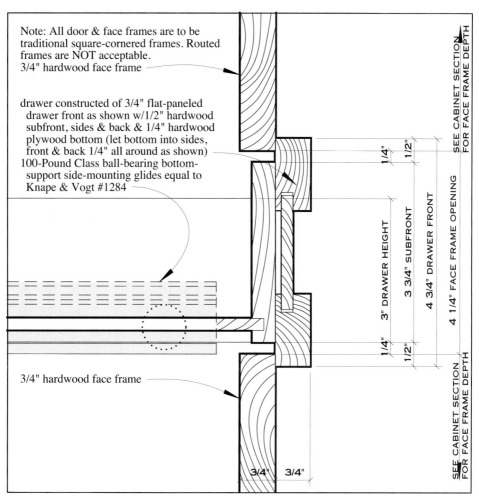

Note: All door & face frames are to be traditional square-cornered frames. Routed frames are NOT acceptable.
3/4" hardwood face frame

drawer constructed of 3/4" flat-paneled drawer front as shown w/1/2" hardwood subfront, sides & back & 1/4" hardwood plywood bottom (let bottom into sides, front & back 1/4" all around as shown) 100-Pound Class ball-bearing bottom-support side-mounting glides equal to Knape & Vogt #1284

3/4" hardwood face frame

SEE CABINET SECTION FOR FACE FRAME DEPTH

1/4"   1/2"

3" DRAWER HEIGHT

3 3/4" SUBFRONT

4 3/4" DRAWER FRONT

4 1/4" FACE FRAME OPENING

1/4"   1/2"

SEE CABINET SECTION FOR FACE FRAME DEPTH

SEE CABINET SECTION FOR FACE FRAME DEPTH

3/4"   3/4"

DRAWING #	Reveal Overlay Cabinet Drawer Detail	SCALE HALF SIZE

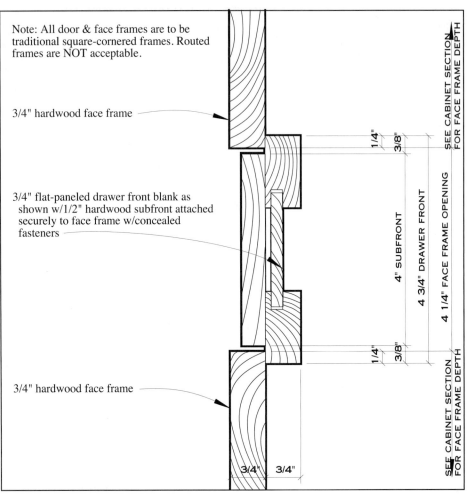

Note: All door & face frames are to be traditional square-cornered frames. Routed frames are NOT acceptable.

3/4" hardwood face frame

3/4" flat-paneled drawer front blank as shown w/1/2" hardwood subfront attached securely to face frame w/concealed fasteners

3/4" hardwood face frame

1/4"
3/8"

1/4"
3/8"

4" SUBFRONT

4 3/4" DRAWER FRONT

4 1/4" FACE FRAME OPENING

SEE CABINET SECTION FOR FACE FRAME DEPTH

SEE CABINET SECTION FOR FACE FRAME DEPTH

3/4" 3/4"

DRAWING #

Reveal Overlay Cabinet Drawer Blank

SCALE
HALF SIZE

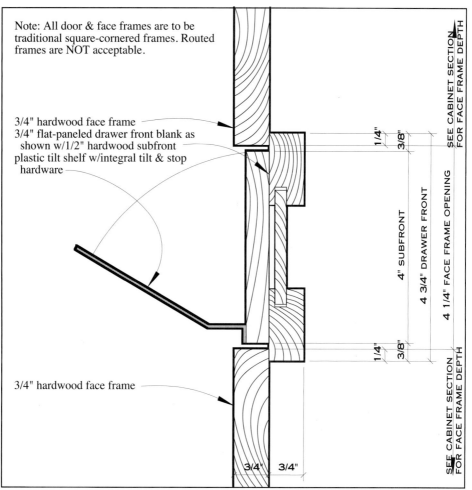

Note: All door & face frames are to be traditional square-cornered frames. Routed frames are NOT acceptable.

3/4" hardwood face frame
3/4" flat-paneled drawer front blank as shown w/1/2" hardwood subfront plastic tilt shelf w/integral tilt & stop hardware

3/4" hardwood face frame

1/4"

3/8"

SEE CABINET SECTION FOR FACE FRAME DEPTH

4" SUBFRONT

4 3/4" DRAWER FRONT

4 1/4" FACE FRAME OPENING

1/4"

3/8"

SEE CABINET SECTION FOR FACE FRAME DEPTH

3/4" 3/4"

DRAWING #

Reveal Overlay Cabinet Tilt Drawer

SCALE
HALF
SIZE

CDRF1006
189

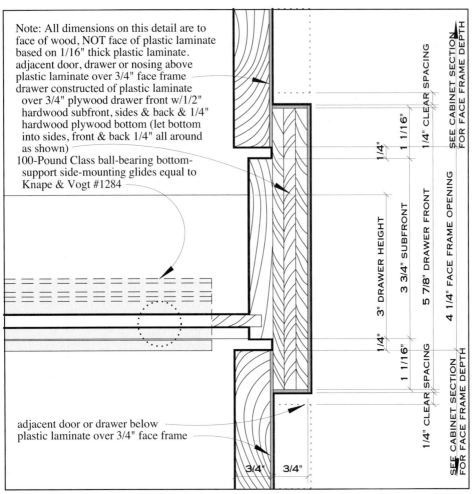

Note: All dimensions on this detail are to face of wood, NOT face of plastic laminate based on 1/16" thick plastic laminate. adjacent door, drawer or nosing above plastic laminate over 3/4" face frame drawer constructed of plastic laminate over 3/4" plywood drawer front w/1/2" hardwood subfront, sides & back & 1/4" hardwood plywood bottom (let bottom into sides, front & back 1/4" all around as shown) 100-Pound Class ball-bearing bottom-support side-mounting glides equal to Knape & Vogt #1284

adjacent door or drawer below plastic laminate over 3/4" face frame

SEE CABINET SECTION FOR FACE FRAME DEPTH

1/4" CLEAR SPACING

1 1/16"

1/4"

3" DRAWER HEIGHT

3 3/4" SUBFRONT

5 7/8" DRAWER FRONT

4 1/4" FACE FRAME OPENING

1/4"

1 1/16"

1/4" CLEAR SPACING

SEE CABINET SECTION FOR FACE FRAME DEPTH

3/4" 3/4"

Flush Overlay Cabinet Drawer Detail

SCALE
HALF
SIZE

DRAWING #

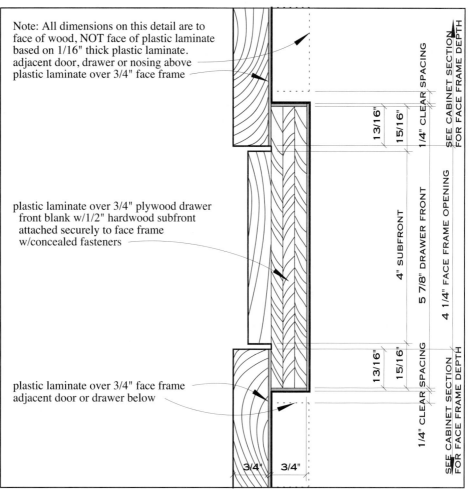

Note: All dimensions on this detail are to
face of wood, NOT face of plastic laminate
based on 1/16" thick plastic laminate.
adjacent door, drawer or nosing above
plastic laminate over 3/4" face frame

plastic laminate over 3/4" plywood drawer
front blank w/1/2" hardwood subfront
attached securely to face frame
w/concealed fasteners

plastic laminate over 3/4" face frame
adjacent door or drawer below

1/4" CLEAR SPACING

15/16"

13/16"

SEE CABINET SECTION
FOR FACE FRAME DEPTH

4" SUBFRONT

5 7/8" DRAWER FRONT

4 1/4" FACE FRAME OPENING

13/16"

15/16"

1/4" CLEAR SPACING

SEE CABINET SECTION
FOR FACE FRAME DEPTH

3/4"   3/4"

DRAWING #

Flush Overlay Cabinet Drawer Blank

SCALE
HALF
SIZE

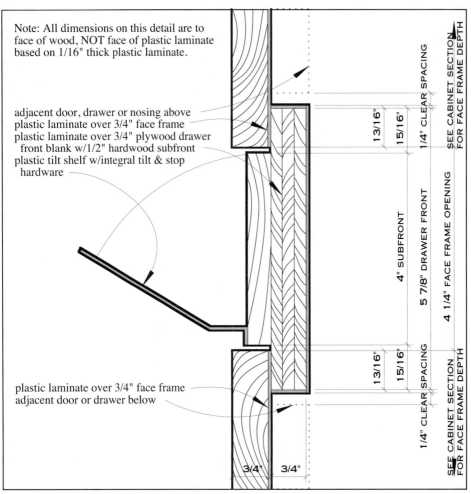

Note: All dimensions on this detail are to face of wood, NOT face of plastic laminate based on 1/16" thick plastic laminate.

adjacent door, drawer or nosing above
plastic laminate over 3/4" face frame
plastic laminate over 3/4" plywood drawer
  front blank w/1/2" hardwood subfront
plastic tilt shelf w/integral tilt & stop
  hardware

plastic laminate over 3/4" face frame
adjacent door or drawer below

13/16"
15/16"
1/4" CLEAR SPACING
SEE CABINET SECTION FOR FACE FRAME DEPTH

4" SUBFRONT
5 7/8" DRAWER FRONT
4 1/4" FACE FRAME OPENING

13/16"
15/16"
1/4" CLEAR SPACING
SEE CABINET SECTION FOR FACE FRAME DEPTH

3/4"   3/4"

Flush Overlay Cabinet Tilt Drawer

DRAWING #

SCALE
HALF SIZE

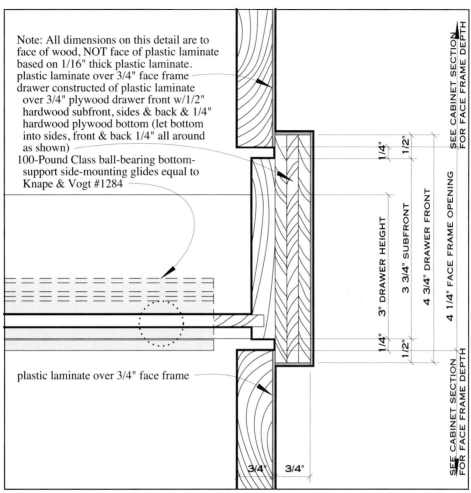

Note: All dimensions on this detail are to face of wood, NOT face of plastic laminate based on 1/16" thick plastic laminate. plastic laminate over 3/4" face frame drawer constructed of plastic laminate over 3/4" plywood drawer front w/1/2" hardwood subfront, sides & back & 1/4" hardwood plywood bottom (let bottom into sides, front & back 1/4" all around as shown)

100-Pound Class ball-bearing bottom-support side-mounting glides equal to Knape & Vogt #1284

plastic laminate over 3/4" face frame

SEE CABINET SECTION FOR FACE FRAME DEPTH

1/4"   1/2"

3" DRAWER HEIGHT

3 3/4" SUBFRONT

4 3/4" DRAWER FRONT

4 1/4" FACE FRAME OPENING

1/4"   1/2"

SEE CABINET SECTION FOR FACE FRAME DEPTH

3/4"   3/4"

DRAWING #

Reveal Overlay Cabinet Drawer Detail

SCALE
**HALF
SIZE**

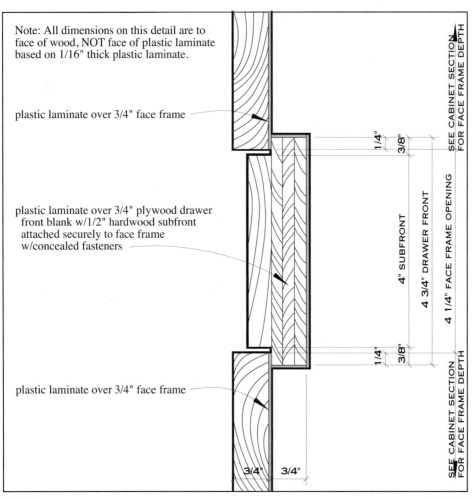

Note: All dimensions on this detail are to face of wood, NOT face of plastic laminate based on 1/16" thick plastic laminate.

plastic laminate over 3/4" face frame

plastic laminate over 3/4" plywood drawer front blank w/1/2" hardwood subfront attached securely to face frame w/concealed fasteners

plastic laminate over 3/4" face frame

1/4"
3/8"

SEE CABINET SECTION FOR FACE FRAME DEPTH

4" SUBFRONT

4 3/4" DRAWER FRONT

4 1/4" FACE FRAME OPENING

1/4"
3/8"

SEE CABINET SECTION FOR FACE FRAME DEPTH

3/4"   3/4"

DRAWING #	Reveal Overlay Cabinet Drawer Blank	SCALE HALF SIZE

Note: All dimensions on this detail are to face of wood, NOT face of plastic laminate based on 1/16" thick plastic laminate.

plastic laminate over 3/4" face frame
plastic laminate over 3/4" plywood drawer front blank w/1/2" hardwood subfront
plastic tilt shelf w/integral tilt & stop hardware

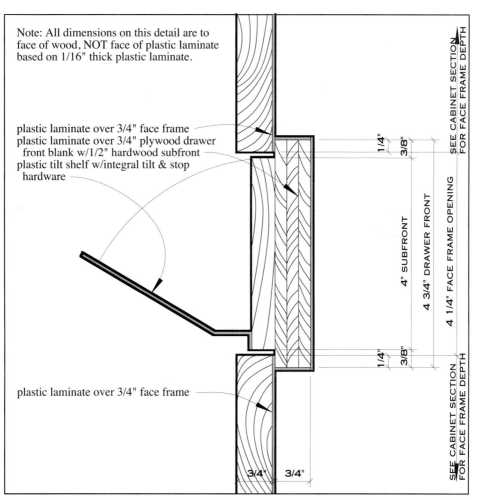

SEE CABINET SECTION FOR FACE FRAME DEPTH

1/4"
3/8"

4" SUBFRONT

4 3/4" DRAWER FRONT

4 1/4" FACE FRAME OPENING

1/4"
3/8"

plastic laminate over 3/4" face frame

SEE CABINET SECTION FOR FACE FRAME DEPTH

3/4"   3/4"

DRAWING #

SCALE
HALF SIZE

Reveal Overlay Cabinet Tilt Drawer

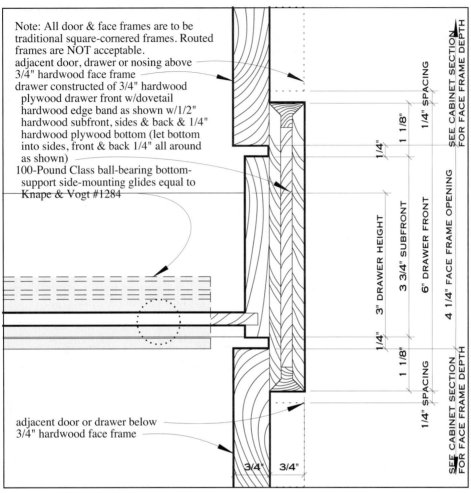

Note: All door & face frames are to be
traditional square-cornered frames. Routed
frames are NOT acceptable.
adjacent door, drawer or nosing above
3/4" hardwood face frame
drawer constructed of 3/4" hardwood
plywood drawer front w/dovetail
hardwood edge band as shown w/1/2"
hardwood subfront, sides & back & 1/4"
hardwood plywood bottom (let bottom
into sides, front & back 1/4" all around
as shown)
100-Pound Class ball-bearing bottom-
support side-mounting glides equal to
Knape & Vogt #1284

adjacent door or drawer below
3/4" hardwood face frame

SEE CABINET SECTION
FOR FACE FRAME DEPTH

1/4" SPACING

1 1/8"

1/4"

3" DRAWER HEIGHT

3 3/4" SUBFRONT

6" DRAWER FRONT

4 1/4" FACE FRAME OPENING

SEE CABINET SECTION
FOR FACE FRAME DEPTH

1/4"

1 1/8"

1/4" SPACING

SEE CABINET SECTION
FOR FACE FRAME DEPTH

3/4"   3/4"

DRAWING #

Flush Overlay Cabinet Drawer Detail

SCALE
HALF
SIZE

CDRF3001
196

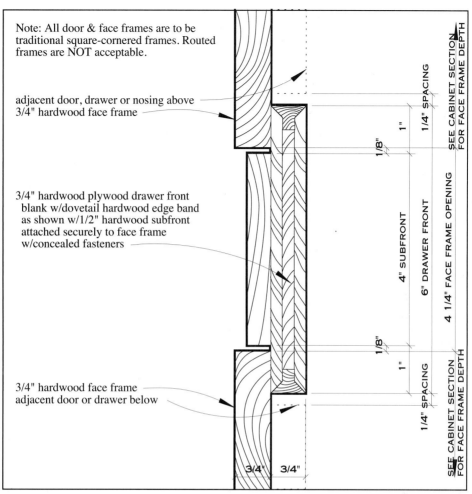

Note: All door & face frames are to be traditional square-cornered frames. Routed frames are NOT acceptable.

adjacent door, drawer or nosing above 3/4" hardwood face frame

3/4" hardwood plywood drawer front blank w/dovetail hardwood edge band as shown w/1/2" hardwood subfront attached securely to face frame w/concealed fasteners

3/4" hardwood face frame adjacent door or drawer below

1/4" SPACING

1"

1/8"

4" SUBFRONT

6" DRAWER FRONT

4 1/4" FACE FRAME OPENING

SEE CABINET SECTION FOR FACE FRAME DEPTH

1/8"

1"

1/4" SPACING

SEE CABINET SECTION FOR FACE FRAME DEPTH

3/4" 3/4"

DRAWING #

Flush Overlay Cabinet Drawer Blank

SCALE

HALF SIZE

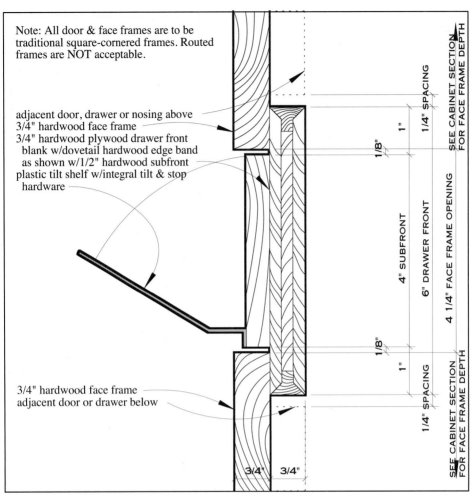

Note: All door & face frames are to be
traditional square-cornered frames. Routed
frames are NOT acceptable.

adjacent door, drawer or nosing above
3/4" hardwood face frame
3/4" hardwood plywood drawer front
  blank w/dovetail hardwood edge band
  as shown w/1/2" hardwood subfront
plastic tilt shelf w/integral tilt & stop
  hardware

3/4" hardwood face frame
adjacent door or drawer below

1/4" SPACING

1"

1/8"

4" SUBFRONT

6" DRAWER FRONT

4 1/4" FACE FRAME OPENING

SEE CABINET SECTION
FOR FACE FRAME DEPTH

1/8"

1"

1/4" SPACING

SEE CABINET SECTION
FOR FACE FRAME DEPTH

3/4"   3/4"

DRAWING #

Flush Overlay Cabinet Tilt Drawer

SCALE
HALF
SIZE

CDRF3003
198

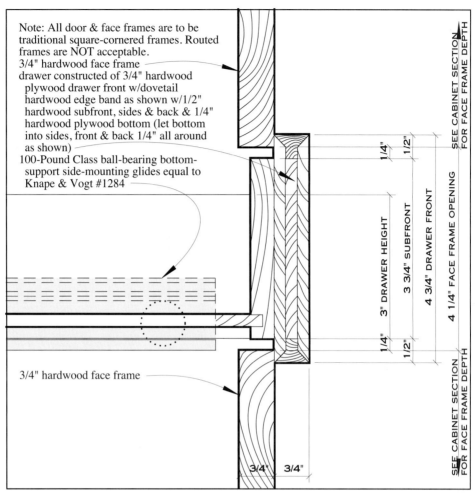

Note: All door & face frames are to be traditional square-cornered frames. Routed frames are NOT acceptable.
3/4" hardwood face frame drawer constructed of 3/4" hardwood plywood drawer front w/dovetail hardwood edge band as shown w/1/2" hardwood subfront, sides & back & 1/4" hardwood plywood bottom (let bottom into sides, front & back 1/4" all around as shown)
100-Pound Class ball-bearing bottom-support side-mounting glides equal to Knape & Vogt #1284

3/4" hardwood face frame

SEE CABINET SECTION
FOR FACE FRAME DEPTH

1/4"   1/2"

3" DRAWER HEIGHT

3 3/4" SUBFRONT

4 3/4" DRAWER FRONT

4 1/4" FACE FRAME OPENING

SEE CABINET SECTION
FOR FACE FRAME DEPTH

1/4"   1/2"

SEE CABINET SECTION
FOR FACE FRAME DEPTH

3/4"   3/4"

DRAWING #

Reveal Overlay Cabinet Drawer Detail

SCALE
HALF
SIZE

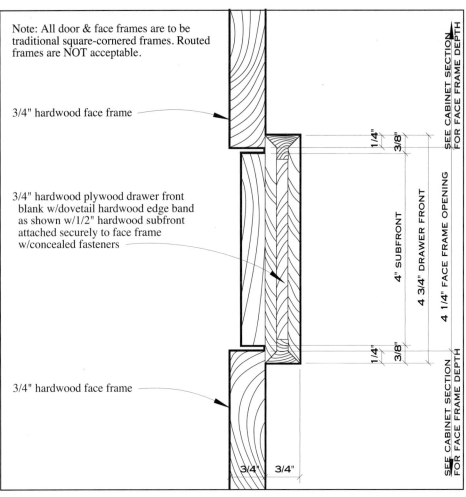

Note: All door & face frames are to be traditional square-cornered frames. Routed frames are NOT acceptable.

3/4" hardwood face frame

3/4" hardwood plywood drawer front blank w/dovetail hardwood edge band as shown w/1/2" hardwood subfront attached securely to face frame w/concealed fasteners

3/4" hardwood face frame

SEE CABINET SECTION FOR FACE FRAME DEPTH

1/4"

3/8"

4" SUBFRONT

4 3/4" DRAWER FRONT

4 1/4" FACE FRAME OPENING

1/4"

3/8"

SEE CABINET SECTION FOR FACE FRAME DEPTH

3/4"   3/4"

DRAWING #		Reveal Overlay Cabinet Drawer Blank	SCALE
			HALF SIZE

CDRF3011
200

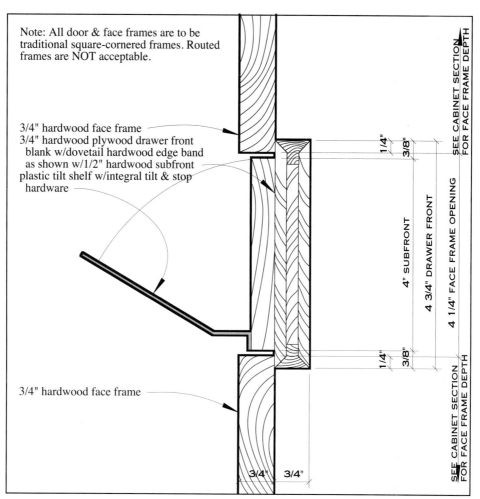

Note: All door & face frames are to be traditional square-cornered frames. Routed frames are NOT acceptable.

3/4" hardwood face frame
3/4" hardwood plywood drawer front blank w/dovetail hardwood edge band as shown w/1/2" hardwood subfront plastic tilt shelf w/integral tilt & stop hardware

3/4" hardwood face frame

SEE CABINET SECTION FOR FACE FRAME DEPTH

1/4"
3/8"

4" SUBFRONT

4 3/4" DRAWER FRONT

4 1/4" FACE FRAME OPENING

1/4"
3/8"

SEE CABINET SECTION FOR FACE FRAME DEPTH

3/4"   3/4"

SEE CABINET SECTION FOR FACE FRAME DEPTH

DRAWING #

Reveal Overlay Cabinet Tilt Drawer

SCALE
HALF SIZE

CDRF3012
201

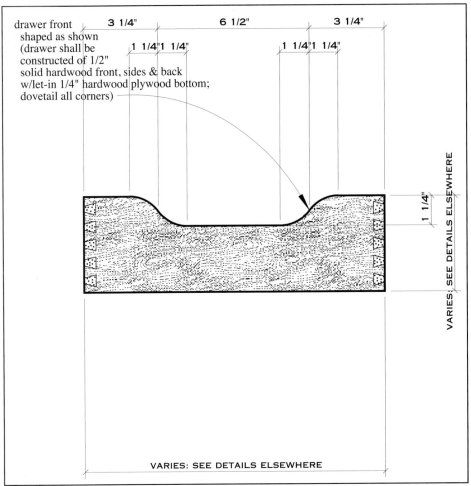

drawer front
shaped as shown
(drawer shall be
constructed of 1/2"
solid hardwood front, sides & back
w/let-in 1/4" hardwood plywood bottom;
dovetail all corners)

3 1/4" 6 1/2" 3 1/4"

1 1/4" 1 1/4" 1 1/4" 1 1/4"

1 1/4"

VARIES; SEE DETAILS ELSEWHERE

VARIES: SEE DETAILS ELSEWHERE

Hidden Drawer Front Elevation

SCALE
3"
1'-0"

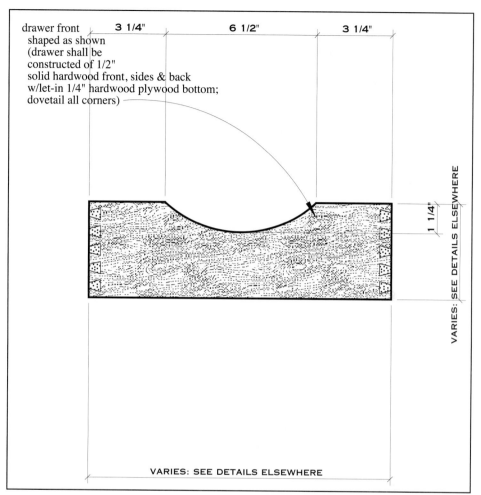

drawer front
shaped as shown
(drawer shall be
constructed of 1/2"
solid hardwood front, sides & back
w/let-in 1/4" hardwood plywood bottom;
dovetail all corners)

3 1/4"   6 1/2"   3 1/4"

1 1/4"

VARIES: SEE DETAILS ELSEWHERE

VARIES: SEE DETAILS ELSEWHERE

DRAWING #

Hidden Drawer Front Elevation

SCALE
3"
1'-0"

CDRH002
203

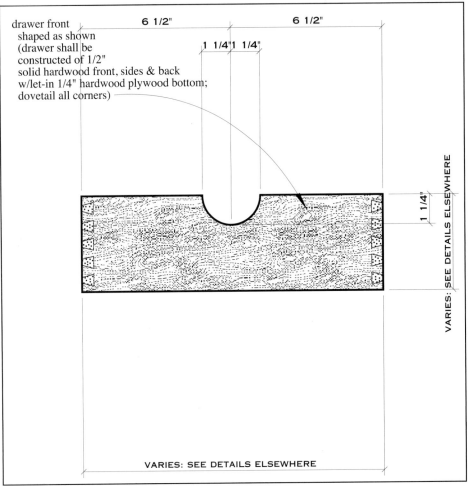

drawer front
shaped as shown
(drawer shall be
constructed of 1/2"
solid hardwood front, sides & back
w/let-in 1/4" hardwood plywood bottom;
dovetail all corners)

6 1/2"   6 1/2"

1 1/4" 1 1/4"

1 1/4"

VARIES: SEE DETAILS ELSEWHERE

VARIES: SEE DETAILS ELSEWHERE

DRAWING #

Hidden Drawer Front Elevation

SCALE
3"
1'-0"

drawer front

6 1/2"   6 1/2"

shaped as shown (drawer shall be
constructed of 1/2" solid hardwood
front, sides & back w/let-in 1/4"
hardwood plywood bottom;
dovetail all corners)
solid brass pull (pull shown is purely
pictoral; see Owner for actual pull style
& finish)

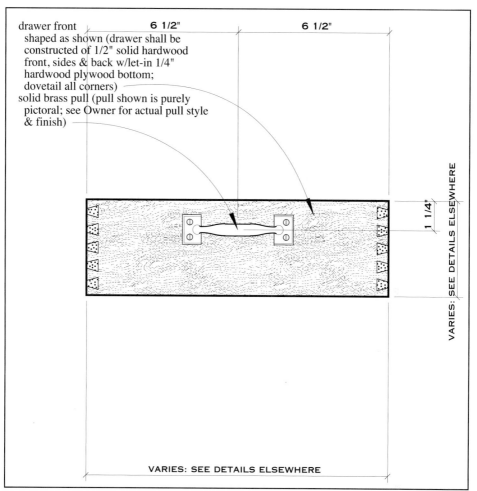

1 1/4"

VARIES: SEE DETAILS ELSEWHERE

VARIES: SEE DETAILS ELSEWHERE

DRAWING #

Hidden Drawer Front Elevation

SCALE

3"
1'-0"

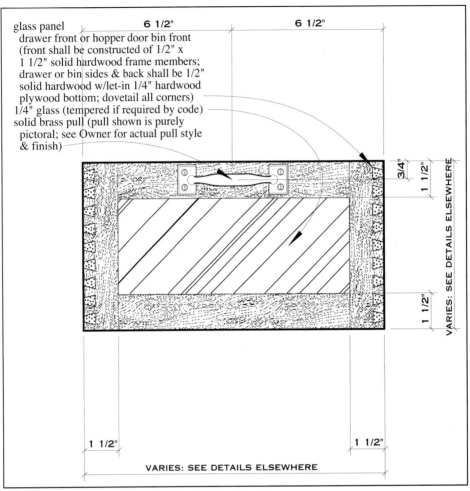

glass panel

drawer front or hopper door bin front
(front shall be constructed of 1/2" x
1 1/2" solid hardwood frame members;
drawer or bin sides & back shall be 1/2"
solid hardwood w/let-in 1/4" hardwood
plywood bottom; dovetail all corners)

1/4" glass (tempered if required by code)

solid brass pull (pull shown is purely
pictoral; see Owner for actual pull style
& finish)

6 1/2"

6 1/2"

3/4"

1 1/2"

1 1/2"

1 1/2"

VARIES: SEE DETAILS ELSEWHERE

1 1/2"

1 1/2"

VARIES: SEE DETAILS ELSEWHERE

DRAWING #

Hidden Drawer or Bin Front Elevation

SCALE

3"
1'-0"

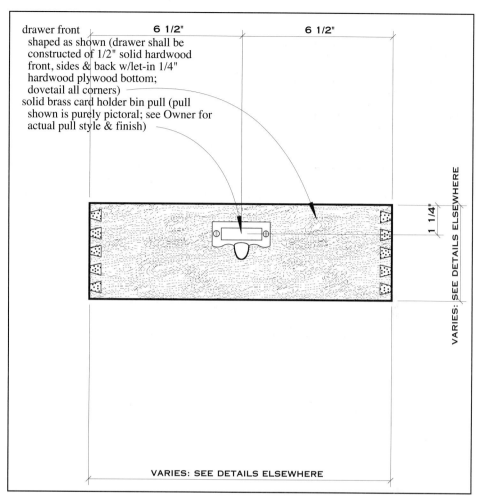

drawer front
  shaped as shown (drawer shall be
  constructed of 1/2" solid hardwood
  front, sides & back w/let-in 1/4"
  hardwood plywood bottom;
  dovetail all corners)
solid brass card holder bin pull (pull
  shown is purely pictoral; see Owner for
  actual pull style & finish)

6 1/2"

6 1/2"

1 1/4"

VARIES: SEE DETAILS ELSEWHERE

VARIES: SEE DETAILS ELSEWHERE

Hidden Drawer Front Elevation

DRAWING #

SCALE
3"
1'-0"

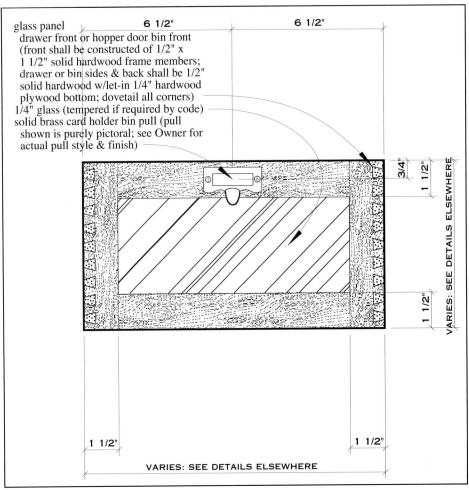

glass panel
  drawer front or hopper door bin front
  (front shall be constructed of 1/2" x
  1 1/2" solid hardwood frame members;
  drawer or bin sides & back shall be 1/2"
  solid hardwood w/let-in 1/4" hardwood
  plywood bottom; dovetail all corners)
1/4" glass (tempered if required by code)
solid brass card holder bin pull (pull
  shown is purely pictoral; see Owner for
  actual pull style & finish)

6 1/2"   6 1/2"

3/4" 1 1/2"

VARIES: SEE DETAILS ELSEWHERE

1 1/2"

1 1/2"   1 1/2"

VARIES: SEE DETAILS ELSEWHERE

DRAWING #

Hidden Drawer or Bin Front Elevation

SCALE
3"
1'-0"

CDRH007
208

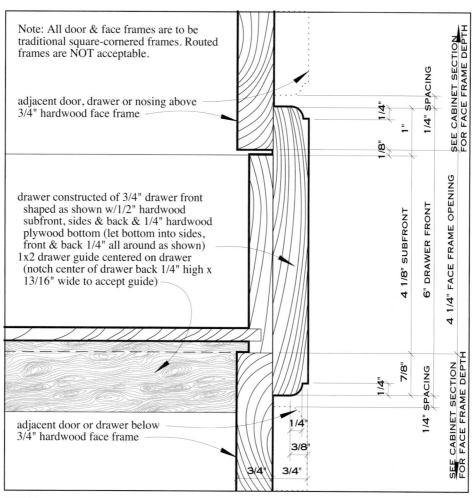

Note: All door & face frames are to be traditional square-cornered frames. Routed frames are NOT acceptable.

adjacent door, drawer or nosing above 3/4" hardwood face frame

drawer constructed of 3/4" drawer front shaped as shown w/1/2" hardwood subfront, sides & back & 1/4" hardwood plywood bottom (let bottom into sides, front & back 1/4" all around as shown) 1x2 drawer guide centered on drawer (notch center of drawer back 1/4" high x 13/16" wide to accept guide)

adjacent door or drawer below 3/4" hardwood face frame

SEE CABINET SECTION FOR FACE FRAME DEPTH

1/4"

1/8" 1" 1/4" SPACING

4 1/8" SUBFRONT

6" DRAWER FRONT

4 1/4" FACE FRAME OPENING

7/8" 1/4" SPACING

1/4"

SEE CABINET SECTION FOR FACE FRAME DEPTH

1/4"
3/8"
3/4" 3/4"

Flush Overlay Cabinet Drawer Detail

DRAWING #

SCALE
HALF SIZE

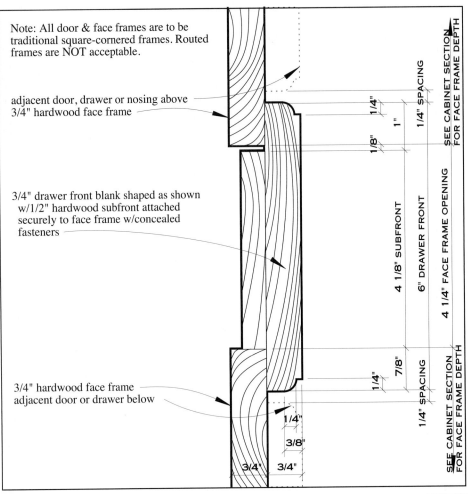

Note: All door & face frames are to be traditional square-cornered frames. Routed frames are NOT acceptable.

adjacent door, drawer or nosing above 3/4" hardwood face frame

3/4" drawer front blank shaped as shown w/1/2" hardwood subfront attached securely to face frame w/concealed fasteners

3/4" hardwood face frame adjacent door or drawer below

1/4"

3/8"

3/4" 3/4"

1/4"

1/8"

1"

1/4" SPACING

SEE CABINET SECTION FOR FACE FRAME DEPTH

4 1/8" SUBFRONT

6" DRAWER FRONT

4 1/4" FACE FRAME OPENING

1/4"

7/8"

1/4" SPACING

SEE CABINET SECTION FOR FACE FRAME DEPTH

DRAWING #

Flush Overlay Cabinet Drawer Blank

SCALE

HALF SIZE

CDRN002
210

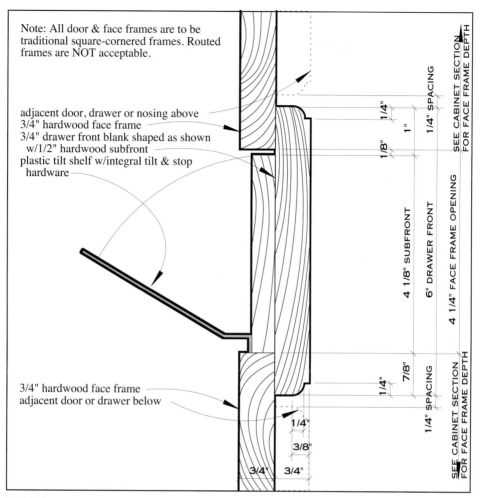

Note: All door & face frames are to be traditional square-cornered frames. Routed frames are NOT acceptable.

adjacent door, drawer or nosing above
3/4" hardwood face frame
3/4" drawer front blank shaped as shown
 w/1/2" hardwood subfront
plastic tilt shelf w/integral tilt & stop
 hardware

3/4" hardwood face frame
adjacent door or drawer below

SEE CABINET SECTION
FOR FACE FRAME DEPTH

1/4"
1"
1/4" SPACING
1/8"

4 1/8" SUBFRONT
6" DRAWER FRONT
4 1/4" FACE FRAME OPENING

1/4"
7/8"
1/4" SPACING

SEE CABINET SECTION
FOR FACE FRAME DEPTH

1/4"
3/8"
3/4"   3/4"

SCALE
HALF SIZE

DRAWING #

Flush Overlay Cabinet Tilt Drawer

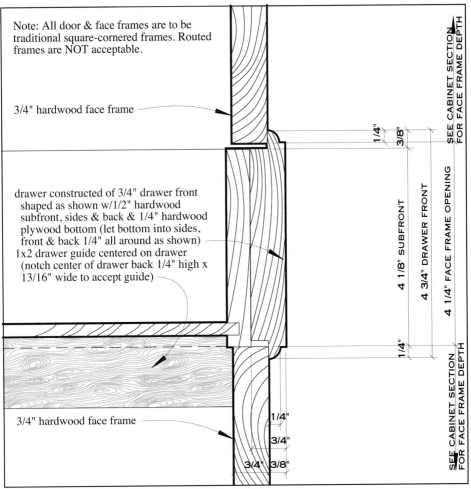

Note: All door & face frames are to be
traditional square-cornered frames. Routed
frames are NOT acceptable.

3/4" hardwood face frame

drawer constructed of 3/4" drawer front
  shaped as shown w/1/2" hardwood
  subfront, sides & back & 1/4" hardwood
  plywood bottom (let bottom into sides,
  front & back 1/4" all around as shown)
1x2 drawer guide centered on drawer
  (notch center of drawer back 1/4" high x
  13/16" wide to accept guide)

3/4" hardwood face frame

1/4"

3/8"

SEE CABINET SECTION
FOR FACE FRAME DEPTH

4 1/8" SUBFRONT

4 3/4" DRAWER FRONT

4 1/4" FACE FRAME OPENING

SEE CABINET SECTION
FOR FACE FRAME DEPTH

1/4"

1/4"

3/4"

3/4" 3/8"

SEE CABINET SECTION
FOR FACE FRAME DEPTH

3/8" Offset Cabinet Drawer Detail

DRAWING #

SCALE
**HALF
SIZE**

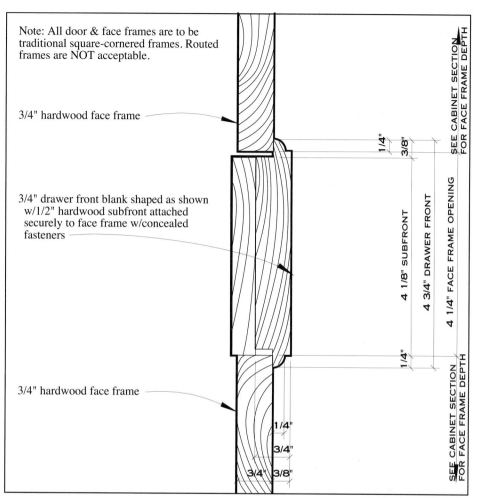

Note: All door & face frames are to be
traditional square-cornered frames. Routed
frames are NOT acceptable.

3/4" hardwood face frame

3/4" drawer front blank shaped as shown
w/1/2" hardwood subfront attached
securely to face frame w/concealed
fasteners

3/4" hardwood face frame

1/4"
3/8"

SEE CABINET SECTION
FOR FACE FRAME DEPTH

4 1/8" SUBFRONT

4 3/4" DRAWER FRONT

4 1/4" FACE FRAME OPENING

1/4"

SEE CABINET SECTION
FOR FACE FRAME DEPTH

1/4"

3/4"

3/4" 3/8"

3/8" Offset Cabinet Drawer Blank

SCALE
**HALF
SIZE**

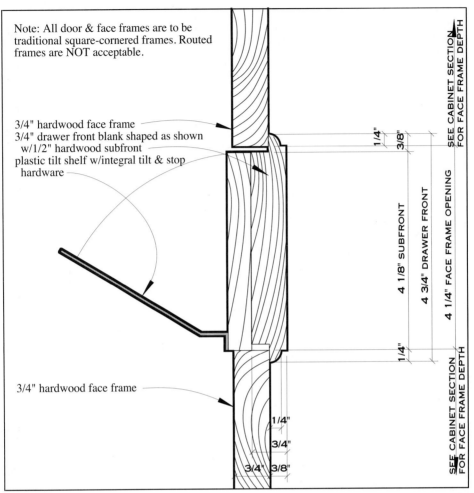

Note: All door & face frames are to be traditional square-cornered frames. Routed frames are NOT acceptable.

3/4" hardwood face frame
3/4" drawer front blank shaped as shown w/1/2" hardwood subfront
plastic tilt shelf w/integral tilt & stop hardware

1/4"
3/8"

SEE CABINET SECTION FOR FACE FRAME DEPTH

4 1/8" SUBFRONT

4 3/4" DRAWER FRONT

4 1/4" FACE FRAME OPENING

3/4" hardwood face frame

1/4"

SEE CABINET SECTION FOR FACE FRAME DEPTH

1/4"
3/4"
3/4" 3/8"

DRAWING #

3/8" Offset Cabinet Tilt Drawer

SCALE
HALF SIZE

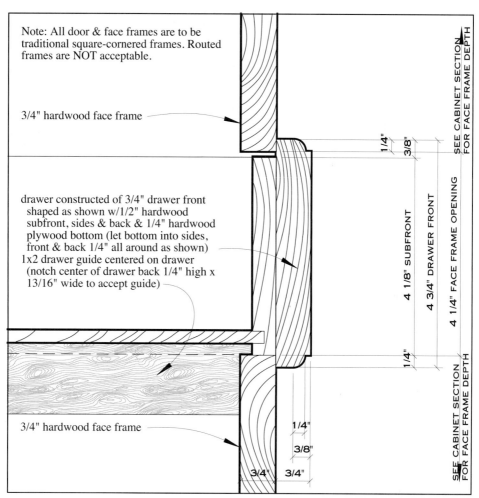

Note: All door & face frames are to be traditional square-cornered frames. Routed frames are NOT acceptable.

3/4" hardwood face frame

drawer constructed of 3/4" drawer front shaped as shown w/1/2" hardwood subfront, sides & back & 1/4" hardwood plywood bottom (let bottom into sides, front & back 1/4" all around as shown) 1x2 drawer guide centered on drawer (notch center of drawer back 1/4" high x 13/16" wide to accept guide)

3/4" hardwood face frame

1/4"
3/8"

SEE CABINET SECTION FOR FACE FRAME DEPTH

4 1/4" FACE FRAME OPENING

4 3/4" DRAWER FRONT

4 1/8" SUBFRONT

1/4"

1/4"
3/8"
3/4"   3/4"

SEE CABINET SECTION FOR FACE FRAME DEPTH

DRAWING #

Reveal Overlay Cabinet Drawer Detail

SCALE
HALF SIZE

CDRN007
215

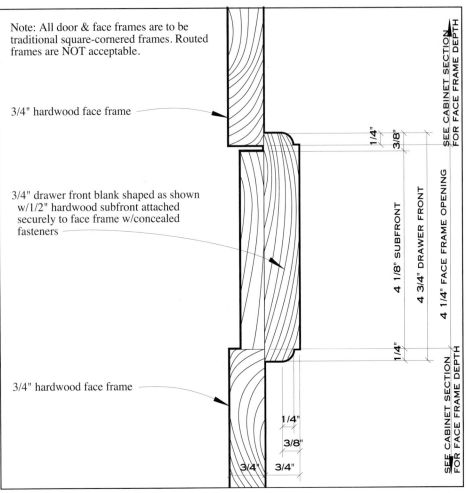

Note: All door & face frames are to be traditional square-cornered frames. Routed frames are NOT acceptable.

3/4" hardwood face frame

3/4" drawer front blank shaped as shown w/1/2" hardwood subfront attached securely to face frame w/concealed fasteners

3/4" hardwood face frame

1/4"

3/8"

4 1/8" SUBFRONT

4 3/4" DRAWER FRONT

4 1/4" FACE FRAME OPENING

SEE CABINET SECTION FOR FACE FRAME DEPTH

1/4"

SEE CABINET SECTION FOR FACE FRAME DEPTH

1/4"

3/8"

3/4"   3/4"

SEE CABINET SECTION FOR FACE FRAME DEPTH

Reveal Overlay Cabinet Drawer Blank

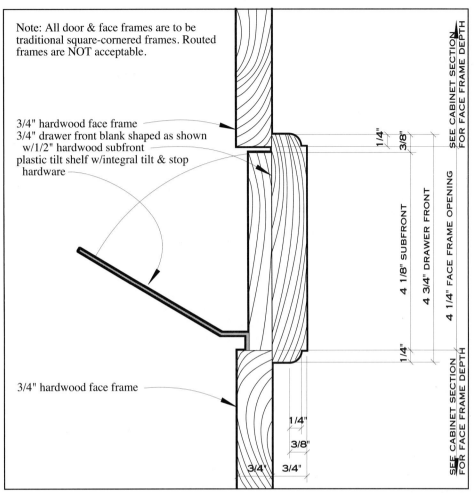

Note: All door & face frames are to be traditional square-cornered frames. Routed frames are NOT acceptable.

3/4" hardwood face frame
3/4" drawer front blank shaped as shown
 w/1/2" hardwood subfront
plastic tilt shelf w/integral tilt & stop
 hardware

3/4" hardwood face frame

1/4"
3/8"

SEE CABINET SECTION
FOR FACE FRAME DEPTH

4 1/8" SUBFRONT

4 3/4" DRAWER FRONT

4 1/4" FACE FRAME OPENING

1/4"

SEE CABINET SECTION
FOR FACE FRAME DEPTH

1/4"
3/8"
3/4"   3/4"

Reveal Overlay Cabinet Tilt Drawer

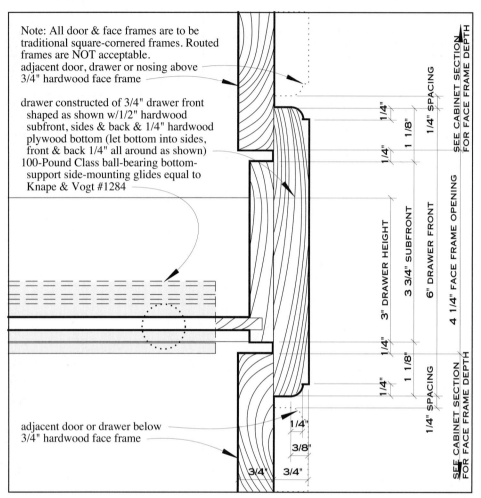

Note: All door & face frames are to be traditional square-cornered frames. Routed frames are NOT acceptable.
adjacent door, drawer or nosing above 3/4" hardwood face frame

drawer constructed of 3/4" drawer front shaped as shown w/1/2" hardwood subfront, sides & back & 1/4" hardwood plywood bottom (let bottom into sides, front & back 1/4" all around as shown)
100-Pound Class ball-bearing bottom-support side-mounting glides equal to Knape & Vogt #1284

adjacent door or drawer below 3/4" hardwood face frame

1/4" 1/4" 1/4" SPACING

SEE CABINET SECTION FOR FACE FRAME DEPTH

1/4"   1 1/8"

3" DRAWER HEIGHT

3 3/4" SUBFRONT

6" DRAWER FRONT

4 1/4" FACE FRAME OPENING

1/4"   1 1/8"

1/4" SPACING

SEE CABINET SECTION FOR FACE FRAME DEPTH

1/4"

3/8"

3/4"   3/4"

Flush Overlay Cabinet Drawer Detail

SCALE
HALF
SIZE

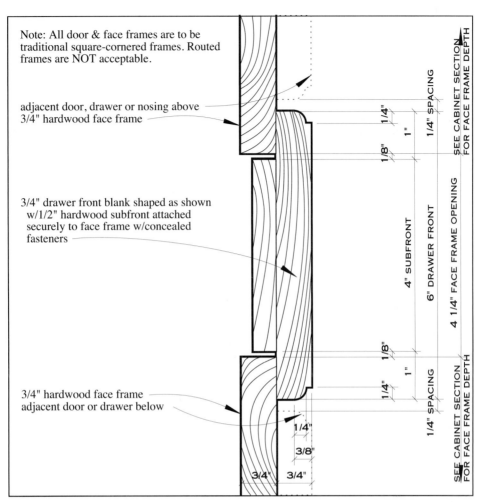

Note: All door & face frames are to be traditional square-cornered frames. Routed frames are NOT acceptable.

adjacent door, drawer or nosing above 3/4" hardwood face frame

3/4" drawer front blank shaped as shown w/1/2" hardwood subfront attached securely to face frame w/concealed fasteners

3/4" hardwood face frame adjacent door or drawer below

1/4" SPACING
1"
1/8"
SEE CABINET SECTION FOR FACE FRAME DEPTH

4" SUBFRONT
6" DRAWER FRONT
4 1/4" FACE FRAME OPENING

1/8"
1"
1/4"
1/4" SPACING
SEE CABINET SECTION FOR FACE FRAME DEPTH

1/4"
3/8"
3/4"   3/4"

DRAWING #

Flush Overlay Cabinet Drawer Blank

SCALE
HALF SIZE

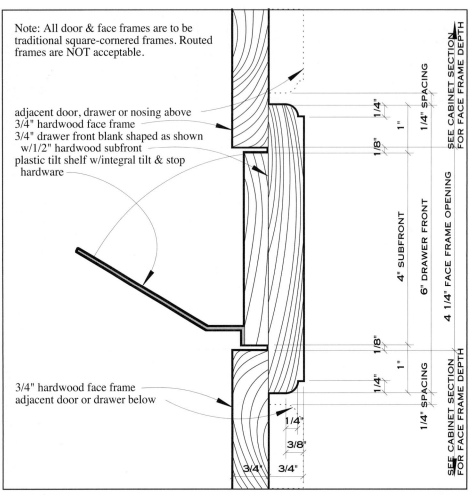

Note: All door & face frames are to be
traditional square-cornered frames. Routed
frames are NOT acceptable.

adjacent door, drawer or nosing above
3/4" hardwood face frame
3/4" drawer front blank shaped as shown
 w/1/2" hardwood subfront
plastic tilt shelf w/integral tilt & stop
 hardware

3/4" hardwood face frame
adjacent door or drawer below

1/4"
1"
1/4" SPACING

1/8"
1"

SEE CABINET SECTION
FOR FACE FRAME DEPTH

4" SUBFRONT

6" DRAWER FRONT

4 1/4" FACE FRAME OPENING

1/8"
1"
1/4"
1/4" SPACING

SEE CABINET SECTION
FOR FACE FRAME DEPTH

1/4"
3/8"
3/4"
3/4"

Flush Overlay Cabinet Tilt Drawer

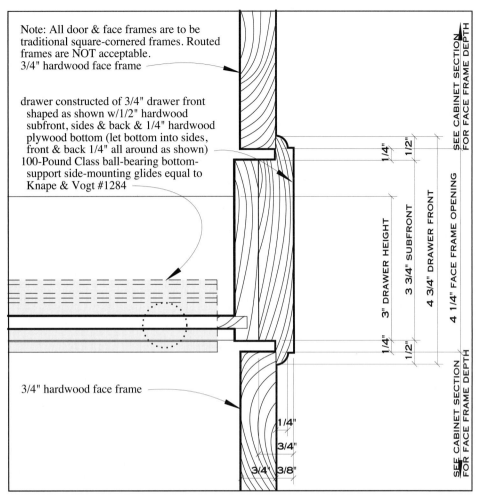

Note: All door & face frames are to be
traditional square-cornered frames. Routed
frames are NOT acceptable.
3/4" hardwood face frame

drawer constructed of 3/4" drawer front
  shaped as shown w/1/2" hardwood
  subfront, sides & back & 1/4" hardwood
  plywood bottom (let bottom into sides,
  front & back 1/4" all around as shown)
100-Pound Class ball-bearing bottom-
  support side-mounting glides equal to
  Knape & Vogt #1284

3/4" hardwood face frame

SEE CABINET SECTION
FOR FACE FRAME DEPTH

1/4" 1/2"

3" DRAWER HEIGHT

3 3/4" SUBFRONT

4 3/4" DRAWER FRONT

4 1/4" FACE FRAME OPENING

1/4"

1/2"

SEE CABINET SECTION
FOR FACE FRAME DEPTH

1/4"
3/4"
3/4" 3/8"

3/8" Offset Cabinet Drawer Detail

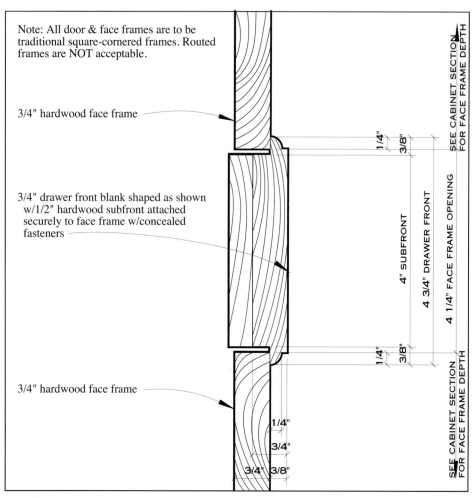

Note: All door & face frames are to be traditional square-cornered frames. Routed frames are NOT acceptable.

3/4" hardwood face frame

3/4" drawer front blank shaped as shown w/1/2" hardwood subfront attached securely to face frame w/concealed fasteners

3/4" hardwood face frame

1/4"

3/8"

SEE CABINET SECTION FOR FACE FRAME DEPTH

4" SUBFRONT

4 3/4" DRAWER FRONT

4 1/4" FACE FRAME OPENING

1/4"

3/8"

SEE CABINET SECTION FOR FACE FRAME DEPTH

1/4"

3/4"

3/4" 3/8"

SEE CABINET SECTION FOR FACE FRAME DEPTH

DRAWING #

3/8" Offset Cabinet Drawer Blank

SCALE
HALF
SIZE

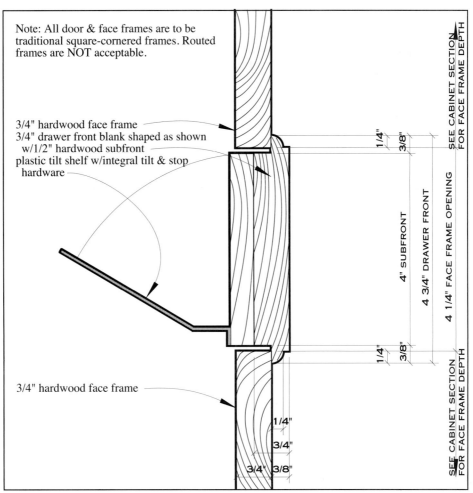

Note: All door & face frames are to be
traditional square-cornered frames. Routed
frames are NOT acceptable.

3/4" hardwood face frame
3/4" drawer front blank shaped as shown
 w/1/2" hardwood subfront
plastic tilt shelf w/integral tilt & stop
 hardware

SEE CABINET SECTION
FOR FACE FRAME DEPTH

1/4"
3/8"

4" SUBFRONT

4 3/4" DRAWER FRONT

4 1/4" FACE FRAME OPENING

1/4"
3/8"

SEE CABINET SECTION
FOR FACE FRAME DEPTH

3/4" hardwood face frame

1/4"

3/4"

3/4"   3/8"

3/8" Offset Cabinet Tilt Drawer

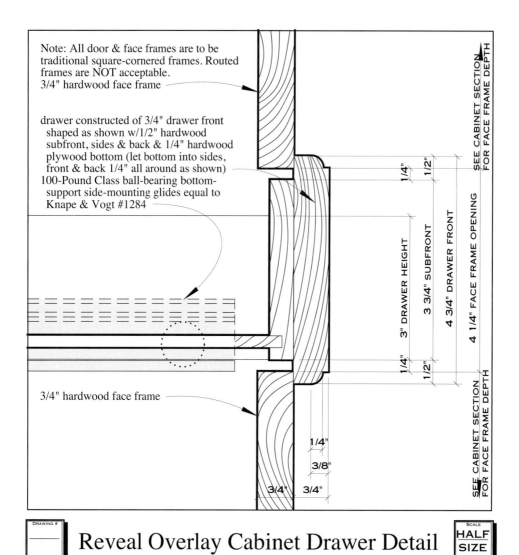

Note: All door & face frames are to be traditional square-cornered frames. Routed frames are NOT acceptable.
3/4" hardwood face frame

drawer constructed of 3/4" drawer front shaped as shown w/1/2" hardwood subfront, sides & back & 1/4" hardwood plywood bottom (let bottom into sides, front & back 1/4" all around as shown) 100-Pound Class ball-bearing bottom-support side-mounting glides equal to Knape & Vogt #1284

3/4" hardwood face frame

SEE CABINET SECTION FOR FACE FRAME DEPTH

1/4"
1/2"
3" DRAWER HEIGHT
3 3/4" SUBFRONT
4 3/4" DRAWER FRONT
4 1/4" FACE FRAME OPENING

1/4"
1/2"

SEE CABINET SECTION FOR FACE FRAME DEPTH

1/4"
3/8"
3/4"   3/4"

DRAWING #

Reveal Overlay Cabinet Drawer Detail

SCALE
HALF SIZE

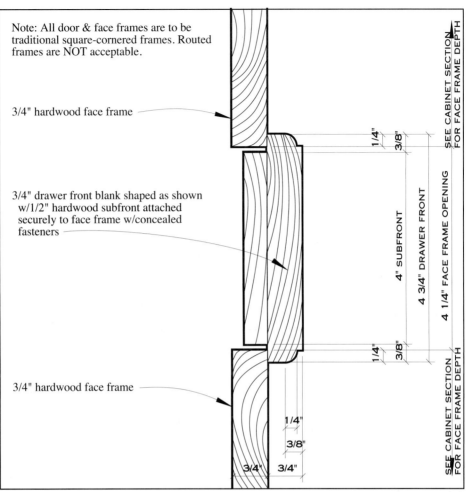

Note: All door & face frames are to be traditional square-cornered frames. Routed frames are NOT acceptable.

3/4" hardwood face frame

3/4" drawer front blank shaped as shown w/1/2" hardwood subfront attached securely to face frame w/concealed fasteners

3/4" hardwood face frame

1/4"

3/8"

SEE CABINET SECTION FOR FACE FRAME DEPTH

4" SUBFRONT

4 3/4" DRAWER FRONT

4 1/4" FACE FRAME OPENING

1/4"

3/8"

SEE CABINET SECTION FOR FACE FRAME DEPTH

1/4"

3/8"

3/4"   3/4"

Reveal Overlay Cabinet Drawer Blank

SCALE
HALF SIZE

DRAWING #

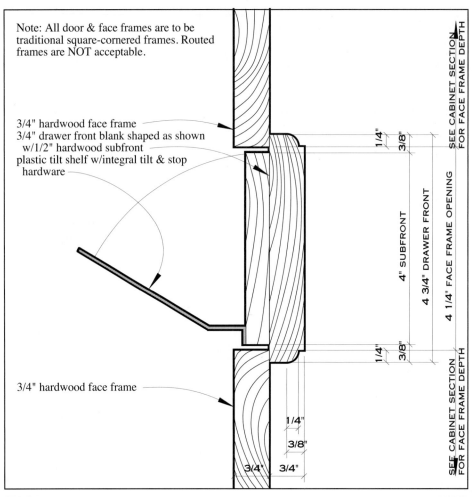

Note: All door & face frames are to be traditional square-cornered frames. Routed frames are NOT acceptable.

3/4" hardwood face frame
3/4" drawer front blank shaped as shown w/1/2" hardwood subfront
plastic tilt shelf w/integral tilt & stop hardware

3/4" hardwood face frame

SEE CABINET SECTION FOR FACE FRAME DEPTH

1/4"
3/8"

4" SUBFRONT

4 3/4" DRAWER FRONT

4 1/4" FACE FRAME OPENING

1/4"
3/8"

SEE CABINET SECTION FOR FACE FRAME DEPTH

SEE CABINET SECTION FOR FACE FRAME DEPTH

1/4"
3/8"
3/4"   3/4"

Reveal Overlay Cabinet Tilt Drawer

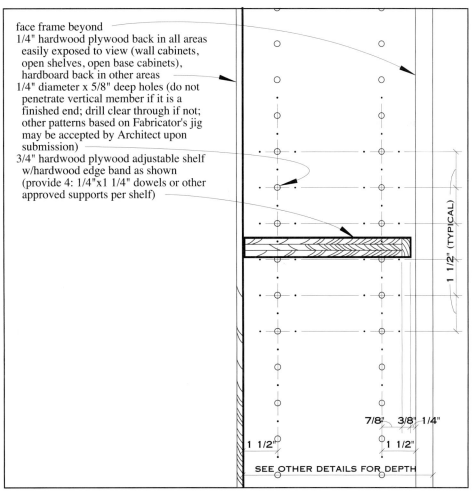

face frame beyond
1/4" hardwood plywood back in all areas
   easily exposed to view (wall cabinets,
   open shelves, open base cabinets),
   hardboard back in other areas
1/4" diameter x 5/8" deep holes (do not
   penetrate vertical member if it is a
   finished end; drill clear through if not;
   other patterns based on Fabricator's jig
   may be accepted by Architect upon
   submission)
3/4" hardwood plywood adjustable shelf
   w/hardwood edge band as shown
   (provide 4: 1/4"x1 1/4" dowels or other
   approved supports per shelf)

1 1/2" (TYPICAL)

7/8"   3/8" 1/4"

1 1/2"   1 1/2"

SEE OTHER DETAILS FOR DEPTH

DRAWING #

Adjustable Plywood Shelf Detail

SCALE
3"
1'-0"

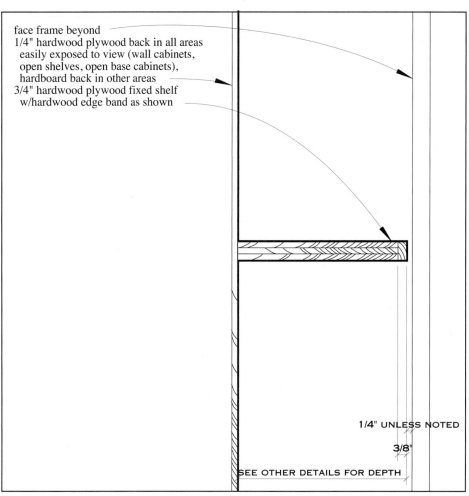

face frame beyond
1/4" hardwood plywood back in all areas
 easily exposed to view (wall cabinets,
 open shelves, open base cabinets),
 hardboard back in other areas
3/4" hardwood plywood fixed shelf
 w/hardwood edge band as shown

1/4" UNLESS NOTED

3/8"

SEE OTHER DETAILS FOR DEPTH

DRAWING #

Fixed Plywood Shelf Detail

SCALE
3"
1'-0"

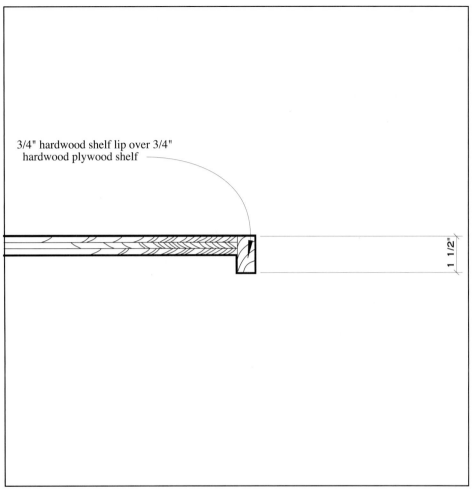

3/4" hardwood shelf lip over 3/4"
hardwood plywood shelf

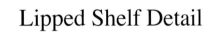

1 1/2"

Lipped Shelf Detail

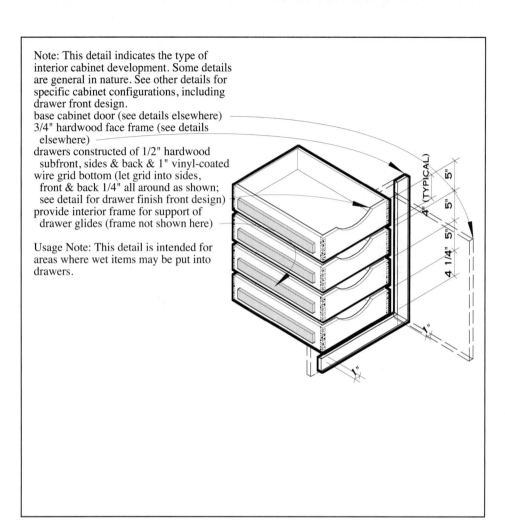

Note: This detail indicates the type of interior cabinet development. Some details are general in nature. See other details for specific cabinet configurations, including drawer front design.

base cabinet door (see details elsewhere)
3/4" hardwood face frame (see details elsewhere)

drawers constructed of 1/2" hardwood subfront, sides & back & 1" vinyl-coated wire grid bottom (let grid into sides, front & back 1/4" all around as shown; see detail for drawer finish front design)

provide interior frame for support of drawer glides (frame not shown here)

Usage Note: This detail is intended for areas where wet items may be put into drawers.

4" (TYPICAL)

5"

5"

5"

4 1/4"

1"

1"

DRAWING #

Base Type 1: 4 Equal Drawers

SCALE

3/4"
1'-0"

Note: This detail indicates the type of
interior cabinet development. Some details
are general in nature. See other details for
specific cabinet configurations, including
drawer front design.
base cabinet door (see details elsewhere)
3/4" hardwood face frame (see details
  elsewhere)
drawers constructed of 1/2" hardwood
  subfront, sides & back & 1" vinyl-coated
  wire grid bottom (let grid into sides,
  front & back 1/4" all around as shown;
  see detail for drawer finish front design)
provide interior frame for support of
  drawer glides (frame not shown here)

Usage: This detail is intended for areas
where wet items may be put into drawers.

Base Type 2: 4 Equal Drawers w/Grid

SCALE
3/4"
1'-0"

CDT002
231

Note: This detail indicates the type of
interior cabinet development. Some details
are general in nature. See other details for
specific cabinet configurations, including
drawer front design.
base cabinet door (see details elsewhere)
3/4" hardwood face frame (see details
  elsewhere)
drawers constructed of 1/2" hardwood
  subfront, sides & back & 1/4" hardwood
  plywood bottom (let bottom into sides,
  front & back 1/4" all around as shown;
  see detail for drawer finish front design)
provide interior frame for support of
  drawer glides (frame not shown here)

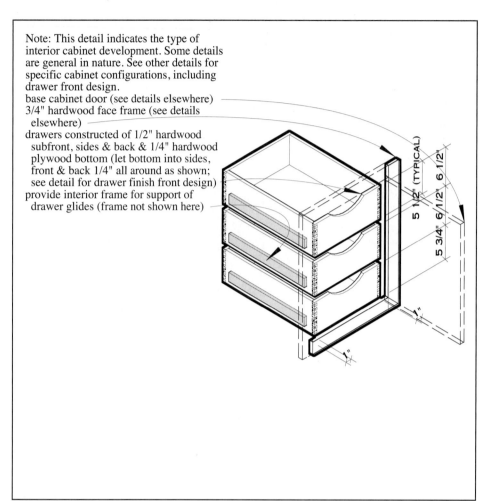

5 1/2" (TYPICAL)

6 1/2"

5 3/4" 6 1/2"

DRAWING #

Base Type 3: 3 Equal Drawers

SCALE

3/4"
1'-0"

Note: This detail indicates the type of
interior cabinet development. Some details
are general in nature. See other details for
specific cabinet configurations, including
drawer front design.

base cabinet door (see details elsewhere)
3/4" hardwood face frame (see details
  elsewhere)

drawers constructed of 1/2" hardwood
  subfront, sides & back & 1" vinyl-coated
  wire grid bottom (let grid into sides,
  front & back 1/4" all around as shown;
  see detail for drawer finish front design)
provide interior frame for support of
  drawer glides (frame not shown here)

Usage: This detail is intended for areas
where wet items may be put into drawers.

5 1/2" (TYPICAL)

6 1/2"

6 1/2"

5 3/4"

1"

1"

Base Type 4: 3 Equal Drawers w/Grid

DRAWING #

SCALE
3/4"
1'-0"

CDT004
233

Note: This detail indicates the type of interior cabinet development. Some details are general in nature. See other details for specific cabinet configurations, including drawer front design.

base cabinet door (see details elsewhere)

3/4" hardwood face frame (see details elsewhere)

drawers constructed of 1/2" hardwood subfront, sides & back & 1/4" hardwood plywood bottom (let bottom into sides, front & back 1/4" all around as shown; see detail for drawer finish front design)

provide interior frame for support of drawer glides (frame not shown here)

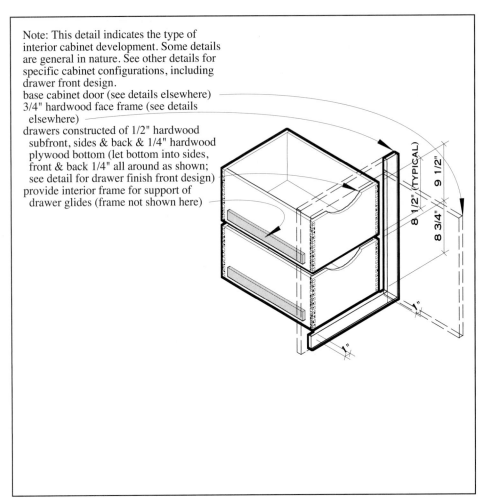

8 1/2" (TYPICAL)

9 1/2"

8 3/4"

1"

1"

Base Type 5: 2 Equal Drawers

SCALE
3/4"
1'-0"

Note: This detail indicates the type of interior cabinet development. Some details are general in nature. See other details for specific cabinet configurations, including drawer front design.

base cabinet door (see details elsewhere)

3/4" hardwood face frame (see details elsewhere)

drawers constructed of 1/2" hardwood subfront, sides & back & 1" vinyl-coated wire grid bottom (let grid into sides, front & back 1/4" all around as shown; see detail for drawer finish front design)

provide interior frame for support of drawer glides (frame not shown here)

Usage: This detail is intended for areas where wet items may be put into drawers.

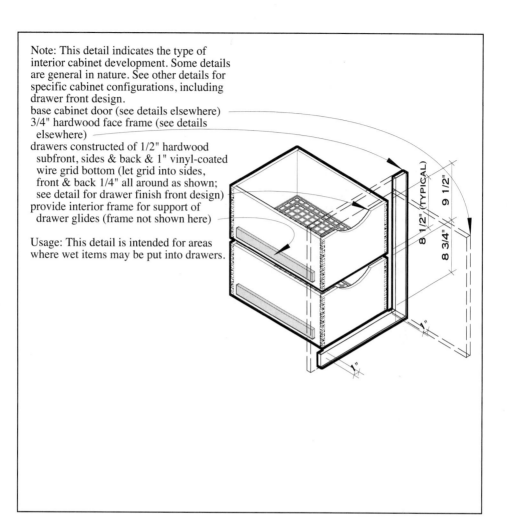

1/2" (TYPICAL)

9 1/2"

8 3/4"

1"

1"

Base Type 6: 2 Equal Drawers w/Grid

 SCALE 3/4" 1'-0"

Note: This detail indicates the type of interior cabinet development. Some details are general in nature. See other details for specific cabinet configurations, including drawer front design.

base cabinet door (see details elsewhere)

3/4" hardwood face frame (see details elsewhere)

trash cans

drawers constructed of 1/2" hardwood subfront, sides & back & 1" vinyl-coated wire grid bottom (let grid into sides, front & back 1/4" all around as shown; see detail for drawer finish front design; provide full-height divider to divide drawer into equal front & back compartments as shown)

provide interior frame for support of drawer glides (frame not shown here)

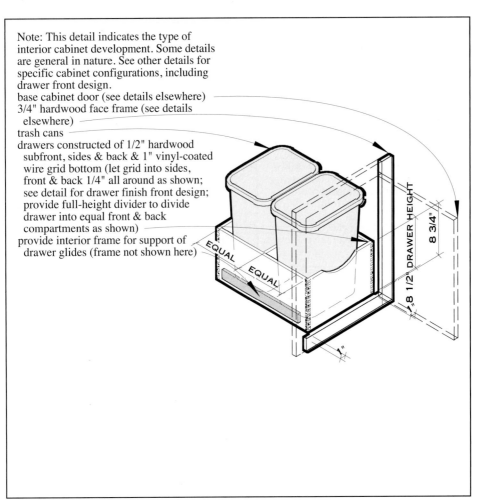

Base Type 7: Trash Containers

SCALE
3/4"
1'-0"

Note: This detail indicates the type of interior cabinet development. Some details are general in nature. See other details for specific cabinet configurations, including drawer front design.

base cabinet door (see details elsewhere)

3/4" hardwood face frame (see details elsewhere)

drawers constructed of 1/2" hardwood subfront, sides & back & 1/4" hardwood plywood bottom (let bottom into sides, front & back 1/4" all around as shown; see detail for drawer finish front design)

provide interior frame for support of drawer glides (frame not shown here)

Usage: This type is intended for face frame openings between 1'-2" & 1'-4" because of typical widths of cereal boxes.

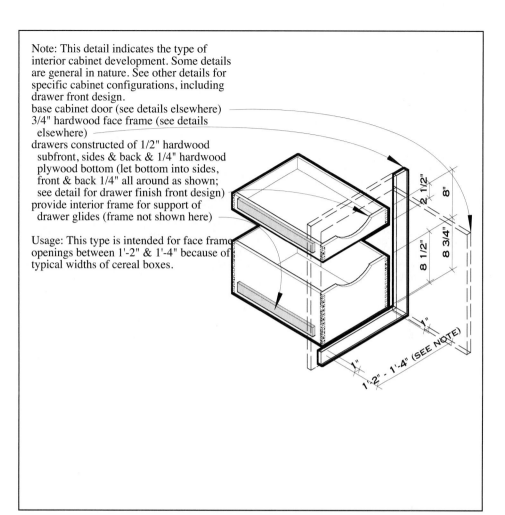

Base Type 8: Soup & Cereal

DRAWING #

SCALE
3/4"
1'-0"

CDT008
237

Note: This detail indicates the type of interior cabinet development. Some details are general in nature. See other details for specific cabinet configurations, including drawer front design.

base cabinet door (see details elsewhere)

3/4" hardwood face frame (see details elsewhere)

drawers constructed of 1/2" hardwood subfront, sides & back & 1" vinyl-coated wire grid bottom (let grid into sides, front & back 1/4" all around as shown; see detail for drawer finish front design)

provide interior frame for support of drawer glides (frame not shown here)

Usage: This detail is intended for drawers for pots & pans or other areas where potentially wet objects in a variety of sizes need to be stored.

Base Type 9: Pots & Pans

DRAWING #

SCALE
3/4"
1'-0"

Note: This detail indicates the type of interior cabinet development. Some details are general in nature. See other details for specific cabinet configurations, including drawer front design.

base cabinet door (see details elsewhere)
3/4" hardwood face frame (see details elsewhere)

drawers constructed of 1/2" hardwood subfront, sides & back & 1/4" hardwood plywood bottom (let bottom into sides, front & back 1/4" all around as shown; see detail for drawer finish front design)
provide interior frame for support of drawer glides (frame not shown here)

Usage: This type is intended for small appliances; low walls on drawers allow appliances to be lifted out easily.

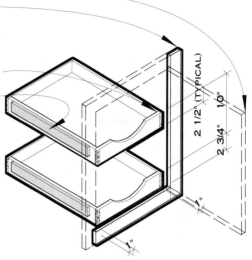

Base Type 10: Small Appliances

Note: This detail indicates the type of
interior cabinet development. Some details
are general in nature. See other details for
specific cabinet configurations, including
drawer front design.
base cabinet door (see details elsewhere)
3/4" hardwood face frame (see details
  elsewhere)
drawers constructed of 1/2" hardwood
  subfront, sides & back & 1/4" hardwood
  plywood bottom (let bottom into sides,
  front & back 1/4" all around as shown;
  see detail for drawer finish front design)
provide interior frame for support of
  drawer glides (frame not shown here)

Usage: This type is intended for large
appliances; low walls on the drawer allows
appliances to be lifted out easily.

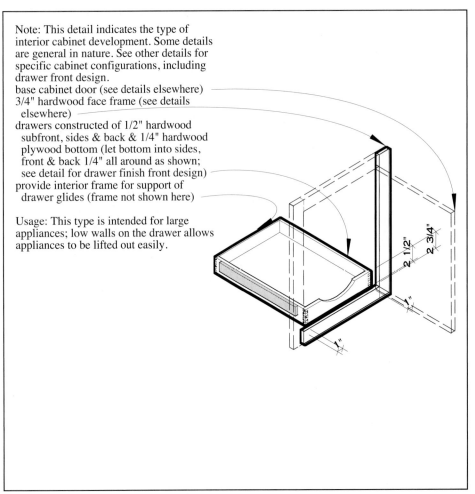

Base Type 11: Large Appliances

Note: This detail indicates the type of
interior cabinet development. Some details
are general in nature. See other details for
specific cabinet configurations, including
drawer front design.
base cabinet door (see details elsewhere)
3/4" hardwood face frame (see details
  elsewhere)
dividers constructed of 1/4" AA hardwood
  plywood plowed 3/8" into hardwood
  plywood bottom w/3/4" hardwood
  quarter round stop & plowed 3/8" into
  hardwood 1x4 guides @ top

Usage: This type is intended for storage of
  cooking sheets & tins

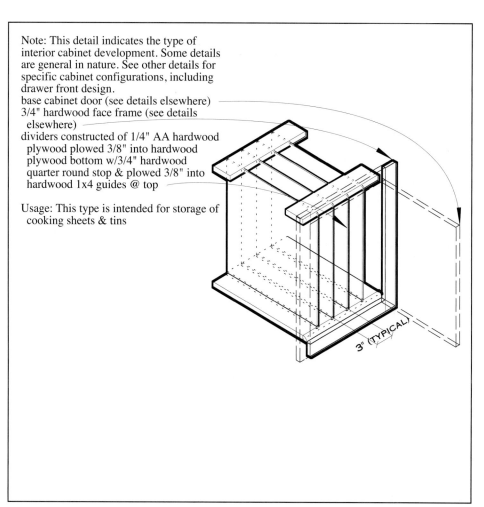

3" (TYPICAL)

DRAWING #

Base Type 12: Sheets & Tins

SCALE
3/4"
1'-0"

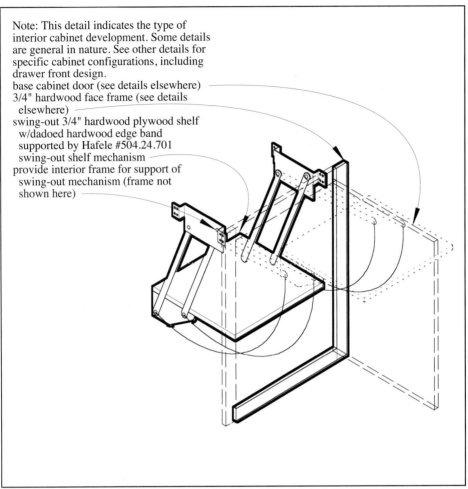

Note: This detail indicates the type of interior cabinet development. Some details are general in nature. See other details for specific cabinet configurations, including drawer front design.

base cabinet door (see details elsewhere)
3/4" hardwood face frame (see details elsewhere)
swing-out 3/4" hardwood plywood shelf w/dadoed hardwood edge band supported by Hafele #504.24.701 swing-out shelf mechanism
provide interior frame for support of swing-out mechanism (frame not shown here)

Base Type 13: Lg. Appliance Swing-Out

DRAWING #

SCALE
3/4"
1'-0"

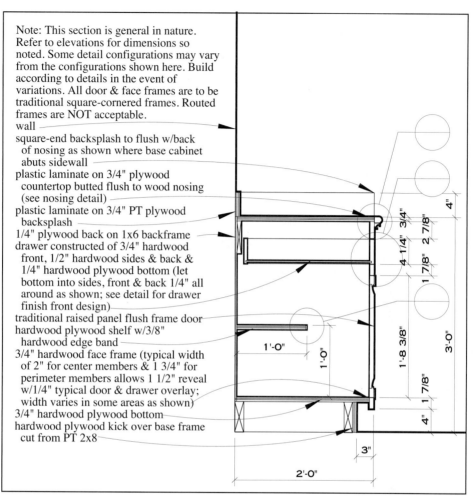

Note: This section is general in nature. Refer to elevations for dimensions so noted. Some detail configurations may vary from the configurations shown here. Build according to details in the event of variations. All door & face frames are to be traditional square-cornered frames. Routed frames are NOT acceptable.

wall

square-end backsplash to flush w/back of nosing as shown where base cabinet abuts sidewall

plastic laminate on 3/4" plywood countertop butted flush to wood nosing (see nosing detail)

plastic laminate on 3/4" PT plywood backsplash

1/4" plywood back on 1x6 backframe

drawer constructed of 3/4" hardwood front, 1/2" hardwood sides & back & 1/4" hardwood plywood bottom (let bottom into sides, front & back 1/4" all around as shown; see detail for drawer finish front design)

traditional raised panel flush frame door

hardwood plywood shelf w/3/8" hardwood edge band

3/4" hardwood face frame (typical width of 2" for center members & 1 3/4" for perimeter members allows 1 1/2" reveal w/1/4" typical door & drawer overlay; width varies in some areas as shown)

3/4" hardwood plywood bottom

hardwood plywood kick over base frame cut from PT 2x8

3/4"

4 1/4"

2 7/8"

4"

1 7/8"

1'-8 3/8"

3'-0"

1 7/8"

4"

1'-0"

1'-0"

3"

2'-0"

Base Cabinet Section

DRAWING #

SCALE
3/4"
1'-0"

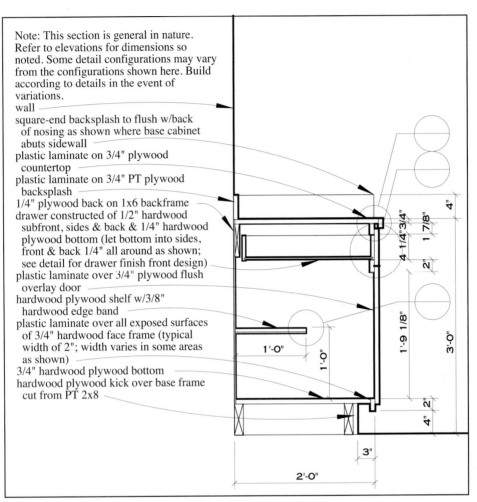

Note: This section is general in nature. Refer to elevations for dimensions so noted. Some detail configurations may vary from the configurations shown here. Build according to details in the event of variations.

wall

square-end backsplash to flush w/back of nosing as shown where base cabinet abuts sidewall

plastic laminate on 3/4" plywood countertop

plastic laminate on 3/4" PT plywood backsplash

1/4" plywood back on 1x6 backframe

drawer constructed of 1/2" hardwood subfront, sides & back & 1/4" hardwood plywood bottom (let bottom into sides, front & back 1/4" all around as shown; see detail for drawer finish front design)

plastic laminate over 3/4" plywood flush overlay door

hardwood plywood shelf w/3/8" hardwood edge band

plastic laminate over all exposed surfaces of 3/4" hardwood face frame (typical width of 2"; width varies in some areas as shown)

3/4" hardwood plywood bottom

hardwood plywood kick over base frame cut from PT 2x8

1'-0"

1'-0"

4 1/4" 3/4"

1 7/8"

2"

4"

1'-9 1/8"

3'-0"

2"

4"

3"

2'-0"

Base Cabinet Section

SCALE
3/4"
1'-0"

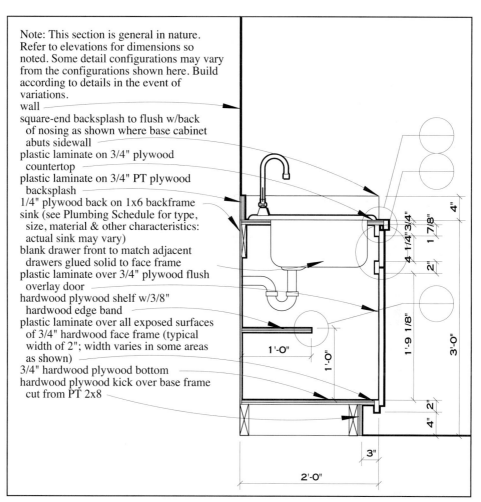

Note: This section is general in nature.
Refer to elevations for dimensions so
noted. Some detail configurations may vary
from the configurations shown here. Build
according to details in the event of
variations.
wall
square-end backsplash to flush w/back
  of nosing as shown where base cabinet
  abuts sidewall
plastic laminate on 3/4" plywood
  countertop
plastic laminate on 3/4" PT plywood
  backsplash
1/4" plywood back on 1x6 backframe
sink (see Plumbing Schedule for type,
  size, material & other characteristics:
  actual sink may vary)
blank drawer front to match adjacent
  drawers glued solid to face frame
plastic laminate over 3/4" plywood flush
  overlay door
hardwood plywood shelf w/3/8"
  hardwood edge band
plastic laminate over all exposed surfaces
  of 3/4" hardwood face frame (typical
  width of 2"; width varies in some areas
  as shown)
3/4" hardwood plywood bottom
hardwood plywood kick over base frame
  cut from PT 2x8

Base Cabinet Section @ Sink

DRAWING #

SCALE
3/4"
1'-0"

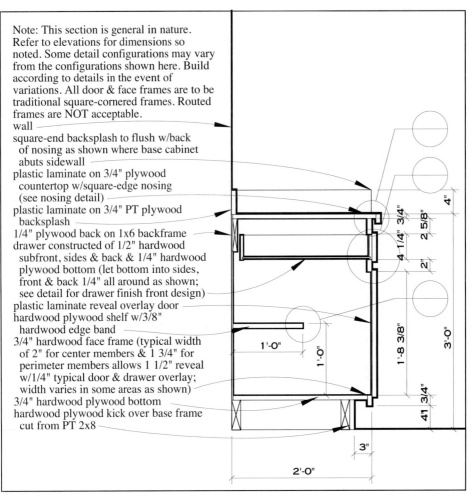

Note: This section is general in nature.
Refer to elevations for dimensions so
noted. Some detail configurations may vary
from the configurations shown here. Build
according to details in the event of
variations. All door & face frames are to be
traditional square-cornered frames. Routed
frames are NOT acceptable.
wall
square-end backsplash to flush w/back
  of nosing as shown where base cabinet
  abuts sidewall
plastic laminate on 3/4" plywood
  countertop w/square-edge nosing
  (see nosing detail)
plastic laminate on 3/4" PT plywood
  backsplash
1/4" plywood back on 1x6 backframe
drawer constructed of 1/2" hardwood
  subfront, sides & back & 1/4" hardwood
  plywood bottom (let bottom into sides,
  front & back 1/4" all around as shown;
  see detail for drawer finish front design)
plastic laminate reveal overlay door
hardwood plywood shelf w/3/8"
  hardwood edge band
3/4" hardwood face frame (typical width
  of 2" for center members & 1 3/4" for
  perimeter members allows 1 1/2" reveal
  w/1/4" typical door & drawer overlay;
  width varies in some areas as shown)
3/4" hardwood plywood bottom
hardwood plywood kick over base frame
  cut from PT 2x8

Base Cabinet Section

DRAWING #

SCALE
3/4"
1'-0"

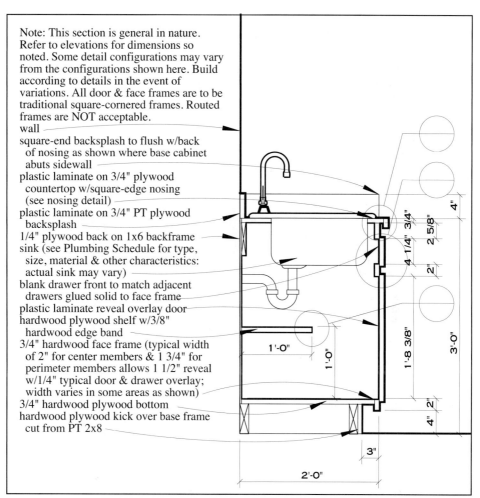

Note: This section is general in nature.
Refer to elevations for dimensions so
noted. Some detail configurations may vary
from the configurations shown here. Build
according to details in the event of
variations. All door & face frames are to be
traditional square-cornered frames. Routed
frames are NOT acceptable.
wall
square-end backsplash to flush w/back
  of nosing as shown where base cabinet
  abuts sidewall
plastic laminate on 3/4" plywood
  countertop w/square-edge nosing
  (see nosing detail)
plastic laminate on 3/4" PT plywood
  backsplash
1/4" plywood back on 1x6 backframe
sink (see Plumbing Schedule for type,
  size, material & other characteristics:
  actual sink may vary)
blank drawer front to match adjacent
  drawers glued solid to face frame
plastic laminate reveal overlay door
hardwood plywood shelf w/3/8"
  hardwood edge band
3/4" hardwood face frame (typical width
  of 2" for center members & 1 3/4" for
  perimeter members allows 1 1/2" reveal
  w/1/4" typical door & drawer overlay;
  width varies in some areas as shown)
3/4" hardwood plywood bottom
hardwood plywood kick over base frame
  cut from PT 2x8

 1'-0"

Base Cabinet Section @ Sink

DRAWING #

SCALE
3/4"
1'-0"

Note: This section is general in nature. Refer to elevations for dimensions so noted. Some detail configurations may vary from the configurations shown here. Build according to details in the event of variations. All door & face frames are to be traditional square-cornered frames. Routed frames are NOT acceptable.

wall

square-end backsplash to flush w/back of nosing as shown where base cabinet abuts sidewall

plastic laminate on 3/4" plywood countertop butted flush to wood nosing (see nosing detail)

plastic laminate on 3/4" PT plywood backsplash

1/4" plywood back on 1x6 backframe

drawer constructed of 1/2" hardwood subfront, sides & back & 1/4" hardwood plywood bottom (let bottom into sides, front & back 1/4" all around as shown; see detail for drawer finish front design)

traditional raised panel reveal overlay door

hardwood plywood shelf w/3/8" hardwood edge band

3/4" hardwood face frame (typical width of 2" for center members & 1 3/4" for perimeter members allows 1 1/2" reveal w/1/4" typical door & drawer overlay; width varies in some areas as shown)

3/4" hardwood plywood bottom

hardwood plywood kick over base frame cut from PT 2x8

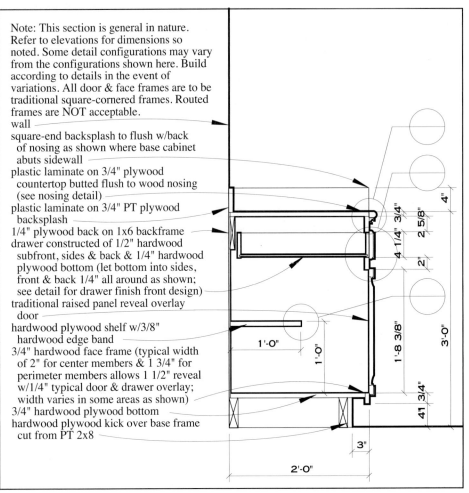

Base Cabinet Section

SCALE
3/4"
1'-0"

Note: This section is general in nature.
Refer to elevations for dimensions so
noted. Some detail configurations may vary
from the configurations shown here. Build
according to details in the event of
variations. All door & face frames are to be
traditional square-cornered frames. Routed
frames are NOT acceptable.
wall
square-end backsplash to flush w/back
  of nosing as shown where base cabinet
  abuts sidewall
plastic laminate on 3/4" plywood
  countertop butted flush to wood nosing
  (see nosing detail)
plastic laminate on 3/4" PT plywood
  backsplash
1/4" plywood back on 1x6 backframe
sink (see Plumbing Schedule for type,
  size, material & other characteristics:
  actual sink may vary)
blank drawer front to match adjacent
  drawers glued solid to face frame
traditional raised panel reveal overlay
  door
hardwood plywood shelf w/3/8"
  hardwood edge band
3/4" hardwood face frame (typical width
  of 2" for center members & 1 3/4" for
  perimeter members allows 1 1/2" reveal
  w/1/4" typical door & drawer overlay;
  width varies in some areas as shown)
3/4" hardwood plywood bottom
hardwood plywood kick over base frame
  cut from PT 2x8

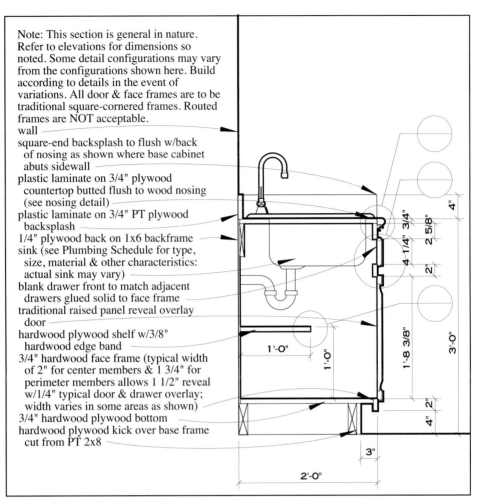

Base Cabinet Section @ Sink

DRAWING #

SCALE
3/4"
1'-0"

Note: This section is general in nature. Refer to elevations for dimensions so noted. Some detail configurations may vary from the configurations shown here. Build according to details in the event of variations.

wall

square-end backsplash to flush w/back of nosing as shown where base cabinet abuts sidewall

plastic laminate on 3/4" plywood countertop

plastic laminate on 3/4" PT plywood backsplash

1/4" plywood back on 1x6 backframe

lavatory (see Plumbing Schedule for type, size, material & other characteristics: actual sink may vary)

blank drawer front to match adjacent drawers glued solid to face frame

plastic laminate over 3/4" plywood flush overlay door

hardwood plywood shelf w/3/8" hardwood edge band

plastic laminate over all exposed surfaces of 3/4" hardwood face frame (typical width of 2"; width varies in some areas as shown)

3/4" hardwood plywood bottom

hardwood plywood kick over base frame cut from PT 2x8

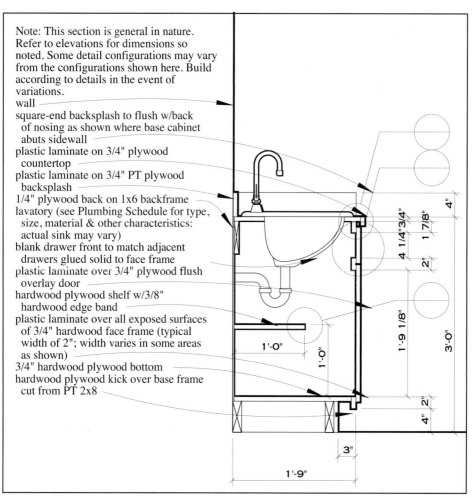

DRAWING #

Vanity Section @ Lavatory

SCALE
3/4"
1'-0"

Note: This section is general in nature.
Refer to elevations for dimensions so
noted. Some detail configurations may vary
from the configurations shown here. Build
according to details in the event of
variations.

wall
square-end backsplash to flush w/back
  of nosing as shown where base cabinet
  abuts sidewall
plastic laminate on 3/4" plywood
  countertop butted flush to wood nosing
  (see nosing detail)
plastic laminate on 3/4" PT plywood
  backsplash
1x6 backframe
sink (see Plumbing Schedule for type,
  size, material & other characteristics:
  actual sink may vary)
insulate pipes to prevent the possibility of
  contact with skin

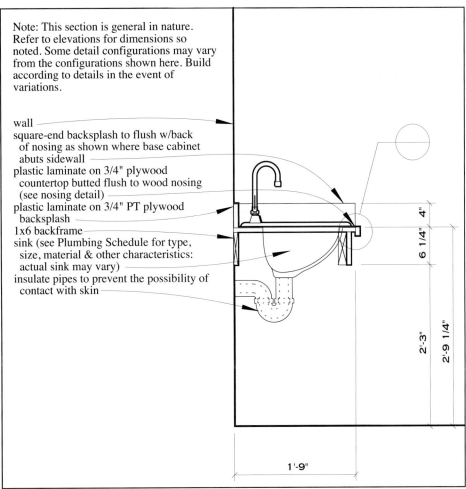

4"
6 1/4"
2'-3"
2'-9 1/4"
1'-9"

Cabinet Section @ Sink

DRAWING #

SCALE
3/4"
1'-0"

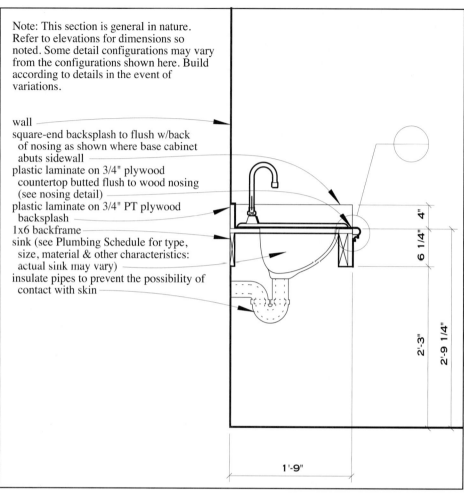

Note: This section is general in nature.
Refer to elevations for dimensions so
noted. Some detail configurations may vary
from the configurations shown here. Build
according to details in the event of
variations.

wall

square-end backsplash to flush w/back
  of nosing as shown where base cabinet
  abuts sidewall

plastic laminate on 3/4" plywood
  countertop butted flush to wood nosing
  (see nosing detail)

plastic laminate on 3/4" PT plywood
  backsplash

1x6 backframe

sink (see Plumbing Schedule for type,
  size, material & other characteristics:
  actual sink may vary)

insulate pipes to prevent the possibility of
  contact with skin

4"

6 1/4"

2'-3"

2'-9 1/4"

1'-9"

DRAWING #

Open Bath Vanity Section

SCALE

3/4"
―――
1'-0"

Note: This section is general in nature. Refer to elevations for dimensions so noted. Some detail configurations may vary from the configurations shown here. Build according to details in the event of variations.

wall

hardwood 1x4 for primary attachment of cabinet to wall framing (use 2 screws per stud of sufficient length to penetrate 1 1/2" into stud; use solid 2x4 blocking if studs or other solid attachment is spaced greater than 24" OC)

3/4" hardwood plywood top

1x6 hardwood face frame head (scribe to ceiling as required)

2 hardwood plywood adjustable shelves per section w/3/8" hardwood edge band

plastic laminate over 3/4" plywood flush overlay door

3/4" hardwood plywood bottom

plastic laminate over all exposed surfaces of 3/4" hardwood face frame (typical width of 2"; width varies in some areas as shown)

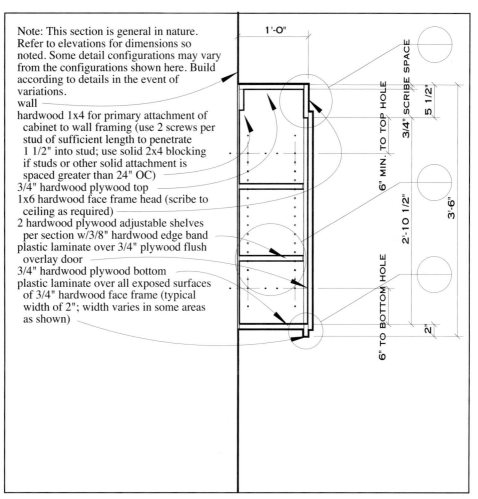

1'-O"

3/4" SCRIBE SPACE

5 1/2"

6" MIN. TO TOP HOLE

2'-10 1/2"

3'-6"

6" TO BOTTOM HOLE

2"

DRAWING #

Wall Cabinet Section

SCALE

3/4"

1'-O"

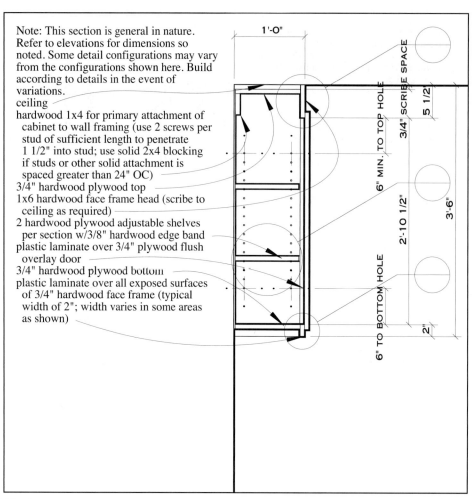

Note: This section is general in nature. Refer to elevations for dimensions so noted. Some detail configurations may vary from the configurations shown here. Build according to details in the event of variations.

ceiling

hardwood 1x4 for primary attachment of cabinet to wall framing (use 2 screws per stud of sufficient length to penetrate 1 1/2" into stud; use solid 2x4 blocking if studs or other solid attachment is spaced greater than 24" OC)

3/4" hardwood plywood top

1x6 hardwood face frame head (scribe to ceiling as required)

2 hardwood plywood adjustable shelves per section w/3/8" hardwood edge band

plastic laminate over 3/4" plywood flush overlay door

3/4" hardwood plywood bottom

plastic laminate over all exposed surfaces of 3/4" hardwood face frame (typical width of 2"; width varies in some areas as shown)

1'-O"

6" MIN. TO TOP HOLE

3/4" SCRIBE SPACE

5 1/2"

2'-10 1/2"

3'-6"

6" TO BOTTOM HOLE

2"

DRAWING #

Wall Cabinet Section @ Ceiling

SCALE

3/4"
1'-O"

Note: This section is general in nature.
Refer to elevations for dimensions so
noted. Some detail configurations may vary
from the configurations shown here. Build
according to details in the event of
variations. All door & face frames are to be
traditional square-cornered frames. Routed
frames are NOT acceptable.

hardwood 1x4 for primary attachment of
  cabinet to wall framing (use 2 screws per
  stud of sufficient length to penetrate
  1 1/2" into stud; use solid 2x4 blocking
  if studs or other solid attachment is
  spaced greater than 24" OC)
3/4" hardwood plywood top
1x6 hardwood face frame head (scribe to
  ceiling as required)
2 hardwood plywood adjustable shelves
  per section w/3/8" hardwood edge band
plastic laminate reveal overlay door
3/4" hardwood plywood bottom
3/4" hardwood face frame

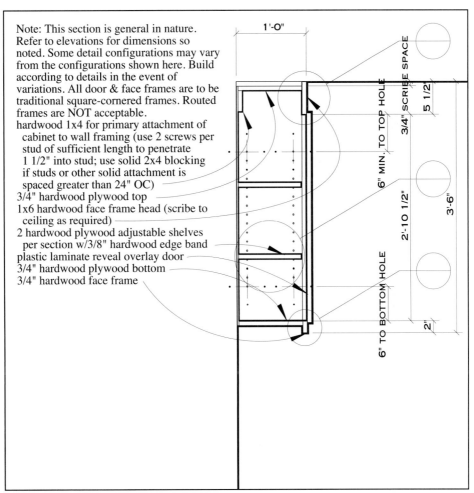

1'-0"

3/4" SCRIBE SPACE

5 1/2"

6" MIN. TO TOP HOLE

2'-10 1/2"

3'-6"

6" TO BOTTOM HOLE

2"

DRAWING #

Wall Cabinet Section

SCALE
3/4"
1'-0"

Note: This section is general in nature.
Refer to elevations for dimensions so
noted. Some detail configurations may vary
from the configurations shown here. Build
according to details in the event of
variations. All door & face frames are to be
traditional square-cornered frames. Routed
frames are NOT acceptable.

hardwood 1x4 for primary attachment of
  cabinet to wall framing (use 2 screws per
  stud of sufficient length to penetrate
  1 1/2" into stud; use solid 2x4 blocking
  if studs or other solid attachment is
  spaced greater than 24" OC)
3/4" hardwood plywood top
1x6 hardwood face frame head (scribe to
  ceiling as required)
2 hardwood plywood adjustable shelves
  per section w/3/8" hardwood edge band
traditional raised panel reveal overlay
  door
3/4" hardwood plywood bottom
3/4" hardwood face frame (typical width
  of 2" for center members & 1 3/4" for
  perimeter members allows 1 1/2" reveal
  w/1/4" typical door & drawer overlay;
  width varies in some areas as shown)

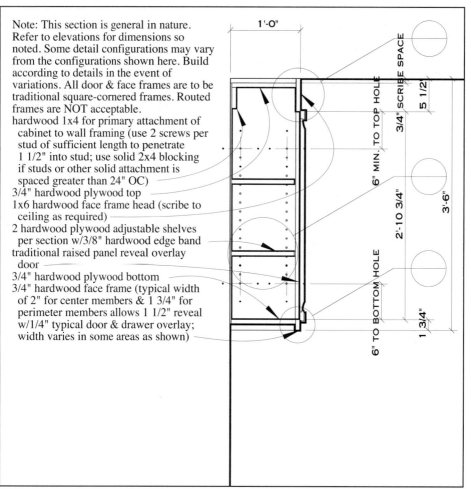

1'-0"

3/4" SCRIBE SPACE

5 1/2"

6" MIN. TO TOP HOLE

2'-10 3/4"

3'-6"

6" TO BOTTOM HOLE

1 3/4"

DRAWING #

Wall Cabinet Section

SCALE

3/4"
1'-0"

Note: This section is general in nature.
Refer to elevations for dimensions so
noted. Some detail configurations may vary
from the configurations shown here. Build
according to details in the event of
variations. All door & face frames are to be
traditional square-cornered frames. Routed
frames are NOT acceptable.
hardwood 1x4 for primary attachment of
  cabinet to wall framing (use 2 screws per
  stud of sufficient length to penetrate
  1 1/2" into stud; use solid 2x4 blocking
  if studs or other solid attachment is
  spaced greater than 24" OC)
3/4" hardwood plywood top
3/4" hardwood face frame head (scribe to
  ceiling as required)
2 hardwood plywood adjustable shelves
  per section w/3/8" hardwood edge band
traditional raised panel cabinet door
3/4" hardwood plywood bottom
3/4" hardwood face frame

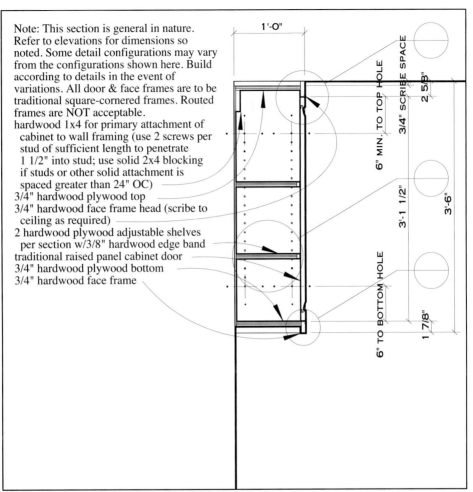

1'-0"

6" MIN. TO TOP HOLE

3/4" SCRIBE SPACE

2 5/8"

3'-1 1/2"

3'-6"

6" TO BOTTOM HOLE

1 7/8"

Wall Cabinet Section

DOOR DETAILS

Details in this section include all door head, jamb, mullion, transom & threshold details. Additionally, it include general opening details & elevations which apply to both doors & windows. The contents of this section are as follows:

Aluminum Door Head Details	260
Aluminum Door Jamb Details	264
Aluminum Door Mullion Details	265
Aluminum Door Transom Details	273
Door, Frame & Window Openings: Brick Jack Arch Elevations	277
Door, Frame & Window Openings: Brick Jack Arch Elevations w/Keystone	280
Door, Frame & Window Openings: Stone Jack Arch Elevations	310
Door, Frame & Window Openings: Stone Jack Arch Elevations w/Keystone	313
Door, Frame & Window Openings: Square Stope Lintel Elevations	343
Door, Frame & Window Openings: Wood Exterior Casing Elevations	344
Door, Frame & Window Openings: Wood Interior Casing Elevations	346
Hollow Metal Door Head Details	349
Hollow Metal Door Jamb Details	364
Hollow Metal Door Transom & Mullion Details	375
Miscellaneous Door Details	380
Special Door Head Details	382
Special Door Jamb Details	383
Door Threshold Details	390
Wood Door Head Details	405
Wood Door Jamb Details	431
Wood Door Mullion Details	443
Wood Door Transom Details	447

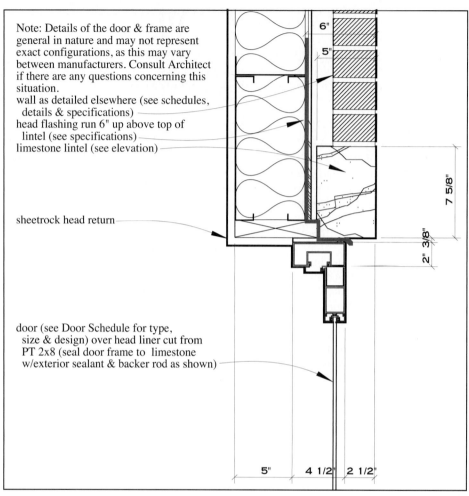

Note: Details of the door & frame are general in nature and may not represent exact configurations, as this may vary between manufacturers. Consult Architect if there are any questions concerning this situation.

wall as detailed elsewhere (see schedules, details & specifications)

head flashing run 6" up above top of lintel (see specifications)

limestone lintel (see elevation)

sheetrock head return

door (see Door Schedule for type, size & design) over head liner cut from PT 2x8 (seal door frame to limestone w/exterior sealant & backer rod as shown)

6"

5"

7 5/8"

2" 3/8"

5"   4 1/2" 2 1/2"

DRAWING #

Door Head Detail w/Stone Lintel

SCALE
1 1/2"
1'-0"

DAH004
260

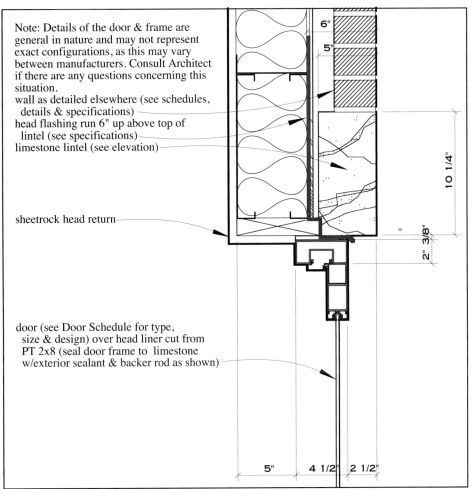

Note: Details of the door & frame are general in nature and may not represent exact configurations, as this may vary between manufacturers. Consult Architect if there are any questions concerning this situation.

wall as detailed elsewhere (see schedules, details & specifications)

head flashing run 6" up above top of lintel (see specifications)

limestone lintel (see elevation)

sheetrock head return

door (see Door Schedule for type, size & design) over head liner cut from PT 2x8 (seal door frame to limestone w/exterior sealant & backer rod as shown)

6"

5"

10 1/4"

2" 3/8"

5"   4 1/2" 2 1/2"

Door Head Detail w/Stone Lintel

SCALE
1 1/2"
1'-0"

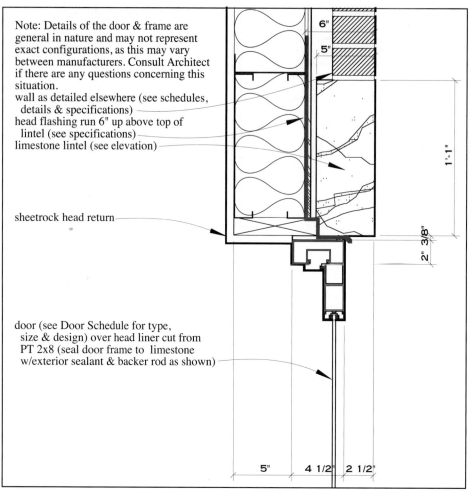

Note: Details of the door & frame are general in nature and may not represent exact configurations, as this may vary between manufacturers. Consult Architect if there are any questions concerning this situation.

wall as detailed elsewhere (see schedules, details & specifications)

head flashing run 6" up above top of lintel (see specifications)

limestone lintel (see elevation)

6"

5"

1'-1"

sheetrock head return

2" 3/8"

door (see Door Schedule for type, size & design) over head liner cut from PT 2x8 (seal door frame to limestone w/exterior sealant & backer rod as shown)

5"   4 1/2"   2 1/2"

DRAWING #

Door Head Detail w/Stone Lintel

SCALE

1 1/2"
1'-0"

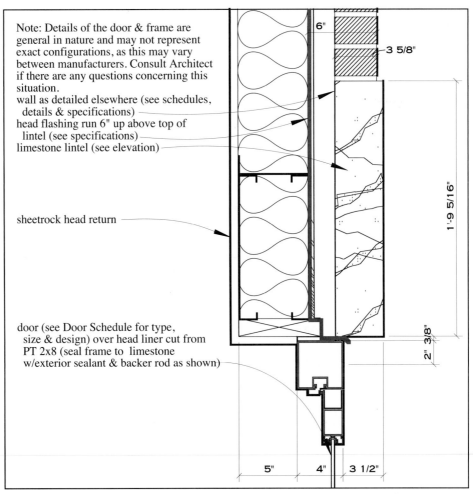

Note: Details of the door & frame are
general in nature and may not represent
exact configurations, as this may vary
between manufacturers. Consult Architect
if there are any questions concerning this
situation.

wall as detailed elsewhere (see schedules,
  details & specifications)

head flashing run 6" up above top of
  lintel (see specifications)

limestone lintel (see elevation)

6"

3 5/8"

1'-9 5/16"

sheetrock head return

2" 3/8"

door (see Door Schedule for type,
  size & design) over head liner cut from
  PT 2x8 (seal frame to limestone
  w/exterior sealant & backer rod as shown)

5"   4"   3 1/2"

DRAWING #

Door Head Detail w/Stone Lintel

SCALE
1 1/2"
1'-0"

DAH007
263

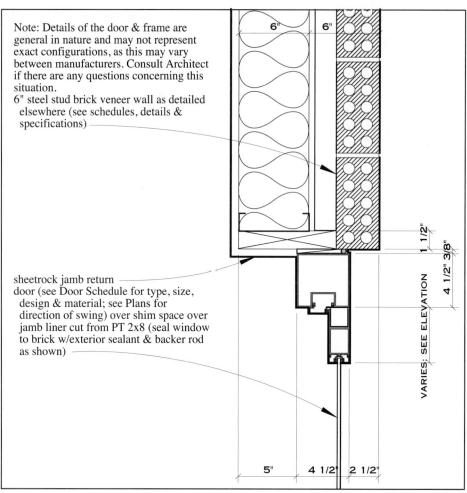

Note: Details of the door & frame are general in nature and may not represent exact configurations, as this may vary between manufacturers. Consult Architect if there are any questions concerning this situation.

6" steel stud brick veneer wall as detailed elsewhere (see schedules, details & specifications)

sheetrock jamb return

door (see Door Schedule for type, size, design & material; see Plans for direction of swing) over shim space over jamb liner cut from PT 2x8 (seal window to brick w/exterior sealant & backer rod as shown)

6"   6"

1 1/2"   3/8"

4 1/2"

VARIES; SEE ELEVATION

5"   4 1/2"   2 1/2"

DRAWING #

Aluminum Door Jamb Detail

SCALE
1 1/2"
1'-0"

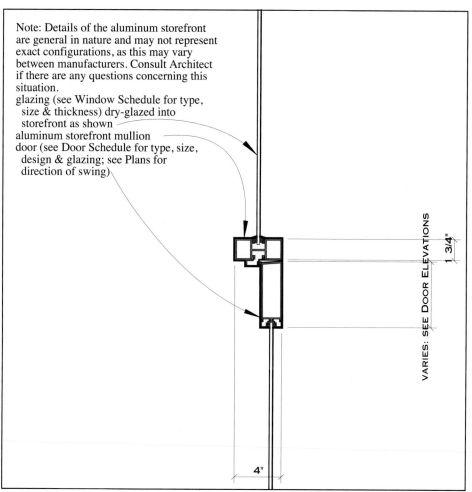

Note: Details of the aluminum storefront are general in nature and may not represent exact configurations, as this may vary between manufacturers. Consult Architect if there are any questions concerning this situation.

glazing (see Window Schedule for type, size & thickness) dry-glazed into storefront as shown

aluminum storefront mullion

door (see Door Schedule for type, size, design & glazing; see Plans for direction of swing)

1 3/4"

VARIES: SEE DOOR ELEVATIONS

4"

Storefront Door/Window Mullion

SCALE
1 1/2"
1'-0"

DAM001
265

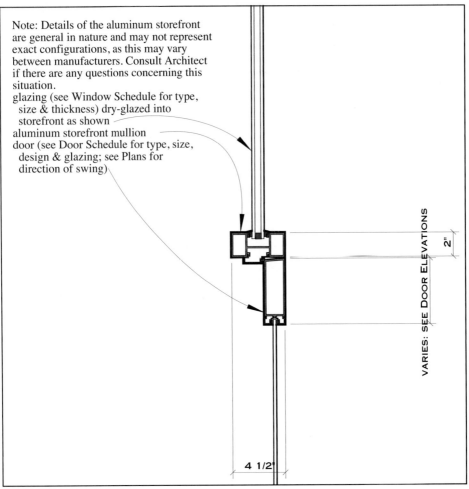

Note: Details of the aluminum storefront are general in nature and may not represent exact configurations, as this may vary between manufacturers. Consult Architect if there are any questions concerning this situation.

glazing (see Window Schedule for type, size & thickness) dry-glazed into storefront as shown

aluminum storefront mullion

door (see Door Schedule for type, size, design & glazing; see Plans for direction of swing)

2"

VARIES: SEE DOOR ELEVATIONS

4 1/2"

Storefront Door/Window Mullion

DAM002
266

Note: Details of the aluminum storefront
are general in nature and may not represent
exact configurations, as this may vary
between manufacturers. Consult Architect
if there are any questions concerning this
situation.
door (see Door Schedule for type, size,
    design & glazing; see Plans for
    direction of swing)
aluminum storefront cornerpost
glazing (see Window Schedule for type,
    size & thickness) dry-glazed into
    storefront as shown

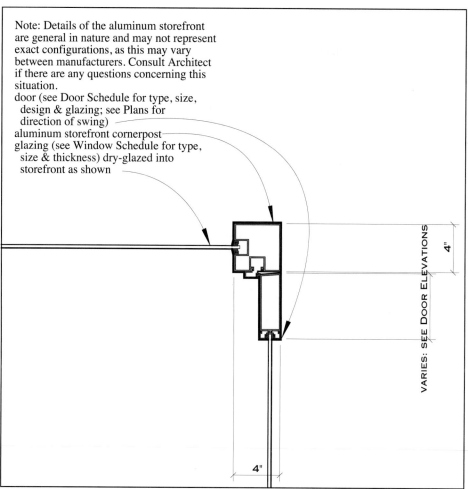

VARIES: SEE DOOR ELEVATIONS

4"

4"

Storefront Door/Window Corner Detail

DRAWING #

SCALE

1 1/2"
1'-0"

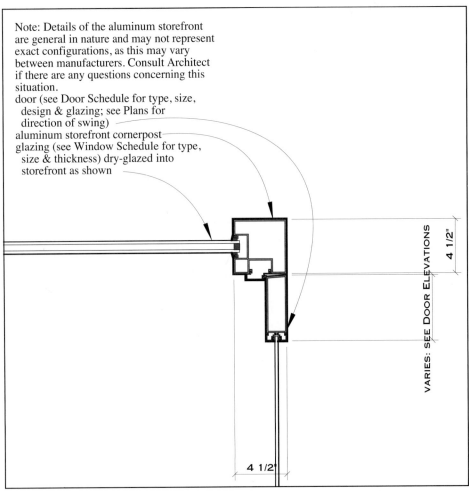

Note: Details of the aluminum storefront are general in nature and may not represent exact configurations, as this may vary between manufacturers. Consult Architect if there are any questions concerning this situation.

door (see Door Schedule for type, size, design & glazing; see Plans for direction of swing)

aluminum storefront cornerpost

glazing (see Window Schedule for type, size & thickness) dry-glazed into storefront as shown

4 1/2"

VARIES: SEE DOOR ELEVATIONS

4 1/2"

DRAWING #

Storefront Door/Window Corner Detail

SCALE

1 1/2"
1'-0"

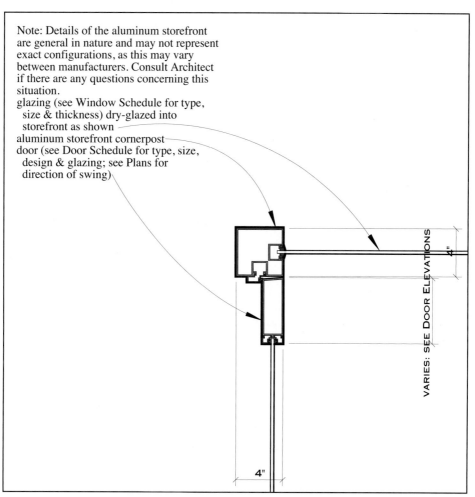

Note: Details of the aluminum storefront are general in nature and may not represent exact configurations, as this may vary between manufacturers. Consult Architect if there are any questions concerning this situation.

glazing (see Window Schedule for type, size & thickness) dry-glazed into storefront as shown

aluminum storefront cornerpost

door (see Door Schedule for type, size, design & glazing; see Plans for direction of swing)

VARIES: SEE DOOR ELEVATIONS

4"

4"

DRAWING #

Storefront Door/Window Corner Detail

SCALE
1 1/2"
1'-0"

DAM005
269

Note: Details of the aluminum storefront
are general in nature and may not represent
exact configurations, as this may vary
between manufacturers. Consult Architect
if there are any questions concerning this
situation.
glazing (see Window Schedule for type,
  size & thickness) dry-glazed into
  storefront as shown
aluminum storefront cornerpost
door (see Door Schedule for type, size,
  design & glazing; see Plans for
  direction of swing)

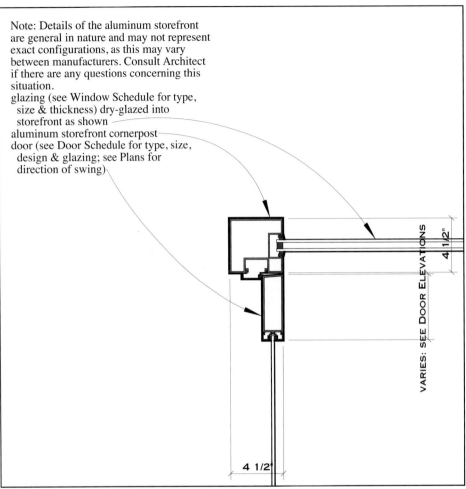

VARIES: SEE DOOR ELEVATIONS

4 1/2"

4 1/2"

DRAWING #

Storefront Door/Window Corner Detail

SCALE

1 1/2"
1'-0"

DAM006
270

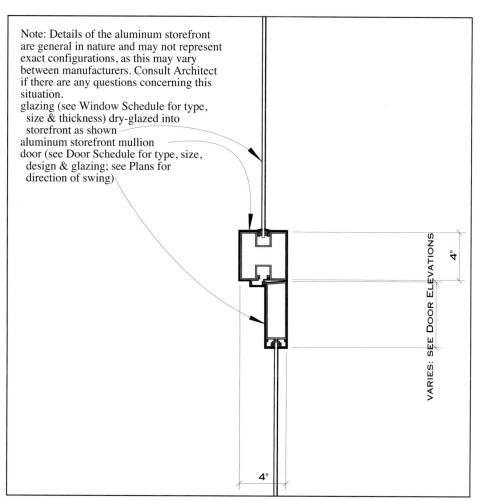

Note: Details of the aluminum storefront are general in nature and may not represent exact configurations, as this may vary between manufacturers. Consult Architect if there are any questions concerning this situation.

glazing (see Window Schedule for type, size & thickness) dry-glazed into storefront as shown

aluminum storefront mullion

door (see Door Schedule for type, size, design & glazing; see Plans for direction of swing)

VARIES: SEE DOOR ELEVATIONS

4"

4"

Storefront Door/Window Mullion

SCALE
1 1/2"
1'-0"

DRAWING #

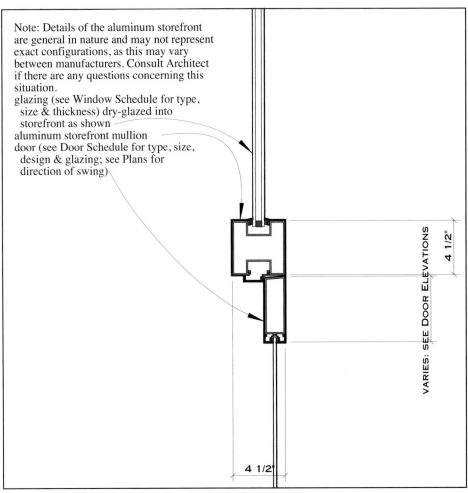

Note: Details of the aluminum storefront are general in nature and may not represent exact configurations, as this may vary between manufacturers. Consult Architect if there are any questions concerning this situation.

glazing (see Window Schedule for type, size & thickness) dry-glazed into storefront as shown

aluminum storefront mullion

door (see Door Schedule for type, size, design & glazing; see Plans for direction of swing)

VARIES: SEE DOOR ELEVATIONS

4 1/2"

4 1/2"

DRAWING #

Storefront Door/Window Mullion

SCALE
1 1/2"
1'-0"

DAM008
272

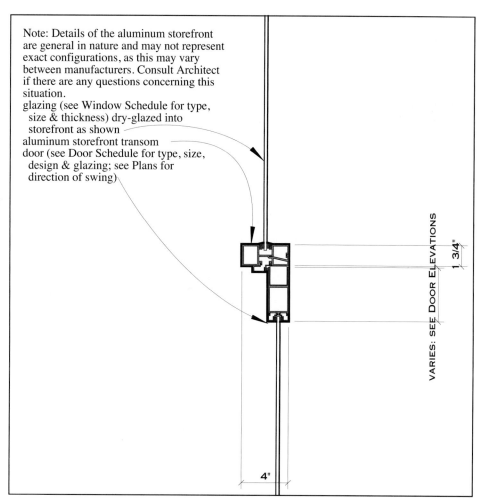

Note: Details of the aluminum storefront
are general in nature and may not represent
exact configurations, as this may vary
between manufacturers. Consult Architect
if there are any questions concerning this
situation.
glazing (see Window Schedule for type,
  size & thickness) dry-glazed into
  storefront as shown
aluminum storefront transom
door (see Door Schedule for type, size,
  design & glazing; see Plans for
  direction of swing)

1 3/4"

VARIES: SEE DOOR ELEVATIONS

4"

Storefront Door/Window Transom

SCALE
1 1/2"
1'-0"

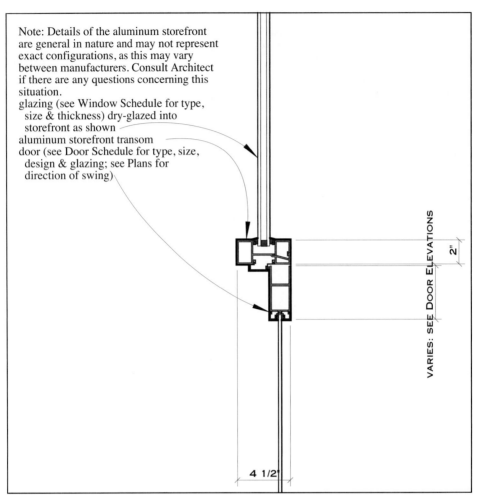

Note: Details of the aluminum storefront
are general in nature and may not represent
exact configurations, as this may vary
between manufacturers. Consult Architect
if there are any questions concerning this
situation.
glazing (see Window Schedule for type,
  size & thickness) dry-glazed into
  storefront as shown
aluminum storefront transom
door (see Door Schedule for type, size,
  design & glazing; see Plans for
  direction of swing)

VARIES: SEE DOOR ELEVATIONS

2"

4 1/2"

DRAWING #

Storefront Door/Window Transom

SCALE

1 1/2"
1'-0"

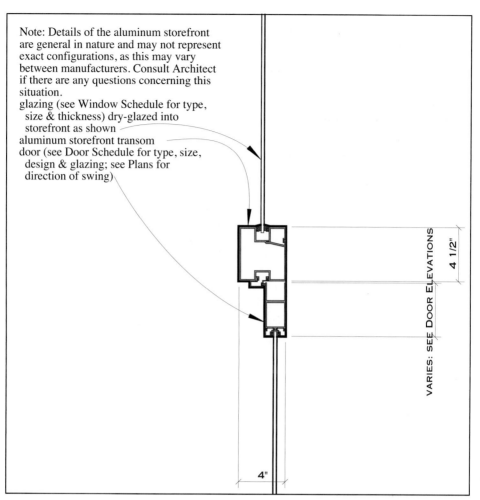

Note: Details of the aluminum storefront
are general in nature and may not represent
exact configurations, as this may vary
between manufacturers. Consult Architect
if there are any questions concerning this
situation.
glazing (see Window Schedule for type,
  size & thickness) dry-glazed into
  storefront as shown
aluminum storefront transom
door (see Door Schedule for type, size,
  design & glazing; see Plans for
  direction of swing)

4 1/2"

VARIES: SEE DOOR ELEVATIONS

4"

DRAWING #

Storefront Door/Window Transom

SCALE

1 1/2"
1'-0"

DAT003
275

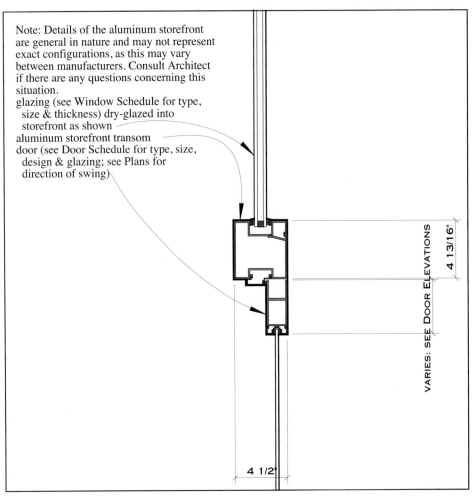

Note: Details of the aluminum storefront are general in nature and may not represent exact configurations, as this may vary between manufacturers. Consult Architect if there are any questions concerning this situation.
glazing (see Window Schedule for type, size & thickness) dry-glazed into storefront as shown
aluminum storefront transom
door (see Door Schedule for type, size, design & glazing; see Plans for direction of swing)

VARIES: SEE DOOR ELEVATIONS

4 13/16"

4 1/2"

Storefront Door/Window Transom

SCALE
1 1/2"
1'-0"

DRAWING #

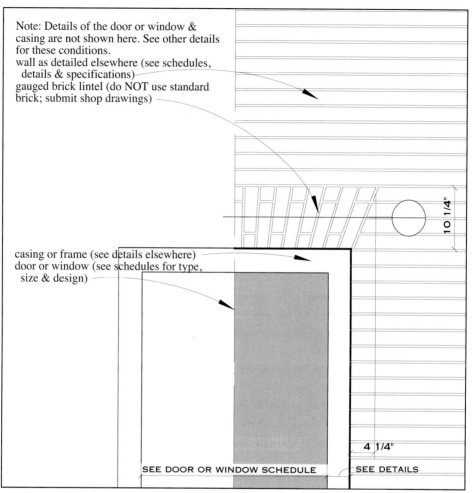

Note: Details of the door or window & casing are not shown here. See other details for these conditions.

wall as detailed elsewhere (see schedules, details & specifications)

gauged brick lintel (do NOT use standard brick; submit shop drawings)

casing or frame (see details elsewhere)

door or window (see schedules for type, size & design)

10 1/4"

4 1/4"

SEE DOOR OR WINDOW SCHEDULE

SEE DETAILS

DRAWING #

Gauged Brick Lintel Elevation

SCALE
3/4"
1'-0"

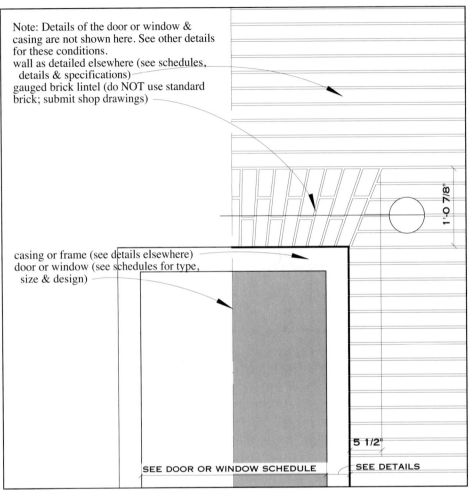

Note: Details of the door or window &
casing are not shown here. See other details
for these conditions.
wall as detailed elsewhere (see schedules,
  details & specifications)
gauged brick lintel (do NOT use standard
brick; submit shop drawings)

1'-0 7/8"

casing or frame (see details elsewhere)
door or window (see schedules for type,
  size & design)

5 1/2"

SEE DOOR OR WINDOW SCHEDULE

SEE DETAILS

DRAWING #

Gauged Brick Lintel Elevation

SCALE
3/4"
1'-0"

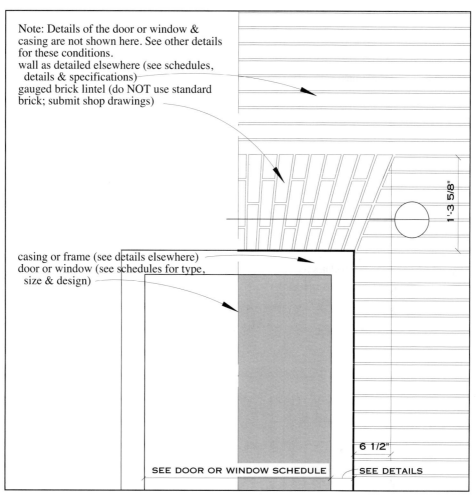

Note: Details of the door or window & casing are not shown here. See other details for these conditions.
wall as detailed elsewhere (see schedules, details & specifications)
gauged brick lintel (do NOT use standard brick; submit shop drawings)

casing or frame (see details elsewhere)
door or window (see schedules for type, size & design)

1'-3 5/8"

6 1/2"

SEE DOOR OR WINDOW SCHEDULE

SEE DETAILS

DRAWING #

Gauged Brick Lintel Elevation

SCALE
3/4"
1'-0"

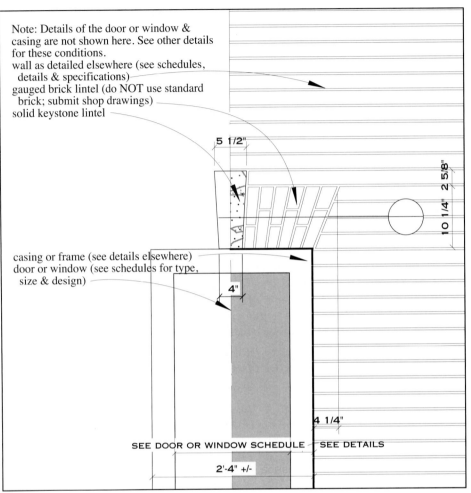

Note: Details of the door or window &
casing are not shown here. See other details
for these conditions.
wall as detailed elsewhere (see schedules,
  details & specifications)
gauged brick lintel (do NOT use standard
  brick; submit shop drawings)
solid keystone lintel

5 1/2"

10 1/4" 2 5/8"

casing or frame (see details elsewhere)
door or window (see schedules for type,
  size & design)

4"

4 1/4"

SEE DOOR OR WINDOW SCHEDULE   SEE DETAILS

2'-4" +/-

Stone Lintel Elevation

SCALE
3/4"
1'-0"

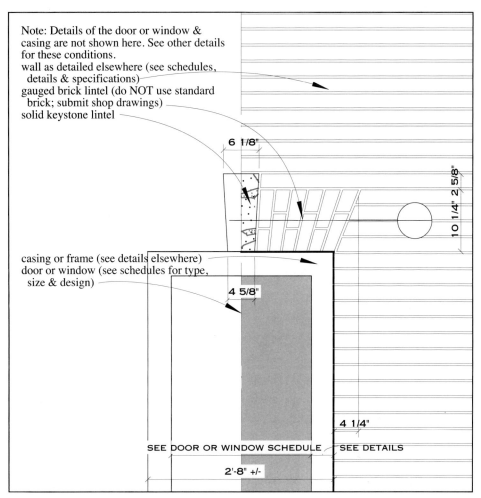

Note: Details of the door or window &
casing are not shown here. See other details
for these conditions.
wall as detailed elsewhere (see schedules,
  details & specifications)
gauged brick lintel (do NOT use standard
  brick; submit shop drawings)
solid keystone lintel

6 1/8"

10 1/4" 2 5/8"

casing or frame (see details elsewhere)
door or window (see schedules for type,
  size & design)

4 5/8"

4 1/4"

SEE DOOR OR WINDOW SCHEDULE   SEE DETAILS

2'-8" +/-

DRAWING #

Stone Lintel Elevation

SCALE
3/4"
1'-0"

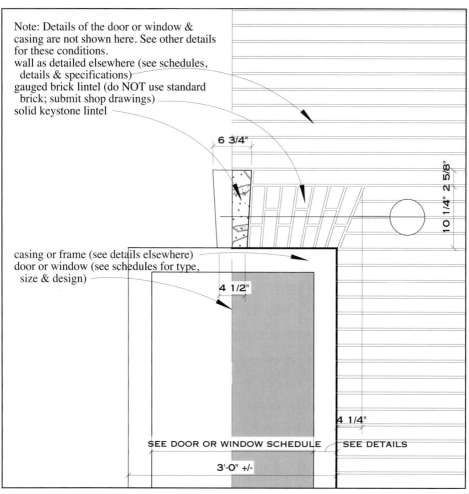

Note: Details of the door or window &
casing are not shown here. See other details
for these conditions.
wall as detailed elsewhere (see schedules,
  details & specifications)
gauged brick lintel (do NOT use standard
  brick; submit shop drawings)
solid keystone lintel

6 3/4"

10 1/4" 2 5/8"

casing or frame (see details elsewhere)
door or window (see schedules for type,
  size & design)

4 1/2"

4 1/4"

SEE DOOR OR WINDOW SCHEDULE   SEE DETAILS

3'-0" +/-

DRAWING #

Stone Lintel Elevation

SCALE
3/4"
1'-0"

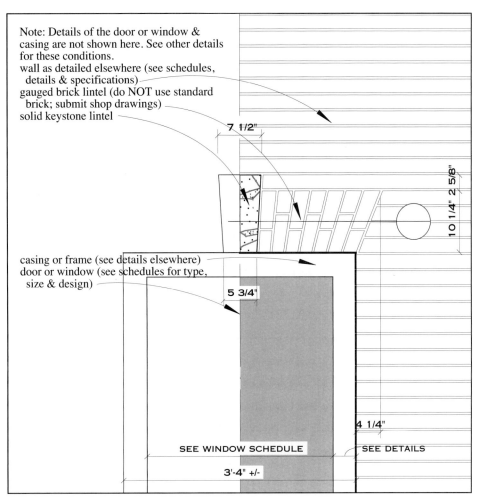

Note: Details of the door or window &
casing are not shown here. See other details
for these conditions.
wall as detailed elsewhere (see schedules,
  details & specifications)
gauged brick lintel (do NOT use standard
  brick; submit shop drawings)
solid keystone lintel

7 1/2"

10 1/4"   2 5/8"

casing or frame (see details elsewhere)
door or window (see schedules for type,
  size & design)

5 3/4"

4 1/4"

SEE WINDOW SCHEDULE

SEE DETAILS

3'-4" +/-

DRAWING #

Stone Lintel Elevation

SCALE
3/4"
1'-0"

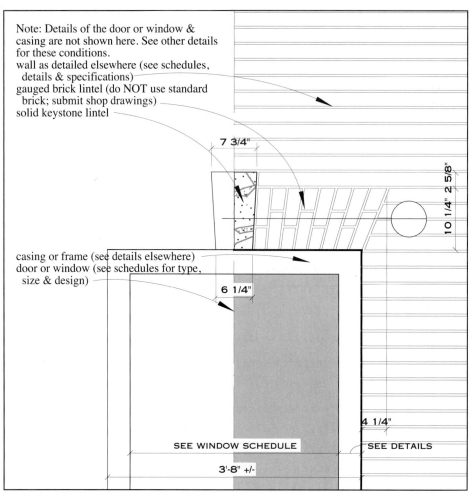

Note: Details of the door or window &
casing are not shown here. See other details
for these conditions.
wall as detailed elsewhere (see schedules,
  details & specifications)
gauged brick lintel (do NOT use standard
  brick; submit shop drawings)
solid keystone lintel

7 3/4"

10 1/4" 2 5/8"

casing or frame (see details elsewhere)
door or window (see schedules for type,
  size & design)

6 1/4"

4 1/4"

SEE WINDOW SCHEDULE

SEE DETAILS

3'-8" +/-

DRAWING #

Stone Lintel Elevation

SCALE
3/4"
1'-0"

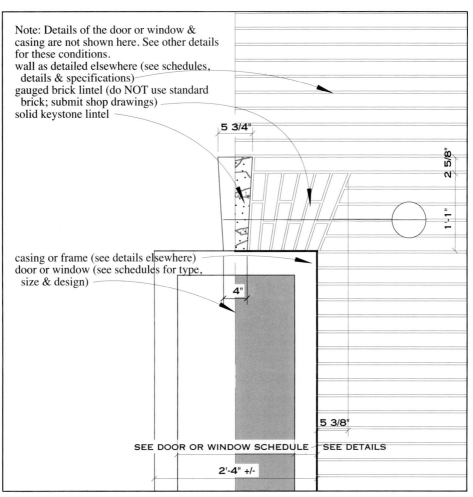

Note: Details of the door or window &
casing are not shown here. See other details
for these conditions.
wall as detailed elsewhere (see schedules,
 details & specifications)
gauged brick lintel (do NOT use standard
 brick; submit shop drawings)
solid keystone lintel

5 3/4"

2 5/8"

1'-1"

casing or frame (see details elsewhere)
door or window (see schedules for type,
 size & design)

4"

5 3/8"

SEE DOOR OR WINDOW SCHEDULE SEE DETAILS

2'-4" +/-

DRAWING #

Stone Lintel Elevation

SCALE
3/4"
1'-0"

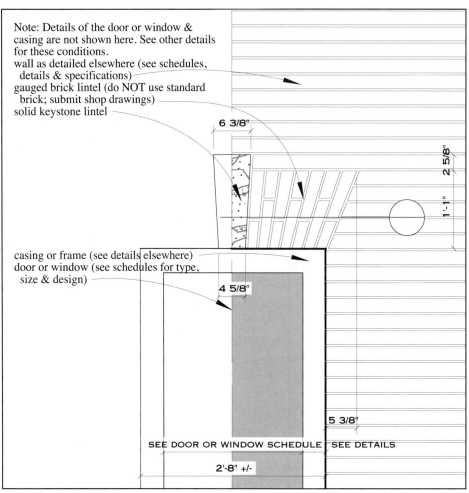

Note: Details of the door or window &
casing are not shown here. See other details
for these conditions.
wall as detailed elsewhere (see schedules,
  details & specifications)
gauged brick lintel (do NOT use standard
  brick; submit shop drawings)
solid keystone lintel

6 3/8"

2 5/8"

1'-1"

casing or frame (see details elsewhere)
door or window (see schedules for type,
  size & design)

4 5/8"

5 3/8"

SEE DOOR OR WINDOW SCHEDULE   SEE DETAILS

2'-8" +/-

DRAWING #

Stone Lintel Elevation

SCALE
3/4"
1'-O"

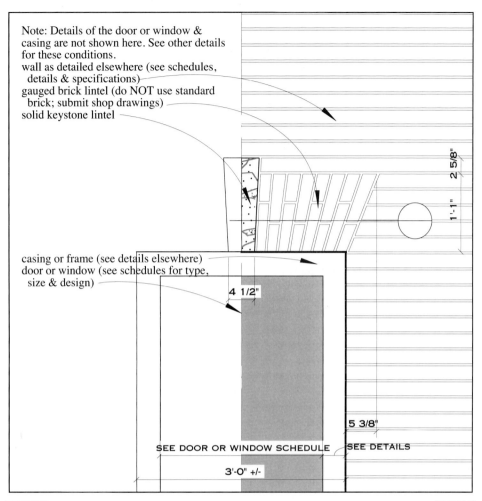

Note: Details of the door or window &
casing are not shown here. See other details
for these conditions.
wall as detailed elsewhere (see schedules,
  details & specifications)
gauged brick lintel (do NOT use standard
  brick; submit shop drawings)
solid keystone lintel

2 5/8"

1'-1"

casing or frame (see details elsewhere)
door or window (see schedules for type,
  size & design)

4 1/2"

5 3/8"

SEE DOOR OR WINDOW SCHEDULE

SEE DETAILS

3'-0" +/-

DRAWING #

Stone Lintel Elevation

SCALE
3/4"
1'-0"

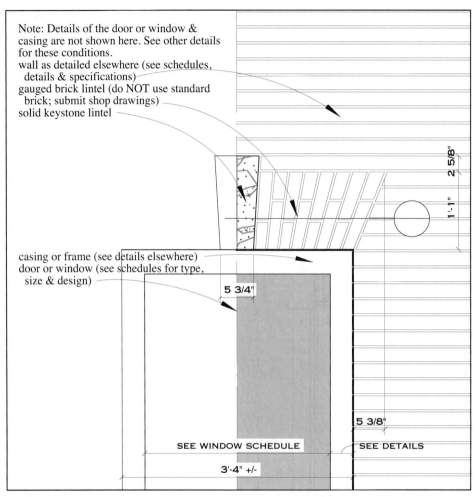

Note: Details of the door or window &
casing are not shown here. See other details
for these conditions.
wall as detailed elsewhere (see schedules,
  details & specifications)
gauged brick lintel (do NOT use standard
  brick; submit shop drawings)
solid keystone lintel

2 5/8"

1'-1"

casing or frame (see details elsewhere)
door or window (see schedules for type,
  size & design)

5 3/4"

5 3/8"

SEE WINDOW SCHEDULE

SEE DETAILS

3'-4" +/-

Stone Lintel Elevation

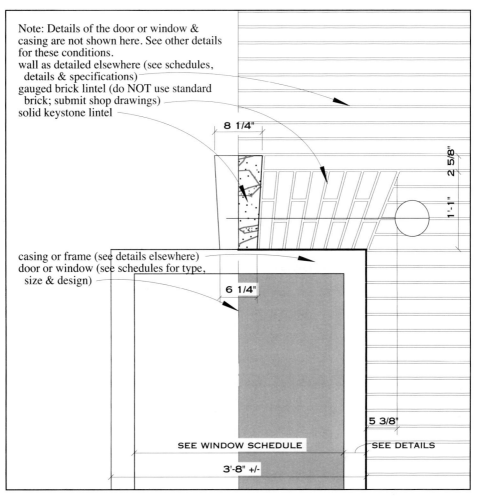

Note: Details of the door or window & casing are not shown here. See other details for these conditions.
wall as detailed elsewhere (see schedules, details & specifications)
gauged brick lintel (do NOT use standard brick; submit shop drawings)
solid keystone lintel

8 1/4"

2 5/8"

1'-1"

casing or frame (see details elsewhere)
door or window (see schedules for type, size & design)

6 1/4"

5 3/8"

SEE WINDOW SCHEDULE

SEE DETAILS

3'-8" +/-

DRAWING #

Stone Lintel Elevation

SCALE
3/4"
1'-0"

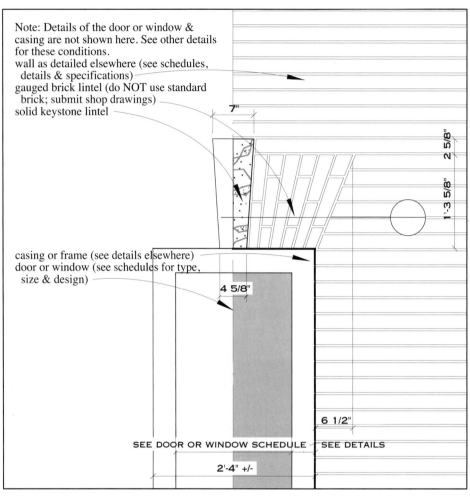

Note: Details of the door or window & casing are not shown here. See other details for these conditions.

wall as detailed elsewhere (see schedules, details & specifications)

gauged brick lintel (do NOT use standard brick; submit shop drawings)

solid keystone lintel

7"

2 5/8"

1'-3 5/8"

casing or frame (see details elsewhere)

door or window (see schedules for type, size & design)

4 5/8"

6 1/2"

SEE DOOR OR WINDOW SCHEDULE   SEE DETAILS

2'-4" +/-

DRAWING #

Stone Lintel Elevation

SCALE

3/4"
1'-O"

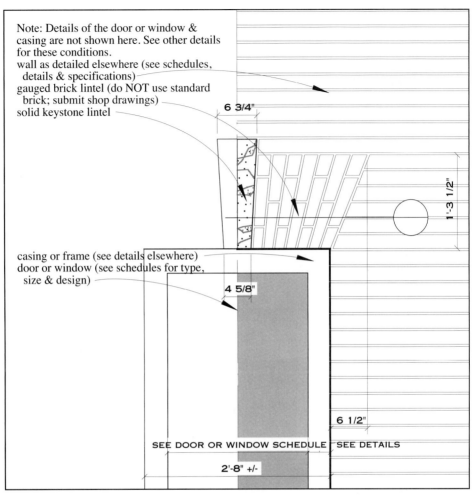

Note: Details of the door or window &
casing are not shown here. See other details
for these conditions.
wall as detailed elsewhere (see schedules,
 details & specifications)
gauged brick lintel (do NOT use standard
 brick; submit shop drawings)
solid keystone lintel

6 3/4"

1'-3 1/2"

casing or frame (see details elsewhere)
door or window (see schedules for type,
 size & design)

4 5/8"

6 1/2"

SEE DOOR OR WINDOW SCHEDULE SEE DETAILS

2'-8" +/-

DRAWING #

Stone Lintel Elevation

SCALE

3/4"
1'-0"

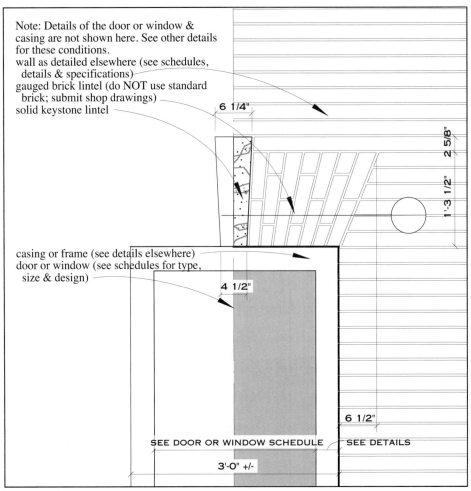

Note: Details of the door or window &
casing are not shown here. See other details
for these conditions.
wall as detailed elsewhere (see schedules,
  details & specifications)
gauged brick lintel (do NOT use standard
  brick; submit shop drawings)
solid keystone lintel

6 1/4"

2 5/8"

1'-3 1/2"

casing or frame (see details elsewhere)
door or window (see schedules for type,
  size & design)

4 1/2"

6 1/2"

SEE DOOR OR WINDOW SCHEDULE   SEE DETAILS

3'-0" +/-

DRAWING #

Stone Lintel Elevation

SCALE

3/4"
1'-0"

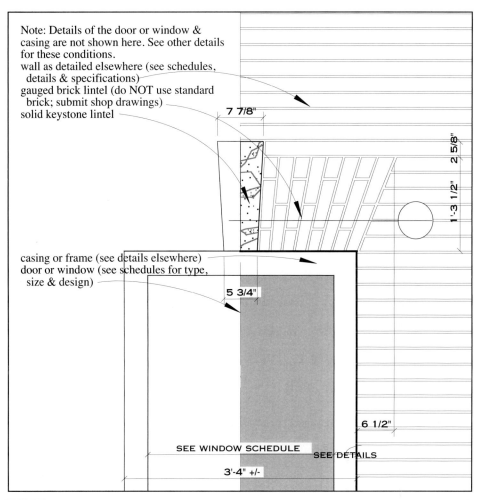

Note: Details of the door or window &
casing are not shown here. See other details
for these conditions.
wall as detailed elsewhere (see schedules,
  details & specifications)
gauged brick lintel (do NOT use standard
  brick; submit shop drawings)
solid keystone lintel

7 7/8"

2 5/8"

1-3 1/2"

casing or frame (see details elsewhere)
door or window (see schedules for type,
  size & design)

5 3/4"

6 1/2"

SEE WINDOW SCHEDULE

SEE DETAILS

3'-4" +/-

DRAWING #

Stone Lintel Elevation

SCALE
3/4"
1'-0"

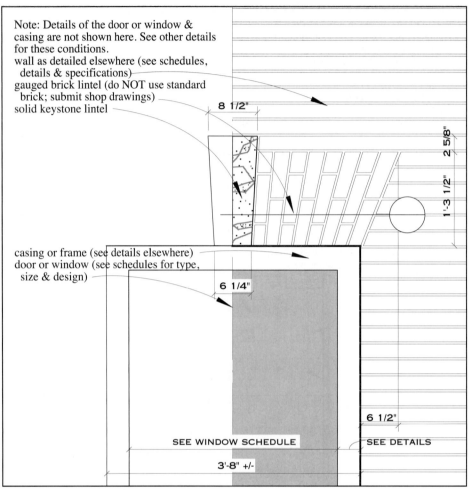

Note: Details of the door or window &
casing are not shown here. See other details
for these conditions.
wall as detailed elsewhere (see schedules,
  details & specifications)
gauged brick lintel (do NOT use standard
  brick; submit shop drawings)
solid keystone lintel

8 1/2"

2 5/8"

1'-3 1/2"

casing or frame (see details elsewhere)
door or window (see schedules for type,
  size & design)

6 1/4"

6 1/2"

SEE WINDOW SCHEDULE

SEE DETAILS

3'-8" +/-

DRAWING #

Stone Lintel Elevation

SCALE
3/4"
1'-0"

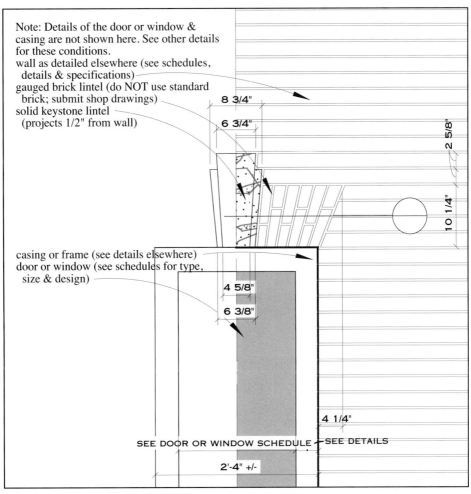

Note: Details of the door or window &
casing are not shown here. See other details
for these conditions.
wall as detailed elsewhere (see schedules,
  details & specifications)
gauged brick lintel (do NOT use standard
  brick; submit shop drawings)
solid keystone lintel
  (projects 1/2" from wall)

8 3/4"

6 3/4"

2 5/8"

10 1/4"

casing or frame (see details elsewhere)
door or window (see schedules for type,
  size & design)

4 5/8"

6 3/8"

4 1/4"

SEE DOOR OR WINDOW SCHEDULE — SEE DETAILS

2'-4" +/-

DRAWING #

Stone Lintel Elevation

SCALE
3/4"
1'-0"

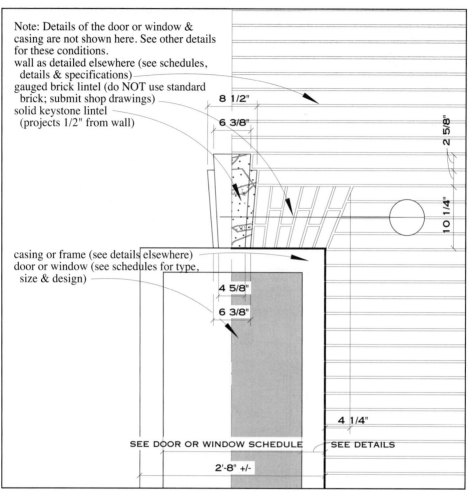

Note: Details of the door or window &
casing are not shown here. See other details
for these conditions.
wall as detailed elsewhere (see schedules,
  details & specifications)
gauged brick lintel (do NOT use standard
  brick; submit shop drawings)
solid keystone lintel
  (projects 1/2" from wall)

8 1/2"

6 3/8"

2 5/8"

10 1/4"

casing or frame (see details elsewhere)
door or window (see schedules for type,
  size & design)

4 5/8"

6 3/8"

4 1/4"

SEE DOOR OR WINDOW SCHEDULE   SEE DETAILS

2'-8" +/-

DRAWING #

Stone Lintel Elevation

SCALE
3/4"
1'-0"

DDEB2002
296

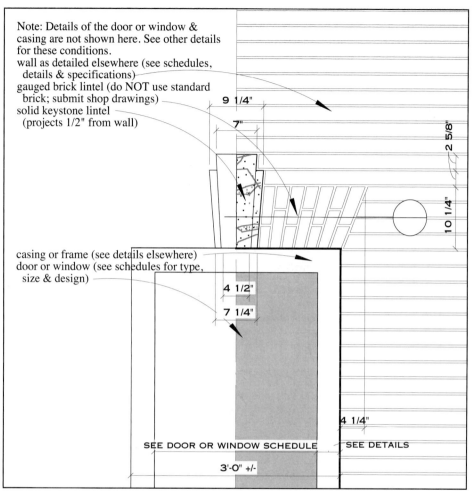

Note: Details of the door or window &
casing are not shown here. See other details
for these conditions.
wall as detailed elsewhere (see schedules,
  details & specifications)
gauged brick lintel (do NOT use standard
  brick; submit shop drawings)
solid keystone lintel
  (projects 1/2" from wall)

9 1/4"

7"

2 5/8"

10 1/4"

casing or frame (see details elsewhere)
door or window (see schedules for type,
  size & design)

4 1/2"

7 1/4"

4 1/4"

SEE DOOR OR WINDOW SCHEDULE   SEE DETAILS

3'-0" +/-

DRAWING #

Stone Lintel Elevation

SCALE
3/4"
1'-0"

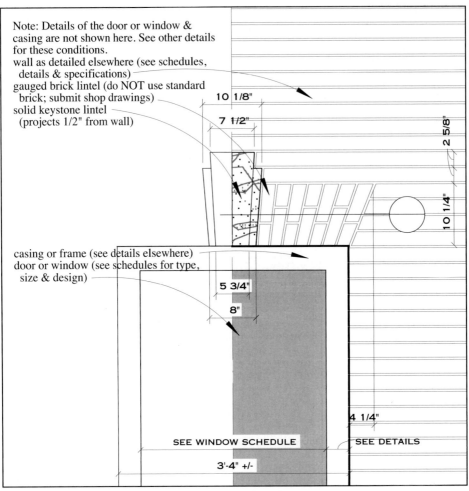

Note: Details of the door or window &
casing are not shown here. See other details
for these conditions.
wall as detailed elsewhere (see schedules,
  details & specifications)
gauged brick lintel (do NOT use standard
  brick; submit shop drawings)
solid keystone lintel
  (projects 1/2" from wall)

10 1/8"

7 1/2"

2 5/8"

10 1/4"

casing or frame (see details elsewhere)
door or window (see schedules for type,
  size & design)

5 3/4"

8"

4 1/4"

SEE WINDOW SCHEDULE

SEE DETAILS

3'-4" +/-

DRAWING #

Stone Lintel Elevation

SCALE
3/4"
1'-0"

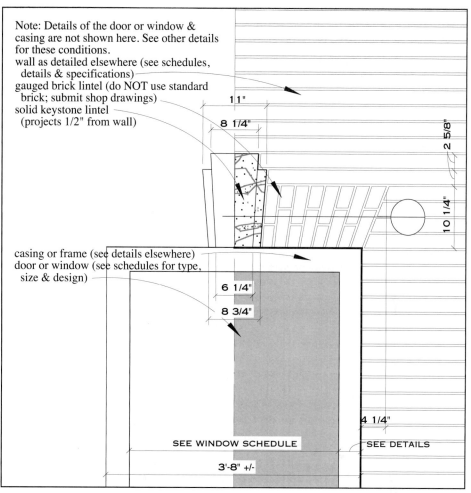

Note: Details of the door or window & casing are not shown here. See other details for these conditions.
wall as detailed elsewhere (see schedules, details & specifications)
gauged brick lintel (do NOT use standard brick; submit shop drawings)
solid keystone lintel (projects 1/2" from wall)

1 1"

8 1/4"

2 5/8"

1 0 1/4"

casing or frame (see details elsewhere)
door or window (see schedules for type, size & design)

6 1/4"

8 3/4"

4 1/4"

SEE WINDOW SCHEDULE

SEE DETAILS

3'-8" +/-

DRAWING #

Stone Lintel Elevation

SCALE
3/4"
1'-0"

Note: Details of the door or window &
casing are not shown here. See other details
for these conditions.
wall as detailed elsewhere (see schedules,
   details & specifications)
gauged brick lintel (do NOT use standard
   brick; submit shop drawings)
solid keystone lintel
   (projects 1/2" from wall)

9 1/4"

7"

2 5/8"

1'-0 7/8"

casing or frame (see details elsewhere)
door or window (see schedules for type,
   size & design)

4 5/8"

6 3/8"

5 3/8"

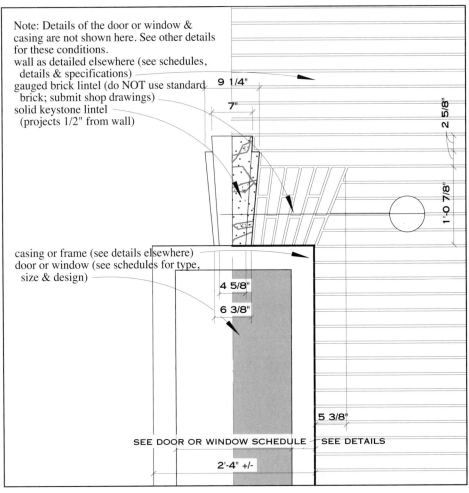

SEE DOOR OR WINDOW SCHEDULE — SEE DETAILS

2'-4" +/-

DRAWING #

Stone Lintel Elevation

SCALE
3/4"
1'-0"

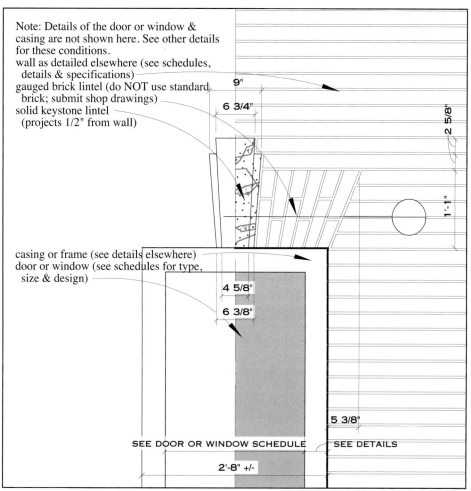

Note: Details of the door or window &
casing are not shown here. See other details
for these conditions.
wall as detailed elsewhere (see schedules,
   details & specifications)
gauged brick lintel (do NOT use standard
   brick; submit shop drawings)
solid keystone lintel
   (projects 1/2" from wall)

9"

6 3/4"

2 5/8"

1'-1"

casing or frame (see details elsewhere)
door or window (see schedules for type,
   size & design)

4 5/8"

6 3/8"

5 3/8"

SEE DOOR OR WINDOW SCHEDULE

SEE DETAILS

2'-8" +/-

DRAWING #

Stone Lintel Elevation

SCALE

$\dfrac{3/4"}{1'-0"}$

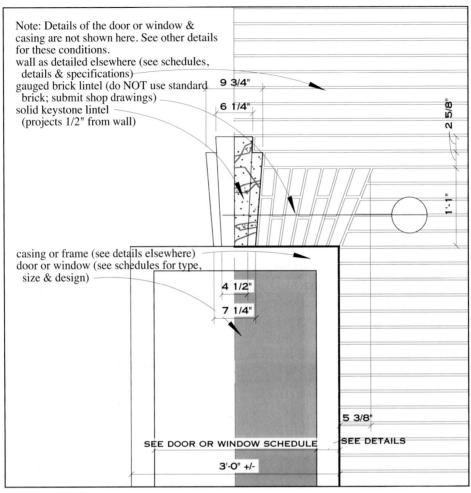

Note: Details of the door or window &
casing are not shown here. See other details
for these conditions.
wall as detailed elsewhere (see schedules,
  details & specifications)
gauged brick lintel (do NOT use standard
  brick; submit shop drawings)
solid keystone lintel
  (projects 1/2" from wall)

9 3/4"

6 1/4"

2 5/8"

1'-1"

casing or frame (see details elsewhere)
door or window (see schedules for type,
  size & design)

4 1/2"

7 1/4"

5 3/8"

SEE DOOR OR WINDOW SCHEDULE

SEE DETAILS

3'-0" +/-

DRAWING #

Stone Lintel Elevation

SCALE
3/4"
1'-0"

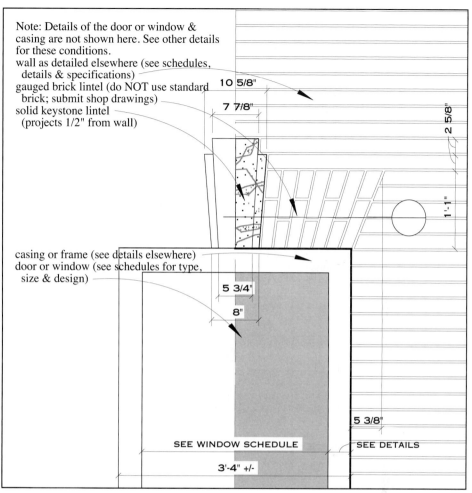

Note: Details of the door or window &
casing are not shown here. See other details
for these conditions.
wall as detailed elsewhere (see schedules,
  details & specifications)
gauged brick lintel (do NOT use standard
  brick; submit shop drawings)
solid keystone lintel
  (projects 1/2" from wall)

10 5/8"

7 7/8"

2 5/8"

1'-1"

casing or frame (see details elsewhere)
door or window (see schedules for type,
  size & design)

5 3/4"

8"

5 3/8"

SEE WINDOW SCHEDULE

SEE DETAILS

3'-4" +/-

Stone Lintel Elevation

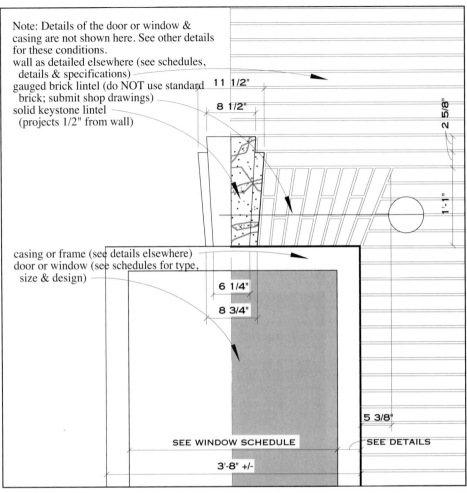

Note: Details of the door or window &
casing are not shown here. See other details
for these conditions.
wall as detailed elsewhere (see schedules,
  details & specifications)
gauged brick lintel (do NOT use standard
  brick; submit shop drawings)
solid keystone lintel
  (projects 1/2" from wall)

11 1/2"

8 1/2"

2 5/8"

1'-1"

casing or frame (see details elsewhere)
door or window (see schedules for type,
  size & design)

6 1/4"

8 3/4"

5 3/8"

SEE WINDOW SCHEDULE

SEE DETAILS

3'-8" +/-

DRAWING #

Stone Lintel Elevation

SCALE
3/4"
1'-0"

DDEB2010
304

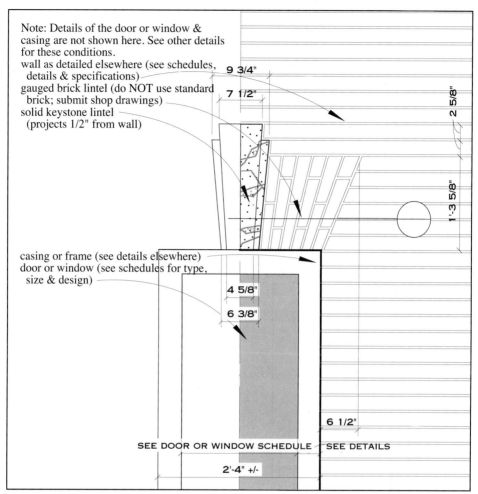

Note: Details of the door or window &
casing are not shown here. See other details
for these conditions.

wall as detailed elsewhere (see schedules,
 details & specifications)

gauged brick lintel (do NOT use standard
 brick; submit shop drawings)

solid keystone lintel
 (projects 1/2" from wall)

9 3/4"

7 1/2"

2 5/8"

1'-3 5/8"

casing or frame (see details elsewhere)

door or window (see schedules for type,
 size & design)

4 5/8"

6 3/8"

6 1/2"

SEE DOOR OR WINDOW SCHEDULE

SEE DETAILS

2'-4" +/-

DRAWING #

Stone Lintel Elevation

SCALE
3/4"
1'-0"

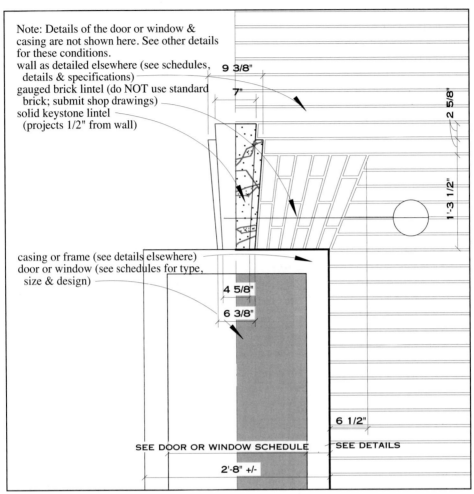

Note: Details of the door or window & casing are not shown here. See other details for these conditions.

wall as detailed elsewhere (see schedules, details & specifications)

gauged brick lintel (do NOT use standard brick; submit shop drawings)

solid keystone lintel (projects 1/2" from wall)

9 3/8"

7"

2 5/8"

1'-3 1/2"

casing or frame (see details elsewhere)
door or window (see schedules for type, size & design)

4 5/8"

6 3/8"

6 1/2"

SEE DOOR OR WINDOW SCHEDULE

SEE DETAILS

2'-8" +/-

DRAWING #

Stone Lintel Elevation

SCALE
3/4"
1'-0"

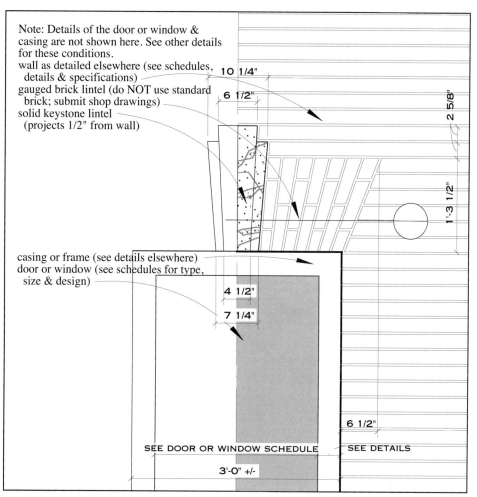

Note: Details of the door or window &
casing are not shown here. See other details
for these conditions.

wall as detailed elsewhere (see schedules,
   details & specifications)

gauged brick lintel (do NOT use standard
   brick; submit shop drawings)

solid keystone lintel
   (projects 1/2" from wall)

10 1/4"

6 1/2"

2 5/8"

1'-3 1/2"

casing or frame (see details elsewhere)

door or window (see schedules for type,
   size & design)

4 1/2"

7 1/4"

6 1/2"

SEE DOOR OR WINDOW SCHEDULE   SEE DETAILS

3'-0" +/-

DRAWING #

Stone Lintel Elevation

SCALE

3/4"
―――
1'-0"

DDEB2013
307

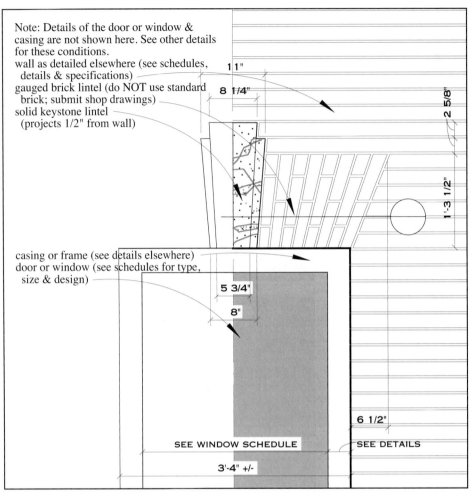

Note: Details of the door or window &
casing are not shown here. See other details
for these conditions.
wall as detailed elsewhere (see schedules,
    details & specifications)
gauged brick lintel (do NOT use standard
    brick; submit shop drawings)
solid keystone lintel
    (projects 1/2" from wall)

1 1"

8 1/4"

2 5/8"

1'-3 1/2"

casing or frame (see details elsewhere)
door or window (see schedules for type,
    size & design)

5 3/4"

8"

6 1/2"

SEE WINDOW SCHEDULE

SEE DETAILS

3'-4" +/-

DRAWING #

Stone Lintel Elevation

SCALE
3/4"
1'-0"

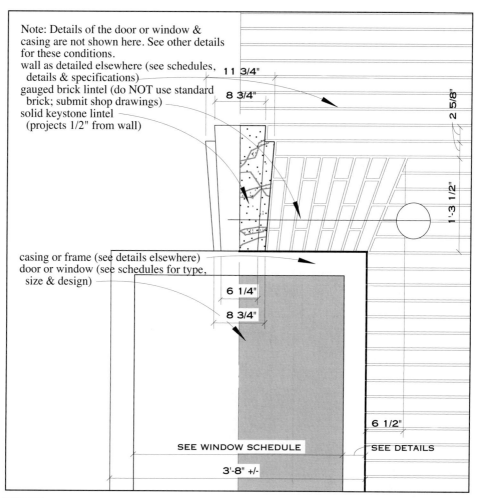

Note: Details of the door or window &
casing are not shown here. See other details
for these conditions.

wall as detailed elsewhere (see schedules,
  details & specifications)

gauged brick lintel (do NOT use standard
  brick; submit shop drawings)

solid keystone lintel
  (projects 1/2" from wall)

11 3/4"

8 3/4"

2 5/8"

1'-3 1/2"

casing or frame (see details elsewhere)
door or window (see schedules for type,
  size & design)

6 1/4"

8 3/4"

SEE WINDOW SCHEDULE

6 1/2"

SEE DETAILS

3'-8" +/-

DRAWING #

Stone Lintel Elevation

SCALE

3/4"
―――
1'-0"

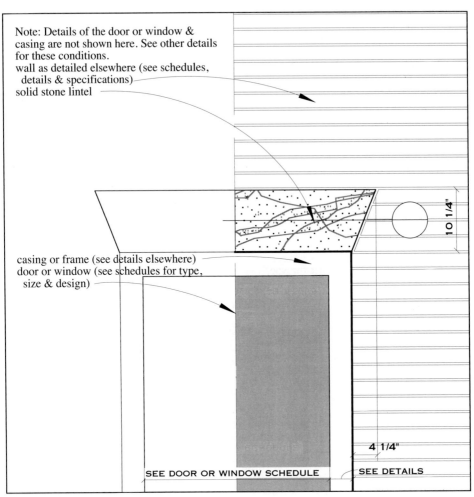

Note: Details of the door or window & casing are not shown here. See other details for these conditions.

wall as detailed elsewhere (see schedules, details & specifications)

solid stone lintel

10 1/4"

casing or frame (see details elsewhere)
door or window (see schedules for type, size & design)

4 1/4"

SEE DOOR OR WINDOW SCHEDULE

SEE DETAILS

DRAWING #

Stone Lintel Elevation

SCALE
3/4"
1'-0"

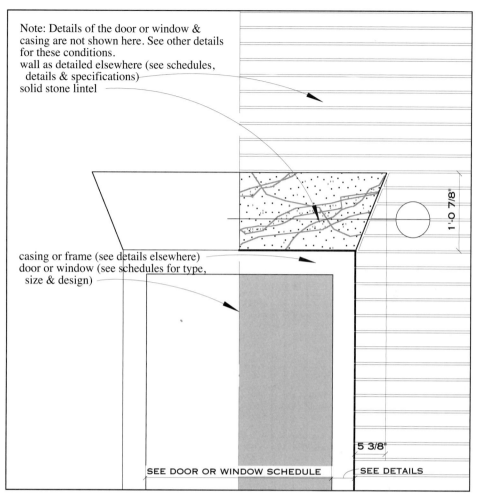

Note: Details of the door or window &
casing are not shown here. See other details
for these conditions.
wall as detailed elsewhere (see schedules,
   details & specifications)
solid stone lintel

1'-0 7/8"

casing or frame (see details elsewhere)
door or window (see schedules for type,
   size & design)

5 3/8"

SEE DOOR OR WINDOW SCHEDULE   SEE DETAILS

DRAWING #

Stone Lintel Elevation

SCALE
3/4"
1'-0"

DDES002
311

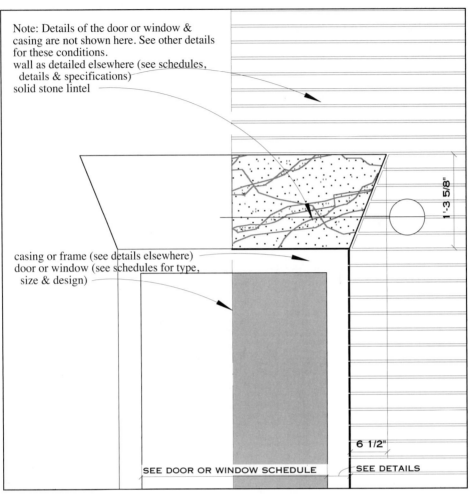

Note: Details of the door or window & casing are not shown here. See other details for these conditions.
wall as detailed elsewhere (see schedules, details & specifications)
solid stone lintel

casing or frame (see details elsewhere)
door or window (see schedules for type, size & design)

1'-3 5/8"

6 1/2"

SEE DOOR OR WINDOW SCHEDULE

SEE DETAILS

DRAWING #

Stone Lintel Elevation

SCALE
3/4"
1'-O"

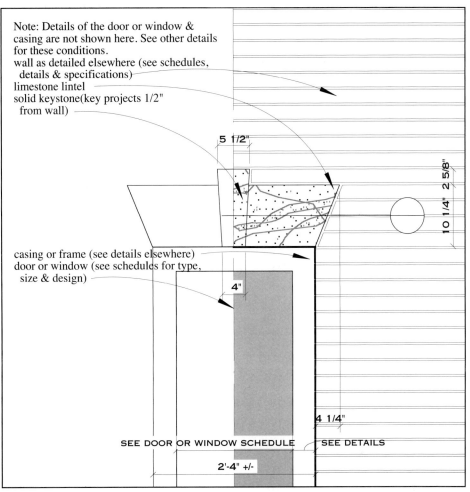

Note: Details of the door or window &
casing are not shown here. See other details
for these conditions.

wall as detailed elsewhere (see schedules,
  details & specifications)

limestone lintel

solid keystone(key projects 1/2"
  from wall)

5 1/2"

10 1/4"   2 5/8"

casing or frame (see details elsewhere)

door or window (see schedules for type,
  size & design)

4"

4 1/4"

SEE DOOR OR WINDOW SCHEDULE   SEE DETAILS

2'-4" +/-

Stone Lintel Elevation

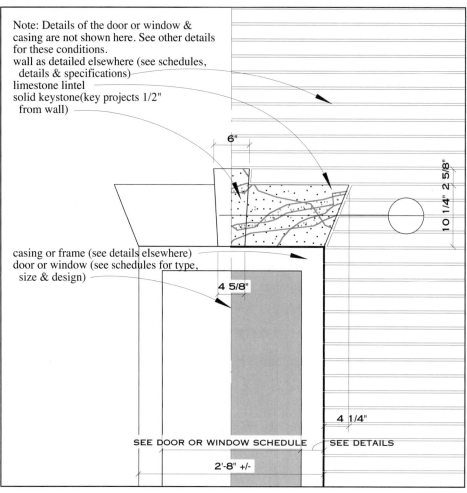

Note: Details of the door or window &
casing are not shown here. See other details
for these conditions.
wall as detailed elsewhere (see schedules,
   details & specifications)
limestone lintel
solid keystone(key projects 1/2"
   from wall)

6"

10 1/4" 2 5/8"

casing or frame (see details elsewhere)
door or window (see schedules for type,
   size & design)

4 5/8"

4 1/4"

SEE DOOR OR WINDOW SCHEDULE

SEE DETAILS

2'-8" +/-

DRAWING #

Stone Lintel Elevation

SCALE
3/4"
1'-O"

DDES1002
314

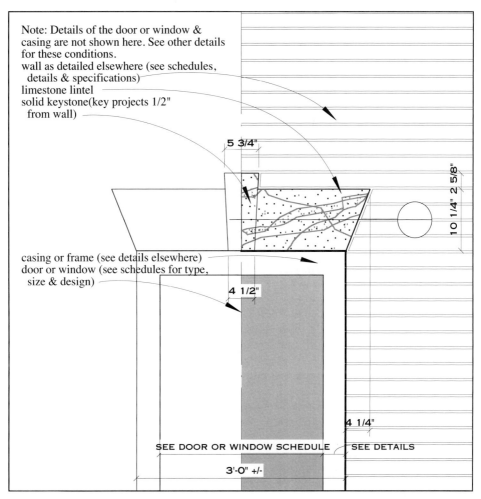

Note: Details of the door or window &
casing are not shown here. See other details
for these conditions.
wall as detailed elsewhere (see schedules,
  details & specifications)
limestone lintel
solid keystone(key projects 1/2"
  from wall)

5 3/4"

10 1/4" 2 5/8"

casing or frame (see details elsewhere)
door or window (see schedules for type,
  size & design)

4 1/2"

4 1/4"

SEE DOOR OR WINDOW SCHEDULE   SEE DETAILS

3'-0" +/-

DRAWING #

Stone Lintel Elevation

SCALE
3/4"
1'-0"

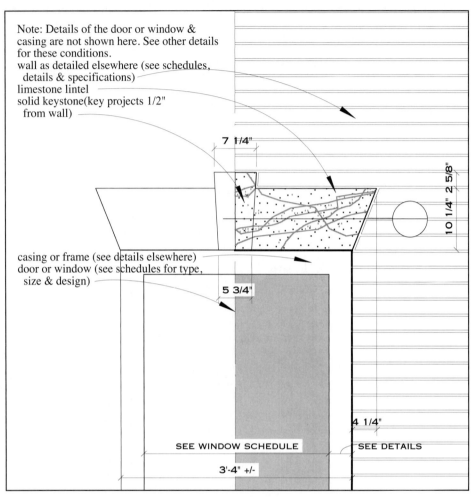

Note: Details of the door or window & casing are not shown here. See other details for these conditions.
wall as detailed elsewhere (see schedules, details & specifications)
limestone lintel
solid keystone(key projects 1/2" from wall)

7 1/4"

10 1/4" 2 5/8"

casing or frame (see details elsewhere)
door or window (see schedules for type, size & design)

5 3/4"

4 1/4"

SEE WINDOW SCHEDULE

SEE DETAILS

3'-4" +/-

DRAWING #

Stone Lintel Elevation

SCALE
3/4"
1'-O"

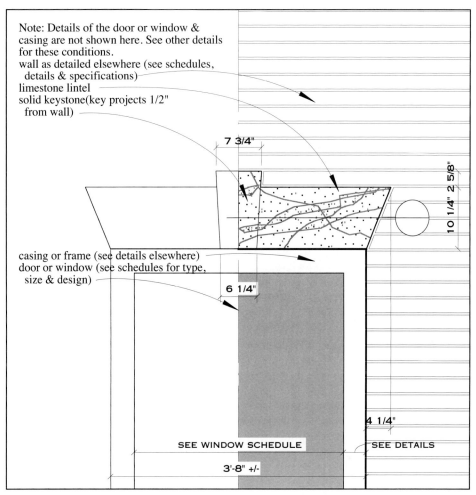

Note: Details of the door or window &
casing are not shown here. See other details
for these conditions.
wall as detailed elsewhere (see schedules,
  details & specifications)
limestone lintel
solid keystone(key projects 1/2"
  from wall)

7 3/4"

10 1/4" 2 5/8"

casing or frame (see details elsewhere)
door or window (see schedules for type,
  size & design)

6 1/4"

4 1/4"

SEE WINDOW SCHEDULE

SEE DETAILS

3'-8" +/-

DRAWING #

Stone Lintel Elevation

SCALE
3/4"
1'-0"

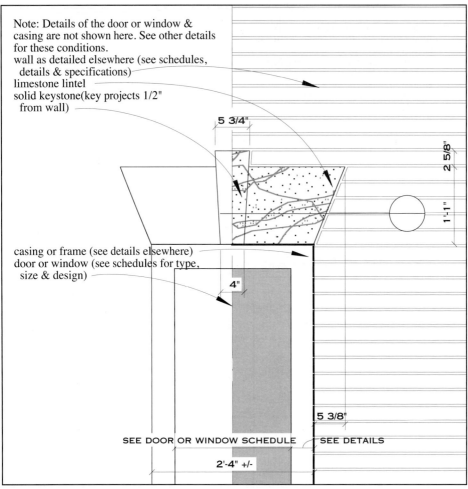

Note: Details of the door or window &
casing are not shown here. See other details
for these conditions.
wall as detailed elsewhere (see schedules,
  details & specifications)
limestone lintel
solid keystone(key projects 1/2"
  from wall)

5 3/4"

2 5/8"

1'-1"

casing or frame (see details elsewhere)
door or window (see schedules for type,
  size & design)

4"

5 3/8"

SEE DOOR OR WINDOW SCHEDULE   SEE DETAILS

2'-4" +/-

DRAWING #

Stone Lintel Elevation

SCALE
3/4"
1'-0"

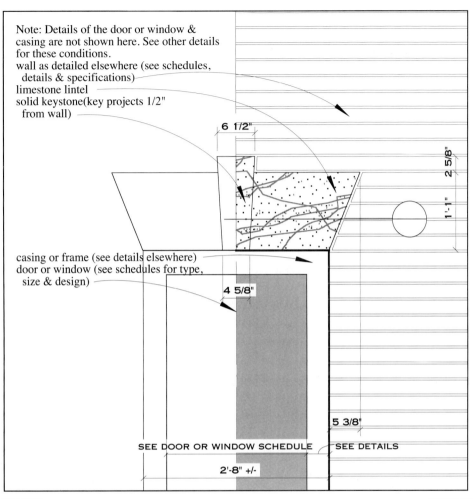

Note: Details of the door or window &
casing are not shown here. See other details
for these conditions.
wall as detailed elsewhere (see schedules,
   details & specifications)
limestone lintel
solid keystone(key projects 1/2"
   from wall)

6 1/2"

2 5/8"

1'-1"

casing or frame (see details elsewhere)
door or window (see schedules for type,
   size & design)

4 5/8"

5 3/8"

SEE DOOR OR WINDOW SCHEDULE   SEE DETAILS

2'-8" +/-

DRAWING #	

Stone Lintel Elevation

SCALE
3/4"
1'-0"

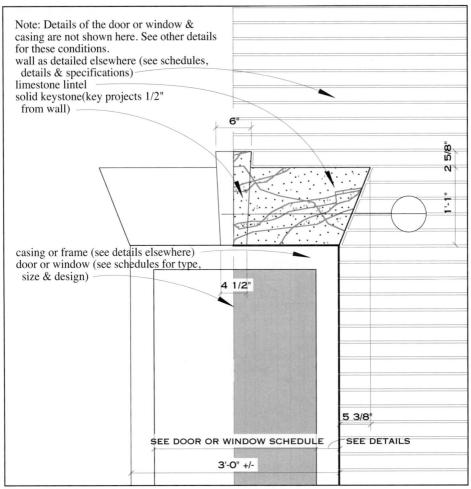

Note: Details of the door or window &
casing are not shown here. See other details
for these conditions.
wall as detailed elsewhere (see schedules,
 details & specifications)
limestone lintel
solid keystone(key projects 1/2"
 from wall)

6"

2 5/8"

1'-1"

casing or frame (see details elsewhere)
door or window (see schedules for type,
 size & design)

4 1/2"

5 3/8"

SEE DOOR OR WINDOW SCHEDULE   SEE DETAILS

3'-0" +/-

DRAWING #

Stone Lintel Elevation

SCALE
3/4"
1'-0"

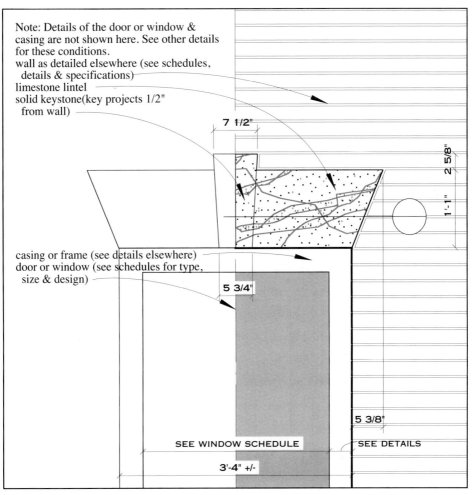

Note: Details of the door or window &
casing are not shown here. See other details
for these conditions.
wall as detailed elsewhere (see schedules,
  details & specifications)
limestone lintel
solid keystone(key projects 1/2"
  from wall)

7 1/2"

2 5/8"

1'-1"

casing or frame (see details elsewhere)
door or window (see schedules for type,
  size & design)

5 3/4"

5 3/8"

SEE WINDOW SCHEDULE

SEE DETAILS

3'-4" +/-

DRAWING #

Stone Lintel Elevation

SCALE
3/4"
1'-0"

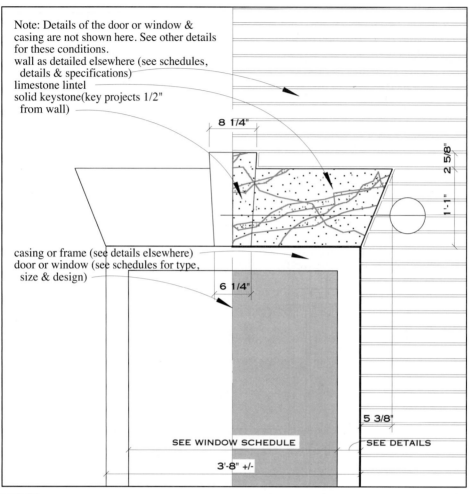

Note: Details of the door or window &
casing are not shown here. See other details
for these conditions.
wall as detailed elsewhere (see schedules,
 details & specifications)
limestone lintel
solid keystone(key projects 1/2"
 from wall)

8 1/4"

2 5/8"

1'-1"

casing or frame (see details elsewhere)
door or window (see schedules for type,
 size & design)

6 1/4"

5 3/8"

SEE WINDOW SCHEDULE

SEE DETAILS

3'-8" +/-

DRAWING #

Stone Lintel Elevation

SCALE
3/4"
1'-0"

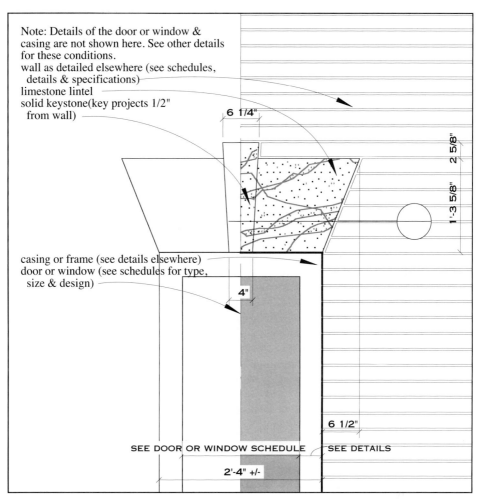

Note: Details of the door or window &
casing are not shown here. See other details
for these conditions.
wall as detailed elsewhere (see schedules,
  details & specifications)
limestone lintel
solid keystone(key projects 1/2"
  from wall)

6 1/4"

2 5/8"

1'-3 5/8"

casing or frame (see details elsewhere)
door or window (see schedules for type,
  size & design)

4"

6 1/2"

SEE DOOR OR WINDOW SCHEDULE   SEE DETAILS

2'-4" +/-

DRAWING #		SCALE
	Stone Lintel Elevation	3/4" / 1'-0"

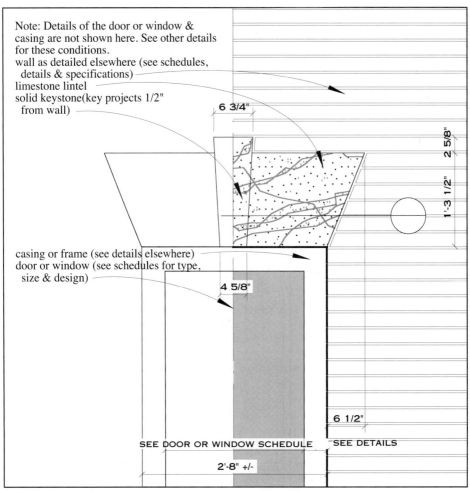

Note: Details of the door or window &
casing are not shown here. See other details
for these conditions.
wall as detailed elsewhere (see schedules,
    details & specifications)
limestone lintel
solid keystone(key projects 1/2"
    from wall)

6 3/4"

2 5/8"

1'-3 1/2"

casing or frame (see details elsewhere)
door or window (see schedules for type,
    size & design)

4 5/8"

6 1/2"

SEE DOOR OR WINDOW SCHEDULE

SEE DETAILS

2'-8" +/-

Stone Lintel Elevation

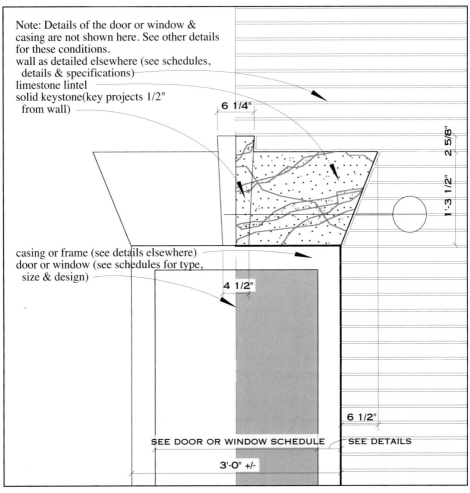

Note: Details of the door or window &
casing are not shown here. See other details
for these conditions.
wall as detailed elsewhere (see schedules,
  details & specifications)
limestone lintel
solid keystone(key projects 1/2"
  from wall)

6 1/4"

2 5/8"

1'-3 1/2"

casing or frame (see details elsewhere)
door or window (see schedules for type,
  size & design)

4 1/2"

6 1/2"

SEE DOOR OR WINDOW SCHEDULE   SEE DETAILS

3'-0" +/-

DRAWING #

Stone Lintel Elevation

SCALE
3/4"
1'-0"

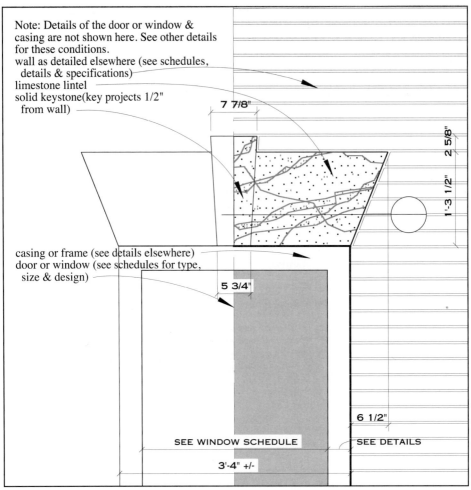

Note: Details of the door or window &
casing are not shown here. See other details
for these conditions.
wall as detailed elsewhere (see schedules,
  details & specifications)
limestone lintel
solid keystone(key projects 1/2"
  from wall)

7 7/8"

2 5/8"

1'-3 1/2"

casing or frame (see details elsewhere)
door or window (see schedules for type,
  size & design)

5 3/4"

6 1/2"

SEE WINDOW SCHEDULE

SEE DETAILS

3'-4" +/-

DRAWING #

Stone Lintel Elevation

SCALE
3/4"
1'-0"

DDES1014
326

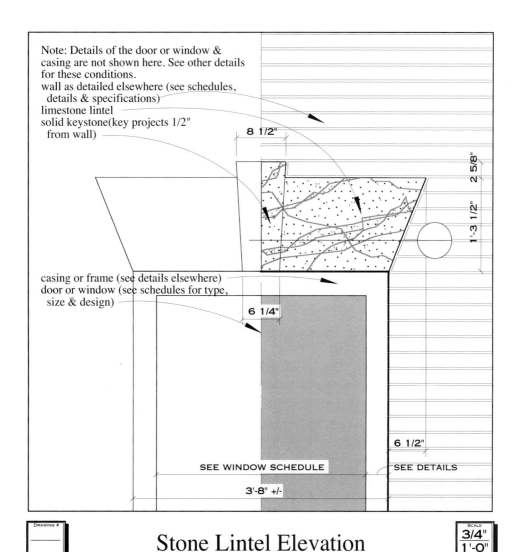

Note: Details of the door or window &
casing are not shown here. See other details
for these conditions.
wall as detailed elsewhere (see schedules,
  details & specifications)
limestone lintel
solid keystone(key projects 1/2"
  from wall)

8 1/2"

2 5/8"

1'-3 1/2"

casing or frame (see details elsewhere)
door or window (see schedules for type,
  size & design)

6 1/4"

6 1/2"

SEE WINDOW SCHEDULE

SEE DETAILS

3'-8" +/-

DRAWING #

Stone Lintel Elevation

SCALE
3/4"
1'-0"

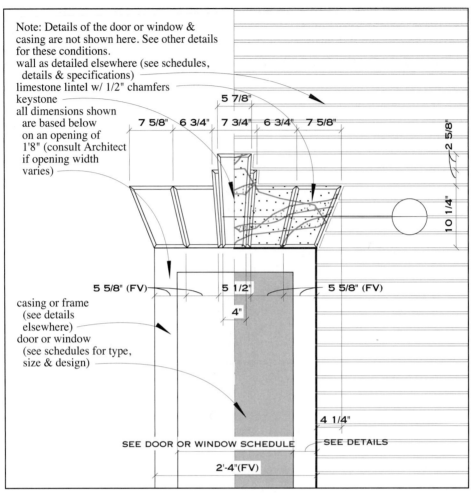

Note: Details of the door or window & casing are not shown here. See other details for these conditions.

wall as detailed elsewhere (see schedules, details & specifications)

limestone lintel w/ 1/2" chamfers

keystone

all dimensions shown are based below on an opening of 1'8" (consult Architect if opening width varies)

5 7/8"

7 5/8" 6 3/4" 7 3/4" 6 3/4" 7 5/8"

2 5/8"

10 1/4"

5 5/8" (FV)   5 1/2"   5 5/8" (FV)

4"

casing or frame (see details elsewhere)

door or window (see schedules for type, size & design)

4 1/4"

SEE DOOR OR WINDOW SCHEDULE

SEE DETAILS

2'-4"(FV)

Stone Lintel Elevation

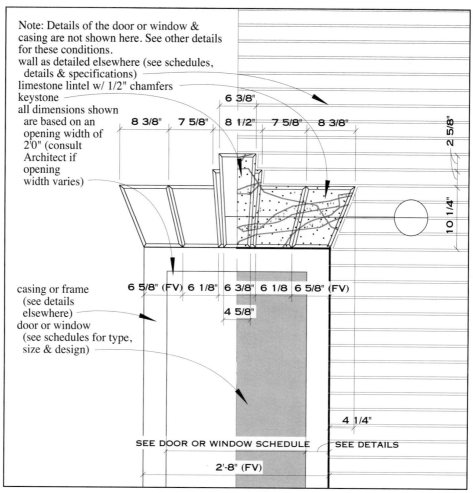

Note: Details of the door or window &
casing are not shown here. See other details
for these conditions.

wall as detailed elsewhere (see schedules,
    details & specifications)

limestone lintel w/ 1/2" chamfers

keystone

all dimensions shown
    are based on an
    opening width of
    2'0" (consult
    Architect if
    opening
    width varies)

8 3/8"   7 5/8"   8 1/2"   7 5/8"   8 3/8"

6 3/8"

2 5/8"

10 1/4"

casing or frame
    (see details
    elsewhere)

door or window
    (see schedules for type,
    size & design)

6 5/8" (FV) 6 1/8" 6 3/8" 6 1/8 6 5/8" (FV)

4 5/8"

4 1/4"

SEE DOOR OR WINDOW SCHEDULE   SEE DETAILS

2'-8" (FV)

Stone Lintel Elevation

SCALE
3/4"
1'-0"

DRAWING #

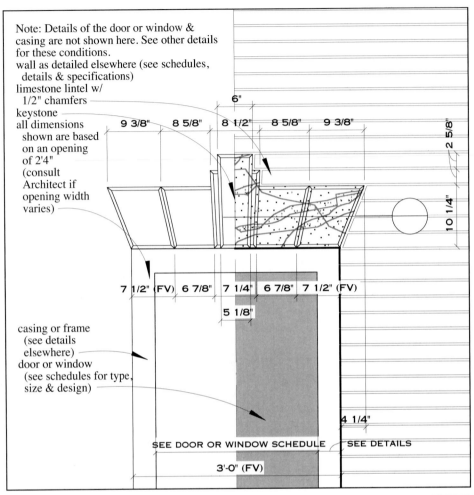

Note: Details of the door or window &
casing are not shown here. See other details
for these conditions.
wall as detailed elsewhere (see schedules,
  details & specifications)
limestone lintel w/
  1/2" chamfers
keystone
all dimensions
  shown are based
  on an opening
  of 2'4"
  (consult
  Architect if
  opening width
  varies)

6"

9 3/8"   8 5/8"   8 1/2"   8 5/8"   9 3/8"

2 5/8"

10 1/4"

7 1/2" (FV)   6 7/8"   7 1/4"   6 7/8"   7 1/2" (FV)

5 1/8"

casing or frame
  (see details
  elsewhere)
door or window
  (see schedules for type,
  size & design)

4 1/4"

SEE DOOR OR WINDOW SCHEDULE   SEE DETAILS

3'-0" (FV)

DRAWING #

Stone Lintel Elevation

SCALE
3/4"
1'-0"

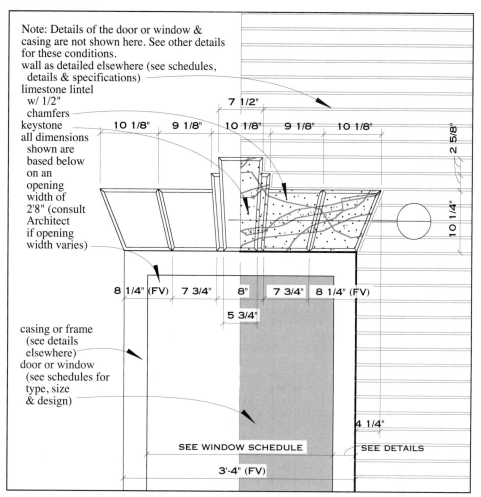

Note: Details of the door or window &
casing are not shown here. See other details
for these conditions.

wall as detailed elsewhere (see schedules,
 details & specifications)

limestone lintel
 w/ 1/2"
 chamfers

keystone

all dimensions
 shown are
 based below
 on an
 opening
 width of
 2'8" (consult
 Architect
 if opening
 width varies)

7 1/2"

10 1/8"   9 1/8"   10 1/8"   9 1/8"   10 1/8"

2 5/8"

10 1/4"

casing or frame
 (see details
 elsewhere)

door or window
 (see schedules for
 type, size
 & design)

8 1/4" (FV)   7 3/4"   8"   7 3/4"   8 1/4" (FV)

5 3/4"

4 1/4"

SEE WINDOW SCHEDULE

SEE DETAILS

3'-4" (FV)

DRAWING #	

Stone Lintel Elevation

SCALE	
3/4"	
1'-0"	

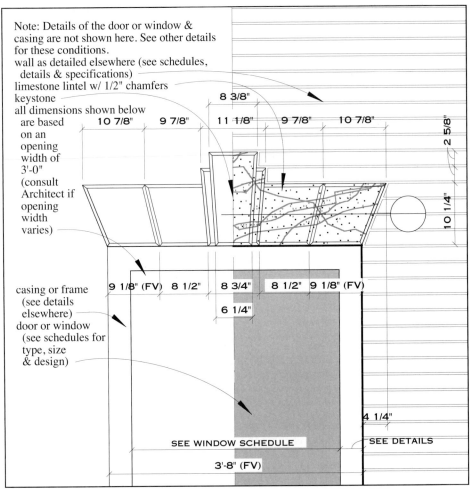

Note: Details of the door or window &
casing are not shown here. See other details
for these conditions.
wall as detailed elsewhere (see schedules,
 details & specifications)
limestone lintel w/ 1/2" chamfers
keystone
all dimensions shown below
 are based
 on an
 opening
 width of
 3'-0"
 (consult
 Architect if
 opening
 width
 varies)

casing or frame
 (see details
 elsewhere)
door or window
 (see schedules for
 type, size
 & design)

8 3/8"

10 7/8"   9 7/8"   11 1/8"   9 7/8"   10 7/8"

2 5/8"

10 1/4"

9 1/8" (FV)   8 1/2"   8 3/4"   8 1/2"   9 1/8" (FV)

6 1/4"

4 1/4"

SEE WINDOW SCHEDULE   SEE DETAILS

3'-8" (FV)

DRAWING #

Stone Lintel Elevation

SCALE
3/4"
1'-0"

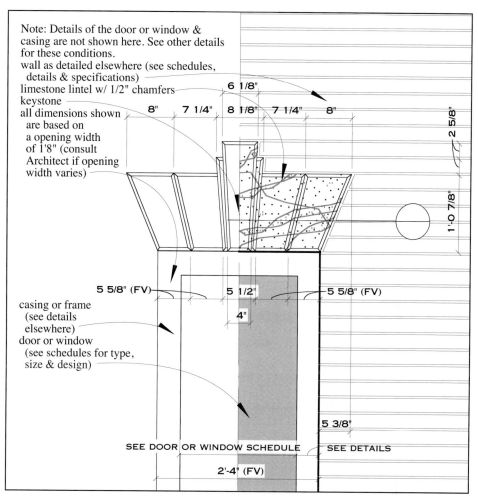

Note: Details of the door or window &
casing are not shown here. See other details
for these conditions.
wall as detailed elsewhere (see schedules,
   details & specifications)
limestone lintel w/ 1/2" chamfers
keystone
all dimensions shown
   are based on
   a opening width
   of 1'8" (consult
   Architect if opening
   width varies)

6 1/8"

8"   7 1/4"   8 1/8"   7 1/4"   8"

2 5/8"

1'-0 7/8"

5 5/8" (FV)   5 1/2"   5 5/8" (FV)

casing or frame
   (see details
   elsewhere)
door or window
   (see schedules for type,
   size & design)

4"

5 3/8"

SEE DOOR OR WINDOW SCHEDULE   SEE DETAILS

2'-4" (FV)

DRAWING #

Stone Lintel Elevation

SCALE
3/4"
1'-0"

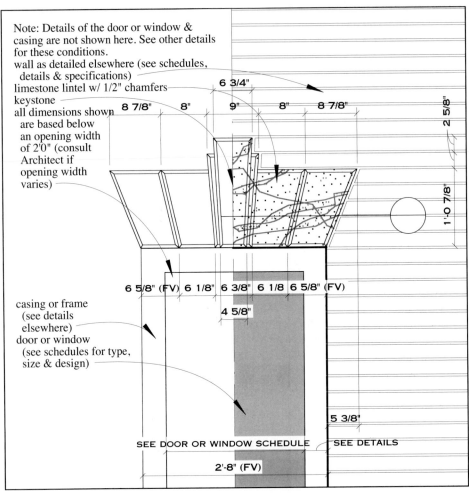

Note: Details of the door or window & casing are not shown here. See other details for these conditions.

wall as detailed elsewhere (see schedules, details & specifications)

limestone lintel w/ 1/2" chamfers

keystone

all dimensions shown are based below an opening width of 2'0" (consult Architect if opening width varies)

6 3/4"

8 7/8"   8"   9"   8"   8 7/8"

2 5/8"

1'-0 7/8"

casing or frame (see details elsewhere)

door or window (see schedules for type, size & design)

6 5/8" (FV) 6 1/8" 6 3/8" 6 1/8 6 5/8" (FV)

4 5/8"

5 3/8"

SEE DOOR OR WINDOW SCHEDULE   SEE DETAILS

2'-8" (FV)

DRAWING #

Stone Lintel Elevation

SCALE
3/4"
1'-0"

DDES3007
334

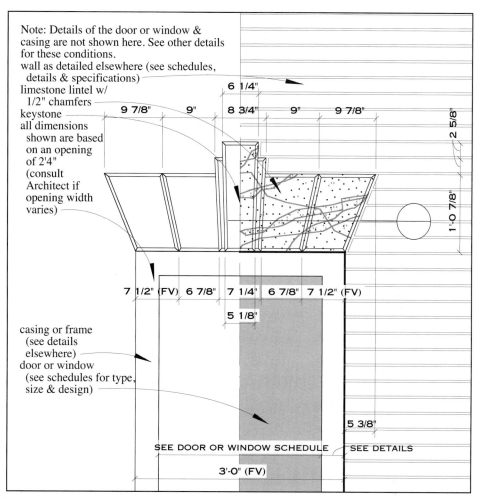

Note: Details of the door or window &
casing are not shown here. See other details
for these conditions.
wall as detailed elsewhere (see schedules,
  details & specifications)
limestone lintel w/
  1/2" chamfers
keystone
all dimensions
  shown are based
  on an opening
  of 2'4"
  (consult
  Architect if
  opening width
  varies)

6 1/4"

9 7/8"   9"   8 3/4"   9"   9 7/8"

2 5/8"

1'-0 7/8"

7 1/2" (FV)   6 7/8"   7 1/4"   6 7/8"   7 1/2" (FV)

5 1/8"

casing or frame
  (see details
  elsewhere)
door or window
  (see schedules for type,
  size & design)

5 3/8"

SEE DOOR OR WINDOW SCHEDULE

SEE DETAILS

3'-0" (FV)

DRAWING #

Stone Lintel Elevation

SCALE
3/4"
1'-0"

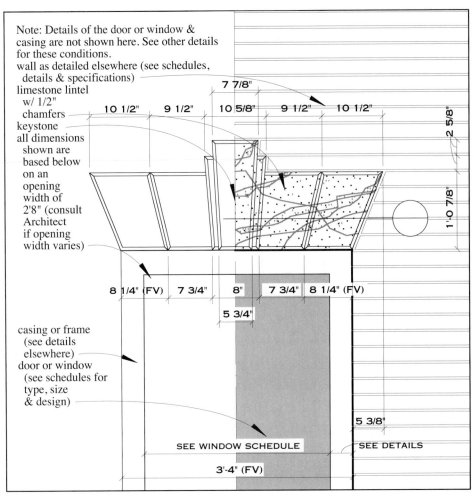

Note: Details of the door or window &
casing are not shown here. See other details
for these conditions.
wall as detailed elsewhere (see schedules,
   details & specifications)
limestone lintel
   w/ 1/2"
   chamfers
keystone
all dimensions
   shown are
   based below
   on an
   opening
   width of
   2'8" (consult
   Architect
   if opening
   width varies)

7 7/8"

10 1/2"   9 1/2"   10 5/8"   9 1/2"   10 1/2"

2 5/8"

1'-0 7/8"

casing or frame
   (see details
   elsewhere)
door or window
   (see schedules for
   type, size
   & design)

8 1/4" (FV)   7 3/4"   8"   7 3/4"   8 1/4" (FV)

5 3/4"

5 3/8"

SEE WINDOW SCHEDULE   SEE DETAILS

3'-4" (FV)

DRAWING #

Stone Lintel Elevation

SCALE
3/4"
1'-0"

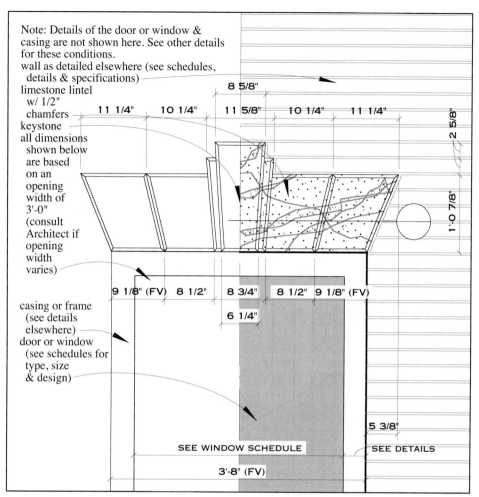

Note: Details of the door or window &
casing are not shown here. See other details
for these conditions.

wall as detailed elsewhere (see schedules,
   details & specifications)

limestone lintel
   w/ 1/2"
   chamfers

keystone

all dimensions
   shown below
   are based
   on an
   opening
   width of
   3'-0"
   (consult
   Architect if
   opening
   width
   varies)

8 5/8"

11 1/4"   10 1/4"   11 5/8"   10 1/4"   11 1/4"

2 5/8"

1'-0 7/8"

casing or frame
   (see details
   elsewhere)

door or window
   (see schedules for
   type, size
   & design)

9 1/8" (FV)   8 1/2"   8 3/4"   8 1/2"   9 1/8" (FV)

6 1/4"

5 3/8"

SEE WINDOW SCHEDULE

SEE DETAILS

3'-8" (FV)

DRAWING #

Stone Lintel Elevation

SCALE
3/4"
1'-0"

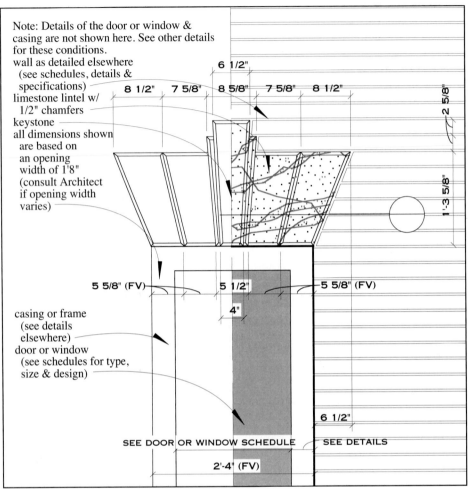

Note: Details of the door or window & casing are not shown here. See other details for these conditions.

wall as detailed elsewhere (see schedules, details & specifications)

limestone lintel w/ 1/2" chamfers

keystone

all dimensions shown are based on an opening width of 1'8" (consult Architect if opening width varies)

6 1/2"

8 1/2" 7 5/8" 8 5/8" 7 5/8" 8 1/2"

2 5/8"

1'-3 5/8"

5 5/8" (FV)

5 1/2"

5 5/8" (FV)

4"

casing or frame (see details elsewhere)

door or window (see schedules for type, size & design)

6 1/2"

SEE DOOR OR WINDOW SCHEDULE

SEE DETAILS

2'-4" (FV)

DRAWING #

Stone Lintel Elevation

SCALE
3/4"
1'-0"

DDES3011
338

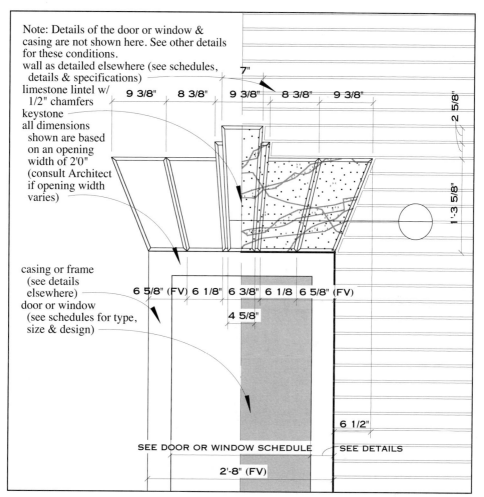

Note: Details of the door or window &
casing are not shown here. See other details
for these conditions.

wall as detailed elsewhere (see schedules,
details & specifications)

limestone lintel w/
1/2" chamfers

keystone

all dimensions
shown are based
on an opening
width of 2'0"
(consult Architect
if opening width
varies)

7"

9 3/8"   8 3/8"   9 3/8"   8 3/8"   9 3/8"

2 5/8"

1'-3 5/8"

casing or frame
(see details
elsewhere)

door or window
(see schedules for type,
size & design)

6 5/8" (FV) 6 1/8" 6 3/8" 6 1/8 6 5/8" (FV)

4 5/8"

6 1/2"

SEE DOOR OR WINDOW SCHEDULE   SEE DETAILS

2'-8" (FV)

DRAWING #

Stone Lintel Elevation

SCALE
3/4"
1'-O"

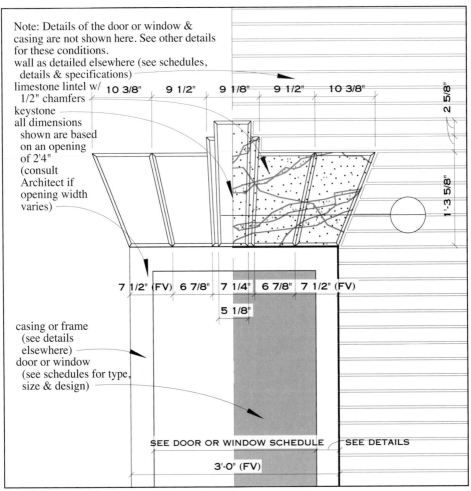

Note: Details of the door or window &
casing are not shown here. See other details
for these conditions.
wall as detailed elsewhere (see schedules,
details & specifications)
limestone lintel w/ 10 3/8"   9 1/2"   9 1/8"   9 1/2"   10 3/8"
1/2" chamfers
keystone
all dimensions
shown are based
on an opening
of 2'4"
(consult
Architect if
opening width
varies)

2 5/8"

1'-3 5/8"

7 1/2" (FV)   6 7/8"   7 1/4"   6 7/8"   7 1/2" (FV)

5 1/8"

casing or frame
(see details
elsewhere)
door or window
(see schedules for type,
size & design)

SEE DOOR OR WINDOW SCHEDULE   SEE DETAILS

3'-0" (FV)

DRAWING #

Stone Lintel Elevation

SCALE
3/4"
1'-0"

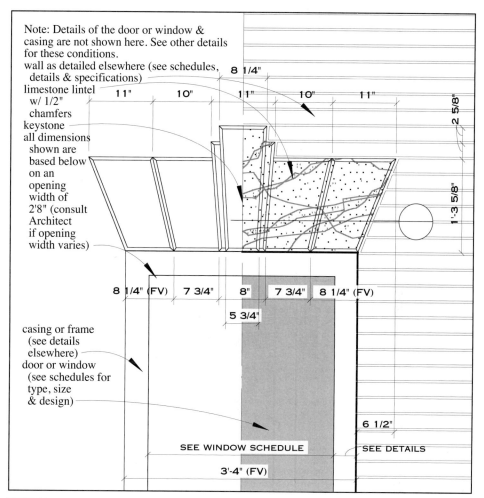

Note: Details of the door or window &
casing are not shown here. See other details
for these conditions.

wall as detailed elsewhere (see schedules,
details & specifications)

limestone lintel
w/ 1/2"
chamfers

keystone

all dimensions
shown are
based below
on an
opening
width of
2'8" (consult
Architect
if opening
width varies)

8 1/4"

11"   10"   11"   10"   11"

2 5/8"

1'-3 5/8"

casing or frame
(see details
elsewhere)
door or window
(see schedules for
type, size
& design)

8 1/4" (FV)   7 3/4"   8"   7 3/4"   8 1/4" (FV)

5 3/4"

6 1/2"

SEE WINDOW SCHEDULE

SEE DETAILS

3'-4" (FV)

Stone Lintel Elevation

SCALE
3/4"
1'-0"

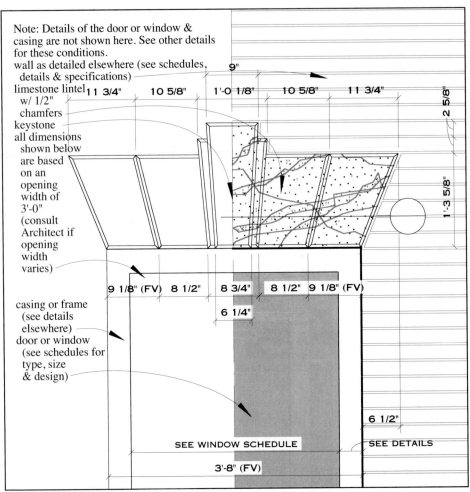

Note: Details of the door or window &
casing are not shown here. See other details
for these conditions.

wall as detailed elsewhere (see schedules,
   details & specifications)

limestone lintel w/ 1/2" chamfers

keystone

all dimensions shown below are based on an opening width of 3'-0" (consult Architect if opening width varies)

9"

11 3/4"   10 5/8"   1'-0 1/8"   10 5/8"   11 3/4"

2 5/8"

1'-3 5/8"

casing or frame (see details elsewhere)

door or window (see schedules for type, size & design)

9 1/8" (FV)   8 1/2"   8 3/4"   8 1/2"   9 1/8" (FV)

6 1/4"

6 1/2"

SEE WINDOW SCHEDULE

SEE DETAILS

3'-8" (FV)

DRAWING #

Stone Lintel Elevation

SCALE
3/4"
1'-0"

DDES3015
342

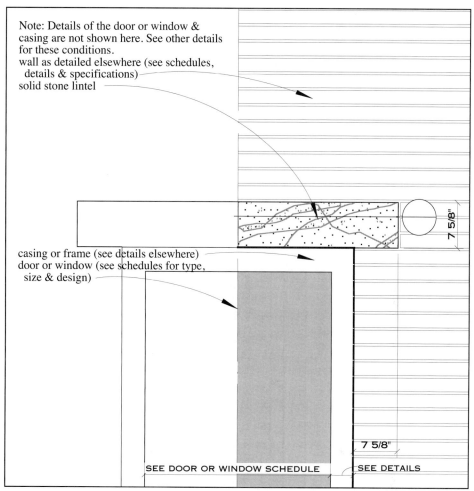

Note: Details of the door or window & casing are not shown here. See other details for these conditions.

wall as detailed elsewhere (see schedules, details & specifications)

solid stone lintel

7 5/8"

casing or frame (see details elsewhere)

door or window (see schedules for type, size & design)

7 5/8"

SEE DOOR OR WINDOW SCHEDULE

SEE DETAILS

DRAWING #

Stone Lintel Elevation

SCALE

3/4"
1'-0"

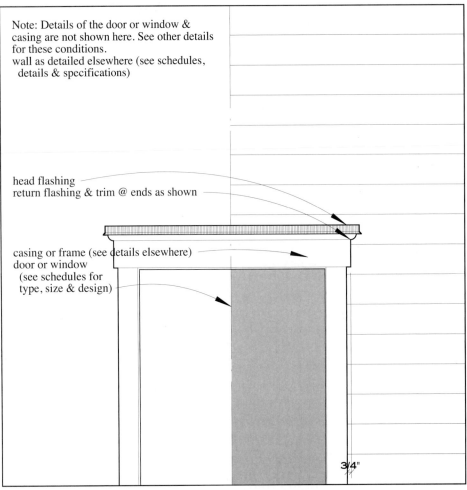

Note: Details of the door or window &
casing are not shown here. See other details
for these conditions.
wall as detailed elsewhere (see schedules,
  details & specifications)

head flashing
return flashing & trim @ ends as shown

casing or frame (see details elsewhere)
door or window
  (see schedules for
  type, size & design)

3/4"

DRAWING #

Wood Head Elevation

SCALE

3/4"
1'-0"

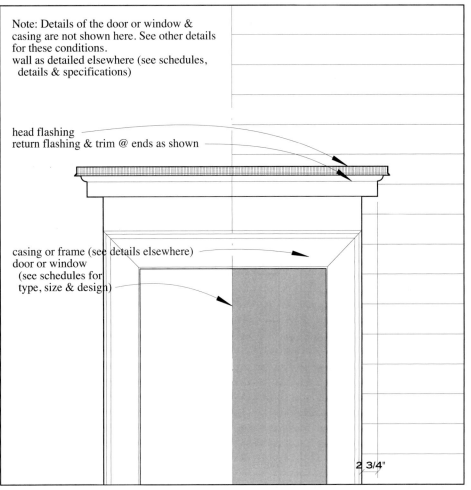

Note: Details of the door or window &
casing are not shown here. See other details
for these conditions.
wall as detailed elsewhere (see schedules,
  details & specifications)

head flashing
return flashing & trim @ ends as shown

casing or frame (see details elsewhere)
door or window
  (see schedules for
  type, size & design)

2 3/4"

Wood Head Elevation

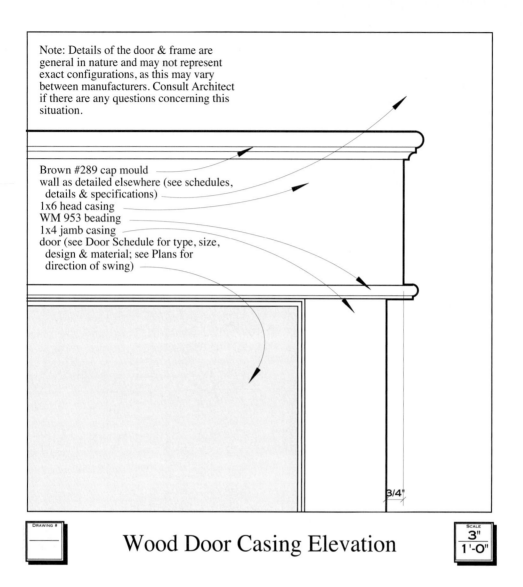

Note: Details of the door & frame are general in nature and may not represent exact configurations, as this may vary between manufacturers. Consult Architect if there are any questions concerning this situation.

Brown #289 cap mould
wall as detailed elsewhere (see schedules, details & specifications)
1x6 head casing
WM 953 beading
1x4 jamb casing
door (see Door Schedule for type, size, design & material; see Plans for direction of swing)

3/4"

DRAWING #

Wood Door Casing Elevation

SCALE
3"
1'-0"

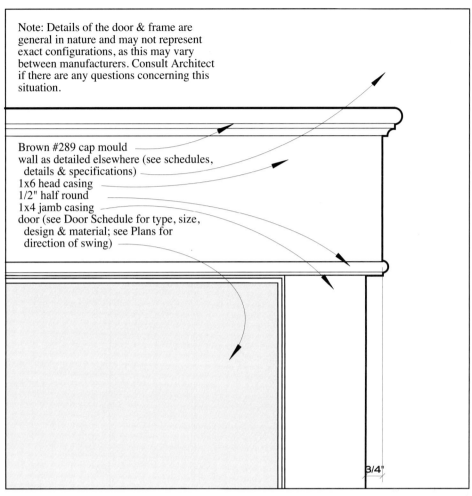

Note: Details of the door & frame are
general in nature and may not represent
exact configurations, as this may vary
between manufacturers. Consult Architect
if there are any questions concerning this
situation.

Brown #289 cap mould
wall as detailed elsewhere (see schedules,
  details & specifications)
1x6 head casing
1/2" half round
1x4 jamb casing
door (see Door Schedule for type, size,
  design & material; see Plans for
  direction of swing)

3/4"

DRAWING #

Wood Door Casing Elevation

SCALE
$\dfrac{3''}{1'\text{-}0''}$

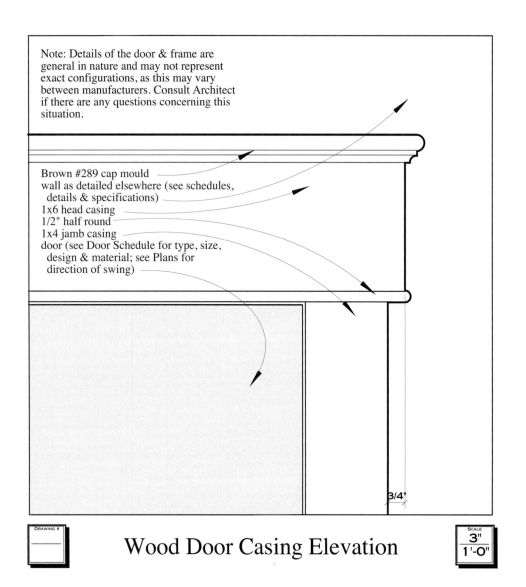

Note: Details of the door & frame are general in nature and may not represent exact configurations, as this may vary between manufacturers. Consult Architect if there are any questions concerning this situation.

Brown #289 cap mould
wall as detailed elsewhere (see schedules, details & specifications)
1x6 head casing
1/2" half round
1x4 jamb casing
door (see Door Schedule for type, size, design & material; see Plans for direction of swing)

3/4"

DRAWING #

SCALE
$\frac{3"}{1'-0"}$

Wood Door Casing Elevation

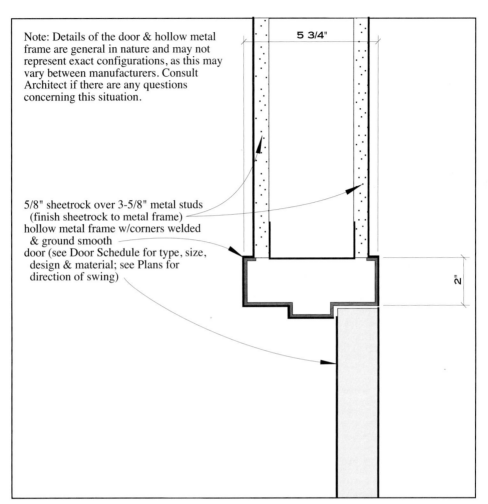

Note: Details of the door & hollow metal frame are general in nature and may not represent exact configurations, as this may vary between manufacturers. Consult Architect if there are any questions concerning this situation.

5/8" sheetrock over 3-5/8" metal studs
  (finish sheetrock to metal frame)
hollow metal frame w/corners welded
  & ground smooth
door (see Door Schedule for type, size,
  design & material; see Plans for
  direction of swing)

5 3/4"

2"

DRAWING #		SCALE

Hollow Metal Frame Head

$\frac{3"}{1'-0"}$

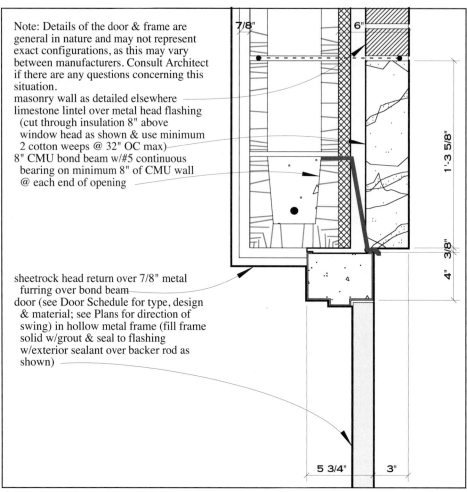

Note: Details of the door & frame are general in nature and may not represent exact configurations, as this may vary between manufacturers. Consult Architect if there are any questions concerning this situation.

masonry wall as detailed elsewhere

limestone lintel over metal head flashing (cut through insulation 8" above window head as shown & use minimum 2 cotton weeps @ 32" OC max)

8" CMU bond beam w/#5 continuous bearing on minimum 8" of CMU wall @ each end of opening

sheetrock head return over 7/8" metal furring over bond beam

door (see Door Schedule for type, design & material; see Plans for direction of swing) in hollow metal frame (fill frame solid w/grout & seal to flashing w/exterior sealant over backer rod as shown)

7/8"   6"

1'-3 5/8"

4"   3/8"

5 3/4"   3"

DRAWING #

Hollow Metal Door Head Detail

SCALE
1 1/2
1'-0"

DHH004
350

Note: Details of the door & frame are general in nature and may not represent exact configurations, as this may vary between manufacturers. Consult Architect if there are any questions concerning this situation.

masonry wall as detailed elsewhere

head flashing (use minimum 2 cotton weeps @ 32" OC max)

8" CMU bond beam w/#5 continuous bearing on minimum 8" of CMU wall @ each end of opening

L6x6x3/8 shelf angle attached to bond beam w/3/4"x6" AB's 16" OC

sheetrock head return over 7/8" metal furring over bond beam

door (see Door Schedule for type, design & material; see Plans for direction of swing) in hollow metal frame (fill frame solid w/grout & seal to bottom of lintel)

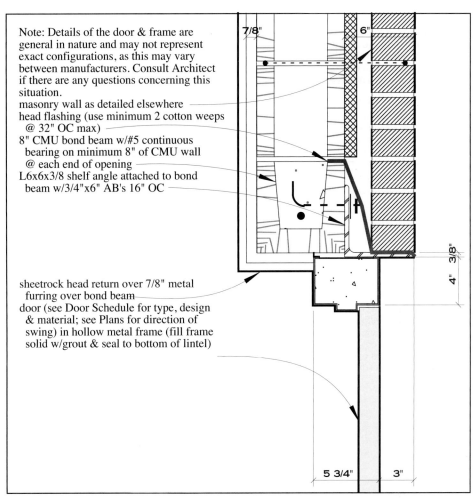

7/8" 6"

3/8"

4"

5 3/4" 3"

Hollow Metal Door Head Detail

DRAWING #

SCALE
1 1/2
1'-0"

DHH005
351

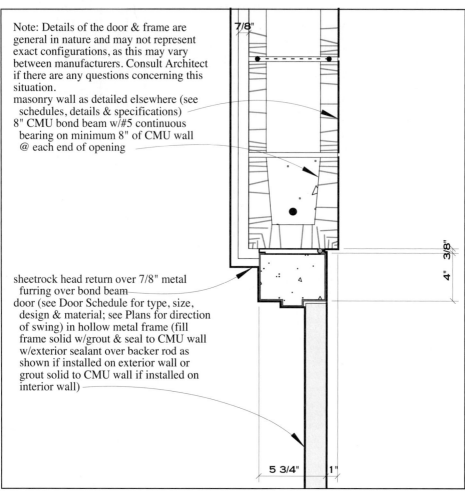

Note: Details of the door & frame are general in nature and may not represent exact configurations, as this may vary between manufacturers. Consult Architect if there are any questions concerning this situation.

masonry wall as detailed elsewhere (see schedules, details & specifications)

8" CMU bond beam w/#5 continuous bearing on minimum 8" of CMU wall @ each end of opening

7/8"

4" 3/8"

sheetrock head return over 7/8" metal furring over bond beam

door (see Door Schedule for type, size, design & material; see Plans for direction of swing) in hollow metal frame (fill frame solid w/grout & seal to CMU wall w/exterior sealant over backer rod as shown if installed on exterior wall or grout solid to CMU wall if installed on interior wall)

5 3/4"   1"

DRAWING #

Hollow Metal Door Head Detail

SCALE
1 1/2
1'-0"

DHH007
352

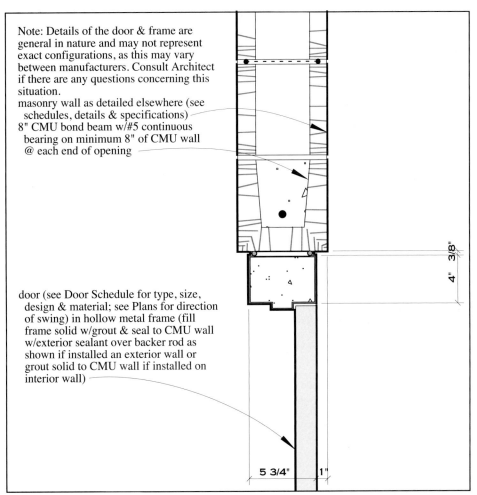

Note: Details of the door & frame are general in nature and may not represent exact configurations, as this may vary between manufacturers. Consult Architect if there are any questions concerning this situation.

masonry wall as detailed elsewhere (see schedules, details & specifications)

8" CMU bond beam w/#5 continuous bearing on minimum 8" of CMU wall @ each end of opening

door (see Door Schedule for type, size, design & material; see Plans for direction of swing) in hollow metal frame (fill frame solid w/grout & seal to CMU wall w/exterior sealant over backer rod as shown if installed an exterior wall or grout solid to CMU wall if installed on interior wall)

4" 3/8"

5 3/4"   1"

Hollow Metal Door Head Detail

DRAWING #

SCALE
1 1/2
1'-0"

DHH008
353

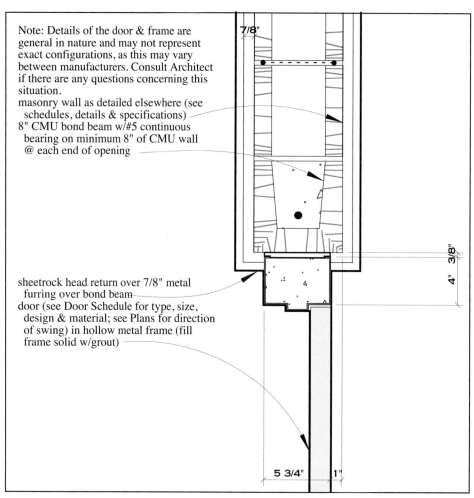

Note: Details of the door & frame are general in nature and may not represent exact configurations, as this may vary between manufacturers. Consult Architect if there are any questions concerning this situation.

masonry wall as detailed elsewhere (see schedules, details & specifications)

8" CMU bond beam w/#5 continuous bearing on minimum 8" of CMU wall @ each end of opening

sheetrock head return over 7/8" metal furring over bond beam

door (see Door Schedule for type, size, design & material; see Plans for direction of swing) in hollow metal frame (fill frame solid w/grout)

7/8"

3/8"

4"

5 3/4"   1"

DRAWING #

Hollow Metal Door Head Detail

SCALE

1 1/2
1'-0"

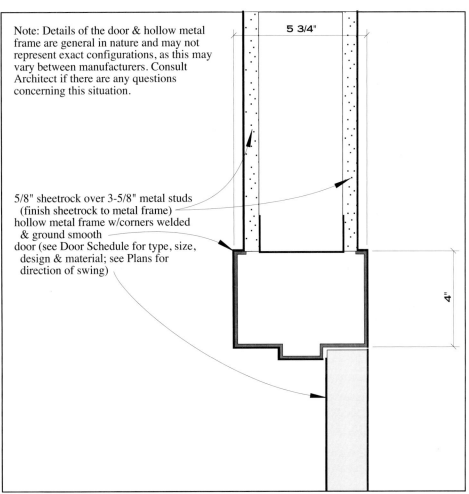

Note: Details of the door & hollow metal
frame are general in nature and may not
represent exact configurations, as this may
vary between manufacturers. Consult
Architect if there are any questions
concerning this situation.

5/8" sheetrock over 3-5/8" metal studs
  (finish sheetrock to metal frame)
hollow metal frame w/corners welded
  & ground smooth
door (see Door Schedule for type, size,
  design & material; see Plans for
  direction of swing)

5 3/4"

4"

DRAWING #

Hollow Metal Frame Head

SCALE
3"
1'-0"

DHH014
355

Note: Details of the door & frame are
general in nature and may not represent
exact configurations, as this may vary
between manufacturers. Consult Architect
if there are any questions concerning this
situation.
steel stud brick veneer wall as detailed
  elsewhere (see schedules, details &
  specifications)
brick soldier course over head flashing
  w/cotton weeps 32" OC max. & 2 per
  door min. over L6x6x3/8" steel
  lintel

door (see Door Schedule for type, size,
  design & material; see Plans for
  direction of swing) in hollow metal
  frame (weld corners & grind smooth)
  sealed to brick w/exterior sealant &
  backer rod as shown

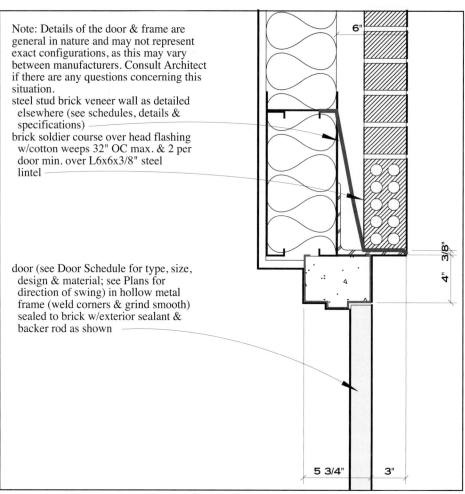

6"

4" 3/8"

5 3/4"   3"

DRAWING #

Hollow Metal Door Head Detail

SCALE
1 1/2
1'-0"

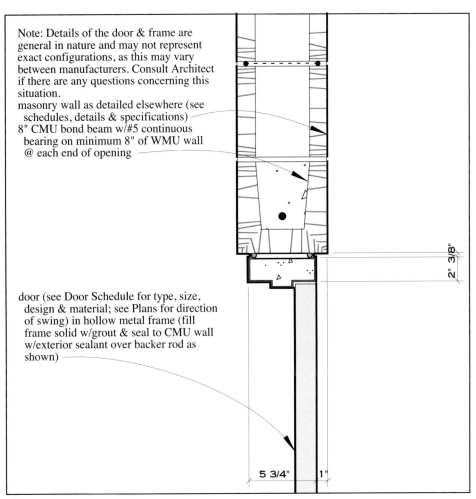

Note: Details of the door & frame are general in nature and may not represent exact configurations, as this may vary between manufacturers. Consult Architect if there are any questions concerning this situation.

masonry wall as detailed elsewhere (see schedules, details & specifications)

8" CMU bond beam w/#5 continuous bearing on minimum 8" of WMU wall @ each end of opening

door (see Door Schedule for type, size, design & material; see Plans for direction of swing) in hollow metal frame (fill frame solid w/grout & seal to CMU wall w/exterior sealant over backer rod as shown)

2" 3/8"

5 3/4"   1"

DRAWING #

Hollow Metal Door Head Detail

SCALE

1 1/2
1'-0"

DHH016
357

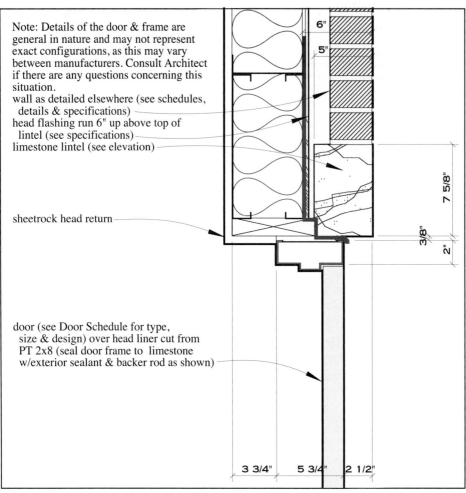

Note: Details of the door & frame are general in nature and may not represent exact configurations, as this may vary between manufacturers. Consult Architect if there are any questions concerning this situation.

wall as detailed elsewhere (see schedules, details & specifications)

head flashing run 6" up above top of lintel (see specifications)

limestone lintel (see elevation)

6"

5"

7 5/8"

3/8"

2"

sheetrock head return

door (see Door Schedule for type, size & design) over head liner cut from PT 2x8 (seal door frame to limestone w/exterior sealant & backer rod as shown)

3 3/4" 5 3/4" 2 1/2"

DRAWING #

Door Head Detail w/Stone Lintel

SCALE
1 1/2"
1'-0"

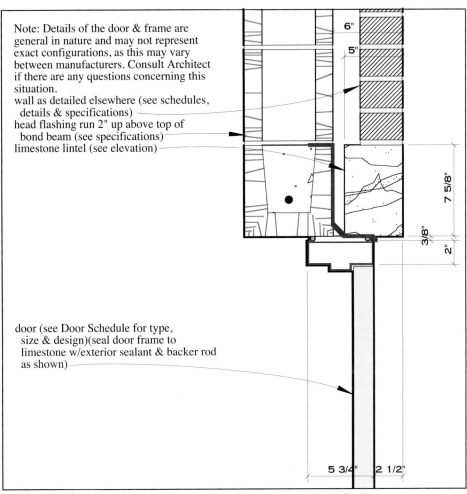

Note: Details of the door & frame are
general in nature and may not represent
exact configurations, as this may vary
between manufacturers. Consult Architect
if there are any questions concerning this
situation.
wall as detailed elsewhere (see schedules,
  details & specifications)
head flashing run 2" up above top of
  bond beam (see specifications)
limestone lintel (see elevation)

6"

5"

7 5/8"

3/8"

2"

door (see Door Schedule for type,
  size & design)(seal door frame to
  limestone w/exterior sealant & backer rod
  as shown)

5 3/4"   2 1/2"

DRAWING #

Door Head Detail w/Stone Lintel

SCALE
1 1/2"
1'-0"

DHH018
359

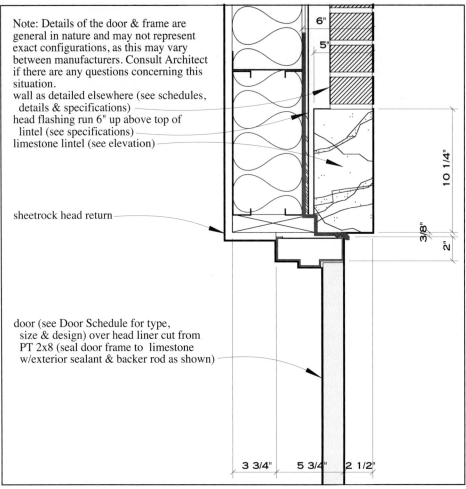

Note: Details of the door & frame are general in nature and may not represent exact configurations, as this may vary between manufacturers. Consult Architect if there are any questions concerning this situation.

wall as detailed elsewhere (see schedules, details & specifications)

head flashing run 6" up above top of lintel (see specifications)

limestone lintel (see elevation)

sheetrock head return

6"

5"

10 1/4"

3/8"

2"

door (see Door Schedule for type, size & design) over head liner cut from PT 2x8 (seal door frame to limestone w/exterior sealant & backer rod as shown)

3 3/4"   5 3/4"   2 1/2"

Door Head Detail w/Stone Lintel

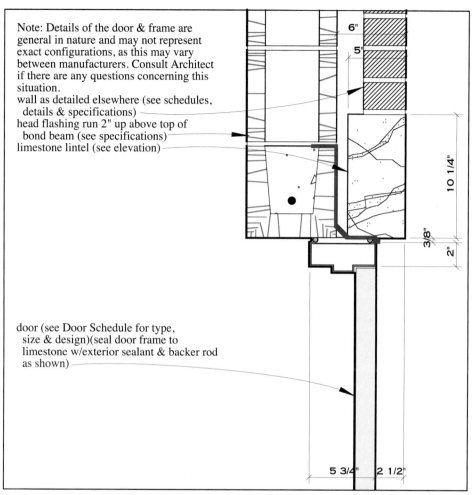

Note: Details of the door & frame are
general in nature and may not represent
exact configurations, as this may vary
between manufacturers. Consult Architect
if there are any questions concerning this
situation.
wall as detailed elsewhere (see schedules,
  details & specifications)
head flashing run 2" up above top of
  bond beam (see specifications)
limestone lintel (see elevation)

6"

5"

10 1/4"

3/8"

2"

door (see Door Schedule for type,
  size & design)(seal door frame to
  limestone w/exterior sealant & backer rod
  as shown)

5 3/4"   2 1/2"

Door Head Detail w/Stone Lintel

SCALE
1 1/2"
1'-0"

DRAWING #

DHH020
361

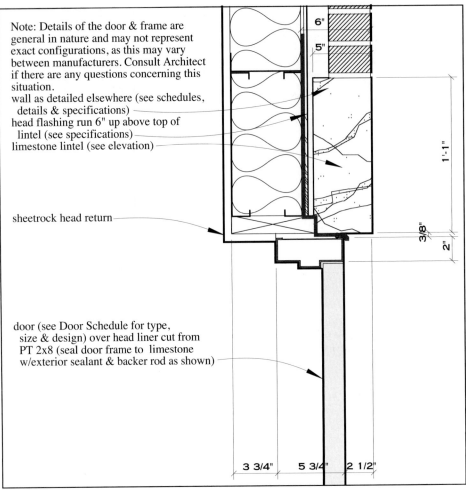

Note: Details of the door & frame are general in nature and may not represent exact configurations, as this may vary between manufacturers. Consult Architect if there are any questions concerning this situation.

wall as detailed elsewhere (see schedules, details & specifications)

head flashing run 6" up above top of lintel (see specifications)

limestone lintel (see elevation)

6"

5"

1'-1"

sheetrock head return

3/8"

2"

door (see Door Schedule for type, size & design) over head liner cut from PT 2x8 (seal door frame to limestone w/exterior sealant & backer rod as shown)

3 3/4"   5 3/4"   2 1/2"

DRAWING #		SCALE

Door Head Detail w/Stone Lintel

1 1/2"
1'-0"

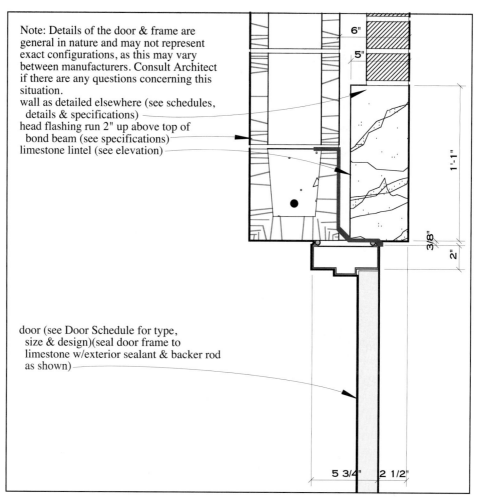

Note: Details of the door & frame are general in nature and may not represent exact configurations, as this may vary between manufacturers. Consult Architect if there are any questions concerning this situation.

wall as detailed elsewhere (see schedules, details & specifications)

head flashing run 2" up above top of bond beam (see specifications)

limestone lintel (see elevation)

door (see Door Schedule for type, size & design)(seal door frame to limestone w/exterior sealant & backer rod as shown)

6"

5"

1'-1"

3/8"

2"

5 3/4"   2 1/2"

DRAWING #

Door Head Detail w/Stone Lintel

SCALE

1 1/2"
1'-0"

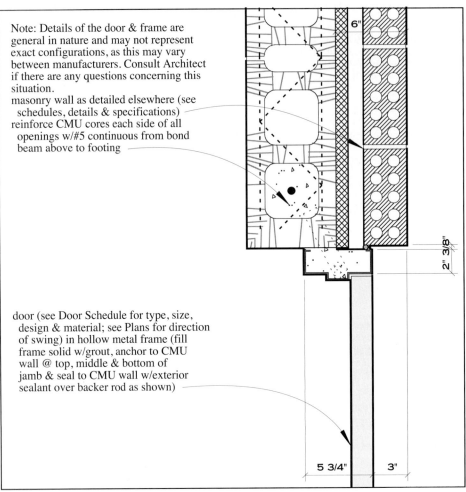

Note: Details of the door & frame are general in nature and may not represent exact configurations, as this may vary between manufacturers. Consult Architect if there are any questions concerning this situation.

masonry wall as detailed elsewhere (see schedules, details & specifications)

reinforce CMU cores each side of all openings w/#5 continuous from bond beam above to footing

6"

2" 3/8"

door (see Door Schedule for type, size, design & material; see Plans for direction of swing) in hollow metal frame (fill frame solid w/grout, anchor to CMU wall @ top, middle & bottom of jamb & seal to CMU wall w/exterior sealant over backer rod as shown)

5 3/4"   3"

DRAWING #

Hollow Metal Door Jamb Detail

SCALE
1 1/2
1'-0"

DHJ001
364

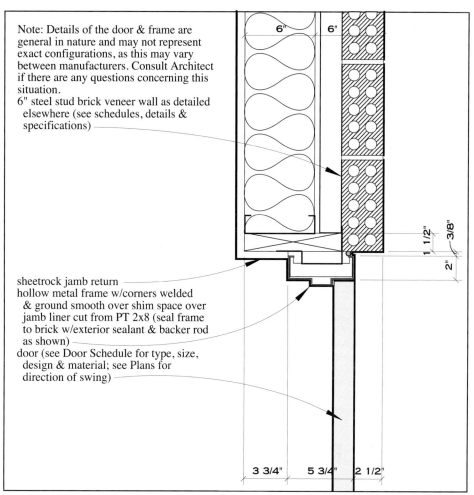

Note: Details of the door & frame are
general in nature and may not represent
exact configurations, as this may vary
between manufacturers. Consult Architect
if there are any questions concerning this
situation.
6" steel stud brick veneer wall as detailed
 elsewhere (see schedules, details &
 specifications)

6" 6"

1 1/2" 3/8"

2"

sheetrock jamb return
hollow metal frame w/corners welded
 & ground smooth over shim space over
 jamb liner cut from PT 2x8 (seal frame
 to brick w/exterior sealant & backer rod
 as shown)
door (see Door Schedule for type, size,
 design & material; see Plans for
 direction of swing)

3 3/4"   5 3/4"   2 1/2"

DRAWING #

Hollow Metal Door Jamb Detail

SCALE
1 1/2"
1'-0"

DHJ002
365

Note: Details of the door & frame are general in nature and may not represent exact configurations, as this may vary between manufacturers. Consult Architect if there are any questions concerning this situation.

masonry wall as detailed elsewhere (see schedules, details & specifications)

reinforce CMU cores each side of all openings w/#5 continuous from bond beam above to footing

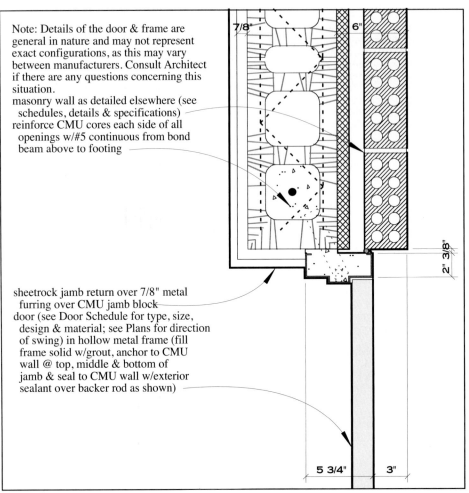

7/8"   6"

2" 3/8"

sheetrock jamb return over 7/8" metal furring over CMU jamb block

door (see Door Schedule for type, size, design & material; see Plans for direction of swing) in hollow metal frame (fill frame solid w/grout, anchor to CMU wall @ top, middle & bottom of jamb & seal to CMU wall w/exterior sealant over backer rod as shown)

5 3/4"   3"

DRAWING #

Hollow Metal Door Jamb Detail

SCALE
$\frac{1\ 1/2}{1'-0"}$

DHJ003
366

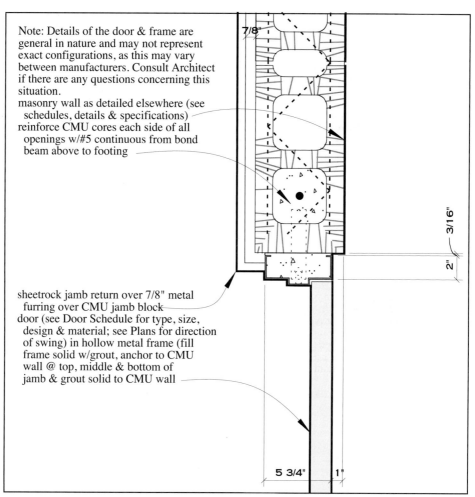

Note: Details of the door & frame are general in nature and may not represent exact configurations, as this may vary between manufacturers. Consult Architect if there are any questions concerning this situation.

masonry wall as detailed elsewhere (see schedules, details & specifications)

reinforce CMU cores each side of all openings w/#5 continuous from bond beam above to footing

sheetrock jamb return over 7/8" metal furring over CMU jamb block

door (see Door Schedule for type, size, design & material; see Plans for direction of swing) in hollow metal frame (fill frame solid w/grout, anchor to CMU wall @ top, middle & bottom of jamb & grout solid to CMU wall

7/8"

3/16"

2"

5 3/4"

1"

DRAWING #

Hollow Metal Door Jamb Detail

SCALE
1 1/2
1'-0"

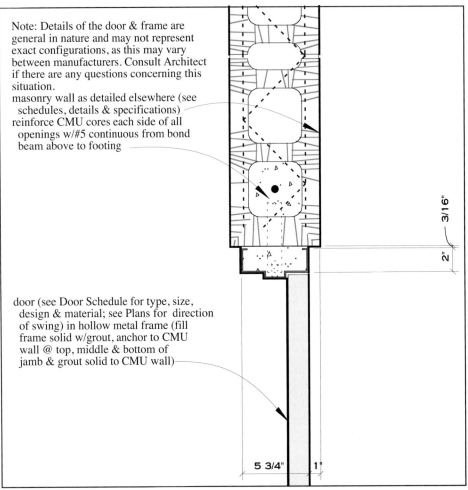

Note: Details of the door & frame are general in nature and may not represent exact configurations, as this may vary between manufacturers. Consult Architect if there are any questions concerning this situation.

masonry wall as detailed elsewhere (see schedules, details & specifications)

reinforce CMU cores each side of all openings w/#5 continuous from bond beam above to footing

3/16"

2"

door (see Door Schedule for type, size, design & material; see Plans for direction of swing) in hollow metal frame (fill frame solid w/grout, anchor to CMU wall @ top, middle & bottom of jamb & grout solid to CMU wall)

5 3/4"   1"

DRAWING #

Hollow Metal Door Jamb Detail

SCALE

1 1/2
1'-0"

DHJ006
368

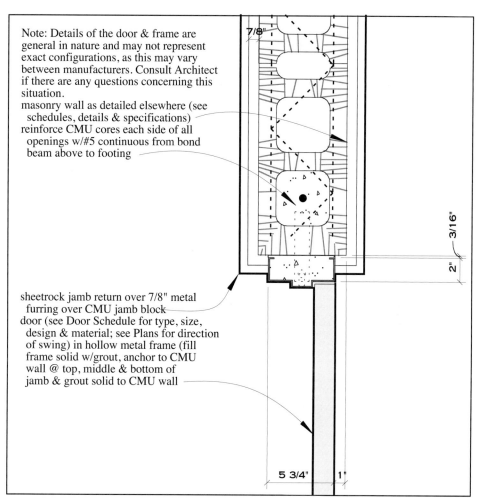

Note: Details of the door & frame are general in nature and may not represent exact configurations, as this may vary between manufacturers. Consult Architect if there are any questions concerning this situation.

masonry wall as detailed elsewhere (see schedules, details & specifications)

reinforce CMU cores each side of all openings w/#5 continuous from bond beam above to footing

7/8"

3/16"

2"

sheetrock jamb return over 7/8" metal furring over CMU jamb block

door (see Door Schedule for type, size, design & material; see Plans for direction of swing) in hollow metal frame (fill frame solid w/grout, anchor to CMU wall @ top, middle & bottom of jamb & grout solid to CMU wall

5 3/4"   1"

Hollow Metal Door Jamb Detail

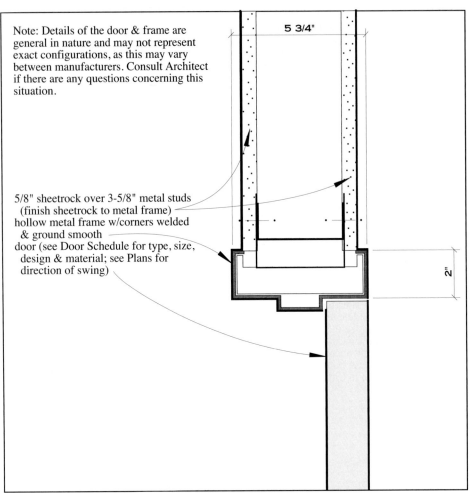

Note: Details of the door & frame are general in nature and may not represent exact configurations, as this may vary between manufacturers. Consult Architect if there are any questions concerning this situation.

5 3/4"

5/8" sheetrock over 3-5/8" metal studs (finish sheetrock to metal frame)
hollow metal frame w/corners welded & ground smooth
door (see Door Schedule for type, size, design & material; see Plans for direction of swing)

2"

DRAWING #

Hollow Metal Frame Jamb

SCALE
3"
1'-0"

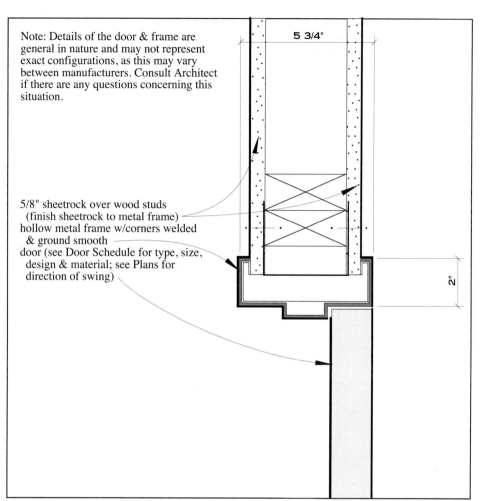

Note: Details of the door & frame are general in nature and may not represent exact configurations, as this may vary between manufacturers. Consult Architect if there are any questions concerning this situation.

5 3/4"

2"

5/8" sheetrock over wood studs
 (finish sheetrock to metal frame)
hollow metal frame w/corners welded
 & ground smooth
door (see Door Schedule for type, size,
 design & material; see Plans for
 direction of swing)

DRAWING #

Hollow Metal Frame Jamb

SCALE
$\dfrac{3"}{1'\text{-}0"}$

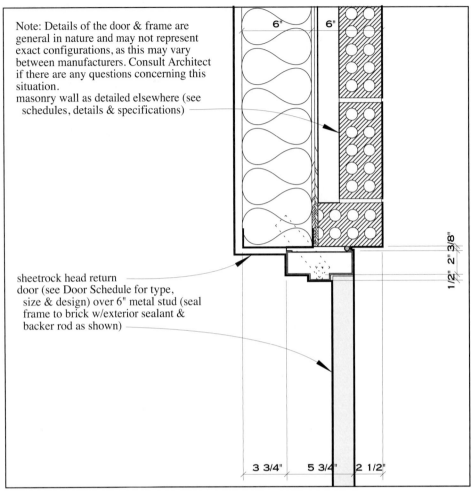

Note: Details of the door & frame are general in nature and may not represent exact configurations, as this may vary between manufacturers. Consult Architect if there are any questions concerning this situation.

masonry wall as detailed elsewhere (see schedules, details & specifications)

6"   6"

1/2" 2" 3/8"

sheetrock head return

door (see Door Schedule for type, size & design) over 6" metal stud (seal frame to brick w/exterior sealant & backer rod as shown)

3 3/4"   5 3/4"   2 1/2"

DRAWING #

Hollow Metal Door Jamb Detail

SCALE

1 1/2"
1'-0"

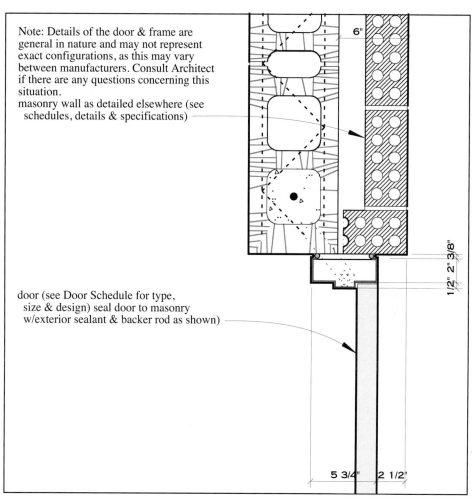

Note: Details of the door & frame are general in nature and may not represent exact configurations, as this may vary between manufacturers. Consult Architect if there are any questions concerning this situation.
masonry wall as detailed elsewhere (see schedules, details & specifications)

6"

1/2" 2" 3/8"

door (see Door Schedule for type, size & design) seal door to masonry w/exterior sealant & backer rod as shown)

5 3/4"   2 1/2"

DRAWING #

Hollow Metal Door Jamb Detail

SCALE

1 1/2"
1'-0"

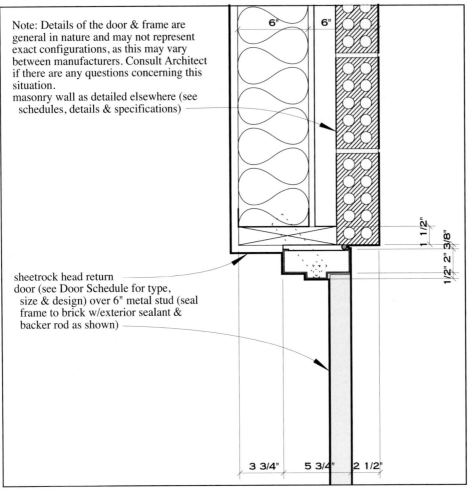

Note: Details of the door & frame are general in nature and may not represent exact configurations, as this may vary between manufacturers. Consult Architect if there are any questions concerning this situation.

masonry wall as detailed elsewhere (see schedules, details & specifications)

6"   6"

1 1/2"
3/8"
2"
1/2"

sheetrock head return
door (see Door Schedule for type, size & design) over 6" metal stud (seal frame to brick w/exterior sealant & backer rod as shown)

3 3/4"   5 3/4"   2 1/2"

DRAWING #

Hollow Metal Door Jamb Detail

SCALE
1 1/2"
1'-0"

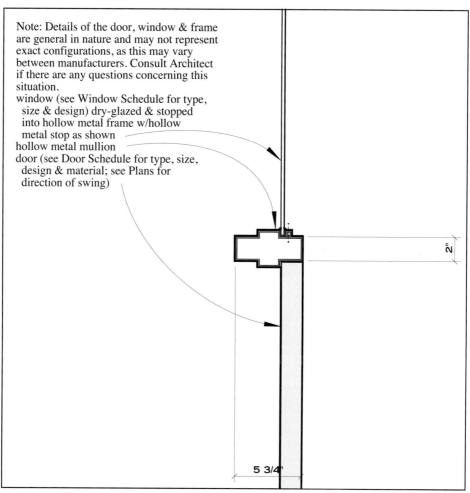

Note: Details of the door, window & frame are general in nature and may not represent exact configurations, as this may vary between manufacturers. Consult Architect if there are any questions concerning this situation.

window (see Window Schedule for type, size & design) dry-glazed & stopped into hollow metal frame w/hollow metal stop as shown

hollow metal mullion

door (see Door Schedule for type, size, design & material; see Plans for direction of swing)

2"

5 3/4"

DRAWING #

Door Transom or Mullion Detail

SCALE
1 1/2"
1'-0"

DHT001
375

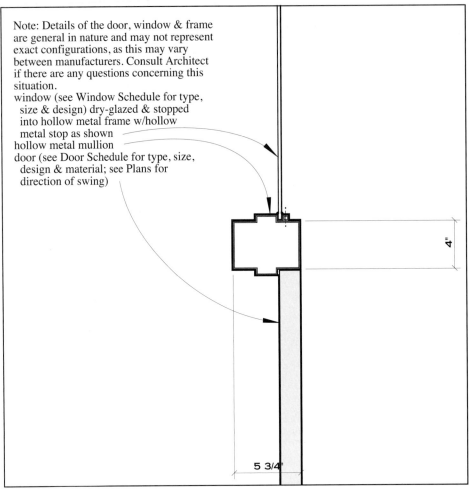

Note: Details of the door, window & frame
are general in nature and may not represent
exact configurations, as this may vary
between manufacturers. Consult Architect
if there are any questions concerning this
situation.
window (see Window Schedule for type,
   size & design) dry-glazed & stopped
   into hollow metal frame w/hollow
   metal stop as shown
hollow metal mullion
door (see Door Schedule for type, size,
   design & material; see Plans for
   direction of swing)

4"

5 3/4"

Door Transom or Mullion Detail

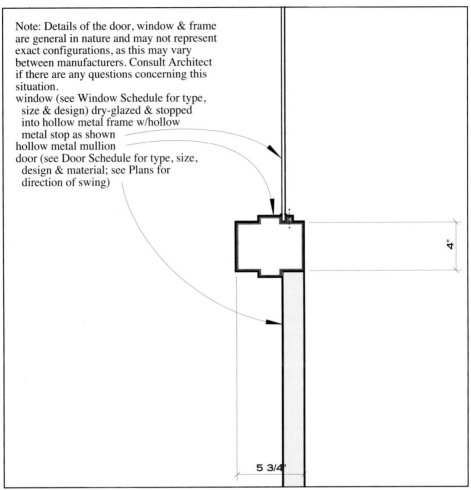

Note: Details of the door, window & frame
are general in nature and may not represent
exact configurations, as this may vary
between manufacturers. Consult Architect
if there are any questions concerning this
situation.
window (see Window Schedule for type,
   size & design) dry-glazed & stopped
   into hollow metal frame w/hollow
   metal stop as shown
hollow metal mullion
door (see Door Schedule for type, size,
   design & material; see Plans for
   direction of swing)

4"

5 3/4"

Door Transom or Mullion Detail

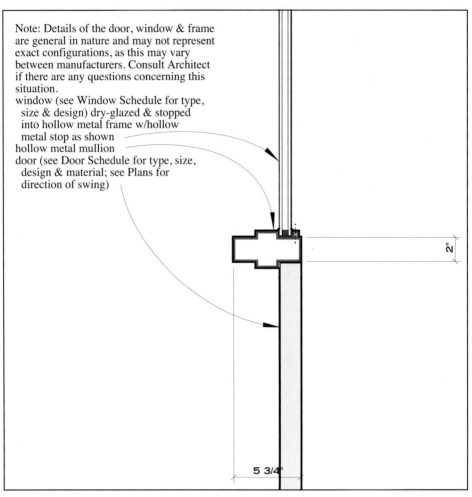

Note: Details of the door, window & frame
are general in nature and may not represent
exact configurations, as this may vary
between manufacturers. Consult Architect
if there are any questions concerning this
situation.
window (see Window Schedule for type,
 size & design) dry-glazed & stopped
 into hollow metal frame w/hollow
 metal stop as shown
hollow metal mullion
door (see Door Schedule for type, size,
 design & material; see Plans for
 direction of swing)

2"

5 3/4"

DRAWING #

Door Transom or Mullion Detail

SCALE

1 1/2"
1'-0"

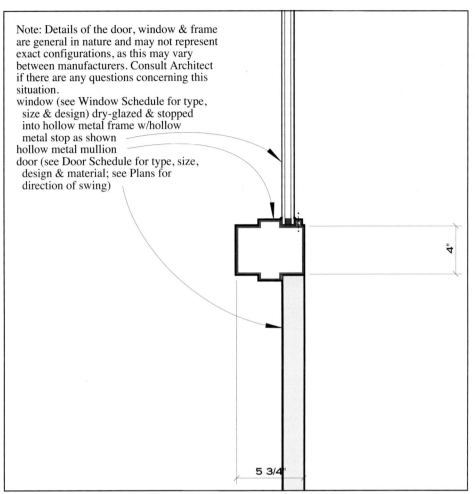

Note: Details of the door, window & frame are general in nature and may not represent exact configurations, as this may vary between manufacturers. Consult Architect if there are any questions concerning this situation.
window (see Window Schedule for type, size & design) dry-glazed & stopped into hollow metal frame w/hollow metal stop as shown
hollow metal mullion
door (see Door Schedule for type, size, design & material; see Plans for direction of swing)

4"

5 3/4"

Door Transom or Mullion Detail

DRAWING #

SCALE
1 1/2"
1'-0"

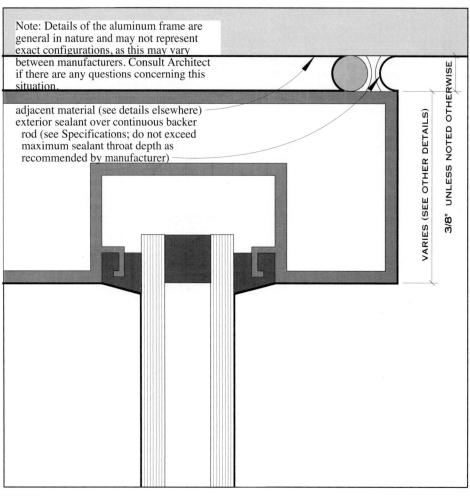

Note: Details of the aluminum frame are general in nature and may not represent exact configurations, as this may vary between manufacturers. Consult Architect if there are any questions concerning this situation.

adjacent material (see details elsewhere)
exterior sealant over continuous backer rod (see Specifications; do not exceed maximum sealant throat depth as recommended by manufacturer)

VARIES (SEE OTHER DETAILS)

3/8" UNLESS NOTED OTHERWISE

DRAWING #

Storefront Edge Sealant Detail

SCALE
FULL SIZE

DM001
380

Note: This detail is typical in nature, and is intended to outline the general procedures for flashing & jamb-wrapping doors & windows. Opening sizes shown here are purely schematic. See Floor Plans and/or Door & Window Schedules & Elevations for sizes of openings. See Wall Sections for thickness of wall.

Step 1: Extend sill flashing 6" minimum each side of opening or 2" past edge of jamb casings (if larger than 6") for wood openings & wrap up over sub-sill

Step 2: Extend 10 mil vinyl jamb wrap 6" minimum each side of opening seal these locations thoroughly with exterior sealant cut jamb wrap at angle as shown where wrap meets sill & extend over sill flashing as shown
Note: Vinyl jamb wrap is not shown on door & window details for clarity, but should be installed on all exterior openings as shown here.

Step 3: Install head flashing over jamb flashing& extend head flashing 6" minimum each side of opening
Note: Head flashing should be run up *behind* wall sheathing whenever possible.

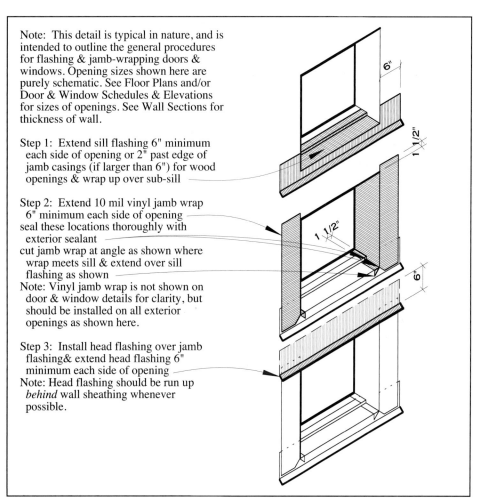

Opening Flashing Detail

DRAWING #

SCALE
NO
SCALE

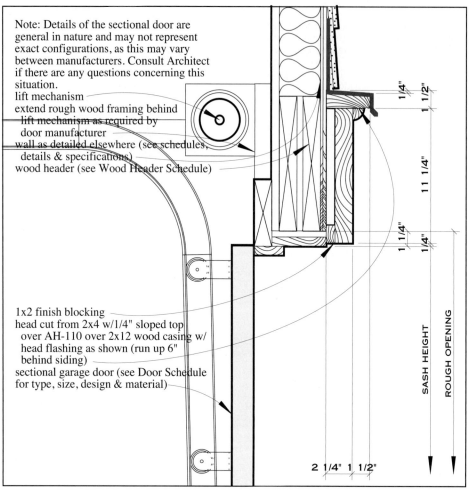

Note: Details of the sectional door are general in nature and may not represent exact configurations, as this may vary between manufacturers. Consult Architect if there are any questions concerning this situation.

lift mechanism
extend rough wood framing behind lift mechanism as required by door manufacturer
wall as detailed elsewhere (see schedules, details & specifications)
wood header (see Wood Header Schedule)

1x2 finish blocking
head cut from 2x4 w/1/4" sloped top over AH-110 over 2x12 wood casing w/ head flashing as shown (run up 6" behind siding)
sectional garage door (see Door Schedule for type, size, design & material)

1/4"

1/2"

11 1/4"

1 1/4"

1/4"

SASH HEIGHT

ROUGH OPENING

2 1/4" 1 1/2"

Sectional Door Head Detail

SCALE
1 1/2"
1'-0"

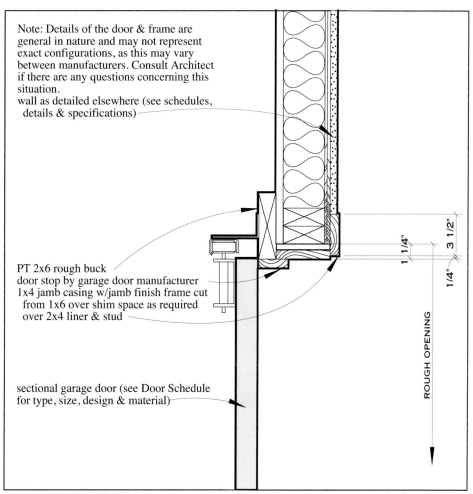

Note: Details of the door & frame are general in nature and may not represent exact configurations, as this may vary between manufacturers. Consult Architect if there are any questions concerning this situation.
wall as detailed elsewhere (see schedules, details & specifications)

PT 2x6 rough buck
door stop by garage door manufacturer
1x4 jamb casing w/jamb finish frame cut from 1x6 over shim space as required over 2x4 liner & stud

sectional garage door (see Door Schedule for type, size, design & material)

1 1/4"
3 1/2"
1/4"
ROUGH OPENING

DRAWING #

Garage Door Jamb Detail

SCALE
1 1/2
1'-0"

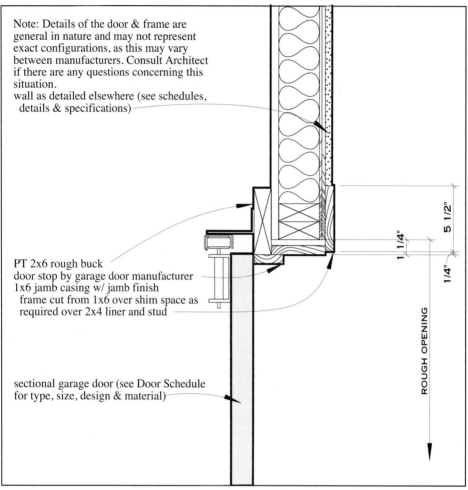

Note: Details of the door & frame are general in nature and may not represent exact configurations, as this may vary between manufacturers. Consult Architect if there are any questions concerning this situation.

wall as detailed elsewhere (see schedules, details & specifications)

PT 2x6 rough buck
door stop by garage door manufacturer
1x6 jamb casing w/ jamb finish
  frame cut from 1x6 over shim space as
  required over 2x4 liner and stud

sectional garage door (see Door Schedule for type, size, design & material)

5 1/2"

1 1/4"

1/4"

ROUGH OPENING

DRAWING #

Garage Door Jamb Detail

SCALE

1 1/2
1'-0"

DSJ004
384

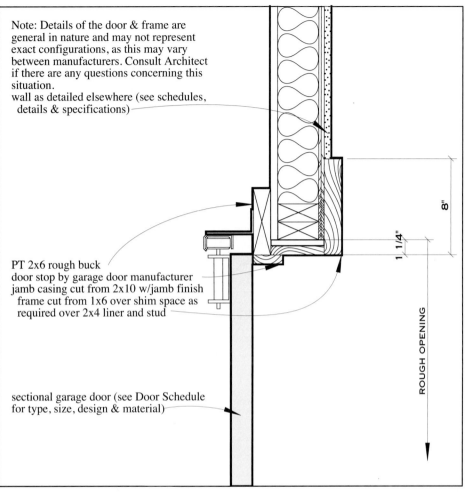

Note: Details of the door & frame are general in nature and may not represent exact configurations, as this may vary between manufacturers. Consult Architect if there are any questions concerning this situation.

wall as detailed elsewhere (see schedules, details & specifications)

PT 2x6 rough buck
door stop by garage door manufacturer
jamb casing cut from 2x10 w/jamb finish
  frame cut from 1x6 over shim space as
  required over 2x4 liner and stud

sectional garage door (see Door Schedule for type, size, design & material)

8"

1 1/4"

ROUGH OPENING

Garage Door Jamb Detail

Note: Details of the door & track are general in nature and may not represent exact configurations, as this may vary between manufacturers. Consult Architect if there are any questions concerning this situation.

face brick over 8" CMU's reinforced w/ horizontal truss-type joint reinforcement every other course

Neenah #4986-C wheel guards @ all sectional door corners

reinforce all cores adjacent to openings w/#5 continuous from footing to top of wall

L4x8x3/8" w/1/2" stud anchors welded to back as shown 16" OC vertically cast into grout fill as shown between brick & CMU's

sectional door & track (see Door Schedule for type, size, design & material)

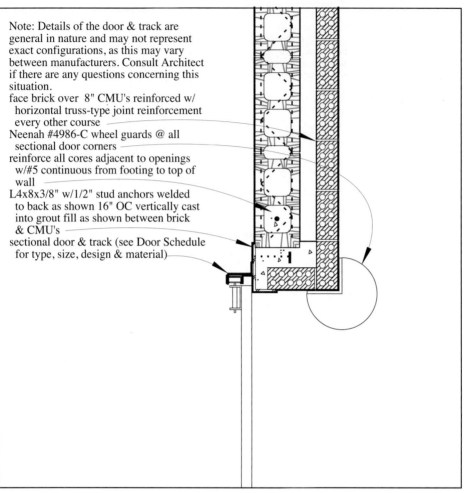

Garage Door Jamb Detail

DRAWING #

SCALE
3/4"
1'-0"

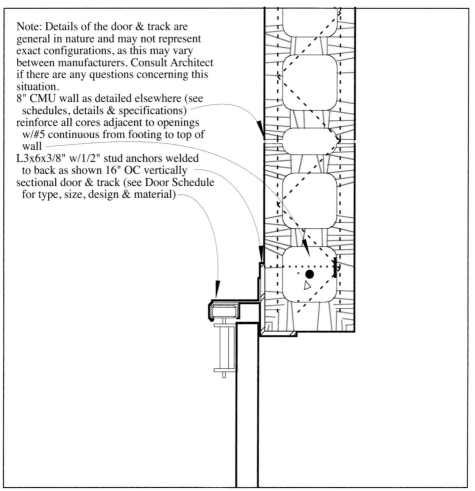

Note: Details of the door & track are
general in nature and may not represent
exact configurations, as this may vary
between manufacturers. Consult Architect
if there are any questions concerning this
situation.
8" CMU wall as detailed elsewhere (see
  schedules, details & specifications)
reinforce all cores adjacent to openings
  w/#5 continuous from footing to top of
  wall
L3x6x3/8" w/1/2" stud anchors welded
  to back as shown 16" OC vertically
sectional door & track (see Door Schedule
  for type, size, design & material)

Garage Door Jamb Detail

Note: Details of the door & track are
general in nature and may not represent
exact configurations, as this may vary
between manufacturers. Consult Architect
if there are any questions concerning this
situation.
face brick over 8" CMU's reinforced w/
   horizontal truss-type joint reinforcement
   every other course
Neenah #4986-C wheel guards @ all
   sectional door corners
reinforce all cores adjacent to openings
   w/#5 continuous from footing to top of
   wall
L4x8x3/8" w/1/2" stud anchors welded
   to back as shown 16" OC vertically cast
   into grout fill as shown between brick
   & CMU's
sectional door & track (see Door Schedule
   for type, size, design & material)

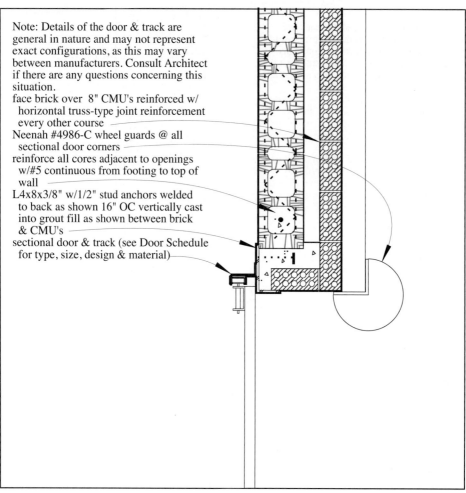

DRAWING #

Garage Door Jamb

SCALE
3/4"
1'-0"

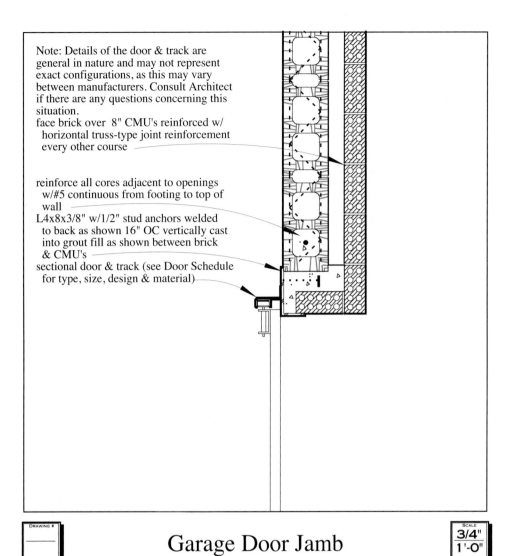

Note: Details of the door & track are general in nature and may not represent exact configurations, as this may vary between manufacturers. Consult Architect if there are any questions concerning this situation.

face brick over 8" CMU's reinforced w/ horizontal truss-type joint reinforcement every other course

reinforce all cores adjacent to openings w/#5 continuous from footing to top of wall

L4x8x3/8" w/1/2" stud anchors welded to back as shown 16" OC vertically cast into grout fill as shown between brick & CMU's

sectional door & track (see Door Schedule for type, size, design & material)

DRAWING #

Garage Door Jamb

SCALE
3/4"
1'-0"

DSJ010
389

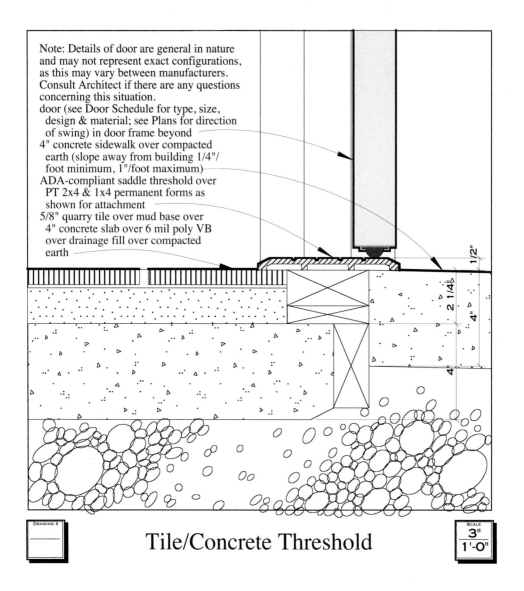

Note: Details of door are general in nature
and may not represent exact configurations,
as this may vary between manufacturers.
Consult Architect if there are any questions
concerning this situation.
door (see Door Schedule for type, size,
  design & material; see Plans for direction
  of swing) in door frame beyond
4" concrete sidewalk over compacted
  earth (slope away from building 1/4"/
  foot minimum, 1"/foot maximum)
ADA-compliant saddle threshold over
  PT 2x4 & 1x4 permanent forms as
  shown for attachment
5/8" quarry tile over mud base over
  4" concrete slab over 6 mil poly VB
  over drainage fill over compacted
  earth

Tile/Concrete Threshold

DRAWING #

SCALE
3"
1'-0"

DT001
390

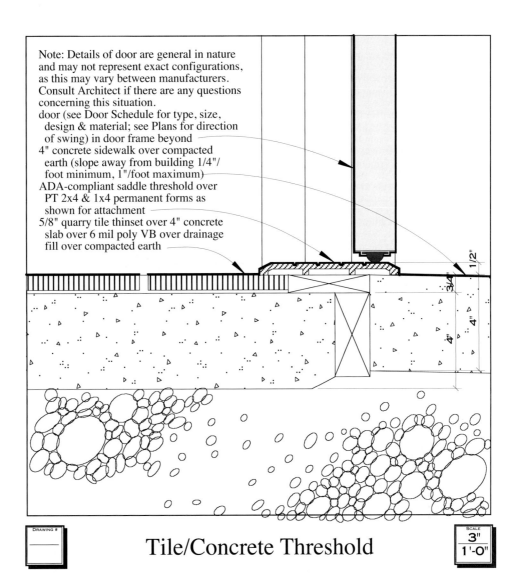

Note: Details of door are general in nature
and may not represent exact configurations,
as this may vary between manufacturers.
Consult Architect if there are any questions
concerning this situation.
door (see Door Schedule for type, size,
  design & material; see Plans for direction
  of swing) in door frame beyond
4" concrete sidewalk over compacted
  earth (slope away from building 1/4"/
  foot minimum, 1"/foot maximum)
ADA-compliant saddle threshold over
  PT 2x4 & 1x4 permanent forms as
  shown for attachment
5/8" quarry tile thinset over 4" concrete
  slab over 6 mil poly VB over drainage
  fill over compacted earth

Tile/Concrete Threshold

DRAWING #

SCALE
3"
1'-0"

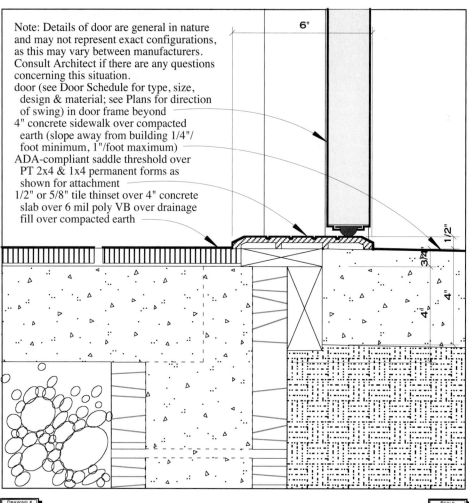

Note: Details of door are general in nature
and may not represent exact configurations,
as this may vary between manufacturers.
Consult Architect if there are any questions
concerning this situation.
door (see Door Schedule for type, size,
  design & material; see Plans for direction
  of swing) in door frame beyond
4" concrete sidewalk over compacted
  earth (slope away from building 1/4"/
  foot minimum, 1"/foot maximum)
ADA-compliant saddle threshold over
  PT 2x4 & 1x4 permanent forms as
  shown for attachment
1/2" or 5/8" tile thinset over 4" concrete
  slab over 6 mil poly VB over drainage
  fill over compacted earth

6"

1/2"

3/4"

4"

4"

DRAWING #

Tile/Concrete Threshold

SCALE
$\dfrac{3"}{1'-0"}$

DT003
392

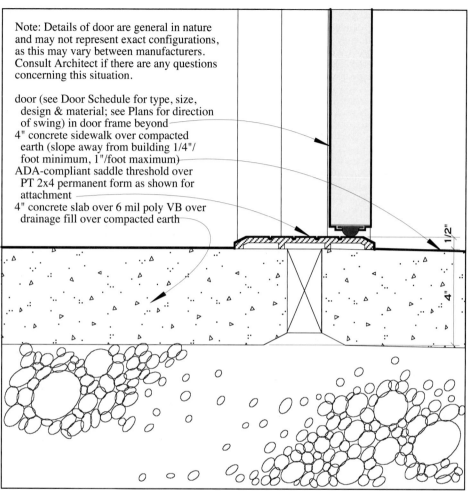

Note: Details of door are general in nature and may not represent exact configurations, as this may vary between manufacturers. Consult Architect if there are any questions concerning this situation.

door (see Door Schedule for type, size, design & material; see Plans for direction of swing) in door frame beyond

4" concrete sidewalk over compacted earth (slope away from building 1/4"/ foot minimum, 1"/foot maximum)

ADA-compliant saddle threshold over PT 2x4 permanent form as shown for attachment

4" concrete slab over 6 mil poly VB over drainage fill over compacted earth

1/2"

4"

DRAWING #

Concrete/Concrete Threshold

SCALE

$\dfrac{3"}{1'\text{-}0"}$

DT004

393

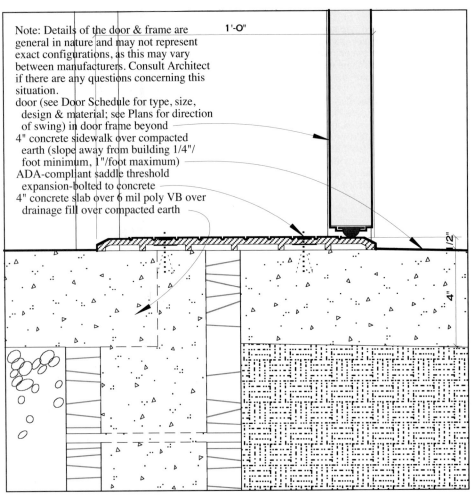

Note: Details of the door & frame are
general in nature and may not represent
exact configurations, as this may vary
between manufacturers. Consult Architect
if there are any questions concerning this
situation.
door (see Door Schedule for type, size,
 design & material; see Plans for direction
 of swing) in door frame beyond
4" concrete sidewalk over compacted
 earth (slope away from building 1/4"/
 foot minimum, 1"/foot maximum)
ADA-compliant saddle threshold
 expansion-bolted to concrete
4" concrete slab over 6 mil poly VB over
 drainage fill over compacted earth

1'-0"

1/2"

4"

DRAWING #

Threshold Detail @ Concrete Slab

SCALE
1 1/2"
1'-0"

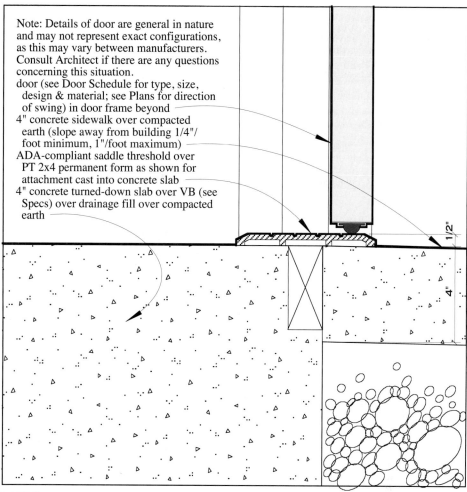

Note: Details of door are general in nature
and may not represent exact configurations,
as this may vary between manufacturers.
Consult Architect if there are any questions
concerning this situation.
door (see Door Schedule for type, size,
  design & material; see Plans for direction
  of swing) in door frame beyond
4" concrete sidewalk over compacted
  earth (slope away from building 1/4"/
  foot minimum, 1"/foot maximum)
ADA-compliant saddle threshold over
  PT 2x4 permanent form as shown for
  attachment cast into concrete slab
4" concrete turned-down slab over VB (see
  Specs) over drainage fill over compacted
  earth

1/2"

4"

DRAWING #

Concrete/Concrete Threshold

SCALE
3"
1'-0"

DT006
395

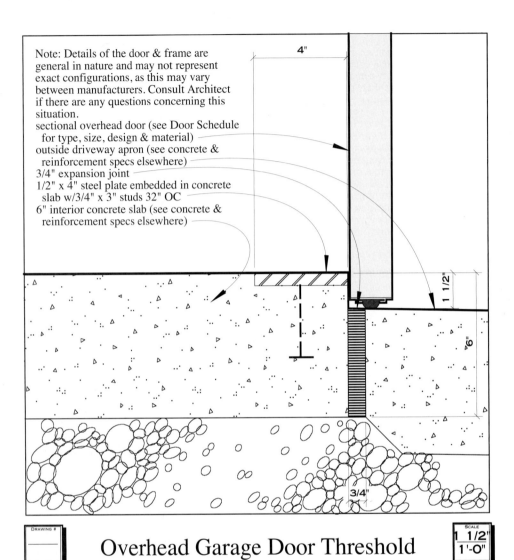

Note: Details of the door & frame are general in nature and may not represent exact configurations, as this may vary between manufacturers. Consult Architect if there are any questions concerning this situation.

sectional overhead door (see Door Schedule for type, size, design & material)

outside driveway apron (see concrete & reinforcement specs elsewhere)

3/4" expansion joint

1/2" x 4" steel plate embedded in concrete slab w/3/4" x 3" studs 32" OC

6" interior concrete slab (see concrete & reinforcement specs elsewhere)

4"

1 1/2"

6"

3/4"

DRAWING #

Overhead Garage Door Threshold

SCALE

1 1/2"
1'-0"

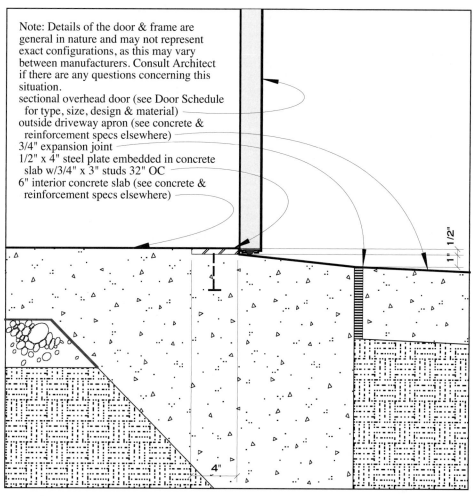

Note: Details of the door & frame are general in nature and may not represent exact configurations, as this may vary between manufacturers. Consult Architect if there are any questions concerning this situation.

sectional overhead door (see Door Schedule for type, size, design & material)

outside driveway apron (see concrete & reinforcement specs elsewhere)

3/4" expansion joint

1/2" x 4" steel plate embedded in concrete slab w/3/4" x 3" studs 32" OC

6" interior concrete slab (see concrete & reinforcement specs elsewhere)

1" 1/2"

4"

DRAWING #

Overhead Garage Door Threshold

SCALE
1 1/2"
1'-0"

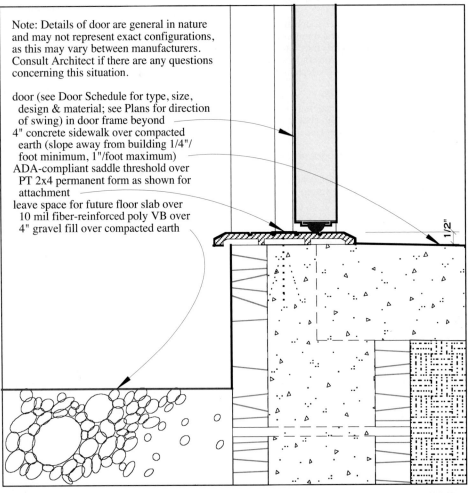

Note: Details of door are general in nature
and may not represent exact configurations,
as this may vary between manufacturers.
Consult Architect if there are any questions
concerning this situation.

door (see Door Schedule for type, size,
  design & material; see Plans for direction
  of swing) in door frame beyond
4" concrete sidewalk over compacted
  earth (slope away from building 1/4"/
  foot minimum, 1"/foot maximum)
ADA-compliant saddle threshold over
  PT 2x4 permanent form as shown for
  attachment
leave space for future floor slab over
  10 mil fiber-reinforced poly VB over
  4" gravel fill over compacted earth

1/2"

Concrete/Concrete Threshold

DRAWING #

SCALE
3"
1'-0"

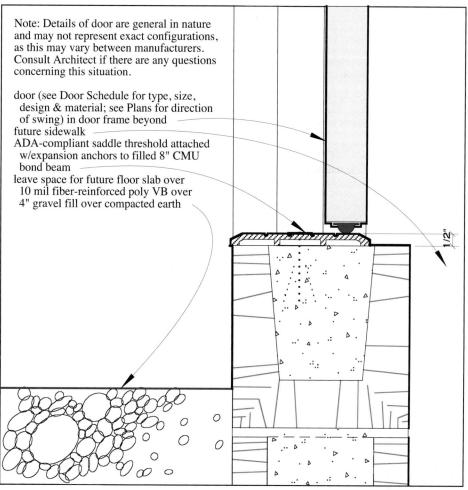

Note: Details of door are general in nature and may not represent exact configurations, as this may vary between manufacturers. Consult Architect if there are any questions concerning this situation.

door (see Door Schedule for type, size, design & material; see Plans for direction of swing) in door frame beyond
future sidewalk
ADA-compliant saddle threshold attached w/expansion anchors to filled 8" CMU bond beam
leave space for future floor slab over 10 mil fiber-reinforced poly VB over 4" gravel fill over compacted earth

1/2"

DRAWING #

Concrete/Concrete Threshold

SCALE
3"
1'-0"

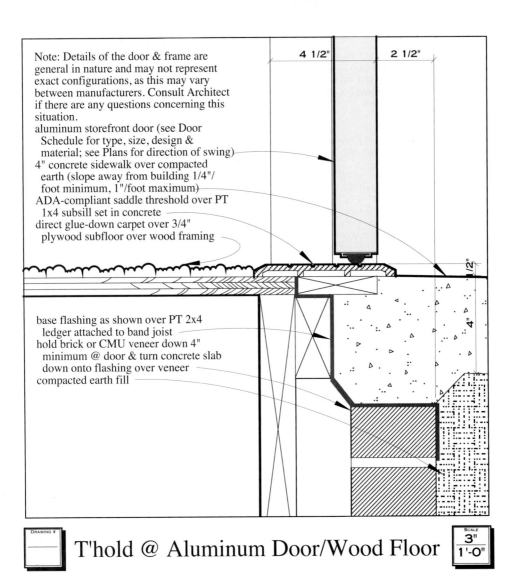

Note: Details of the door & frame are general in nature and may not represent exact configurations, as this may vary between manufacturers. Consult Architect if there are any questions concerning this situation.

aluminum storefront door (see Door Schedule for type, size, design & material; see Plans for direction of swing)

4" concrete sidewalk over compacted earth (slope away from building 1/4"/ foot minimum, 1"/foot maximum)

ADA-compliant saddle threshold over PT 1x4 subsill set in concrete

direct glue-down carpet over 3/4" plywood subfloor over wood framing

base flashing as shown over PT 2x4 ledger attached to band joist

hold brick or CMU veneer down 4" minimum @ door & turn concrete slab down onto flashing over veneer

compacted earth fill

4 1/2"   2 1/2"

1/2"

4"

T'hold @ Aluminum Door/Wood Floor

DRAWING #

SCALE
$\frac{3"}{1'-0"}$

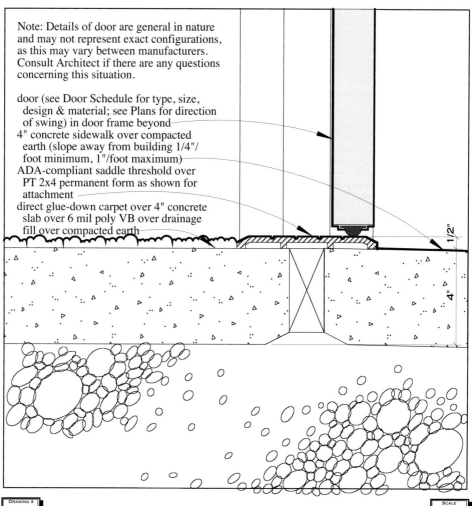

Note: Details of door are general in nature
and may not represent exact configurations,
as this may vary between manufacturers.
Consult Architect if there are any questions
concerning this situation.

door (see Door Schedule for type, size,
  design & material; see Plans for direction
  of swing) in door frame beyond
4" concrete sidewalk over compacted
  earth (slope away from building 1/4"/
  foot minimum, 1"/foot maximum)
ADA-compliant saddle threshold over
  PT 2x4 permanent form as shown for
  attachment
direct glue-down carpet over 4" concrete
  slab over 6 mil poly VB over drainage
  fill over compacted earth

1/2"

4"

DRAWING #		

Concrete/Concrete Threshold

SCALE
$\dfrac{3"}{1'-0"}$

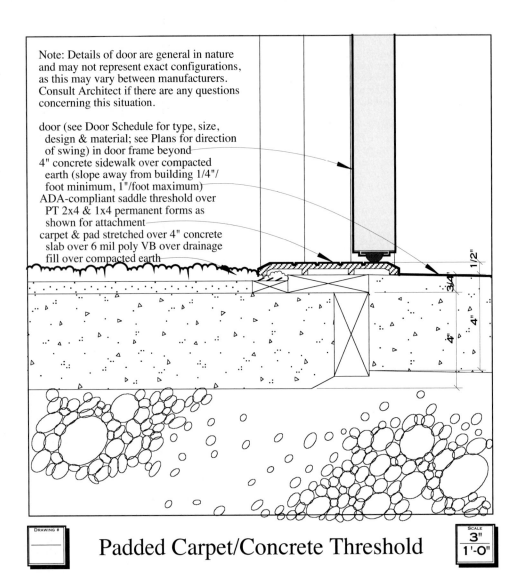

Note: Details of door are general in nature
and may not represent exact configurations,
as this may vary between manufacturers.
Consult Architect if there are any questions
concerning this situation.

door (see Door Schedule for type, size,
   design & material; see Plans for direction
   of swing) in door frame beyond
4" concrete sidewalk over compacted
   earth (slope away from building 1/4"/
   foot minimum, 1"/foot maximum)
ADA-compliant saddle threshold over
   PT 2x4 & 1x4 permanent forms as
   shown for attachment
carpet & pad stretched over 4" concrete
   slab over 6 mil poly VB over drainage
   fill over compacted earth

Padded Carpet/Concrete Threshold

DRAWING #

SCALE
3"
1'-0"

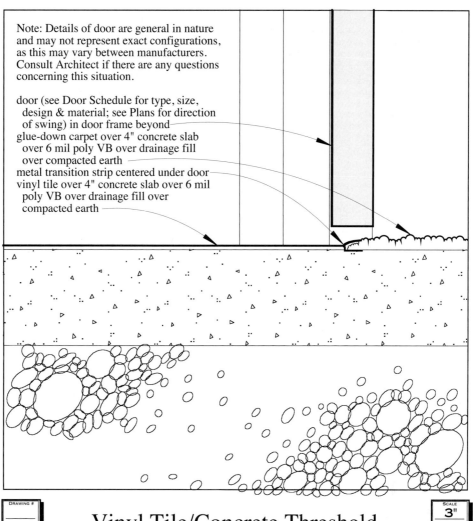

Note: Details of door are general in nature
and may not represent exact configurations,
as this may vary between manufacturers.
Consult Architect if there are any questions
concerning this situation.

door (see Door Schedule for type, size,
   design & material; see Plans for direction
   of swing) in door frame beyond
glue-down carpet over 4" concrete slab
   over 6 mil poly VB over drainage fill
   over compacted earth
metal transition strip centered under door
vinyl tile over 4" concrete slab over 6 mil
   poly VB over drainage fill over
   compacted earth

DRAWING #

SCALE
3"
1'-0"

Vinyl Tile/Concrete Threshold

DT014
403

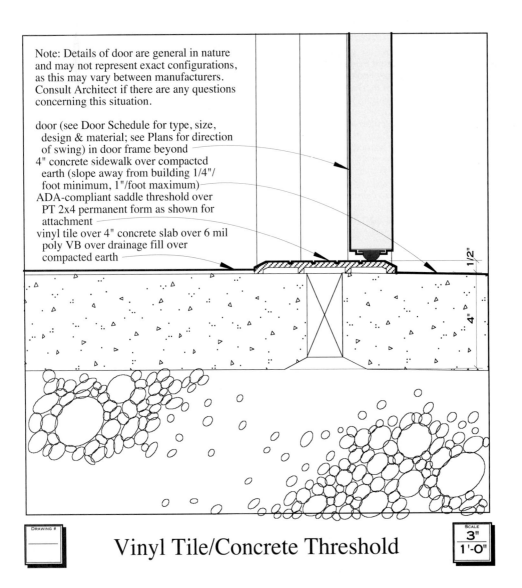

Note: Details of door are general in nature
and may not represent exact configurations,
as this may vary between manufacturers.
Consult Architect if there are any questions
concerning this situation.

door (see Door Schedule for type, size,
  design & material; see Plans for direction
  of swing) in door frame beyond
4" concrete sidewalk over compacted
  earth (slope away from building 1/4"/
  foot minimum, 1"/foot maximum)
ADA-compliant saddle threshold over
  PT 2x4 permanent form as shown for
  attachment
vinyl tile over 4" concrete slab over 6 mil
  poly VB over drainage fill over
  compacted earth

DRAWING #

Vinyl Tile/Concrete Threshold

SCALE
3"
1'-0"

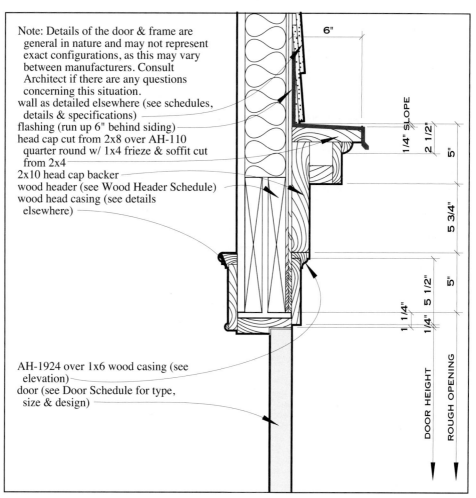

Note: Details of the door & frame are
general in nature and may not represent
exact configurations, as this may vary
between manufacturers. Consult
Architect if there are any questions
concerning this situation.

wall as detailed elsewhere (see schedules,
details & specifications)

flashing (run up 6" behind siding)

head cap cut from 2x8 over AH-110
quarter round w/ 1x4 frieze & soffit cut
from 2x4

2x10 head cap backer

wood header (see Wood Header Schedule)

wood head casing (see details
elsewhere)

AH-1924 over 1x6 wood casing (see
elevation)

door (see Door Schedule for type,
size & design)

6"

1/4" SLOPE

2 1/2"

5"

5 3/4"

5"

1 1/4" 5 1/2"

1/4"

DOOR HEIGHT

ROUGH OPENING

DRAWING #

Door Head Detail @ Frieze

SCALE

1 1/2"
1'-0"

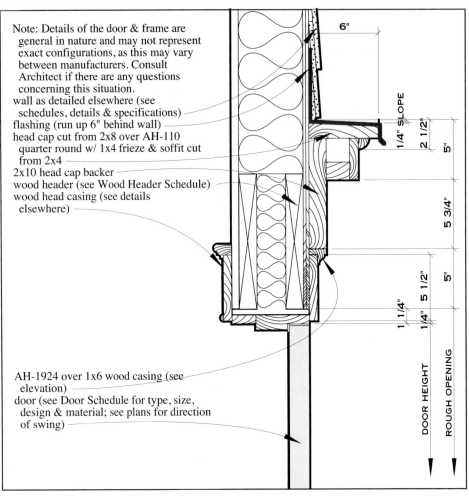

Note: Details of the door & frame are
general in nature and may not represent
exact configurations, as this may vary
between manufacturers. Consult
Architect if there are any questions
concerning this situation.
wall as detailed elsewhere (see
schedules, details & specifications)
flashing (run up 6" behind wall)
head cap cut from 2x8 over AH-110
quarter round w/ 1x4 frieze & soffit cut
from 2x4
2x10 head cap backer
wood header (see Wood Header Schedule)
wood head casing (see details
elsewhere)

6"

1/4" SLOPE

2 1/2"

5"

5 3/4"

5"

5 1/2"

1 1/4"

1/4"

DOOR HEIGHT

ROUGH OPENING

AH-1924 over 1x6 wood casing (see
elevation)
door (see Door Schedule for type, size,
design & material; see plans for direction
of swing)

DRAWING #

Door Head Detail

SCALE

1 1/2"
1'-0"

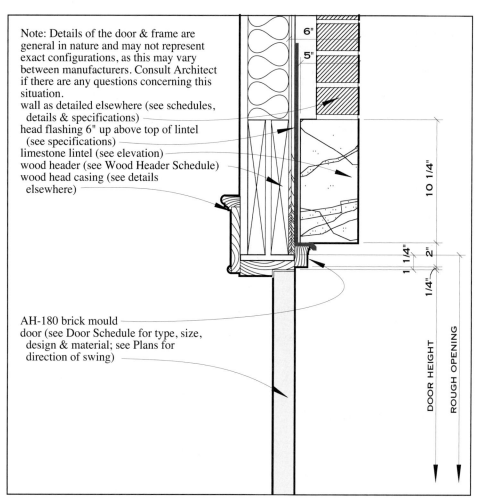

Note: Details of the door & frame are general in nature and may not represent exact configurations, as this may vary between manufacturers. Consult Architect if there are any questions concerning this situation.

wall as detailed elsewhere (see schedules, details & specifications)

head flashing 6" up above top of lintel (see specifications)

limestone lintel (see elevation)

wood header (see Wood Header Schedule)

wood head casing (see details elsewhere)

AH-180 brick mould

door (see Door Schedule for type, size, design & material; see Plans for direction of swing)

6"

5"

10 1/4"

1 1/4"

2"

1/4"

DOOR HEIGHT

ROUGH OPENING

Door Head Detail w/Stone Lintel

SCALE

1 1/2"
1'-0"

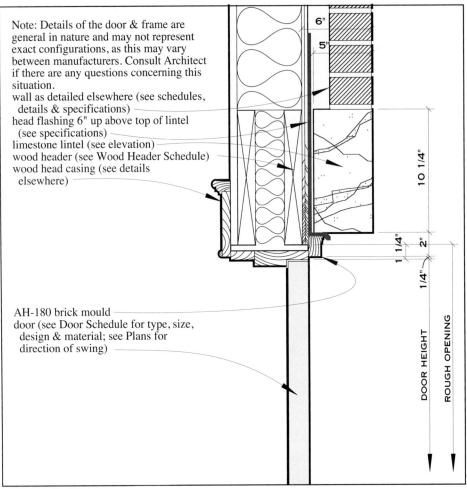

Note: Details of the door & frame are general in nature and may not represent exact configurations, as this may vary between manufacturers. Consult Architect if there are any questions concerning this situation.

wall as detailed elsewhere (see schedules, details & specifications)

head flashing 6" up above top of lintel (see specifications)

limestone lintel (see elevation)

wood header (see Wood Header Schedule)

wood head casing (see details elsewhere)

AH-180 brick mould

door (see Door Schedule for type, size, design & material; see Plans for direction of swing)

6"

5"

10 1/4"

1 1/4"   2"

1/4"

DOOR HEIGHT

ROUGH OPENING

DRAWING #

Door Head Detail w/Stone Lintel

SCALE
1 1/2"
1'-0"

DWH004
408

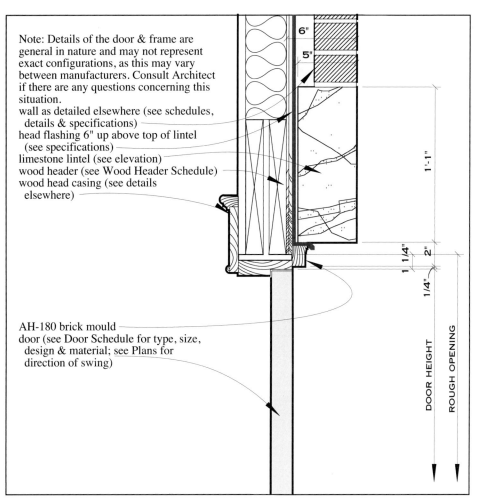

Note: Details of the door & frame are general in nature and may not represent exact configurations, as this may vary between manufacturers. Consult Architect if there are any questions concerning this situation.

wall as detailed elsewhere (see schedules, details & specifications)

head flashing 6" up above top of lintel (see specifications)

limestone lintel (see elevation)

wood header (see Wood Header Schedule)

wood head casing (see details elsewhere)

6"

5"

1'-1"

1 1/4"

2"

1/4"

AH-180 brick mould

door (see Door Schedule for type, size, design & material; see Plans for direction of swing)

DOOR HEIGHT

ROUGH OPENING

DRAWING #
_____

Door Head Detail w/Stone Lintel

SCALE
1 1/2"
1'-0"

DWH005
409

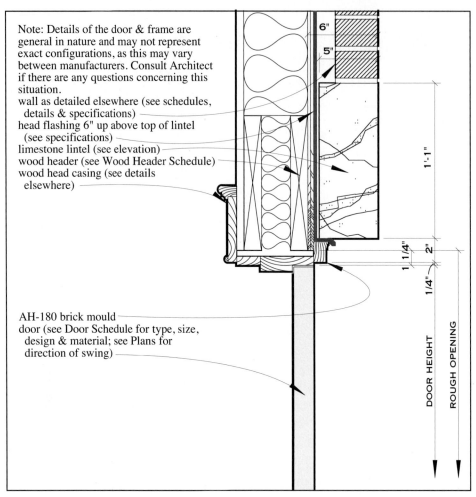

Note: Details of the door & frame are general in nature and may not represent exact configurations, as this may vary between manufacturers. Consult Architect if there are any questions concerning this situation.

wall as detailed elsewhere (see schedules, details & specifications)

head flashing 6" up above top of lintel (see specifications)

limestone lintel (see elevation)

wood header (see Wood Header Schedule)

wood head casing (see details elsewhere)

AH-180 brick mould

door (see Door Schedule for type, size, design & material; see Plans for direction of swing)

6"

5"

1'-1"

1 1/4"

2"

1/4"

DOOR HEIGHT

ROUGH OPENING

Door Head Detail w/Stone Lintel

DRAWING #

SCALE
1 1/2"
1'-0"

DWH006
410

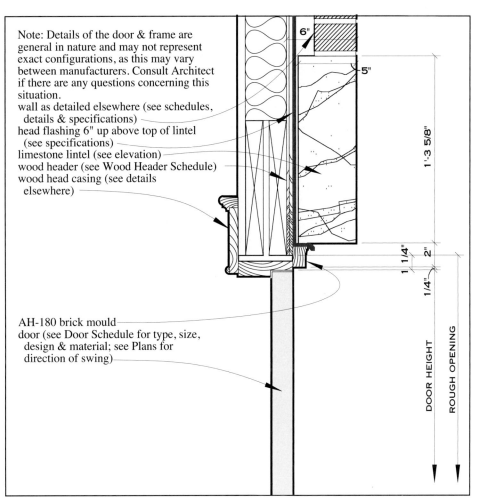

Note: Details of the door & frame are
general in nature and may not represent
exact configurations, as this may vary
between manufacturers. Consult Architect
if there are any questions concerning this
situation.
wall as detailed elsewhere (see schedules,
   details & specifications)
head flashing 6" up above top of lintel
   (see specifications)
limestone lintel (see elevation)
wood header (see Wood Header Schedule)
wood head casing (see details
   elsewhere)

6"

5"

1'-3 5/8"

1 1/4"

2"

1/4"

DOOR HEIGHT

ROUGH OPENING

AH-180 brick mould
door (see Door Schedule for type, size,
   design & material; see Plans for
   direction of swing)

DRAWING #

Door Head Detail w/Stone Lintel

SCALE

1 1/2"
1'-0"

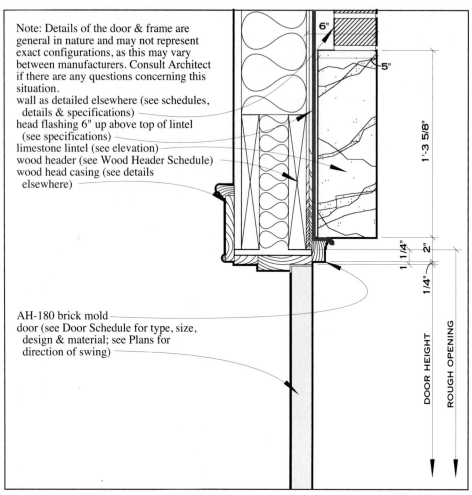

Note: Details of the door & frame are general in nature and may not represent exact configurations, as this may vary between manufacturers. Consult Architect if there are any questions concerning this situation.

wall as detailed elsewhere (see schedules, details & specifications)

head flashing 6" up above top of lintel (see specifications)

limestone lintel (see elevation)

wood header (see Wood Header Schedule)

wood head casing (see details elsewhere)

6"

5"

1'-3 5/8"

1 1/4"

2"

1/4"

DOOR HEIGHT

ROUGH OPENING

AH-180 brick mold

door (see Door Schedule for type, size, design & material; see Plans for direction of swing)

Door Head Detail w/Stone Lintel

DRAWING #

SCALE
1 1/2"
1'-0"

DWH008
412

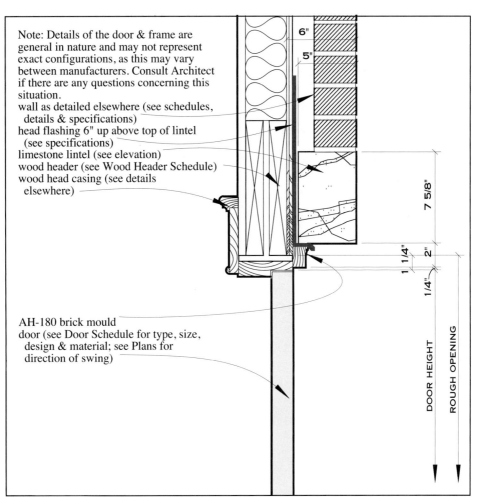

Note: Details of the door & frame are general in nature and may not represent exact configurations, as this may vary between manufacturers. Consult Architect if there are any questions concerning this situation.

wall as detailed elsewhere (see schedules, details & specifications)

head flashing 6" up above top of lintel (see specifications)

limestone lintel (see elevation)

wood header (see Wood Header Schedule)

wood head casing (see details elsewhere)

AH-180 brick mould

door (see Door Schedule for type, size, design & material; see Plans for direction of swing)

6"

5"

7 5/8"

1 1/4"

2"

1/4"

DOOR HEIGHT

ROUGH OPENING

Door Head Detail w/Stone Lintel

SCALE
1 1/2"
1'-0"

DWH009
413

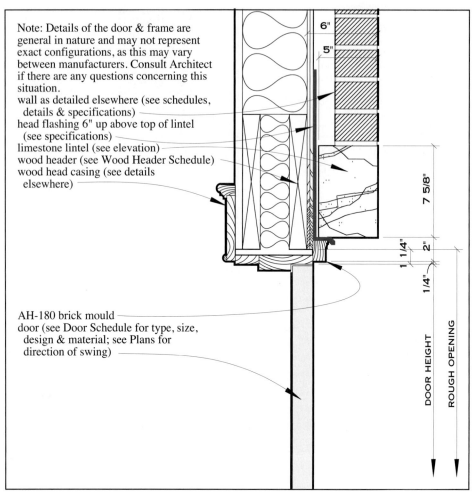

Note: Details of the door & frame are general in nature and may not represent exact configurations, as this may vary between manufacturers. Consult Architect if there are any questions concerning this situation.

wall as detailed elsewhere (see schedules, details & specifications)

head flashing 6" up above top of lintel (see specifications)

limestone lintel (see elevation)

wood header (see Wood Header Schedule)

wood head casing (see details elsewhere)

6"

5"

7 5/8"

1 1/4"

2"

1/4"

AH-180 brick mould

door (see Door Schedule for type, size, design & material; see Plans for direction of swing)

DOOR HEIGHT

ROUGH OPENING

DRAWING #

Door Head Detail w/Stone Lintel

SCALE

1 1/2"
1'-0"

DWH010
414

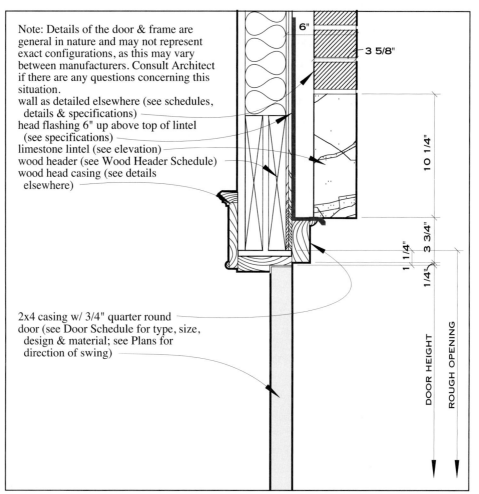

Note: Details of the door & frame are general in nature and may not represent exact configurations, as this may vary between manufacturers. Consult Architect if there are any questions concerning this situation.

wall as detailed elsewhere (see schedules, details & specifications)

head flashing 6" up above top of lintel (see specifications)

limestone lintel (see elevation)

wood header (see Wood Header Schedule)

wood head casing (see details elsewhere)

6"

3 5/8"

10 1/4"

3 3/4"

1 1/4"

1/4"

2x4 casing w/ 3/4" quarter round

door (see Door Schedule for type, size, design & material; see Plans for direction of swing)

DOOR HEIGHT

ROUGH OPENING

DRAWING #

Door Head Detail w/Stone Lintel

SCALE
1 1/2"
1'-0"

DWH011
415

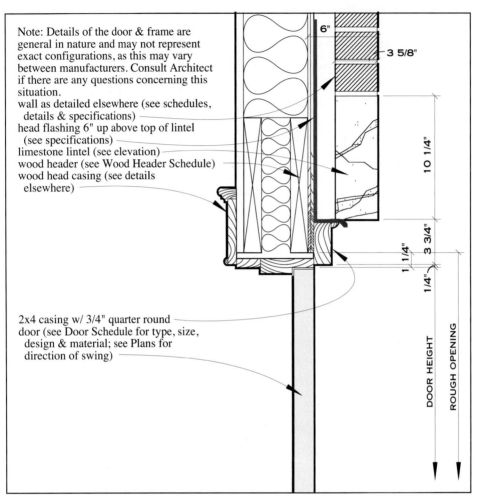

Note: Details of the door & frame are general in nature and may not represent exact configurations, as this may vary between manufacturers. Consult Architect if there are any questions concerning this situation.

wall as detailed elsewhere (see schedules, details & specifications)

head flashing 6" up above top of lintel (see specifications)

limestone lintel (see elevation)

wood header (see Wood Header Schedule)

wood head casing (see details elsewhere)

2x4 casing w/ 3/4" quarter round

door (see Door Schedule for type, size, design & material; see Plans for direction of swing)

6"

3 5/8"

10 1/4"

3 3/4"

1 1/4"

1/4"

DOOR HEIGHT

ROUGH OPENING

DRAWING #

Door Head Detail w/Stone Lintel

SCALE
1 1/2"
1'-0"

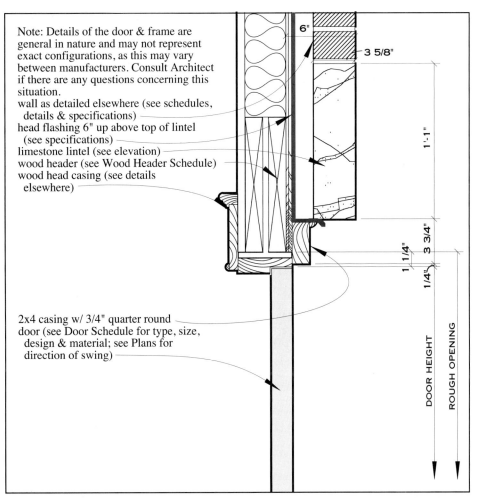

Note: Details of the door & frame are general in nature and may not represent exact configurations, as this may vary between manufacturers. Consult Architect if there are any questions concerning this situation.

wall as detailed elsewhere (see schedules, details & specifications)

head flashing 6" up above top of lintel (see specifications)

limestone lintel (see elevation)

wood header (see Wood Header Schedule)

wood head casing (see details elsewhere)

2x4 casing w/ 3/4" quarter round

door (see Door Schedule for type, size, design & material; see Plans for direction of swing)

6"

3 5/8"

1'-1"

3 3/4"

1 1/4"

1/4"

DOOR HEIGHT

ROUGH OPENING

Door Head Detail w/Stone Lintel

SCALE
1 1/2"
1'-0"

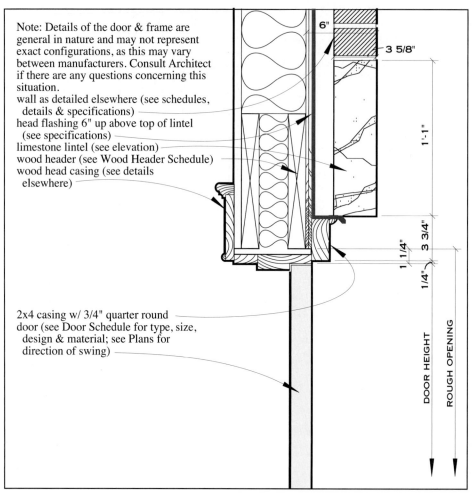

Note: Details of the door & frame are
general in nature and may not represent
exact configurations, as this may vary
between manufacturers. Consult Architect
if there are any questions concerning this
situation.

wall as detailed elsewhere (see schedules,
   details & specifications)

head flashing 6" up above top of lintel
   (see specifications)

limestone lintel (see elevation)

wood header (see Wood Header Schedule)

wood head casing (see details
   elsewhere)

2x4 casing w/ 3/4" quarter round

door (see Door Schedule for type, size,
   design & material; see Plans for
   direction of swing)

6"

3 5/8"

1'-1"

3 3/4"

1 1/4"

1/4"

DOOR HEIGHT

ROUGH OPENING

Door Head Detail w/Stone Lintel

DRAWING #

SCALE

1 1/2"
1'-0"

DWH014
418

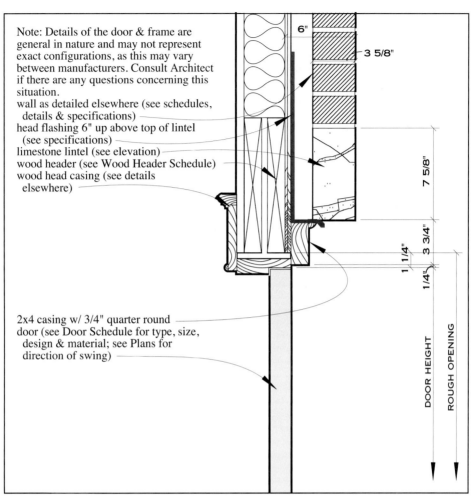

Note: Details of the door & frame are general in nature and may not represent exact configurations, as this may vary between manufacturers. Consult Architect if there are any questions concerning this situation.

wall as detailed elsewhere (see schedules, details & specifications)

head flashing 6" up above top of lintel (see specifications)

limestone lintel (see elevation)

wood header (see Wood Header Schedule)

wood head casing (see details elsewhere)

6"

3 5/8"

7 5/8"

3 3/4"

1 1/4"

1/4"

DOOR HEIGHT

ROUGH OPENING

2x4 casing w/ 3/4" quarter round

door (see Door Schedule for type, size, design & material; see Plans for direction of swing)

DRAWING #

Door Head Detail w/Stone Lintel

SCALE

1 1/2"
1'-0"

DWH015!
419

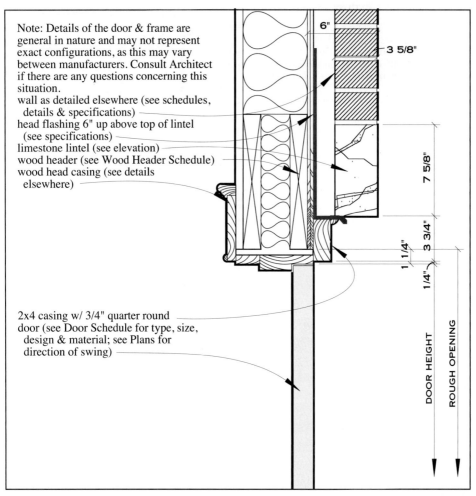

Note: Details of the door & frame are general in nature and may not represent exact configurations, as this may vary between manufacturers. Consult Architect if there are any questions concerning this situation.

wall as detailed elsewhere (see schedules, details & specifications)

head flashing 6" up above top of lintel (see specifications)

limestone lintel (see elevation)

wood header (see Wood Header Schedule)

wood head casing (see details elsewhere)

6"

3 5/8"

7 5/8"

3 3/4"

1 1/4"

1/4"

DOOR HEIGHT

ROUGH OPENING

2x4 casing w/ 3/4" quarter round

door (see Door Schedule for type, size, design & material; see Plans for direction of swing)

DRAWING #

Door Head Detail w/Stone Lintel

SCALE
1 1/2"
1'-0"

DWH016
420

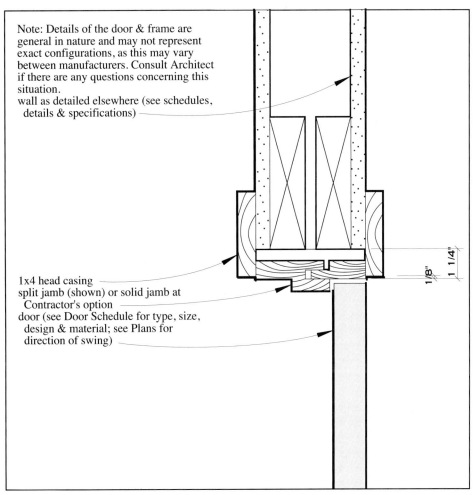

Note: Details of the door & frame are general in nature and may not represent exact configurations, as this may vary between manufacturers. Consult Architect if there are any questions concerning this situation.
wall as detailed elsewhere (see schedules, details & specifications)

1x4 head casing
split jamb (shown) or solid jamb at Contractor's option
door (see Door Schedule for type, size, design & material; see Plans for direction of swing)

1 1/4"

1/8"

Door Head Detail w/Wood Casing

SCALE
3"
1'-0"

DRAWING #

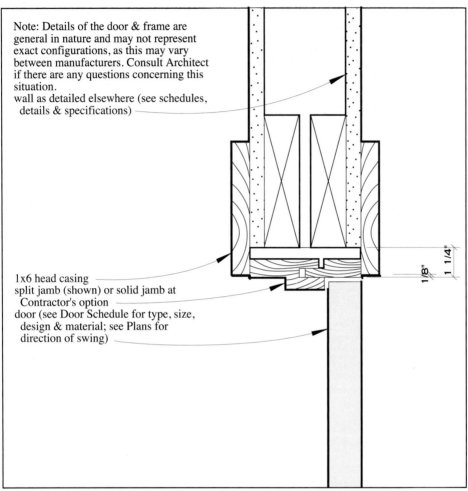

Note: Details of the door & frame are general in nature and may not represent exact configurations, as this may vary between manufacturers. Consult Architect if there are any questions concerning this situation.
wall as detailed elsewhere (see schedules, details & specifications)

1x6 head casing
split jamb (shown) or solid jamb at Contractor's option
door (see Door Schedule for type, size, design & material; see Plans for direction of swing)

Door Head Detail w/Wood Casing

SCALE
3"
1'-0"

DWH018
422

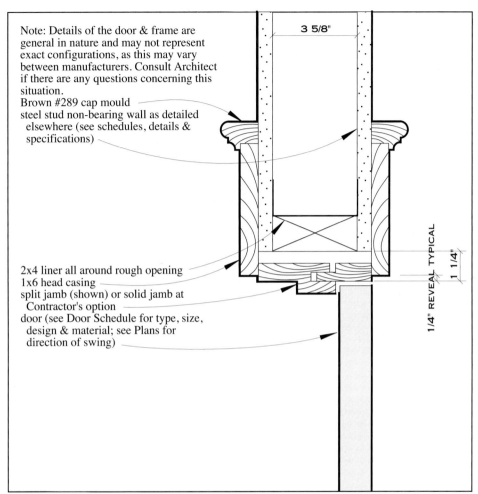

Note: Details of the door & frame are general in nature and may not represent exact configurations, as this may vary between manufacturers. Consult Architect if there are any questions concerning this situation.

Brown #289 cap mould

steel stud non-bearing wall as detailed elsewhere (see schedules, details & specifications)

3 5/8"

2x4 liner all around rough opening

1x6 head casing

split jamb (shown) or solid jamb at Contractor's option

door (see Door Schedule for type, size, design & material; see Plans for direction of swing)

1/4" REVEAL TYPICAL

1 1/4"

Door Head Detail w/Wood Casing

SCALE
3"
1'-0"

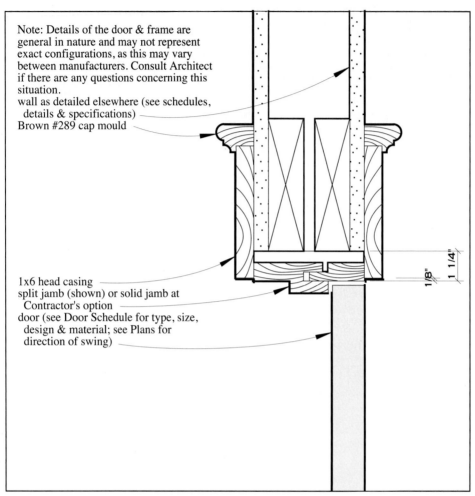

Note: Details of the door & frame are
general in nature and may not represent
exact configurations, as this may vary
between manufacturers. Consult Architect
if there are any questions concerning this
situation.
wall as detailed elsewhere (see schedules,
 details & specifications)
Brown #289 cap mould

1x6 head casing
split jamb (shown) or solid jamb at
 Contractor's option
door (see Door Schedule for type, size,
 design & material; see Plans for
 direction of swing)

1 1/4"

1/8"

Door Head Detail w/Wood Casing

SCALE
3"
1'-0"

DRAWING #

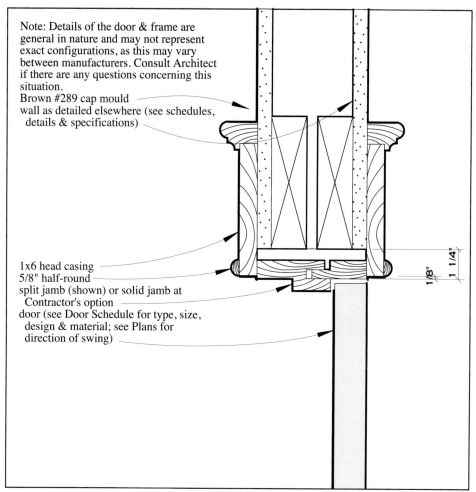

Note: Details of the door & frame are general in nature and may not represent exact configurations, as this may vary between manufacturers. Consult Architect if there are any questions concerning this situation.

Brown #289 cap mould

wall as detailed elsewhere (see schedules, details & specifications)

1x6 head casing

5/8" half-round

split jamb (shown) or solid jamb at Contractor's option

door (see Door Schedule for type, size, design & material; see Plans for direction of swing)

1 1/4"

1/8"

Door Head Detail w/Wood Casing

SCALE
3"
1'-0"

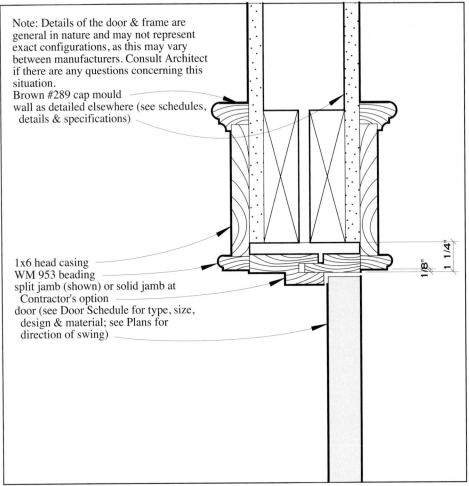

Note: Details of the door & frame are
general in nature and may not represent
exact configurations, as this may vary
between manufacturers. Consult Architect
if there are any questions concerning this
situation.
Brown #289 cap mould
wall as detailed elsewhere (see schedules,
  details & specifications)

1x6 head casing
WM 953 beading
split jamb (shown) or solid jamb at
  Contractor's option
door (see Door Schedule for type, size,
  design & material; see Plans for
  direction of swing)

1 1/4"

1/8"

DRAWING #

Door Head Detail w/Wood Casing

SCALE
$\frac{3"}{1'-0"}$

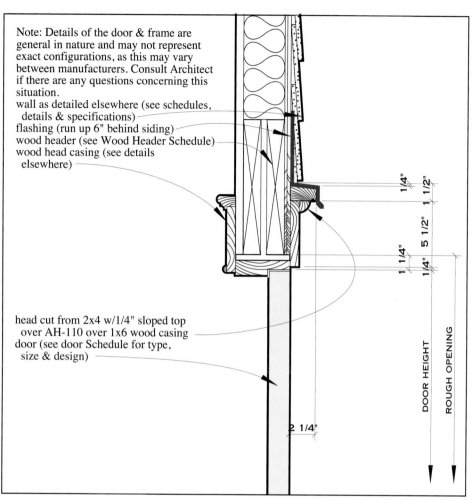

Note: Details of the door & frame are general in nature and may not represent exact configurations, as this may vary between manufacturers. Consult Architect if there are any questions concerning this situation.

wall as detailed elsewhere (see schedules, details & specifications)

flashing (run up 6" behind siding)

wood header (see Wood Header Schedule)

wood head casing (see details elsewhere)

head cut from 2x4 w/1/4" sloped top over AH-110 over 1x6 wood casing

door (see door Schedule for type, size & design)

1/4"

1 1/2"

1"

1 1/4"

5 1/2"

1/4"

2 1/4"

DOOR HEIGHT

ROUGH OPENING

DRAWING #

Door Head Detail

SCALE

1 1/2"
1'-0"

DWH023
427

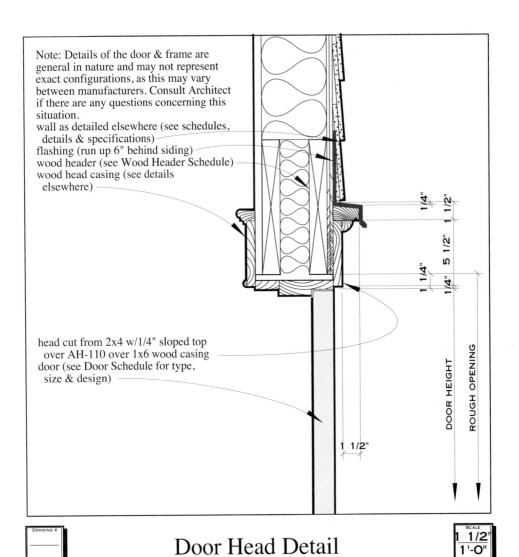

Note: Details of the door & frame are
general in nature and may not represent
exact configurations, as this may vary
between manufacturers. Consult Architect
if there are any questions concerning this
situation.

wall as detailed elsewhere (see schedules,
  details & specifications)
flashing (run up 6" behind siding)
wood header (see Wood Header Schedule)
wood head casing (see details
  elsewhere)

head cut from 2x4 w/1/4" sloped top
  over AH-110 over 1x6 wood casing
door (see Door Schedule for type,
  size & design)

1/4"
1 1/2"
1 1/4"
1/4"
5 1/2"

DOOR HEIGHT
ROUGH OPENING

1 1/2"

Door Head Detail

DRAWING #

SCALE
1 1/2"
1'-0"

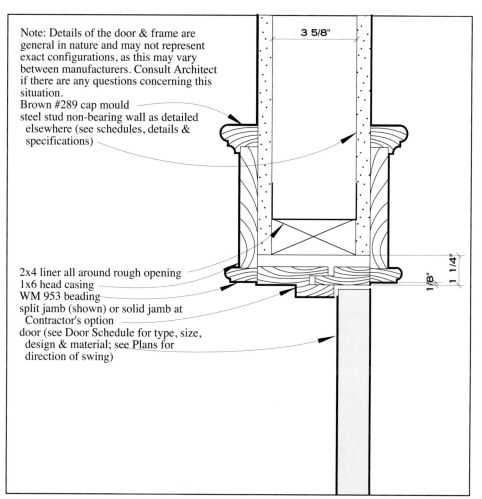

Note: Details of the door & frame are general in nature and may not represent exact configurations, as this may vary between manufacturers. Consult Architect if there are any questions concerning this situation.

Brown #289 cap mould

steel stud non-bearing wall as detailed elsewhere (see schedules, details & specifications)

3 5/8"

2x4 liner all around rough opening

1x6 head casing

WM 953 beading

split jamb (shown) or solid jamb at Contractor's option

door (see Door Schedule for type, size, design & material; see Plans for direction of swing)

1 1/4"

1/8"

Door Head Detail w/Wood Casing

SCALE
$\frac{3"}{1'\text{-}0"}$

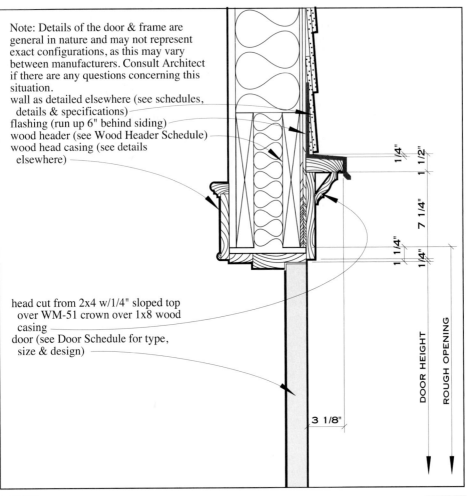

Note: Details of the door & frame are general in nature and may not represent exact configurations, as this may vary between manufacturers. Consult Architect if there are any questions concerning this situation.

wall as detailed elsewhere (see schedules, details & specifications)

flashing (run up 6" behind siding)

wood header (see Wood Header Schedule)

wood head casing (see details elsewhere)

head cut from 2x4 w/1/4" sloped top over WM-51 crown over 1x8 wood casing

door (see Door Schedule for type, size & design)

1/4"

1 1/2"

7 1/4"

1 1/4"

1/4"

3 1/8"

DOOR HEIGHT

ROUGH OPENING

Door Head Detail

DRAWING #

SCALE

1 1/2"
1'-0"

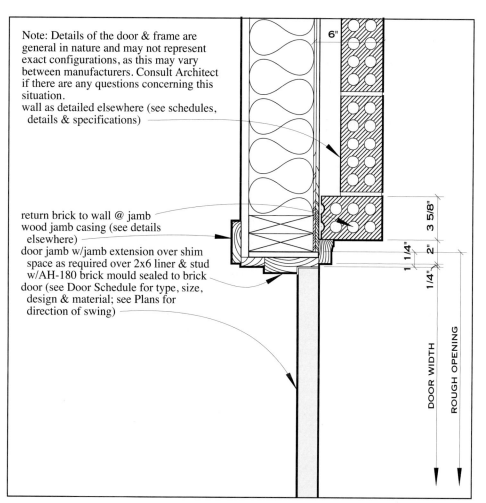

Note: Details of the door & frame are
general in nature and may not represent
exact configurations, as this may vary
between manufacturers. Consult Architect
if there are any questions concerning this
situation.
wall as detailed elsewhere (see schedules,
    details & specifications)

6"

3 5/8"

return brick to wall @ jamb
wood jamb casing (see details
    elsewhere)
door jamb w/jamb extension over shim
    space as required over 2x6 liner & stud
    w/AH-180 brick mould sealed to brick
door (see Door Schedule for type, size,
    design & material; see Plans for
    direction of swing)

1 1/4"
2"
1/4"

DOOR WIDTH

ROUGH OPENING

Door Jamb Detail @ Brick Veneer

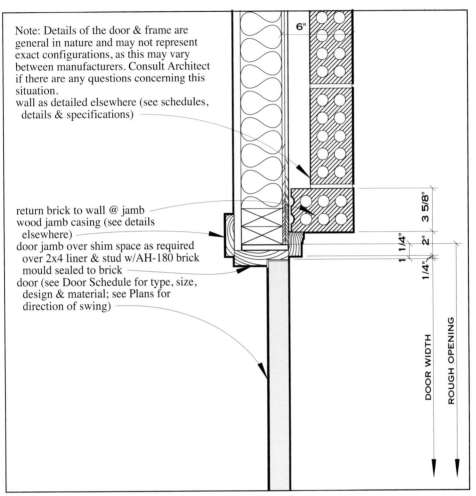

Note: Details of the door & frame are general in nature and may not represent exact configurations, as this may vary between manufacturers. Consult Architect if there are any questions concerning this situation.

wall as detailed elsewhere (see schedules, details & specifications)

6"

return brick to wall @ jamb
wood jamb casing (see details elsewhere)
door jamb over shim space as required over 2x4 liner & stud w/AH-180 brick mould sealed to brick
door (see Door Schedule for type, size, design & material; see Plans for direction of swing)

3 5/8"

1 1/4"

2"

1/4"

DOOR WIDTH

ROUGH OPENING

DRAWING #

Door Jamb Detail @ Brick Veneer

SCALE
1 1/2
1'-0"

DWJ004
432

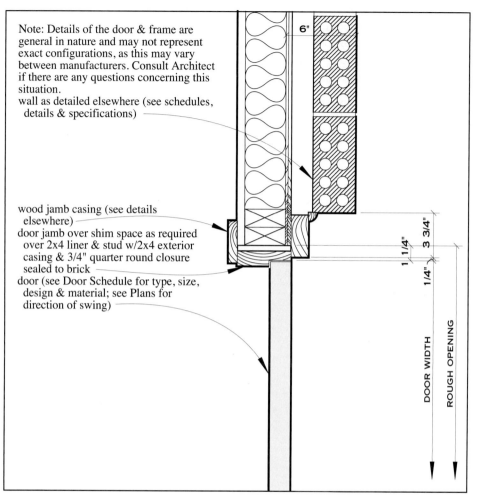

Note: Details of the door & frame are general in nature and may not represent exact configurations, as this may vary between manufacturers. Consult Architect if there are any questions concerning this situation.

wall as detailed elsewhere (see schedules, details & specifications)

6"

wood jamb casing (see details elsewhere)

door jamb over shim space as required over 2x4 liner & stud w/2x4 exterior casing & 3/4" quarter round closure sealed to brick

door (see Door Schedule for type, size, design & material; see Plans for direction of swing)

3 3/4"

1 1/4"

1/4"

DOOR WIDTH

ROUGH OPENING

Door Jamb Detail @ Brick Veneer

SCALE
1 1/2
1'-0"

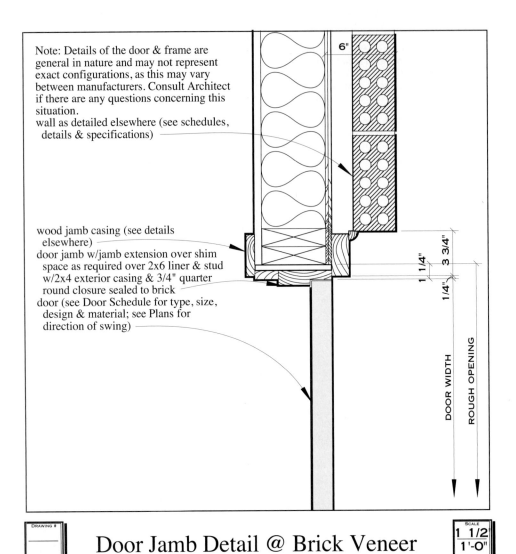

Note: Details of the door & frame are
general in nature and may not represent
exact configurations, as this may vary
between manufacturers. Consult Architect
if there are any questions concerning this
situation.
wall as detailed elsewhere (see schedules,
   details & specifications)

6"

wood jamb casing (see details
   elsewhere)
door jamb w/jamb extension over shim
   space as required over 2x6 liner & stud
   w/2x4 exterior casing & 3/4" quarter
   round closure sealed to brick
door (see Door Schedule for type, size,
   design & material; see Plans for
   direction of swing)

1 1/4"

3 3/4"

1/4"

DOOR WIDTH

ROUGH OPENING

DRAWING #

Door Jamb Detail @ Brick Veneer

SCALE
1 1/2
1'-0"

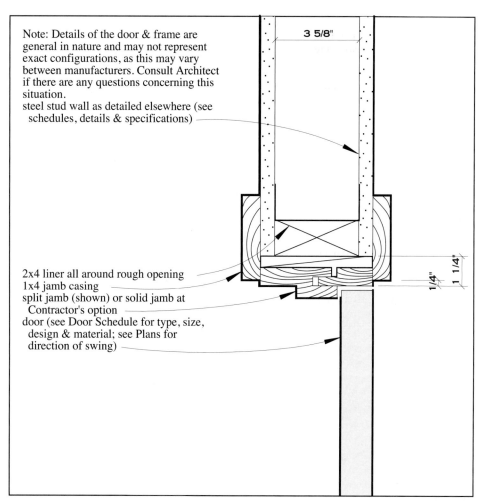

Note: Details of the door & frame are general in nature and may not represent exact configurations, as this may vary between manufacturers. Consult Architect if there are any questions concerning this situation.

steel stud wall as detailed elsewhere (see schedules, details & specifications)

3 5/8"

2x4 liner all around rough opening
1x4 jamb casing
split jamb (shown) or solid jamb at Contractor's option
door (see Door Schedule for type, size, design & material; see Plans for direction of swing)

1 1/4"

1/4"

DRAWING #

Door Jamb Detail w/Wood Casing

SCALE
3"
1'-0"

DWJ007
435

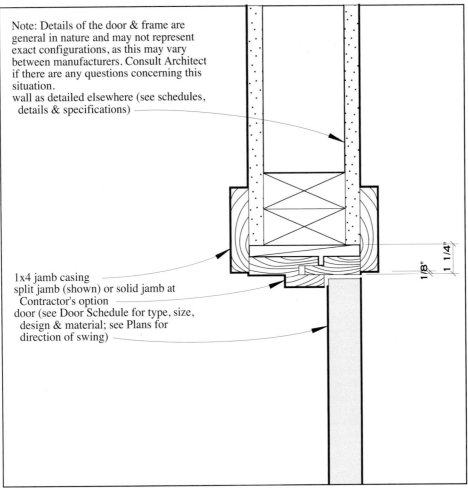

Note: Details of the door & frame are general in nature and may not represent exact configurations, as this may vary between manufacturers. Consult Architect if there are any questions concerning this situation.
wall as detailed elsewhere (see schedules, details & specifications)

1x4 jamb casing
split jamb (shown) or solid jamb at Contractor's option
door (see Door Schedule for type, size, design & material; see Plans for direction of swing)

1 1/4"

1/8"

DRAWING #

Door Jamb Detail w/Wood Casing

SCALE
3"
1'-0"

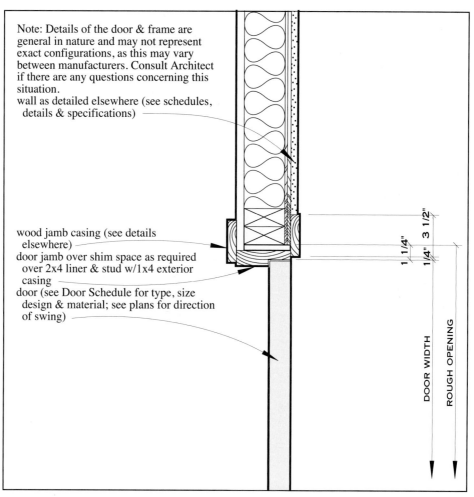

Note: Details of the door & frame are general in nature and may not represent exact configurations, as this may vary between manufacturers. Consult Architect if there are any questions concerning this situation.
wall as detailed elsewhere (see schedules, details & specifications)

wood jamb casing (see details elsewhere)
door jamb over shim space as required over 2x4 liner & stud w/1x4 exterior casing
door (see Door Schedule for type, size design & material; see plans for direction of swing)

1 1/4"   3 1/2"
1/4"

DOOR WIDTH

ROUGH OPENING

DRAWING #

Door Jamb Detail

SCALE
1 1/2
1'-0"

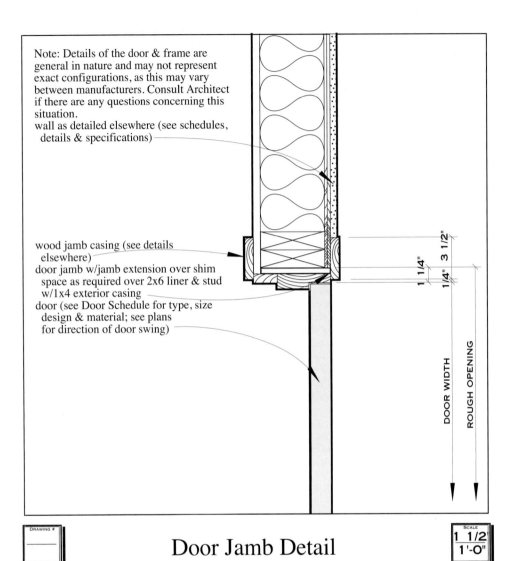

Note: Details of the door & frame are general in nature and may not represent exact configurations, as this may vary between manufacturers. Consult Architect if there are any questions concerning this situation.

wall as detailed elsewhere (see schedules, details & specifications)

wood jamb casing (see details elsewhere)

door jamb w/jamb extension over shim space as required over 2x6 liner & stud w/1x4 exterior casing

door (see Door Schedule for type, size design & material; see plans for direction of door swing)

1 1/4"

3 1/2"

1/4"

DOOR WIDTH

ROUGH OPENING

DRAWING #

Door Jamb Detail

SCALE
1 1/2"
1'-0"

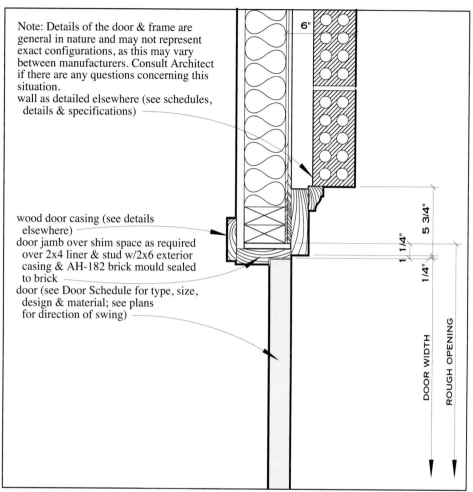

Note: Details of the door & frame are general in nature and may not represent exact configurations, as this may vary between manufacturers. Consult Architect if there are any questions concerning this situation.

wall as detailed elsewhere (see schedules, details & specifications)

6"

wood door casing (see details elsewhere)

door jamb over shim space as required over 2x4 liner & stud w/2x6 exterior casing & AH-182 brick mould sealed to brick

door (see Door Schedule for type, size, design & material; see plans for direction of swing)

5 3/4"

1 1/4"

1/4"

DOOR WIDTH

ROUGH OPENING

DRAWING #

Door Jamb Detail @ Brick Veneer

SCALE
1 1/2
1'-0"

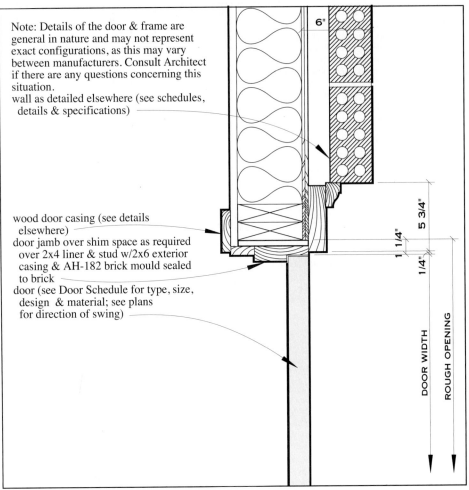

Note: Details of the door & frame are general in nature and may not represent exact configurations, as this may vary between manufacturers. Consult Architect if there are any questions concerning this situation.

wall as detailed elsewhere (see schedules, details & specifications)

6"

wood door casing (see details elsewhere)

door jamb over shim space as required over 2x4 liner & stud w/2x6 exterior casing & AH-182 brick mould sealed to brick

door (see Door Schedule for type, size, design & material; see plans for direction of swing)

5 3/4"

1 1/4"

1/4"

DOOR WIDTH

ROUGH OPENING

Door Jamb Detail @ Brick Veneer

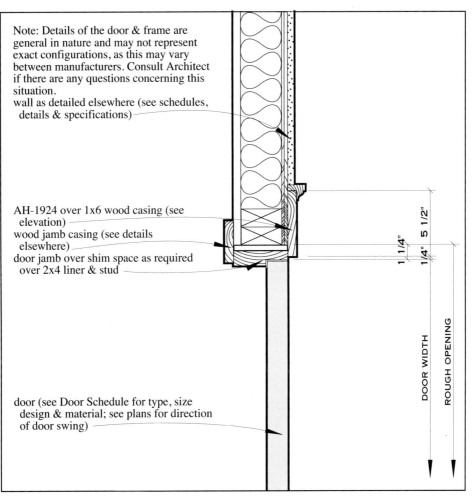

Note: Details of the door & frame are general in nature and may not represent exact configurations, as this may vary between manufacturers. Consult Architect if there are any questions concerning this situation.

wall as detailed elsewhere (see schedules, details & specifications)

AH-1924 over 1x6 wood casing (see elevation)

wood jamb casing (see details elsewhere)

door jamb over shim space as required over 2x4 liner & stud

door (see Door Schedule for type, size design & material; see plans for direction of door swing)

1 1/4"

1/4"

5 1/2"

DOOR WIDTH

ROUGH OPENING

DRAWING #

Door Jamb Detail

SCALE

1 1/2 / 1'-0"

0441 DWJ013
441

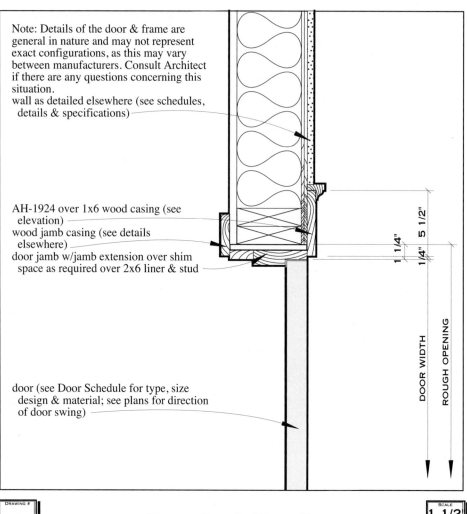

Note: Details of the door & frame are general in nature and may not represent exact configurations, as this may vary between manufacturers. Consult Architect if there are any questions concerning this situation.

wall as detailed elsewhere (see schedules, details & specifications)

AH-1924 over 1x6 wood casing (see elevation)

wood jamb casing (see details elsewhere)

door jamb w/jamb extension over shim space as required over 2x6 liner & stud

door (see Door Schedule for type, size design & material; see plans for direction of door swing)

1 1/4"

1/4" 5 1/2"

DOOR WIDTH

ROUGH OPENING

Door Jamb Detail

DRAWING #

SCALE
1 1/2
1'-0"

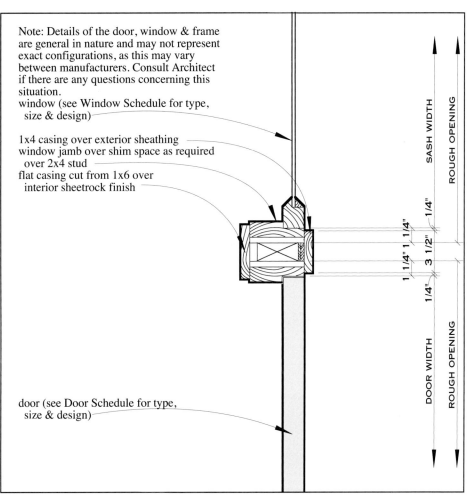

Note: Details of the door, window & frame
are general in nature and may not represent
exact configurations, as this may vary
between manufacturers. Consult Architect
if there are any questions concerning this
situation.
window (see Window Schedule for type,
  size & design)

1x4 casing over exterior sheathing
window jamb over shim space as required
  over 2x4 stud
flat casing cut from 1x6 over
  interior sheetrock finish

SASH WIDTH

ROUGH OPENING

1/4"

1 1/4" 1 1/4"

3 1/2"

1/4"

DOOR WIDTH

ROUGH OPENING

door (see Door Schedule for type,
  size & design)

DRAWING #

Door Mullion Detail

SCALE

1 1/2"

1'-0

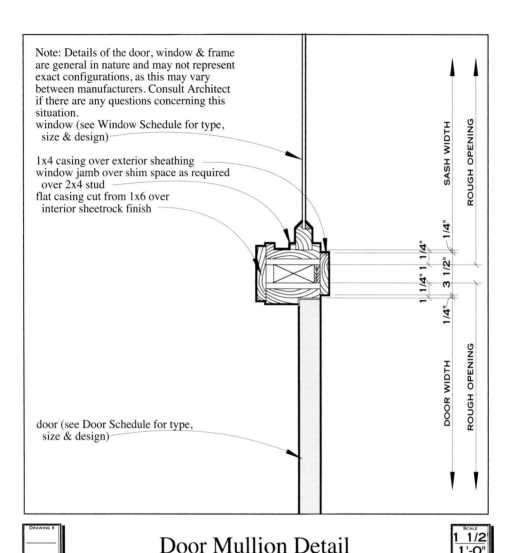

Note: Details of the door, window & frame are general in nature and may not represent exact configurations, as this may vary between manufacturers. Consult Architect if there are any questions concerning this situation.

window (see Window Schedule for type, size & design)

1x4 casing over exterior sheathing
window jamb over shim space as required over 2x4 stud
flat casing cut from 1x6 over interior sheetrock finish

door (see Door Schedule for type, size & design)

SASH WIDTH

ROUGH OPENING

1/4"

1 1/4" 1 1/4"

1 1/4" 1

3 1/2"

1/4"

DOOR WIDTH

ROUGH OPENING

DRAWING #

Door Mullion Detail

SCALE
1 1/2
1'-0"

DWM002
444

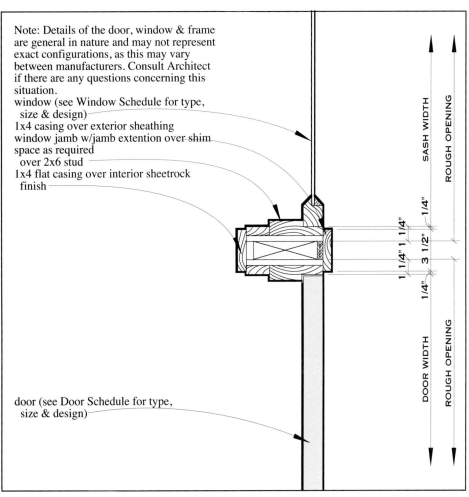

Note: Details of the door, window & frame
are general in nature and may not represent
exact configurations, as this may vary
between manufacturers. Consult Architect
if there are any questions concerning this
situation.
window (see Window Schedule for type,
  size & design)
1x4 casing over exterior sheathing
window jamb w/jamb extention over shim
space as required
  over 2x6 stud
1x4 flat casing over interior sheetrock
  finish

door (see Door Schedule for type,
  size & design)

SASH WIDTH

ROUGH OPENING

1/4"

1 1/4"

1 1/4"

3 1/2"

1/4"

DOOR WIDTH

ROUGH OPENING

DRAWING #

Door Mullion Detail

SCALE

1 1/2
1'-0"

Note: Details of the door, window & frame
are general in nature and may not represent
exact configurations, as this may vary
between manufacturers. Consult Architect
if there are any questions concerning this
situation.
window (see Window Schedule for type,
  size & design)

1x4 casing over exterior sheathing
window jamb w/jamb extension over shim
  space as required over 2x6 stud
1x4 flat casing over interior sheetrock
  finish

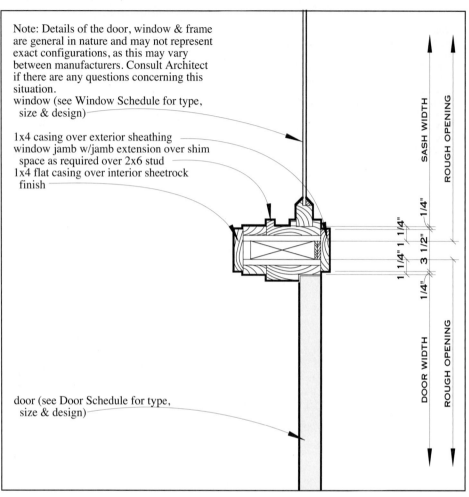

SASH WIDTH

ROUGH OPENING

1/4"

1 1/4" 1 1/4"

3 1/2"

1/4"

DOOR WIDTH

ROUGH OPENING

door (see Door Schedule for type,
  size & design)

Door Mullion Detail

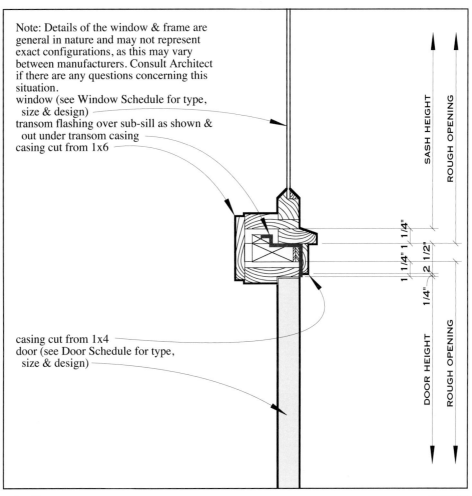

Note: Details of the window & frame are general in nature and may not represent exact configurations, as this may vary between manufacturers. Consult Architect if there are any questions concerning this situation.

window (see Window Schedule for type, size & design)

transom flashing over sub-sill as shown & out under transom casing

casing cut from 1x6

casing cut from 1x4

door (see Door Schedule for type, size & design)

SASH HEIGHT

ROUGH OPENING

1 1/4" 1 1/4"

1 1/4" 1 2 1/2"

1/4"

DOOR HEIGHT

ROUGH OPENING

DRAWING #

Door Transom Detail

SCALE

1 1/2"

1'-0"

DWT001

447

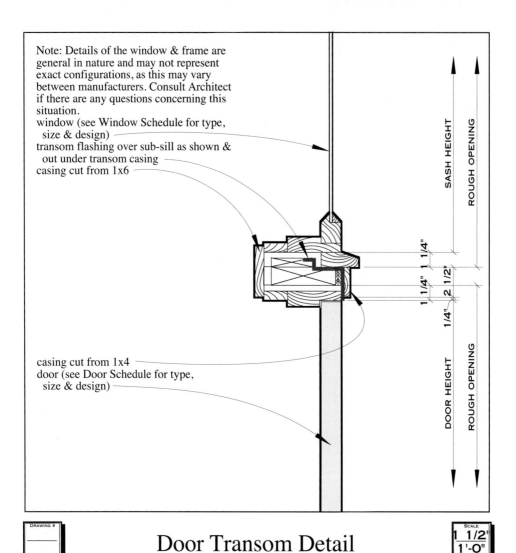

Note: Details of the window & frame are
general in nature and may not represent
exact configurations, as this may vary
between manufacturers. Consult Architect
if there are any questions concerning this
situation.
window (see Window Schedule for type,
  size & design)
transom flashing over sub-sill as shown &
  out under transom casing
casing cut from 1x6

casing cut from 1x4
door (see Door Schedule for type,
  size & design)

SASH HEIGHT

ROUGH OPENING

1 1/4"

1 1/4"

2 1/2"

1/4"

DOOR HEIGHT

ROUGH OPENING

DRAWING #

Door Transom Detail

SCALE

1 1/2"

1'-0"

DWT002
448

BUILDING ENVELOPE DETAILS

Details in this section include all general construction of the building envelope or shell except for doors & windows. Many of these details are either structural in nature or concern moisture protection. The contents of this section are as follows:

EIFS Details	450
Masonry Details	465
Roof Details: Eave Conditions	468
Roof Details: Flashing	469
Roof Details: Miscellaneous	477
Roof Details: Parapet Conditions	478
Roof Details: Ridge Conditions	481
Structural Details: Flitch Beams	485
Structural Details: Wood Decks	493
Structural Details: Concrete Floor Joints	502
Structural Details: Concrete Floor Plan Details	504
Structural Details: Wood Floor Details	512
Structural Details: Miscellaneous Subgrade & Foundation Details	522
Structural Details: Foundation Pier Details	525
Structural Details: Foundation Sections	540
Structural Details: Wall Conditions	548
Firewall Details	554
Wall Plan Details	563
Wall Section Details	569

449

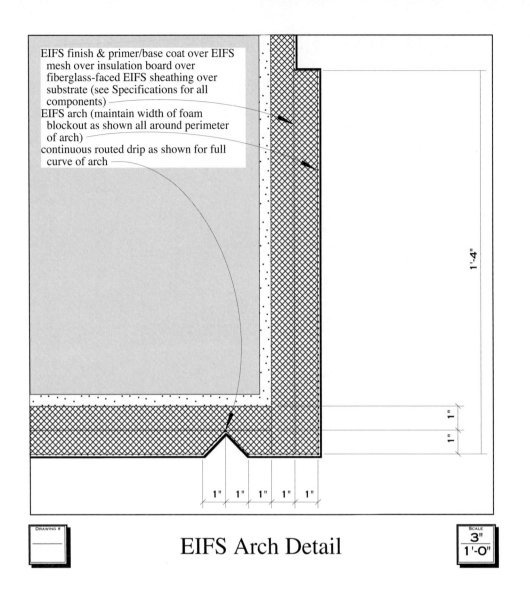

EIFS finish & primer/base coat over EIFS
   mesh over insulation board over
   fiberglass-faced EIFS sheathing over
   substrate (see Specifications for all
   components)
EIFS arch (maintain width of foam
   blockout as shown all around perimeter
   of arch)
continuous routed drip as shown for full
   curve of arch

1'-4"

1"
1"

1" 1" 1" 1" 1"

EIFS Arch Detail

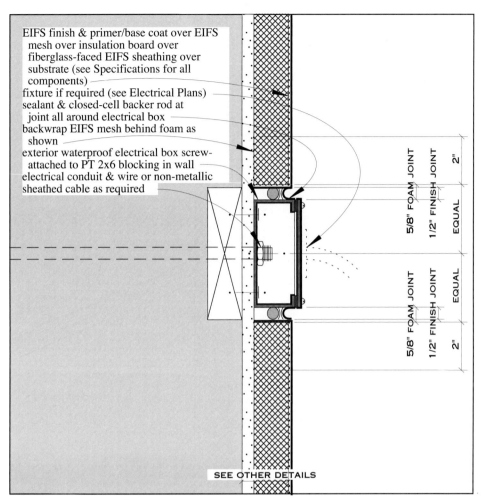

EIFS finish & primer/base coat over EIFS
mesh over insulation board over
fiberglass-faced EIFS sheathing over
substrate (see Specifications for all
components)
fixture if required (see Electrical Plans)
sealant & closed-cell backer rod at
joint all around electrical box
backwrap EIFS mesh behind foam as
shown
exterior waterproof electrical box screw-
attached to PT 2x6 blocking in wall
electrical conduit & wire or non-metallic
sheathed cable as required

5/8" FOAM JOINT
1/2" FINISH JOINT
2"
EQUAL

5/8" FOAM JOINT
1/2" FINISH JOINT
2"
EQUAL

SEE OTHER DETAILS

DRAWING #

EIFS Electrical Box Detail

SCALE
$\dfrac{3"}{1'\text{-}0"}$

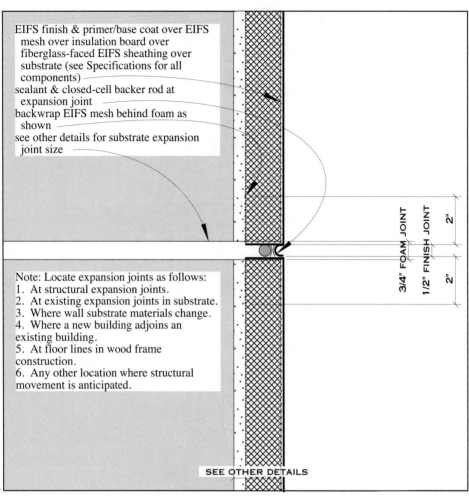

EIFS finish & primer/base coat over EIFS
 mesh over insulation board over
 fiberglass-faced EIFS sheathing over
 substrate (see Specifications for all
 components)
sealant & closed-cell backer rod at
 expansion joint
backwrap EIFS mesh behind foam as
 shown
see other details for substrate expansion
 joint size

3/4" FOAM JOINT

1/2" FINISH JOINT

2"

2"

Note: Locate expansion joints as follows:
1. At structural expansion joints.
2. At existing expansion joints in substrate.
3. Where wall substrate materials change.
4. Where a new building adjoins an
existing building.
5. At floor lines in wood frame
construction.
6. Any other location where structural
movement is anticipated.

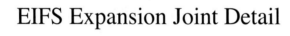

SEE OTHER DETAILS

DRAWING #

EIFS Expansion Joint Detail

SCALE
3"
1'-0"

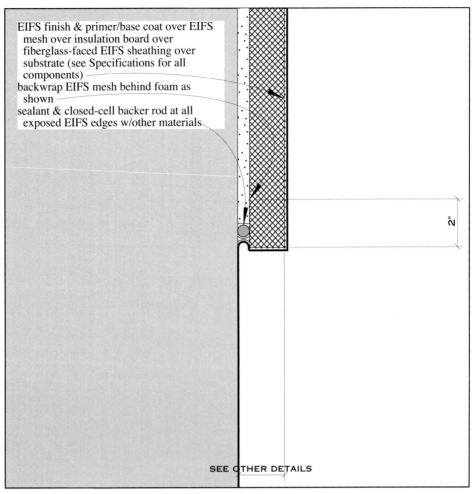

EIFS finish & primer/base coat over EIFS mesh over insulation board over fiberglass-faced EIFS sheathing over substrate (see Specifications for all components)

backwrap EIFS mesh behind foam as shown

sealant & closed-cell backer rod at all exposed EIFS edges w/other materials

2"

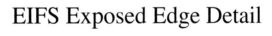
SEE OTHER DETAILS

DRAWING #
_____

EIFS Exposed Edge Detail

SCALE
3"
1'-0"

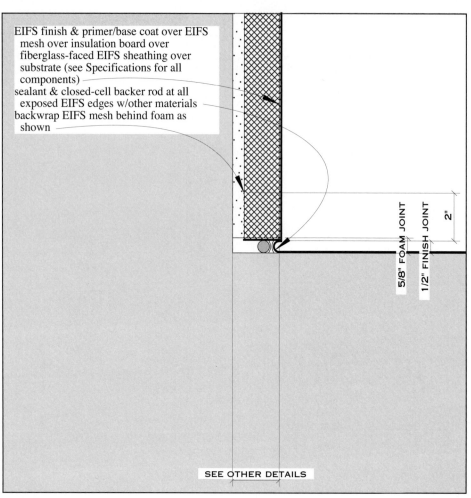

EIFS finish & primer/base coat over EIFS
mesh over insulation board over
fiberglass-faced EIFS sheathing over
substrate (see Specifications for all
components)

sealant & closed-cell backer rod at all
exposed EIFS edges w/other materials

backwrap EIFS mesh behind foam as
shown

5/8" FOAM JOINT

1/2" FINISH JOINT

2"

SEE OTHER DETAILS

EIFS Exposed Edge Detail

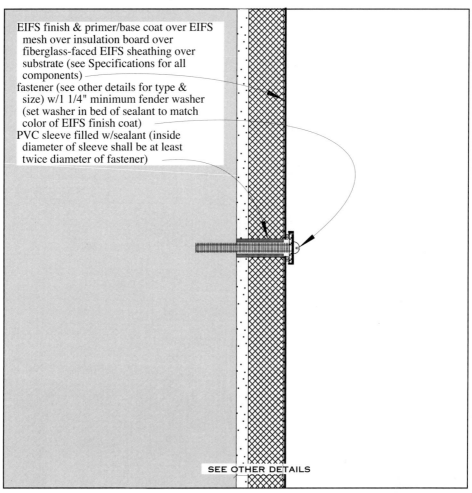

EIFS finish & primer/base coat over EIFS
mesh over insulation board over
fiberglass-faced EIFS sheathing over
substrate (see Specifications for all
components)
fastener (see other details for type &
size) w/1 1/4" minimum fender washer
(set washer in bed of sealant to match
color of EIFS finish coat)
PVC sleeve filled w/sealant (inside
diameter of sleeve shall be at least
twice diameter of fastener)

SEE OTHER DETAILS

EIFS Connector Detail

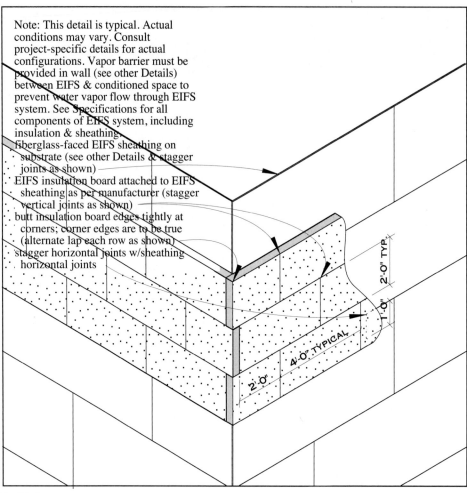

Note: This detail is typical. Actual conditions may vary. Consult project-specific details for actual configurations. Vapor barrier must be provided in wall (see other Details) between EIFS & conditioned space to prevent water vapor flow through EIFS system. See Specifications for all components of EIFS system, including insulation & sheathing.

· fiberglass-faced EIFS sheathing on substrate (see other Details & stagger joints as shown)
· EIFS insulation board attached to EIFS sheathing as per manufacturer (stagger vertical joints as shown)
· butt insulation board edges tightly at corners; corner edges are to be true (alternate lap each row as shown)
· stagger horizontal joints w/sheathing horizontal joints

2'-0" TYP.

1'-0"

2'-0"

4'-0" TYPICAL

 DRAWING #

EIFS Insulation Board Layout Detail

 SCALE $\frac{1/4"}{1'-0"}$

EE008
456

Note: This detail is typical in nature, and is intended to outline the general procedures for reinforcing EIFS mesh in the corners of doors & windows. Opening sizes shown here are purely schematic. See Floor Plans and/or Door & Window Schedules & Elevations for sizes of openings. See Wall Sections for thickness of foam.

Step 1: Install mesh over foam to cover wall. Cut out mesh at window, leaving flap of mesh equal to foam thickness plus 2" @ head & sill as shown for backwrapping foam

Step 2: Backwrap head & sill. Cut strips of mesh equal in width to thickness of foam plus 4" for jamb reinforcement. Front- and backwrap jamb as shown

Step 3: Reinforce corners w/12" square section of mesh as shown. Several EIFS manufacturers make mesh specifically for this purpose. Verify availability w/manufacturer.

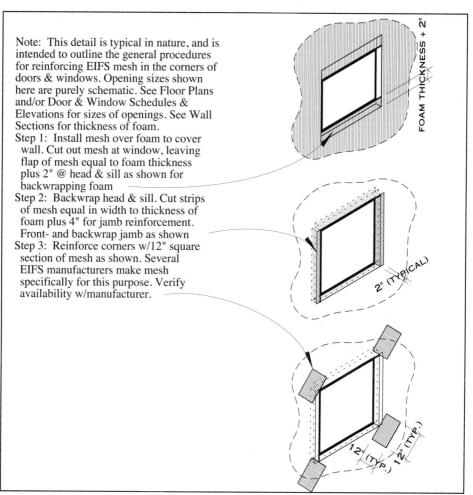

EIFS Mesh Corner Opening Reinforcing

DRAWING #

SCALE
NO SCALE

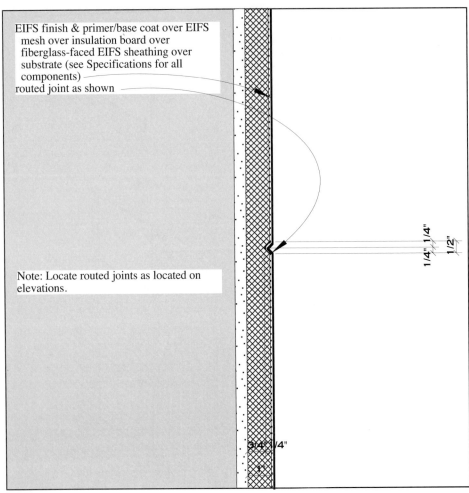

EIFS finish & primer/base coat over EIFS
mesh over insulation board over
fiberglass-faced EIFS sheathing over
substrate (see Specifications for all
components)
routed joint as shown

Note: Locate routed joints as located on
elevations.

1/4" 1/4"

1/2"

3/4" 1/4"

1"

Routed 1" EIFS Joint Detail

DRAWING #

SCALE
$\dfrac{3"}{1'\text{-}0"}$

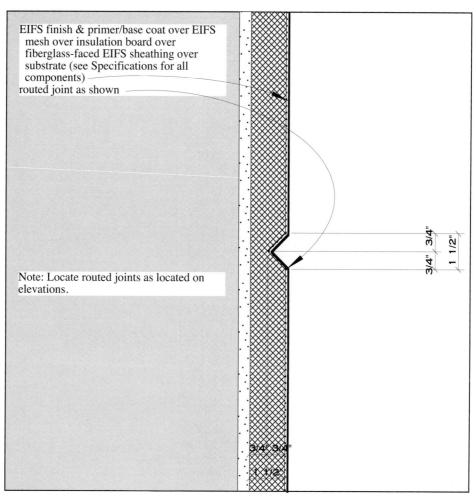

EIFS finish & primer/base coat over EIFS
mesh over insulation board over
fiberglass-faced EIFS sheathing over
substrate (see Specifications for all
components)
routed joint as shown

Note: Locate routed joints as located on
elevations.

3/4" 3/4"

1 1/2"

Routed 1 1/2" EIFS Joint Detail

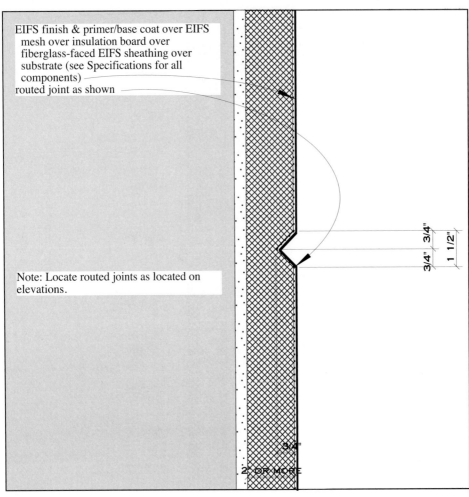

EIFS finish & primer/base coat over EIFS
mesh over insulation board over
fiberglass-faced EIFS sheathing over
substrate (see Specifications for all
components)
routed joint as shown

3/4" 3/4"

3/4"

1 1/2"

Note: Locate routed joints as located on
elevations.

3/4"

2" OR MORE

DRAWING #

Routed 2"+ EIFS Joint Detail

SCALE

3"
———
1'-0"

EE013
460

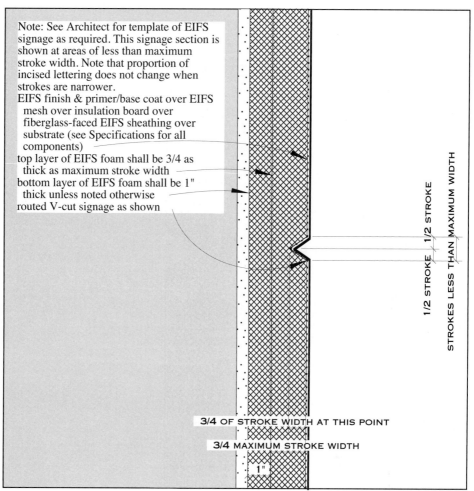

Note: See Architect for template of EIFS signage as required. This signage section is shown at areas of less than maximum stroke width. Note that proportion of incised lettering does not change when strokes are narrower.

EIFS finish & primer/base coat over EIFS mesh over insulation board over fiberglass-faced EIFS sheathing over substrate (see Specifications for all components)

top layer of EIFS foam shall be 3/4 as thick as maximum stroke width

bottom layer of EIFS foam shall be 1" thick unless noted otherwise

routed V-cut signage as shown

1/2 STROKE 1/2 STROKE

STROKES LESS THAN MAXIMUM WIDTH

3/4 OF STROKE WIDTH AT THIS POINT

3/4 MAXIMUM STROKE WIDTH

1"

DRAWING #

Routed EIFS V-Cut Signage Detail

SCALE

3"
1'-0"

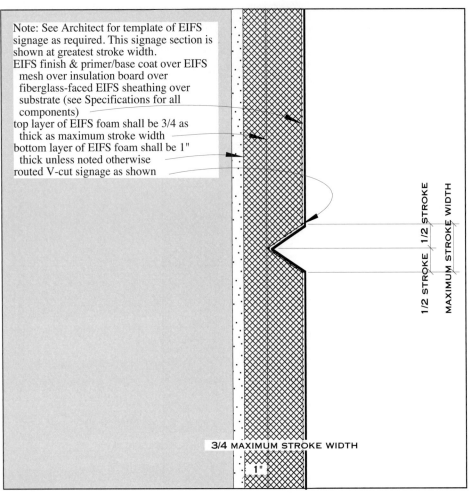

Note: See Architect for template of EIFS signage as required. This signage section is shown at greatest stroke width.

EIFS finish & primer/base coat over EIFS mesh over insulation board over fiberglass-faced EIFS sheathing over substrate (see Specifications for all components)

top layer of EIFS foam shall be 3/4 as thick as maximum stroke width

bottom layer of EIFS foam shall be 1" thick unless noted otherwise

routed V-cut signage as shown

1/2 STROKE | 1/2 STROKE

MAXIMUM STROKE WIDTH

3/4 MAXIMUM STROKE WIDTH

1"

DRAWING #

Routed EIFS V-Cut Signage Detail

SCALE
3"
1'-0"

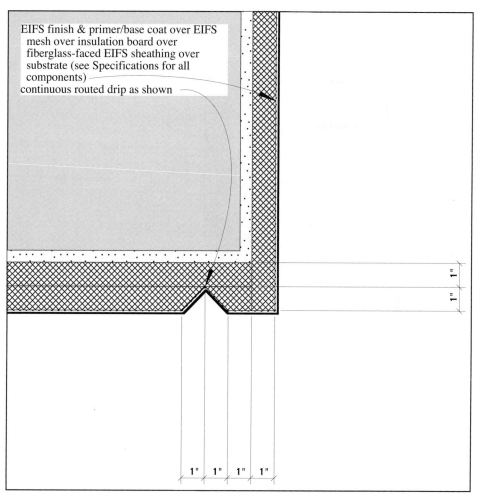

EIFS finish & primer/base coat over EIFS
mesh over insulation board over
fiberglass-faced EIFS sheathing over
substrate (see Specifications for all
components)

continuous routed drip as shown

1"

1"

1"

1"   1"   1"   1"

DRAWING #

EIFS Soffit Detail

SCALE
3"
1'-0"

EIFS finish & primer/base coat over EIFS mesh over insulation board over fiberglass-faced EIFS sheathing over substrate (see Specifications for all components)
continuous square-edged drip as shown

1/2" 1"

1"

DRAWING #

EIFS Square-Edge Soffit Detail

SCALE
3"
1'-0"

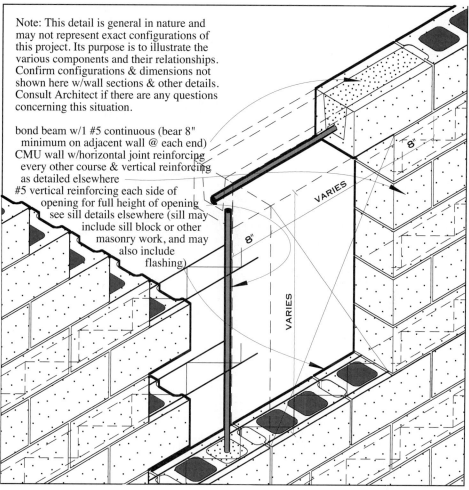

Note: This detail is general in nature and may not represent exact configurations of this project. Its purpose is to illustrate the various components and their relationships. Confirm configurations & dimensions not shown here w/wall sections & other details. Consult Architect if there are any questions concerning this situation.

bond beam w/1 #5 continuous (bear 8" minimum on adjacent wall @ each end)
CMU wall w/horizontal joint reinforcing every other course & vertical reinforcing as detailed elsewhere
#5 vertical reinforcing each side of opening for full height of opening see sill details elsewhere (sill may include sill block or other masonry work, and may also include flashing)

VARIES

8"

8"

VARIES

CMU Opening Reinforcing Detail

SCALE
3/4"
1'-O"

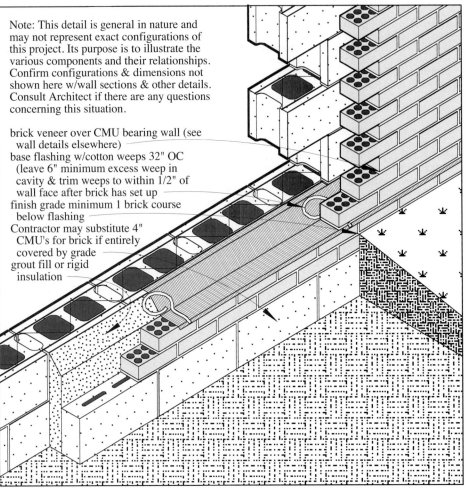

Note: This detail is general in nature and may not represent exact configurations of this project. Its purpose is to illustrate the various components and their relationships. Confirm configurations & dimensions not shown here w/wall sections & other details. Consult Architect if there are any questions concerning this situation.

brick veneer over CMU bearing wall (see wall details elsewhere)

base flashing w/cotton weeps 32" OC (leave 6" minimum excess weep in cavity & trim weeps to within 1/2" of wall face after brick has set up

finish grade minimum 1 brick course below flashing

Contractor may substitute 4" CMU's for brick if entirely covered by grade

grout fill or rigid insulation

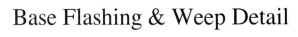

DRAWING #		

Base Flashing & Weep Detail

SCALE
3/4"
1'-0"

EM002
466

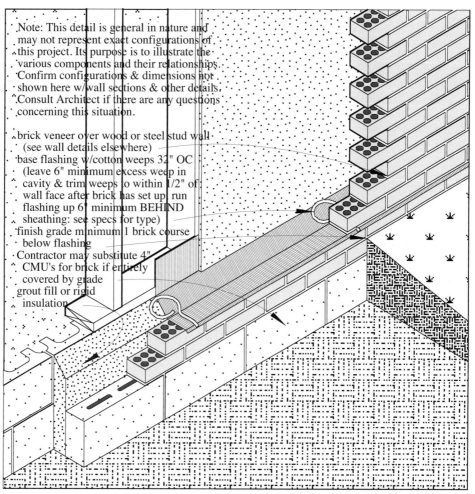

Note: This detail is general in nature and
may not represent exact configurations of
this project. Its purpose is to illustrate the
various components and their relationships.
Confirm configurations & dimensions not
shown here w/wall sections & other details.
Consult Architect if there are any questions
concerning this situation.

brick veneer over wood or steel stud wall
(see wall details elsewhere)
base flashing w/cotton weeps 32" OC
(leave 6" minimum excess weep in
cavity & trim weeps to within 1/2" of
wall face after brick has set up; run
flashing up 6" minimum BEHIND
sheathing: see specs for type)
finish grade minimum 1 brick course
below flashing
Contractor may substitute 4"
CMU's for brick if entirely
covered by grade
grout fill or rigid
insulation

DRAWING #	Base Flashing & Weep Detail	SCALE 3/4" / 1'-0"

EM003
467

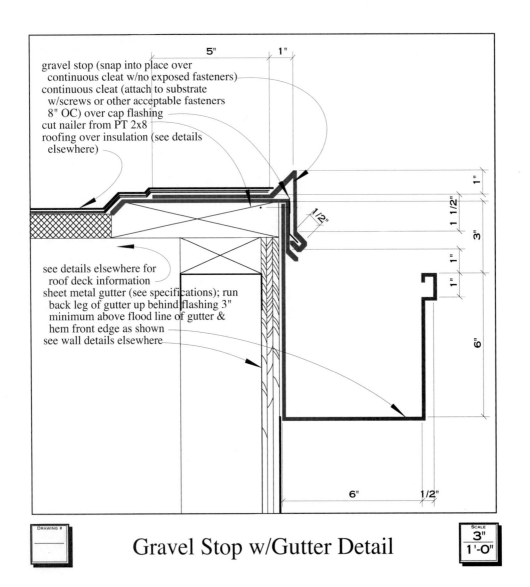

gravel stop (snap into place over
  continuous cleat w/no exposed fasteners)
continuous cleat (attach to substrate
  w/screws or other acceptable fasteners
  8" OC) over cap flashing
cut nailer from PT 2x8
roofing over insulation (see details
  elsewhere)

see details elsewhere for
  roof deck information
sheet metal gutter (see specifications); run
  back leg of gutter up behind flashing 3"
  minimum above flood line of gutter &
  hem front edge as shown
see wall details elsewhere

5"   1"

1"
1 1/2"
3"
1"
1"
6"

1/2"

6"   1/2"

| DRAWING # | | SCALE |
| --- | | --- |

Gravel Stop w/Gutter Detail

SCALE
3"
1'-0"

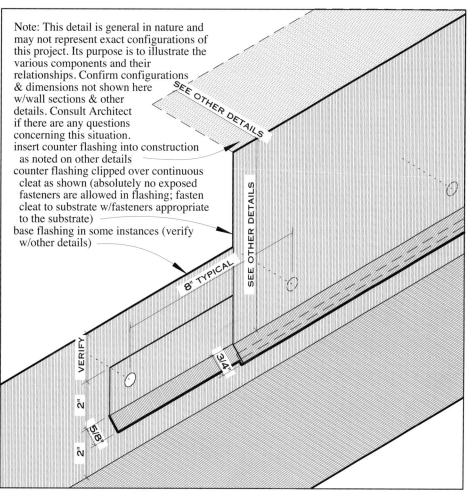

Note: This detail is general in nature and may not represent exact configurations of this project. Its purpose is to illustrate the various components and their relationships. Confirm configurations & dimensions not shown here w/wall sections & other details. Consult Architect if there are any questions concerning this situation.

insert counter flashing into construction as noted on other details

counter flashing clipped over continuous cleat as shown (absolutely no exposed fasteners are allowed in flashing; fasten cleat to substrate w/fasteners appropriate to the substrate)

base flashing in some instances (verify w/other details)

SEE OTHER DETAILS

SEE OTHER DETAILS

8" TYPICAL

VERIFY

2"

5/8"

2"

3/4"

Flashing & Concealed Cleat Attachment

DRAWING #

SCALE
3"
1'-0"

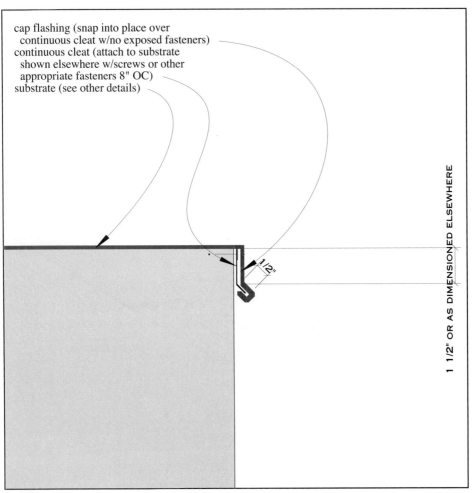

cap flashing (snap into place over
 continuous cleat w/no exposed fasteners)
continuous cleat (attach to substrate
 shown elsewhere w/screws or other
 appropriate fasteners 8" OC)
substrate (see other details)

1/2"

1 1/2" OR AS DIMENSIONED ELSEWHERE

DRAWING #

Concealed Cleat Detail

SCALE
3"
1'-0"

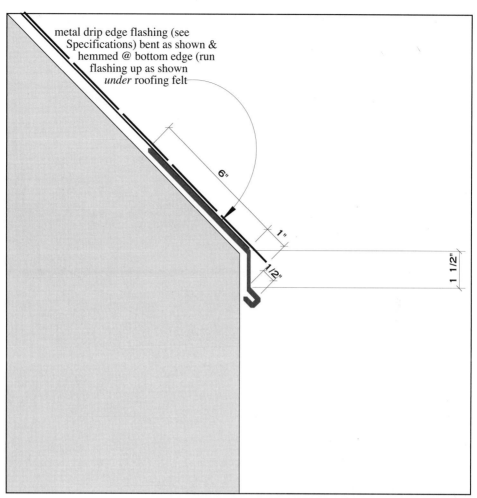

metal drip edge flashing (see
Specifications) bent as shown &
hemmed @ bottom edge (run
flashing up as shown
under roofing felt

6"

1"

1/2"

1 1/2"

Drip Edge Flashing Detail

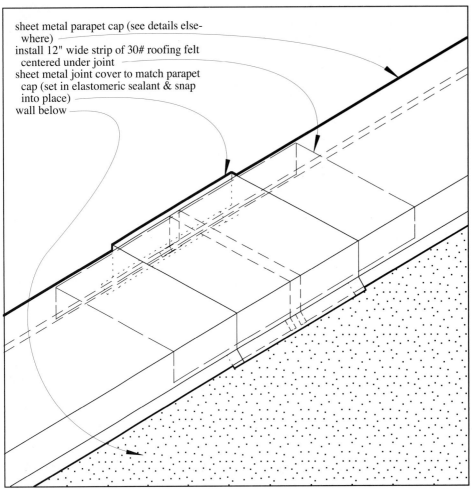

sheet metal parapet cap (see details elsewhere)

install 12" wide strip of 30# roofing felt
centered under joint

sheet metal joint cover to match parapet
cap (set in elastomeric sealant & snap
into place)

wall below

Parapet Cap Joint

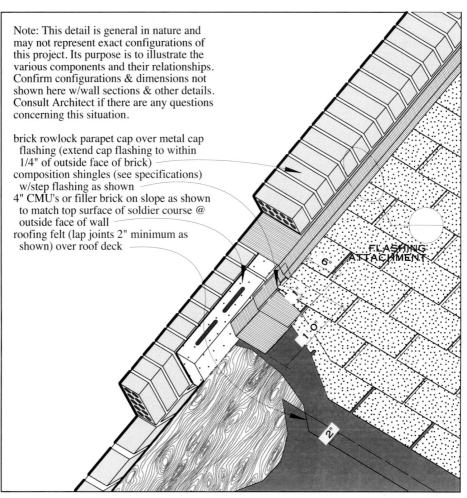

Note: This detail is general in nature and may not represent exact configurations of this project. Its purpose is to illustrate the various components and their relationships. Confirm configurations & dimensions not shown here w/wall sections & other details. Consult Architect if there are any questions concerning this situation.

brick rowlock parapet cap over metal cap flashing (extend cap flashing to within 1/4" of outside face of brick)
composition shingles (see specifications) w/step flashing as shown
4" CMU's or filler brick on slope as shown to match top surface of soldier course @ outside face of wall
roofing felt (lap joints 2" minimum as shown) over roof deck

FLASHING ATTACHMENT

6"

DRAWING #

Parapet Flashing Detail

SCALE
3/4"
1'-O"

ERF007
473

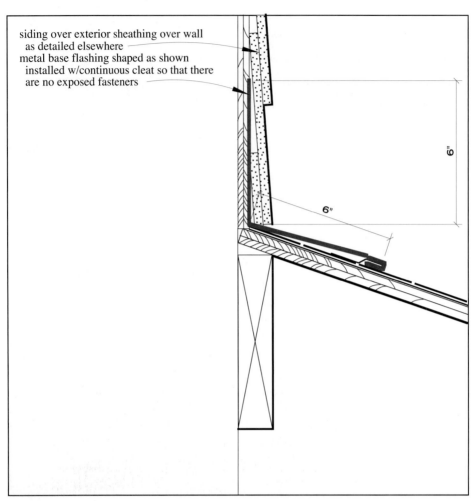

siding over exterior sheathing over wall
  as detailed elsewhere
metal base flashing shaped as shown
  installed w/continuous cleat so that there
  are no exposed fasteners

6"

6"

Roof to Wall Flashing Detail

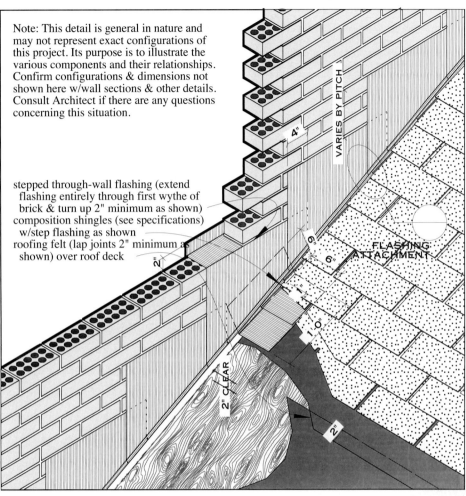

Note: This detail is general in nature and may not represent exact configurations of this project. Its purpose is to illustrate the various components and their relationships. Confirm configurations & dimensions not shown here w/wall sections & other details. Consult Architect if there are any questions concerning this situation.

stepped through-wall flashing (extend flashing entirely through first wythe of brick & turn up 2" minimum as shown)
composition shingles (see specifications) w/step flashing as shown
roofing felt (lap joints 2" minimum as shown) over roof deck

VARIES BY PITCH

4"

2"

FLASHING ATTACHMENT

6"

6"

1'-0"

2" CLEAR

2"

DRAWING #	Roof to Wall Flashing Detail	SCALE $\frac{3/4"}{1'-0"}$

ERF009
475

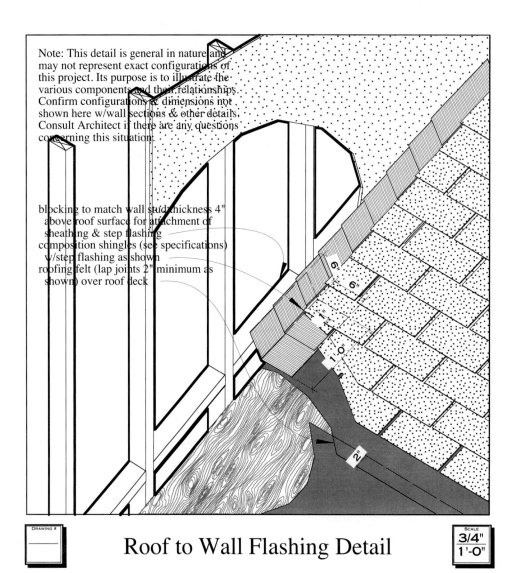

Note: This detail is general in nature and may not represent exact configurations of this project. Its purpose is to illustrate the various components and their relationships. Confirm configurations & dimensions not shown here w/wall sections & other details. Consult Architect if there are any questions concerning this situation.

blocking to match wall stud thickness 4" above roof surface for attachment of sheathing & step flashing
composition shingles (see specifications) w/step flashing as shown
roofing felt (lap joints 2" minimum as shown) over roof deck

6"

6"

1"

1'-0"

2"

DRAWING #

Roof to Wall Flashing Detail

SCALE
3/4"
1'-0"

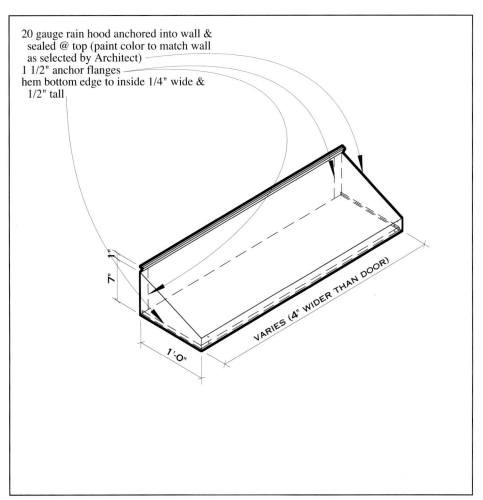

20 gauge rain hood anchored into wall &
   sealed @ top (paint color to match wall
   as selected by Architect)
1 1/2" anchor flanges
hem bottom edge to inside 1/4" wide &
   1/2" tall

7"

1"

1'-0"

VARIES (4" WIDER THAN DOOR)

DRAWING #

Rain Hood Detail

SCALE
3/4"
1'-0"

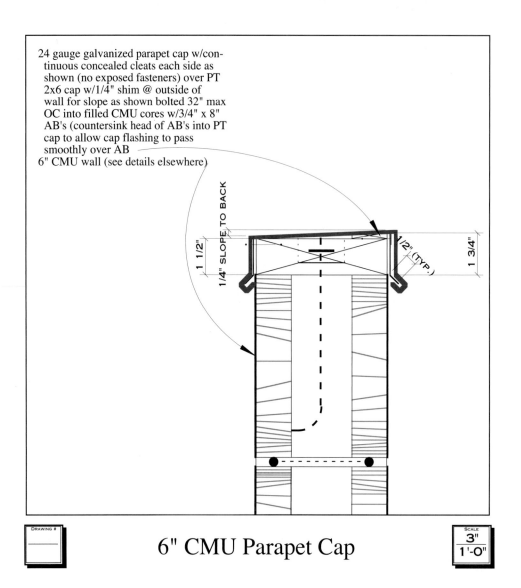

24 gauge galvanized parapet cap w/continuous concealed cleats each side as shown (no exposed fasteners) over PT 2x6 cap w/1/4" shim @ outside of wall for slope as shown bolted 32" max OC into filled CMU cores w/3/4" x 8" AB's (countersink head of AB's into PT cap to allow cap flashing to pass smoothly over AB

6" CMU wall (see details elsewhere)

1 1/2"

1/4" SLOPE TO BACK

1/2" (TYP.)

1 3/4"

DRAWING #		SCALE
		3"
		1'-0"

6" CMU Parapet Cap

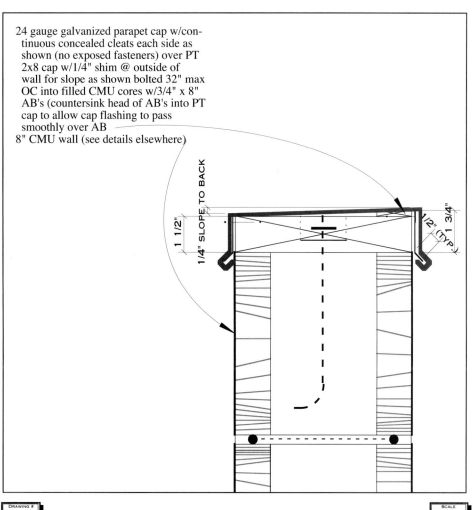

24 gauge galvanized parapet cap w/con-
tinuous concealed cleats each side as
shown (no exposed fasteners) over PT
2x8 cap w/1/4" shim @ outside of
wall for slope as shown bolted 32" max
OC into filled CMU cores w/3/4" x 8"
AB's (countersink head of AB's into PT
cap to allow cap flashing to pass
smoothly over AB

8" CMU wall (see details elsewhere)

SLOPE TO BACK

1 1/2"

1/4" SLOPE TO BACK

1/2" (TYP)

1 3/4"

8" CMU Parapet Cap

SCALE
3"
1'-0"

24 gauge galvanized parapet cap w/con-
  tinuous concealed cleats each side as
  shown (no exposed fasteners) over cap
  cut from PT 2x10 w/1/4" shim @ outside
  of wall for slope as shown screwed 32"
  max OC into top track of lightgauge
  metal parapet wall
bed flashing to 26 gauge backsheeting
  w/exterior sealant
backsheeting finish on exterior sheathing
  on metal stud wall (see details elsewhere)

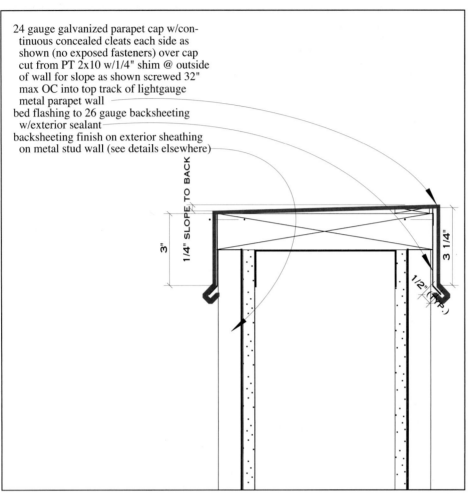

1/4" SLOPE TO BACK

3"

3 1/4"

1/2" (TYP.)

DRAWING #	Backsheet Parapet Cap	SCALE $\dfrac{3"}{1'-0"}$

ERP006
480

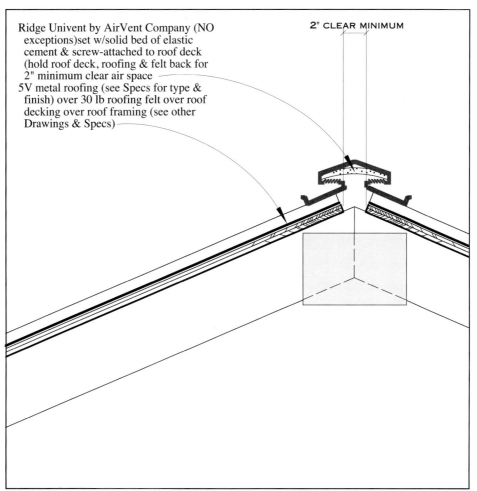

Ridge Univent by AirVent Company (NO
  exceptions)set w/solid bed of elastic
  cement & screw-attached to roof deck
  (hold roof deck, roofing & felt back for
  2" minimum clear air space
5V metal roofing (see Specs for type &
  finish) over 30 lb roofing felt over roof
  decking over roof framing (see other
  Drawings & Specs)

2" CLEAR MINIMUM

Ridge Vent Detail on 5V Roofing

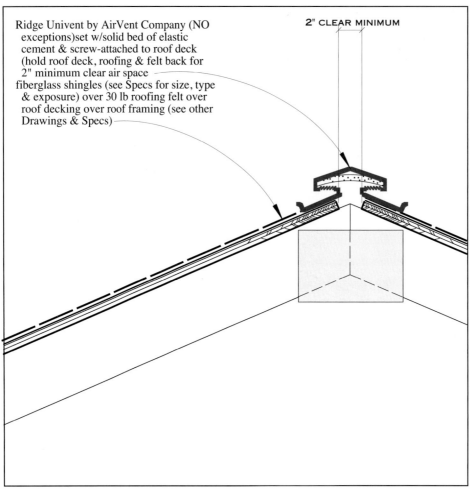

Ridge Univent by AirVent Company (NO
exceptions) set w/solid bed of elastic
cement & screw-attached to roof deck
(hold roof deck, roofing & felt back for
2" minimum clear air space

fiberglass shingles (see Specs for size, type
& exposure) over 30 lb roofing felt over
roof decking over roof framing (see other
Drawings & Specs)

2" CLEAR MINIMUM

DRAWING #

Ridge Vent Detail on Fiberglass Roofing

SCALE
1 1/2"
1'-0"

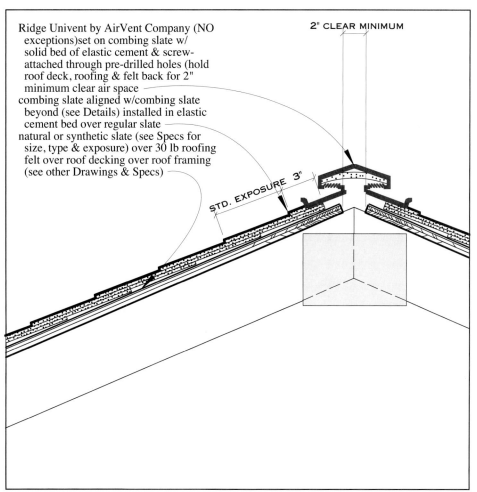

Ridge Univent by AirVent Company (NO
  exceptions)set on combing slate w/
  solid bed of elastic cement & screw-
  attached through pre-drilled holes (hold
  roof deck, roofing & felt back for 2"
  minimum clear air space
combing slate aligned w/combing slate
  beyond (see Details) installed in elastic
  cement bed over regular slate
natural or synthetic slate (see Specs for
  size, type & exposure) over 30 lb roofing
  felt over roof decking over roof framing
  (see other Drawings & Specs)

2" CLEAR MINIMUM

STD. EXPOSURE 3"

DRAWING #

Ridge Vent Detail on Slate Roofing

SCALE
1 1/2"
1'-0"

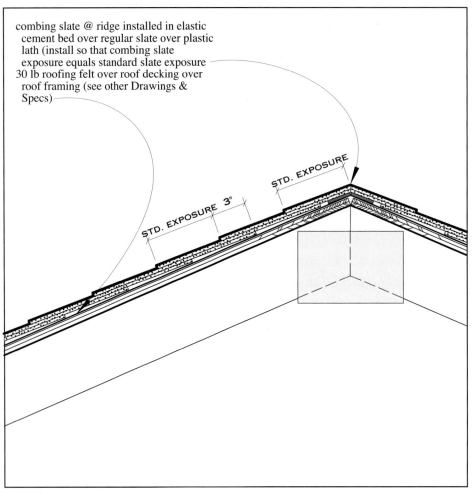

combing slate @ ridge installed in elastic
  cement bed over regular slate over plastic
  lath (install so that combing slate
  exposure equals standard slate exposure
30 lb roofing felt over roof decking over
  roof framing (see other Drawings &
  Specs)

STD. EXPOSURE

STD. EXPOSURE   3"

Slate Ridge Detail

DRAWING #

SCALE
1 1/2"
1'-0"

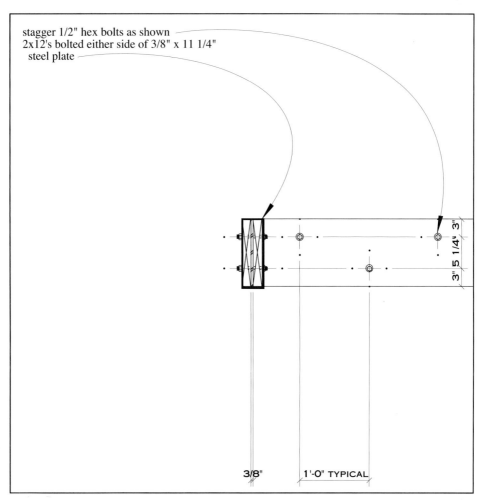

stagger 1/2" hex bolts as shown
2x12's bolted either side of 3/8" x 11 1/4"
  steel plate

3"

5 1/4"

3"

3/8"

1'-0" TYPICAL

3/8" Flitch Beam Section/Elevation

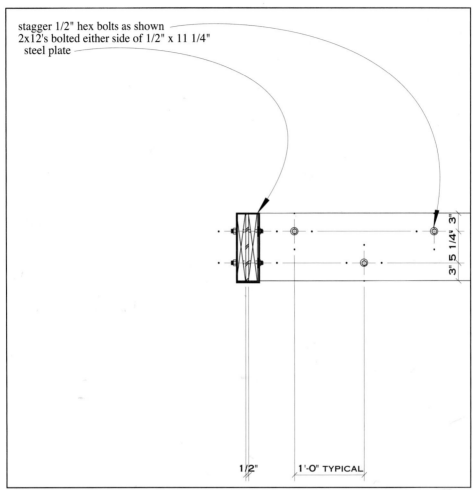

stagger 1/2" hex bolts as shown
2x12's bolted either side of 1/2" x 11 1/4"
  steel plate

3"
5 1/4"
3"

1/2"   1'-0" TYPICAL

1/2" Flitch Beam Section/Elevation

3/4"
1'-0"

ESBF002
486

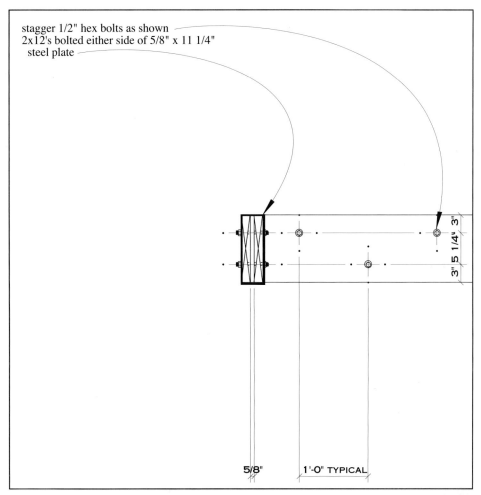

stagger 1/2" hex bolts as shown
2x12's bolted either side of 5/8" x 11 1/4"
  steel plate

3"
5 1/4"
3"

5/8"

1'-0" TYPICAL

5/8" Flitch Beam Section/Elevation

SCALE
3/4"
1'-0"

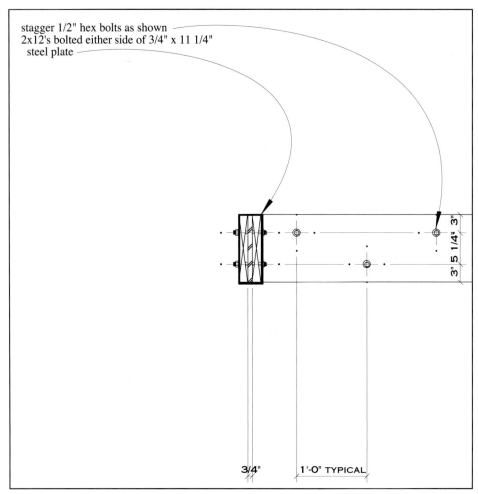

stagger 1/2" hex bolts as shown
2x12's bolted either side of 3/4" x 11 1/4"
  steel plate

3"
5 1/4"
3"

3/4"

1'-0" TYPICAL

3/4" Flitch Beam Section/Elevation

DRAWING #

SCALE
3/4"
1'-0"

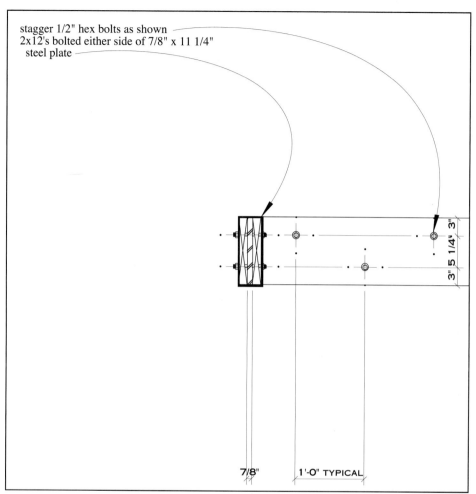

stagger 1/2" hex bolts as shown
2x12's bolted either side of 7/8" x 11 1/4"
  steel plate

3" 5 1/4" 3"

7/8"   1'-0" TYPICAL

DRAWING #

7/8" Flitch Beam Section/Elevation

SCALE
3/4"
1'-0"

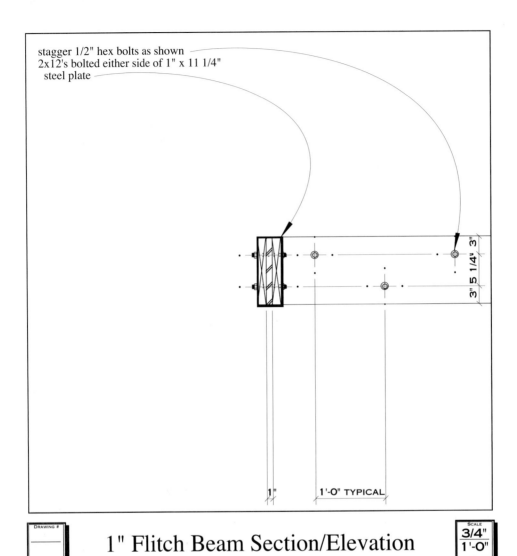

stagger 1/2" hex bolts as shown
2x12's bolted either side of 1" x 11 1/4"
  steel plate

1"

1'-0" TYPICAL

3" 5 1/4" 3"

3"

1" Flitch Beam Section/Elevation

DRAWING #

SCALE
3/4"
1'-0"

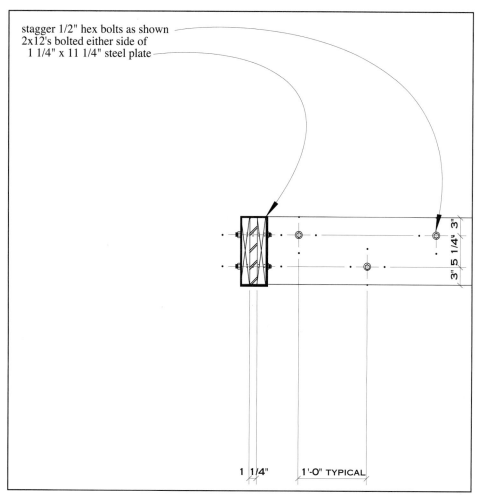

stagger 1/2" hex bolts as shown
2x12's bolted either side of
1 1/4" x 11 1/4" steel plate

1 1/4"   1'-0" TYPICAL

1 1/4" Flitch Beam Section/Elevation

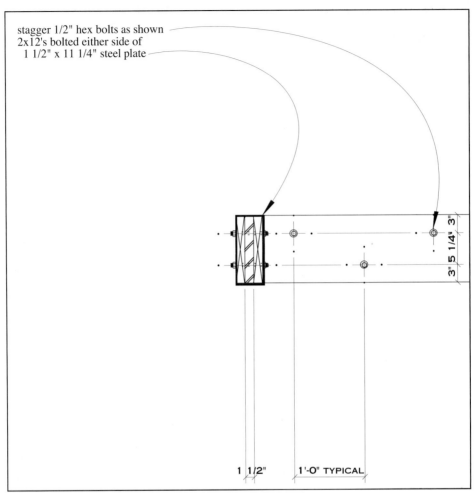

stagger 1/2" hex bolts as shown
2x12's bolted either side of
 1 1/2" x 11 1/4" steel plate

3"

5 1/4"

3"

1 1/2"

1'-0" TYPICAL

1 1/2" Flitch Beam Section/Elevation

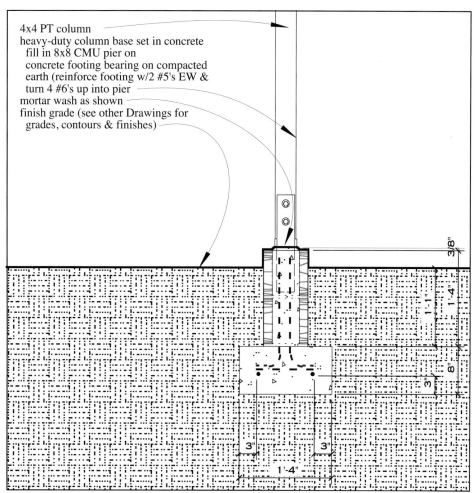

4x4 PT column
heavy-duty column base set in concrete
  fill in 8x8 CMU pier on
  concrete footing bearing on compacted
  earth (reinforce footing w/2 #5's EW &
  turn 4 #6's up into pier
mortar wash as shown
finish grade (see other Drawings for
  grades, contours & finishes)

3/8"
1-1
1'-4"
8"
3"
3"
3"
1'-4"

4x4 Column Base Detail

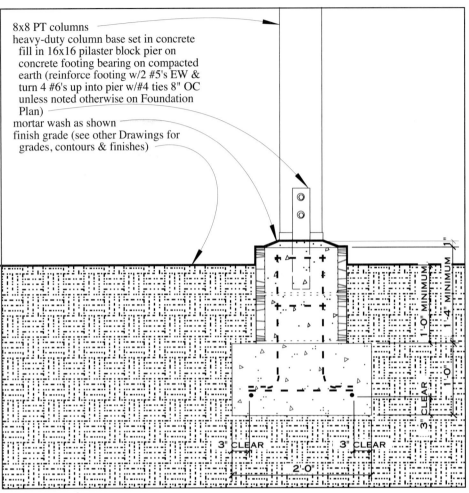

8x8 PT columns

heavy-duty column base set in concrete
fill in 16x16 pilaster block pier on
concrete footing bearing on compacted
earth (reinforce footing w/2 #5's EW &
turn 4 #6's up into pier w/#4 ties 8" OC
unless noted otherwise on Foundation
Plan)

mortar wash as shown

finish grade (see other Drawings for
grades, contours & finishes)

1'-0" MINIMUM

1'-4" MINIMUM

1"

3" CLEAR

1'-0"

3" CLEAR   3" CLEAR

2'-0"

DRAWING #

8x8 Column Base Detail

SCALE
3/4"
1'-0"

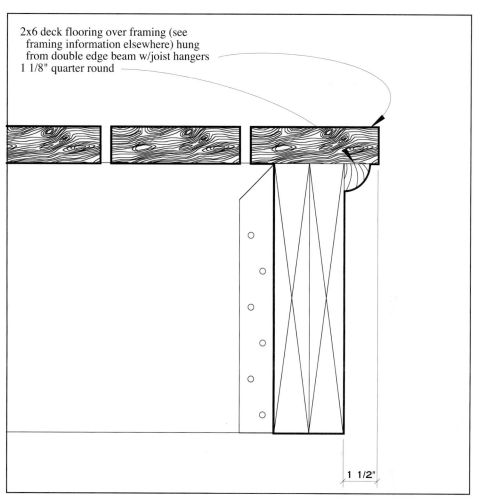

2x6 deck flooring over framing (see
  framing information elsewhere) hung
  from double edge beam w/joist hangers
1 1/8" quarter round

1 1/2"

Deck Edge Detail

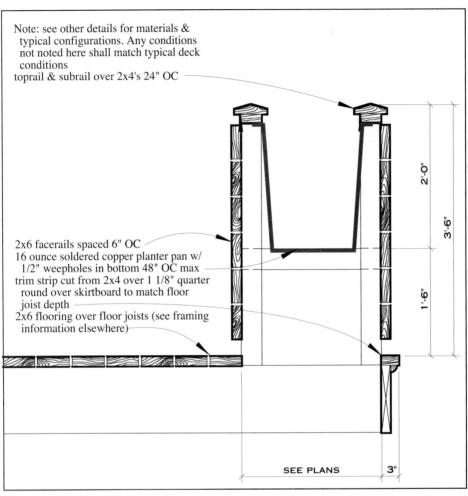

Note: see other details for materials &
  typical configurations. Any conditions
  not noted here shall match typical deck
  conditions
toprail & subrail over 2x4's 24" OC

2x6 facerails spaced 6" OC
16 ounce soldered copper planter pan w/
  1/2" weepholes in bottom 48" OC max
trim strip cut from 2x4 over 1 1/8" quarter
  round over skirtboard to match floor
  joist depth
2x6 flooring over floor joists (see framing
  information elsewhere)

2'-0"

3'-6"

1'-6"

SEE PLANS

3"

DRAWING #		SCALE

Deck Planter Detail

3/4"
1'-0"

ESD004
496

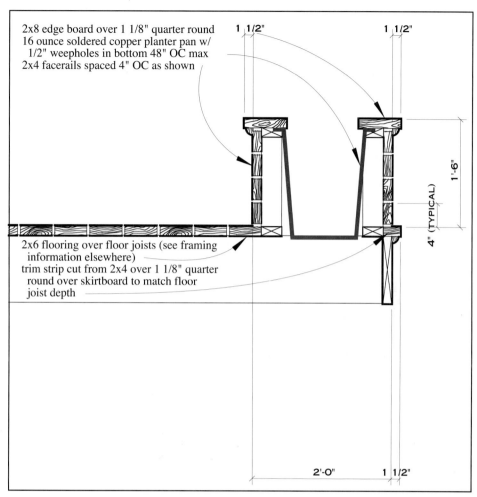

2x8 edge board over 1 1/8" quarter round
16 ounce soldered copper planter pan w/
1/2" weepholes in bottom 48" OC max
2x4 facerails spaced 4" OC as shown

1 1/2"   1 1/2"

1'-6"

4" (TYPICAL)

2x6 flooring over floor joists (see framing
information elsewhere)
trim strip cut from 2x4 over 1 1/8" quarter
round over skirtboard to match floor
joist depth

2'-0"   1 1/2"

DRAWING #

Deck Planter Detail

SCALE
3/4"
1'-0"

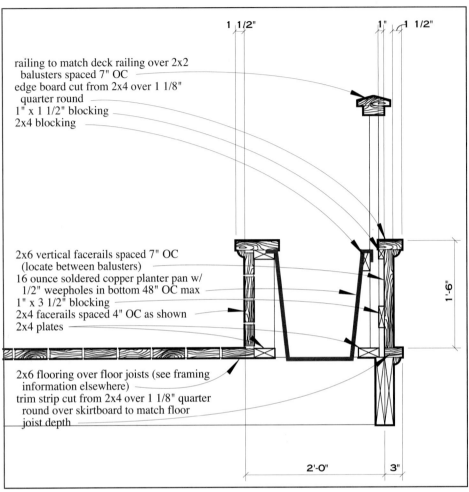

1 1/2"

1" 1 1/2"

railing to match deck railing over 2x2
  balusters spaced 7" OC
edge board cut from 2x4 over 1 1/8"
  quarter round
1" x 1 1/2" blocking
2x4 blocking

2x6 vertical facerails spaced 7" OC
  (locate between balusters)
16 ounce soldered copper planter pan w/
  1/2" weepholes in bottom 48" OC max
1" x 3 1/2" blocking
2x4 facerails spaced 4" OC as shown
2x4 plates

2x6 flooring over floor joists (see framing
  information elsewhere)
trim strip cut from 2x4 over 1 1/8" quarter
  round over skirtboard to match floor
  joist depth

1'-6"

2'-0"

3"

DRAWING #

Deck Planter Detail

SCALE
3/4"
1'-0"

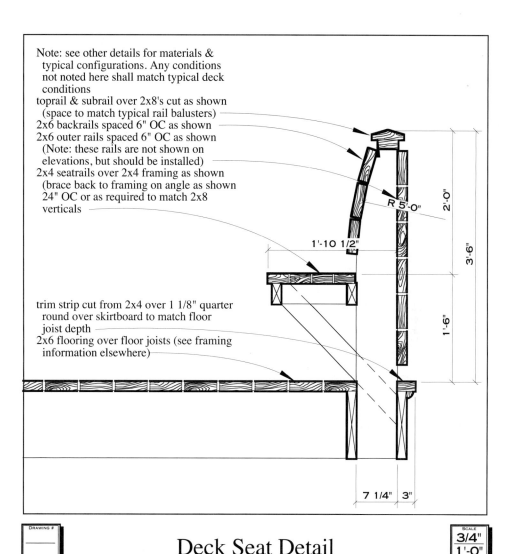

Note: see other details for materials &
  typical configurations. Any conditions
  not noted here shall match typical deck
  conditions
toprail & subrail over 2x8's cut as shown
  (space to match typical rail balusters)
2x6 backrails spaced 6" OC as shown
2x6 outer rails spaced 6" OC as shown
  (Note: these rails are not shown on
  elevations, but should be installed)
2x4 seatrails over 2x4 framing as shown
  (brace back to framing on angle as shown
  24" OC or as required to match 2x8
  verticals

trim strip cut from 2x4 over 1 1/8" quarter
  round over skirtboard to match floor
  joist depth
2x6 flooring over floor joists (see framing
  information elsewhere)

R 5'-0"

2'-0"

3'-6"

1'-10 1/2"

1'-6"

7 1/4"   3"

DRAWING #

SCALE
3/4"
1'-0"

Deck Seat Detail

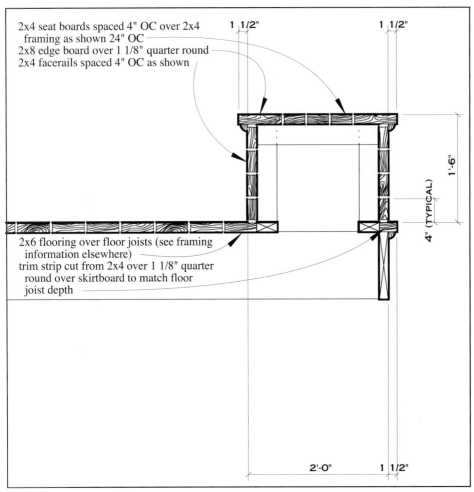

2x4 seat boards spaced 4" OC over 2x4
  framing as shown 24" OC
2x8 edge board over 1 1/8" quarter round
2x4 facerails spaced 4" OC as shown

1 1/2"

1 1/2"

1'-6"

4" (TYPICAL)

2x6 flooring over floor joists (see framing
  information elsewhere)
trim strip cut from 2x4 over 1 1/8" quarter
  round over skirtboard to match floor
  joist depth

2'-0"

1 1/2"

DRAWING #

Deck Seat Detail

SCALE
3/4"
1'-0"

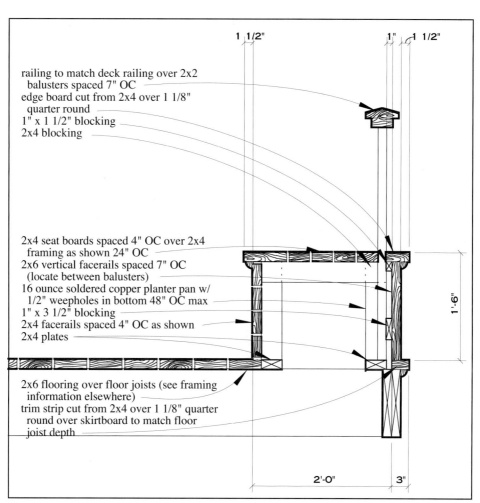

railing to match deck railing over 2x2
  balusters spaced 7" OC
edge board cut from 2x4 over 1 1/8"
  quarter round
1" x 1 1/2" blocking
2x4 blocking

2x4 seat boards spaced 4" OC over 2x4
  framing as shown 24" OC
2x6 vertical facerails spaced 7" OC
  (locate between balusters)
16 ounce soldered copper planter pan w/
  1/2" weepholes in bottom 48" OC max
1" x 3 1/2" blocking
2x4 facerails spaced 4" OC as shown
2x4 plates

2x6 flooring over floor joists (see framing
  information elsewhere)
trim strip cut from 2x4 over 1 1/8" quarter
  round over skirtboard to match floor
  joist depth

1 1/2"   1"   1 1/2"

1'-6"

2'-0"   3"

DRAWING #

Deck Planter Detail

SCALE
3/4"
1'-0"

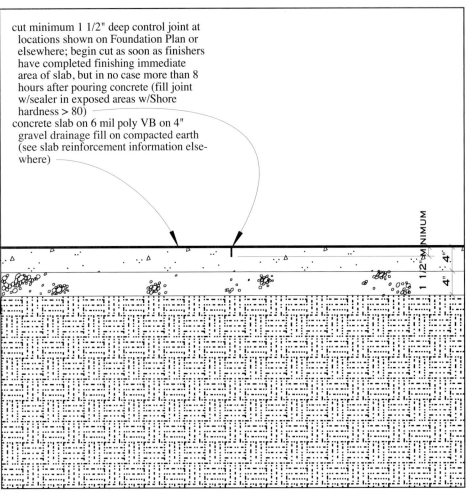

cut minimum 1 1/2" deep control joint at locations shown on Foundation Plan or elsewhere; begin cut as soon as finishers have completed finishing immediate area of slab, but in no case more than 8 hours after pouring concrete (fill joint w/sealer in exposed areas w/Shore hardness > 80)

concrete slab on 6 mil poly VB on 4" gravel drainage fill on compacted earth (see slab reinforcement information else-where)

1 1/2" MINIMUM

4"

4"

DRAWING #

Control Joint Detail

SCALE

3/4"
1'-0"

ESFCJ001
502

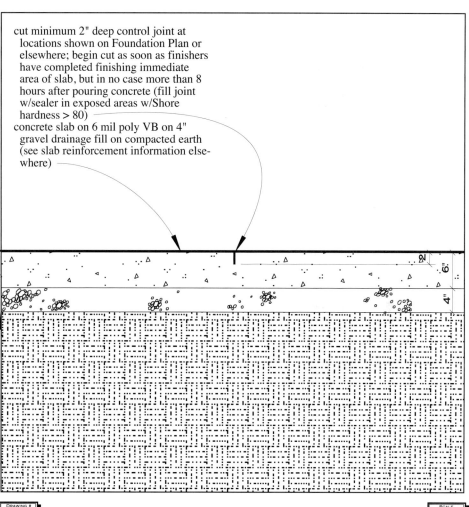

cut minimum 2" deep control joint at
    locations shown on Foundation Plan or
    elsewhere; begin cut as soon as finishers
    have completed finishing immediate
    area of slab, but in no case more than 8
    hours after pouring concrete (fill joint
    w/sealer in exposed areas w/Shore
    hardness > 80)
concrete slab on 6 mil poly VB on 4"
    gravel drainage fill on compacted earth
    (see slab reinforcement information else-
    where)

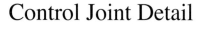

DRAWING #

Control Joint Detail

SCALE
3/4"
1'-0"

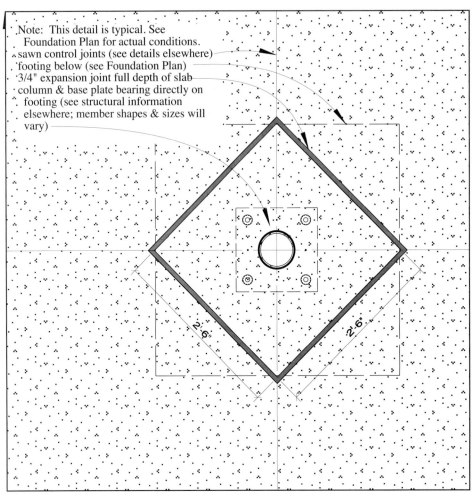

Note: This detail is typical. See
Foundation Plan for actual conditions.
sawn control joints (see details elsewhere)
footing below (see Foundation Plan)
3/4" expansion joint full depth of slab
column & base plate bearing directly on
footing (see structural information
elsewhere; member shapes & sizes will
vary)

2'-6"

2'-6"

Slab Detail @ Column

DRAWING #

SCALE
3/4"
1'-0"

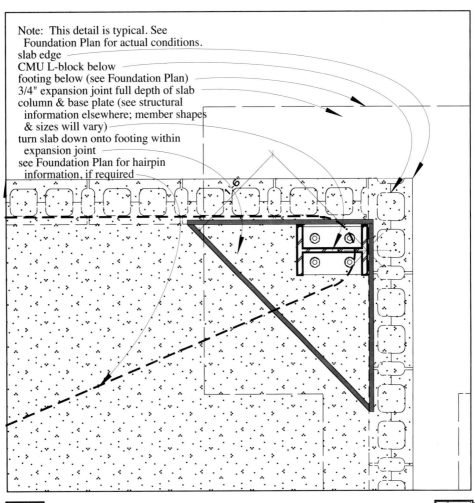

Note: This detail is typical. See
  Foundation Plan for actual conditions.
slab edge
CMU L-block below
footing below (see Foundation Plan)
3/4" expansion joint full depth of slab
column & base plate (see structural
  information elsewhere; member shapes
  & sizes will vary)
turn slab down onto footing within
  expansion joint
see Foundation Plan for hairpin
  information, if required

1'-6"

Slab Corner @ Metal Bldg. Column

DRAWING #

SCALE
3/4"
1'-0"

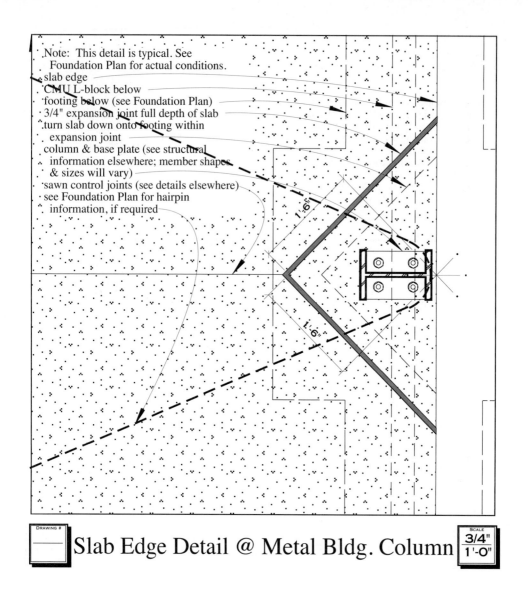

Note: This detail is typical. See
  Foundation Plan for actual conditions.
slab edge
CMU L-block below
footing below (see Foundation Plan)
3/4" expansion joint full depth of slab
turn slab down onto footing within
  expansion joint
column & base plate (see structural
  information elsewhere; member shapes
  & sizes will vary)
sawn control joints (see details elsewhere)
see Foundation Plan for hairpin
  information, if required

1'-6"

1'-6"

DRAWING #

Slab Edge Detail @ Metal Bldg. Column

SCALE
3/4"
1'-0"

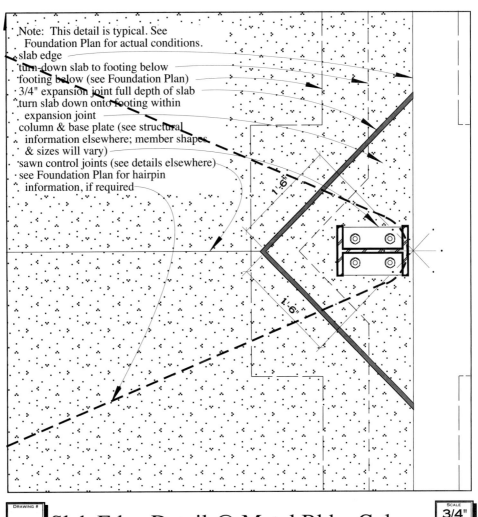

Note: This detail is typical. See
    Foundation Plan for actual conditions.
slab edge
turn-down slab to footing below
footing below (see Foundation Plan)
3/4" expansion joint full depth of slab
turn slab down onto footing within
    expansion joint
column & base plate (see structural
    information elsewhere; member shapes
    & sizes will vary)
sawn control joints (see details elsewhere)
see Foundation Plan for hairpin
    information, if required

1'-6"

1'-6"

| DRAWING # | Slab Edge Detail @ Metal Bldg. Column | SCALE 3/4" 1'-0" |

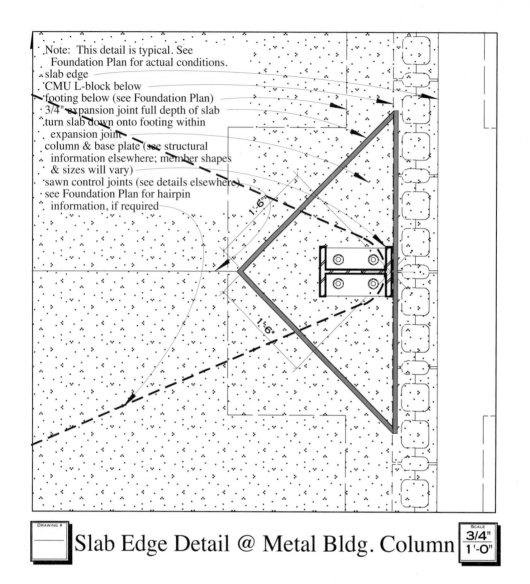

Note: This detail is typical. See
  Foundation Plan for actual conditions.
slab edge
CMU L-block below
footing below (see Foundation Plan)
3/4" expansion joint full depth of slab
turn slab down onto footing within
  expansion joint
column & base plate (see structural
  information elsewhere; member shapes
  & sizes will vary)
sawn control joints (see details elsewhere)
see Foundation Plan for hairpin
  information, if required

1'-6"

1'-6"

Slab Edge Detail @ Metal Bldg. Column

DRAWING #

SCALE
3/4"
1'-0"

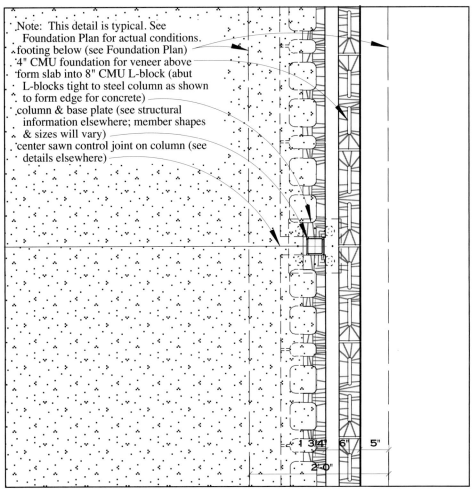

Note: This detail is typical. See
  Foundation Plan for actual conditions.
footing below (see Foundation Plan)
4" CMU foundation for veneer above
form slab into 8" CMU L-block (abut
  L-blocks tight to steel column as shown
  to form edge for concrete)
column & base plate (see structural
  information elsewhere; member shapes
  & sizes will vary)
center sawn control joint on column (see
  details elsewhere)

3/4" 6" 5"

2'-0"

DRAWING #		SCALE
	Slab Detail @ Column	3/4" / 1'-0"

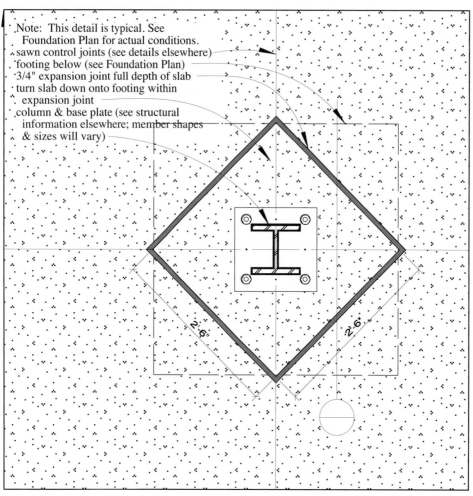

Note: This detail is typical. See
 Foundation Plan for actual conditions.
sawn control joints (see details elsewhere)
footing below (see Foundation Plan)
3/4" expansion joint full depth of slab
turn slab down onto footing within
 expansion joint
column & base plate (see structural
 information elsewhere; member shapes
 & sizes will vary)

2'-6"   2'-6"

DRAWING #

SCALE
3/4"
1'-0"

Slab Detail @ Column

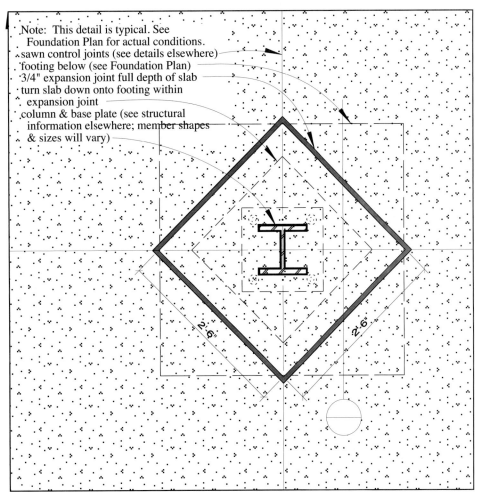

Note: This detail is typical. See
   Foundation Plan for actual conditions.
sawn control joints (see details elsewhere)
footing below (see Foundation Plan)
3/4" expansion joint full depth of slab
turn slab down onto footing within
   expansion joint
column & base plate (see structural
   information elsewhere; member shapes
   & sizes will vary)

2'-6"

2'-6"

Slab Detail @ Column

DRAWING #

SCALE
3/4"
1'-0"

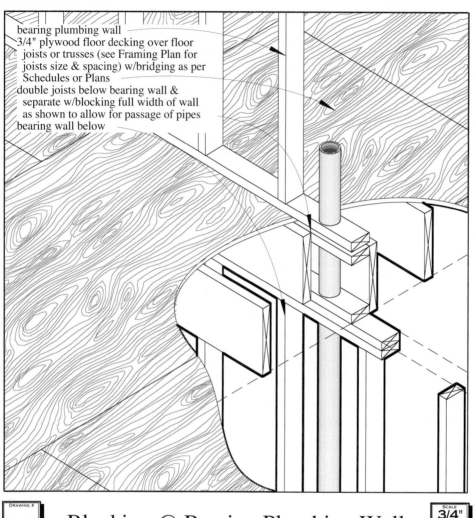

bearing plumbing wall
3/4" plywood floor decking over floor
joists or trusses (see Framing Plan for
joists size & spacing) w/bridging as per
Schedules or Plans
double joists below bearing wall &
separate w/blocking full width of wall
as shown to allow for passage of pipes
bearing wall below

Blocking @ Bearing Plumbing Wall

DRAWING #

SCALE
3/4"
1'-0"

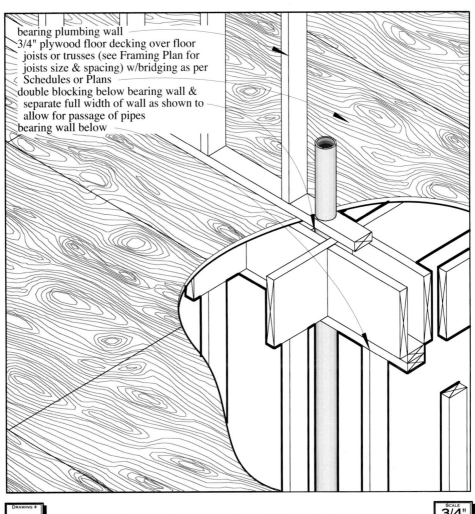

bearing plumbing wall
3/4" plywood floor decking over floor
joists or trusses (see Framing Plan for
joists size & spacing) w/bridging as per
Schedules or Plans
double blocking below bearing wall &
separate full width of wall as shown to
allow for passage of pipes
bearing wall below

Blocking @ Bearing Plumbing Wall

DRAWING #

SCALE
$\frac{3/4"}{1'-0"}$

bearing wall
3/4" plywood floor decking over floor
joists or trusses (see Framing Plan for
joists size & spacing) w/bridging as per
Schedules or Plans
girder below bearing wall (see Floor
Framing Plan for type & size)

DRAWING #

Floor Joists @ Bearing Wall

SCALE
3/4"
1'-0"

bearing wall
3/4" plywood floor decking over floor
joists or trusses (see Framing Plan for
joists size & spacing) w/bridging as per
Schedules or Plans
double joists below bearing wall &
separate to catch ceiling board below
bearing wall below

3/4"
3/4"

DRAWING #

Blocking @ Bearing Wall

SCALE
3/4"
1'-0"

ESFWI004
515

bearing wall
3/4" plywood floor decking over floor
 joists or trusses (see Framing Plan for
 joists size & spacing) w/bridging as per
 Schedules or Plans
double blocking below bearing wall &
 separate to catch ceiling board below
bearing wall below

3/4" 3/4"

Blocking @ Bearing Wall

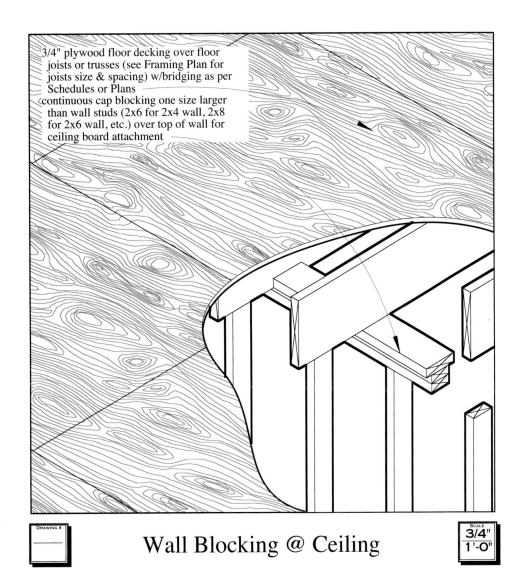

3/4" plywood floor decking over floor joists or trusses (see Framing Plan for joists size & spacing) w/bridging as per Schedules or Plans

continuous cap blocking one size larger than wall studs (2x6 for 2x4 wall, 2x8 for 2x6 wall, etc.) over top of wall for ceiling board attachment

Wall Blocking @ Ceiling

SCALE
3/4"
1'-0"

non-bearing wall
3/4" plywood floor decking over floor
joists or trusses (see Framing Plan for
joists size & spacing) w/bridging as per
Schedules or Plans
double joists below non-bearing wall

Floor Joists @ Non-Bearing Wall

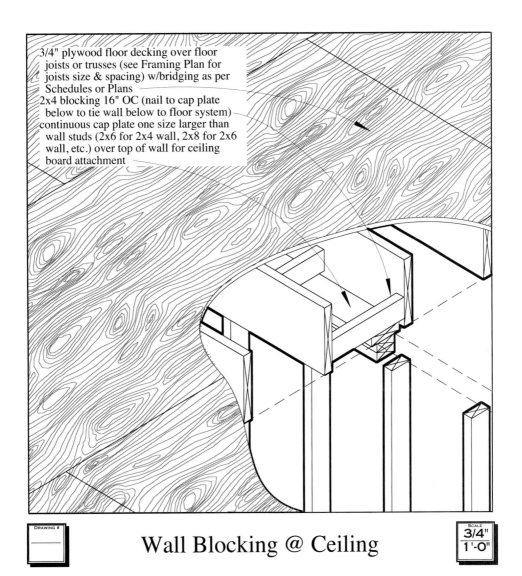

3/4" plywood floor decking over floor joists or trusses (see Framing Plan for joists size & spacing) w/bridging as per Schedules or Plans

2x4 blocking 16" OC (nail to cap plate below to tie wall below to floor system)

continuous cap plate one size larger than wall studs (2x6 for 2x4 wall, 2x8 for 2x6 wall, etc.) over top of wall for ceiling board attachment

Wall Blocking @ Ceiling

DRAWING #

SCALE
3/4"
1'-0"

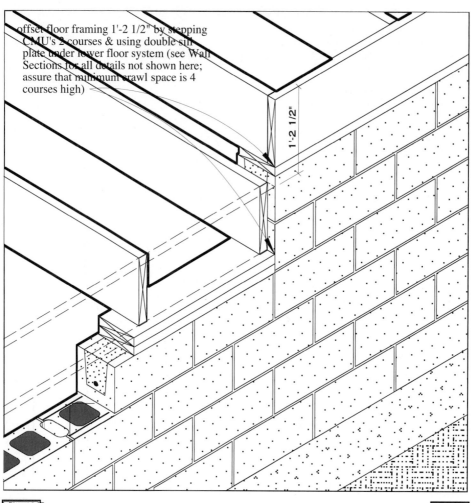

offset floor framing 1'-2 1/2" by stepping CMU's 2 courses & using double sill plate under lower floor system (see Wall Sections for all details not shown here; assure that minimum crawl space is 4 courses high)

1'-2 1/2"

2-Course Floor System Offset

DRAWING #

SCALE
3/4"
1'-O"

ESFWI009
520

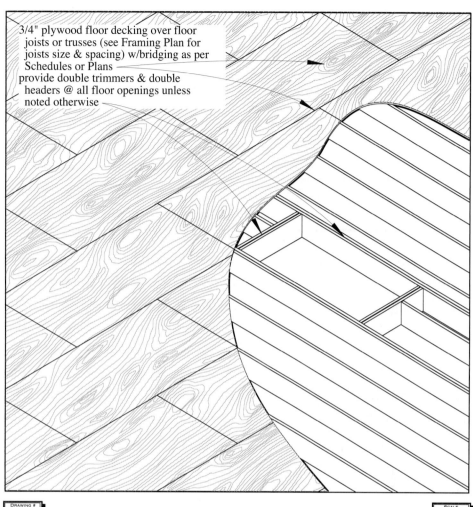

3/4" plywood floor decking over floor
joists or trusses (see Framing Plan for
joists size & spacing) w/bridging as per
Schedules or Plans
provide double trimmers & double
headers @ all floor openings unless
noted otherwise

Floor Opening Detail

SCALE
1/4"
1'-0"

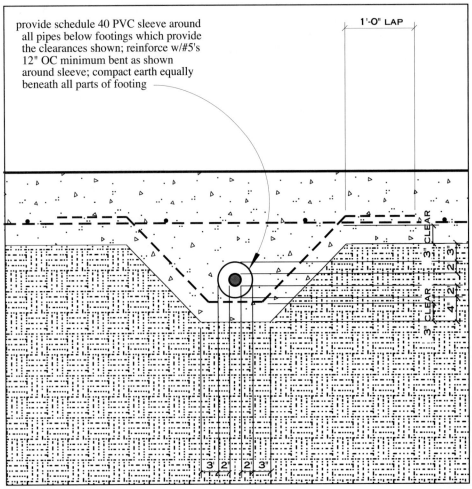

provide schedule 40 PVC sleeve around
all pipes below footings which provide
the clearances shown; reinforce w/#5's
12" OC minimum bent as shown
around sleeve; compact earth equally
beneath all parts of footing

1'-0" LAP

3" CLEAR

3" CLEAR

Pipe Sleeve Detail Below Footing

DRAWING #

SCALE
3/4"
1'-0"

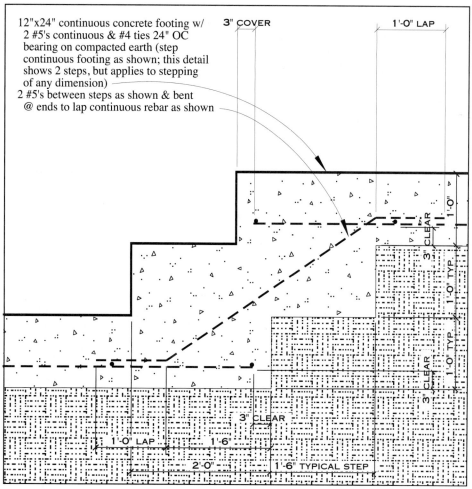

12"x24" continuous concrete footing w/
2 #5's continuous & #4 ties 24" OC
bearing on compacted earth (step
continuous footing as shown; this detail
shows 2 steps, but applies to stepping
of any dimension)
2 #5's between steps as shown & bent
@ ends to lap continuous rebar as shown

3" COVER

1'-0" LAP

1'-0"

3" CLEAR

1'-0" TYP

1'-0" TYP

3" CLEAR

3" CLEAR

1'-0" LAP

1'-6"

2'-0"

1'-6" TYPICAL STEP

Multiple-Stepped Footing Detail

SCALE
3/4"
1'-0"

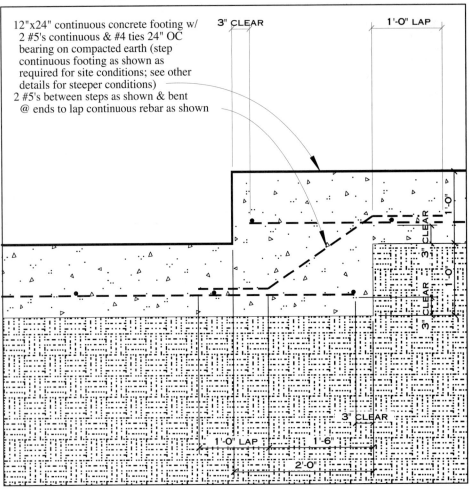

12"x24" continuous concrete footing w/
  2 #5's continuous & #4 ties 24" OC
  bearing on compacted earth (step
  continuous footing as shown as
  required for site conditions; see other
  details for steeper conditions)
2 #5's between steps as shown & bent
  @ ends to lap continuous rebar as shown

3" CLEAR

1'-0" LAP

1'-0"

CLEAR

3" CLEAR

1'-0"

3" CLEAR

1'-0"

3" CLEAR

1'-0" LAP   1'-6"

2'-0"

DRAWING #

Single-Stepped Footing Detail

SCALE
3/4"
1'-0"

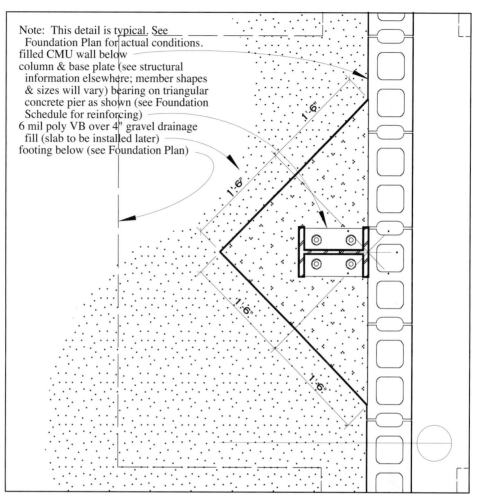

Note: This detail is typical. See
  Foundation Plan for actual conditions.
filled CMU wall below
column & base plate (see structural
  information elsewhere; member shapes
  & sizes will vary) bearing on triangular
  concrete pier as shown (see Foundation
  Schedule for reinforcing)
6 mil poly VB over 4" gravel drainage
  fill (slab to be installed later)
footing below (see Foundation Plan)

1'-6"

1'-6"

1'-6"

1'-6"

DRAWING #

Pier Detail @ Metal Building Column

SCALE
3/4"
1'-0"

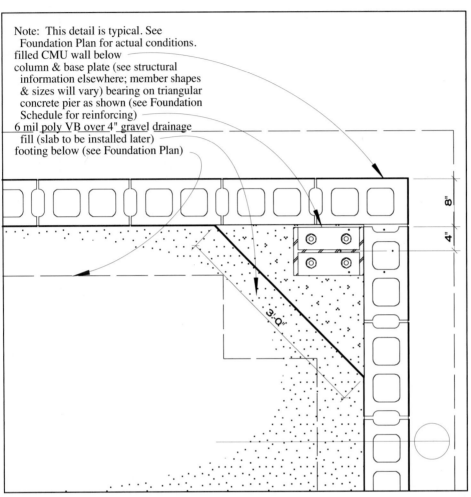

Note: This detail is typical. See
  Foundation Plan for actual conditions.
filled CMU wall below
column & base plate (see structural
  information elsewhere; member shapes
  & sizes will vary) bearing on triangular
  concrete pier as shown (see Foundation
  Schedule for reinforcing)
6 mil poly VB over 4" gravel drainage
  fill (slab to be installed later)
footing below (see Foundation Plan)

8"

4"

3'-0"

| DRAWING # | | Pier Detail @ Metal Building Column | SCALE 3/4" / 1'-0" |

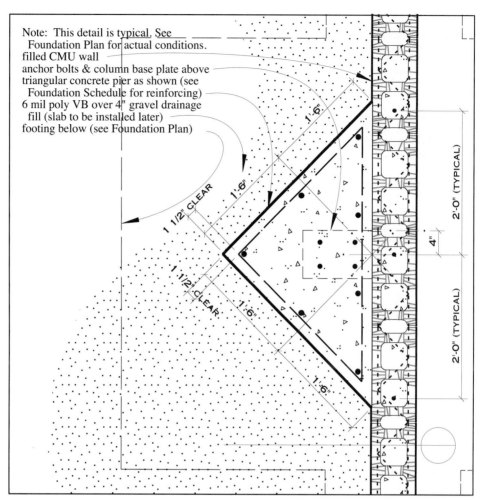

Note: This detail is typical. See
  Foundation Plan for actual conditions.
filled CMU wall
anchor bolts & column base plate above
triangular concrete pier as shown (see
  Foundation Schedule for reinforcing)
6 mil poly VB over 4" gravel drainage
  fill (slab to be installed later)
footing below (see Foundation Plan)

1 1/2" CLEAR

1 1/2" CLEAR

1'-6"

1'-6"

1'-6"

1'-6"

2'-0" (TYPICAL)

2'-0" (TYPICAL)

4"

DRAWING #

Pier Section @ Metal Building Column

SCALE
3/4"
1'-0"

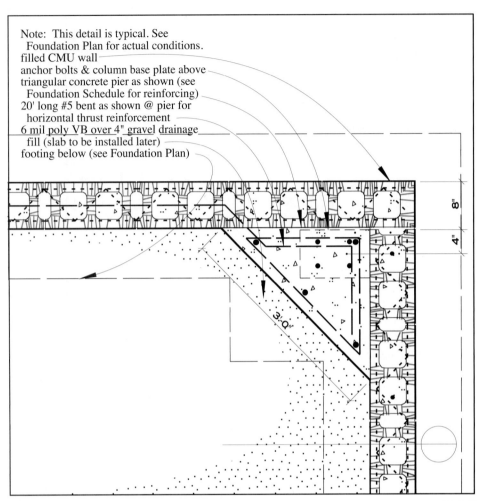

Note: This detail is typical. See
  Foundation Plan for actual conditions.
filled CMU wall
anchor bolts & column base plate above
triangular concrete pier as shown (see
  Foundation Schedule for reinforcing)
20' long #5 bent as shown @ pier for
  horizontal thrust reinforcement
6 mil poly VB over 4" gravel drainage
  fill (slab to be installed later)
footing below (see Foundation Plan)

8"

4"

3'-0"

Pier Detail @ Metal Building Column

SCALE
3/4"
1'-0"

DRAWING #

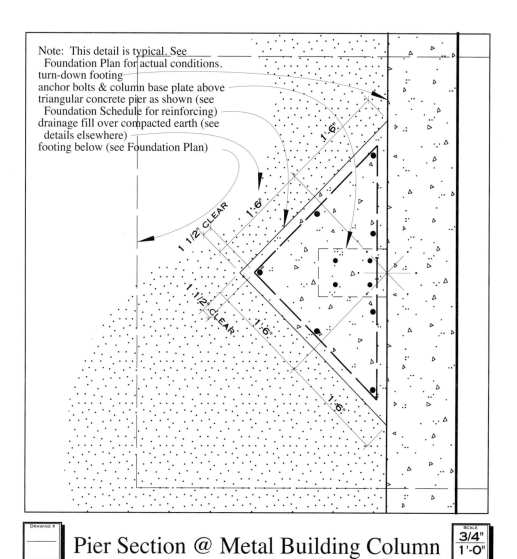

Note: This detail is typical. See
 Foundation Plan for actual conditions.
turn-down footing
anchor bolts & column base plate above
triangular concrete pier as shown (see
 Foundation Schedule for reinforcing)
drainage fill over compacted earth (see
 details elsewhere)
footing below (see Foundation Plan)

1'-6"
1'-6"
1 1/2" CLEAR
1 1/2" CLEAR
1'-6"
1'-6"

DRAWING #

Pier Section @ Metal Building Column

SCALE
3/4"
1'-0"

ESSP005
529

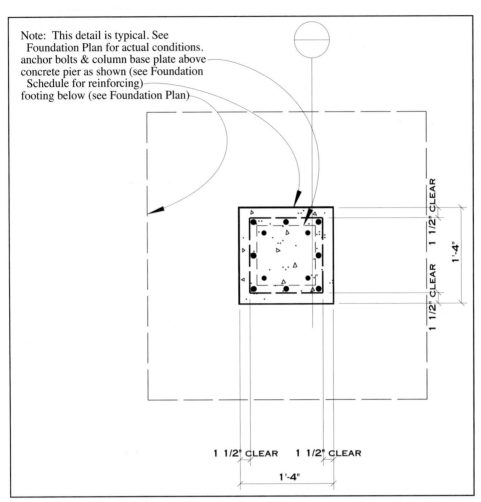

Note: This detail is typical. See
  Foundation Plan for actual conditions.
anchor bolts & column base plate above
concrete pier as shown (see Foundation
  Schedule for reinforcing)
footing below (see Foundation Plan)

1 1/2" CLEAR

1 1/2" CLEAR

1'-4"

1 1/2" CLEAR   1 1/2" CLEAR

1'-4"

DRAWING #

Typical Pier Plan Section

SCALE
3/4"
1'-0"

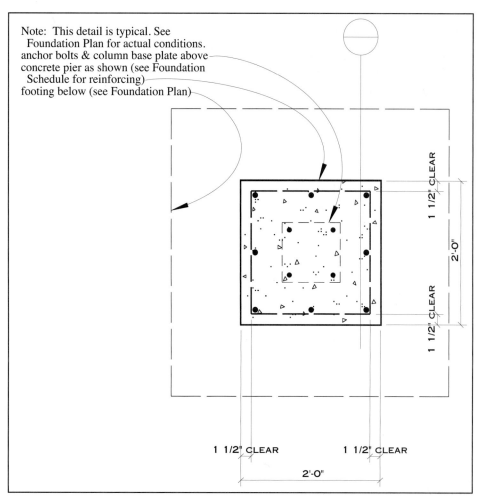

Note: This detail is typical. See
  Foundation Plan for actual conditions.
anchor bolts & column base plate above
concrete pier as shown (see Foundation
  Schedule for reinforcing)
footing below (see Foundation Plan)

1 1/2" CLEAR

2'-0"

1 1/2" CLEAR

1 1/2" CLEAR   1 1/2" CLEAR

2'-0"

DRAWING #

Typical Pier Plan Section

SCALE
3/4"
1'-0"

ESSP007
531

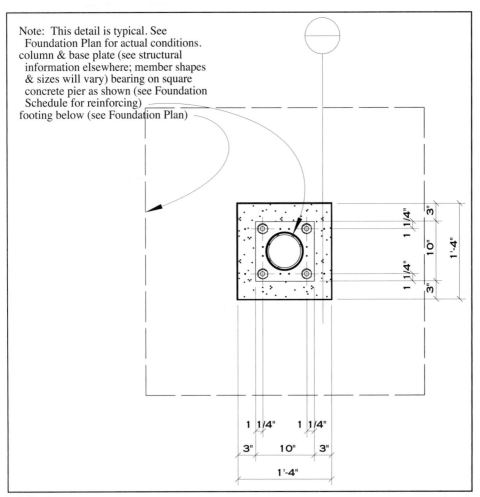

Note: This detail is typical. See
  Foundation Plan for actual conditions.
column & base plate (see structural
  information elsewhere; member shapes
  & sizes will vary) bearing on square
  concrete pier as shown (see Foundation
  Schedule for reinforcing)
footing below (see Foundation Plan)

3"
1 1/4"
10"
1'-4"
1 1/4"
3"

1 1/4"   1 1/4"

3"   10"   3"

1'-4"

Typical Pier Plan Detail

DRAWING #

SCALE
3/4"
1'-0"

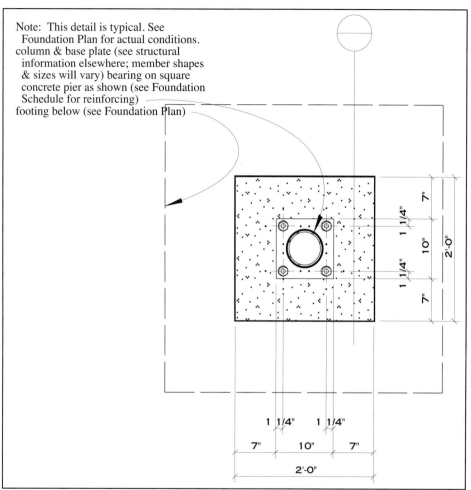

Note: This detail is typical. See
  Foundation Plan for actual conditions.
column & base plate (see structural
  information elsewhere; member shapes
  & sizes will vary) bearing on square
  concrete pier as shown (see Foundation
  Schedule for reinforcing)
footing below (see Foundation Plan)

7"
1 1/4"
10"
1 1/4"
7"
2'-0"

1 1/4"   1 1/4"
7"   10"   7"
2'-0"

Typical Pier Plan Detail

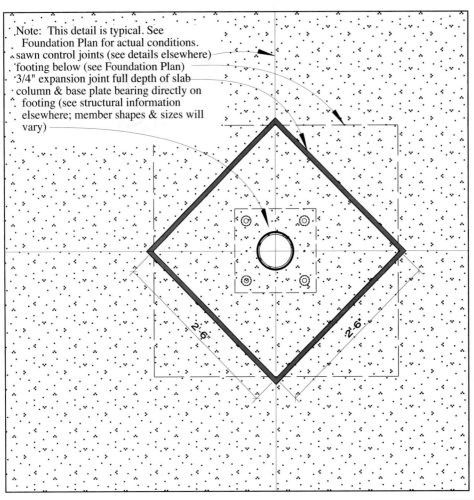

Note: This detail is typical. See
Foundation Plan for actual conditions.
sawn control joints (see details elsewhere)
footing below (see Foundation Plan)
3/4" expansion joint full depth of slab
column & base plate bearing directly on
footing (see structural information
elsewhere; member shapes & sizes will
vary)

2'-6"

2'-6"

DRAWING #	Slab Detail @ Column	SCALE 3/4" 1'-0"

ESSP010
534

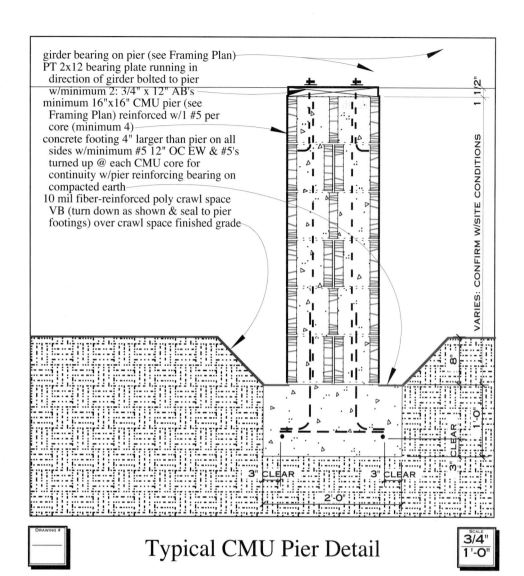

girder bearing on pier (see Framing Plan)
PT 2x12 bearing plate running in
  direction of girder bolted to pier
  w/minimum 2: 3/4" x 12" AB's
minimum 16"x16" CMU pier (see
  Framing Plan) reinforced w/1 #5 per
  core (minimum 4)
concrete footing 4" larger than pier on all
  sides w/minimum #5 12" OC EW & #5's
  turned up @ each CMU core for
  continuity w/pier reinforcing bearing on
  compacted earth
10 mil fiber-reinforced poly crawl space
  VB (turn down as shown & seal to pier
  footings) over crawl space finished grade

1 1/2"

VARIES: CONFIRM W/SITE CONDITIONS

8"

1'-0"

3" CLEAR

3" CLEAR

3" CLEAR

2'-0"

Typical CMU Pier Detail

DRAWING #

SCALE
3/4"
1'-0"

ESSP012
535

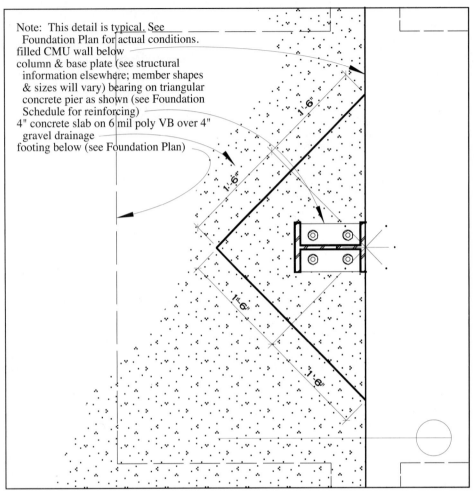

Note: This detail is typical. See
 Foundation Plan for actual conditions.
filled CMU wall below
column & base plate (see structural
 information elsewhere; member shapes
 & sizes will vary) bearing on triangular
 concrete pier as shown (see Foundation
 Schedule for reinforcing)
4" concrete slab on 6 mil poly VB over 4"
 gravel drainage
footing below (see Foundation Plan)

1'-6"

1'-6"

1'-6"

1'-6"

Pier Detail @ Metal Building Column

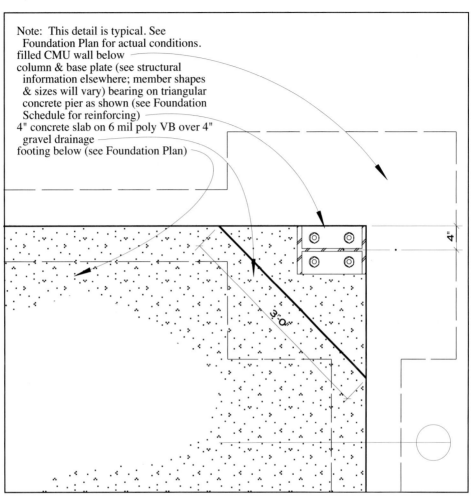

Note: This detail is typical. See
   Foundation Plan for actual conditions.
filled CMU wall below
column & base plate (see structural
   information elsewhere; member shapes
   & sizes will vary) bearing on triangular
   concrete pier as shown (see Foundation
   Schedule for reinforcing)
4" concrete slab on 6 mil poly VB over 4"
   gravel drainage
footing below (see Foundation Plan)

3'-0"

4"

Pier Detail @ Metal Building Column

DRAWING #

SCALE
3/4"
1'-0"

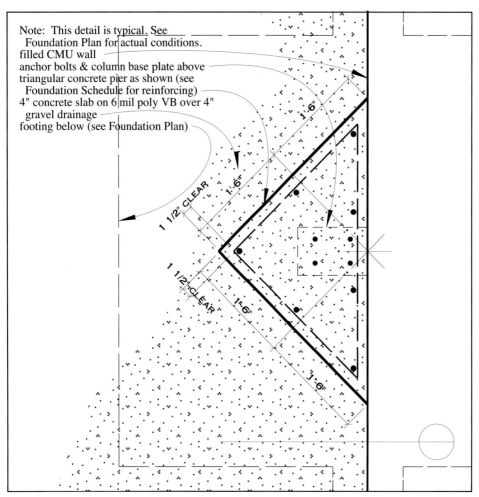

Note: This detail is typical. See
   Foundation Plan for actual conditions.
filled CMU wall
anchor bolts & column base plate above
triangular concrete pier as shown (see
   Foundation Schedule for reinforcing)
4" concrete slab on 6 mil poly VB over 4"
   gravel drainage
footing below (see Foundation Plan)

1'-6"

1 1/2" CLEAR

1'-6"

1 1/2" CLEAR

1'-6"

1'-6"

| DRAWING # | Pier Section @ Metal Building Column | SCALE 3/4" 1'-0" |

ESSP018
538

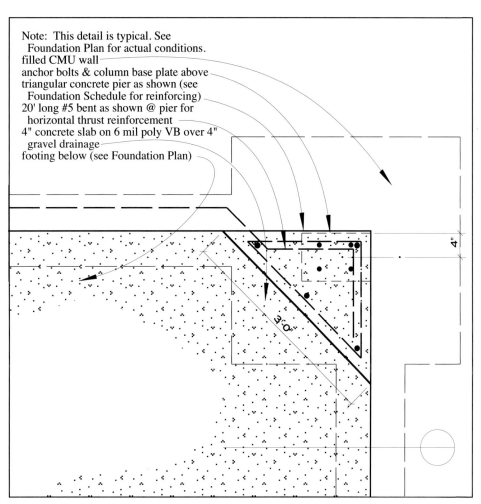

Note: This detail is typical. See
  Foundation Plan for actual conditions.
filled CMU wall
anchor bolts & column base plate above
triangular concrete pier as shown (see
  Foundation Schedule for reinforcing)
20' long #5 bent as shown @ pier for
  horizontal thrust reinforcement
4" concrete slab on 6 mil poly VB over 4"
  gravel drainage
footing below (see Foundation Plan)

3'-0"

4"

DRAWING #	Pier Detail @ Metal Building Column	SCALE 3/4" 1'-0"

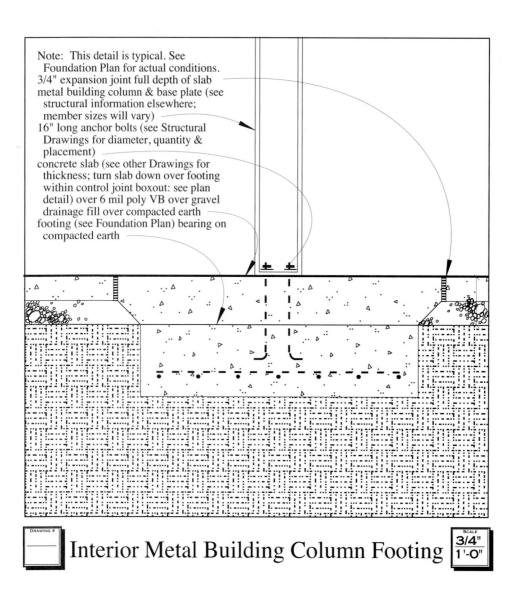

Note: This detail is typical. See
Foundation Plan for actual conditions.
3/4" expansion joint full depth of slab
metal building column & base plate (see
structural information elsewhere;
member sizes will vary)
16" long anchor bolts (see Structural
Drawings for diameter, quantity &
placement)
concrete slab (see other Drawings for
thickness; turn slab down over footing
within control joint boxout: see plan
detail) over 6 mil poly VB over gravel
drainage fill over compacted earth
footing (see Foundation Plan) bearing on
compacted earth

Interior Metal Building Column Footing

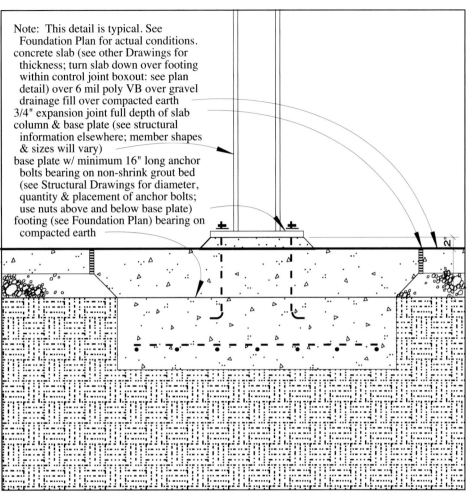

Note: This detail is typical. See
   Foundation Plan for actual conditions.
concrete slab (see other Drawings for
   thickness; turn slab down over footing
   within control joint boxout: see plan
   detail) over 6 mil poly VB over gravel
   drainage fill over compacted earth
3/4" expansion joint full depth of slab
column & base plate (see structural
   information elsewhere; member shapes
   & sizes will vary)
base plate w/ minimum 16" long anchor
   bolts bearing on non-shrink grout bed
   (see Structural Drawings for diameter,
   quantity & placement of anchor bolts;
   use nuts above and below base plate)
footing (see Foundation Plan) bearing on
   compacted earth

2"

Interior Steel Column Footing

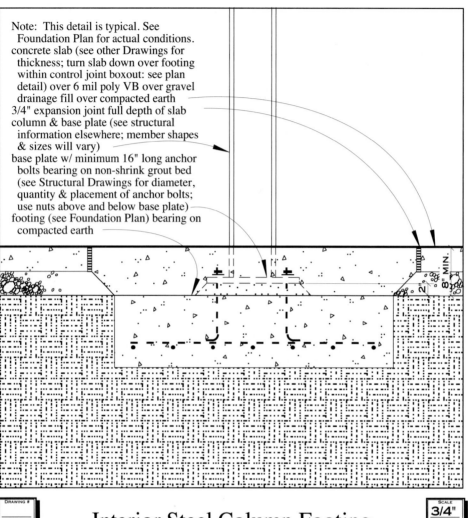

Note: This detail is typical. See
  Foundation Plan for actual conditions.
concrete slab (see other Drawings for
  thickness; turn slab down over footing
  within control joint boxout: see plan
  detail) over 6 mil poly VB over gravel
  drainage fill over compacted earth
3/4" expansion joint full depth of slab
column & base plate (see structural
  information elsewhere; member shapes
  & sizes will vary)
base plate w/ minimum 16" long anchor
  bolts bearing on non-shrink grout bed
  (see Structural Drawings for diameter,
  quantity & placement of anchor bolts;
  use nuts above and below base plate)
footing (see Foundation Plan) bearing on
  compacted earth

8" MIN.

2"

DRAWING #

Interior Steel Column Footing

SCALE
3/4"
1'-0"

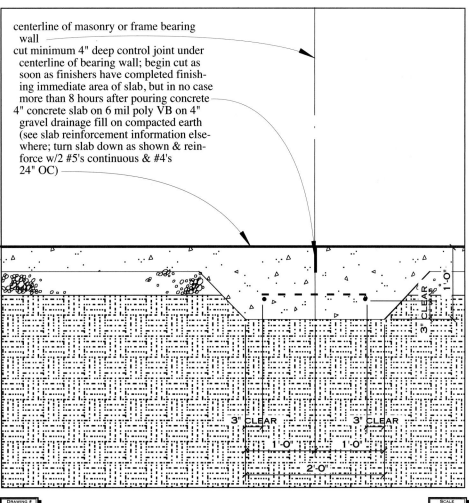

centerline of masonry or frame bearing
  wall

cut minimum 4" deep control joint under
  centerline of bearing wall; begin cut as
  soon as finishers have completed finishing immediate area of slab, but in no case
  more than 8 hours after pouring concrete

4" concrete slab on 6 mil poly VB on 4"
  gravel drainage fill on compacted earth
  (see slab reinforcement information elsewhere; turn slab down as shown & reinforce w/2 #5's continuous & #4's
  24" OC)

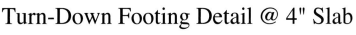

1'-0"

3" CLEAR

3" CLEAR   3" CLEAR

1'-0"   1'-0"

2'-0"

Turn-Down Footing Detail @ 4" Slab

SCALE
3/4"
1'-0"

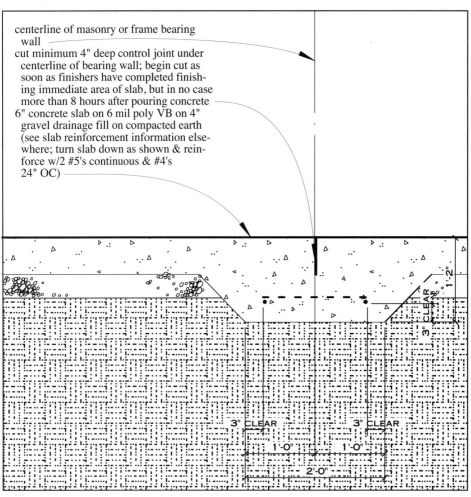

centerline of masonry or frame bearing
wall

cut minimum 4" deep control joint under
centerline of bearing wall; begin cut as
soon as finishers have completed finishing immediate area of slab, but in no case
more than 8 hours after pouring concrete

6" concrete slab on 6 mil poly VB on 4"
gravel drainage fill on compacted earth
(see slab reinforcement information elsewhere; turn slab down as shown & reinforce w/2 #5's continuous & #4's
24" OC)

3" CLEAR

3" CLEAR

1'-0"

1'-0"

2'-0"

3" CLEAR

1'-2"

DRAWING #

Turn-Down Footing Detail @ 6" Slab

SCALE
3/4"
1'-0"

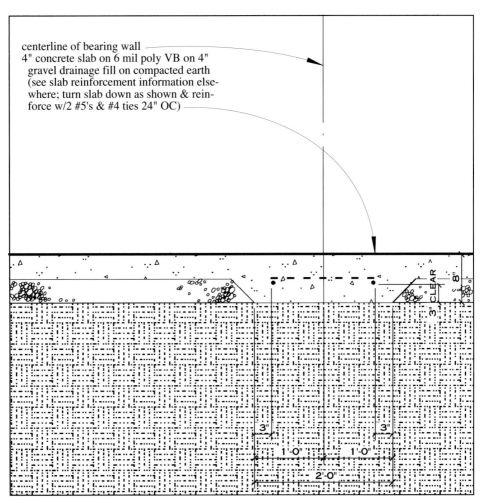

centerline of bearing wall
4" concrete slab on 6 mil poly VB on 4"
gravel drainage fill on compacted earth
(see slab reinforcement information elsewhere; turn slab down as shown & reinforce w/2 #5's & #4 ties 24" OC)

8"

3" CLEAR

3"

1'-0"

1'-0"

3"

2'-0"

DRAWING #

Thickened 4" Slab Detail

SCALE
3/4"
1'-0"

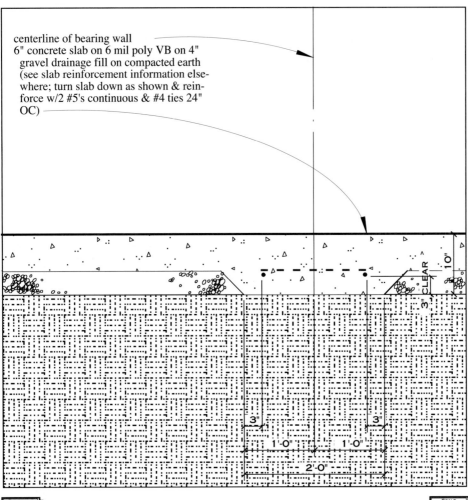

centerline of bearing wall
6" concrete slab on 6 mil poly VB on 4"
    gravel drainage fill on compacted earth
    (see slab reinforcement information else-
    where; turn slab down as shown & rein-
    force w/2 #5's continuous & #4 ties 24"
    OC)

3" CLEAR

10"

3"

3"

1'-0"

1'-0"

2'-0"

Thickened 6" Slab Detail

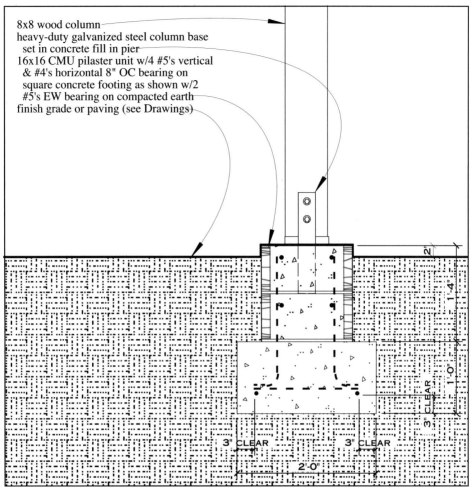

8x8 wood column
heavy-duty galvanized steel column base
  set in concrete fill in pier
16x16 CMU pilaster unit w/4 #5's vertical
  & #4's horizontal 8" OC bearing on
  square concrete footing as shown w/2
  #5's EW bearing on compacted earth
finish grade or paving (see Drawings)

2"

1'-4"

1'-0"

3" CLEAR

3" CLEAR

3" CLEAR

2'-0"

DRAWING #

8x8 Wood Column Foundation Detail

SCALE

3/4"
1'-0"

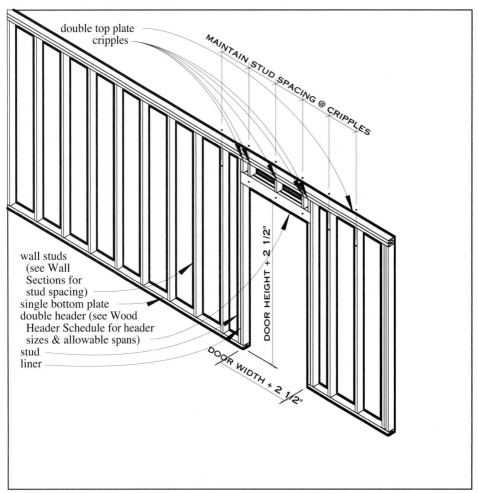

double top plate
cripples

MAINTAIN STUD SPACING @ CRIPPLES

DOOR HEIGHT + 2 1/2"

DOOR WIDTH + 2 1/2"

wall studs
  (see Wall
   Sections for
   stud spacing)
single bottom plate
double header (see Wood
  Header Schedule for header
  sizes & allowable spans)
stud
liner

DRAWING #

Door Framing @ Loadbearing Wall

SCALE

1/4"
1'-0"

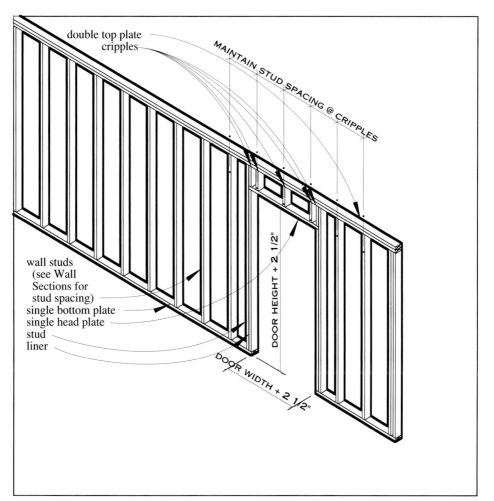

double top plate
cripples

MAINTAIN STUD SPACING @ CRIPPLES

wall studs
(see Wall
Sections for
stud spacing)
single bottom plate
single head plate
stud
liner

DOOR HEIGHT + 2 1/2"

DOOR WIDTH + 2 1/2"

Door Framing @ Partition Wall

DRAWING #

SCALE
1/4"
1'-0"

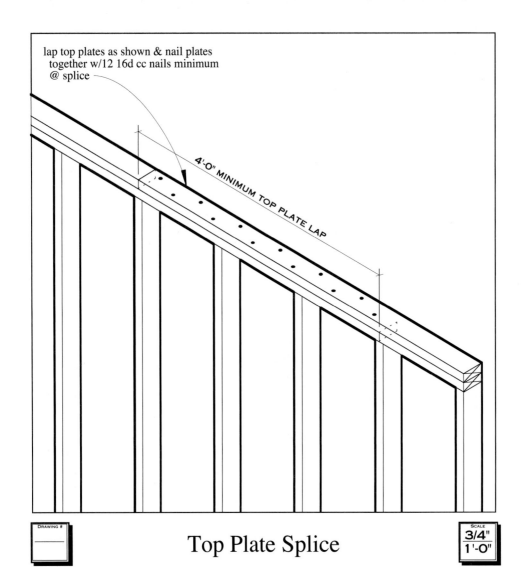

lap top plates as shown & nail plates
together w/12 16d cc nails minimum
@ splice

4'-0" MINIMUM TOP PLATE LAP

Top Plate Splice

DRAWING #

SCALE
3/4"
1'-0"

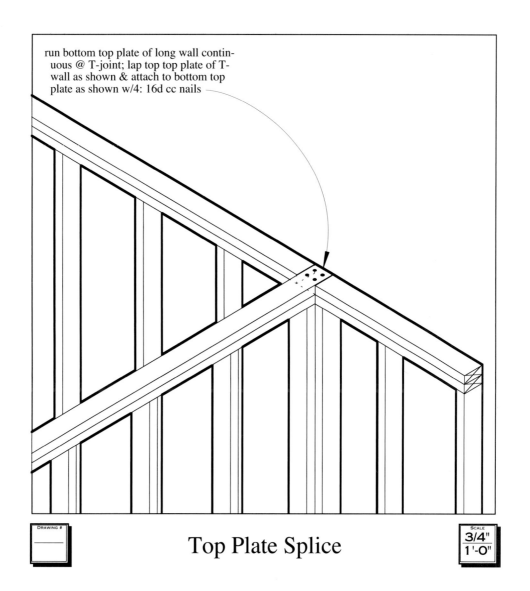

run bottom top plate of long wall continuous @ T-joint; lap top top plate of T-
wall as shown & attach to bottom top
plate as shown w/4: 16d cc nails

Top Plate Splice

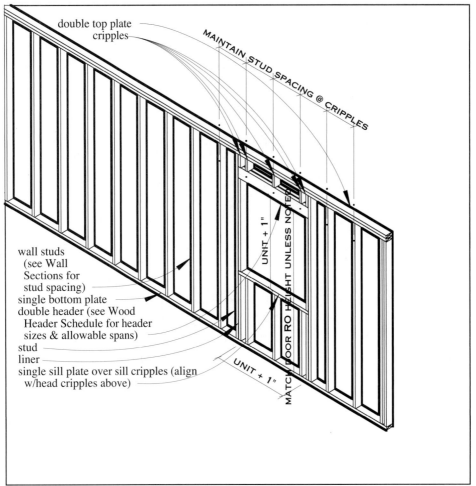

double top plate
cripples

MAINTAIN STUD SPACING @ CRIPPLES

UNIT + 1"

MATCH DOOR RO HEIGHT UNLESS NOTED

wall studs
(see Wall
Sections for
stud spacing)
single bottom plate
double header (see Wood
Header Schedule for header
sizes & allowable spans)
stud
liner
single sill plate over sill cripples (align
w/head cripples above)

UNIT + 1"

DRAWING #

Window Framing @ Loadbearing Wall

SCALE
1/4"
1'-O"

ESW005
552

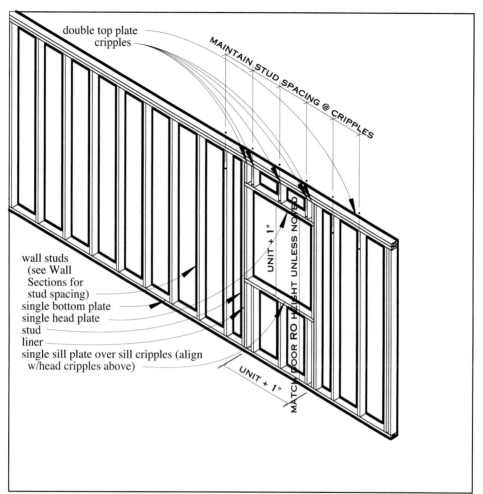

double top plate
cripples

MAINTAIN STUD SPACING @ CRIPPLES

UNIT + 1"

MATCH DOOR RO HEIGHT UNLESS NOTED

wall studs
  (see Wall
   Sections for
   stud spacing)
single bottom plate
single head plate
stud
liner
single sill plate over sill cripples (align
  w/head cripples above)

UNIT + 1"

DRAWING #

Window Framing @ Partition Wall

SCALE
1/4"
1'-O"

ESW006
553

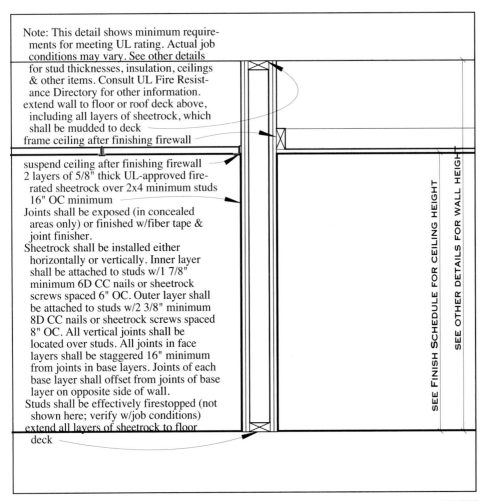

Note: This detail shows minimum requirements for meeting UL rating. Actual job
conditions may vary. See other details
for stud thicknesses, insulation, ceilings
& other items. Consult UL Fire Resistance Directory for other information.
extend wall to floor or roof deck above,
including all layers of sheetrock, which
shall be mudded to deck
frame ceiling after finishing firewall

suspend ceiling after finishing firewall
2 layers of 5/8" thick UL-approved fire-
rated sheetrock over 2x4 minimum studs
16" OC minimum
Joints shall be exposed (in concealed
areas only) or finished w/fiber tape &
joint finisher.
Sheetrock shall be installed either
horizontally or vertically. Inner layer
shall be attached to studs w/1 7/8"
minimum 6D CC nails or sheetrock
screws spaced 6" OC. Outer layer shall
be attached to studs w/2 3/8" minimum
8D CC nails or sheetrock screws spaced
8" OC. All vertical joints shall be
located over studs. All joints in face
layers shall be staggered 16" minimum
from joints in base layers. Joints of each
base layer shall offset from joints of base
layer on opposite side of wall.
Studs shall be effectively firestopped (not
shown here; verify w/job conditions)
extend all layers of sheetrock to floor
deck

SEE FINISH SCHEDULE FOR CEILING HEIGHT

SEE OTHER DETAILS FOR WALL HEIGHT

U301 2 Hour Wood Bearing Wall

SCALE
3/4"
1'-0"

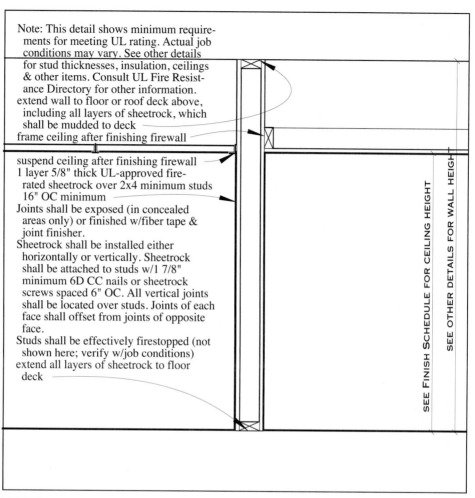

Note: This detail shows minimum requirements for meeting UL rating. Actual job conditions may vary. See other details for stud thicknesses, insulation, ceilings & other items. Consult UL Fire Resistance Directory for other information.

extend wall to floor or roof deck above, including all layers of sheetrock, which shall be mudded to deck

frame ceiling after finishing firewall

suspend ceiling after finishing firewall

1 layer 5/8" thick UL-approved fire-rated sheetrock over 2x4 minimum studs 16" OC minimum

Joints shall be exposed (in concealed areas only) or finished w/fiber tape & joint finisher.

Sheetrock shall be installed either horizontally or vertically. Sheetrock shall be attached to studs w/1 7/8" minimum 6D CC nails or sheetrock screws spaced 6" OC. All vertical joints shall be located over studs. Joints of each face shall offset from joints of opposite face.

Studs shall be effectively firestopped (not shown here; verify w/job conditions)

extend all layers of sheetrock to floor deck

SEE FINISH SCHEDULE FOR CEILING HEIGHT

SEE OTHER DETAILS FOR WALL HEIGHT

DRAWING #

U305 1 Hour Wood Bearing Wall

SCALE
3/4"
1'-0"

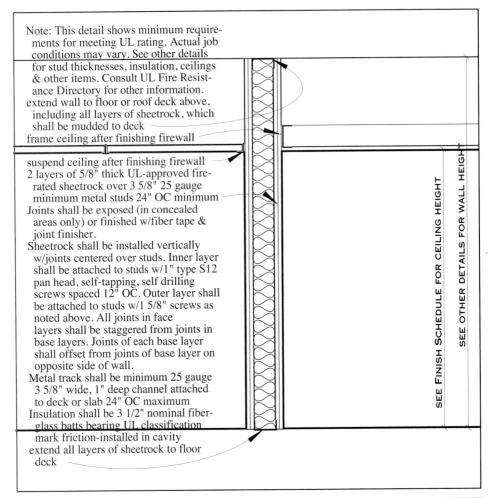

Note: This detail shows minimum requirements for meeting UL rating. Actual job
conditions may vary. See other details
for stud thicknesses, insulation, ceilings
& other items. Consult UL Fire Resistance Directory for other information.

extend wall to floor or roof deck above,
including all layers of sheetrock, which
shall be mudded to deck

frame ceiling after finishing firewall

suspend ceiling after finishing firewall

2 layers of 5/8" thick UL-approved fire-
rated sheetrock over 3 5/8" 25 gauge
minimum metal studs 24" OC minimum

Joints shall be exposed (in concealed
areas only) or finished w/fiber tape &
joint finisher.

Sheetrock shall be installed vertically
w/joints centered over studs. Inner layer
shall be attached to studs w/1" type S12
pan head, self-tapping, self drilling
screws spaced 12" OC. Outer layer shall
be attached to studs w/1 5/8" screws as
noted above. All joints in face
layers shall be staggered from joints in
base layers. Joints of each base layer
shall offset from joints of base layer on
opposite side of wall.

Metal track shall be minimum 25 gauge
3 5/8" wide, 1" deep channel attached
to deck or slab 24" OC maximum

Insulation shall be 3 1/2" nominal fiberglass batts bearing UL classification
mark friction-installed in cavity

extend all layers of sheetrock to floor
deck

SEE FINISH SCHEDULE FOR CEILING HEIGHT

SEE OTHER DETAILS FOR WALL HEIGHT

DRAWING #

U411 2 Hour Metal Nonbearing Wall

SCALE
3/4"
1'-0"

Note: This detail shows minimum requirements for meeting UL rating. Actual job
conditions may vary. See other details
for stud thicknesses, insulation, ceilings
& other items. Consult UL Fire Resistance Directory for other information.
extend wall to floor or roof deck above,
including all layers of sheetrock, which
shall be mudded to deck
frame ceiling after finishing firewall

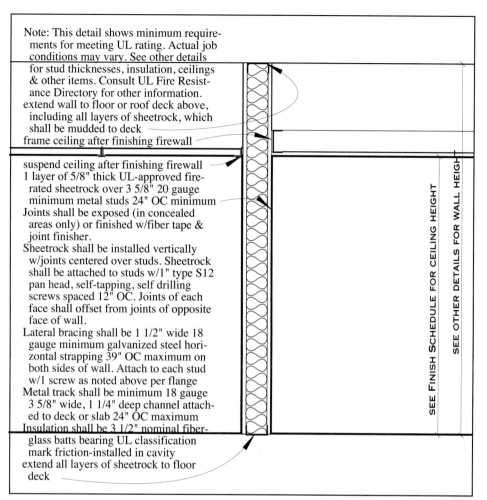

suspend ceiling after finishing firewall
1 layer of 5/8" thick UL-approved fire-
rated sheetrock over 3 5/8" 20 gauge
minimum metal studs 24" OC minimum
Joints shall be exposed (in concealed
areas only) or finished w/fiber tape &
joint finisher.
Sheetrock shall be installed vertically
w/joints centered over studs. Sheetrock
shall be attached to studs w/1" type S12
pan head, self-tapping, self drilling
screws spaced 12" OC. Joints of each
face shall offset from joints of opposite
face of wall.
Lateral bracing shall be 1 1/2" wide 18
gauge minimum galvanized steel horizontal strapping 39" OC maximum on
both sides of wall. Attach to each stud
w/1 screw as noted above per flange
Metal track shall be minimum 18 gauge
3 5/8" wide, 1 1/4" deep channel attached to deck or slab 24" OC maximum
Insulation shall be 3 1/2" nominal fiberglass batts bearing UL classification
mark friction-installed in cavity
extend all layers of sheetrock to floor
deck

SEE FINISH SCHEDULE FOR CEILING HEIGHT

SEE OTHER DETAILS FOR WALL HEIGHT

DRAWING #

U464 1 Hour Metal Bearing Wall

SCALE
3/4"
1'-0"

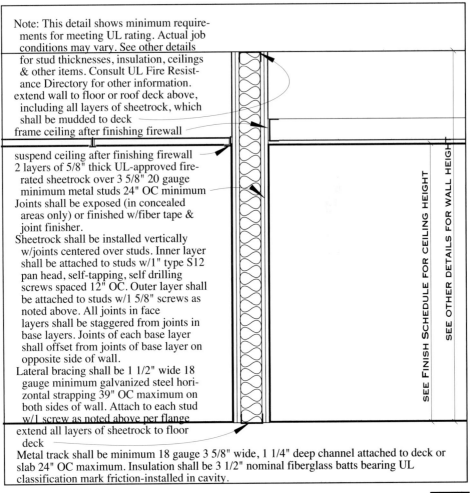

Note: This detail shows minimum requirements for meeting UL rating. Actual job
  conditions may vary. See other details
  for stud thicknesses, insulation, ceilings
  & other items. Consult UL Fire Resistance Directory for other information.
extend wall to floor or roof deck above,
  including all layers of sheetrock, which
  shall be mudded to deck
frame ceiling after finishing firewall

suspend ceiling after finishing firewall
2 layers of 5/8" thick UL-approved fire-
  rated sheetrock over 3 5/8" 20 gauge
  minimum metal studs 24" OC minimum
Joints shall be exposed (in concealed
  areas only) or finished w/fiber tape &
  joint finisher.
Sheetrock shall be installed vertically
  w/joints centered over studs. Inner layer
  shall be attached to studs w/1" type S12
  pan head, self-tapping, self drilling
  screws spaced 12" OC. Outer layer shall
  be attached to studs w/1 5/8" screws as
  noted above. All joints in face
  layers shall be staggered from joints in
  base layers. Joints of each base layer
  shall offset from joints of base layer on
  opposite side of wall.
Lateral bracing shall be 1 1/2" wide 18
  gauge minimum galvanized steel horizontal strapping 39" OC maximum on
  both sides of wall. Attach to each stud
  w/1 screw as noted above per flange.
extend all layers of sheetrock to floor
  deck
Metal track shall be minimum 18 gauge 3 5/8" wide, 1 1/4" deep channel attached to deck or
slab 24" OC maximum. Insulation shall be 3 1/2" nominal fiberglass batts bearing UL
classification mark friction-installed in cavity.

SEE FINISH SCHEDULE FOR CEILING HEIGHT

SEE OTHER DETAILS FOR WALL HEIGHT

DRAWING #

U464 2 Hour Metal Bearing Wall

SCALE
3/4"
1'-0"

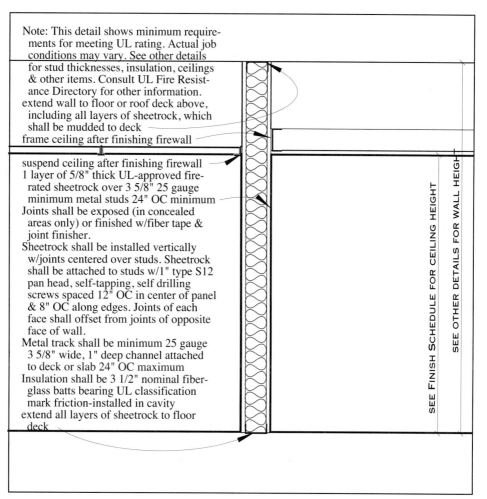

Note: This detail shows minimum requirements for meeting UL rating. Actual job
conditions may vary. See other details
for stud thicknesses, insulation, ceilings
& other items. Consult UL Fire Resistance Directory for other information.
extend wall to floor or roof deck above,
including all layers of sheetrock, which
shall be mudded to deck
frame ceiling after finishing firewall

suspend ceiling after finishing firewall
1 layer of 5/8" thick UL-approved fire-
rated sheetrock over 3 5/8" 25 gauge
minimum metal studs 24" OC minimum
Joints shall be exposed (in concealed
areas only) or finished w/fiber tape &
joint finisher.
Sheetrock shall be installed vertically
w/joints centered over studs. Sheetrock
shall be attached to studs w/1" type S12
pan head, self-tapping, self drilling
screws spaced 12" OC in center of panel
& 8" OC along edges. Joints of each
face shall offset from joints of opposite
face of wall.
Metal track shall be minimum 25 gauge
3 5/8" wide, 1" deep channel attached
to deck or slab 24" OC maximum
Insulation shall be 3 1/2" nominal fiberglass batts bearing UL classification
mark friction-installed in cavity
extend all layers of sheetrock to floor
deck

SEE FINISH SCHEDULE FOR CEILING HEIGHT

SEE OTHER DETAILS FOR WALL HEIGHT

U468 1 Hour Metal Nonbearing Wall

SCALE
3/4"
1'-0"

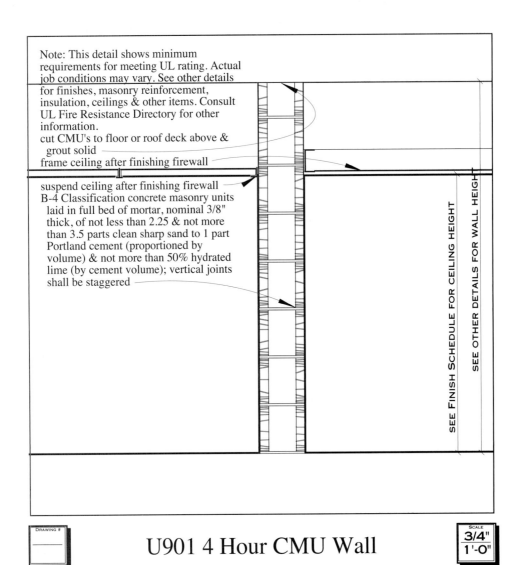

Note: This detail shows minimum requirements for meeting UL rating. Actual job conditions may vary. See other details for finishes, masonry reinforcement, insulation, ceilings & other items. Consult UL Fire Resistance Directory for other information.
cut CMU's to floor or roof deck above & grout solid
frame ceiling after finishing firewall

suspend ceiling after finishing firewall
B-4 Classification concrete masonry units laid in full bed of mortar, nominal 3/8" thick, of not less than 2.25 & not more than 3.5 parts clean sharp sand to 1 part Portland cement (proportioned by volume) & not more than 50% hydrated lime (by cement volume); vertical joints shall be staggered

SEE FINISH SCHEDULE FOR CEILING HEIGHT

SEE OTHER DETAILS FOR WALL HEIGHT

DRAWING #

U901 4 Hour CMU Wall

SCALE
3/4"
1'-0"

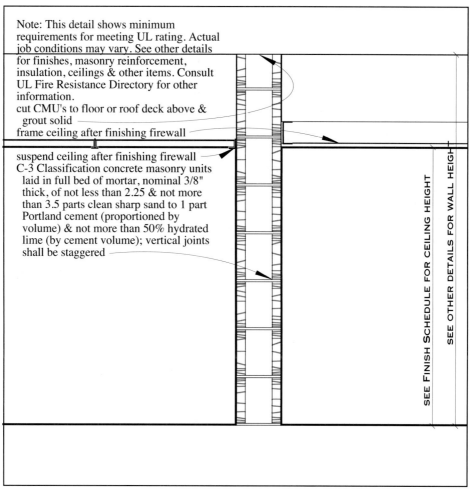

Note: This detail shows minimum requirements for meeting UL rating. Actual job conditions may vary. See other details for finishes, masonry reinforcement, insulation, ceilings & other items. Consult UL Fire Resistance Directory for other information.

cut CMU's to floor or roof deck above & grout solid

frame ceiling after finishing firewall

suspend ceiling after finishing firewall

C-3 Classification concrete masonry units laid in full bed of mortar, nominal 3/8" thick, of not less than 2.25 & not more than 3.5 parts clean sharp sand to 1 part Portland cement (proportioned by volume) & not more than 50% hydrated lime (by cement volume); vertical joints shall be staggered

SEE FINISH SCHEDULE FOR CEILING HEIGHT

SEE OTHER DETAILS FOR WALL HEIGHT

DRAWING #

U904 3 Hour CMU Wall

SCALE
3/4"
1'-0"

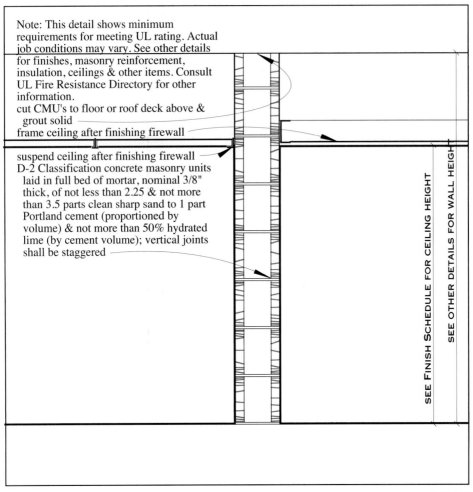

Note: This detail shows minimum requirements for meeting UL rating. Actual job conditions may vary. See other details for finishes, masonry reinforcement, insulation, ceilings & other items. Consult UL Fire Resistance Directory for other information.

cut CMU's to floor or roof deck above & grout solid

frame ceiling after finishing firewall

suspend ceiling after finishing firewall

D-2 Classification concrete masonry units laid in full bed of mortar, nominal 3/8" thick, of not less than 2.25 & not more than 3.5 parts clean sharp sand to 1 part Portland cement (proportioned by volume) & not more than 50% hydrated lime (by cement volume); vertical joints shall be staggered

SEE FINISH SCHEDULE FOR CEILING HEIGHT

SEE OTHER DETAILS FOR WALL HEIGHT

DRAWING #

U905 2 Hour CMU Wall

SCALE
3/4"
1'-0"

Note: This detail includes only the CMU
control joint. There may be other veneers
or finishes associated with this wall which
are not shown here. See Floor Plan & other
details for these components

rigid pre-formed insulating CMU inserts
  (see Specifications)

8" CMU slotted sash block (reinforce
  cores each side of joint w/#5 from
  footing to top of wall)

preformed neoprene control joint full
  height of wall w/sealant closure on both
  sides of joint (use backer rod if neoprene
  joint is not wide enough to serve as
  proper backer)

discontinue all horizontal joint
  reinforcement & bond beams @ control
  joint

Control Joint Placement Criteria:
A. 60' maximum along wall
B. @ changes in wall height
C. @ changes in wall thickness
D. @ openings (1 side of opening for
   openings less than 6' wide, both sides
   of opening for larger openings)
E. @ location of joints in floor or roof
   above, or in floor or foundation
   beneath

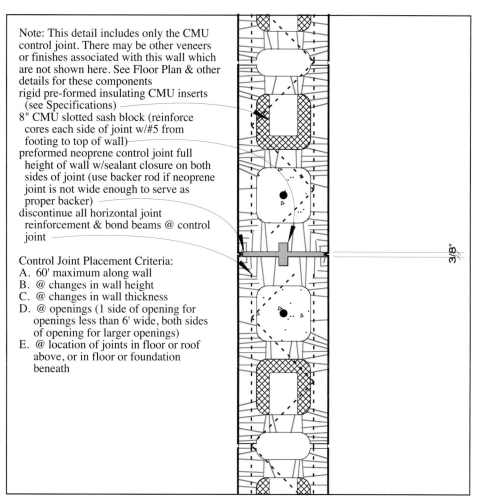

3/8"

CMU Control Joint Detail

Note: This detail includes only the CMU
control joint. There may be other veneers
or finishes associated with this wall which
are not shown here. See Floor Plan & other
details for these components
8" CMU slotted sash block (reinforce
  cores each side of joint w/#5 from
  footing to top of wall)
preformed neoprene control joint full
  height of wall w/sealant closure on both
  sides of joint (use backer rod if neoprene
  joint is not wide enough to serve as
  proper backer)
discontinue all horizontal joint
  reinforcement & bond beams @ control
  joint

Control Joint Placement Criteria:
A. 60' maximum along wall
B. @ changes in wall height
C. @ changes in wall thickness
D. @ openings (1 side of opening for
    openings less than 6' wide, both sides
    of opening for larger openings)
E. @ location of joints in floor or roof
    above, or in floor or foundation
    beneath

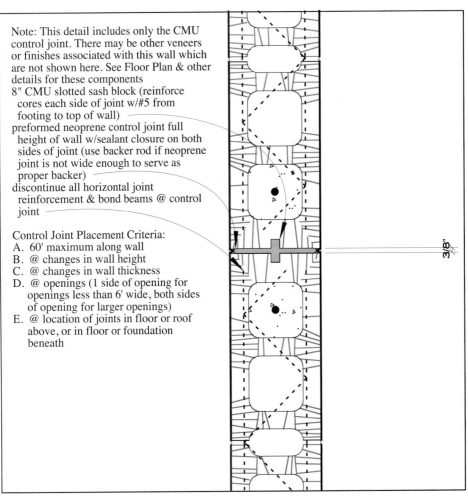

3/8"

DRAWING #

CMU Control Joint Detail

SCALE

1 1/2"
1'-0"

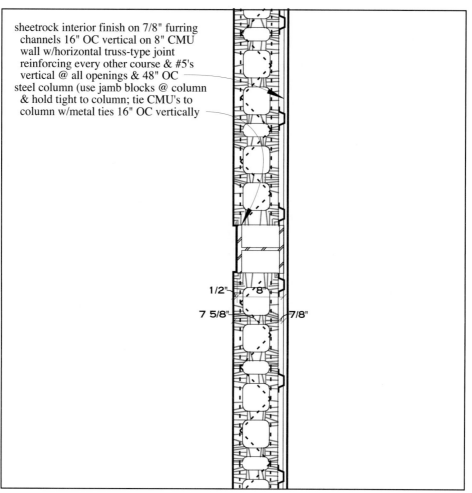

sheetrock interior finish on 7/8" furring
channels 16" OC vertical on 8" CMU
wall w/horizontal truss-type joint
reinforcing every other course & #5's
vertical @ all openings & 48" OC

steel column (use jamb blocks @ column
& hold tight to column; tie CMU's to
column w/metal ties 16" OC vertically

1/2"   8"

7 5/8"   7/8"

Plan Detail @ Column in 8" CMU Wall

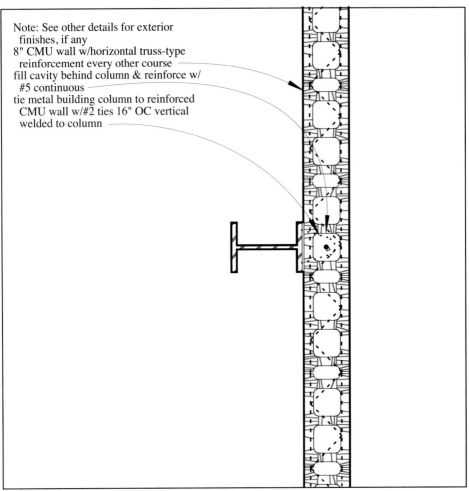

Note: See other details for exterior
  finishes, if any
8" CMU wall w/horizontal truss-type
  reinforcement every other course
fill cavity behind column & reinforce w/
  #5 continuous
tie metal building column to reinforced
  CMU wall w/#2 ties 16" OC vertical
  welded to column

 Plan Detail @ Metal Building Column

SCALE
3/4"
1'-0"

EWP005
566

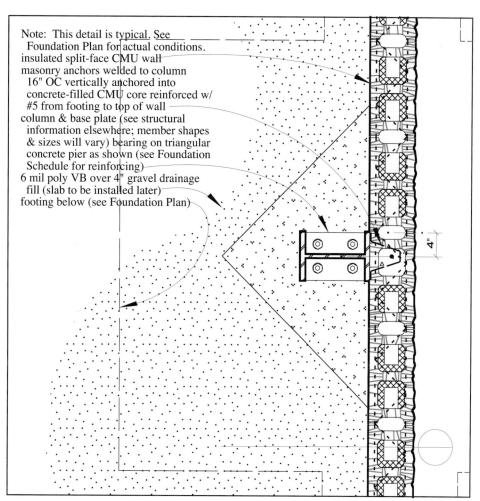

Note: This detail is typical. See
  Foundation Plan for actual conditions.
insulated split-face CMU wall
masonry anchors welded to column
  16" OC vertically anchored into
  concrete-filled CMU core reinforced w/
  #5 from footing to top of wall
column & base plate (see structural
  information elsewhere; member shapes
  & sizes will vary) bearing on triangular
  concrete pier as shown (see Foundation
  Schedule for reinforcing)
6 mil poly VB over 4" gravel drainage
  fill (slab to be installed later)
footing below (see Foundation Plan)

4"

DRAWING #

Plan Detail @ Metal Building Column

SCALE
3/4"
1'-0"

Note: This detail includes only the CMU
control joint. There may be other veneers
or finishes associated with this wall which
are not shown here. See Floor Plan & other
details for these components

rigid pre-formed insulating CMU inserts
  (see Specifications)

8" split-face CMU slotted sash block
  (reinforce cores each side of joint w/#5
  from footing to top of wall)

preformed neoprene control joint full
  height of wall w/sealant closure on both
  sides of joint (use backer rod if neoprene
  joint is not wide enough to serve as
  proper backer)

discontinue all horizontal joint
  reinforcement & bond beams @ control
  joint

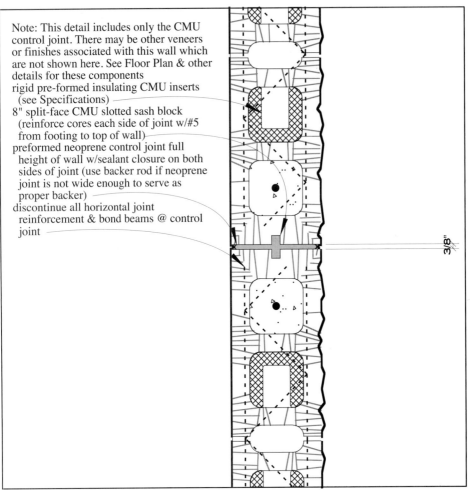

3/8"

DRAWING #

Split-Face CMU Control Joint Detail

SCALE

1 1/2"
1'-0"

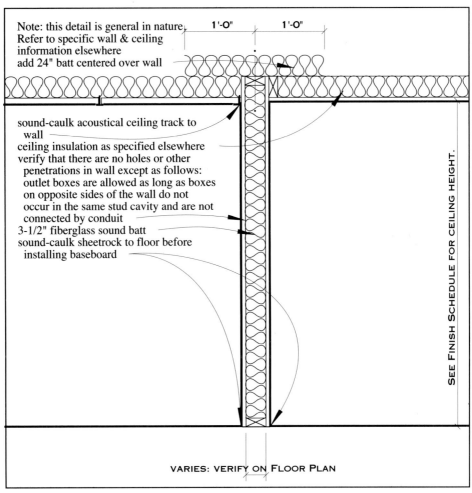

Note: this detail is general in nature
Refer to specific wall & ceiling
information elsewhere
add 24" batt centered over wall

1'-0"   1'-0"

sound-caulk acoustical ceiling track to
  wall
ceiling insulation as specified elsewhere
verify that there are no holes or other
  penetrations in wall except as follows:
  outlet boxes are allowed as long as boxes
  on opposite sides of the wall do not
  occur in the same stud cavity and are not
  connected by conduit
3-1/2" fiberglass sound batt
sound-caulk sheetrock to floor before
  installing baseboard

SEE FINISH SCHEDULE FOR CEILING HEIGHT.

VARIES: VERIFY ON FLOOR PLAN

DRAWING #	Interior Sound Attenuation Detail	SCALE 3/4" 1'-0"

DETAILS OF FINISHES

Details in this section are limited to only those interior finish-related details which do not occur elsewhere. Millwork-related finish work occurs in the Trim Details section. These details primarily include floor tile details.

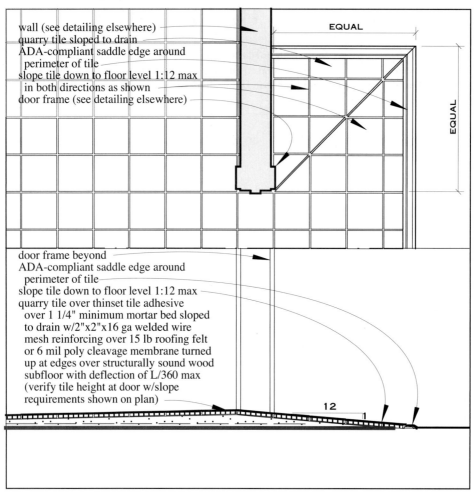

wall (see detailing elsewhere)
quarry tile sloped to drain
ADA-compliant saddle edge around
  perimeter of tile
slope tile down to floor level 1:12 max
  in both directions as shown
door frame (see detailing elsewhere)

EQUAL

EQUAL

door frame beyond
ADA-compliant saddle edge around
  perimeter of tile
slope tile down to floor level 1:12 max
quarry tile over thinset tile adhesive
  over 1 1/4" minimum mortar bed sloped
  to drain w/2"x2"x16 ga welded wire
  mesh reinforcing over 15 lb roofing felt
  or 6 mil poly cleavage membrane turned
  up at edges over structurally sound wood
  subfloor with deflection of L/360 max
  (verify tile height at door w/slope
  requirements shown on plan)

12

1

DRAWING #

Quarry Tile Plan/Section @ Door

SCALE

3/4"
‾‾‾‾
1'-0"

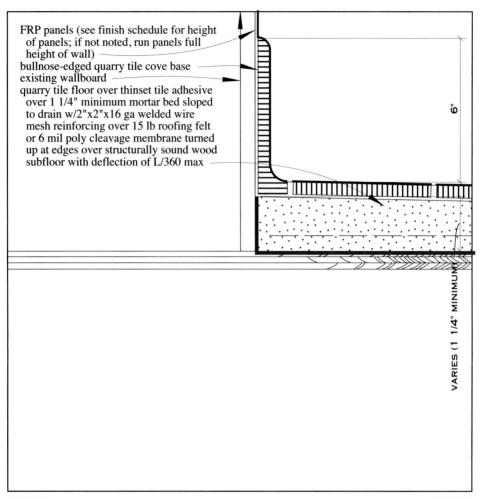

FRP panels (see finish schedule for height
of panels; if not noted, run panels full
height of wall)
bullnose-edged quarry tile cove base
existing wallboard
quarry tile floor over thinset tile adhesive
over 1 1/4" minimum mortar bed sloped
to drain w/2"x2"x16 ga welded wire
mesh reinforcing over 15 lb roofing felt
or 6 mil poly cleavage membrane turned
up at edges over structurally sound wood
subfloor with deflection of L/360 max

6"

VARIES (1 1/4" MINIMUM)

DRAWING #

Quarry Tile & Base @ Existing Wall

SCALE
3"
1'-0"

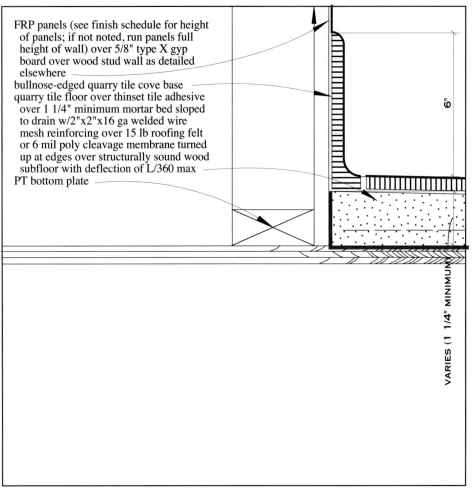

FRP panels (see finish schedule for height
  of panels; if not noted, run panels full
  height of wall) over 5/8" type X gyp
  board over wood stud wall as detailed
  elsewhere
bullnose-edged quarry tile cove base
quarry tile floor over thinset tile adhesive
  over 1 1/4" minimum mortar bed sloped
  to drain w/2"x2"x16 ga welded wire
  mesh reinforcing over 15 lb roofing felt
  or 6 mil poly cleavage membrane turned
  up at edges over structurally sound wood
  subfloor with deflection of L/360 max
PT bottom plate

6"

VARIES (1 1/4" MINIMUM)

DRAWING #	Quarry Tile & Base @ New Wall	SCALE $\dfrac{3"}{1'\text{-}0"}$

FF003
574

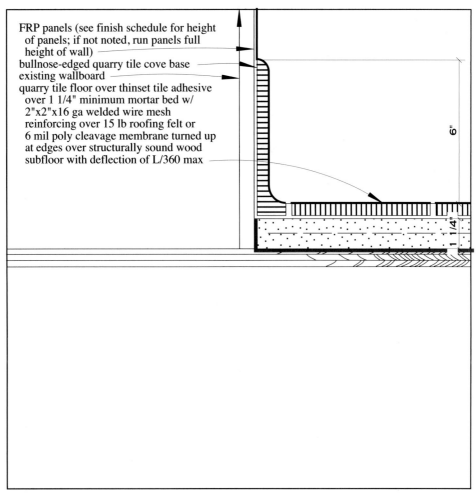

FRP panels (see finish schedule for height of panels; if not noted, run panels full height of wall)

bullnose-edged quarry tile cove base

existing wallboard

quarry tile floor over thinset tile adhesive over 1 1/4" minimum mortar bed w/ 2"x2"x16 ga welded wire mesh reinforcing over 15 lb roofing felt or 6 mil poly cleavage membrane turned up at edges over structurally sound wood subfloor with deflection of L/360 max

6"

1 1/4"

Flat Quarry Tile & Base @ Exist. Wall

SCALE
3"
1'-0"

FF004
575

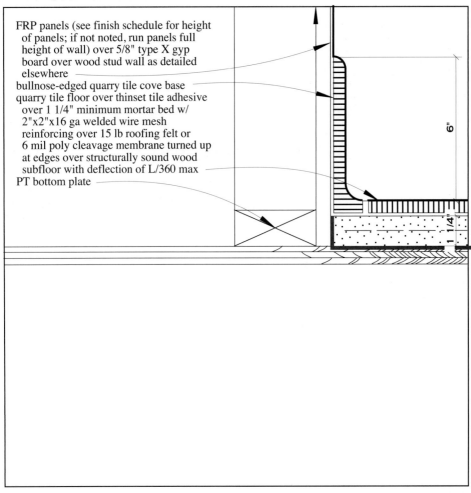

FRP panels (see finish schedule for height
  of panels; if not noted, run panels full
  height of wall) over 5/8" type X gyp
  board over wood stud wall as detailed
  elsewhere
bullnose-edged quarry tile cove base
quarry tile floor over thinset tile adhesive
  over 1 1/4" minimum mortar bed w/
  2"x2"x16 ga welded wire mesh
  reinforcing over 15 lb roofing felt or
  6 mil poly cleavage membrane turned up
  at edges over structurally sound wood
  subfloor with deflection of L/360 max
PT bottom plate

6"

1 1/4"

Flat Quarry Tile & Base @ New Wall

DRAWING #

SCALE
3"
1'-0"

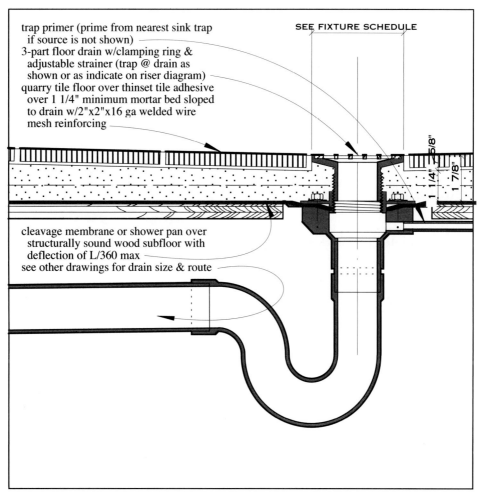

trap primer (prime from nearest sink trap
  if source is not shown)

3-part floor drain w/clamping ring &
  adjustable strainer (trap @ drain as
  shown or as indicate on riser diagram)

quarry tile floor over thinset tile adhesive
  over 1 1/4" minimum mortar bed sloped
  to drain w/2"x2"x16 ga welded wire
  mesh reinforcing

SEE FIXTURE SCHEDULE

cleavage membrane or shower pan over
  structurally sound wood subfloor with
  deflection of L/360 max

see other drawings for drain size & route

| DRAWING # | | Floor Drain in Mudset Tile Floor | SCALE 3" / 1'-0" |

FF006

577

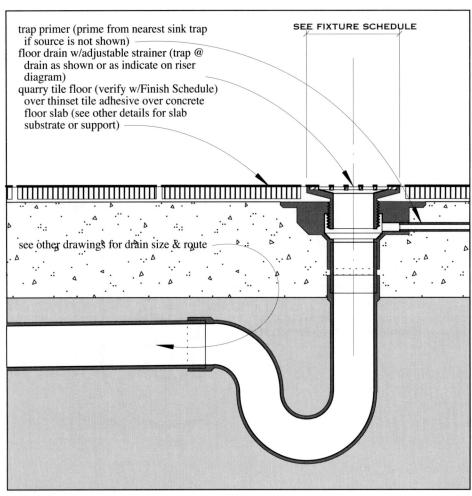

trap primer (prime from nearest sink trap
  if source is not shown)

floor drain w/adjustable strainer (trap @
  drain as shown or as indicate on riser
  diagram)

quarry tile floor (verify w/Finish Schedule)
  over thinset tile adhesive over concrete
  floor slab (see other details for slab
  substrate or support)

SEE FIXTURE SCHEDULE

see other drawings for drain size & route

DRAWING #	Floor Drain in Thinset Tile Floor	SCALE $\frac{3"}{1'-0"}$

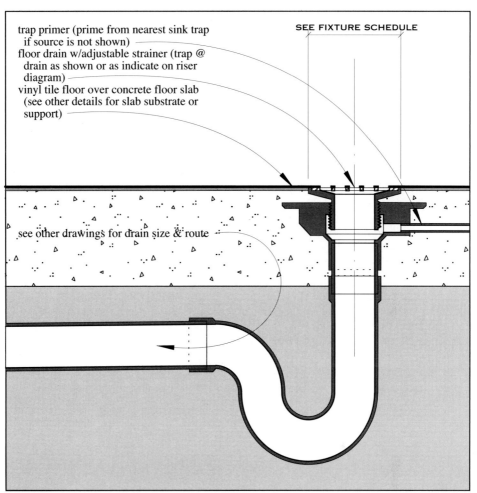

trap primer (prime from nearest sink trap
   if source is not shown)
floor drain w/adjustable strainer (trap @
   drain as shown or as indicate on riser
   diagram)
vinyl tile floor over concrete floor slab
   (see other details for slab substrate or
   support)

SEE FIXTURE SCHEDULE

see other drawings for drain size & route

DRAWING #

Floor Drain in Vinyl Tile Floor

SCALE
3"
1'-0"

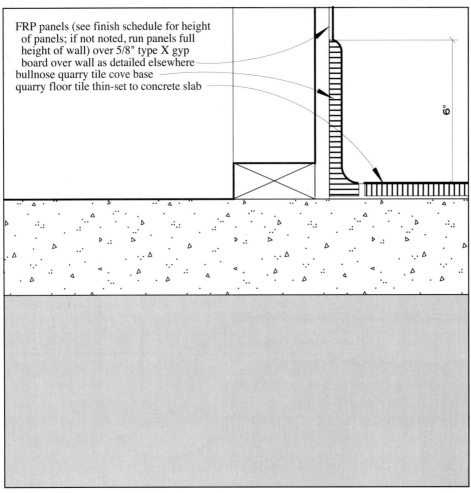

FRP panels (see finish schedule for height
  of panels; if not noted, run panels full
  height of wall) over 5/8" type X gyp
  board over wall as detailed elsewhere
bullnose quarry tile cove base
quarry floor tile thin-set to concrete slab

6"

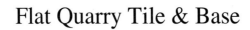

DRAWING #

Flat Quarry Tile & Base

SCALE
3"
1'-0"

GRAPHICS DETAILS

This section includes ADA signage details.

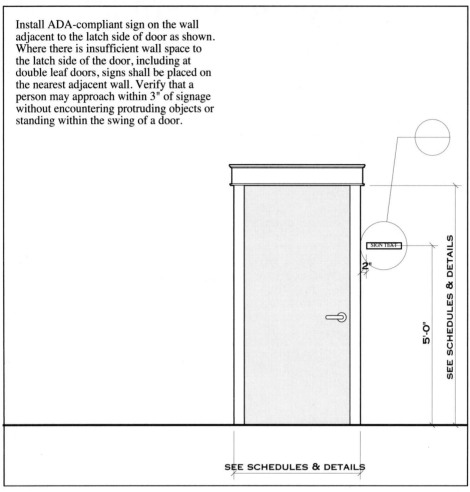

Install ADA-compliant sign on the wall adjacent to the latch side of door as shown. Where there is insufficient wall space to the latch side of the door, including at double leaf doors, signs shall be placed on the nearest adjacent wall. Verify that a person may approach within 3" of signage without encountering protruding objects or standing within the swing of a door.

SIGN TEXT

2"

5'-0"

SEE SCHEDULES & DETAILS

SEE SCHEDULES & DETAILS

Door Sign Elevation

Note: All signage shall meet all ADA
requirements, including the 70% color
contrast requirement. See Specifications
for sign & panel colors. See Door Schedule
for text.
acrylic sign panel w/eggshell matte finish
  adhesively attached to substrate
  w/commercial-grade double-sided foam
  tape (see Elevations for locations)
1/32" raised characters or symbols
  centered in sign panel (font is Helvetica,
  characters are all uppercase)
computer-engraved raised Grade II Braille
  signage conforming to Specification
  #800, National Library Service, Library
  of Congress, in this area

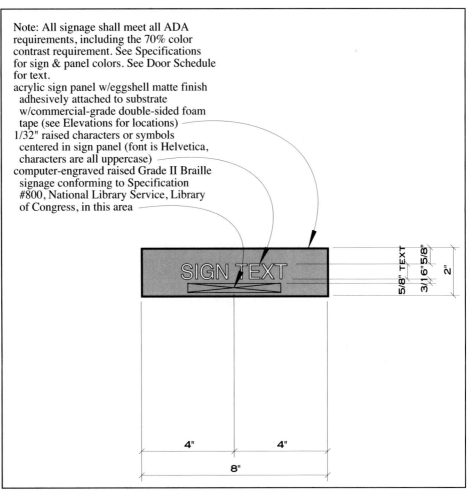

SIGN TEXT

5/8" TEXT
3/16" 5/8"
2"

4"   4"
8"

Room Sign Detail

Note: All signage shall meet all ADA
requirements, including the 70% color
contrast requirement. See Specifications
for sign & panel colors.
acrylic sign panel w/eggshell matte finish
  adhesively attached to substrate
  w/commercial-grade double-sided foam
  tape (see Elevations for locations)
1/32" raised characters or symbols
  centered in sign panel (font is Times,
  characters are all uppercase)
computer-engraved raised Grade II Braille
  signage conforming to Specification
  #800, National Library Service, Library
  of Congress, in this area

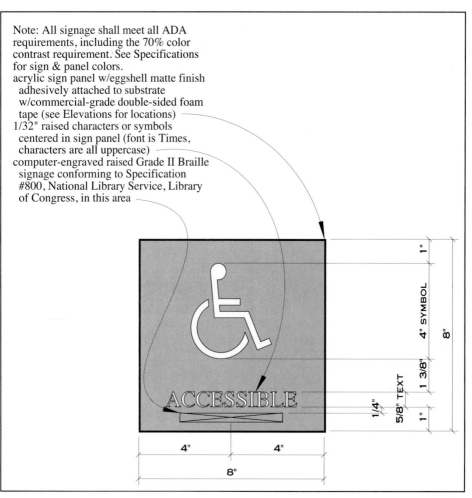

ACCESSIBLE

1"

4" SYMBOL

8"

1 3/8"

1/4"

5/8" TEXT

1"

4"   4"

8"

DRAWING #

Accessibility Sign Detail

SCALE
3"
1'-O"

Note: All signage shall meet all ADA
requirements, including the 70% color
contrast requirement. See Specifications
for sign & panel colors.
acrylic sign panel w/eggshell matte finish
  adhesively attached to substrate
  w/commercial-grade double-sided foam
  tape (see Elevations for locations)
1/32" raised characters or symbols
  centered in sign panel (font is Times,
  characters are all uppercase)
computer-engraved raised Grade II Braille
  signage conforming to Specification
  #800, National Library Service, Library
  of Congress, in this area

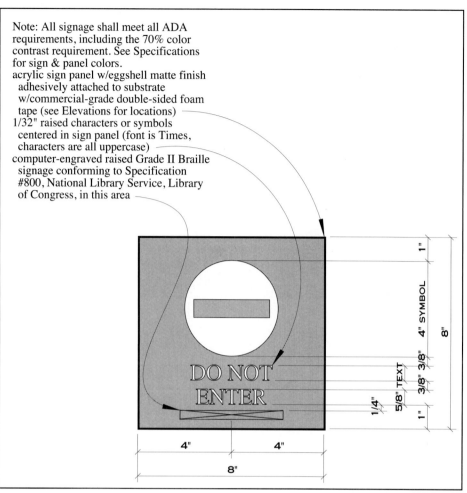

Do Not Enter Sign Detail

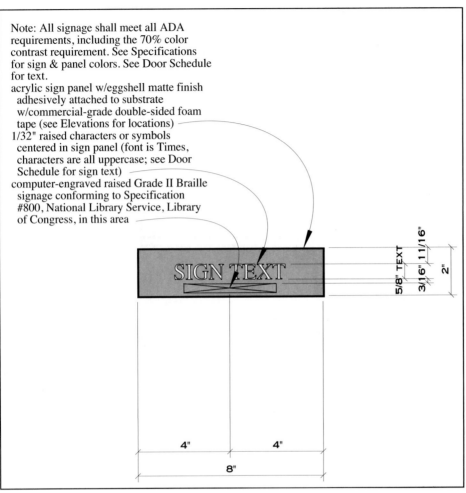

Note: All signage shall meet all ADA
requirements, including the 70% color
contrast requirement. See Specifications
for sign & panel colors. See Door Schedule
for text.
acrylic sign panel w/eggshell matte finish
   adhesively attached to substrate
   w/commercial-grade double-sided foam
   tape (see Elevations for locations)
1/32" raised characters or symbols
   centered in sign panel (font is Times,
   characters are all uppercase; see Door
   Schedule for sign text)
computer-engraved raised Grade II Braille
   signage conforming to Specification
   #800, National Library Service, Library
   of Congress, in this area

SIGN TEXT

5/8" TEXT
3/16" 11/16"
2"

4"   4"

8"

Room Sign Detail

Note: All signage shall meet all ADA
requirements, including the 70% color
contrast requirement. See Specifications
for sign & panel colors. See Door Schedule
for text.
acrylic sign panel w/eggshell matte finish
  adhesively attached to substrate
  w/commercial-grade double-sided foam
  tape (see Elevations for locations)
1/32" raised characters or symbols
  centered in sign panel (font is Times,
  characters are all uppercase; see Door
  Schedule for sign text)
computer-engraved raised Grade II Braille
  signage conforming to Specification
  #800, National Library Service, Library
  of Congress, in this area

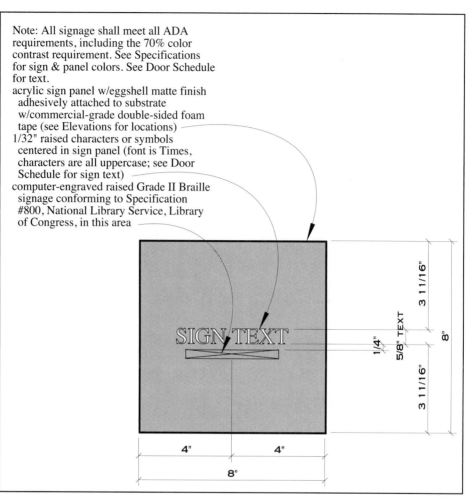

SIGN TEXT

3 11/16"

1/4"

5/8" TEXT

8"

3 11/16"

4"   4"

8"

DRAWING #

1-Line Room Sign Detail

SCALE
3"
1'-0"

Note: All signage shall meet all ADA requirements, including the 70% color contrast requirement. See Specifications for sign & panel colors. See Door Schedule for text.

acrylic sign panel w/eggshell matte finish adhesively attached to substrate w/commercial-grade double-sided foam tape (see Elevations for locations)

1/32" raised characters or symbols centered in sign panel (font is Times, characters are all uppercase; see Door Schedule for sign text)

computer-engraved raised Grade II Braille signage conforming to Specification #800, National Library Service, Library of Congress, in this area

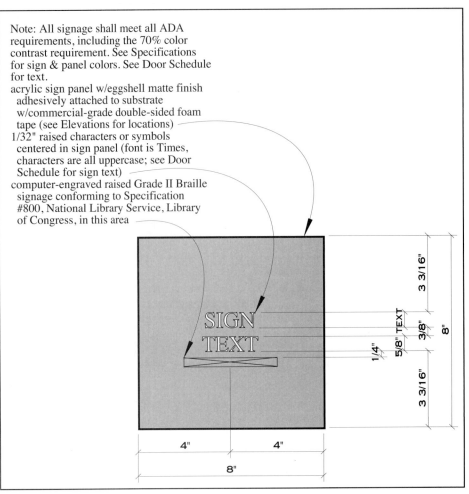

2-Line Room Sign Detail

DRAWING #

SCALE
3"
1'-0"

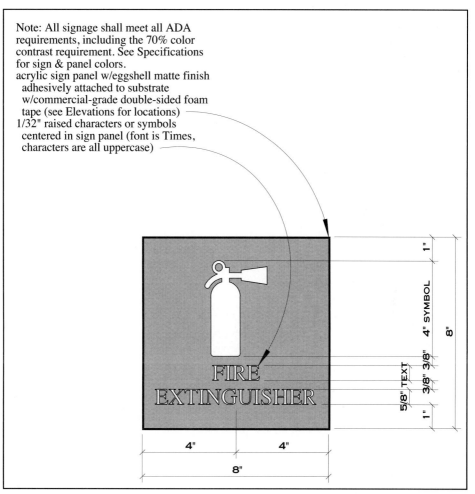

Note: All signage shall meet all ADA requirements, including the 70% color contrast requirement. See Specifications for sign & panel colors.

acrylic sign panel w/eggshell matte finish adhesively attached to substrate w/commercial-grade double-sided foam tape (see Elevations for locations)

1/32" raised characters or symbols centered in sign panel (font is Times, characters are all uppercase)

1"

4" SYMBOL

8"

3/8"

3/8"

5/8" TEXT

1"

FIRE EXTINGUISHER

4"   4"

8"

DRAWING #

Fire Extinguisher Sign Detail

SCALE
3"
1'-0"

Note: All signage shall meet all ADA
requirements, including the 70% color
contrast requirement. See Specifications
for sign & panel colors.
acrylic sign panel w/eggshell matte finish
  adhesively attached to substrate
  w/commercial-grade double-sided foam
  tape (see Elevations for locations)
1/32" raised characters or symbols
  centered in sign panel (font is Times,
  characters are all uppercase)

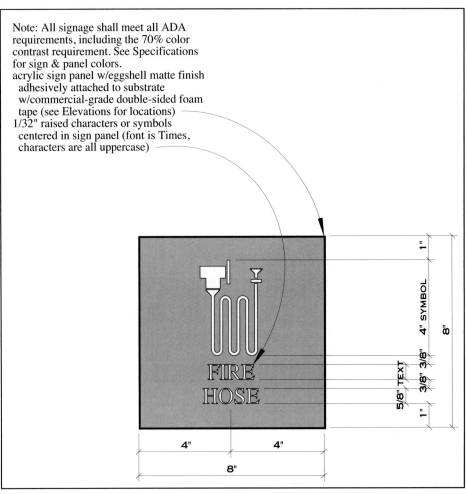

Fire Hose Sign Detail

DRAWING #

SCALE
3"
1'-0"

Note: All signage shall meet all ADA
requirements, including the 70% color
contrast requirement. See Specifications
for sign & panel colors.
acrylic sign panel w/eggshell matte finish
  adhesively attached to substrate
  w/commercial-grade double-sided foam
  tape (see Elevations for locations)
1/32" raised characters or symbols
  centered in sign panel (font is Times,
  characters are all uppercase)

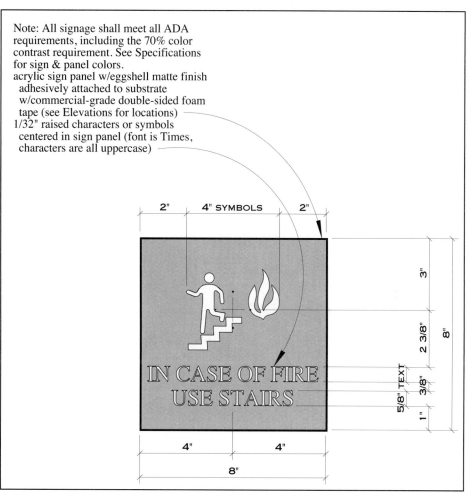

2"   4" SYMBOLS   2"

3"

2 3/8"   8"

5/8" TEXT   3/8"   1"

IN CASE OF FIRE
USE STAIRS

4"   4"

8"

DRAWING #

In Case of Fire Sign Detail

SCALE
$\frac{3"}{1'-0"}$

Note: All signage shall meet all ADA
requirements, including the 70% color
contrast requirement. See Specifications
for sign & panel colors.
acrylic sign panel w/eggshell matte finish
  adhesively attached to substrate
  w/commercial-grade double-sided foam
  tape (see Elevations for locations)
1/32" raised characters or symbols
  centered in sign panel (font is Times,
  characters are all uppercase)
computer-engraved raised Grade II Braille
  signage conforming to Specification
  #800, National Library Service, Library
  of Congress, in this area

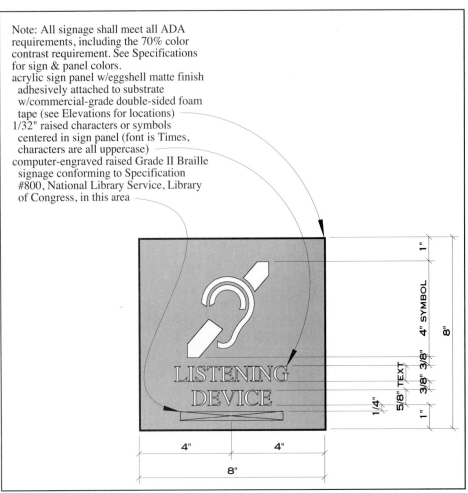

Listening Device Sign Detail

Note: All signage shall meet all ADA
requirements, including the 70% color
contrast requirement. See Specifications
for sign & panel colors.
acrylic sign panel w/eggshell matte finish
 adhesively attached to substrate
 w/commercial-grade double-sided foam
 tape (see Elevations for locations)
1/32" raised characters or symbols
 centered in sign panel (font is Times,
 characters are all uppercase)
computer-engraved raised Grade II Braille
 signage conforming to Specification
 #800, National Library Service, Library
 of Congress, in this area

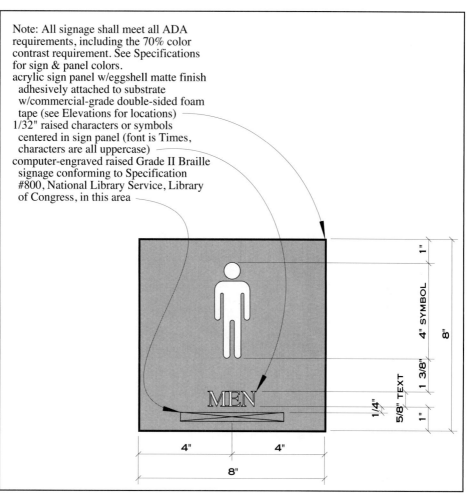

Men's Restroom Sign Detail

Note: All signage shall meet all ADA
requirements, including the 70% color
contrast requirement. See Specifications
for sign & panel colors.
acrylic sign panel w/eggshell matte finish
  adhesively attached to substrate
  w/commercial-grade double-sided foam
  tape (see Elevations for locations)
1/32" raised characters or symbols
  centered in sign panel (font is Times,
  characters are all uppercase)
computer-engraved raised Grade II Braille
  signage conforming to Specification
  #800, National Library Service, Library
  of Congress, in this area

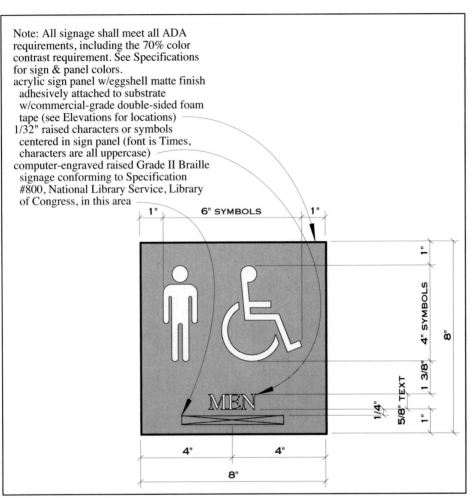

 Men's Accessible Restroom Sign Detail

Note: All signage shall meet all ADA
requirements, including the 70% color
contrast requirement. See Specifications
for sign & panel colors.
acrylic sign panel w/eggshell matte finish
  adhesively attached to substrate
  w/commercial-grade double-sided foam
  tape (see Elevations for locations)
1/32" raised characters or symbols
  centered in sign panel (font is Times,
  characters are all uppercase)

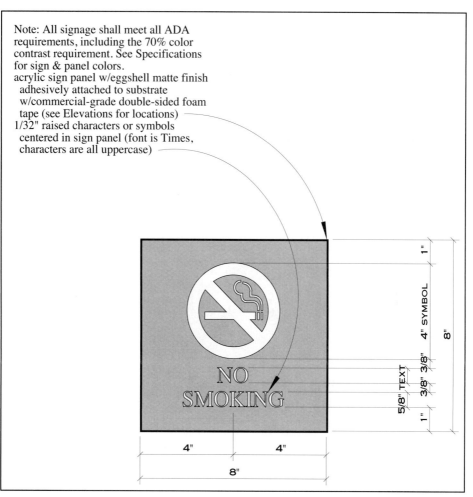

No Smoking Sign Detail

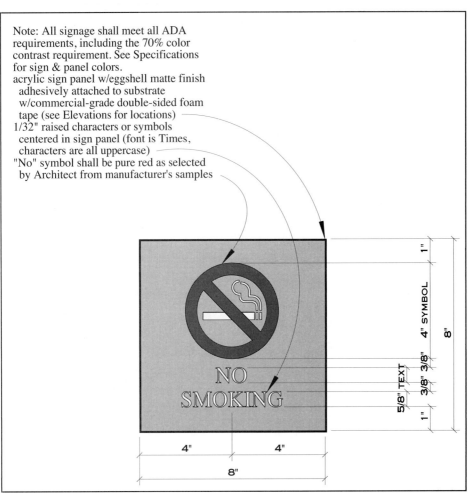

Note: All signage shall meet all ADA requirements, including the 70% color contrast requirement. See Specifications for sign & panel colors.

acrylic sign panel w/eggshell matte finish adhesively attached to substrate w/commercial-grade double-sided foam tape (see Elevations for locations)

1/32" raised characters or symbols centered in sign panel (font is Times, characters are all uppercase)

"No" symbol shall be pure red as selected by Architect from manufacturer's samples

NO
SMOKING

1"

4" SYMBOL

8"

3/8" 3/8"

5/8" TEXT

1"

4"   4"

8"

DRAWING #

No Smoking Sign Detail

SCALE
3"
1'-0"

Note: All signage shall meet all ADA
requirements, including the 70% color
contrast requirement. See Specifications
for sign & panel colors.
acrylic sign panel w/eggshell matte finish
  adhesively attached to substrate
  w/commercial-grade double-sided foam
  tape (see Elevations for locations)
1/32" raised characters or symbols
  centered in sign panel (font is Times,
  characters are all uppercase)
computer-engraved raised Grade II Braille
  signage conforming to Specification
  #800, National Library Service, Library
  of Congress, in this area

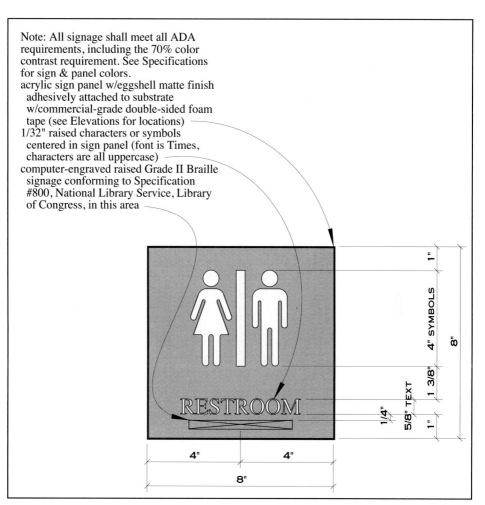

Restroom Sign Detail

Note: All signage shall meet all ADA
requirements, including the 70% color
contrast requirement. See Specifications
for sign & panel colors.
acrylic sign panel w/eggshell matte finish
  adhesively attached to substrate
  w/commercial-grade double-sided foam
  tape (see Elevations for locations)
1/32" raised characters or symbols
  centered in sign panel (font is Times,
  characters are all uppercase)
computer-engraved raised Grade II Braille
  signage conforming to Specification
  #800, National Library Service, Library
  of Congress, in this area

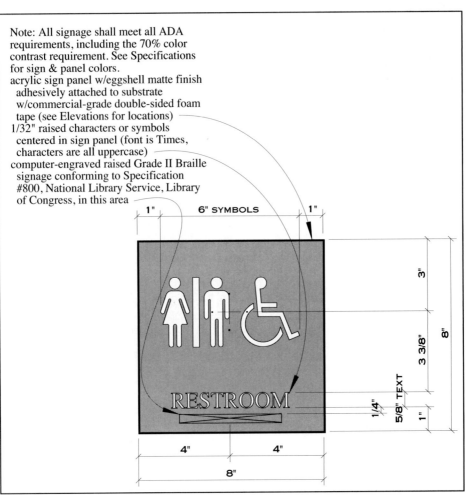

Accessible Restroom Sign Detail

DRAWING #

SCALE
3"
1'-0"

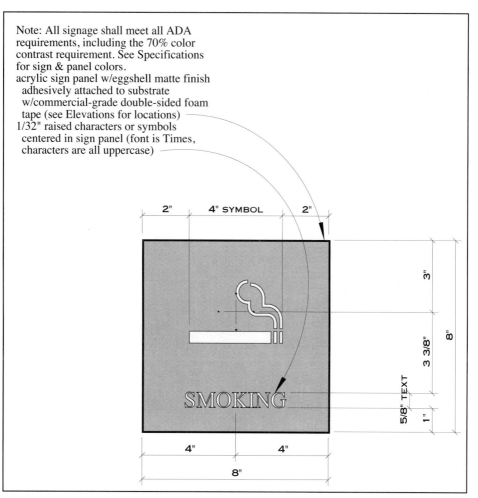

Note: All signage shall meet all ADA
requirements, including the 70% color
contrast requirement. See Specifications
for sign & panel colors.
acrylic sign panel w/eggshell matte finish
  adhesively attached to substrate
  w/commercial-grade double-sided foam
  tape (see Elevations for locations)
1/32" raised characters or symbols
  centered in sign panel (font is Times,
  characters are all uppercase)

2"   4" SYMBOL   2"

3"

8"

3 3/8"

5/8" TEXT

1"

SMOKING

4"   4"

8"

DRAWING #

Smoking Sign Detail

SCALE
3"
―――
1'-0"

Note: All signage shall meet all ADA
requirements, including the 70% color
contrast requirement. See Specifications
for sign & panel colors.
acrylic sign panel w/eggshell matte finish
  adhesively attached to substrate
  w/commercial-grade double-sided foam
  tape (see Elevations for locations)
1/32" raised characters or symbols
  centered in sign panel (font is Times,
  characters are all uppercase)
computer-engraved raised Grade II Braille
  signage conforming to Specification
  #800, National Library Service, Library
  of Congress, in this area

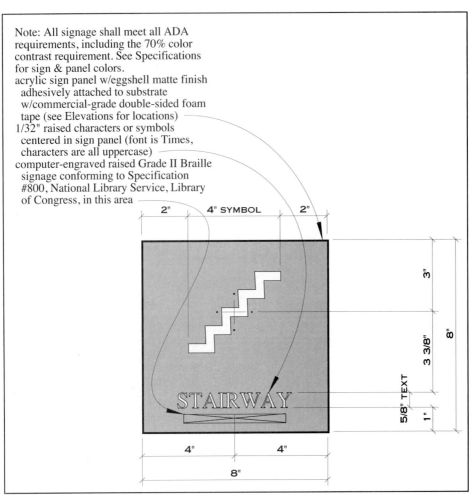

| 2" | 4" SYMBOL | 2" |

STAIRWAY

3"

8"

3 3/8"

5/8" TEXT

1"

| 4" | 4" |
| 8" | |

DRAWING #

Stairway Sign Detail

SCALE
3"
1'-0"

G019
600

Note: All signage shall meet all ADA
requirements, including the 70% color
contrast requirement. See Specifications
for sign & panel colors.
acrylic sign panel w/eggshell matte finish
  adhesively attached to substrate
  w/commercial-grade double-sided foam
  tape (see Elevations for locations)
1/32" raised characters or symbols
  centered in sign panel (font is Times,
  characters are all uppercase)
computer-engraved raised Grade II Braille
  signage conforming to Specification
  #800, National Library Service, Library
  of Congress, in this area

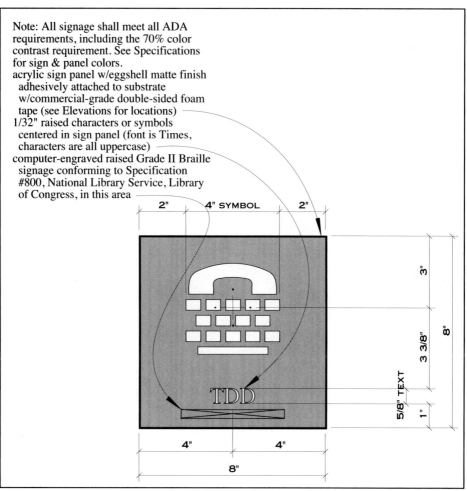

TDD Sign Detail

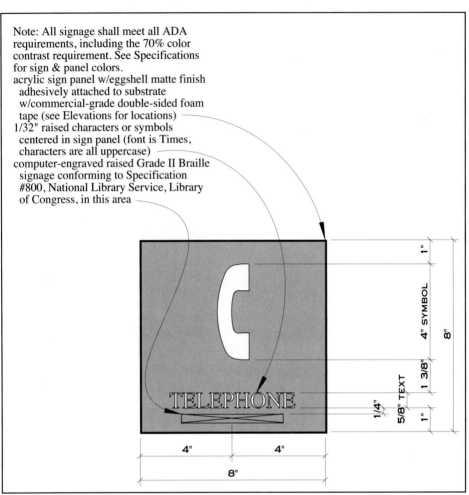

Note: All signage shall meet all ADA requirements, including the 70% color contrast requirement. See Specifications for sign & panel colors.

acrylic sign panel w/eggshell matte finish adhesively attached to substrate w/commercial-grade double-sided foam tape (see Elevations for locations)

1/32" raised characters or symbols centered in sign panel (font is Times, characters are all uppercase)

computer-engraved raised Grade II Braille signage conforming to Specification #800, National Library Service, Library of Congress, in this area

TELEPHONE

1"

4" SYMBOL

8"

1 3/8"

1/4"

5/8" TEXT

1"

4" 4"

8"

DRAWING #

Telephone Sign Detail

SCALE

$\dfrac{3"}{1'\text{-}0"}$

Note: All signage shall meet all ADA
requirements, including the 70% color
contrast requirement. See Specifications
for sign & panel colors.
acrylic sign panel w/eggshell matte finish
    adhesively attached to substrate
    w/commercial-grade double-sided foam
    tape (see Elevations for locations)
1/32" raised characters or symbols
    centered in sign panel (font is Times,
    characters are all uppercase)
computer-engraved raised Grade II Braille
    signage conforming to Specification
    #800, National Library Service, Library
    of Congress, in this area

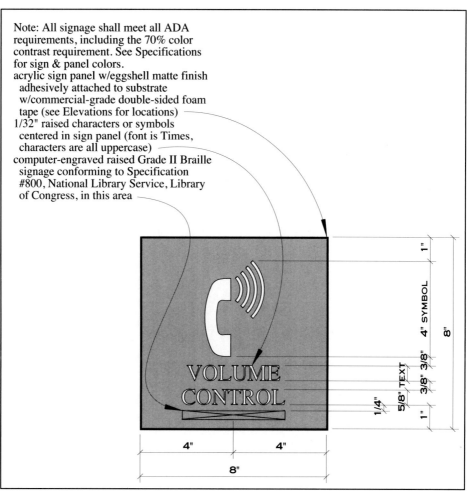

 Volume Control Telephone Sign Detail

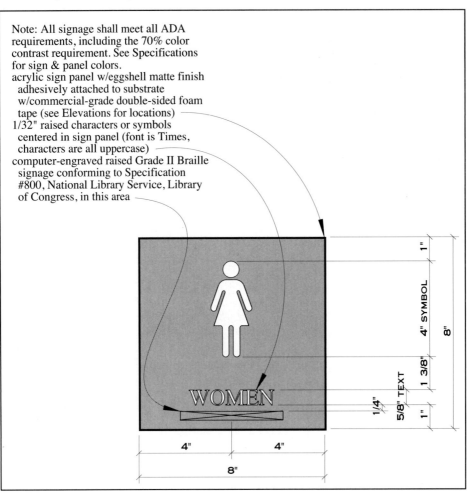

Note: All signage shall meet all ADA
requirements, including the 70% color
contrast requirement. See Specifications
for sign & panel colors.
acrylic sign panel w/eggshell matte finish
  adhesively attached to substrate
  w/commercial-grade double-sided foam
  tape (see Elevations for locations)
1/32" raised characters or symbols
  centered in sign panel (font is Times,
  characters are all uppercase)
computer-engraved raised Grade II Braille
  signage conforming to Specification
  #800, National Library Service, Library
  of Congress, in this area

WOMEN

1"
4" SYMBOL
8"
1 3/8"
5/8" TEXT
1/4"
1"

4"   4"
8"

Women's Restroom Sign Detail

Note: All signage shall meet all ADA
requirements, including the 70% color
contrast requirement. See Specifications
for sign & panel colors.
acrylic sign panel w/eggshell matte finish
  adhesively attached to substrate
  w/commercial-grade double-sided foam
  tape (see Elevations for locations)
1/32" raised characters or symbols
  centered in sign panel (font is Times,
  characters are all uppercase)
computer-engraved raised Grade II Braille
  signage conforming to Specification
  #800, National Library Service, Library
  of Congress, in this area

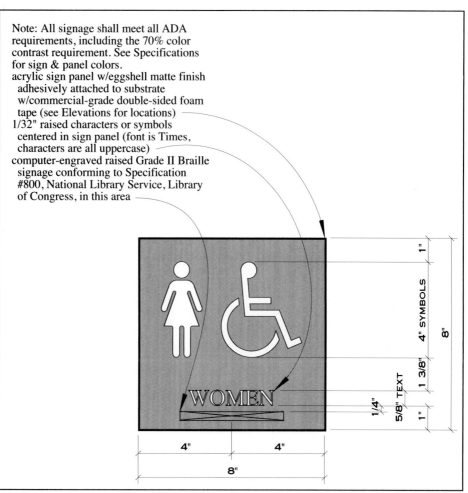

Women's Accessible Bath Sign Detail

DRAWING #

SCALE
3"
1'-0"

HVAC, PLUMBING & ELECTRICAL DETAILS

This section includes general HVAC, plumbing & electrical details. The contents of this section are as follows:

Electrical Details 608
HVAC Details 615
Plumbing Details 624

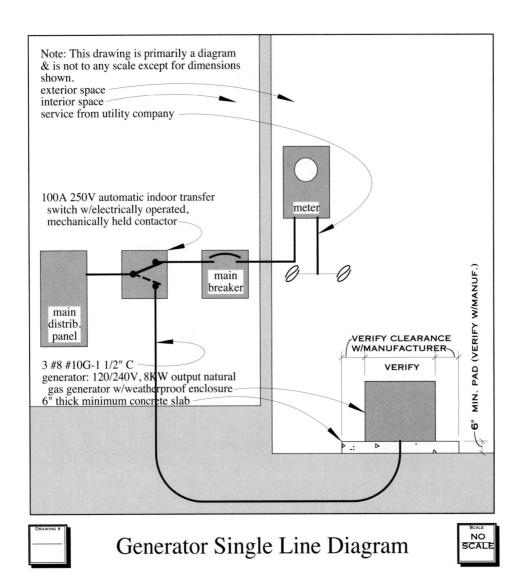

Note: This drawing is primarily a diagram & is not to any scale except for dimensions shown.
exterior space
interior space
service from utility company

meter

100A 250V automatic indoor transfer switch w/electrically operated, mechanically held contactor

main breaker

main distrib. panel

3 #8 #10G-1 1/2" C
generator: 120/240V, 8KW output natural gas generator w/weatherproof enclosure
6" thick minimum concrete slab

VERIFY CLEARANCE W/MANUFACTURER

VERIFY

6" MIN. PAD (VERIFY W/MANUF.)

Generator Single Line Diagram

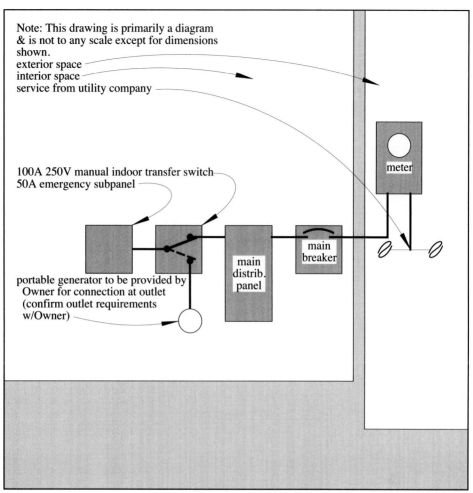

Note: This drawing is primarily a diagram
& is not to any scale except for dimensions
shown.
exterior space
interior space
service from utility company

meter

100A 250V manual indoor transfer switch
50A emergency subpanel

main
distrib.
panel

main
breaker

portable generator to be provided by
Owner for connection at outlet
(confirm outlet requirements
w/Owner)

Generator Single Line Diagram

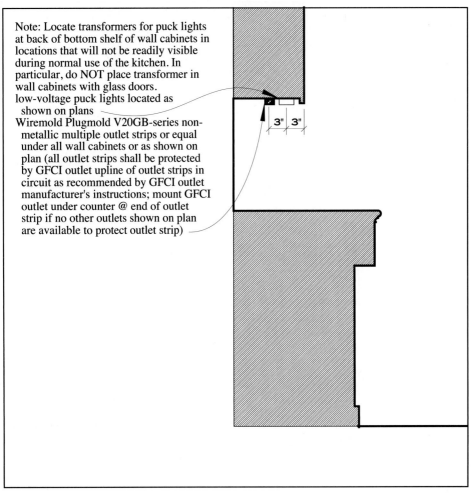

Note: Locate transformers for puck lights at back of bottom shelf of wall cabinets in locations that will not be readily visible during normal use of the kitchen. In particular, do NOT place transformer in wall cabinets with glass doors.

low-voltage puck lights located as shown on plans

Wiremold Plugmold V20GB-series non-metallic multiple outlet strips or equal under all wall cabinets or as shown on plan (all outlet strips shall be protected by GFCI outlet upline of outlet strips in circuit as recommended by GFCI outlet manufacturer's instructions; mount GFCI outlet under counter @ end of outlet strip if no other outlets shown on plan are available to protect outlet strip)

3" 3"

DRAWING #

Kitchen Electrical Locations Diagram

SCALE
3/4"
1'-0"

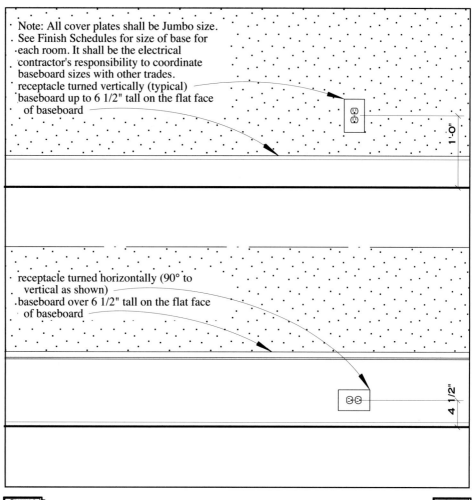

Note: All cover plates shall be Jumbo size.
See Finish Schedules for size of base for
each room. It shall be the electrical
contractor's responsibility to coordinate
baseboard sizes with other trades.
receptacle turned vertically (typical)
baseboard up to 6 1/2" tall on the flat face
  of baseboard

1'-0"

receptacle turned horizontally (90° to
  vertical as shown)
baseboard over 6 1/2" tall on the flat face
  of baseboard

4 1/2"

Electrical Outlet Locations Diagram

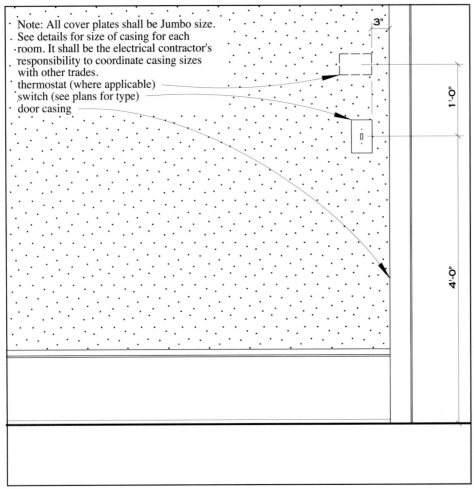

Note: All cover plates shall be Jumbo size.
See details for size of casing for each
room. It shall be the electrical contractor's
responsibility to coordinate casing sizes
with other trades.
thermostat (where applicable)
switch (see plans for type)
door casing

3"

1'-0"

4'-0"

DRAWING #	Switch Locations Diagram	SCALE 3/4" 1'-0"

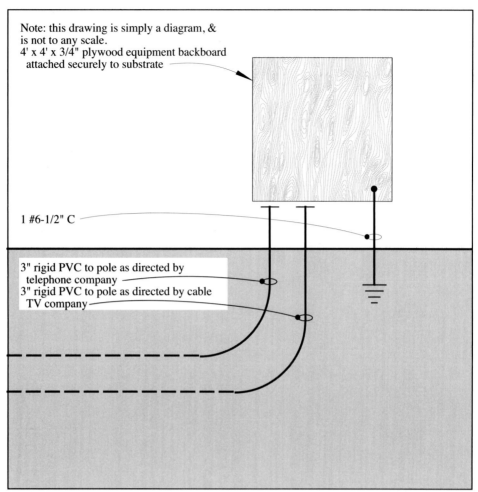

Note: this drawing is simply a diagram, &
is not to any scale.
4' x 4' x 3/4" plywood equipment backboard
 attached securely to substrate

1 #6-1/2" C

3" rigid PVC to pole as directed by
 telephone company
3" rigid PVC to pole as directed by cable
 TV company

Telephone & TV Single Line Diagram

DRAWING #

SCALE
NO
SCALE

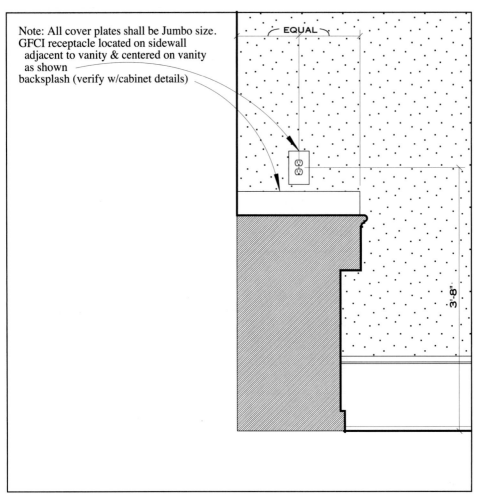

Note: All cover plates shall be Jumbo size.
GFCI receptacle located on sidewall
  adjacent to vanity & centered on vanity
  as shown
backsplash (verify w/cabinet details)

EQUAL

3'-8"

Vanity Electrical Location Diagram

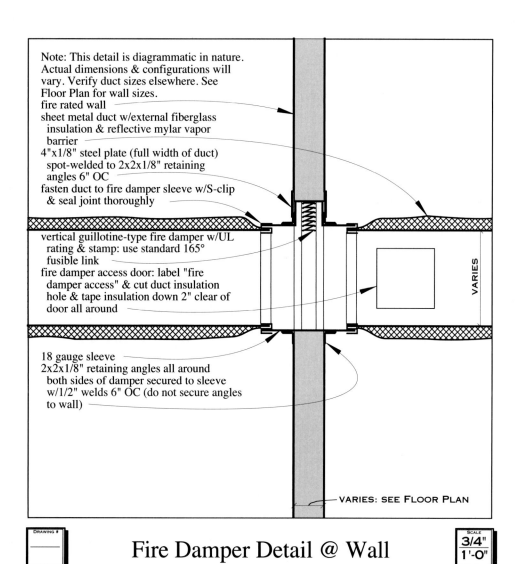

Note: This detail is diagrammatic in nature.
Actual dimensions & configurations will
vary. Verify duct sizes elsewhere. See
Floor Plan for wall sizes.

fire rated wall

sheet metal duct w/external fiberglass
  insulation & reflective mylar vapor
  barrier

4"x1/8" steel plate (full width of duct)
  spot-welded to 2x2x1/8" retaining
  angles 6" OC

fasten duct to fire damper sleeve w/S-clip
  & seal joint thoroughly

vertical guillotine-type fire damper w/UL
  rating & stamp: use standard 165°
  fusible link

fire damper access door: label "fire
  damper access" & cut duct insulation
  hole & tape insulation down 2" clear of
  door all around

18 gauge sleeve

2x2x1/8" retaining angles all around
  both sides of damper secured to sleeve
  w/1/2" welds 6" OC (do not secure angles
  to wall)

VARIES

VARIES: SEE FLOOR PLAN

DRAWING #

Fire Damper Detail @ Wall

SCALE
3/4"
1'-0"

HH001
615

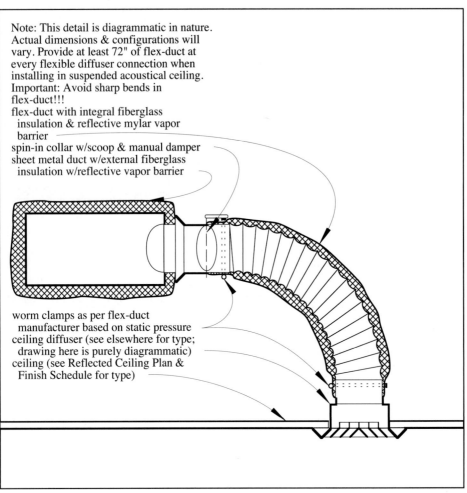

Note: This detail is diagrammatic in nature. Actual dimensions & configurations will vary. Provide at least 72" of flex-duct at every flexible diffuser connection when installing in suspended acoustical ceiling. Important: Avoid sharp bends in flex-duct!!!
flex-duct with integral fiberglass insulation & reflective mylar vapor barrier
spin-in collar w/scoop & manual damper
sheet metal duct w/external fiberglass insulation w/reflective vapor barrier

worm clamps as per flex-duct manufacturer based on static pressure
ceiling diffuser (see elsewhere for type; drawing here is purely diagrammatic)
ceiling (see Reflected Ceiling Plan & Finish Schedule for type)

DRAWING #

Flexible Duct Connection

SCALE
3/4"
1'-0"

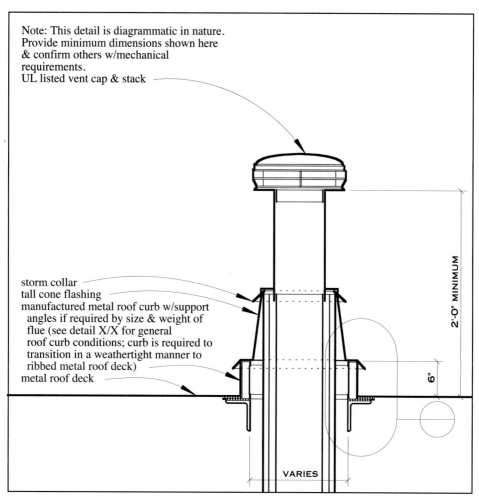

Note: This detail is diagrammatic in nature.
Provide minimum dimensions shown here
& confirm others w/mechanical
requirements.
UL listed vent cap & stack

storm collar
tall cone flashing
manufactured metal roof curb w/support
  angles if required by size & weight of
  flue (see detail X/X for general
  roof curb conditions; curb is required to
  transition in a weathertight manner to
  ribbed metal roof deck)
metal roof deck

2'-0" MINIMUM

6"

VARIES

DRAWING #

Gas Vent Detail @ Metal Roof

SCALE
3/4"
1'-0"

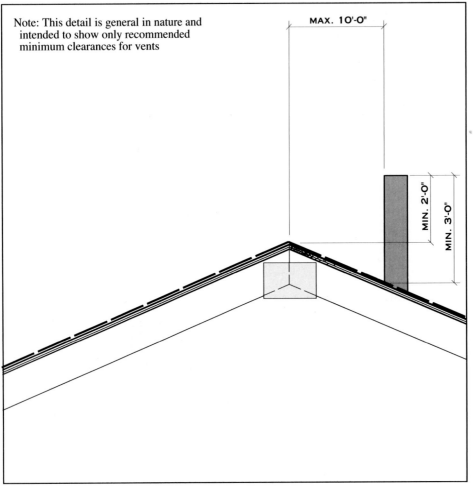

Note: This detail is general in nature and
intended to show only recommended
minimum clearances for vents

MAX. 10'-0"

MIN. 2'-0"

MIN. 3'-0"

DRAWING #

Typical Gas Vent Requirements

SCALE
NO
SCALE

HH004
618

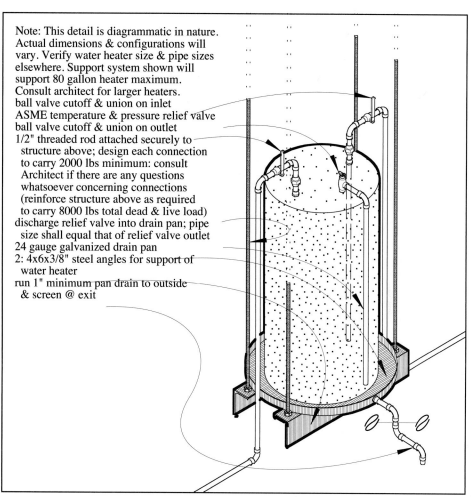

Note: This detail is diagrammatic in nature. Actual dimensions & configurations will vary. Verify water heater size & pipe sizes elsewhere. Support system shown will support 80 gallon heater maximum. Consult architect for larger heaters.

ball valve cutoff & union on inlet

ASME temperature & pressure relief valve

ball valve cutoff & union on outlet

1/2" threaded rod attached securely to structure above; design each connection to carry 2000 lbs minimum: consult Architect if there are any questions whatsoever concerning connections (reinforce structure above as required to carry 8000 lbs total dead & live load)

discharge relief valve into drain pan; pipe size shall equal that of relief valve outlet

24 gauge galvanized drain pan

2: 4x6x3/8" steel angles for support of water heater

run 1" minimum pan drain to outside & screen @ exit

DRAWING #

Suspended Electric Water Heater Detail

SCALE
1/2"
1'-0"

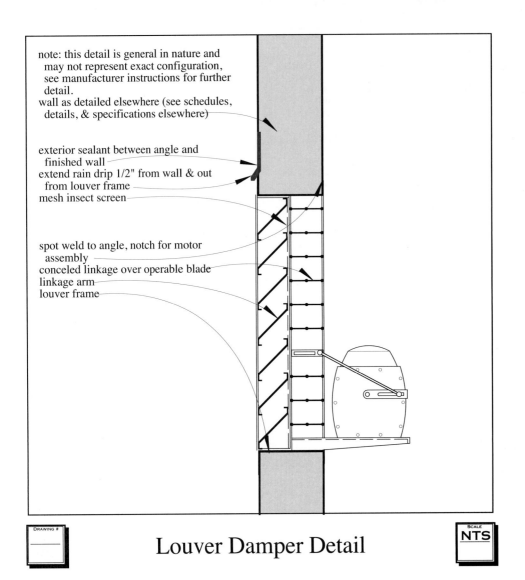

note: this detail is general in nature and
  may not represent exact configuration,
  see manufacturer instructions for further
  detail.
wall as detailed elsewhere (see schedules,
  details, & specifications elsewhere)

exterior sealant between angle and
  finished wall
extend rain drip 1/2" from wall & out
  from louver frame
mesh insect screen

spot weld to angle, notch for motor
  assembly
conceled linkage over operable blade
linkage arm
louver frame

Louver Damper Detail

DRAWING #

SCALE
NTS

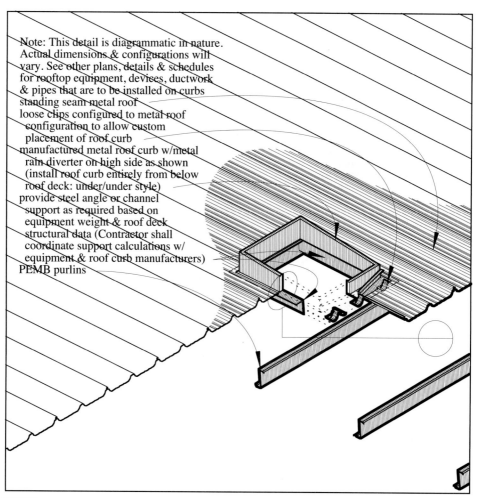

Note: This detail is diagrammatic in nature. Actual dimensions & configurations will vary. See other plans, details & schedules for rooftop equipment, devices, ductwork & pipes that are to be installed on curbs

standing seam metal roof

loose clips configured to metal roof configuration to allow custom placement of roof curb

manufactured metal roof curb w/metal rain diverter on high side as shown (install roof curb entirely from below roof deck: under/under style)

provide steel angle or channel support as required based on equipment weight & roof deck structural data (Contractor shall coordinate support calculations w/ equipment & roof curb manufacturers)

PEMB purlins

 DRAWING #

Metal Roof Curb Detail on Metal Roof

 SCALE
1/4"
1'-0"

HH007
621

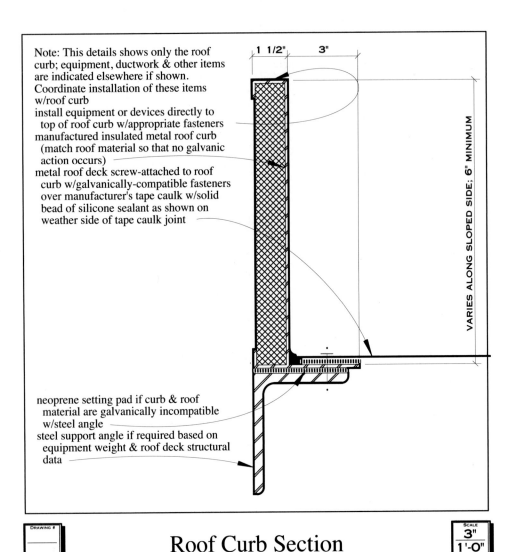

Note: This details shows only the roof curb; equipment, ductwork & other items are indicated elsewhere if shown. Coordinate installation of these items w/roof curb

install equipment or devices directly to top of roof curb w/appropriate fasteners

manufactured insulated metal roof curb (match roof material so that no galvanic action occurs)

metal roof deck screw-attached to roof curb w/galvanically-compatible fasteners over manufacturer's tape caulk w/solid bead of silicone sealant as shown on weather side of tape caulk joint

neoprene setting pad if curb & roof material are galvanically incompatible w/steel angle

steel support angle if required based on equipment weight & roof deck structural data

1 1/2"   3"

VARIES ALONG SLOPED SIDE; 6" MINIMUM

Roof Curb Section

DRAWING #

SCALE
3"
1'-0"

HH008
622

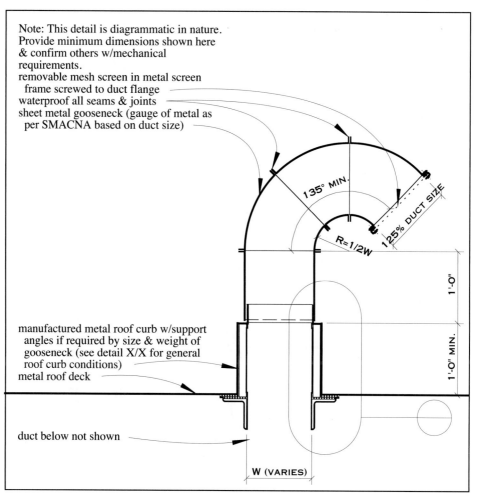

Note: This detail is diagrammatic in nature.
Provide minimum dimensions shown here
& confirm others w/mechanical
requirements.
removable mesh screen in metal screen
  frame screwed to duct flange
waterproof all seams & joints
sheet metal gooseneck (gauge of metal as
  per SMACNA based on duct size)

135° MIN.

125% DUCT SIZE

R=1/2W

1'-0"

1'-0" MIN.

manufactured metal roof curb w/support
  angles if required by size & weight of
  gooseneck (see detail X/X for general
  roof curb conditions)
metal roof deck

duct below not shown

W (VARIES)

Gooseneck Detail @ Metal Roof

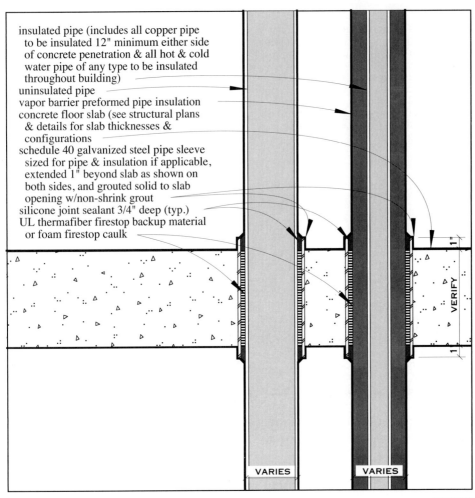

insulated pipe (includes all copper pipe
  to be insulated 12" minimum either side
  of concrete penetration & all hot & cold
  water pipe of any type to be insulated
  throughout building)
uninsulated pipe
vapor barrier preformed pipe insulation
concrete floor slab (see structural plans
  & details for slab thicknesses &
  configurations
schedule 40 galvanized steel pipe sleeve
  sized for pipe & insulation if applicable,
  extended 1" beyond slab as shown on
  both sides, and grouted solid to slab
  opening w/non-shrink grout
silicone joint sealant 3/4" deep (typ.)
UL thermafiber firestop backup material
  or foam firestop caulk

VARIES   VARIES

1"
VERIFY
1'-0"
1"

Pipe Sleeve Details @ Concrete Slab

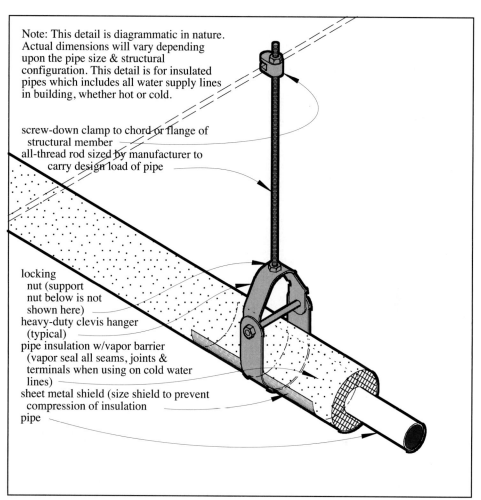

Note: This detail is diagrammatic in nature. Actual dimensions will vary depending upon the pipe size & structural configuration. This detail is for insulated pipes which includes all water supply lines in building, whether hot or cold.

screw-down clamp to chord or flange of structural member

all-thread rod sized by manufacturer to carry design load of pipe

locking nut (support nut below is not shown here)

heavy-duty clevis hanger (typical)

pipe insulation w/vapor barrier (vapor seal all seams, joints & terminals when using on cold water lines)

sheet metal shield (size shield to prevent compression of insulation

pipe

Insulated Pipe Support Detail

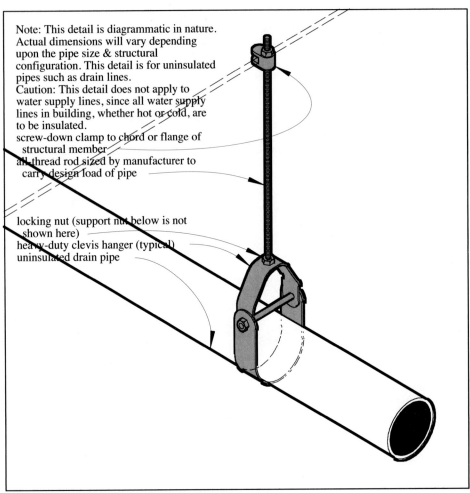

Note: This detail is diagrammatic in nature. Actual dimensions will vary depending upon the pipe size & structural configuration. This detail is for uninsulated pipes such as drain lines.

Caution: This detail does not apply to water supply lines, since all water supply lines in building, whether hot or cold, are to be insulated.

screw-down clamp to chord or flange of structural member

all-thread rod sized by manufacturer to carry design load of pipe

locking nut (support nut below is not shown here)

heavy-duty clevis hanger (typical)

uninsulated drain pipe

Uninsulated Pipe Support Detail

DRAWING #

SCALE
NO
SCALE

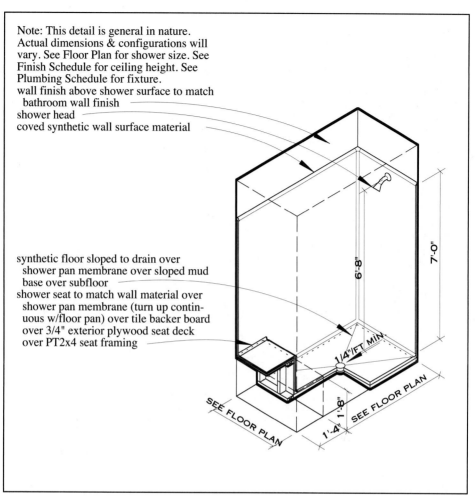

Note: This detail is general in nature.
Actual dimensions & configurations will
vary. See Floor Plan for shower size. See
Finish Schedule for ceiling height. See
Plumbing Schedule for fixture.

wall finish above shower surface to match
  bathroom wall finish

shower head

coved synthetic wall surface material

synthetic floor sloped to drain over
  shower pan membrane over sloped mud
  base over subfloor

shower seat to match wall material over
  shower pan membrane (turn up continuous w/floor pan) over tile backer board
  over 3/4" exterior plywood seat deck
  over PT2x4 seat framing

6'-8"

7'-0"

1/4"/FT MIN.

SEE FLOOR PLAN

SEE FLOOR PLAN

1'-4"   1'-8"

DRAWING #

Custom Synthetic Shower Detail

SCALE
1/4"
1'-0"

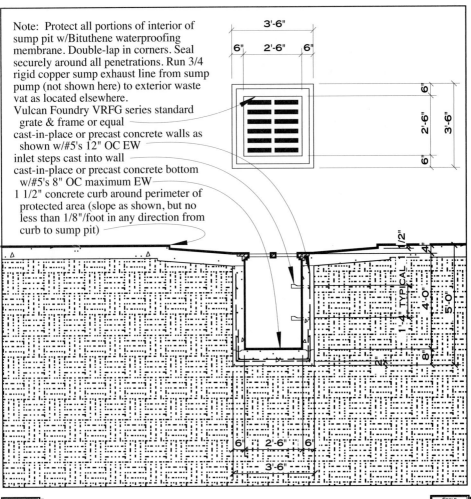

Note: Protect all portions of interior of sump pit w/Bituthene waterproofing membrane. Double-lap in corners. Seal securely around all penetrations. Run 3/4 rigid copper sump exhaust line from sump pump (not shown here) to exterior waste vat as located elsewhere.

Vulcan Foundry VRFG series standard grate & frame or equal

cast-in-place or precast concrete walls as shown w/#5's 12" OC EW

inlet steps cast into wall

cast-in-place or precast concrete bottom w/#5's 8" OC maximum EW

1 1/2" concrete curb around perimeter of protected area (slope as shown, but no less than 1/8"/foot in any direction from curb to sump pit)

Waste Sump Pit Detail

DRAWING #

SCALE
1/4"
1'-0"

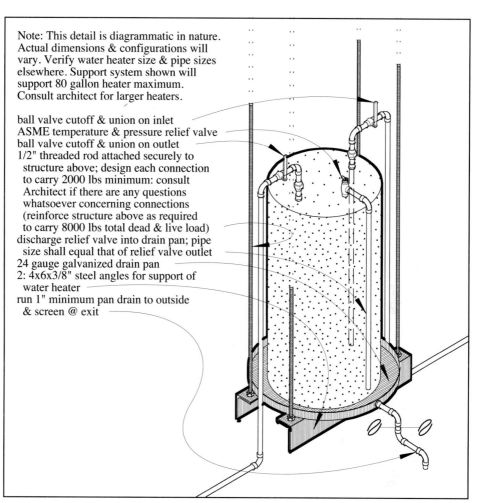

Note: This detail is diagrammatic in nature.
Actual dimensions & configurations will
vary. Verify water heater size & pipe sizes
elsewhere. Support system shown will
support 80 gallon heater maximum.
Consult architect for larger heaters.

ball valve cutoff & union on inlet
ASME temperature & pressure relief valve
ball valve cutoff & union on outlet
1/2" threaded rod attached securely to
   structure above; design each connection
   to carry 2000 lbs minimum: consult
   Architect if there are any questions
   whatsoever concerning connections
   (reinforce structure above as required
   to carry 8000 lbs total dead & live load)
discharge relief valve into drain pan; pipe
   size shall equal that of relief valve outlet
24 gauge galvanized drain pan
2: 4x6x3/8" steel angles for support of
   water heater
run 1" minimum pan drain to outside
   & screen @ exit

DRAWING #

Suspended Electric Water Heater Detail

SCALE
1/2"
1'-0"

MISCELLANEOUS DETAILS

This section includes all details which did not fit appropriately into another section. The contents of this section are as follows:

Chimney Details 632
Expansion Joint Details 637
Ladder Details 643
Specialty Details 646

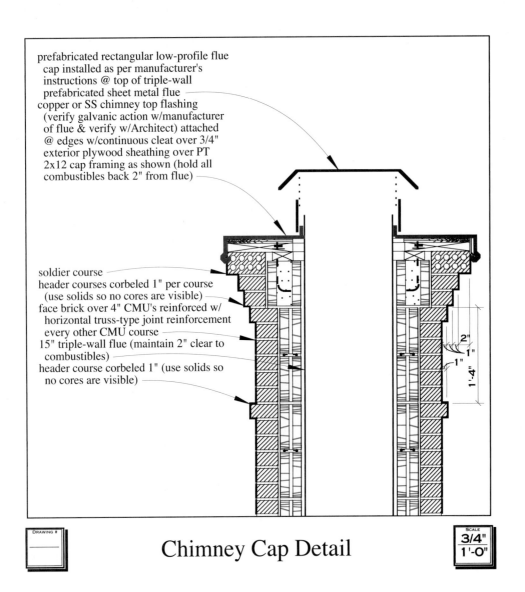

prefabricated rectangular low-profile flue
  cap installed as per manufacturer's
  instructions @ top of triple-wall
  prefabricated sheet metal flue
copper or SS chimney top flashing
  (verify galvanic action w/manufacturer
  of flue & verify w/Architect) attached
  @ edges w/continuous cleat over 3/4"
  exterior plywood sheathing over PT
  2x12 cap framing as shown (hold all
  combustibles back 2" from flue)

soldier course
header courses corbeled 1" per course
  (use solids so no cores are visible)
face brick over 4" CMU's reinforced w/
  horizontal truss-type joint reinforcement
  every other CMU course
15" triple-wall flue (maintain 2" clear to
  combustibles)
header course corbeled 1" (use solids so
  no cores are visible)

2"
1"
1"
1'-4"

DRAWING #

Chimney Cap Detail

SCALE
3/4"
1'-0"

MCB001
632

face brick over 4" CMU's reinforced w/
horizontal truss-type joint reinforcement
every other CMU course
15" triple-wall flue

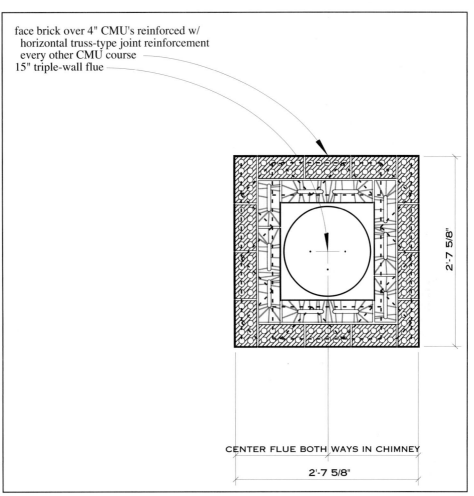

2'-7 5/8"

CENTER FLUE BOTH WAYS IN CHIMNEY

2'-7 5/8"

DRAWING #

Chimney Section

SCALE

3/4"
1'-0"

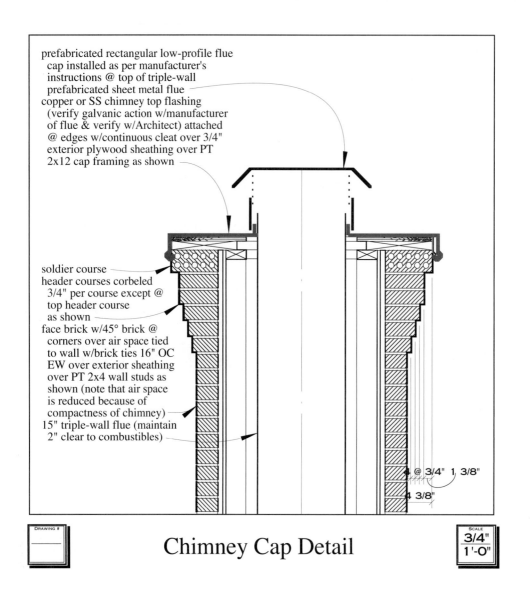

prefabricated rectangular low-profile flue
  cap installed as per manufacturer's
  instructions @ top of triple-wall
  prefabricated sheet metal flue
copper or SS chimney top flashing
  (verify galvanic action w/manufacturer
  of flue & verify w/Architect) attached
  @ edges w/continuous cleat over 3/4"
  exterior plywood sheathing over PT
  2x12 cap framing as shown

soldier course
header courses corbeled
  3/4" per course except @
  top header course
  as shown
face brick w/45° brick @
  corners over air space tied
  to wall w/brick ties 16" OC
  EW over exterior sheathing
  over PT 2x4 wall studs as
  shown (note that air space
  is reduced because of
  compactness of chimney)
15" triple-wall flue (maintain
  2" clear to combustibles)

4 @ 3/4" 1 3/8"

4 3/8"

Chimney Cap Detail

DRAWING #

SCALE
3/4"
1'-0"

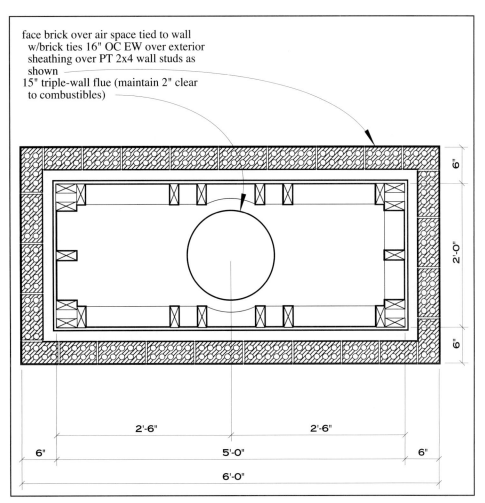

face brick over air space tied to wall
  w/brick ties 16" OC EW over exterior
  sheathing over PT 2x4 wall studs as
  shown
15" triple-wall flue (maintain 2" clear
  to combustibles)

6"

2'-0"

6"

2'-6"

2'-6"

6"

5'-0"

6"

6'-0"

DRAWING #

Lower Chimney Section

SCALE
3/4"
1'-0"

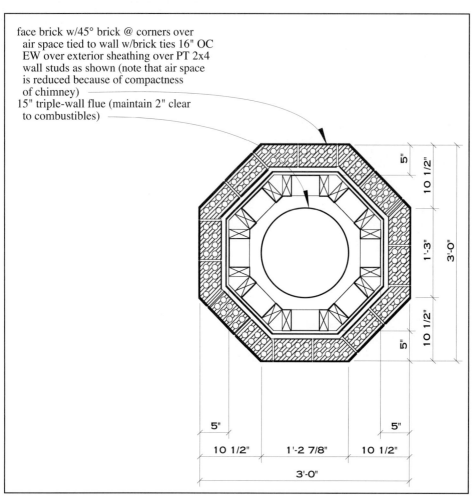

face brick w/45° brick @ corners over
  air space tied to wall w/brick ties 16" OC
  EW over exterior sheathing over PT 2x4
  wall studs as shown (note that air space
  is reduced because of compactness
  of chimney)
15" triple-wall flue (maintain 2" clear
  to combustibles)

5"   10 1/2"   1'-3"   10 1/2"   5"   3'-0"

5"   5"
10 1/2"   1'-2 7/8"   10 1/2"
3'-0"

Chimney Top Section

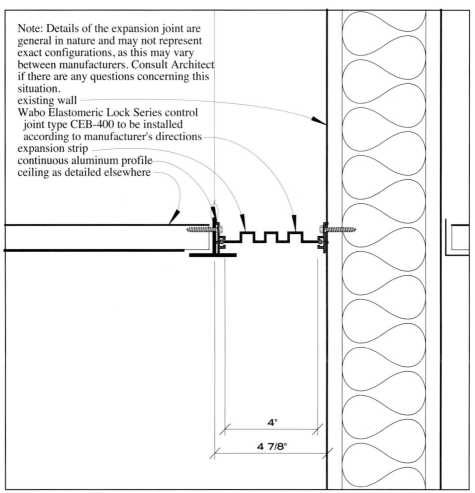

Note: Details of the expansion joint are general in nature and may not represent exact configurations, as this may vary between manufacturers. Consult Architect if there are any questions concerning this situation.
existing wall
Wabo Elastomeric Lock Series control joint type CEB-400 to be installed according to manufacturer's directions
expansion strip
continuous aluminum profile
ceiling as detailed elsewhere

4"

4 7/8"

DRAWING #

Ceiling Expansion Joint @ Ceiling/Wall

SCALE
3"
1'-0"

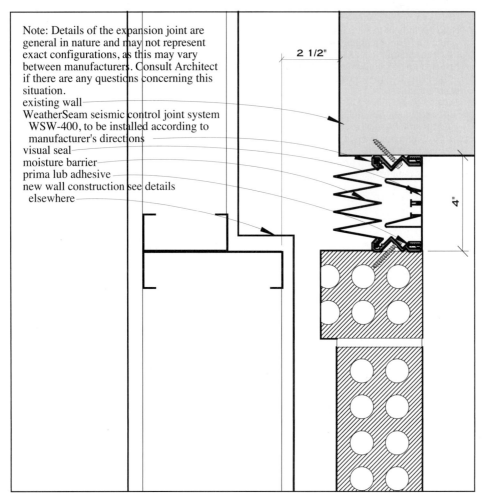

Note: Details of the expansion joint are
general in nature and may not represent
exact configurations, as this may vary
between manufacturers. Consult Architect
if there are any questions concerning this
situation.
existing wall
WeatherSeam seismic control joint system
  WSW-400, to be installed according to
  manufacturer's directions
visual seal
moisture barrier
prima lub adhesive
new wall construction see details
  elsewhere

2 1/2"

4"

DRAWING #	Ext. Wall Expansion Joint @ New/Old	SCALE 3" 1'-0"

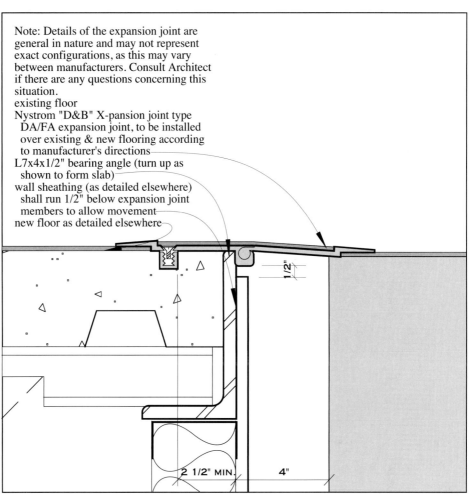

Note: Details of the expansion joint are
general in nature and may not represent
exact configurations, as this may vary
between manufacturers. Consult Architect
if there are any questions concerning this
situation.
existing floor
Nystrom "D&B" X-pansion joint type
   DA/FA expansion joint, to be installed
   over existing & new flooring according
   to manufacturer's directions
L7x4x1/2" bearing angle (turn up as
   shown to form slab)
wall sheathing (as detailed elsewhere)
   shall run 1/2" below expansion joint
   members to allow movement
new floor as detailed elsewhere

1/2"

2 1/2" MIN.   4"

Floor Expansion Joint Detail New/Old

SCALE
3"
1'-0"

ME003
639

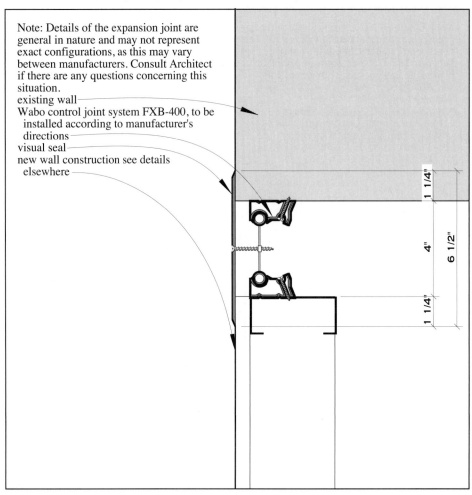

Note: Details of the expansion joint are general in nature and may not represent exact configurations, as this may vary between manufacturers. Consult Architect if there are any questions concerning this situation.

existing wall

Wabo control joint system FXB-400, to be installed according to manufacturer's directions

visual seal

new wall construction see details elsewhere

1 1/4"

4"

6 1/2"

1 1/4"

Int. Wall Expansion Joint @ New/Old

SCALE
$\dfrac{3"}{1'-0"}$

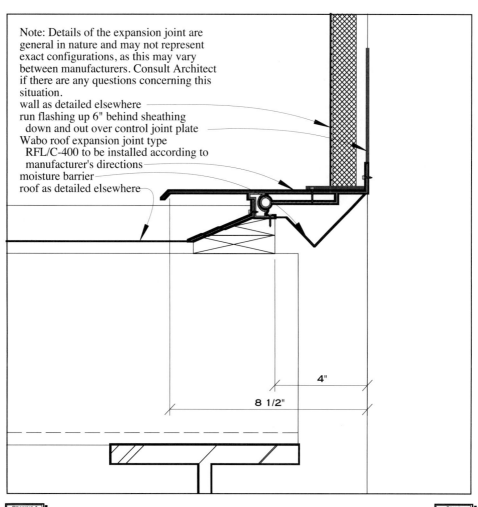

Note: Details of the expansion joint are
general in nature and may not represent
exact configurations, as this may vary
between manufacturers. Consult Architect
if there are any questions concerning this
situation.
wall as detailed elsewhere
run flashing up 6" behind sheathing
  down and out over control joint plate
Wabo roof expansion joint type
  RFL/C-400 to be installed according to
  manufacturer's directions
moisture barrier
roof as detailed elsewhere

4"

8 1/2"

DRAWING #

Ext.Expansion Joint New Roof/Old Wall

SCALE
3"
1'-0"

ME005
641

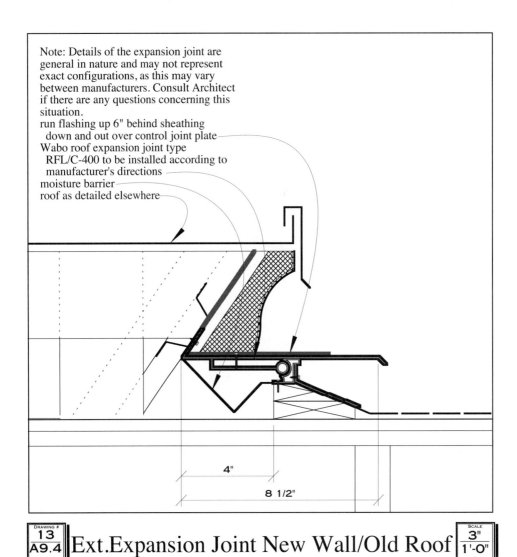

Note: Details of the expansion joint are general in nature and may not represent exact configurations, as this may vary between manufacturers. Consult Architect if there are any questions concerning this situation.

run flashing up 6" behind sheathing down and out over control joint plate

Wabo roof expansion joint type RFL/C-400 to be installed according to manufacturer's directions

moisture barrier

roof as detailed elsewhere

4"

8 1/2"

DRAWING #
13
A9.4

Ext.Expansion Joint New Wall/Old Roof

SCALE
3"
1'-0"

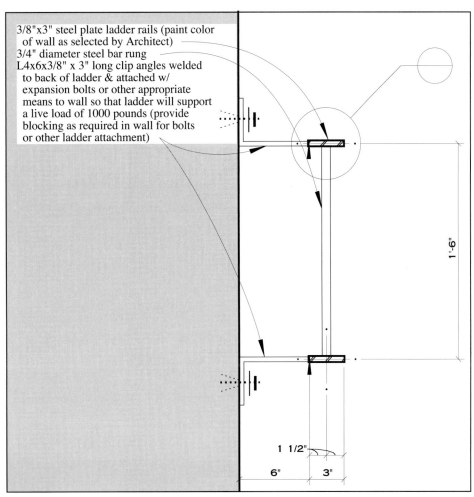

3/8"x3" steel plate ladder rails (paint color of wall as selected by Architect)
3/4" diameter steel bar rung
L4x6x3/8" x 3" long clip angles welded to back of ladder & attached w/ expansion bolts or other appropriate means to wall so that ladder will support a live load of 1000 pounds (provide blocking as required in wall for bolts or other ladder attachment)

1'-6"

1 1/2"

6" 3"

Typical Ladder Section

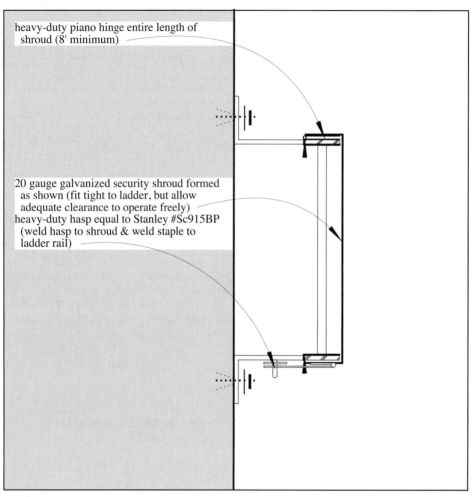

heavy-duty piano hinge entire length of
 shroud (8' minimum)

20 gauge galvanized security shroud formed
 as shown (fit tight to ladder, but allow
 adequate clearance to operate freely)
heavy-duty hasp equal to Stanley #Sc915BP
 (weld hasp to shroud & weld staple to
 ladder rail)

DRAWING #

Ladder Security Shroud Section

SCALE

1 1/2"
1'-0"

ML004
644

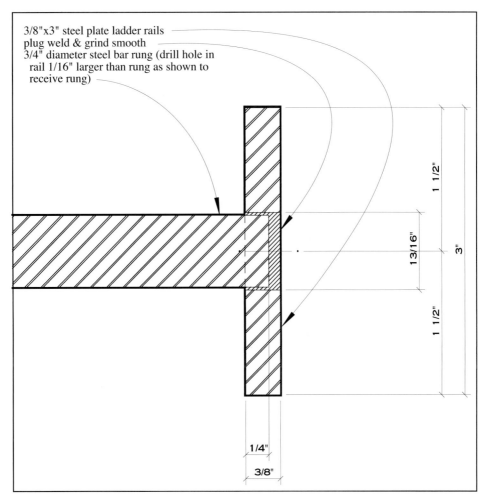

3/8"x3" steel plate ladder rails
plug weld & grind smooth
3/4" diameter steel bar rung (drill hole in
 rail 1/16" larger than rung as shown to
 receive rung)

1 1/2"

13/16"

3"

1 1/2"

1/4"

3/8"

Rung Connection Detail

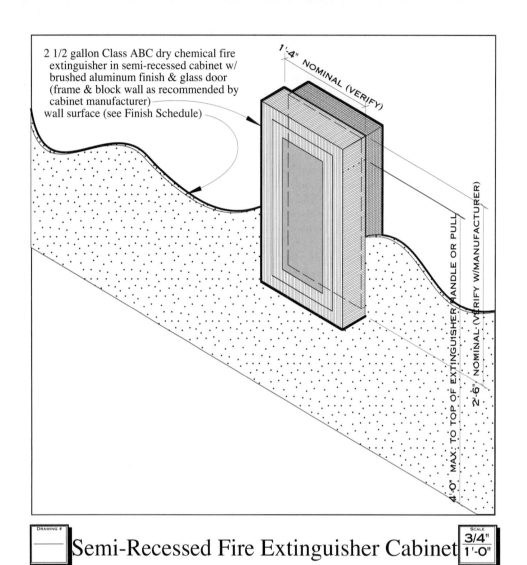

2 1/2 gallon Class ABC dry chemical fire extinguisher in semi-recessed cabinet w/ brushed aluminum finish & glass door (frame & block wall as recommended by cabinet manufacturer)
wall surface (see Finish Schedule)

1'-4" NOMINAL (VERIFY)

4'-0" MAX. TO TOP OF EXTINGUISHER HANDLE OR PULL

2'-6" NOMINAL (VERIFY W/MANUFACTURER)

Semi-Recessed Fire Extinguisher Cabinet

SCALE
3/4"
1'-0"

PORCH DETAILS

Details in this section include all parts of porches and other structures open to the exterior. The contents of this section are as follows:

Column Flashing Details 5
Wood Column Details 6
Porch Floor Details 8
Porch Lattice & Infill Details 10

Note: This detail is typical in nature, and is intended to outline the general procedures for flashing penetrations of waterproof membranes with posts and columns. Post sizes shown here are purely schematic. See details elsewhere for roofing or waterproofing materials.

Step 1: Slit membrane at approximate center of post to allow placement around post. Cut membrane diagonally @ each corner of post., fitting down around post in the process. Adhere membrane to decking. Adhere flaps to post.

Step 2: Cut strip of membrane 7" high x 5 times width of post. Fit around post to extend 4" up post. Split as shown @ corners. Fit around post, adhering to post & decking in the process.

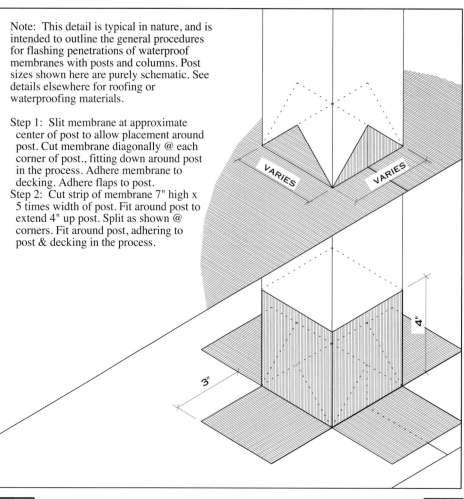

Post Base Flashing Detail

SCALE
3"
1'-0"

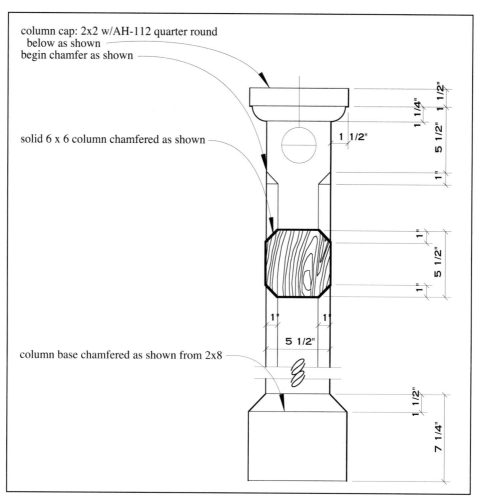

column cap: 2x2 w/AH-112 quarter round
  below as shown
begin chamfer as shown

solid 6 x 6 column chamfered as shown

column base chamfered as shown from 2x8

1 1/2"

1 1/2"
1 1/4"
5 1/2"
1"

1"
5 1/2"
1"

1"
1"
5 1/2"

1 1/2"
7 1/4"

Chamfered 6" Column Details

DRAWING #
____

SCALE
1 1/2"
1'-O"

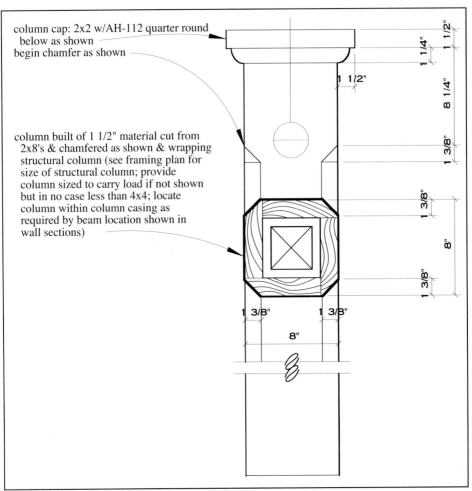

column cap: 2x2 w/AH-112 quarter round
  below as shown
begin chamfer as shown

column built of 1 1/2" material cut from
  2x8's & chamfered as shown & wrapping
  structural column (see framing plan for
  size of structural column; provide
  column sized to carry load if not shown
  but in no case less than 4x4; locate
  column within column casing as
  required by beam location shown in
  wall sections)

1 1/2"

1 1/2"

1 1/4"

1 1/2"

8 1/4"

1 3/8"

1 3/8"

8"

1 3/8"

1 3/8"   1 3/8"

8"

DRAWING #

Chamfered 8" Column Detail

SCALE

1 1/2"
1'-0"

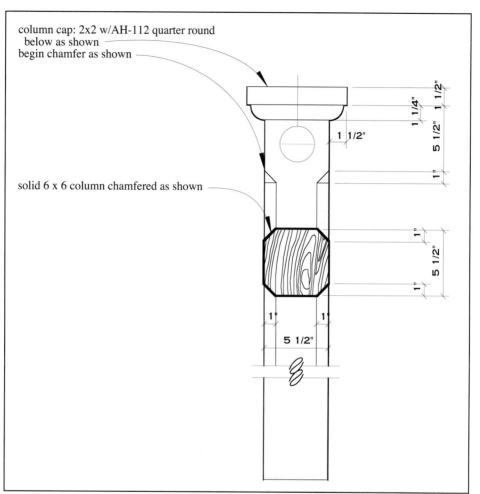

column cap: 2x2 w/AH-112 quarter round
  below as shown
begin chamfer as shown

1 1/2"

1 1/4"

1 1/2"

5 1/2"

1 1/2"

1"

solid 6 x 6 column chamfered as shown

1"

5 1/2"

1"

1"

1"

5 1/2"

DRAWING #

Chamfered 6" Column Detail

SCALE

1 1/2"
1'-0"

PCW003
651

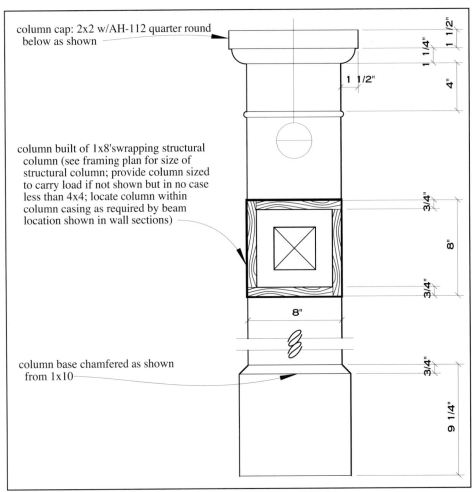

column cap: 2x2 w/AH-112 quarter round below as shown

1 1/2"

1 1/4"

1 1/2"

4"

column built of 1x8's wrapping structural column (see framing plan for size of structural column; provide column sized to carry load if not shown but in no case less than 4x4; locate column within column casing as required by beam location shown in wall sections)

3/4"

8"

3/4"

8"

column base chamfered as shown from 1x10

3/4"

9 1/4"

Chamfered 8" Column Detail

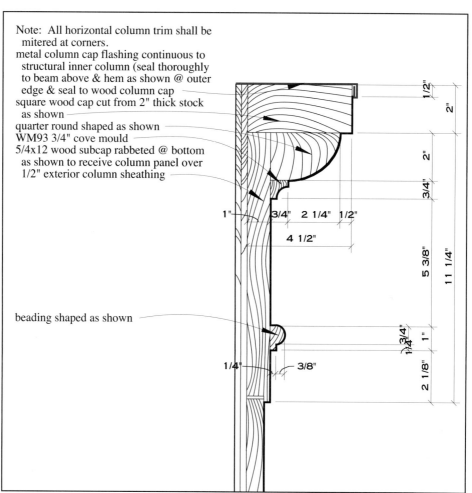

Note: All horizontal column trim shall be
   mitered at corners.
metal column cap flashing continuous to
   structural inner column (seal thoroughly
   to beam above & hem as shown @ outer
   edge & seal to wood column cap
square wood cap cut from 2" thick stock
   as shown
quarter round shaped as shown
WM93 3/4" cove mould
5/4x12 wood subcap rabbeted @ bottom
   as shown to receive column panel over
   1/2" exterior column sheathing

beading shaped as shown

1"   3/4"   2 1/4" 1/2"

4 1/2"

1/4"   3/8"

1/2"
2"
2"
3/4"
5 3/8"
11 1/4"
3/4"
1"
2 1/8"

Column Capital Detail

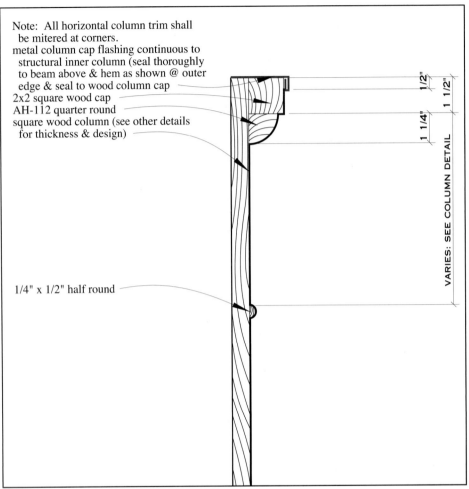

Note: All horizontal column trim shall
  be mitered at corners.
metal column cap flashing continuous to
  structural inner column (seal thoroughly
  to beam above & hem as shown @ outer
  edge & seal to wood column cap
2x2 square wood cap
AH-112 quarter round
square wood column (see other details
  for thickness & design)

1/4" x 1/2" half round

1/2"

1 1/2"

1 1/4"

VARIES: SEE COLUMN DETAIL

Column Capital Detail

DRAWING #

SCALE
3"
1'-0"

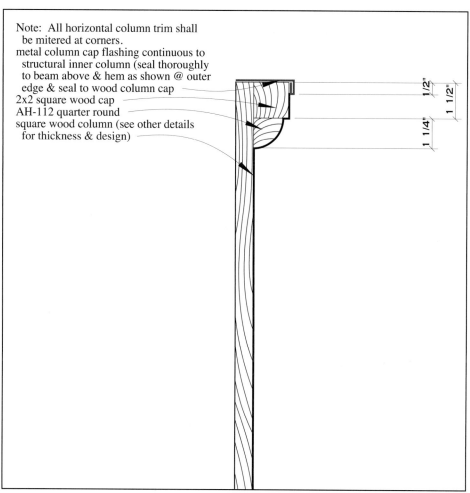

Note: All horizontal column trim shall
  be mitered at corners.
metal column cap flashing continuous to
  structural inner column (seal thoroughly
  to beam above & hem as shown @ outer
  edge & seal to wood column cap
2x2 square wood cap
AH-112 quarter round
square wood column (see other details
  for thickness & design)

1/2"

1 1/2"

1 1/4"

Column Capital Detail

SCALE
3"
1'-0"

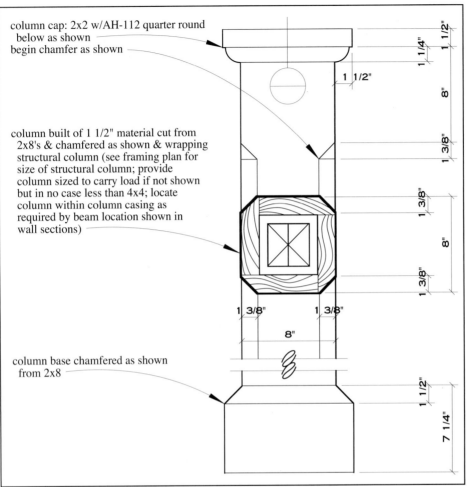

column cap: 2x2 w/AH-112 quarter round
  below as shown
begin chamfer as shown

1 1/2"

1 1/4"

1 1/2"

8"

1 3/8"

column built of 1 1/2" material cut from
  2x8's & chamfered as shown & wrapping
  structural column (see framing plan for
  size of structural column; provide
  column sized to carry load if not shown
  but in no case less than 4x4; locate
  column within column casing as
  required by beam location shown in
  wall sections)

1 3/8"

8"

1 3/8"

1 3/8"   1 3/8"

8"

column base chamfered as shown
  from 2x8

1 1/2"

7 1/4"

Chamfered Column Detail

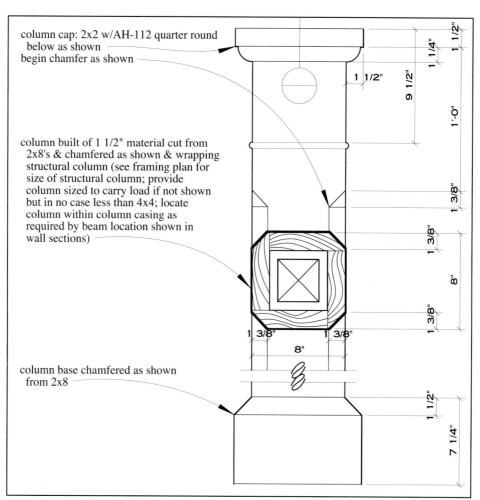

column cap: 2x2 w/AH-112 quarter round
  below as shown
begin chamfer as shown

column built of 1 1/2" material cut from
  2x8's & chamfered as shown & wrapping
  structural column (see framing plan for
  size of structural column; provide
  column sized to carry load if not shown
  but in no case less than 4x4; locate
  column within column casing as
  required by beam location shown in
  wall sections)

column base chamfered as shown
  from 2x8

1 1/2"

1 1/4"

1 1/2"

9 1/2"

1'-0"

1 3/8"

1 3/8"

8"

1 3/8"

1 3/8"   1 3/8"

8"

1 1/2"

7 1/4"

Chamfered Column Detail

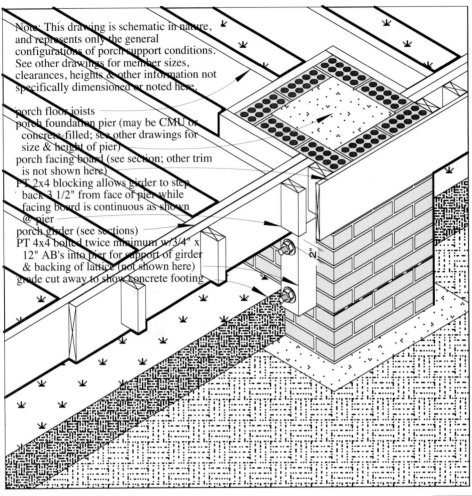

Note: This drawing is schematic in nature, and represents only the general configurations of porch support conditions. See other drawings for member sizes, clearances, heights & other information not specifically dimensioned or noted here.

porch floor joists
porch foundation pier (may be CMU or concrete-filled; see other drawings for size & height of pier)
porch facing board (see section; other trim is not shown here)
PT 2x4 blocking allows girder to step back 3 1/2" from face of pier while facing board is continuous as shown @ pier
porch girder (see sections)
PT 4x4 bolted twice minimum w/3/4" x 12" AB's into pier for support of girder & backing of lattice (not shown here)
grade cut away to show concrete footing

DRAWING #	Porch Floor Support Detail	SCALE 3/4" 1'-0"

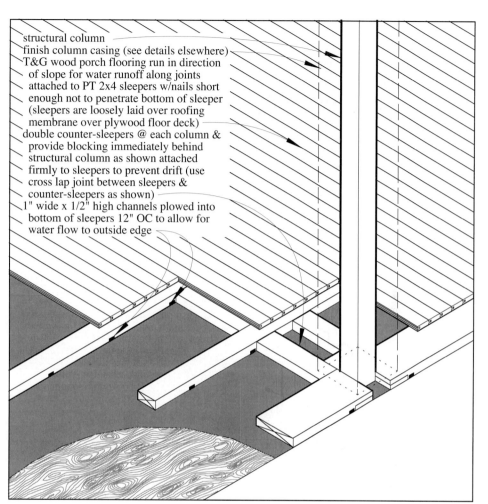

structural column
finish column casing (see details elsewhere)
T&G wood porch flooring run in direction
of slope for water runoff along joints
attached to PT 2x4 sleepers w/nails short
enough not to penetrate bottom of sleeper
(sleepers are loosely laid over roofing
membrane over plywood floor deck)
double counter-sleepers @ each column &
provide blocking immediately behind
structural column as shown attached
firmly to sleepers to prevent drift (use
cross lap joint between sleepers &
counter-sleepers as shown)
1" wide x 1/2" high channels plowed into
bottom of sleepers 12" OC to allow for
water flow to outside edge

DRAWING #

Waterproof Wood Porch Flooring Detail

SCALE
3/4"
1'-0"

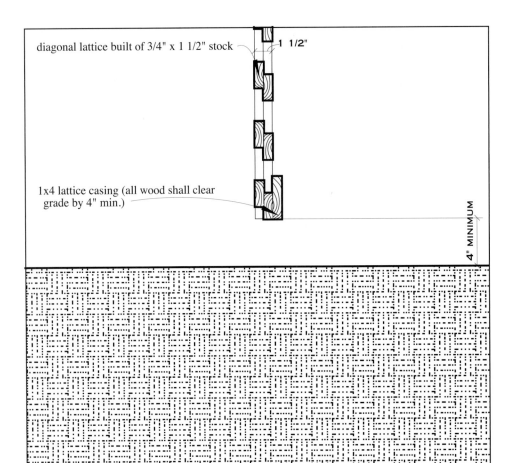

diagonal lattice built of 3/4" x 1 1/2" stock

1 1/2"

1x4 lattice casing (all wood shall clear grade by 4" min.)

4" MINIMUM

Lattice Bottom Detail

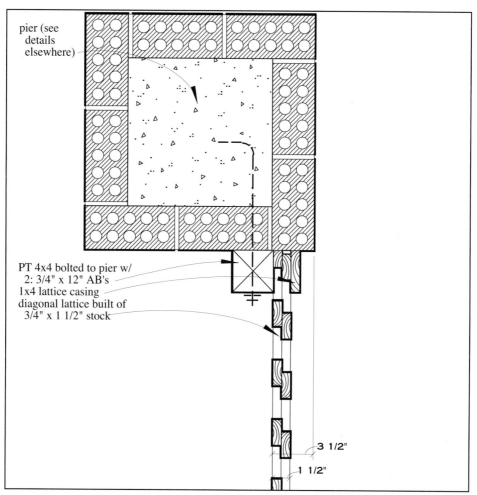

pier (see
details
elsewhere)

PT 4x4 bolted to pier w/
2: 3/4" x 12" AB's
1x4 lattice casing
diagonal lattice built of
3/4" x 1 1/2" stock

3 1/2"

1 1/2"

Lattice Plan Detail @ Pier

SCALE

1 1/2"
1'-0"

DRAWING #

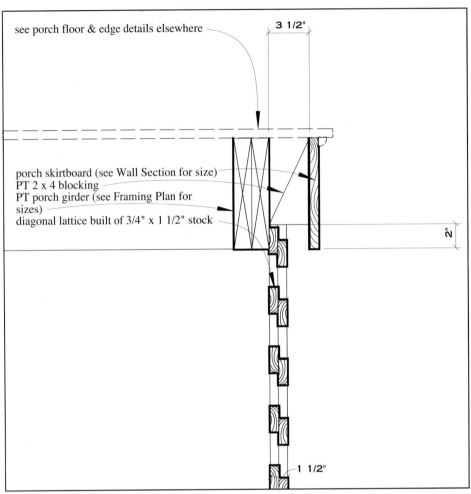

see porch floor & edge details elsewhere

3 1/2"

porch skirtboard (see Wall Section for size)
PT 2 x 4 blocking
PT porch girder (see Framing Plan for sizes)
diagonal lattice built of 3/4" x 1 1/2" stock

2"

1 1/2"

Lattice Top Detail

SCALE
1 1/2"
1'-0"

RAILING DETAILS

Details in this section both exterior & interior commercial & residential railings. The contents of this section are as follows:

Brass Over Steel Railing Details 664
Fypon Railing Details 673
Wood Over Glass Railing Details 674
Wood Over Steel Railing Details 676
Wood Railing Details 679

Note: All steel components of rail shall
  be galvanized.
traditional brass handrail equal to Julius
  Blum #4530 over 3/16"x1 1/2" subrail
  over 1/2" square tubular frame (attach
  rail to frame w/screws from underside
  as shown)

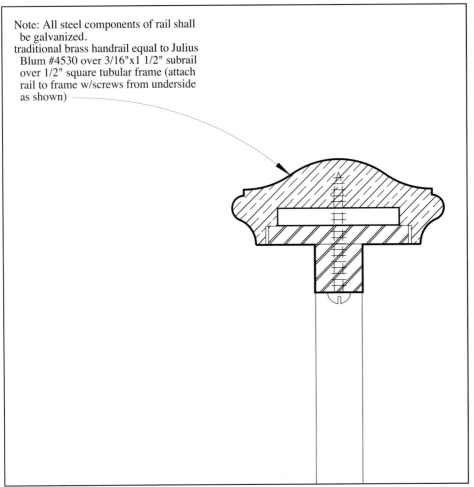

DRAWING #

Brass Railing Detail

SCALE
FULL
SIZE

Note: All steel components of rail shall
  be galvanized.
4"x4"x3/16" steel tube newel post
6 1/2" diameter x 1/4" thick steel base
  plate welded to bottom of column over
  7" diameter x 1/4" thick steel sub-base
  plate welded to base plate
bolts @ each side (see anchorage detail)

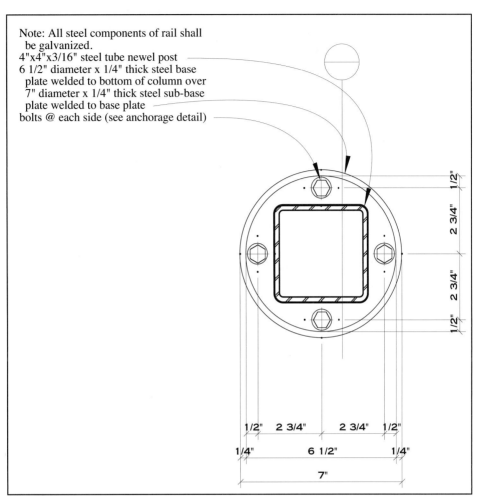

1/2" | 2 3/4" | 2 3/4" | 1/2"
1/4" | 6 1/2" | 1/4"
7"

1/2"
2 3/4"
2 3/4"
1/2"

Newel Base Plan Section

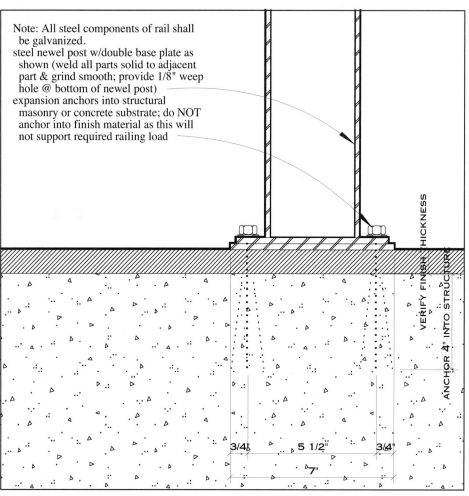

Note: All steel components of rail shall
   be galvanized.
steel newel post w/double base plate as
   shown (weld all parts solid to adjacent
   part & grind smooth; provide 1/8" weep
   hole @ bottom of newel post)
expansion anchors into structural
   masonry or concrete substrate; do NOT
   anchor into finish material as this will
   not support required railing load

VERIFY FINISH THICKNESS

ANCHOR 4" INTO STRUCTURE

3/4"   5 1/2"   3/4"

7"

DRAWING #

Newel Base Section @ Masonry

SCALE
3"
1'-0"

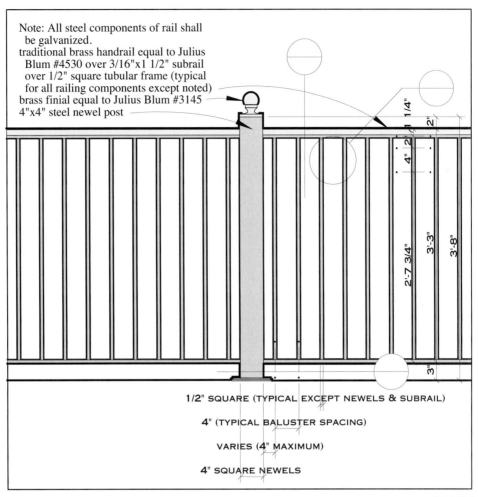

Note: All steel components of rail shall
  be galvanized.
traditional brass handrail equal to Julius
  Blum #4530 over 3/16"x1 1/2" subrail
  over 1/2" square tubular frame (typical
  for all railing components except noted)
brass finial equal to Julius Blum #3145
4"x4" steel newel post

1 1/4"

2"

4" 2"

2'-7 3/4"

3'-3"

3'-8"

3"

1/2" SQUARE (TYPICAL EXCEPT NEWELS & SUBRAIL)

4" (TYPICAL BALUSTER SPACING)

VARIES (4" MAXIMUM)

4" SQUARE NEWELS

DRAWING #

Metal Railing Elevation

SCALE
3/4"
1'-0"

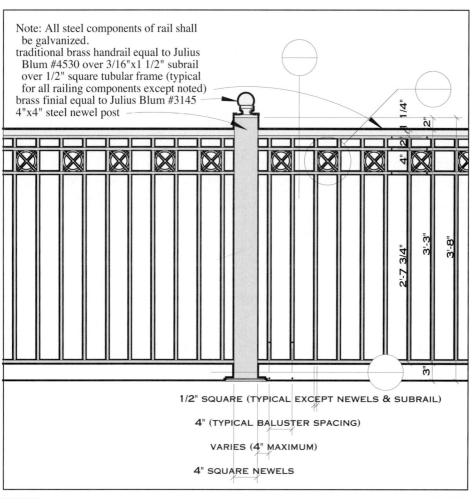

Note: All steel components of rail shall
  be galvanized.
traditional brass handrail equal to Julius
  Blum #4530 over 3/16"x1 1/2" subrail
  over 1/2" square tubular frame (typical
  for all railing components except noted)
brass finial equal to Julius Blum #3145
4"x4" steel newel post

1 1/4"
2"
4"
2'-7 3/4"
3'-3"
3'-8"
3"

1/2" SQUARE (TYPICAL EXCEPT NEWELS & SUBRAIL)

4" (TYPICAL BALUSTER SPACING)

VARIES (4" MAXIMUM)

4" SQUARE NEWELS

DRAWING #		SCALE

Metal Railing Elevation

SCALE
3/4"
1'-0"

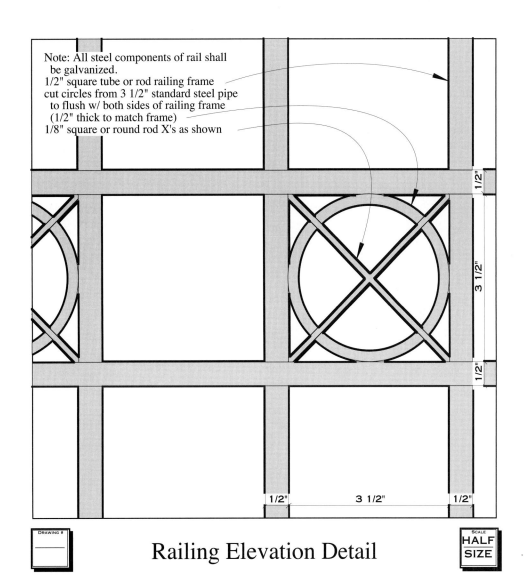

Note: All steel components of rail shall
  be galvanized.
1/2" square tube or rod railing frame
cut circles from 3 1/2" standard steel pipe
  to flush w/ both sides of railing frame
  (1/2" thick to match frame)
1/8" square or round rod X's as shown

1/2"

3 1/2"

1/2"

1/2"   3 1/2"   1/2"

DRAWING #

Railing Elevation Detail

SCALE
HALF
SIZE

RBS02002
669

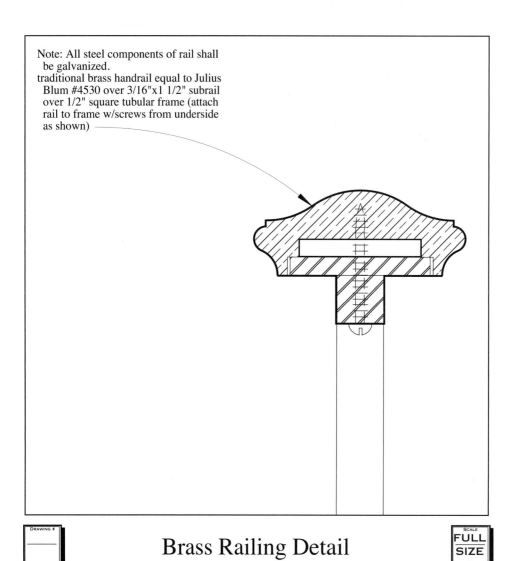

Note: All steel components of rail shall
  be galvanized.
traditional brass handrail equal to Julius
  Blum #4530 over 3/16"x1 1/2" subrail
  over 1/2" square tubular frame (attach
  rail to frame w/screws from underside
  as shown)

Brass Railing Detail

DRAWING #

SCALE
FULL
SIZE

Note: All steel components of rail shall
  be galvanized.
4"x4"x3/16" steel tube newel post
6 1/2" diameter x 1/4" thick steel base
  plate welded to bottom of column over
  7" diameter x 1/4" thick steel sub-base
  plate welded to base plate
bolts @ each side (see anchorage detail)

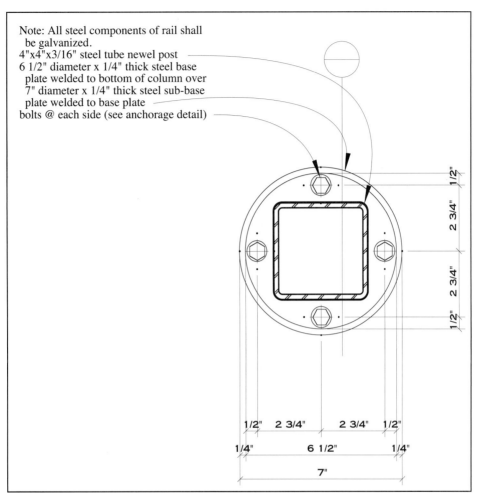

Newel Base Plan Section

DRAWING #

SCALE
3"
1'-0"

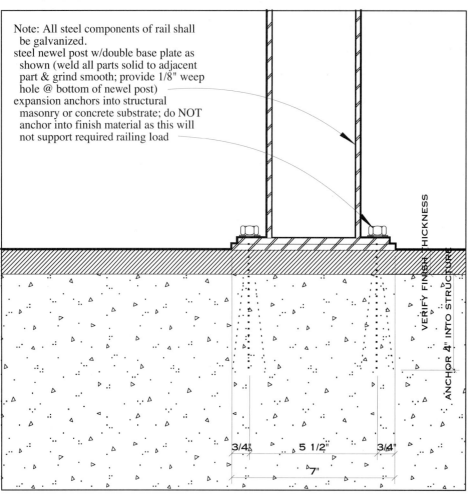

Note: All steel components of rail shall
be galvanized.
steel newel post w/double base plate as
shown (weld all parts solid to adjacent
part & grind smooth; provide 1/8" weep
hole @ bottom of newel post)
expansion anchors into structural
masonry or concrete substrate; do NOT
anchor into finish material as this will
not support required railing load

VERIFY FINISH THICKNESS

ANCHOR 4" INTO STRUCTURE

3/4"   5 1/2"   3/4"

7"

DRAWING #

Newel Base Section @ Masonry

SCALE
3"
1'-0"

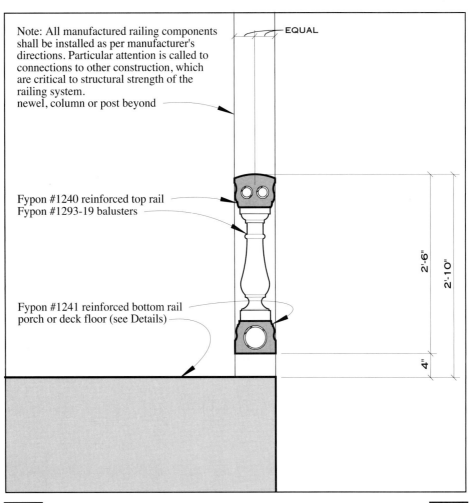

Note: All manufactured railing components shall be installed as per manufacturer's directions. Particular attention is called to connections to other construction, which are critical to structural strength of the railing system.
newel, column or post beyond

EQUAL

Fypon #1240 reinforced top rail
Fypon #1293-19 balusters

Fypon #1241 reinforced bottom rail
porch or deck floor (see Details)

2'-6"

2'-10"

4"

DRAWING #

Fypon Balustrade Detail

SCALE
3/4"
1'-0"

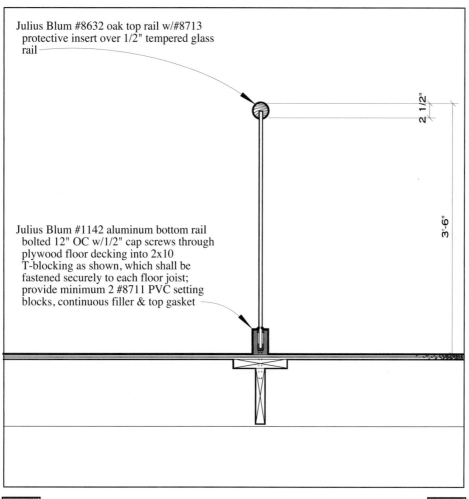

Julius Blum #8632 oak top rail w/#8713
protective insert over 1/2" tempered glass
rail

2 1/2"

3'-6"

Julius Blum #1142 aluminum bottom rail
bolted 12" OC w/1/2" cap screws through
plywood floor decking into 2x10
T-blocking as shown, which shall be
fastened securely to each floor joist;
provide minimum 2 #8711 PVC setting
blocks, continuous filler & top gasket

DRAWING #

Wood/Glass Handrail Detail

SCALE
3/4"
1'-0"

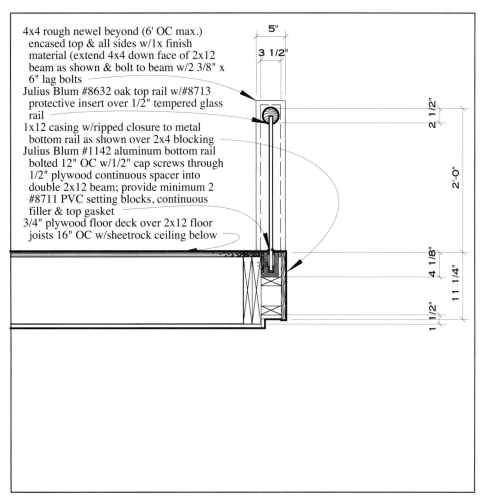

4x4 rough newel beyond (6' OC max.) encased top & all sides w/1x finish material (extend 4x4 down face of 2x12 beam as shown & bolt to beam w/2 3/8" x 6" lag bolts

Julius Blum #8632 oak top rail w/#8713 protective insert over 1/2" tempered glass rail

1x12 casing w/ripped closure to metal bottom rail as shown over 2x4 blocking

Julius Blum #1142 aluminum bottom rail bolted 12" OC w/1/2" cap screws through 1/2" plywood continuous spacer into double 2x12 beam; provide minimum 2 #8711 PVC setting blocks, continuous filler & top gasket

3/4" plywood floor deck over 2x12 floor joists 16" OC w/sheetrock ceiling below

5"

3 1/2"

2 1/2"

2'-0"

4 1/8"

11 1/4"

1 1/2"

DRAWING #

Sleeping Loft Edge Detail

SCALE
3/4"
1'-0"

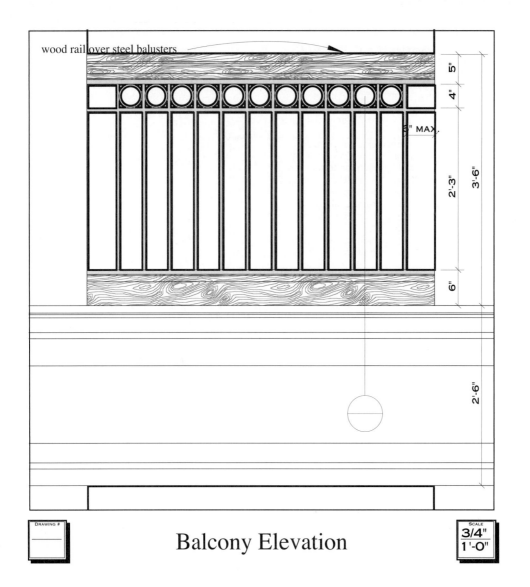

wood rail over steel balusters

5"

4"

3" MAX.

2'-3"

3'-6"

6"

2'-6"

Balcony Elevation

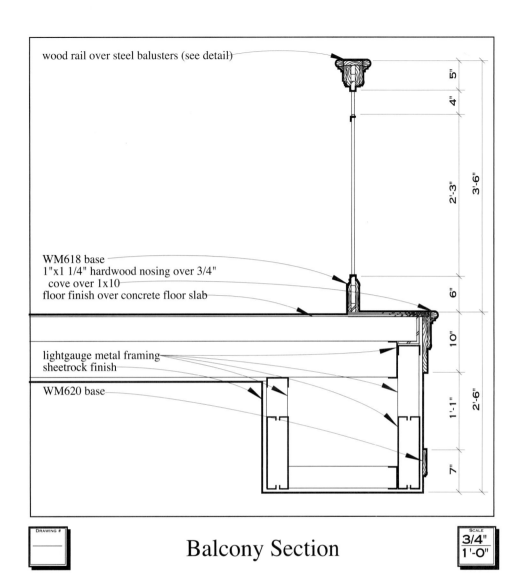

wood rail over steel balusters (see detail)

5"
4"
2'-3"
3'-6"

WM618 base
1"x1 1/4" hardwood nosing over 3/4"
 cove over 1x10
floor finish over concrete floor slab

6"

lightgauge metal framing
sheetrock finish

10"

WM620 base

1'-1"
2'-6"

7"

DRAWING #

Balcony Section

SCALE
3/4"
1'-0"

cut top rail from hardwood 1x4
1" x 1 1/4" hardwood nosing over 3/4"
  cove mould
WM 623 base over 1x4 (bolt 1x4 to
  steel structure before attaching base
  so that rough fasteners are hidden)

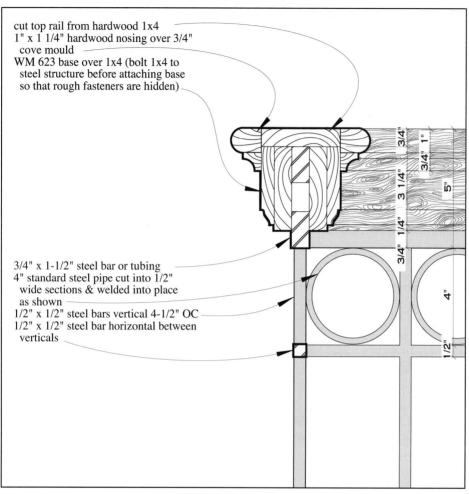

3/4" x 1-1/2" steel bar or tubing
4" standard steel pipe cut into 1/2"
  wide sections & welded into place
  as shown
1/2" x 1/2" steel bars vertical 4-1/2" OC
1/2" x 1/2" steel bar horizontal between
  verticals

DRAWING #

Railing Detail/Elevation

SCALE
3"
1'-0"

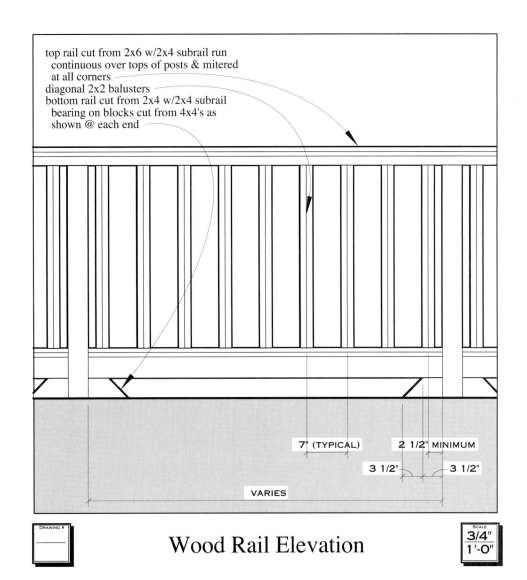

top rail cut from 2x6 w/2x4 subrail run
  continuous over tops of posts & mitered
  at all corners
diagonal 2x2 balusters
bottom rail cut from 2x4 w/2x4 subrail
  bearing on blocks cut from 4x4's as
  shown @ each end

7" (TYPICAL)

2 1/2" MINIMUM

3 1/2"   3 1/2"

VARIES

DRAWING #

Wood Rail Elevation

SCALE
3/4"
1'-0"

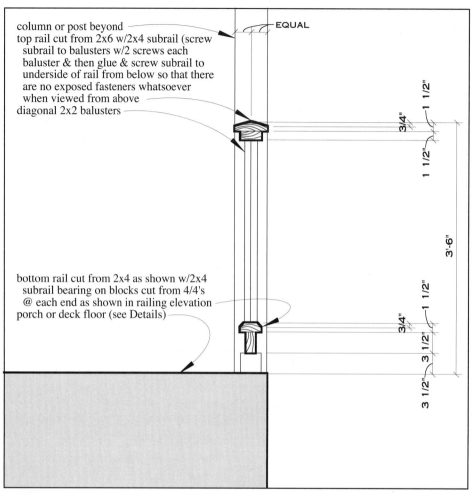

column or post beyond

top rail cut from 2x6 w/2x4 subrail (screw
  subrail to balusters w/2 screws each
  baluster & then glue & screw subrail to
  underside of rail from below so that there
  are no exposed fasteners whatsoever
  when viewed from above

diagonal 2x2 balusters

EQUAL

1 1/2"

3/4"

1 1/2"

3'-6"

bottom rail cut from 2x4 as shown w/2x4
  subrail bearing on blocks cut from 4/4's
  @ each end as shown in railing elevation

porch or deck floor (see Details)

3/4"

1 1/2"

3 1/2"

3 1/2"

DRAWING #

Wood Rail Section

SCALE

3/4"
1'-0"

Note: All horizontal newel cap trim shall
be mitered at corners.

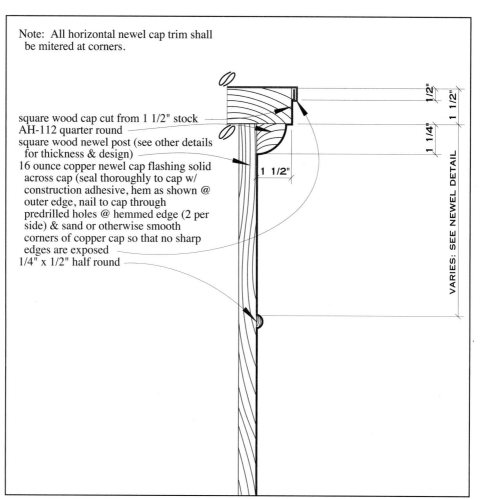

square wood cap cut from 1 1/2" stock
AH-112 quarter round
square wood newel post (see other details
for thickness & design)
16 ounce copper newel cap flashing solid
across cap (seal thoroughly to cap w/
construction adhesive, hem as shown @
outer edge, nail to cap through
predrilled holes @ hemmed edge (2 per
side) & sand or otherwise smooth
corners of copper cap so that no sharp
edges are exposed
1/4" x 1/2" half round

1 1/2"

1/2"

1 1/4"

1 1/2"

VARIES: SEE NEWEL DETAIL

DRAWING #

Newel Cap Detail

SCALE
3"
1'-0"

Note: All horizontal newel cap trim shall
  be mitered at corners.

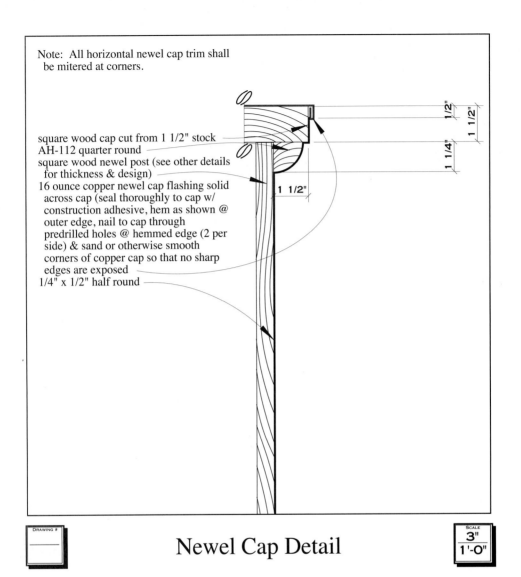

square wood cap cut from 1 1/2" stock
AH-112 quarter round
square wood newel post (see other details
  for thickness & design)
16 ounce copper newel cap flashing solid
  across cap (seal thoroughly to cap w/
  construction adhesive, hem as shown @
  outer edge, nail to cap through
  predrilled holes @ hemmed edge (2 per
  side) & sand or otherwise smooth
  corners of copper cap so that no sharp
  edges are exposed
1/4" x 1/2" half round

1/2"
1 1/2"
1 1/4"
1 1/2"

DRAWING #

SCALE
3"
1'-0"

Newel Cap Detail

RWW02002
682

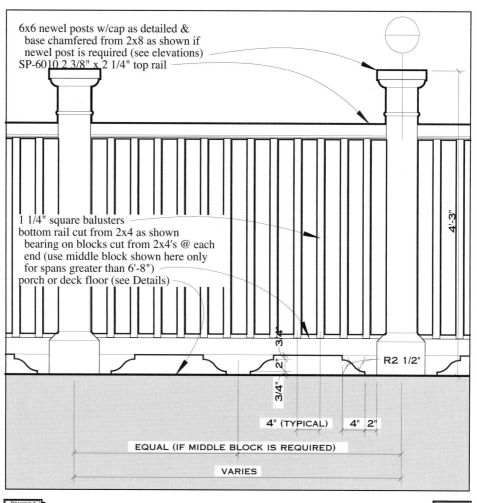

6x6 newel posts w/cap as detailed &
  base chamfered from 2x8 as shown if
  newel post is required (see elevations)
SP-6010 2 3/8" x 2 1/4" top rail

1 1/4" square balusters
bottom rail cut from 2x4 as shown
  bearing on blocks cut from 2x4's @ each
  end (use middle block shown here only
  for spans greater than 6'-8")
porch or deck floor (see Details)

4'-3"

3/4"

2"

3/4"

R2 1/2"

4" (TYPICAL)

4" 2"

EQUAL (IF MIDDLE BLOCK IS REQUIRED)

VARIES

DRAWING #

Wood Rail Elevation

SCALE
3/4"
1'-0"

RWW02003
683

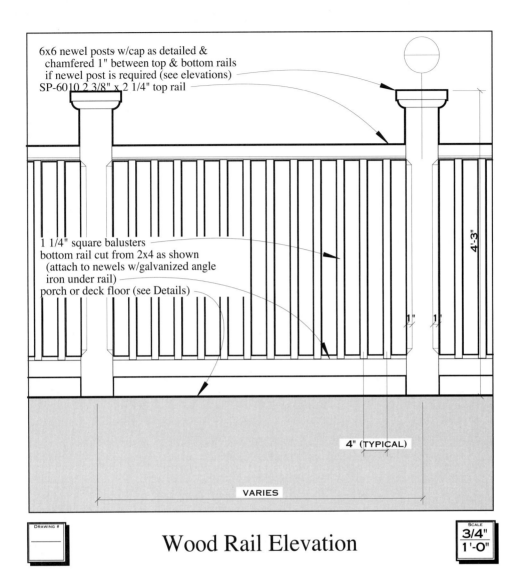

6x6 newel posts w/cap as detailed &
  chamfered 1" between top & bottom rails
  if newel post is required (see elevations)
SP-6010 2 3/8" x 2 1/4" top rail

1 1/4" square balusters
bottom rail cut from 2x4 as shown
  (attach to newels w/galvanized angle
  iron under rail)
porch or deck floor (see Details)

4'-3"

1" 1"

4" (TYPICAL)

VARIES

DRAWING #

Wood Rail Elevation

SCALE
3/4"
1'-0"

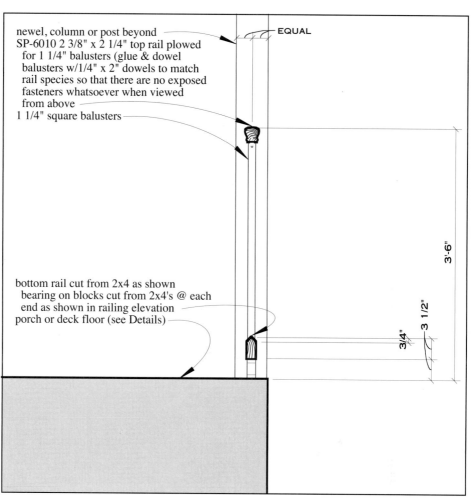

newel, column or post beyond
SP-6010 2 3/8" x 2 1/4" top rail plowed
for 1 1/4" balusters (glue & dowel
balusters w/1/4" x 2" dowels to match
rail species so that there are no exposed
fasteners whatsoever when viewed
from above
1 1/4" square balusters

EQUAL

3'-6"

bottom rail cut from 2x4 as shown
bearing on blocks cut from 2x4's @ each
end as shown in railing elevation
porch or deck floor (see Details)

3 1/2"

3/4"

Wood Rail Section

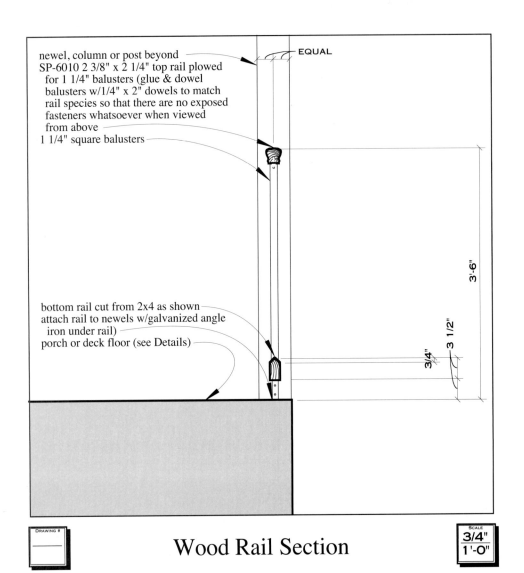

newel, column or post beyond
SP-6010 2 3/8" x 2 1/4" top rail plowed
for 1 1/4" balusters (glue & dowel
balusters w/1/4" x 2" dowels to match
rail species so that there are no exposed
fasteners whatsoever when viewed
from above
1 1/4" square balusters

bottom rail cut from 2x4 as shown
attach rail to newels w/galvanized angle
iron under rail)
porch or deck floor (see Details)

EQUAL

3'-6"

3 1/2"

3/4"

Wood Rail Section

DRAWING #

SCALE
3/4"
1'-0"

SITEWORK DETAILS

Details in this section include all conditions outside the perimeter of a building. The contents of this section are as follows:

ADA Parking Details. 688
Bed Details 700
Drainage Details 706
Erosion Control Details 718
Fencing Details 723
Landscaping Details 730
Paving Details 735
Structural Sitework Details 744
Electric Utility Details 746
Gas Utility Details 748
HVAC Utility Details. 750
Site Lighting Details 751
Sewer Details 752
Domestic Water Utility Details 755
Water Feature Details 757

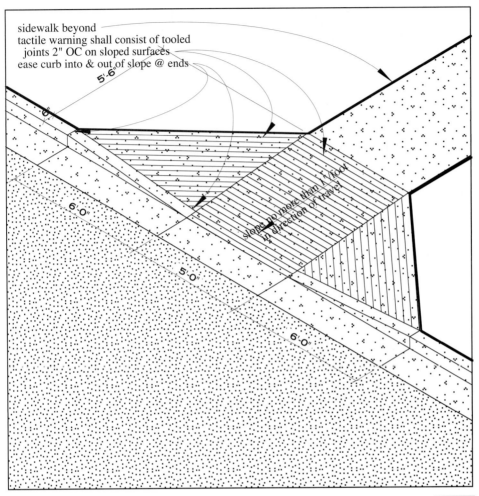

sidewalk beyond
tactile warning shall consist of tooled
  joints 2" OC on sloped surfaces
ease curb into & out of slope @ ends

5'-6"

6'-0"

5'-0"

6'-0"

slope no more than 1/foot
in direction of travel

Handicap Curb Cut @ End of Sidewalk

DRAWING #

SCALE
1/4"
1'-0"

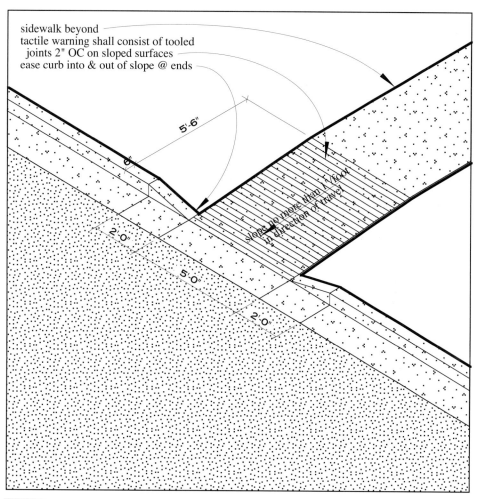

sidewalk beyond
tactile warning shall consist of tooled
 joints 2" OC on sloped surfaces
ease curb into & out of slope @ ends

5'-6"

2'-0"

5'-0"

2'-0"

slope no more than ¼"/foot
in direction of travel

Handicap Curb Cut @ End of Sidewalk

DRAWING #

SCALE
1/4"
1'-0"

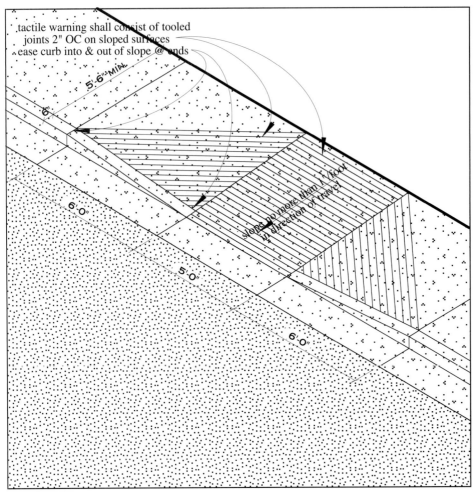

tactile warning shall consist of tooled
joints 2" OC on sloped surfaces

ease curb into & out of slope @ ends

5'-6" MIN.

6"

6'-0"

5'-0"

slope no more than ¼"/foot
in direction of travel

6'-0"

Handicap Curb Cut Into Sidewalk

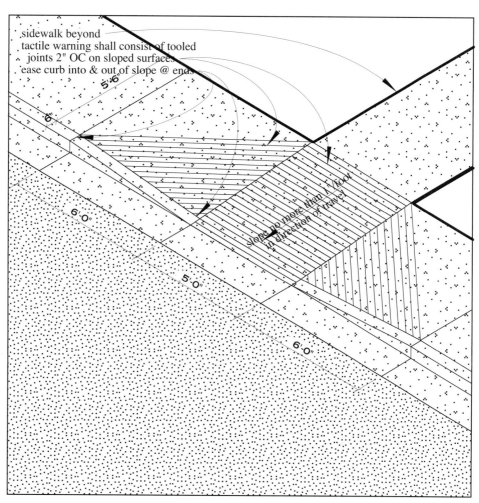

sidewalk beyond
tactile warning shall consist of tooled
joints 2" OC on sloped surfaces
ease curb into & out of slope @ ends

5'-6"

6"

6'-0"

5'-0"

6'-0"

slope no more than ¼"/foot
in direction of travel

DRAWING #

Handicap Curb Cut Into Sidewalk

SCALE
1/4"
1'-0"

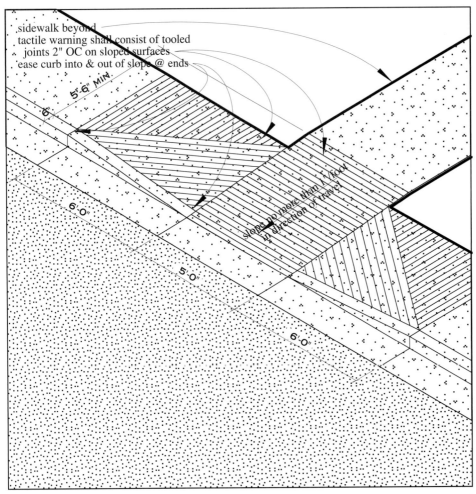

sidewalk beyond
tactile warning shall consist of tooled
joints 2" OC on sloped surfaces
ease curb into & out of slope @ ends

5'-6" MIN.

6"

slope no more than 1 foot
in direction of travel

6'-0"

5'-0"

6'-0"

DRAWING #

Handicap Curb Cut Into Sidewalk

SCALE
1/4"
1'-0"

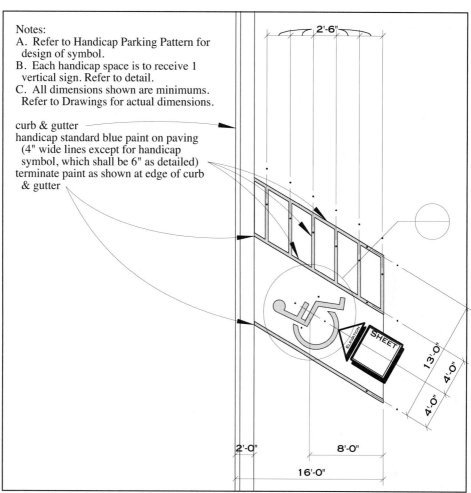

Notes:
A. Refer to Handicap Parking Pattern for design of symbol.
B. Each handicap space is to receive 1 vertical sign. Refer to detail.
C. All dimensions shown are minimums. Refer to Drawings for actual dimensions.

curb & gutter
handicap standard blue paint on paving (4" wide lines except for handicap symbol, which shall be 6" as detailed)
terminate paint as shown at edge of curb & gutter

2'-6"

13'-0"

4'-0"

4'-0"

2'-0"

8'-0"

16'-0"

ELEVATION

SHEET

DRAWING #

Single 60° Handicap Parking Detail

SCALE
$\frac{1"}{10'}$

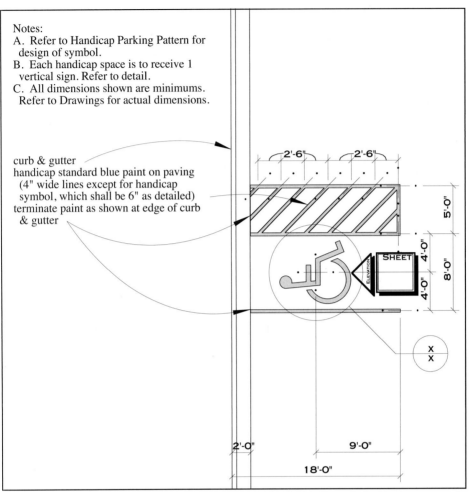

Notes:
A. Refer to Handicap Parking Pattern for design of symbol.
B. Each handicap space is to receive 1 vertical sign. Refer to detail.
C. All dimensions shown are minimums. Refer to Drawings for actual dimensions.

curb & gutter
handicap standard blue paint on paving (4" wide lines except for handicap symbol, which shall be 6" as detailed)
terminate paint as shown at edge of curb & gutter

2'-6"   2'-6"

5'-0"

4'-0"

8'-0"

SHEET

ELEVATION

4'-0"

X
X

2'-0"   9'-0"

18'-0"

DRAWING #
_____

Single 90° Handicap Parking Detail

SCALE
1"
10'

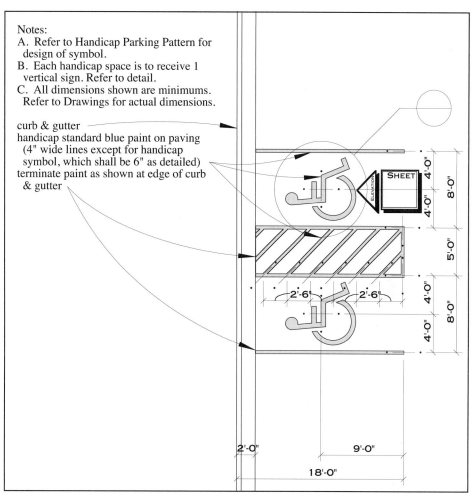

Notes:
A. Refer to Handicap Parking Pattern for design of symbol.
B. Each handicap space is to receive 1 vertical sign. Refer to detail.
C. All dimensions shown are minimums. Refer to Drawings for actual dimensions.

curb & gutter
handicap standard blue paint on paving (4" wide lines except for handicap symbol, which shall be 6" as detailed)
terminate paint as shown at edge of curb & gutter

SHEET

ELEVATION

4'-0"
4'-0"
8'-0"
5'-0"
4'-0"
8'-0"
4'-0"

2'-6"
2'-6"

2'-0"
9'-0"
18'-0"

Double 90° Handicap Parking Detail

DRAWING #

SCALE
$\frac{1"}{10'}$

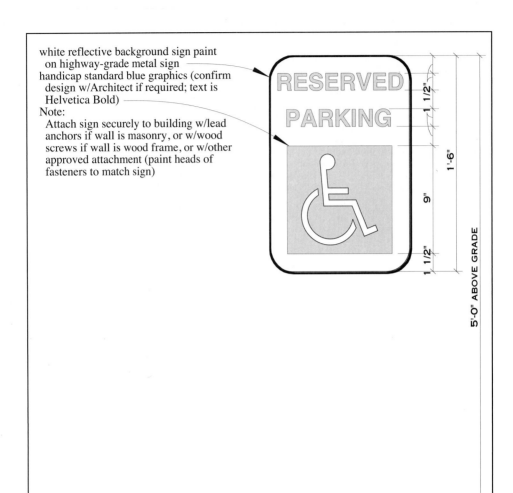

white reflective background sign paint on highway-grade metal sign

handicap standard blue graphics (confirm design w/Architect if required; text is Helvetica Bold)

Note:

Attach sign securely to building w/lead anchors if wall is masonry, or w/wood screws if wall is wood frame, or w/other approved attachment (paint heads of fasteners to match sign)

RESERVED PARKING

1 1/2"

1'-6"

9"

1 1/2"

5'-0" ABOVE GRADE

Handicap Sign on Tubular Post

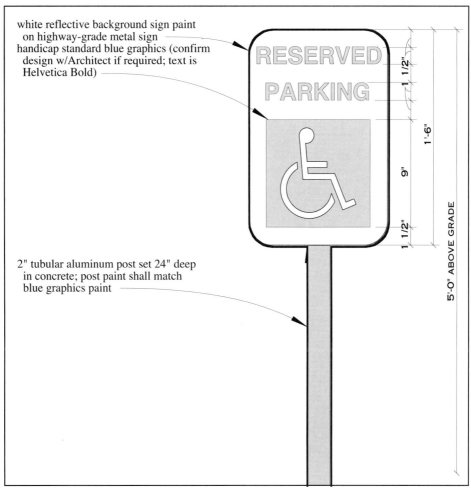

white reflective background sign paint on highway-grade metal sign handicap standard blue graphics (confirm design w/Architect if required; text is Helvetica Bold)

RESERVED PARKING

1 1/2"

1'-6"

9"

1 1/2"

5'-0" ABOVE GRADE

2" tubular aluminum post set 24" deep in concrete; post paint shall match blue graphics paint

Handicap Sign on Tubular Post

DRAWING #

SCALE
1 1/2
1'-0"

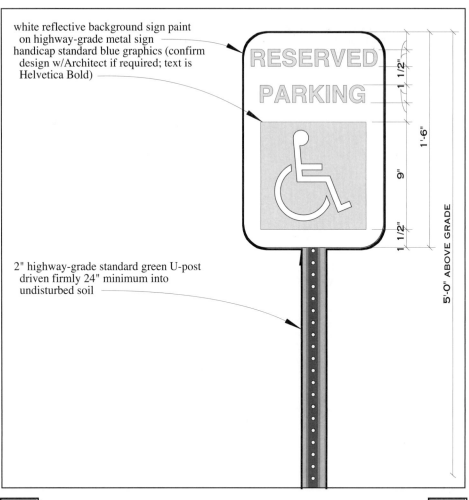

white reflective background sign paint on highway-grade metal sign handicap standard blue graphics (confirm design w/Architect if required; text is Helvetica Bold)

RESERVED PARKING

1 1/2"

1'-6"

9"

1 1/2"

5'-0" ABOVE GRADE

2" highway-grade standard green U-post driven firmly 24" minimum into undisturbed soil

Handicap Sign on U-Post

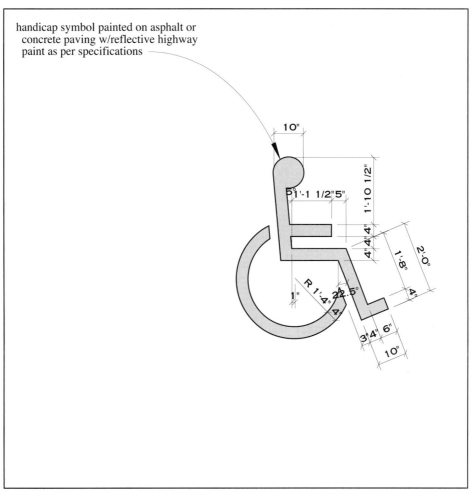

handicap symbol painted on asphalt or
concrete paving w/reflective highway
paint as per specifications

10"

5" 1'-1 1/2" 5"

1'-10 1/2"

4" 4"

2'-0"

1'-8"

4"

R 1'-4" 22.5°

1"

4"

3" 4" 6"

10"

DRAWING #

Handicap Parking Symbol Pattern

SCALE
3/8"
1'-0"

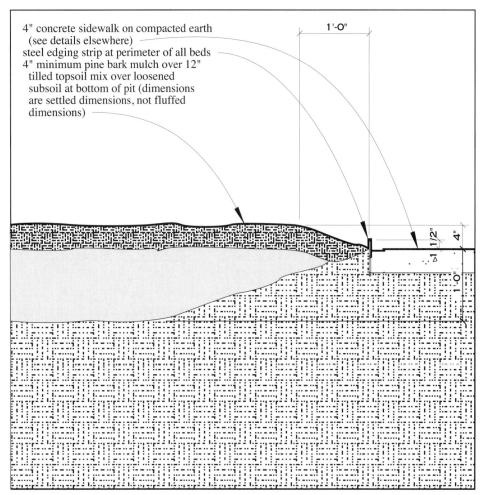

4" concrete sidewalk on compacted earth
(see details elsewhere)
steel edging strip at perimeter of all beds
4" minimum pine bark mulch over 12"
tilled topsoil mix over loosened
subsoil at bottom of pit (dimensions
are settled dimensions, not fluffed
dimensions)

1'-0"

1 1/2"

4"

1'-0"

DRAWING #

Planting Bed Detail @ Sidewalk

SCALE

3/4"
1'-0"

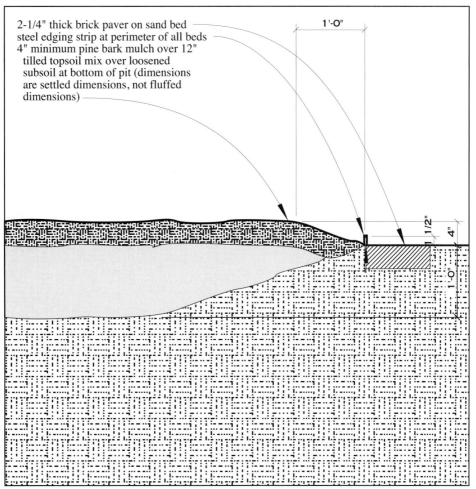

2-1/4" thick brick paver on sand bed
steel edging strip at perimeter of all beds
4" minimum pine bark mulch over 12"
   tilled topsoil mix over loosened
   subsoil at bottom of pit (dimensions
   are settled dimensions, not fluffed
   dimensions)

1'-0"

1 1/2"

4"

1'-0"

Planting Bed Detail w/Metal Edge

3/4"
1'-0"

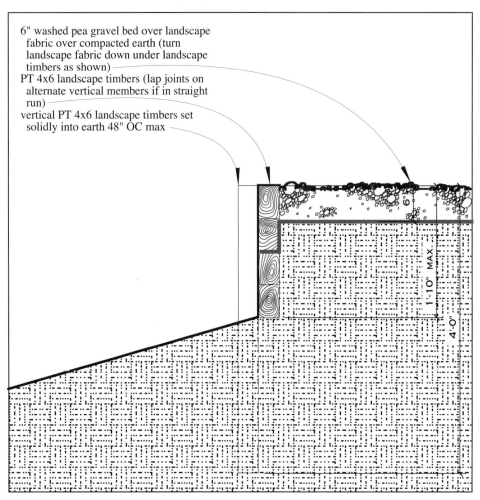

6" washed pea gravel bed over landscape
  fabric over compacted earth (turn
  landscape fabric down under landscape
  timbers as shown)
PT 4x6 landscape timbers (lap joints on
  alternate vertical members if in straight
  run)
vertical PT 4x6 landscape timbers set
  solidly into earth 48" OC max

6"

1'-10" MAX.

4'-0"

DRAWING #

Gravel Bed Edge Detail

SCALE

3/4"
1'-0"

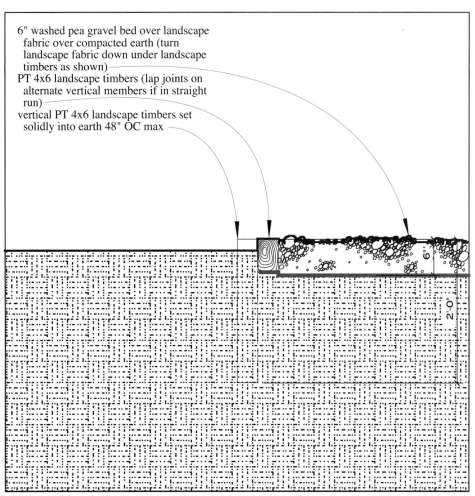

6" washed pea gravel bed over landscape
 fabric over compacted earth (turn
 landscape fabric down under landscape
 timbers as shown)

PT 4x6 landscape timbers (lap joints on
 alternate vertical members if in straight
 run)

vertical PT 4x6 landscape timbers set
 solidly into earth 48" OC max

6"

2'-0"

DRAWING #

Flat Gravel Bed Edge Detail

SCALE
3/4"
1'-0"

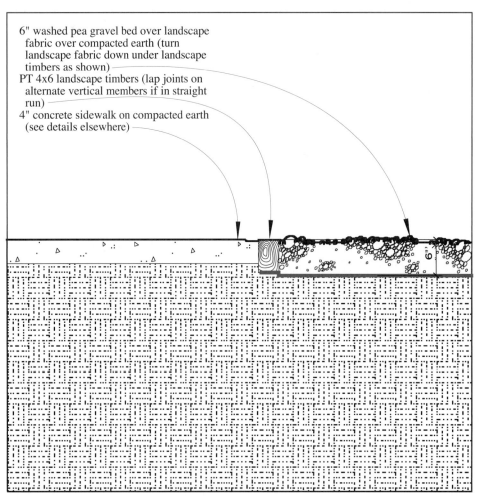

6" washed pea gravel bed over landscape fabric over compacted earth (turn landscape fabric down under landscape timbers as shown)

PT 4x6 landscape timbers (lap joints on alternate vertical members if in straight run)

4" concrete sidewalk on compacted earth (see details elsewhere)

6"

DRAWING #		SCALE
	Flat Gravel Bed Edge Detail	3/4" 1'-0"

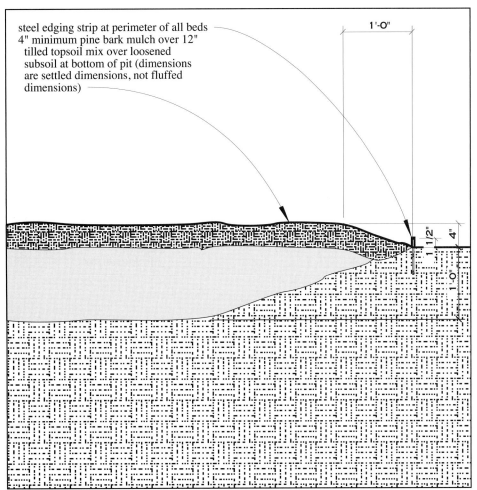

steel edging strip at perimeter of all beds
4" minimum pine bark mulch over 12"
tilled topsoil mix over loosened
subsoil at bottom of pit (dimensions
are settled dimensions, not fluffed
dimensions)

1'-0"

1 1/2"

4"

1'-0"

DRAWING #

Planting Bed Detail w/Metal Edge

SCALE

3/4"
―――
1'-0"

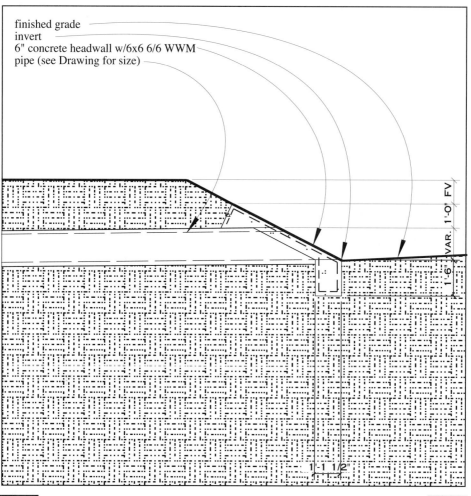

finished grade
invert
6" concrete headwall w/6x6 6/6 WWM
pipe (see Drawing for size)

VAR. 1'-0" FV

1'-6"

1'-1 1/2"

Beveled Pipe Inlet

DRAWING #

SCALE
1/4"
1'-0"

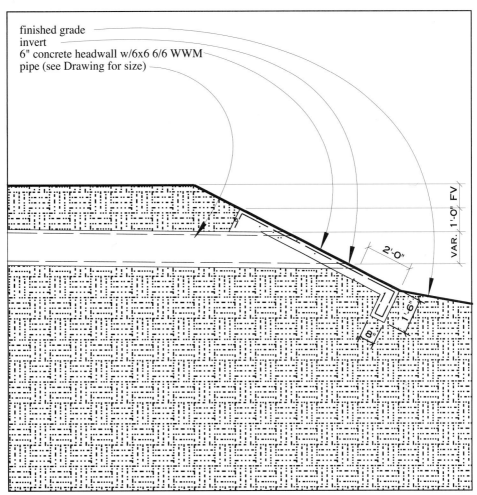

finished grade
invert
6" concrete headwall w/6x6 6/6 WWM
pipe (see Drawing for size)

VAR. 1'-0" FV

2'-0"

1'-6"

8"

Beveled Pipe Outlet

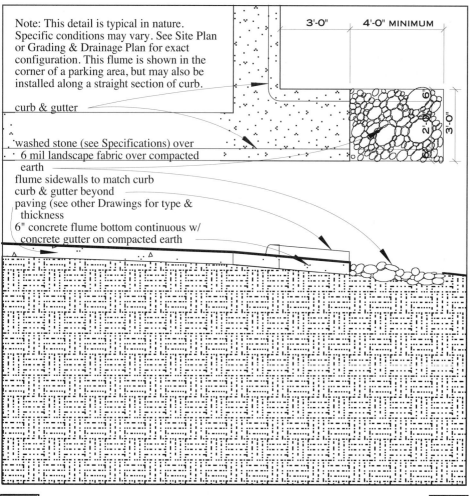

Note: This detail is typical in nature. Specific conditions may vary. See Site Plan or Grading & Drainage Plan for exact configuration. This flume is shown in the corner of a parking area, but may also be installed along a straight section of curb.

curb & gutter

3'-0"   4'-0" MINIMUM

3'-0"

6"   2'-0"   6"

washed stone (see Specifications) over 6 mil landscape fabric over compacted earth

flume sidewalls to match curb

curb & gutter beyond

paving (see other Drawings for type & thickness

6" concrete flume bottom continuous w/ concrete gutter on compacted earth

DRAWING #

Concrete Flume Detail

SCALE
1/4"
1'-0"

SD003
708

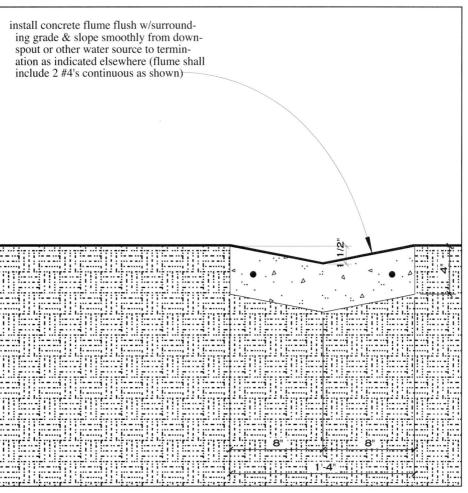

install concrete flume flush w/surround-
  ing grade & slope smoothly from down-
  spout or other water source to termin-
  ation as indicated elsewhere (flume shall
  include 2 #4's continuous as shown)

1 1/2"

4"

8"   8"

1'-4"

Downspout Flume Detail

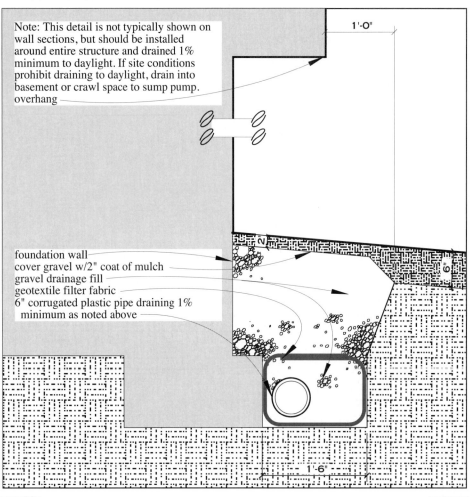

Note: This detail is not typically shown on wall sections, but should be installed around entire structure and drained 1% minimum to daylight. If site conditions prohibit draining to daylight, drain into basement or crawl space to sump pump. overhang

1'-0"

foundation wall
cover gravel w/2" coat of mulch
gravel drainage fill
geotextile filter fabric
6" corrugated plastic pipe draining 1% minimum as noted above

6"

1'-6"

DRAWING #

French Drain Detail

SCALE
3/4"
1'-0"

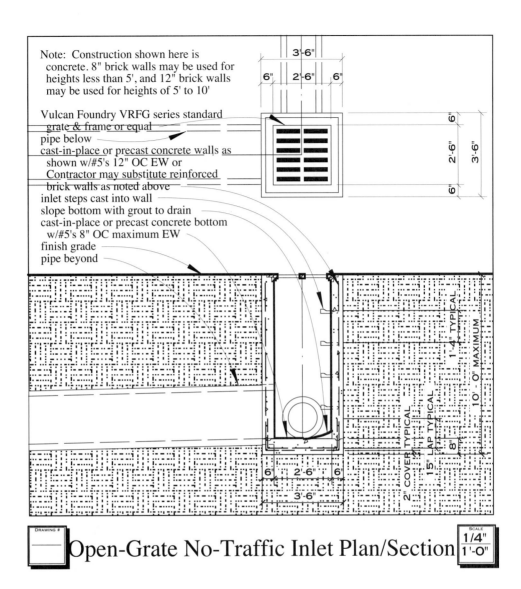

Note: Construction shown here is
concrete. 8" brick walls may be used for
heights less than 5', and 12" brick walls
may be used for heights of 5' to 10'

Vulcan Foundry VRFG series standard
grate & frame or equal
pipe below
cast-in-place or precast concrete walls as
shown w/#5's 12" OC EW or
Contractor may substitute reinforced
brick walls as noted above
inlet steps cast into wall
slope bottom with grout to drain
cast-in-place or precast concrete bottom
w/#5's 8" OC maximum EW
finish grade
pipe beyond

Open-Grate No-Traffic Inlet Plan/Section

DRAWING #

SCALE
1/4"
1'-0"

SD006
711

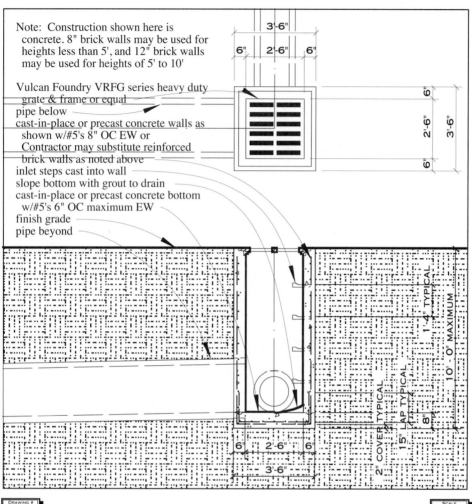

Note: Construction shown here is
concrete. 8" brick walls may be used for
heights less than 5', and 12" brick walls
may be used for heights of 5' to 10'

Vulcan Foundry VRFG series heavy duty
grate & frame or equal
pipe below
cast-in-place or precast concrete walls as
shown w/#5's 8" OC EW or
Contractor may substitute reinforced
brick walls as noted above
inlet steps cast into wall
slope bottom with grout to drain
cast-in-place or precast concrete bottom
w/#5's 6" OC maximum EW
finish grade
pipe beyond

3'-6"

6" | 2'-6" | 6"

6"

2'-6"

3'-6"

6"

2" COVER TYPICAL

15" LAP TYPICAL

8"

1'-4" TYPICAL

10'-0" MAXIMUM

6" | 2'-6" | 6"

3'-6"

DRAWING #

Open-Grate Traffic Inlet Plan/Section

SCALE
1/4"
1'-0"

SD007
712

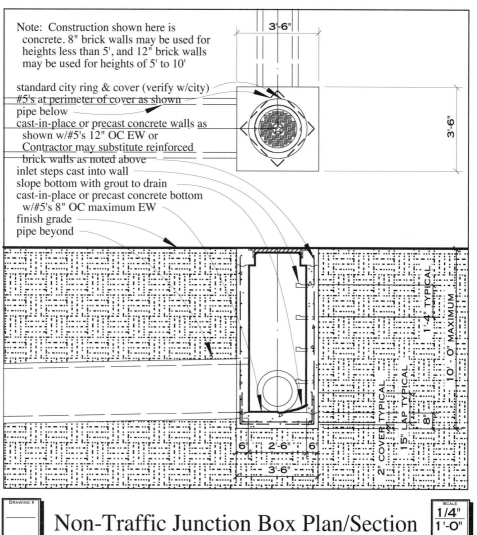

Note: Construction shown here is
concrete. 8" brick walls may be used for
heights less than 5', and 12" brick walls
may be used for heights of 5' to 10'

standard city ring & cover (verify w/city)
#5's at perimeter of cover as shown
pipe below
cast-in-place or precast concrete walls as
shown w/#5's 12" OC EW or
Contractor may substitute reinforced
brick walls as noted above
inlet steps cast into wall
slope bottom with grout to drain
cast-in-place or precast concrete bottom
w/#5's 8" OC maximum EW
finish grade
pipe beyond

3'-6"

3'-6"

1'-4" TYPICAL
10' - 0" MAXIMUM
15" LAP TYPICAL
2" COVER TYPICAL
8"

6"   2'-6"   6"
3'-6"

Non-Traffic Junction Box Plan/Section

DRAWING #

SCALE
1/4"
1'-0"

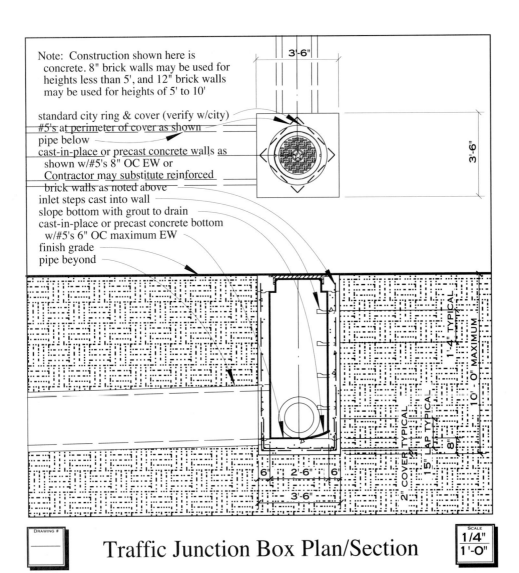

Note: Construction shown here is
  concrete. 8" brick walls may be used for
  heights less than 5', and 12" brick walls
  may be used for heights of 5' to 10'

standard city ring & cover (verify w/city)
#5's at perimeter of cover as shown
pipe below
cast-in-place or precast concrete walls as
  shown w/#5's 8" OC EW or
Contractor may substitute reinforced
  brick walls as noted above
inlet steps cast into wall
slope bottom with grout to drain
cast-in-place or precast concrete bottom
  w/#5's 6" OC maximum EW
finish grade
pipe beyond

3'-6"

3'-6"

1'-4" TYPICAL
10'-0" MAXIMUM
15" LAP TYPICAL
8"
2" COVER TYPICAL

6"   2'-6"   6"
3'-6"

DRAWING #

Traffic Junction Box Plan/Section

SCALE
1/4"
1'-0"

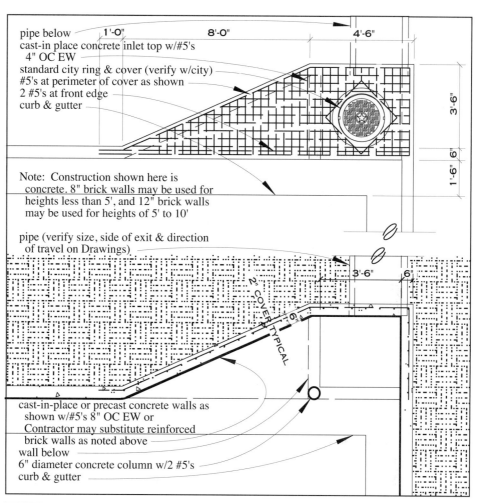

pipe below
cast-in place concrete inlet top w/#5's
  4" OC EW
standard city ring & cover (verify w/city)
#5's at perimeter of cover as shown
2 #5's at front edge
curb & gutter

1'-0"   8'-0"   4'-6"

3'-6"

6"

1'-6"

Note: Construction shown here is
concrete. 8" brick walls may be used for
  heights less than 5', and 12" brick walls
  may be used for heights of 5' to 10'

pipe (verify size, side of exit & direction
  of travel on Drawings)

3'-6"   6"

2" COVER TYPICAL

cast-in-place or precast concrete walls as
  shown w/#5's 8" OC EW or
  Contractor may substitute reinforced
  brick walls as noted above
wall below
6" diameter concrete column w/2 #5's
curb & gutter

DRAWING #

Corner S Inlet Plans

SCALE
1/4"
1'-0"

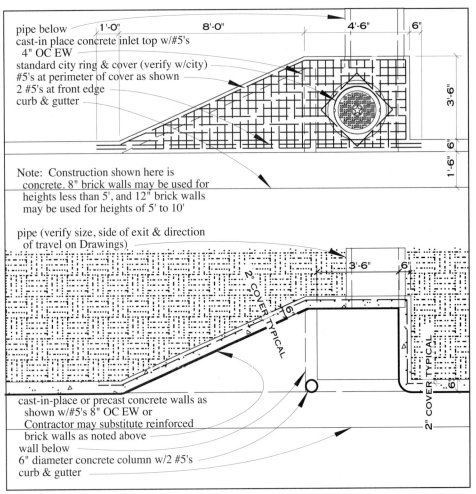

pipe below
cast-in place concrete inlet top w/#5's
  4" OC EW
standard city ring & cover (verify w/city)
#5's at perimeter of cover as shown
2 #5's at front edge
curb & gutter

1'-0"   8'-0"   4'-6"   6"

3'-6"

6"

1'-6"

Note: Construction shown here is
concrete. 8" brick walls may be used for
heights less than 5', and 12" brick walls
may be used for heights of 5' to 10'

pipe (verify size, side of exit & direction
  of travel on Drawings)

3'-6"   6"

2" COVER TYPICAL

2" COVER TYPICAL

6"

cast-in-place or precast concrete walls as
  shown w/#5's 8" OC EW or
  Contractor may substitute reinforced
  brick walls as noted above
wall below
6" diameter concrete column w/2 #5's
curb & gutter

DRAWING #

S Inlet Plans

SCALE
1/4"
1'-0"

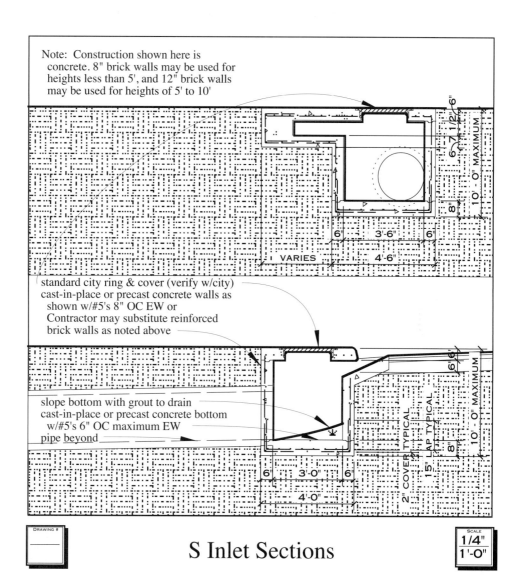

Note: Construction shown here is concrete. 8" brick walls may be used for heights less than 5', and 12" brick walls may be used for heights of 5' to 10'

standard city ring & cover (verify w/city)
cast-in-place or precast concrete walls as shown w/#5's 8" OC EW or
Contractor may substitute reinforced brick walls as noted above

slope bottom with grout to drain
cast-in-place or precast concrete bottom w/#5's 6" OC maximum EW
pipe beyond

VARIES

6" 3'-6" 6"

4'-6"

6" 7 1/2" 6"

8"

10' - 0" MAXIMUM

6" 6"

8"

10' - 0" MAXIMUM

2" COVER TYPICAL

15" LAP TYPICAL

6" 3'-0" 6"

4'-0"

DRAWING #

SCALE
1/4"
1'-0"

S Inlet Sections

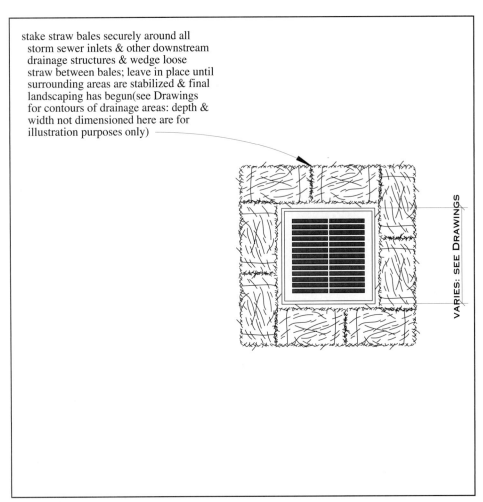

stake straw bales securely around all
storm sewer inlets & other downstream
drainage structures & wedge loose
straw between bales; leave in place until
surrounding areas are stabilized & final
landscaping has begun(see Drawings
for contours of drainage areas: depth &
width not dimensioned here are for
illustration purposes only)

VARIES: SEE DRAWINGS

DRAWING #

Storm Sewer Inlet Sediment Barrier

SCALE
1/4"
1'-0"

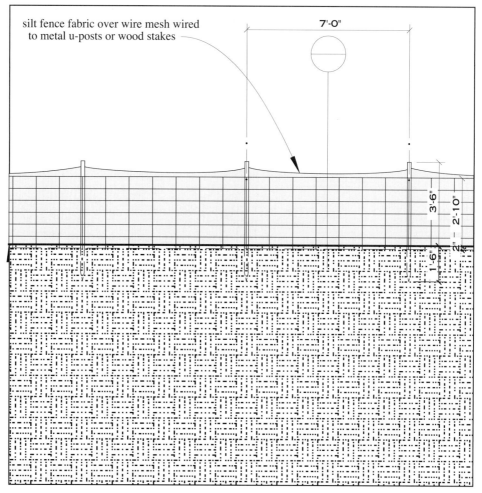

silt fence fabric over wire mesh wired
to metal u-posts or wood stakes

7'-0"

3'-6"

2'-10"

1'-6"

2"

Silt Fence Elevation

SCALE
1/4"
1'-0"

DRAWING #

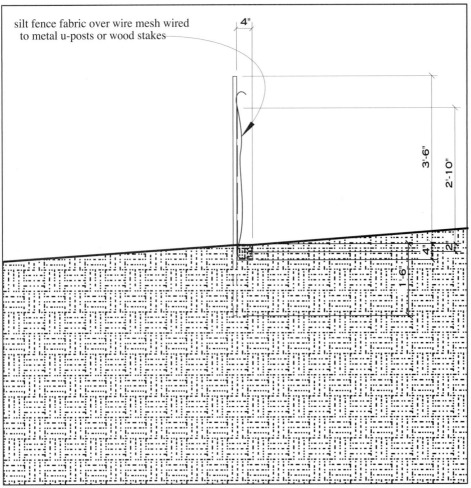

silt fence fabric over wire mesh wired to metal u-posts or wood stakes

4"

3'-6"

2'-10"

1'-6"

4"

2"

Silt Fence Section

DRAWING #

SE003
720

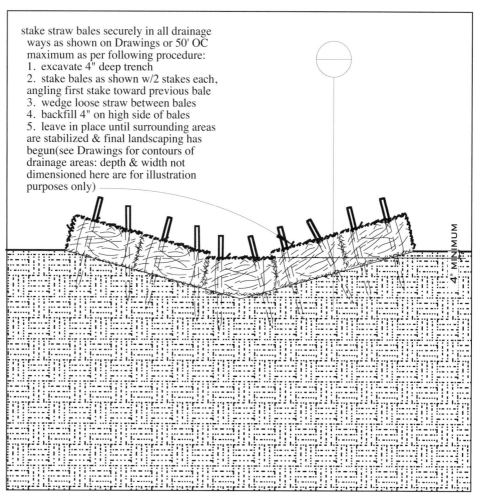

stake straw bales securely in all drainage
ways as shown on Drawings or 50' OC
maximum as per following procedure:
1. excavate 4" deep trench
2. stake bales as shown w/2 stakes each,
angling first stake toward previous bale
3. wedge loose straw between bales
4. backfill 4" on high side of bales
5. leave in place until surrounding areas
are stabilized & final landscaping has
begun(see Drawings for contours of
drainage areas: depth & width not
dimensioned here are for illustration
purposes only)

4" MINIMUM

DRAWING #

Swale Erosion Control Elevation

SCALE
1/4"
1'-0"

SE004
721

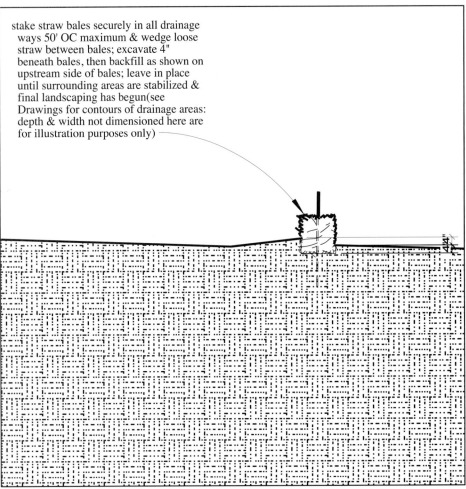

stake straw bales securely in all drainage
ways 50' OC maximum & wedge loose
straw between bales; excavate 4"
beneath bales, then backfill as shown on
upstream side of bales; leave in place
until surrounding areas are stabilized &
final landscaping has begun(see
Drawings for contours of drainage areas:
depth & width not dimensioned here are
for illustration purposes only)

4"

DRAWING #

Swale Erosion Control Section

SCALE
1/4"
1'-0"

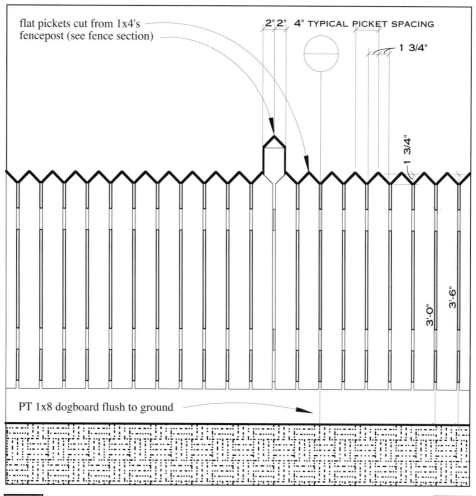

flat pickets cut from 1x4's
fencepost (see fence section)

2" 2" 4" TYPICAL PICKET SPACING

1 3/4"

1 3/4"

3'-0"

3'-6"

PT 1x8 dogboard flush to ground

Picket Fence Elevation

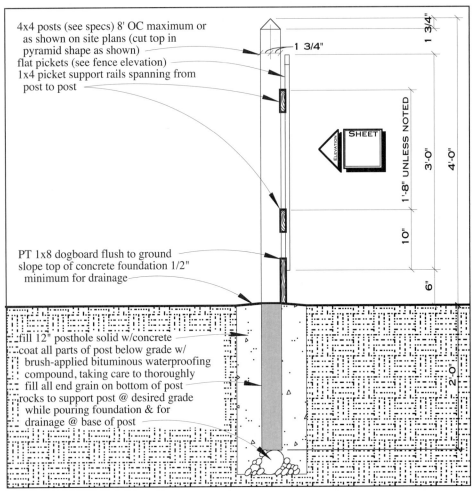

4x4 posts (see specs) 8' OC maximum or
as shown on site plans (cut top in
pyramid shape as shown)

flat pickets (see fence elevation)

1x4 picket support rails spanning from
post to post

1 3/4"

1 3/4"

1 3/4"

3'-0"

4'-0"

1'-8" UNLESS NOTED

10"

6"

ELEVATION

SHEET

PT 1x8 dogboard flush to ground
slope top of concrete foundation 1/2"
minimum for drainage

fill 12" posthole solid w/concrete
coat all parts of post below grade w/
brush-applied bituminous waterproofing
compound, taking care to thoroughly
fill all end grain on bottom of post
rocks to support post @ desired grade
while pouring foundation & for
drainage @ base of post

2'-0"

Picket Fence Section (Flat Pickets)

DRAWING #

SCALE
3/4"
1'-0"

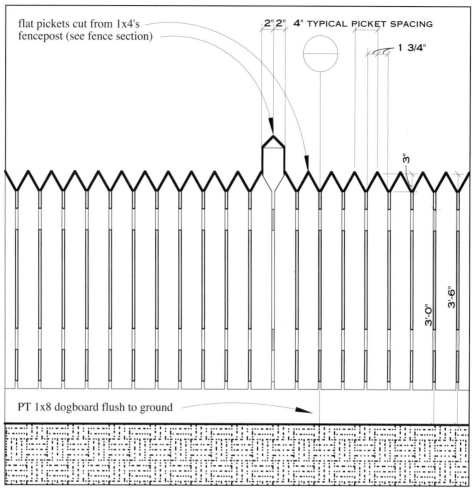

flat pickets cut from 1x4's
fencepost (see fence section)

2" 2" 4" TYPICAL PICKET SPACING

1 3/4"

3"

3'-0"

3'-6"

PT 1x8 dogboard flush to ground

Picket Fence Elevation

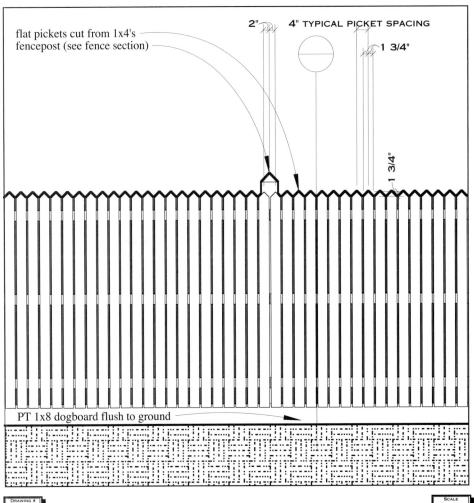

flat pickets cut from 1x4's
fencepost (see fence section)

2"   4" TYPICAL PICKET SPACING

1 3/4"

1 3/4"

PT 1x8 dogboard flush to ground

DRAWING #		SCALE
	Picket Fence Elevation	3/8" 1'-0"

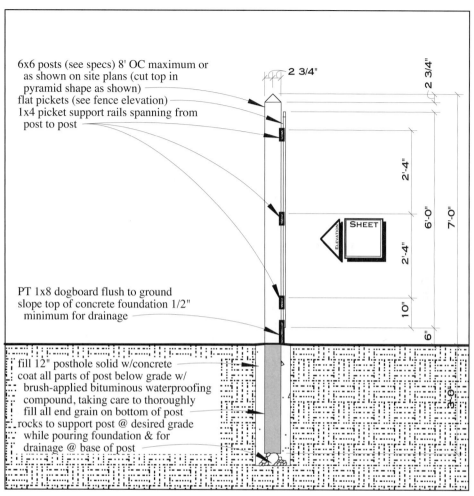

6x6 posts (see specs) 8' OC maximum or
as shown on site plans (cut top in
pyramid shape as shown)
flat pickets (see fence elevation)
1x4 picket support rails spanning from
post to post

2 3/4"

2 3/4"

2 3/4"

2'-4"

6'-0"

7'-0"

SHEET

ELEVATION

2'-4"

10"

6"

PT 1x8 dogboard flush to ground
slope top of concrete foundation 1/2"
minimum for drainage

fill 12" posthole solid w/concrete
coat all parts of post below grade w/
brush-applied bituminous waterproofing
compound, taking care to thoroughly
fill all end grain on bottom of post
rocks to support post @ desired grade
while pouring foundation & for
drainage @ base of post

3'-0"

DRAWING #

6' Picket Fence Section (Flat Pickets)

SCALE
3/8"
1'-0"

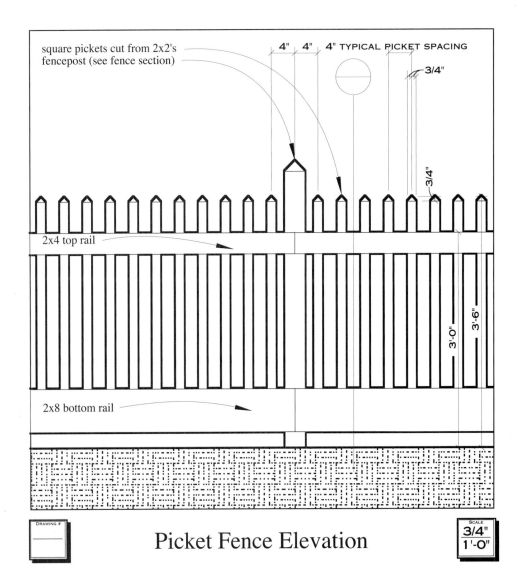

square pickets cut from 2x2's
fencepost (see fence section)

4"   4"   4" TYPICAL PICKET SPACING

3/4"

3/4"

2x4 top rail

3'-0"   3'-6"

2x8 bottom rail

DRAWING #

Picket Fence Elevation

SCALE
3/4"
1'-0"

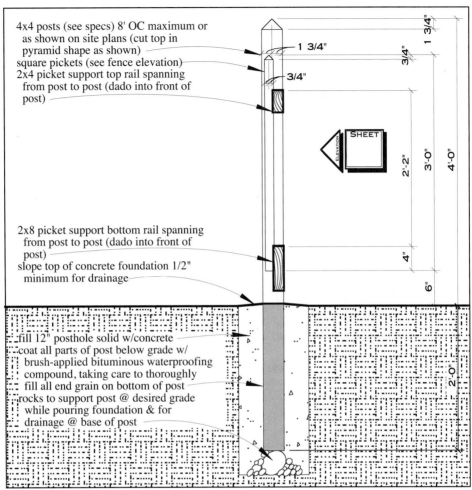

4x4 posts (see specs) 8' OC maximum or
as shown on site plans (cut top in
pyramid shape as shown)

square pickets (see fence elevation)

2x4 picket support top rail spanning
from post to post (dado into front of
post)

1 3/4"

3/4"

1 3/4"

3/4"

SHEET

2'-2"

3'-0"

4'-0"

2x8 picket support bottom rail spanning
from post to post (dado into front of
post)

slope top of concrete foundation 1/2"
minimum for drainage

4"

6"

fill 12" posthole solid w/concrete

coat all parts of post below grade w/
brush-applied bituminous waterproofing
compound, taking care to thoroughly
fill all end grain on bottom of post

rocks to support post @ desired grade
while pouring foundation & for
drainage @ base of post

2'-0"

DRAWING #		SCALE

Picket Fence Section (Square Pickets)

SCALE 3/4" / 1'-0"

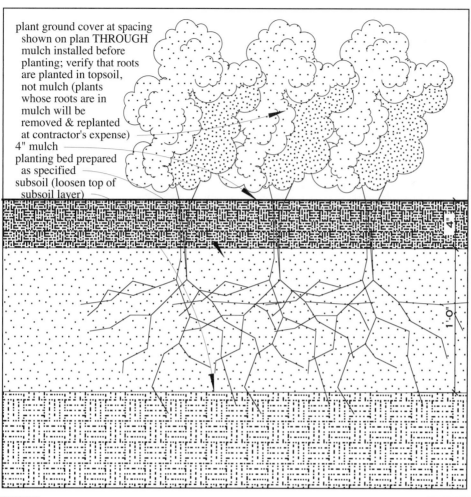

plant ground cover at spacing
  shown on plan THROUGH
  mulch installed before
  planting; verify that roots
  are planted in topsoil,
  not mulch (plants
  whose roots are in
  mulch will be
  removed & replanted
  at contractor's expense)
4" mulch
planting bed prepared
  as specified
subsoil (loosen top of
  subsoil layer)

4"

1'-0"

Ground Cover Planting Detail

SCALE
1/2"
1'-0"

DRAWING #

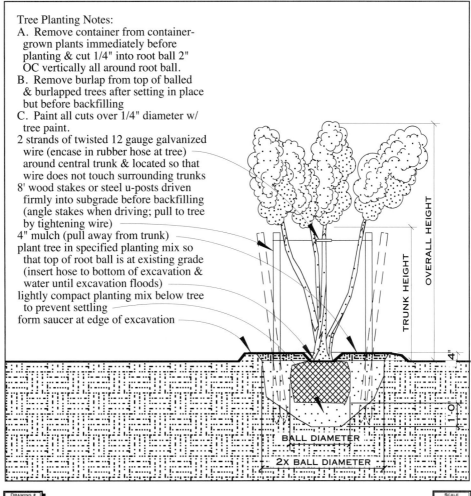

Tree Planting Notes:
A. Remove container from container-grown plants immediately before planting & cut 1/4" into root ball 2" OC vertically all around root ball.
B. Remove burlap from top of balled & burlapped trees after setting in place but before backfilling
C. Paint all cuts over 1/4" diameter w/ tree paint.

2 strands of twisted 12 gauge galvanized wire (encase in rubber hose at tree) around central trunk & located so that wire does not touch surrounding trunks

8' wood stakes or steel u-posts driven firmly into subgrade before backfilling (angle stakes when driving; pull to tree by tightening wire)

4" mulch (pull away from trunk)

plant tree in specified planting mix so that top of root ball is at existing grade (insert hose to bottom of excavation & water until excavation floods)

lightly compact planting mix below tree to prevent settling

form saucer at edge of excavation

OVERALL HEIGHT

TRUNK HEIGHT

4"

1'-0

BALL DIAMETER

2X BALL DIAMETER

DRAWING #

Tree Planting Detail

SCALE
1/4"
1'-0"

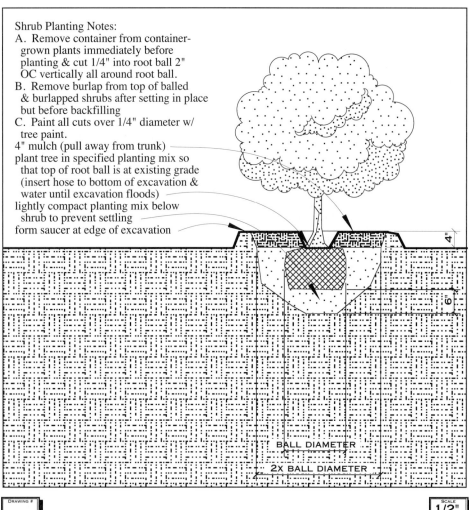

Shrub Planting Notes:
A. Remove container from container-
   grown plants immediately before
   planting & cut 1/4" into root ball 2"
   OC vertically all around root ball.
B. Remove burlap from top of balled
   & burlapped shrubs after setting in place
   but before backfilling
C. Paint all cuts over 1/4" diameter w/
   tree paint.
4" mulch (pull away from trunk)
plant tree in specified planting mix so
   that top of root ball is at existing grade
   (insert hose to bottom of excavation &
   water until excavation floods)
lightly compact planting mix below
   shrub to prevent settling
form saucer at edge of excavation

4"

6"

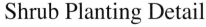

BALL DIAMETER

2X BALL DIAMETER

DRAWING #

Shrub Planting Detail

SCALE
1/2"
―――
1'-0"

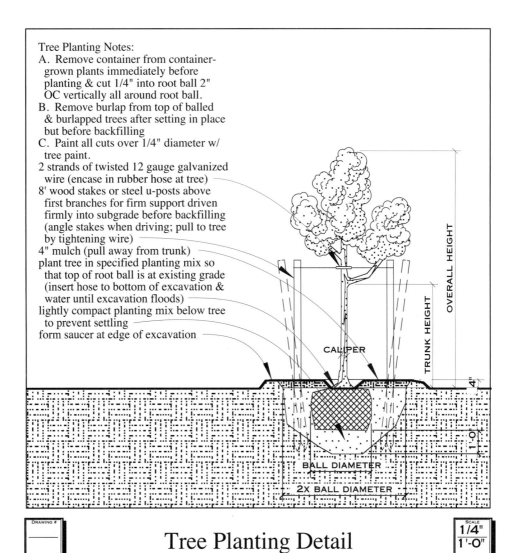

Tree Planting Notes:
A. Remove container from container-grown plants immediately before planting & cut 1/4" into root ball 2" OC vertically all around root ball.
B. Remove burlap from top of balled & burlapped trees after setting in place but before backfilling
C. Paint all cuts over 1/4" diameter w/ tree paint.

2 strands of twisted 12 gauge galvanized wire (encase in rubber hose at tree)

8' wood stakes or steel u-posts above first branches for firm support driven firmly into subgrade before backfilling (angle stakes when driving; pull to tree by tightening wire)

4" mulch (pull away from trunk)

plant tree in specified planting mix so that top of root ball is at existing grade (insert hose to bottom of excavation & water until excavation floods)

lightly compact planting mix below tree to prevent settling

form saucer at edge of excavation

OVERALL HEIGHT

TRUNK HEIGHT

CALIPER

4"

1'-0"

BALL DIAMETER

2X BALL DIAMETER

DRAWING #

Tree Planting Detail

SCALE
1/4"
1'-0"

SL004
733

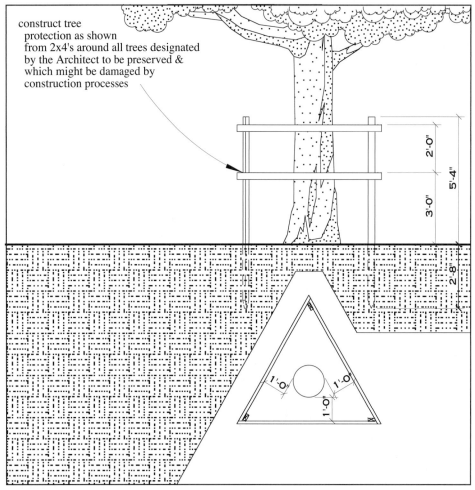

construct tree
  protection as shown
  from 2x4's around all trees designated
  by the Architect to be preserved &
  which might be damaged by
  construction processes

2'-0"

5'-4"

3'-0"

2'-8"

 1'-0"

 1'-0"

1'-0"

DRAWING #

Tree Protection Elevation & Plan

SCALE
1/4"
1'-0"

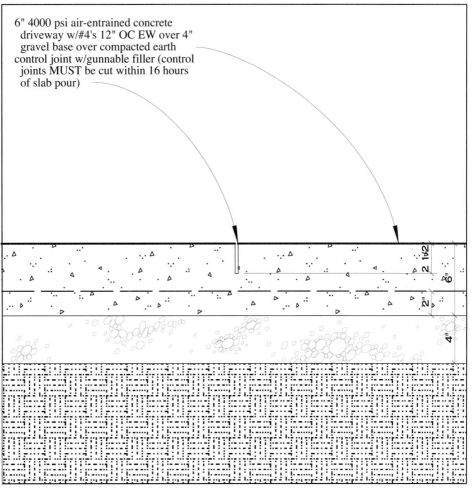

6" 4000 psi air-entrained concrete
  driveway w/#4's 12" OC EW over 4"
  gravel base over compacted earth
control joint w/gunnable filler (control
  joints MUST be cut within 16 hours
  of slab pour)

Control Joint Detail @ 6" Driveway

DRAWING #

SCALE

1 1/2
1'-0"

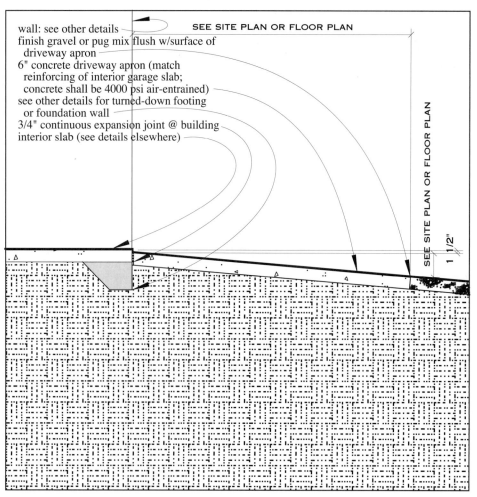

wall: see other details
finish gravel or pug mix flush w/surface of
  driveway apron
6" concrete driveway apron (match
  reinforcing of interior garage slab;
  concrete shall be 4000 psi air-entrained)
see other details for turned-down footing
  or foundation wall
3/4" continuous expansion joint @ building
interior slab (see details elsewhere)

SEE SITE PLAN OR FLOOR PLAN

SEE SITE PLAN OR FLOOR PLAN

1 1/2"

6" Driveway Apron Detail

DRAWING #

SCALE

1/4"
1'-0"

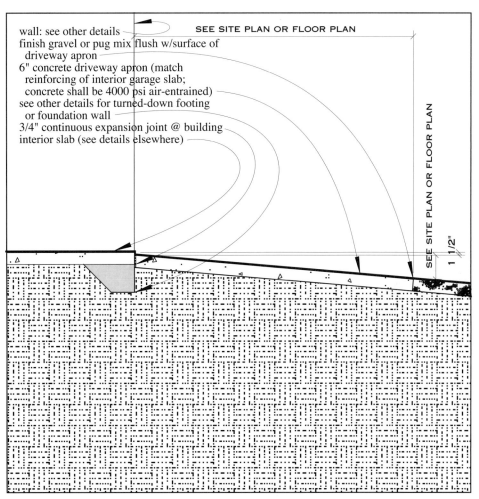

wall: see other details

finish gravel or pug mix flush w/surface of driveway apron

6" concrete driveway apron (match reinforcing of interior garage slab; concrete shall be 4000 psi air-entrained)

see other details for turned-down footing or foundation wall

3/4" continuous expansion joint @ building interior slab (see details elsewhere)

SEE SITE PLAN OR FLOOR PLAN

SEE SITE PLAN OR FLOOR PLAN

1 1/2"

6" Driveway Apron Detail

DRAWING #

SCALE
1/4"
1'-0"

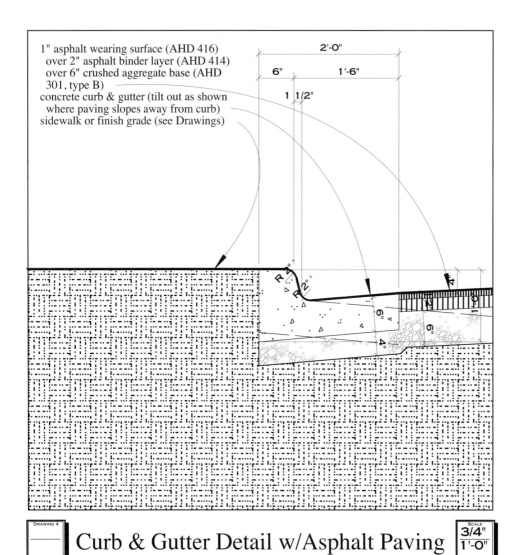

1" asphalt wearing surface (AHD 416)
  over 2" asphalt binder layer (AHD 414)
  over 6" crushed aggregate base (AHD
  301, type B)
concrete curb & gutter (tilt out as shown
  where paving slopes away from curb)
sidewalk or finish grade (see Drawings)

2'-0"
6"
1'-6"
1 1/2"

R 2"
R 2"
6"
4"
6"
4"

DRAWING #

Curb & Gutter Detail w/Asphalt Paving

SCALE
3/4"
1'-0"

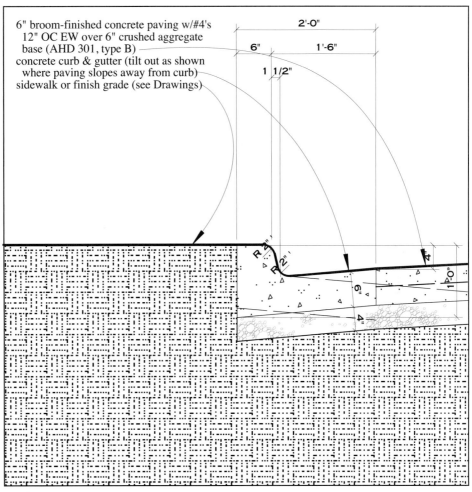

6" broom-finished concrete paving w/#4's
  12" OC EW over 6" crushed aggregate
  base (AHD 301, type B)
concrete curb & gutter (tilt out as shown
  where paving slopes away from curb)
sidewalk or finish grade (see Drawings)

2'-0"
6"   1'-6"
1 1/2"

R 2"   R 2"   4"
6"   1'-0"
4"

Curb & Gutter Detail w/Concrete Paving

SCALE 3/4" 1'-0"

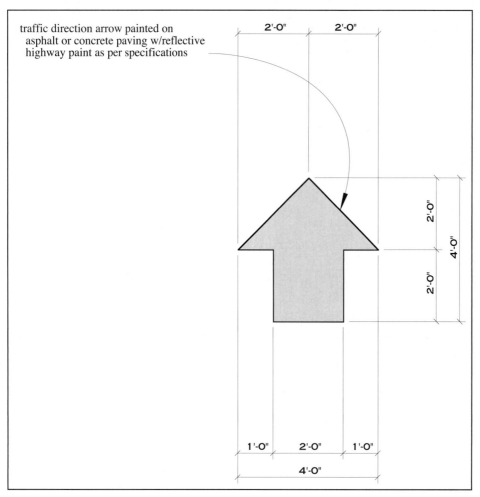

traffic direction arrow painted on
 asphalt or concrete paving w/reflective
 highway paint as per specifications

2'-0" 2'-0"

2'-0"

4'-0"

2'-0"

1'-0" 2'-0" 1'-0"

4'-0"

DRAWING #

Traffic Direction Arrow Detail

SCALE
3/8"
1'-0"

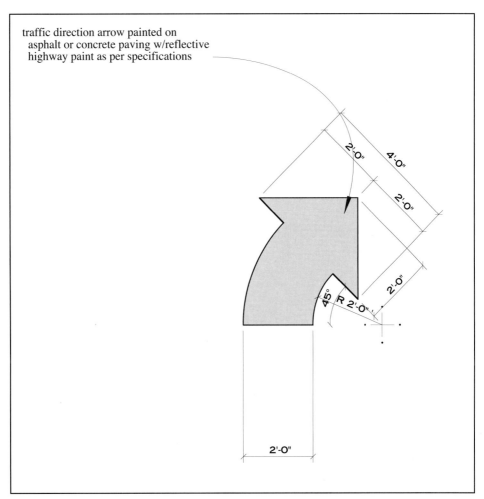

traffic direction arrow painted on
  asphalt or concrete paving w/reflective
  highway paint as per specifications

2'-0"

4'-0"

2'-0"

2'-0"

45° R 2'-0"

2'-0"

Traffic Direction Arrow Detail

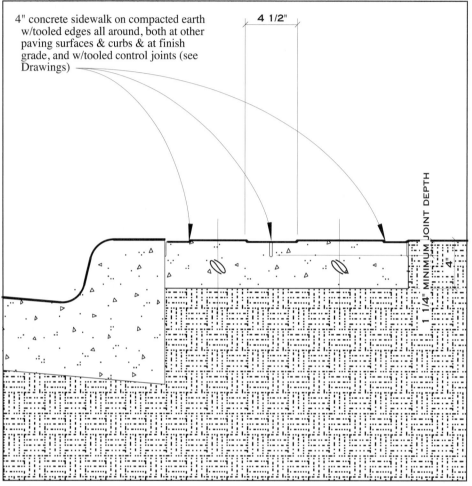

4" concrete sidewalk on compacted earth w/tooled edges all around, both at other paving surfaces & curbs & at finish grade, and w/tooled control joints (see Drawings)

4 1/2"

1 1/4" MINIMUM JOINT DEPTH

4"

Sidewalk Joint & Edge Details

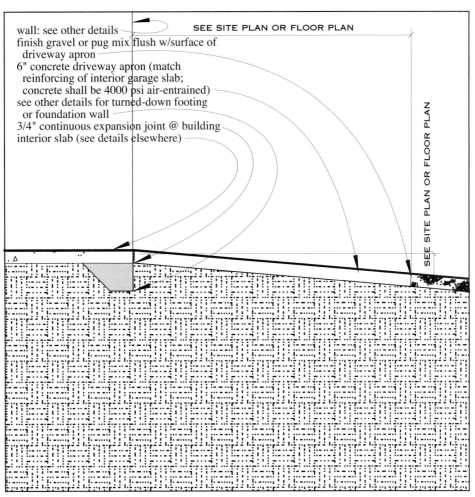

wall: see other details

finish gravel or pug mix flush w/surface of
driveway apron

6" concrete driveway apron (match
reinforcing of interior garage slab;
concrete shall be 4000 psi air-entrained)

see other details for turned-down footing
or foundation wall

3/4" continuous expansion joint @ building
interior slab (see details elsewhere)

SEE SITE PLAN OR FLOOR PLAN

SEE SITE PLAN OR FLOOR PLAN

DRAWING #		SCALE

6" Driveway Apron Detail

1/4"
1'-0"

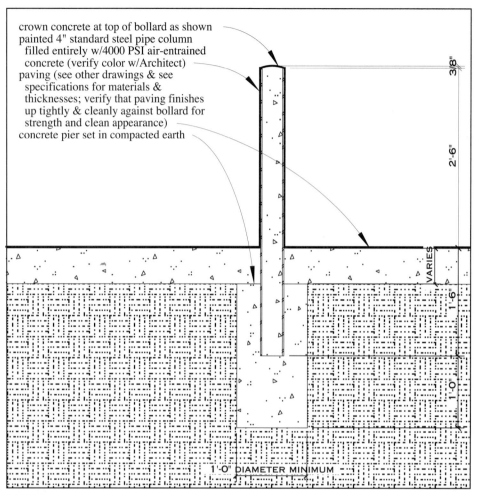

crown concrete at top of bollard as shown
painted 4" standard steel pipe column
   filled entirely w/4000 PSI air-entrained
   concrete (verify color w/Architect)
paving (see other drawings & see
   specifications for materials &
   thicknesses; verify that paving finishes
   up tightly & cleanly against bollard for
   strength and clean appearance)
concrete pier set in compacted earth

3/8"

2'-6"

VARIES

1'-6"

1'-0"

1'-0" DIAMETER MINIMUM

4" Bollard Detail

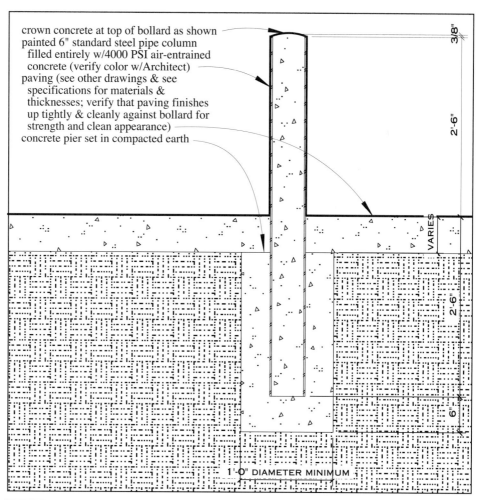

crown concrete at top of bollard as shown
painted 6" standard steel pipe column
    filled entirely w/4000 PSI air-entrained
    concrete (verify color w/Architect)
paving (see other drawings & see
    specifications for materials &
    thicknesses; verify that paving finishes
    up tightly & cleanly against bollard for
    strength and clean appearance)
concrete pier set in compacted earth

3/8"

2'-6"

VARIES

2'-6"

6"

1'-0" DIAMETER MINIMUM

DRAWING #

SCALE
3/4"
1'-0"

6" Bollard Detail

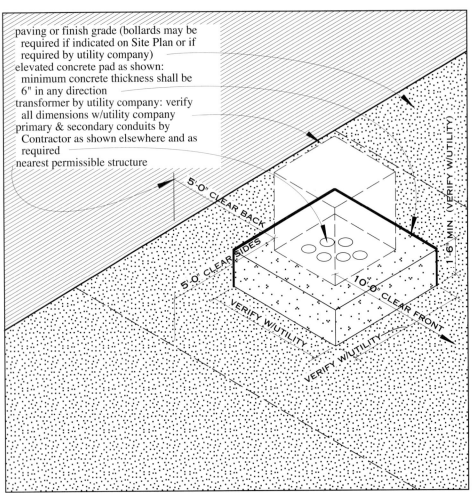

paving or finish grade (bollards may be
required if indicated on Site Plan or if
required by utility company)
elevated concrete pad as shown:
minimum concrete thickness shall be
6" in any direction
transformer by utility company: verify
all dimensions w/utility company
primary & secondary conduits by
Contractor as shown elsewhere and as
required
nearest permissible structure

5'-0" CLEAR BACK

5'-0" CLEAR SIDES

10'-0" CLEAR FRONT

1'-6" MIN. (VERIFY W/UTILITY)

VERIFY W/UTILITY

VERIFY W/UTILITY

DRAWING #

Transformer Pad Detail

SCALE
1/4"
1'-0"

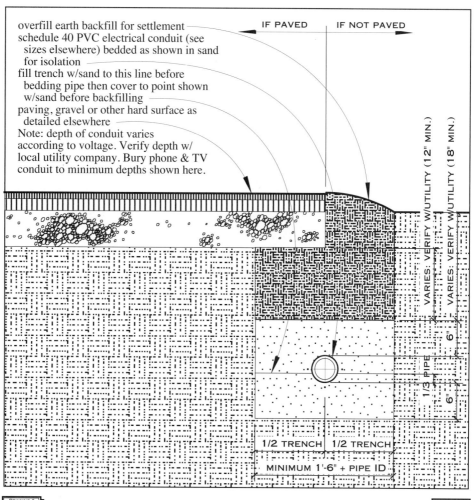

overfill earth backfill for settlement
schedule 40 PVC electrical conduit (see
  sizes elsewhere) bedded as shown in sand
  for isolation
fill trench w/sand to this line before
  bedding pipe then cover to point shown
  w/sand before backfilling
paving, gravel or other hard surface as
  detailed elsewhere
Note: depth of conduit varies
according to voltage. Verify depth w/
local utility company. Bury phone & TV
conduit to minimum depths shown here.

IF PAVED | IF NOT PAVED

VARIES: VERIFY W/UTILITY (12" MIN.)

VARIES: VERIFY W/UTILITY (18" MIN.)

6"

1/3 PIPE

6"

1/2 TRENCH | 1/2 TRENCH

MINIMUM 1'-6" + PIPE ID

DRAWING #

Elect./Auxiliary Conduit Trench Detail

SCALE
3/4"
1'-0"

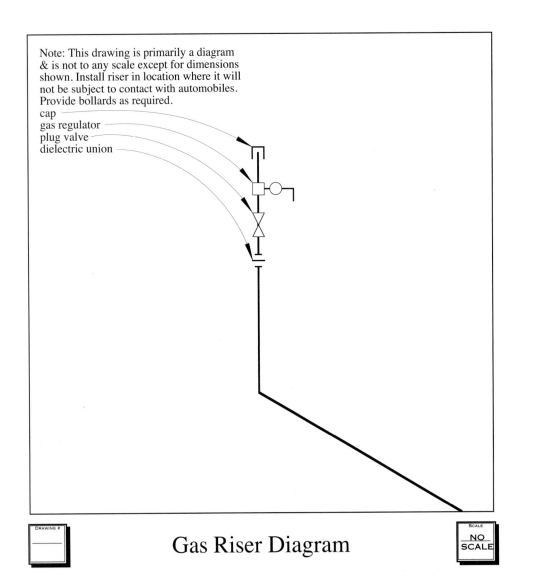

Note: This drawing is primarily a diagram
& is not to any scale except for dimensions
shown. Install riser in location where it will
not be subject to contact with automobiles.
Provide bollards as required.

cap
gas regulator
plug valve
dielectric union

Gas Riser Diagram

DRAWING #

SCALE
NO
SCALE

SUG001
748

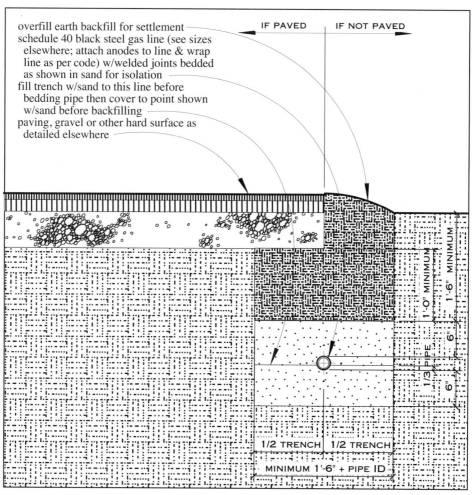

overfill earth backfill for settlement
schedule 40 black steel gas line (see sizes
  elsewhere; attach anodes to line & wrap
  line as per code) w/welded joints bedded
  as shown in sand for isolation
fill trench w/sand to this line before
  bedding pipe then cover to point shown
  w/sand before backfilling
paving, gravel or other hard surface as
  detailed elsewhere

IF PAVED   IF NOT PAVED

1'-0" MINIMUM
1'-6" MINIMUM
1/3 PIPE
6"
6"

1/2 TRENCH   1/2 TRENCH

MINIMUM 1'-6" + PIPE ID

DRAWING #

SCALE
3/4"
1'-0"

Gas Line Trench Paved/Unpaved

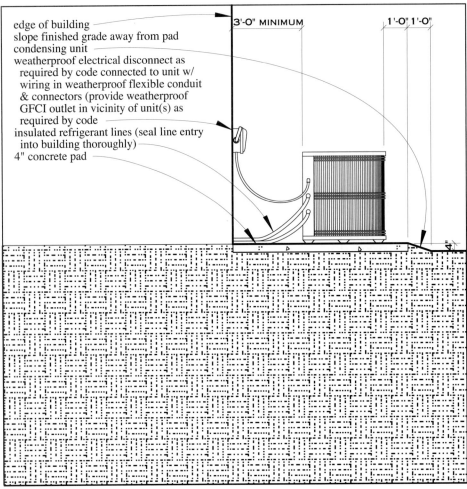

edge of building
slope finished grade away from pad
condensing unit
weatherproof electrical disconnect as
  required by code connected to unit w/
  wiring in weatherproof flexible conduit
  & connectors (provide weatherproof
  GFCI outlet in vicinity of unit(s) as
  required by code
insulated refrigerant lines (seal line entry
  into building thoroughly)
4" concrete pad

3'-0" MINIMUM   1'-0" 1'-0"

DRAWING #

Condensing Unit Detail

SCALE
1/4"
1'-0"

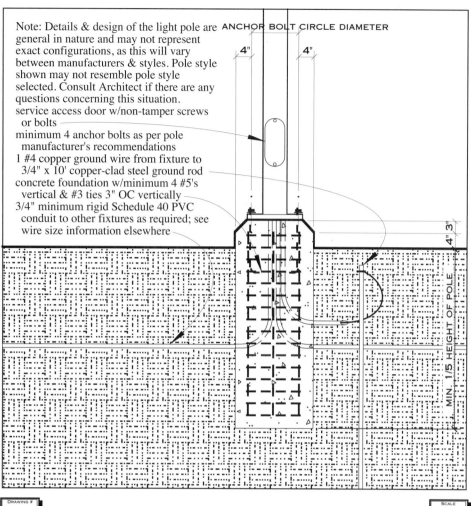

Note: Details & design of the light pole are general in nature and may not represent exact configurations, as this will vary between manufacturers & styles. Pole style shown may not resemble pole style selected. Consult Architect if there are any questions concerning this situation.

service access door w/non-tamper screws or bolts

minimum 4 anchor bolts as per pole manufacturer's recommendations

1 #4 copper ground wire from fixture to 3/4" x 10' copper-clad steel ground rod

concrete foundation w/minimum 4 #5's vertical & #3 ties 3" OC vertically

3/4" minimum rigid Schedule 40 PVC conduit to other fixtures as required; see wire size information elsewhere

ANCHOR BOLT CIRCLE DIAMETER

4"   4"

4" 3"

MIN. 1/5 HEIGHT OF POLE

Light Pole Foundation Detail

DRAWING #

SCALE
1/2"
1'-0"

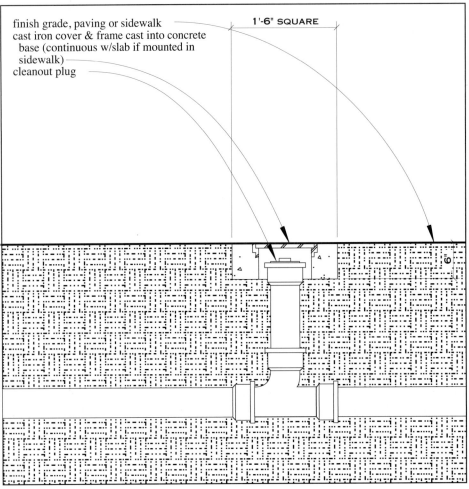

finish grade, paving or sidewalk
cast iron cover & frame cast into concrete
   base (continuous w/slab if mounted in
   sidewalk)
cleanout plug

1'-6" SQUARE

6"

DRAWING #

Exterior Cleanout Detail

SCALE
3/4"
1'-0"

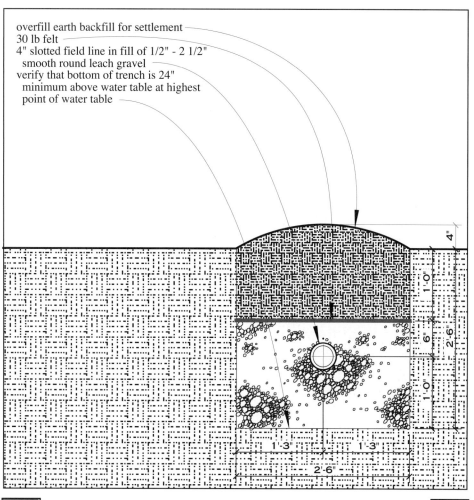

overfill earth backfill for settlement
30 lb felt
4" slotted field line in fill of 1/2" - 2 1/2"
  smooth round leach gravel
verify that bottom of trench is 24"
  minimum above water table at highest
  point of water table

4"

1'-0"

6"

2'-6"

1'-0"

1'-3"

1'-3"

2'-6"

Field Line Detail

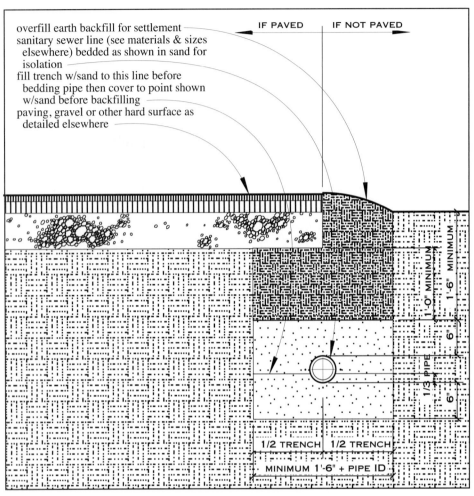

overfill earth backfill for settlement
sanitary sewer line (see materials & sizes
   elsewhere) bedded as shown in sand for
   isolation
fill trench w/sand to this line before
   bedding pipe then cover to point shown
   w/sand before backfilling
paving, gravel or other hard surface as
   detailed elsewhere

IF PAVED   IF NOT PAVED

1'-0" MINIMUM
1'-6" MINIMUM
6"
1/3 PIPE
6"

1/2 TRENCH | 1/2 TRENCH
MINIMUM 1'-6" + PIPE ID

DRAWING #

Sanitary Sewer Trench Detail

SCALE
3/4"
1'-0"

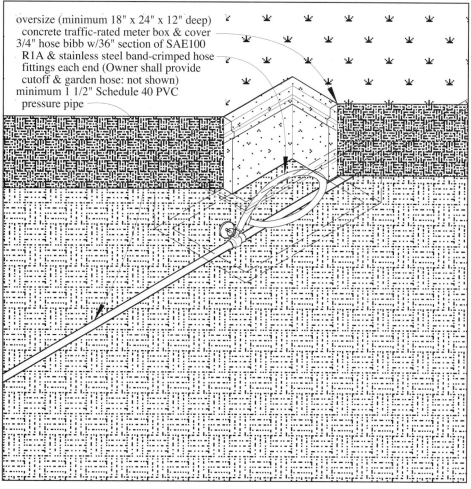

oversize (minimum 18" x 24" x 12" deep)
  concrete traffic-rated meter box & cover
3/4" hose bibb w/36" section of SAE100
  R1A & stainless steel band-crimped hose
  fittings each end (Owner shall provide
  cutoff & garden hose: not shown)
minimum 1 1/2" Schedule 40 PVC
  pressure pipe

DRAWING #

Underground Hose Bibb Detail

SCALE
3/4"
1'-0"

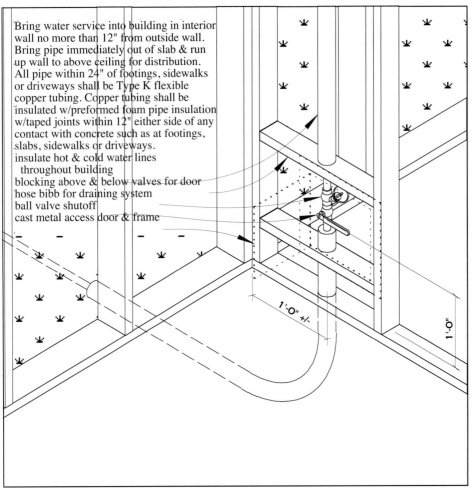

Bring water service into building in interior
wall no more than 12" from outside wall.
Bring pipe immediately out of slab & run
up wall to above ceiling for distribution.
All pipe within 24" of footings, sidewalks
or driveways shall be Type K flexible
copper tubing. Copper tubing shall be
insulated w/preformed foam pipe insulation
w/taped joints within 12" either side of any
contact with concrete such as at footings,
slabs, sidewalks or driveways.
insulate hot & cold water lines
  throughout building
blocking above & below valves for door
hose bibb for draining system
ball valve shutoff
cast metal access door & frame

1'-O" +/-

1'-O"

DRAWING #		

Water Service Entrance

SCALE
3/4"
1'-O"

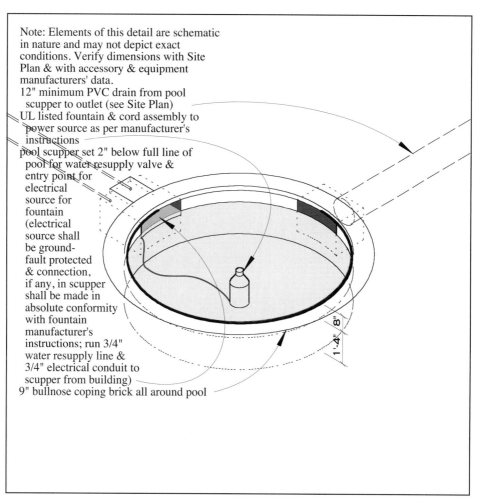

Note: Elements of this detail are schematic in nature and may not depict exact conditions. Verify dimensions with Site Plan & with accessory & equipment manufacturers' data.

12" minimum PVC drain from pool scupper to outlet (see Site Plan)

UL listed fountain & cord assembly to power source as per manufacturer's instructions

pool scupper set 2" below full line of pool for water resupply valve & entry point for electrical source for fountain (electrical source shall be ground-fault protected & connection, if any, in scupper shall be made in absolute conformity with fountain manufacturer's instructions; run 3/4" water resupply line & 3/4" electrical conduit to scupper from building)

9" bullnose coping brick all around pool

1'-4" 8"

| DRAWING # | | Reflecting Pool Detail | SCALE 1/4" 1'-O" |

TRIMWORK DETAILS

This section includes primarily interior trim, millwork & architectural woodwork details. The contents of this section are as follows:

Column Details 760
Entablature Details 764
Pilaster Details 770
Crown Details 789
Ceiling Surface Details 793
Door, Window, Frame & Opening Details: Head Casing 794
Door, Window, Frame & Opening Details: Jamb Casing 798
Door, Window, Frame & Opening Details: Sill Casing 800
Baseboard Details 807
Chair Rail Details 822
Wall Cap Details. 827

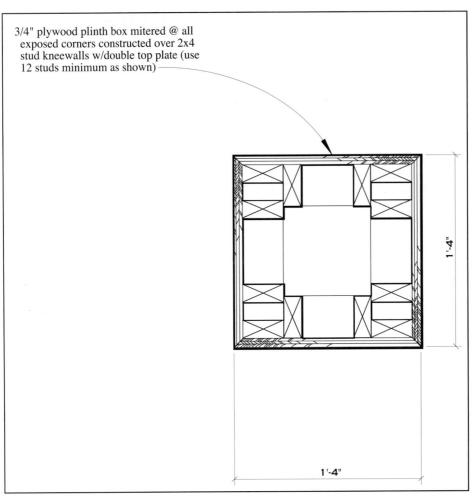

3/4" plywood plinth box mitered @ all
exposed corners constructed over 2x4
stud kneewalls w/double top plate (use
12 studs minimum as shown)

1'-4"

1'-4"

16" Square Pedestal Section

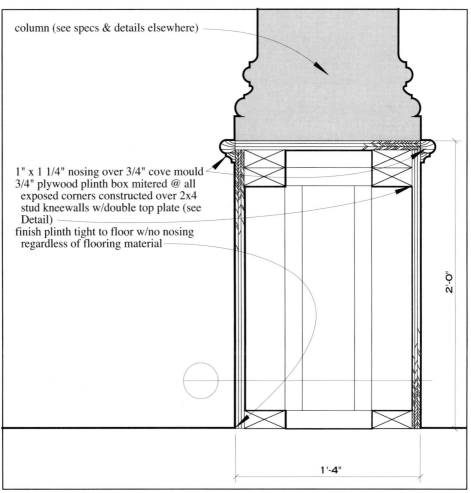

column (see specs & details elsewhere)

1" x 1 1/4" nosing over 3/4" cove mould
3/4" plywood plinth box mitered @ all
  exposed corners constructed over 2x4
  stud kneewalls w/double top plate (see
  Detail)
finish plinth tight to floor w/no nosing
  regardless of flooring material

2'-0"

1'-4"

Roman Doric Column Pedestal Detail

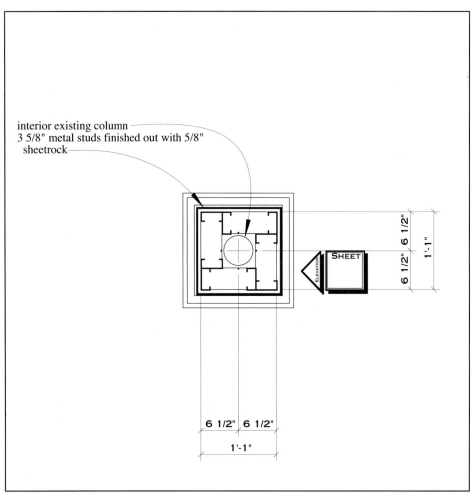

interior existing column
3 5/8" metal studs finished out with 5/8"
sheetrock

6 1/2" 6 1/2"
1'-1"

SHEET

ELEVATION

6 1/2" 6 1/2"
1'-1"

Existing Column Finish Detail

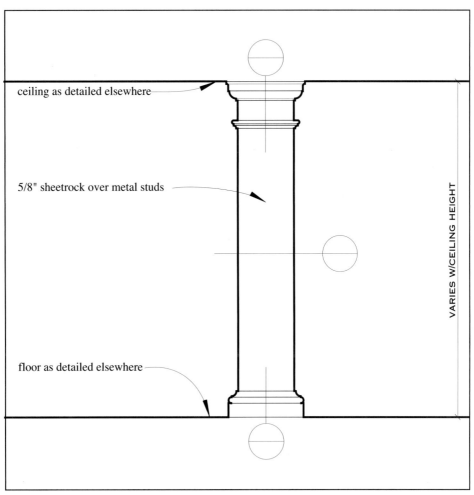

ceiling as detailed elsewhere

5/8" sheetrock over metal studs

floor as detailed elsewhere

VARIES W/CEILING HEIGHT

Existing Column Finish Detail

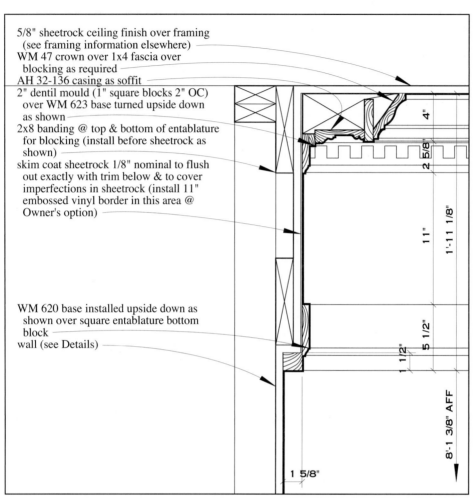

5/8" sheetrock ceiling finish over framing
(see framing information elsewhere)
WM 47 crown over 1x4 fascia over
blocking as required
AH 32-136 casing as soffit

2" dentil mould (1" square blocks 2" OC)
over WM 623 base turned upside down
as shown
2x8 banding @ top & bottom of entablature
for blocking (install before sheetrock as
shown)
skim coat sheetrock 1/8" nominal to flush
out exactly with trim below & to cover
imperfections in sheetrock (install 11"
embossed vinyl border in this area @
Owner's option)

WM 620 base installed upside down as
shown over square entablature bottom
block
wall (see Details)

4"

2 5/8"

11"

1'-11 1/8"

1 1/2"

5 1/2"

8'-1 3/8" AFF

1 5/8"

DRAWING #

24" Entablature @ Ceiling

SCALE
1 1/2"
1'-0"

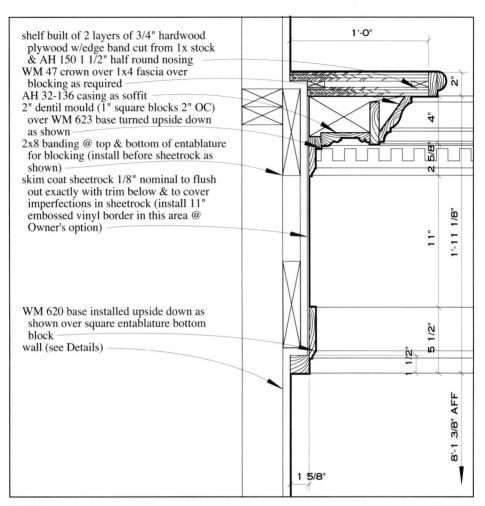

shelf built of 2 layers of 3/4" hardwood
  plywood w/edge band cut from 1x stock
  & AH 150 1 1/2" half round nosing
WM 47 crown over 1x4 fascia over
  blocking as required
AH 32-136 casing as soffit
2" dentil mould (1" square blocks 2" OC)
  over WM 623 base turned upside down
  as shown
2x8 banding @ top & bottom of entablature
  for blocking (install before sheetrock as
  shown)
skim coat sheetrock 1/8" nominal to flush
  out exactly with trim below & to cover
  imperfections in sheetrock (install 11"
  embossed vinyl border in this area @
  Owner's option)

WM 620 base installed upside down as
  shown over square entablature bottom
  block
wall (see Details)

1'-0"

2"

4"

2 5/8"

11"

1'-11 1/8"

5 1/2"

1 1/2"

8'-1 3/8" AFF

1 5/8"

24" Entablature @ Wall

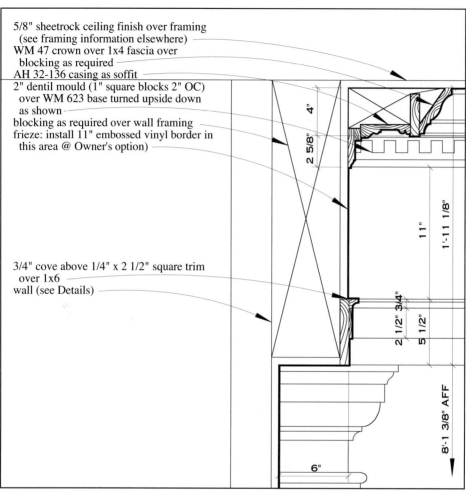

5/8" sheetrock ceiling finish over framing
(see framing information elsewhere)
WM 47 crown over 1x4 fascia over
blocking as required
AH 32-136 casing as soffit

2" dentil mould (1" square blocks 2" OC)
over WM 623 base turned upside down
as shown
blocking as required over wall framing
frieze: install 11" embossed vinyl border in
this area @ Owner's option)

3/4" cove above 1/4" x 2 1/2" square trim
over 1x6
wall (see Details)

4"

2 5/8"

11"

1'-11 1/8"

2 1/2" 3/4"

5 1/2"

8'-1 3/8" AFF

6"

24" Entablature @ Ceiling

DRAWING #

SCALE
1 1/2"
1'-0"

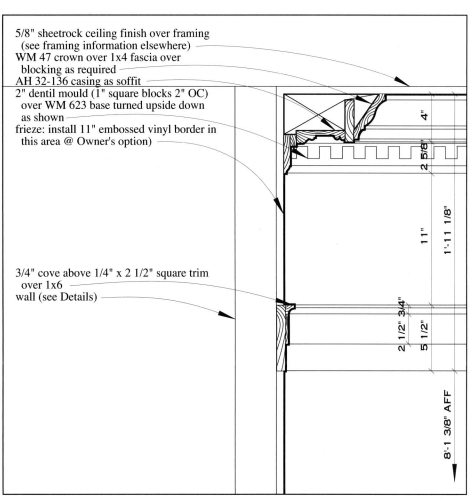

5/8" sheetrock ceiling finish over framing
  (see framing information elsewhere)
WM 47 crown over 1x4 fascia over
  blocking as required
AH 32-136 casing as soffit

2" dentil mould (1" square blocks 2" OC)
  over WM 623 base turned upside down
  as shown
frieze: install 11" embossed vinyl border in
  this area @ Owner's option)

3/4" cove above 1/4" x 2 1/2" square trim
  over 1x6
wall (see Details)

4"

2 5/8"

11"

1'-11 1/8"

2 1/2" 3/4"

5 1/2"

8'-1 3/8" AFF

DRAWING #

24" Entablature @ Ceiling

SCALE

1 1/2"
1'-0"

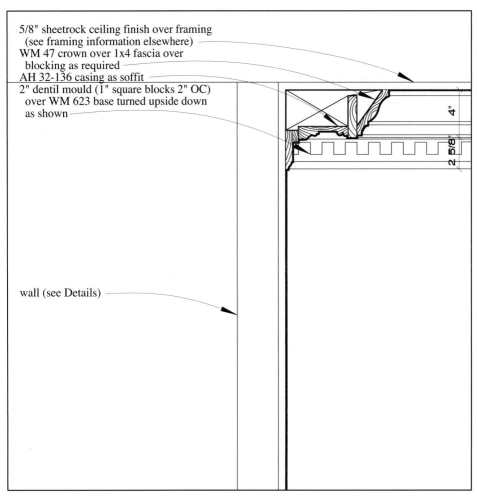

5/8" sheetrock ceiling finish over framing
  (see framing information elsewhere)
WM 47 crown over 1x4 fascia over
  blocking as required
AH 32-136 casing as soffit
2" dentil mould (1" square blocks 2" OC)
  over WM 623 base turned upside down
  as shown

4"

2 5/8"

wall (see Details)

5-Part Crown to Match Entablature

SCALE
1 1/2"
1'-0"

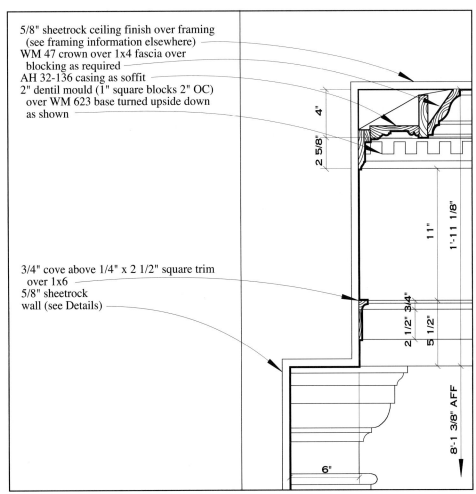

5/8" sheetrock ceiling finish over framing
 (see framing information elsewhere)
WM 47 crown over 1x4 fascia over
 blocking as required
AH 32-136 casing as soffit
2" dentil mould (1" square blocks 2" OC)
 over WM 623 base turned upside down
 as shown

3/4" cove above 1/4" x 2 1/2" square trim
 over 1x6
5/8" sheetrock
wall (see Details)

4"

2 5/8"

11"

1'-11 1/8"

2 1/2"

3/4"

5 1/2"

8'-1 3/8" AFF

6"

 DRAWING #

24" Entablature @ Ceiling

 SCALE
1 1/2"
1'-0"

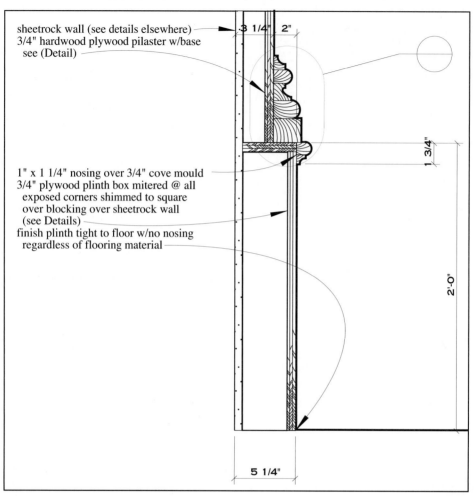

sheetrock wall (see details elsewhere)
3/4" hardwood plywood pilaster w/base
see (Detail)

3 1/4"   2"

1 3/4"

1" x 1 1/4" nosing over 3/4" cove mould
3/4" plywood plinth box mitered @ all
exposed corners shimmed to square
over blocking over sheetrock wall
(see Details)
finish plinth tight to floor w/no nosing
regardless of flooring material

2'-0"

5 1/4"

| DRAWING # | Roman Doric 10" Pilaster Plinth Detail | SCALE 3/4" 1'-0" |

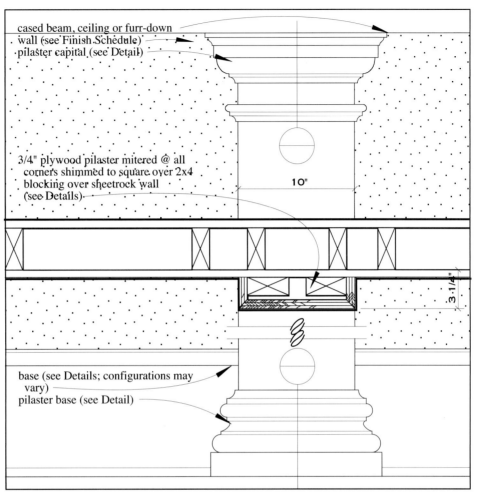

cased beam, ceiling or furr-down
wall (see Finish Schedule)
pilaster capital (see Detail)

3/4" plywood pilaster mitered @ all
corners shimmed to square over 2x4
blocking over sheetrock wall
(see Details)

10"

3-1/4"

base (see Details; configurations may
vary)
pilaster base (see Detail)

DRAWING #

Roman Doric 10" Pilaster Detail

SCALE
1 1/2"
1'-0"

TBP003
771

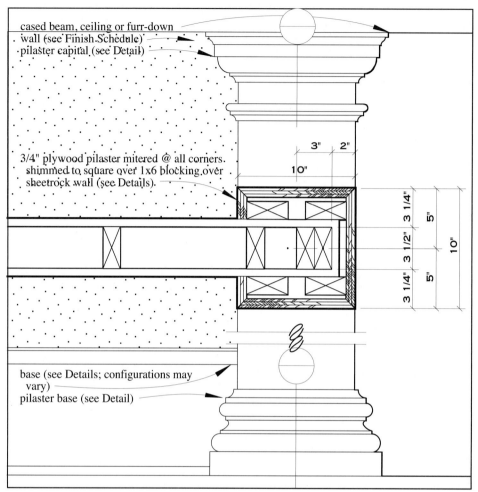

cased beam, ceiling or furr-down

wall (see Finish Schedule)

pilaster capital (see Detail)

3/4" plywood pilaster mitered @ all corners,
shimmed to square over 1x6 blocking over
sheetrock wall (see Details).

3"   2"

10"

3 1/4"   5"

3 1/2"   5"   10"

3 1/4"   5"

base (see Details; configurations may
vary)

pilaster base (see Detail)

  DRAWING #

Roman Doric 10" Pilaster Detail

  SCALE
1 1/2"
1'-0"

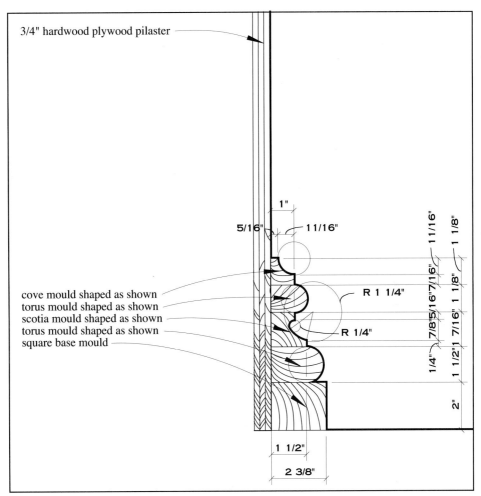

3/4" hardwood plywood pilaster

1"

5/16"   11/16"

11/16"

1 1/8"

cove mould shaped as shown
torus mould shaped as shown
scotia mould shaped as shown
torus mould shaped as shown
square base mould

R 1 1/4"

R 1/4"

7/16"   1 1/8"

5/16"   1 1/8"

7/8"   1 7/16"

1/4"   1 1/2"

2"

1 1/2"

2 3/8"

Roman Doric Pilaster Base Detail

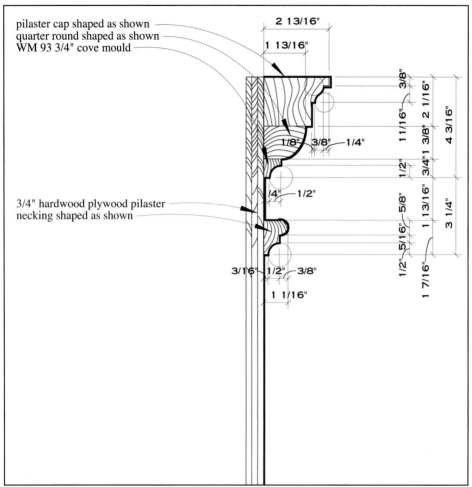

pilaster cap shaped as shown
quarter round shaped as shown
WM 93 3/4" cove mould

2 13/16"

1 13/16"

3/8"

2 1/16"

11/16"

4 3/16"

1/8" 3/8" 1/4"

3/8"

1/2"

3/4" 1

3 1/4"

3/4" hardwood plywood pilaster
necking shaped as shown

1/4" 1/2"

5/8"

1 13/16"

5/16"

1/2"

3/16" 1/2" 3/8"

1 7/16"

1 1/16"

DRAWING #

Roman Doric Pilaster Capital Detail

SCALE
3"
1'-0"

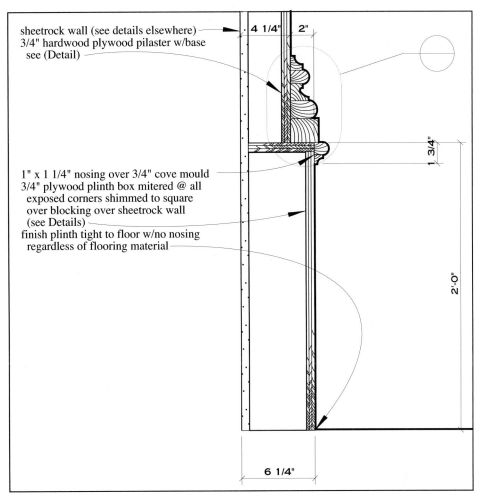

sheetrock wall (see details elsewhere)
3/4" hardwood plywood pilaster w/base
see (Detail)

4 1/4"   2"

1 3/4"

1" x 1 1/4" nosing over 3/4" cove mould
3/4" plywood plinth box mitered @ all
exposed corners shimmed to square
over blocking over sheetrock wall
(see Details)
finish plinth tight to floor w/no nosing
regardless of flooring material

2'-0"

6 1/4"

Roman Doric 12" Pilaster Plinth Detail

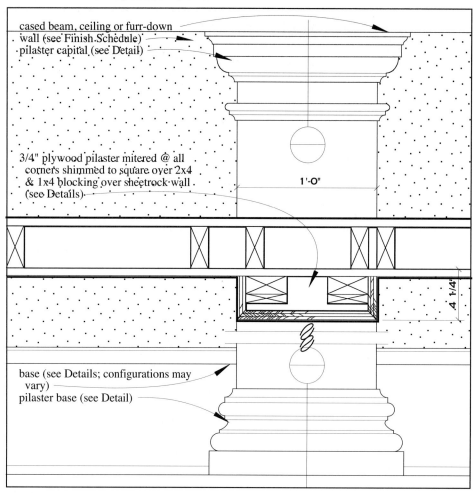

cased beam, ceiling or furr-down
wall (see Finish Schedule)
pilaster capital (see Detail)

3/4" plywood pilaster mitered @ all
corners shimmed to square over 2x4
& 1x4 blocking over sheetrock wall
(see Details)

1'-0"

4 1/4"

base (see Details; configurations may
vary)
pilaster base (see Detail)

DRAWING #

Roman Doric 12" Pilaster Detail

SCALE

1 1/2"
1'-0"

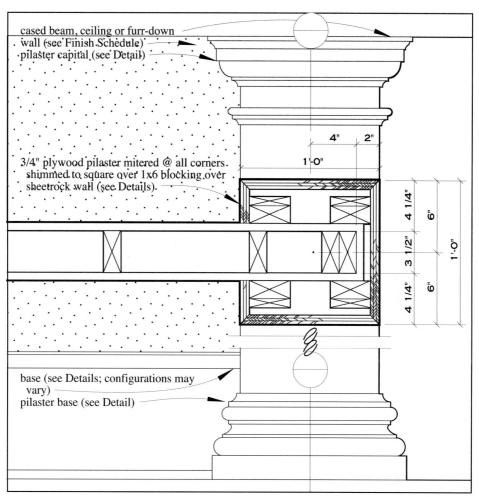

cased beam, ceiling or furr-down
wall (see Finish Schedule)
pilaster capital (see Detail)

3/4" plywood pilaster mitered @ all corners,
shimmed to square over 1x6 blocking over
sheetrock wall (see Details).

4" 2"

1'-0"

4 1/4"

6"

3 1/2"

1'-0"

4 1/4"

6"

base (see Details; configurations may
vary)
pilaster base (see Detail)

Roman Doric 12" Pilaster Detail

DRAWING #

SCALE
1 1/2"
1'-0"

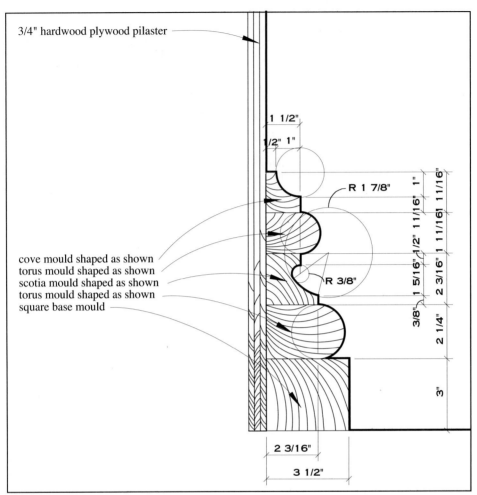

3/4" hardwood plywood pilaster

1 1/2"

1/2" 1"

R 1 7/8"

R 3/8"

1"
11/16"
11/16"
1 11/16"
1/2"
1 5/16"
2 3/16"
3/8"
2 1/4"
3"

cove mould shaped as shown
torus mould shaped as shown
scotia mould shaped as shown
torus mould shaped as shown
square base mould

2 3/16"

3 1/2"

DRAWING #	

Roman Doric Pilaster Base Detail

SCALE	
3"	
1'-0"	

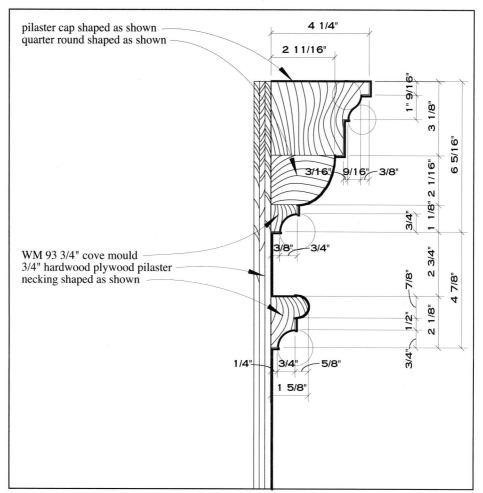

pilaster cap shaped as shown
quarter round shaped as shown

WM 93 3/4" cove mould
3/4" hardwood plywood pilaster
necking shaped as shown

4 1/4"
2 11/16"

1" 9/16"
3 1/8"
6 5/16"

3/16" 9/16" 3/8"
2 1/16"
1 1/8"
3/4"
1 1/8"

3/8" 3/4"

7/8"
2 3/4"
4 7/8"

1/2"
2 1/8"

3/4"

1/4" 3/4" 5/8"
1 5/8"

Roman Doric Pilaster Capital Detail

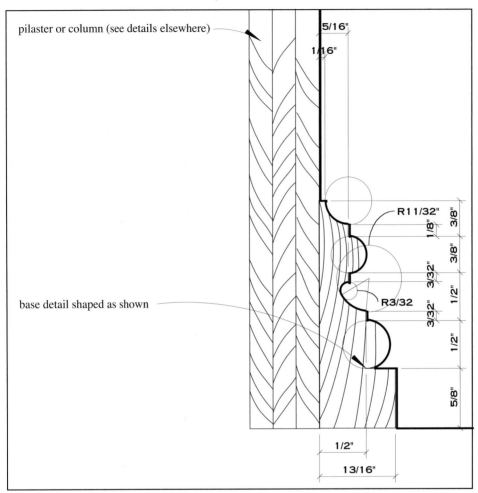

pilaster or column (see details elsewhere)

5/16"

1/16"

R11/32"

3/8"

1/8"

3/8"

3/32"

base detail shaped as shown

1/2"

R3/32

3/32"

1/2"

5/8"

1/2"

13/16"

DRAWING #

Roman Doric Pilaster Base Detail

SCALE
FULL
SIZE

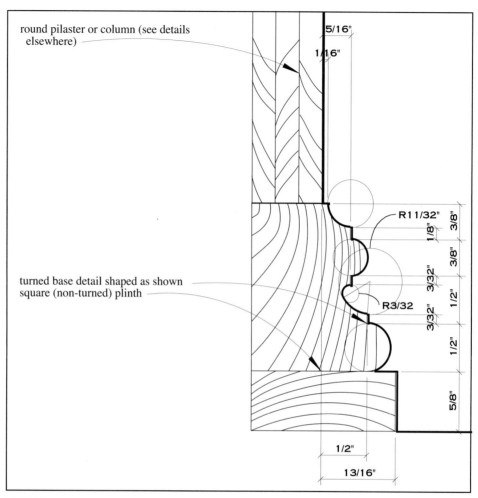

round pilaster or column (see details elsewhere)

5/16"

1/16"

R1 1/32"

3/8"

1/8"

3/8"

turned base detail shaped as shown
square (non-turned) plinth

3/32"

3/8"

R3/32

1/2"

3/32"

1/2"

5/8"

1/2"

13/16"

Roman Doric Pilaster Turned Base Detail

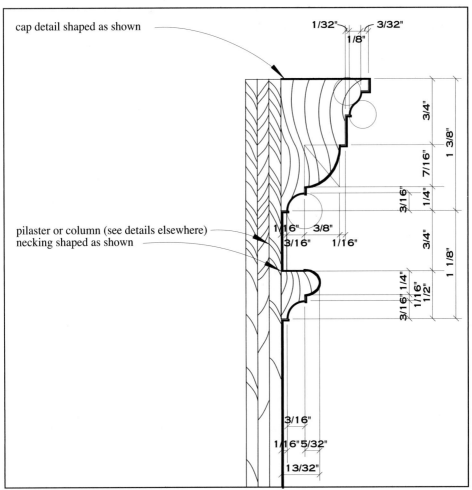

cap detail shaped as shown

1/32"   3/32"
1/8"

3/4"
1 3/8"
7/16"
3/16" 1/4"

pilaster or column (see details elsewhere)
necking shaped as shown

1/16" 3/8"
3/16" 1/16"

3/4"
1 1/8"

3/16" 1/4"
1/16"
1/2"

3/16"
1/16" 5/32"
13/32"

Roman Doric Pilaster Capital Detail

DRAWING #

SCALE
FULL SIZE

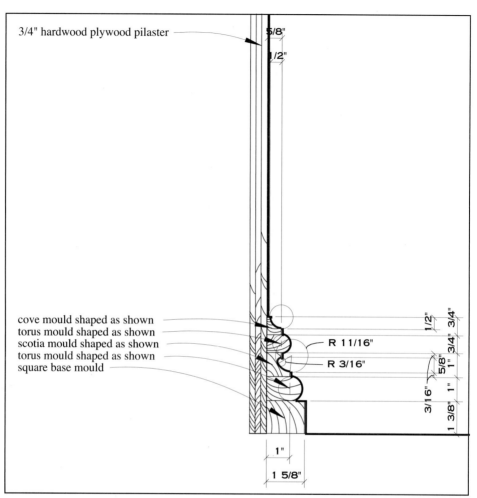

3/4" hardwood plywood pilaster

5/8"

1/2"

cove mould shaped as shown
torus mould shaped as shown
scotia mould shaped as shown
torus mould shaped as shown
square base mould

R 11/16"

R 3/16"

1/2" 3/4"

3/4"

5/8" 1"

3/16" 1"

1 3/8" 1"

1"

1 5/8"

DRAWING #

Roman Doric Pilaster Base Detail

SCALE

$\dfrac{3"}{1'-0"}$

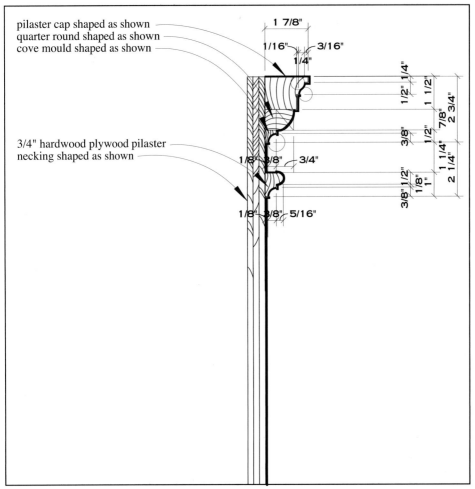

pilaster cap shaped as shown
quarter round shaped as shown
cove mould shaped as shown

1 7/8"

1/16"   3/16"
1/4"

1/4"
1/2" 1 1/2"
7/8" 2 3/4"
3/8" 1/2"

3/4" hardwood plywood pilaster
necking shaped as shown

1/8" 3/8"   3/4"

1 1/4"
2 1/4"

3/8" 1/2"
1/8"
1"
2 1/8"

1/8" 3/8" 5/16"

DRAWING #		SCALE

Roman Doric Pilaster Capital Detail

SCALE
3"
1'-0"

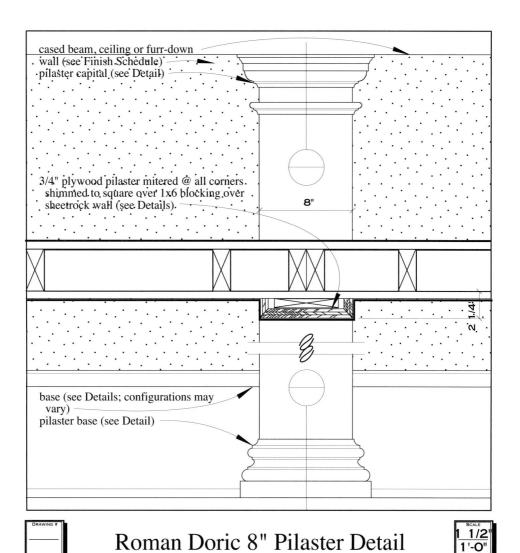

cased beam, ceiling or furr-down

wall (see Finish Schedule)

pilaster capital (see Detail)

3/4" plywood pilaster mitered @ all corners,
shimmed to square over 1x6 blocking over
sheetrock wall (see Details).

8"

2 1/4"

base (see Details; configurations may
vary)

pilaster base (see Detail)

Roman Doric 8" Pilaster Detail

DRAWING #

SCALE
1 1/2"
1'-0"

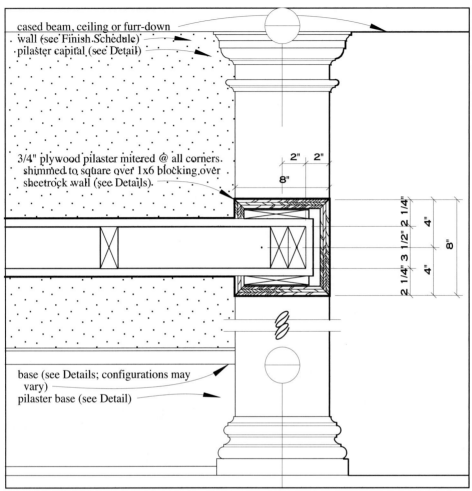

cased beam, ceiling or furr-down

wall (see Finish Schedule)

pilaster capital (see Detail)

3/4" plywood pilaster mitered @ all corners. shimmed to square over 1x6 blocking over sheetrock wall (see Details).

2" 2"

8"

2 1/4" 2 1/4"

4"

3 1/2"

8"

2 1/4" 3 1/2" 2 1/4"

4"

base (see Details; configurations may vary)

pilaster base (see Detail)

DRAWING #

Roman Doric 8" Pilaster Detail

SCALE

1 1/2"
1'-0"

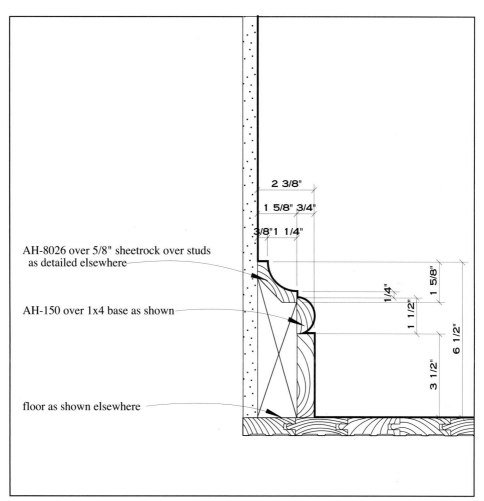

AH-8026 over 5/8" sheetrock over studs
as detailed elsewhere

AH-150 over 1x4 base as shown

floor as shown elsewhere

2 3/8"

1 5/8" 3/4"

3/8" 1 1/4"

1 5/8"

1/4"

1 1/2"

6 1/2"

3 1/2"

Pilaster Section Detail

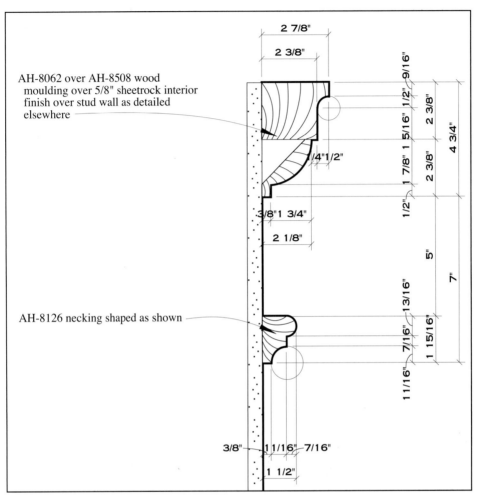

AH-8062 over AH-8508 wood moulding over 5/8" sheetrock interior finish over stud wall as detailed elsewhere

AH-8126 necking shaped as shown

2 7/8"

2 3/8"

9/16"

1/2"

2 3/8"

4 3/4"

1 5/16"

1 7/8"

2 3/8"

1/4" 1/2"

1/2"

3/8" 1 3/4"

2 1/8"

5"

7"

13/16"

1 15/16"

7/16"

11/16"

1

3/8" 1 1/16" 7/16"

1 1/2"

DRAWING #

Pilaster Section Detail

SCALE

3"
───
1'-0"

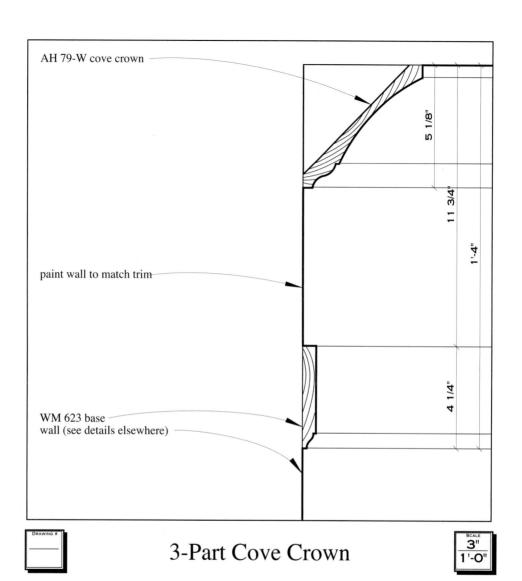

AH 79-W cove crown

5 1/8"

11 3/4"

1'-4"

paint wall to match trim

4 1/4"

WM 623 base
wall (see details elsewhere)

DRAWING #

3-Part Cove Crown

SCALE
3"
1'-0"

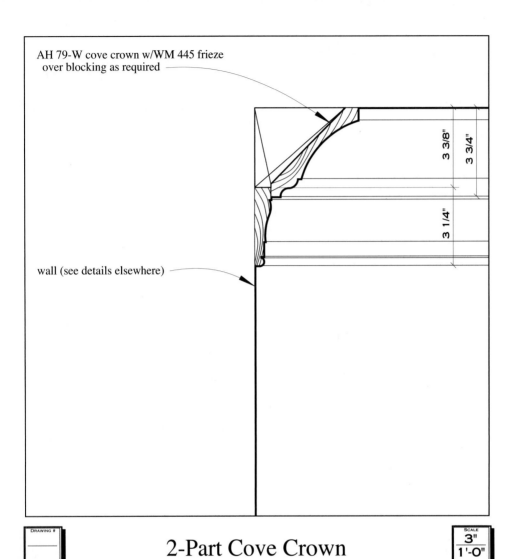

AH 79-W cove crown w/WM 445 frieze
  over blocking as required

3 3/8"

3 3/4"

3 1/4"

wall (see details elsewhere)

2-Part Cove Crown

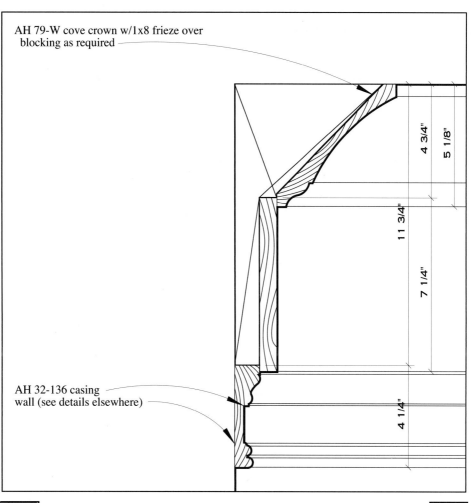

AH 79-W cove crown w/1x8 frieze over
   blocking as required

4 3/4"

5 1/8"

11 3/4"

7 1/4"

AH 32-136 casing
wall (see details elsewhere)

4 1/4"

3-Part Cove Crown

SCALE
$\dfrac{3"}{1'\text{-}0"}$

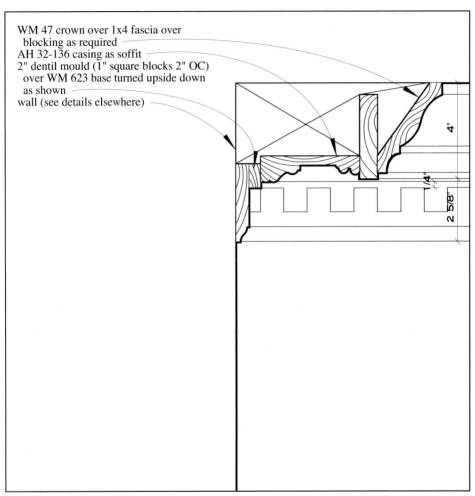

WM 47 crown over 1x4 fascia over
   blocking as required
AH 32-136 casing as soffit
2" dentil mould (1" square blocks 2" OC)
   over WM 623 base turned upside down
   as shown
wall (see details elsewhere)

4"

1/4"

2 5/8"

Crown to Match 24" Entablature

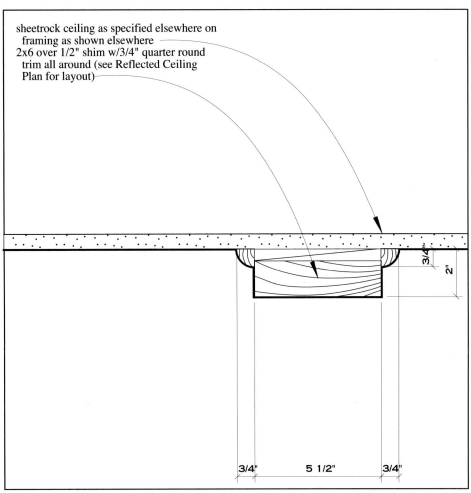

sheetrock ceiling as specified elsewhere on
  framing as shown elsewhere
2x6 over 1/2" shim w/3/4" quarter round
  trim all around (see Reflected Ceiling
  Plan for layout)

3/4"

2"

3/4"   5 1/2"   3/4"

DRAWING #

Coffered Ceiling Minor Beam

SCALE
$\dfrac{3"}{1'-0"}$

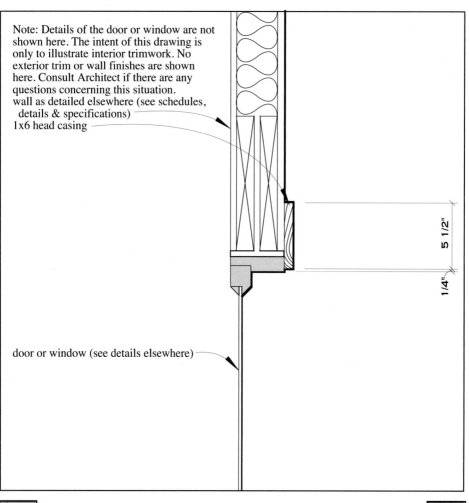

Note: Details of the door or window are not shown here. The intent of this drawing is only to illustrate interior trimwork. No exterior trim or wall finishes are shown here. Consult Architect if there are any questions concerning this situation.
wall as detailed elsewhere (see schedules, details & specifications)
1x6 head casing

5 1/2"

1/4"

door or window (see details elsewhere)

DRAWING #

Head Trim Detail

SCALE

1 1/2"
1'-0"

TDH001
794

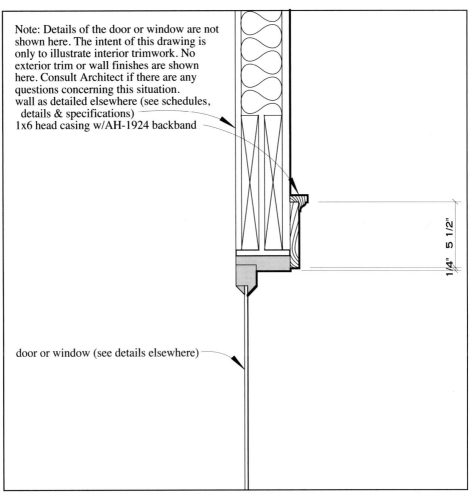

Note: Details of the door or window are not shown here. The intent of this drawing is only to illustrate interior trimwork. No exterior trim or wall finishes are shown here. Consult Architect if there are any questions concerning this situation.

wall as detailed elsewhere (see schedules, details & specifications)

1x6 head casing w/AH-1924 backband

5 1/2"

1/4"

door or window (see details elsewhere)

DRAWING #

Head Trim Detail

SCALE

1 1/2"
1'-0"

TDH002
795

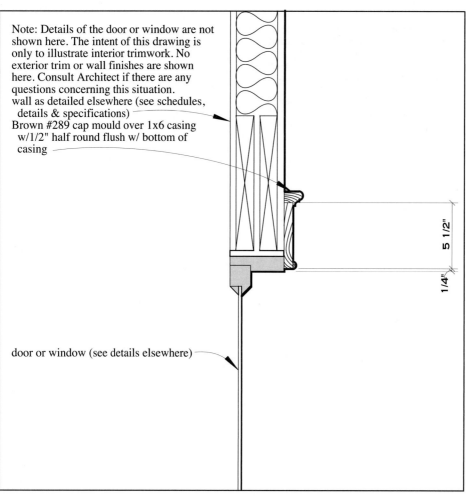

Note: Details of the door or window are not shown here. The intent of this drawing is only to illustrate interior trimwork. No exterior trim or wall finishes are shown here. Consult Architect if there are any questions concerning this situation.
wall as detailed elsewhere (see schedules, details & specifications)
Brown #289 cap mould over 1x6 casing w/1/2" half round flush w/ bottom of casing

5 1/2"

1/4"

door or window (see details elsewhere)

DRAWING #

Head Trim Detail

SCALE

1 1/2"
1'-0"

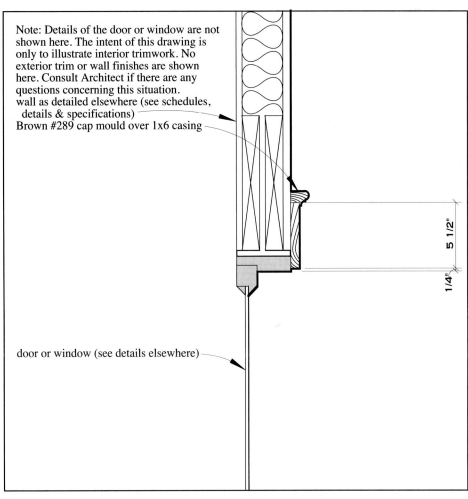

Note: Details of the door or window are not
shown here. The intent of this drawing is
only to illustrate interior trimwork. No
exterior trim or wall finishes are shown
here. Consult Architect if there are any
questions concerning this situation.
wall as detailed elsewhere (see schedules,
  details & specifications)
Brown #289 cap mould over 1x6 casing

5 1/2"

1/4"

door or window (see details elsewhere)

Head Trim Detail

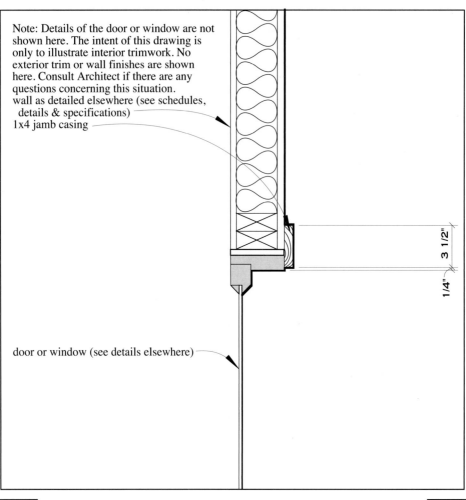

Note: Details of the door or window are not
shown here. The intent of this drawing is
only to illustrate interior trimwork. No
exterior trim or wall finishes are shown
here. Consult Architect if there are any
questions concerning this situation.
wall as detailed elsewhere (see schedules,
  details & specifications)
1x4 jamb casing

3 1/2"

1/4"

door or window (see details elsewhere)

Jamb Trim Detail

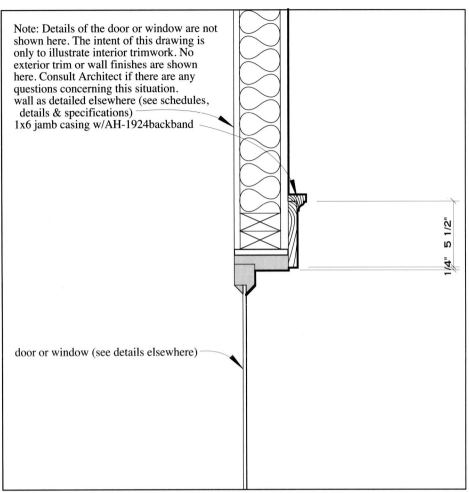

Note: Details of the door or window are not
shown here. The intent of this drawing is
only to illustrate interior trimwork. No
exterior trim or wall finishes are shown
here. Consult Architect if there are any
questions concerning this situation.
wall as detailed elsewhere (see schedules,
  details & specifications)
1x6 jamb casing w/AH-1924backband

5 1/2"

1/4"

door or window (see details elsewhere)

DRAWING #

Jamb Trim Detail

SCALE

1 1/2"
―――
1'-0"

TDJ002
799

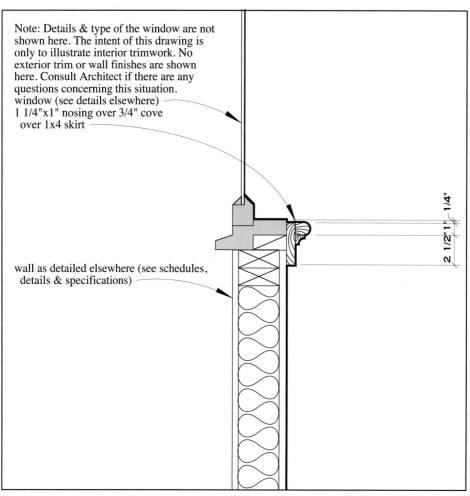

Note: Details & type of the window are not
shown here. The intent of this drawing is
only to illustrate interior trimwork. No
exterior trim or wall finishes are shown
here. Consult Architect if there are any
questions concerning this situation.
window (see details elsewhere)
1 1/4"x1" nosing over 3/4" cove
   over 1x4 skirt

wall as detailed elsewhere (see schedules,
   details & specifications)

2 1/2" 1" 1/4"

Window Sill Trim Detail

DRAWING #

SCALE

1 1/2"
1'-0"

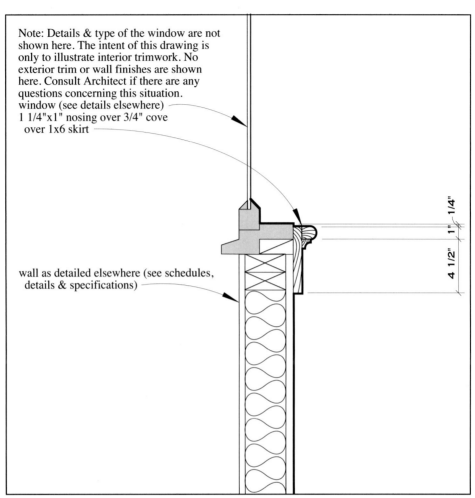

Note: Details & type of the window are not shown here. The intent of this drawing is only to illustrate interior trimwork. No exterior trim or wall finishes are shown here. Consult Architect if there are any questions concerning this situation.
window (see details elsewhere)
1 1/4"x1" nosing over 3/4" cove
  over 1x6 skirt

wall as detailed elsewhere (see schedules,
  details & specifications)

4 1/2"   1"   1/4"

DRAWING #

Window Sill Trim Detail

SCALE
1 1/2"
1'-0"

TDS002
801

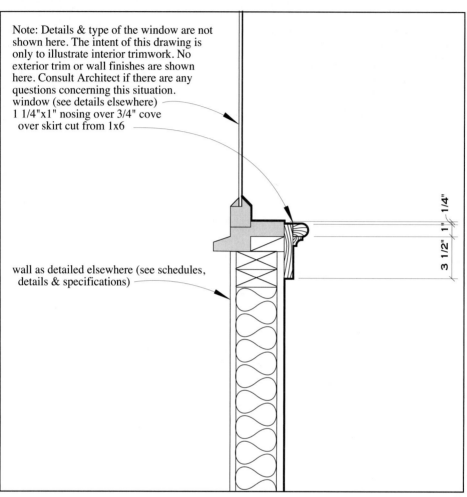

Note: Details & type of the window are not
shown here. The intent of this drawing is
only to illustrate interior trimwork. No
exterior trim or wall finishes are shown
here. Consult Architect if there are any
questions concerning this situation.
window (see details elsewhere)
1 1/4"x1" nosing over 3/4" cove
  over skirt cut from 1x6

wall as detailed elsewhere (see schedules,
  details & specifications)

Window Sill Trim Detail

DRAWING #

SCALE
1 1/2"
1'-0"

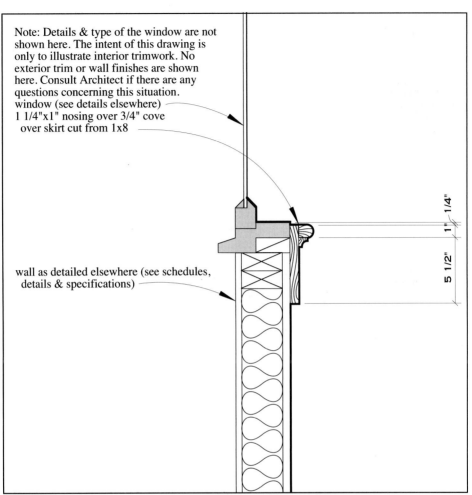

Note: Details & type of the window are not shown here. The intent of this drawing is only to illustrate interior trimwork. No exterior trim or wall finishes are shown here. Consult Architect if there are any questions concerning this situation.
window (see details elsewhere)
 1 1/4"x1" nosing over 3/4" cove
  over skirt cut from 1x8

wall as detailed elsewhere (see schedules, details & specifications)

1" 1/4"

5 1/2"

DRAWING #

Window Sill Trim Detail

SCALE
1 1/2"
1'-O"

TDS004
803

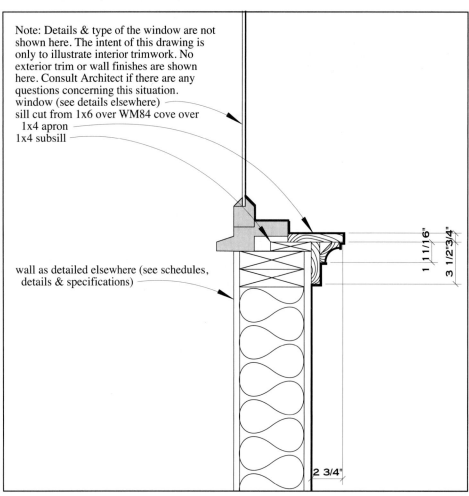

Note: Details & type of the window are not shown here. The intent of this drawing is only to illustrate interior trimwork. No exterior trim or wall finishes are shown here. Consult Architect if there are any questions concerning this situation.

window (see details elsewhere)
sill cut from 1x6 over WM84 cove over
 1x4 apron
1x4 subsill

wall as detailed elsewhere (see schedules,
 details & specifications)

1 11/16"

3 1/2"3/4"

2 3/4"

DRAWING #

Window Sill Trim Detail

SCALE

1 1/2"
1'-0"

TDS005
804

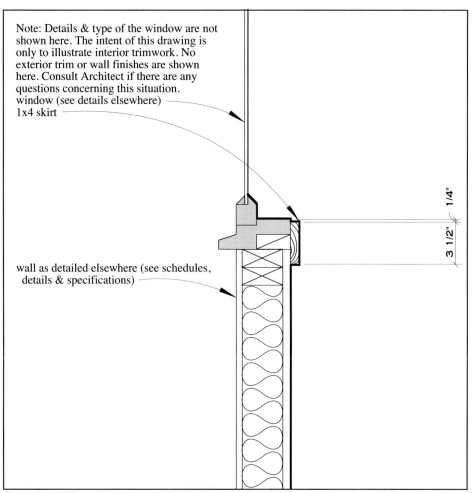

Note: Details & type of the window are not shown here. The intent of this drawing is only to illustrate interior trimwork. No exterior trim or wall finishes are shown here. Consult Architect if there are any questions concerning this situation.
window (see details elsewhere) ————
1x4 skirt ————

1/4"

3 1/2"

wall as detailed elsewhere (see schedules, details & specifications) ————

DRAWING #

Window Sill Trim Detail

SCALE
1 1/2"
1'-0"

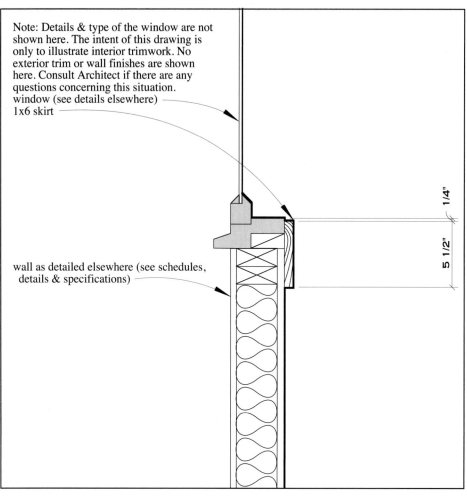

Note: Details & type of the window are not shown here. The intent of this drawing is only to illustrate interior trimwork. No exterior trim or wall finishes are shown here. Consult Architect if there are any questions concerning this situation.
window (see details elsewhere)
1x6 skirt

wall as detailed elsewhere (see schedules, details & specifications)

1/4"

5 1/2"

Window Sill Trim Detail

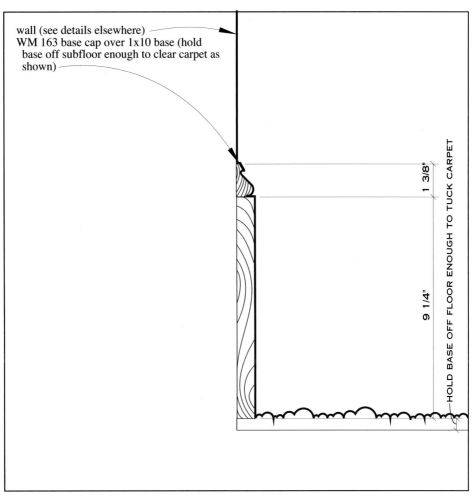

wall (see details elsewhere)
WM 163 base cap over 1x10 base (hold
  base off subfloor enough to clear carpet as
  shown)

1 3/8"

9 1/4"

HOLD BASE OFF FLOOR ENOUGH TO TUCK CARPET

DRAWING #

1x10 Base w/Cap on Carpet

SCALE
3"
1'-0"

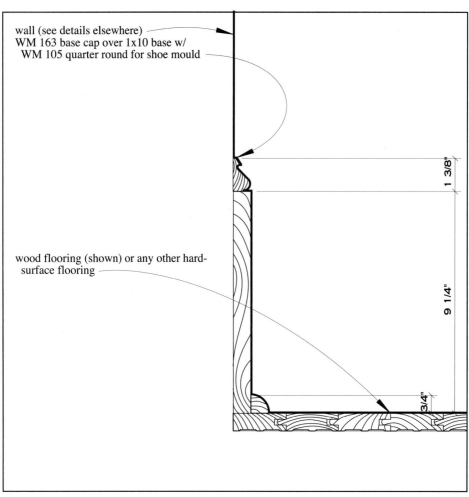

wall (see details elsewhere)
WM 163 base cap over 1x10 base w/
 WM 105 quarter round for shoe mould

wood flooring (shown) or any other hard-
 surface flooring

1 3/8"

9 1/4"

3/4"

DRAWING #	1x10 Base w/Cap on Hard Flooring	SCALE 3" / 1'-0"

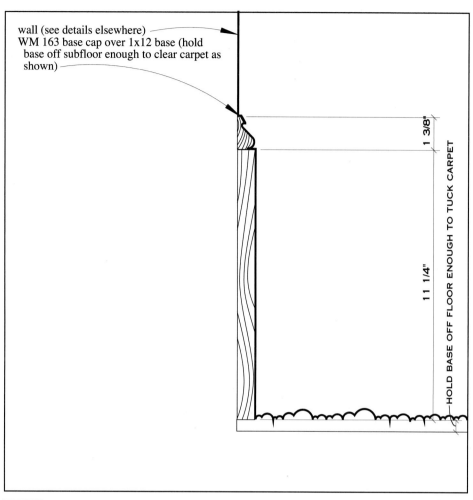

wall (see details elsewhere)
WM 163 base cap over 1x12 base (hold
  base off subfloor enough to clear carpet as
  shown)

1 3/8"

11 1/4"

HOLD BASE OFF FLOOR ENOUGH TO TUCK CARPET

1x12 Base w/Cap on Carpet

DRAWING #

SCALE
3"
1'-0"

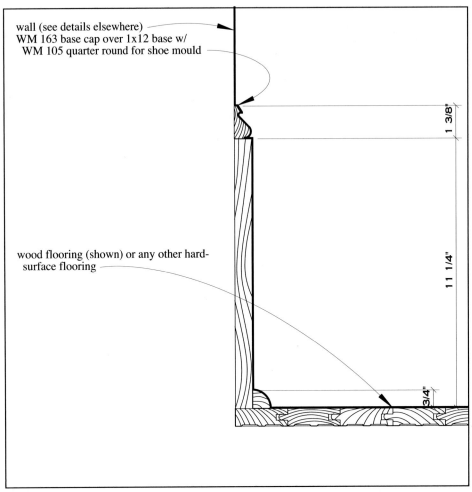

wall (see details elsewhere)
WM 163 base cap over 1x12 base w/
 WM 105 quarter round for shoe mould

1 3/8"

11 1/4"

wood flooring (shown) or any other hard-
 surface flooring

3/4"

DRAWING #

1x12 Base w/Cap on Hard Flooring

SCALE
3"
1'-0"

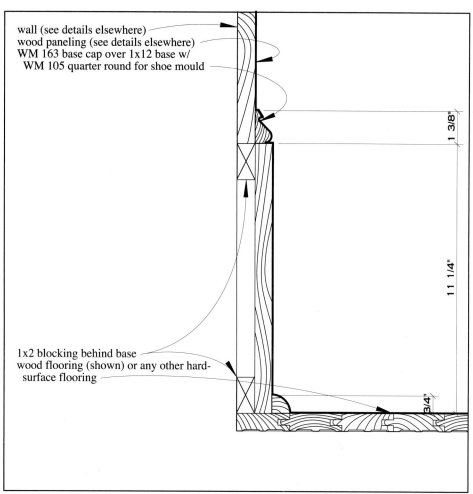

wall (see details elsewhere)
wood paneling (see details elsewhere)
WM 163 base cap over 1x12 base w/
    WM 105 quarter round for shoe mould

1 3/8"

11 1/4"

1x2 blocking behind base
wood flooring (shown) or any other hard-
    surface flooring

3/4"

1x12 Base w/Cap on Hard Floor @ Panel

SCALE
3"
1'-0"

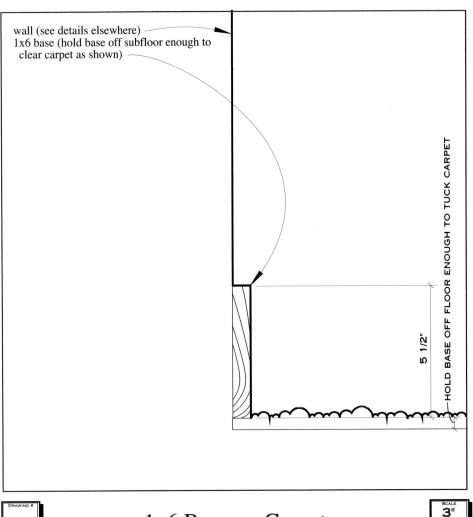

wall (see details elsewhere)
1x6 base (hold base off subfloor enough to
    clear carpet as shown)

5 1/2"

HOLD BASE OFF FLOOR ENOUGH TO TUCK CARPET

1x6 Base on Carpet

DRAWING #

SCALE
$\frac{3"}{1'-0"}$

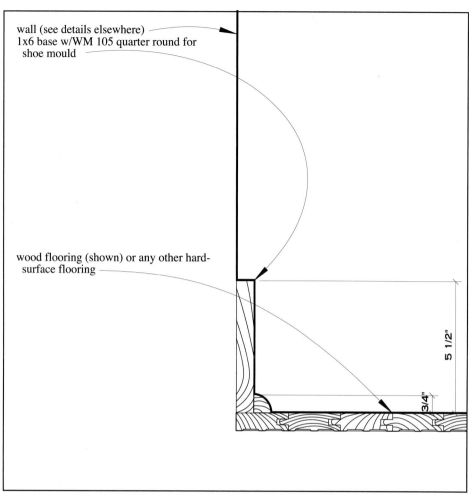

wall (see details elsewhere)
1x6 base w/WM 105 quarter round for
  shoe mould

wood flooring (shown) or any other hard-
  surface flooring

5 1/2"

3/4"

1x6 Base on Hard Flooring

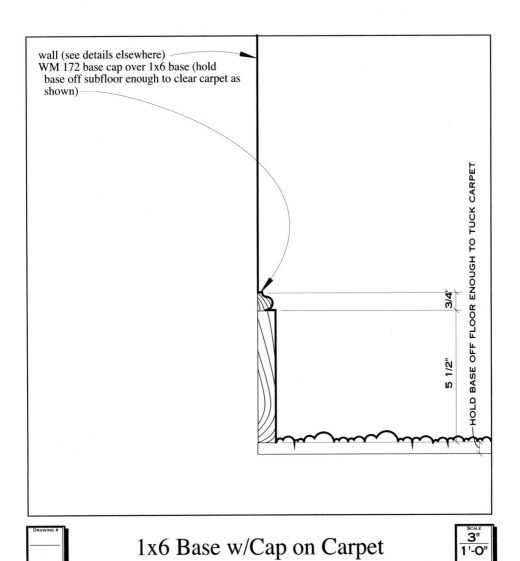

wall (see details elsewhere)
WM 172 base cap over 1x6 base (hold base off subfloor enough to clear carpet as shown)

3/4"

5 1/2"

HOLD BASE OFF FLOOR ENOUGH TO TUCK CARPET

1x6 Base w/Cap on Carpet

DRAWING #

SCALE
3"
1'-0"

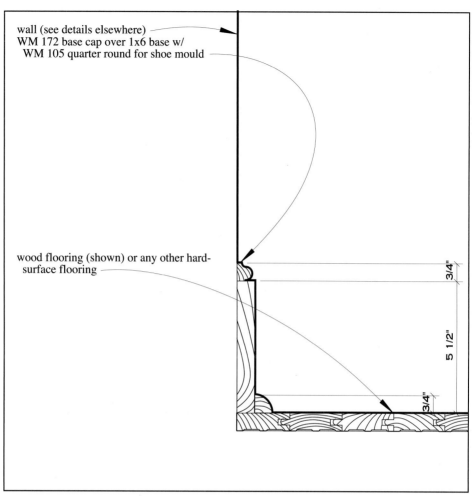

wall (see details elsewhere)
WM 172 base cap over 1x6 base w/
  WM 105 quarter round for shoe mould

wood flooring (shown) or any other hard-
  surface flooring

3/4"

5 1/2"

3/4"

1x6 Base w/Cap on Hard Flooring

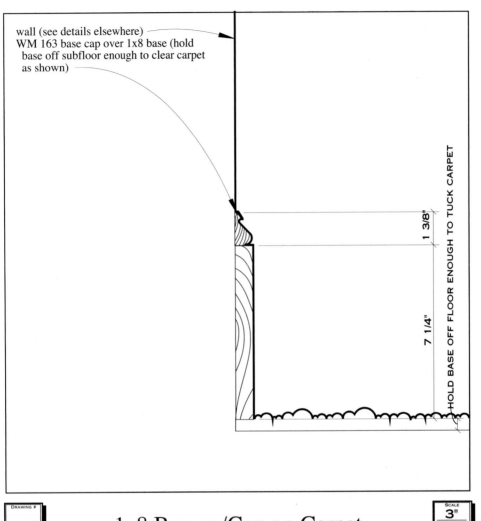

wall (see details elsewhere)
WM 163 base cap over 1x8 base (hold
 base off subfloor enough to clear carpet
 as shown)

1 3/8"

7 1/4"

HOLD BASE OFF FLOOR ENOUGH TO TUCK CARPET

p

DRAWING #

SCALE
3"
1'-0"

1x8 Base w/Cap on Carpet

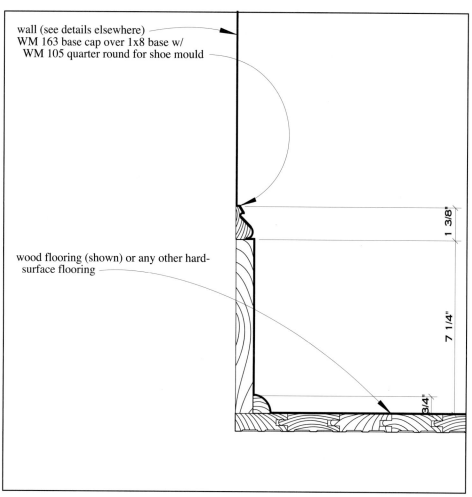

wall (see details elsewhere)
WM 163 base cap over 1x8 base w/
    WM 105 quarter round for shoe mould

wood flooring (shown) or any other hard-
    surface flooring

1 3/8"

7 1/4"

3/4"

1x8 Base w/Cap on Hard Flooring

SCALE
$\frac{3"}{1'-0"}$

DRAWING #

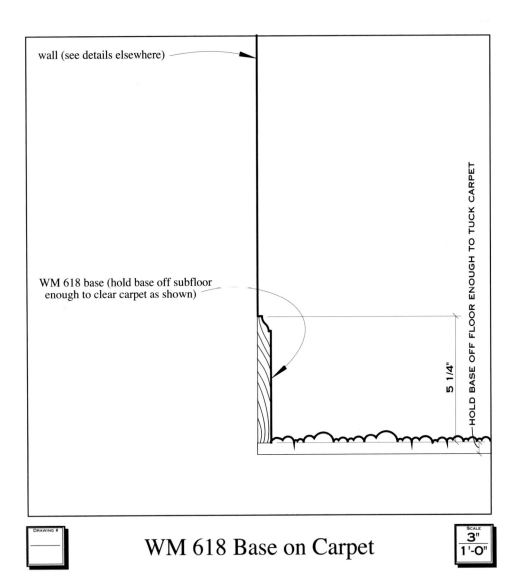

wall (see details elsewhere)

WM 618 base (hold base off subfloor
enough to clear carpet as shown)

5 1/4"

HOLD BASE OFF FLOOR ENOUGH TO TUCK CARPET

DRAWING #

WM 618 Base on Carpet

SCALE
$\frac{3"}{1'-0"}$

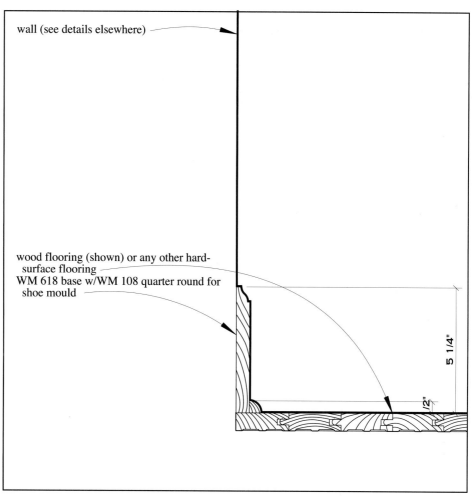

wall (see details elsewhere)

wood flooring (shown) or any other hard-
surface flooring
WM 618 base w/WM 108 quarter round for
shoe mould

5 1/4"

1/2"

WM 618 Base on Hard Flooring

SCALE
3"
1'-0"

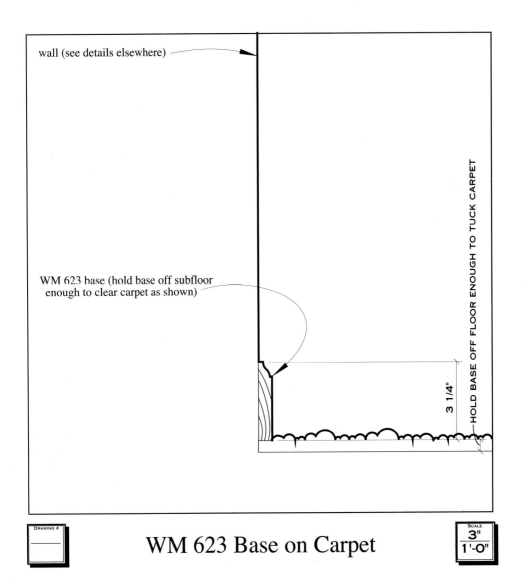

wall (see details elsewhere)

WM 623 base (hold base off subfloor enough to clear carpet as shown)

HOLD BASE OFF FLOOR ENOUGH TO TUCK CARPET

3 1/4"

DRAWING #

WM 623 Base on Carpet

SCALE
3"
1'-0"

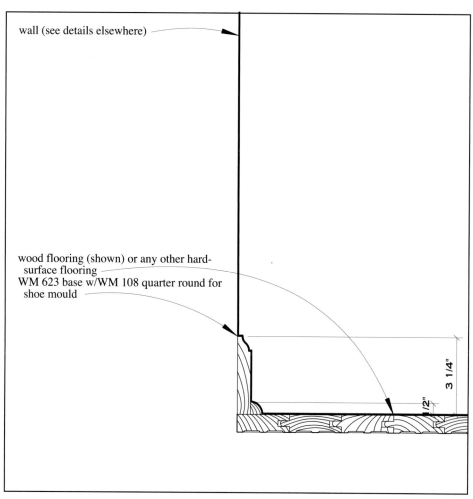

wall (see details elsewhere)

wood flooring (shown) or any other hard-
  surface flooring
WM 623 base w/WM 108 quarter round for
  shoe mould

3 1/4"

1/2"

WM 623 Base on Hard Flooring

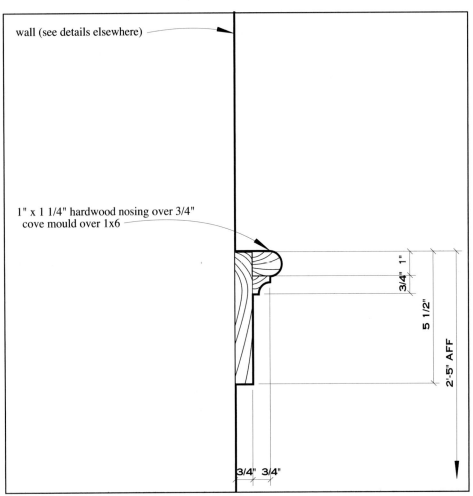

wall (see details elsewhere)

1" x 1 1/4" hardwood nosing over 3/4"
cove mould over 1x6

3/4" 1"

5 1/2"

2'-5" AFF

3/4" 3/4"

DRAWING #

Nosing & Cove Chair Rail

SCALE
3"
1'-0"

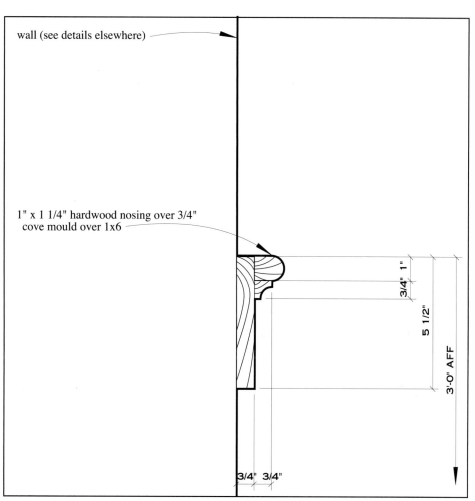

wall (see details elsewhere)

1" x 1 1/4" hardwood nosing over 3/4"
cove mould over 1x6

1"
3/4"

5 1/2"

3'-0" AFF

3/4" 3/4"

DRAWING #

Nosing & Cove Chair Rail

SCALE
3"
1'-0"

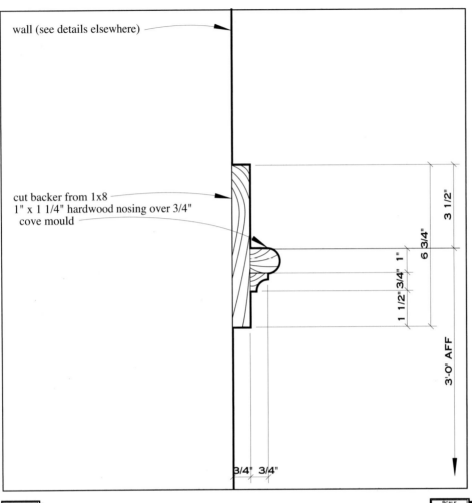

wall (see details elsewhere)

cut backer from 1x8
1" x 1 1/4" hardwood nosing over 3/4"
cove mould

3 1/2"

6 3/4"

1"

3/4"

1 1/2"

3'-0" AFF

3/4"   3/4"

Chair Rail to Match Cabinet

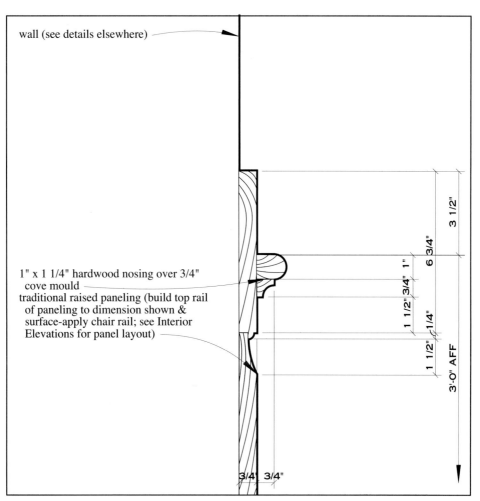

wall (see details elsewhere)

1" x 1 1/4" hardwood nosing over 3/4"
cove mould
traditional raised paneling (build top rail
of paneling to dimension shown &
surface-apply chair rail; see Interior
Elevations for panel layout)

3 1/2"

6 3/4"

1 1/2" 3/4" 1"

1 1/4"

1 1/2"

3'-0" AFF

3/4" 3/4"

Chair Rail/Paneling to Match Cabinet

SCALE
3"
1'-0"

DRAWING #

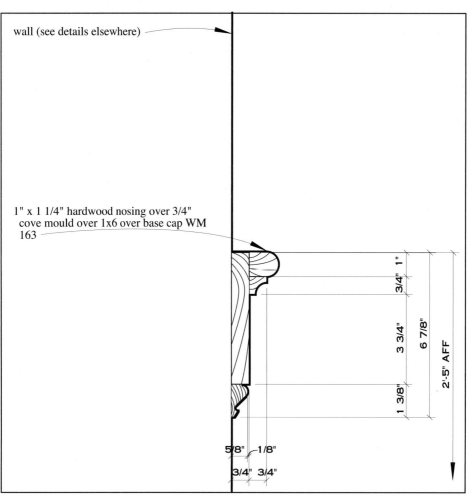

wall (see details elsewhere)

1" x 1 1/4" hardwood nosing over 3/4"
  cove mould over 1x6 over base cap WM
  163

1"

3/4"

3 3/4"

6 7/8"

1 3/8"

2'-5" AFF

5/8"   1/8"

3/4"   3/4"

Nosing & Cove Chair Rail

DRAWING #

SCALE
3"
1'-0"

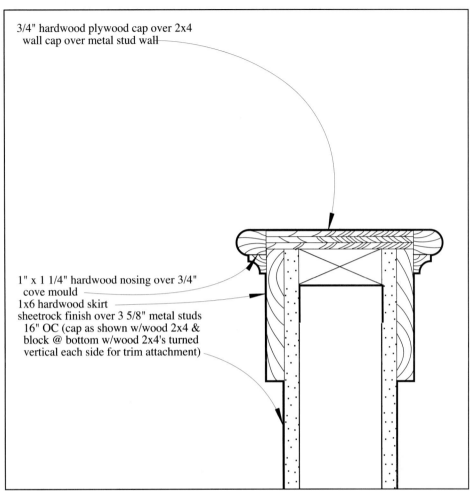

3/4" hardwood plywood cap over 2x4
wall cap over metal stud wall

1" x 1 1/4" hardwood nosing over 3/4"
cove mould

1x6 hardwood skirt

sheetrock finish over 3 5/8" metal studs
16" OC (cap as shown w/wood 2x4 &
block @ bottom w/wood 2x4's turned
vertical each side for trim attachment)

Metal Wall Cap Detail

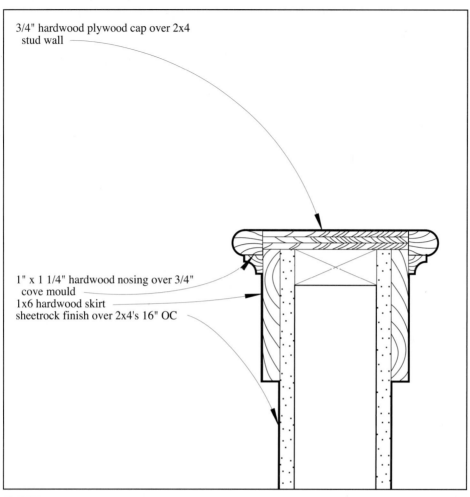

3/4" hardwood plywood cap over 2x4
   stud wall

1" x 1 1/4" hardwood nosing over 3/4"
   cove mould
1x6 hardwood skirt
sheetrock finish over 2x4's 16" OC

DRAWING #

Wood Wall Cap Detail

SCALE
3"
1'-0"

TWS003
828

VERTICAL CIRCULATION DETAILS

This section includes primarily stair details. The contents of this section are as follows:

Brick Stair Details 830
Wood Stair Details 841

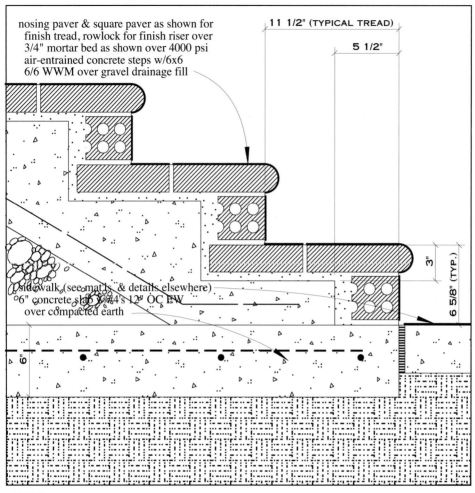

nosing paver & square paver as shown for
finish tread, rowlock for finish riser over
3/4" mortar bed as shown over 4000 psi
air-entrained concrete steps w/6x6
6/6 WWM over gravel drainage fill

11 1/2" (TYPICAL TREAD)

5 1/2"

3"

6 5/8" (TYP.)

sidewalk (see mat'ls & details elsewhere)
6" concrete slab w/#4's 12" OC EW
over compacted earth

6"

Brick Exterior Stair Bottom Landing

DRAWING #

SCALE
1 1/2
1'-0"

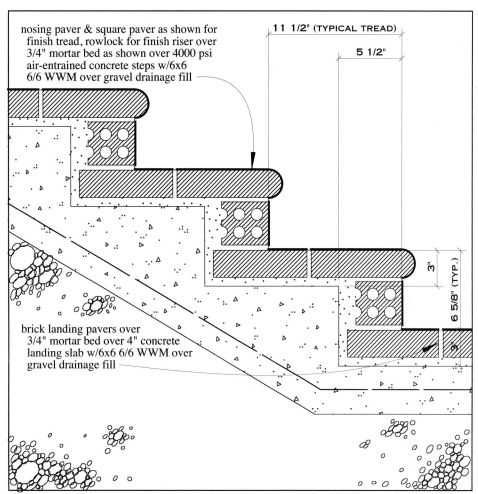

nosing paver & square paver as shown for
finish tread, rowlock for finish riser over
3/4" mortar bed as shown over 4000 psi
air-entrained concrete steps w/6x6
6/6 WWM over gravel drainage fill

11 1/2" (TYPICAL TREAD)

5 1/2"

3"

6 5/8" (TYP.)

3"

brick landing pavers over
3/4" mortar bed over 4" concrete
landing slab w/6x6 6/6 WWM over
gravel drainage fill

DRAWING #

Brick Stair Intermediate Landing

SCALE
1 1/2
1'-0"

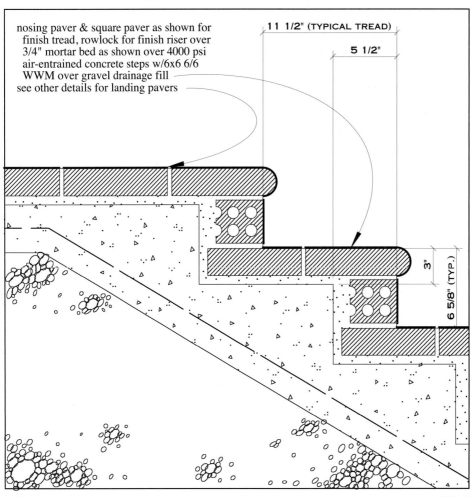

nosing paver & square paver as shown for
finish tread, rowlock for finish riser over
3/4" mortar bed as shown over 4000 psi
air-entrained concrete steps w/6x6 6/6
WWM over gravel drainage fill
see other details for landing pavers

11 1/2" (TYPICAL TREAD)

5 1/2"

3"

6 5/8" (TYP.)

DRAWING #

Brick Exterior Stair @ Top Landing

SCALE
1 1/2
1'-0"

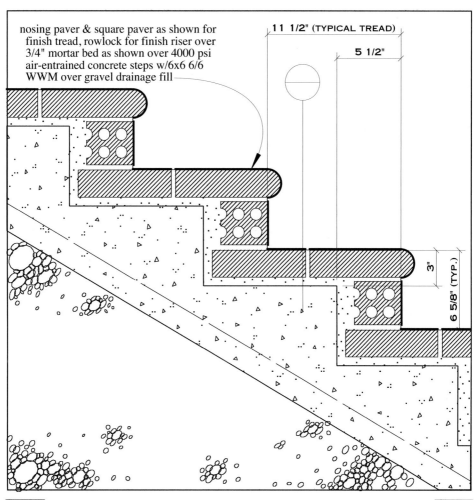

nosing paver & square paver as shown for finish tread, rowlock for finish riser over 3/4" mortar bed as shown over 4000 psi air-entrained concrete steps w/6x6 6/6 WWM over gravel drainage fill

11 1/2" (TYPICAL TREAD)

5 1/2"

3"

6 5/8" (TYP.)

DRAWING #

Brick Exterior Stair Detail

SCALE
1 1/2
1'-0"

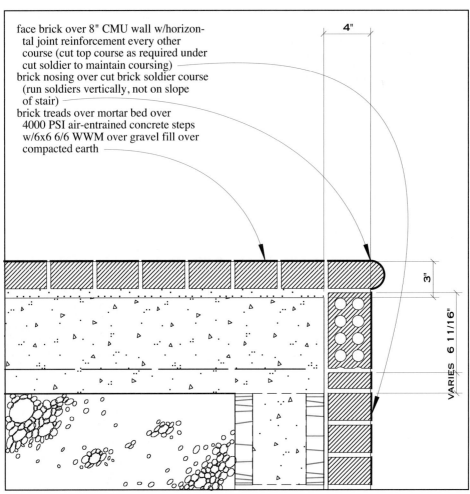

face brick over 8" CMU wall w/horizon-
tal joint reinforcement every other
course (cut top course as required under
cut soldier to maintain coursing)
brick nosing over cut brick soldier course
(run soldiers vertically, not on slope
of stair)
brick treads over mortar bed over
4000 PSI air-entrained concrete steps
w/6x6 6/6 WWM over gravel fill over
compacted earth

4"

3"

VARIES 6 11/16"

DRAWING #

Brick Exterior Stair Stringer Section

SCALE
1 1/2"
1'-0"

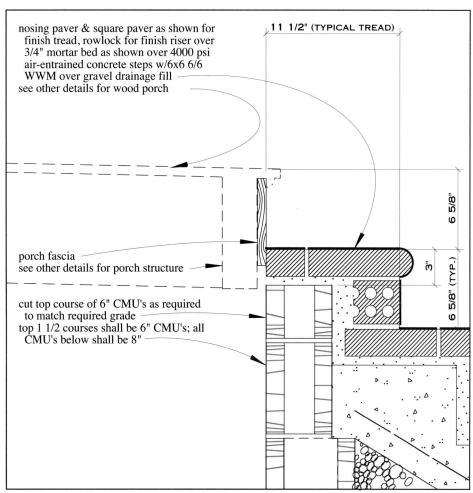

nosing paver & square paver as shown for
 finish tread, rowlock for finish riser over
 3/4" mortar bed as shown over 4000 psi
 air-entrained concrete steps w/6x6 6/6
 WWM over gravel drainage fill
see other details for wood porch

11 1/2" (TYPICAL TREAD)

6 5/8"

3"

6 5/8" (TYP.)

porch fascia
see other details for porch structure

cut top course of 6" CMU's as required
 to match required grade
top 1 1/2 courses shall be 6" CMU's; all
 CMU's below shall be 8"

Brick Exterior Stair @ Porch

SCALE
1 1/2
1'-0"

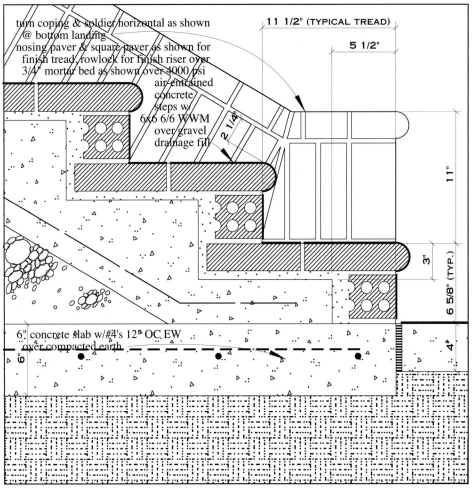

turn coping & soldier horizontal as shown
@ bottom landing
nosing paver & square paver as shown for
finish tread, rowlock for finish riser over
3/4" mortar bed as shown over 4000 psi
air-entrained
concrete
steps w/
6x6 6/6 WWM
over gravel
drainage fill

11 1/2" (TYPICAL TREAD)

5 1/2"

2 1/4"

11"

3" (TYP.)

6 5/8" (TYP.)

6" concrete slab w/#4's 12" OC EW
over compacted earth

6"

4"

| DRAWING # | Brick Exterior Stair Detail | SCALE 1 1/2 / 1'-0" |

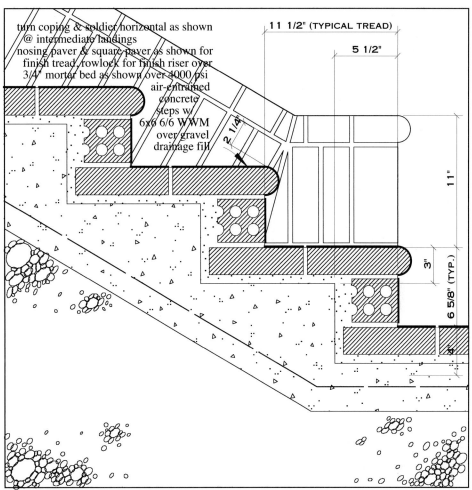

turn coping & soldier horizontal as shown
@ intermediate landings
nosing paver & square paver as shown for
finish tread, rowlock for finish riser over
3/4" mortar bed as shown over 4000 psi
air-entrained
concrete
steps w/
6x6 6/6 WWM
over gravel
drainage fill

11 1/2" (TYPICAL TREAD)

5 1/2"

2 1/4"

11"

3"

6 5/8" (TYP.)

| DRAWING # | Brick Exterior Stair Landing Detail | SCALE 1 1/2 / 1'-0" |

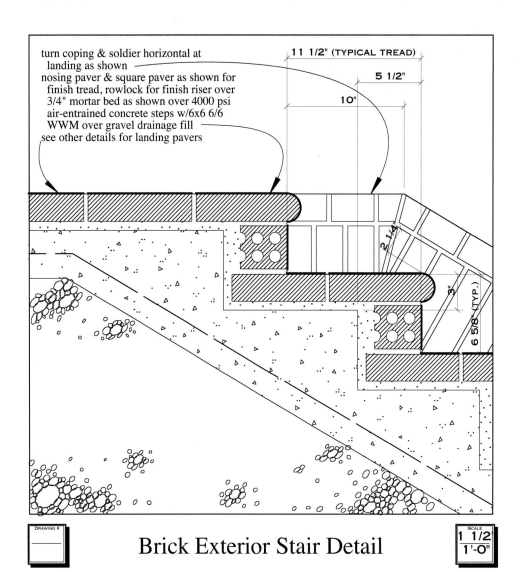

turn coping & soldier horizontal at
landing as shown
nosing paver & square paver as shown for
finish tread, rowlock for finish riser over
3/4" mortar bed as shown over 4000 psi
air-entrained concrete steps w/6x6 6/6
WWM over gravel drainage fill
see other details for landing pavers

11 1/2" (TYPICAL TREAD)

5 1/2"

10"

2 1/4"

3"

6 5/8" (TYP.)

DRAWING #

Brick Exterior Stair Detail

SCALE
1 1/2
1'-0"

VSB02003
838

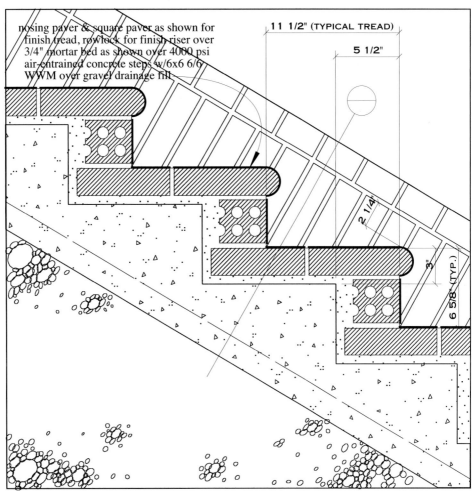

nosing paver & square paver as shown for finish tread, rowlock for finish riser over 3/4" mortar bed as shown over 4000 psi air-entrained concrete steps w/6x6 6/6 WWM over gravel drainage fill

11 1/2" (TYPICAL TREAD)

5 1/2"

2 1/4"

3"

6 5/8" (TYP.)

Brick Exterior Stair Detail

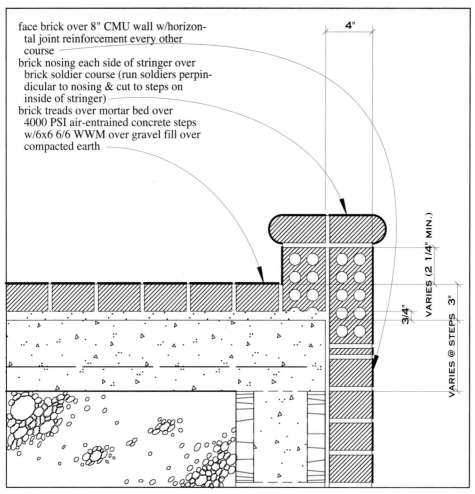

face brick over 8" CMU wall w/horizon-
tal joint reinforcement every other
course

brick nosing each side of stringer over
brick soldier course (run soldiers perpin-
dicular to nosing & cut to steps on
inside of stringer)

brick treads over mortar bed over
4000 PSI air-entrained concrete steps
w/6x6 6/6 WWM over gravel fill over
compacted earth

4"

VARIES (2 1/4" MIN.)

3/4"

VARIES @ STEPS   3"

DRAWING #		SCALE	
	Brick Exterior Stair Stringer Section	1 1/2"	1'-0"

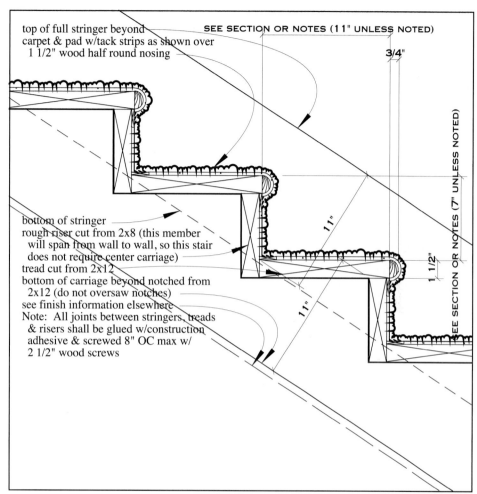

top of full stringer beyond
carpet & pad w/tack strips as shown over
  1 1/2" wood half round nosing

SEE SECTION OR NOTES (11" UNLESS NOTED)

3/4"

SEE SECTION OR NOTES (7" UNLESS NOTED)

11"

1 1/2"

11"

11"

bottom of stringer
rough riser cut from 2x8 (this member
  will span from wall to wall, so this stair
  does not require center carriage)
tread cut from 2x12
bottom of carriage beyond notched from
  2x12 (do not oversaw notches)
see finish information elsewhere
Note: All joints between stringers, treads
  & risers shall be glued w/construction
  adhesive & screwed 8" OC max w/
  2 1/2" wood screws

DRAWING #

Carpeted Stair Detail

SCALE
1 1/2
1'-0"

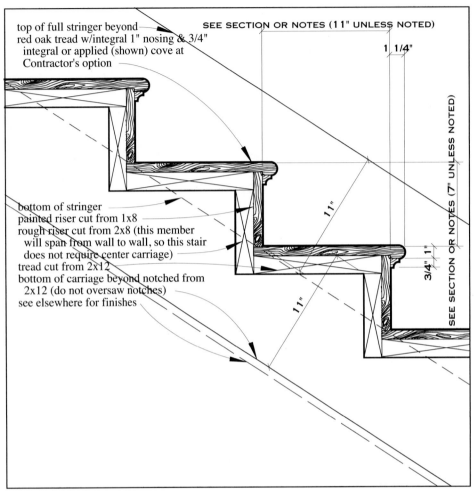

top of full stringer beyond
red oak tread w/integral 1" nosing & 3/4"
  integral or applied (shown) cove at
  Contractor's option

SEE SECTION OR NOTES (11" UNLESS NOTED)

1 1/4"

SEE SECTION OR NOTES (7" UNLESS NOTED)

11"

11"

11"

3/4" 1"

bottom of stringer
painted riser cut from 1x8
rough riser cut from 2x8 (this member
  will span from wall to wall, so this stair
  does not require center carriage)
tread cut from 2x12
bottom of carriage beyond notched from
  2x12 (do not oversaw notches)
see elsewhere for finishes

DRAWING #

Wood Stair Detail

SCALE
1 1/2
1'-0"

WINDOW DETAILS

Details in this section include all window head, jamb, mullion, transom & sill details. Refer to the Door Details section for general opening details & elevations which apply to both doors & windows. The contents of this section are as follows:

Aluminum Window Head Details 844
Aluminum Window Jamb Details 853
Aluminum Window Mullion Details 856
Aluminum Window Sill Details 862
Aluminum Window Transom Details 867
Hollow Metal Window Head Details 871
Hollow Metal Window Jamb Details 878
Hollow Metal Window Mullion Details 883
Hollow Metal Window Sill Details 884
Hollow Metal Window Transom Details 890
Special Window Head Details 894
Special Window Jamb Details 895
Special Window Sill Details 896
Wood Dormer Jamb Details 898
Wood Dormer Sill Details 902
Wood Window Elevation Details 903
Wood Window Head Details 904
Wood Window Jamb Details 967
Wood Window Mullion Details 996
Wood Window Sill Details 1002
Wood Window Transom Details 1032

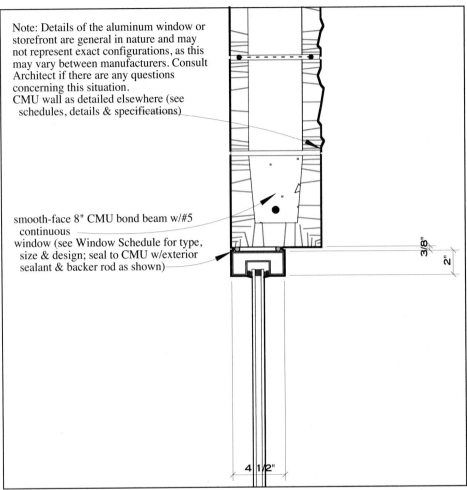

Note: Details of the aluminum window or storefront are general in nature and may not represent exact configurations, as this may vary between manufacturers. Consult Architect if there are any questions concerning this situation.
CMU wall as detailed elsewhere (see schedules, details & specifications)

smooth-face 8" CMU bond beam w/#5 continuous
window (see Window Schedule for type, size & design; seal to CMU w/exterior sealant & backer rod as shown)

3/8"

2"

4 1/2"

DRAWING #

Aluminum Window Head Detail

SCALE

1 1/2"
1'-0"

WAH001
844

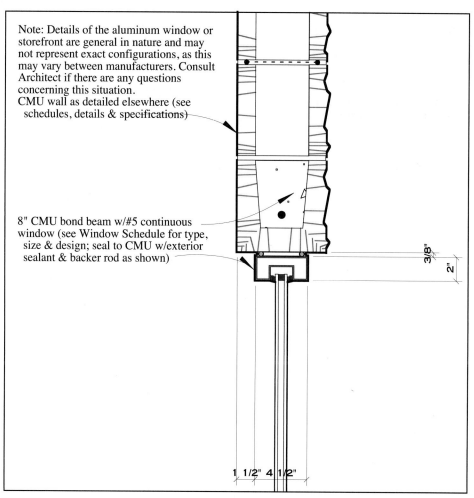

Note: Details of the aluminum window or
storefront are general in nature and may
not represent exact configurations, as this
may vary between manufacturers. Consult
Architect if there are any questions
concerning this situation.
CMU wall as detailed elsewhere (see
  schedules, details & specifications)

8" CMU bond beam w/#5 continuous
window (see Window Schedule for type,
  size & design; seal to CMU w/exterior
  sealant & backer rod as shown)

3/8"

2"

1 1/2" 4 1/2"

Aluminum Window Head Detail

WAH002
845

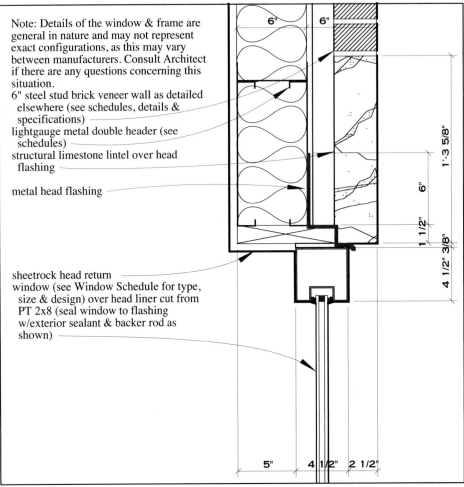

Note: Details of the window & frame are general in nature and may not represent exact configurations, as this may vary between manufacturers. Consult Architect if there are any questions concerning this situation.

6" steel stud brick veneer wall as detailed elsewhere (see schedules, details & specifications)

lightgauge metal double header (see schedules)

structural limestone lintel over head flashing

metal head flashing

sheetrock head return

window (see Window Schedule for type, size & design) over head liner cut from PT 2x8 (seal window to flashing w/exterior sealant & backer rod as shown)

6"   6"

1'-3 5/8"

6"

1 1/2"   3/8"

4 1/2"

5"   4 1/2"   2 1/2"

DRAWING #

Aluminum Window Head Detail

SCALE
1 1/2"
1'-0"

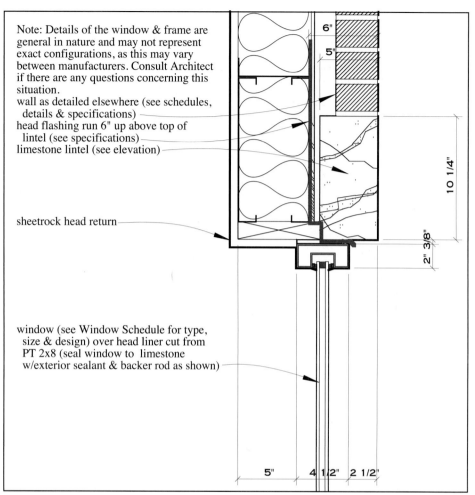

Note: Details of the window & frame are general in nature and may not represent exact configurations, as this may vary between manufacturers. Consult Architect if there are any questions concerning this situation.

wall as detailed elsewhere (see schedules, details & specifications)

head flashing run 6" up above top of lintel (see specifications)

limestone lintel (see elevation)

sheetrock head return

window (see Window Schedule for type, size & design) over head liner cut from PT 2x8 (seal window to limestone w/exterior sealant & backer rod as shown)

6"

5"

10 1/4"

2 3/8"

5"   4 1/2"   2 1/2"

Window Head Detail w/Stone Lintel

DRAWING #

SCALE
1 1/2"
1'-0"

WAH010
847

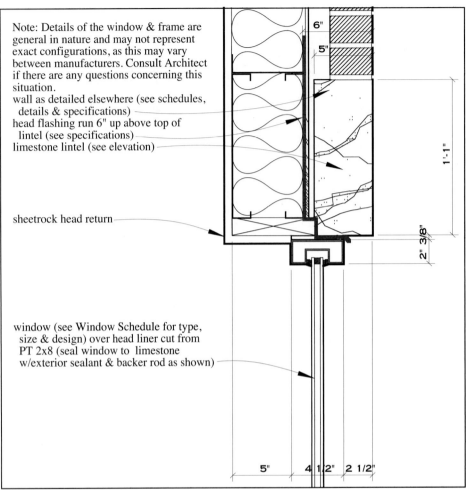

Note: Details of the window & frame are
general in nature and may not represent
exact configurations, as this may vary
between manufacturers. Consult Architect
if there are any questions concerning this
situation.
wall as detailed elsewhere (see schedules,
  details & specifications)
head flashing run 6" up above top of
  lintel (see specifications)
limestone lintel (see elevation)

6"

5"

1'-1"

sheetrock head return

2" 3/8"

window (see Window Schedule for type,
  size & design) over head liner cut from
  PT 2x8 (seal window to limestone
  w/exterior sealant & backer rod as shown)

5"   4 1/2"   2 1/2"

DRAWING #

Window Head Detail w/Stone Lintel

SCALE
1 1/2"
1'-0"

WAH011
848

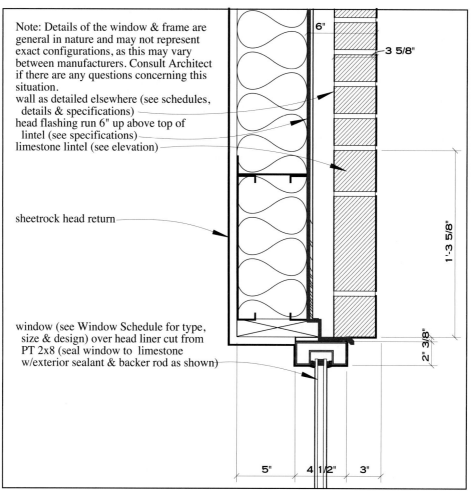

Note: Details of the window & frame are general in nature and may not represent exact configurations, as this may vary between manufacturers. Consult Architect if there are any questions concerning this situation.

wall as detailed elsewhere (see schedules, details & specifications)

head flashing run 6" up above top of lintel (see specifications)

limestone lintel (see elevation)

sheetrock head return

window (see Window Schedule for type, size & design) over head liner cut from PT 2x8 (seal window to limestone w/exterior sealant & backer rod as shown)

6"

3 5/8"

1'-3 5/8"

2" 3/8"

5"   4 1/2"   3"

Window Head Detail w/Brick Lintel

SCALE
1 1/2"
1'-0"

DRAWING #

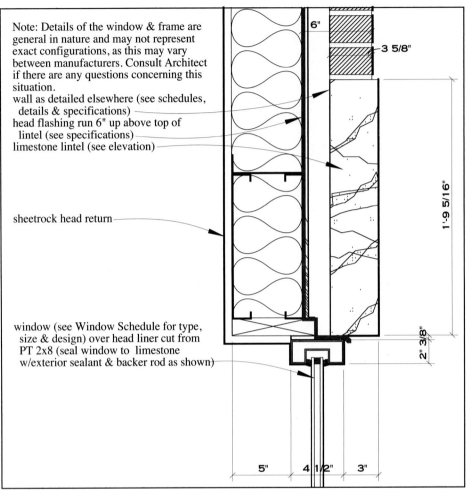

Note: Details of the window & frame are
general in nature and may not represent
exact configurations, as this may vary
between manufacturers. Consult Architect
if there are any questions concerning this
situation.
wall as detailed elsewhere (see schedules,
 details & specifications)
head flashing run 6" up above top of
 lintel (see specifications)
limestone lintel (see elevation)

sheetrock head return

window (see Window Schedule for type,
 size & design) over head liner cut from
 PT 2x8 (seal window to limestone
 w/exterior sealant & backer rod as shown)

6"

3 5/8"

1'-9 5/16"

2" 3/8"

5"   4 1/2"   3"

Window Head Detail w/Stone Lintel

WAH013
850

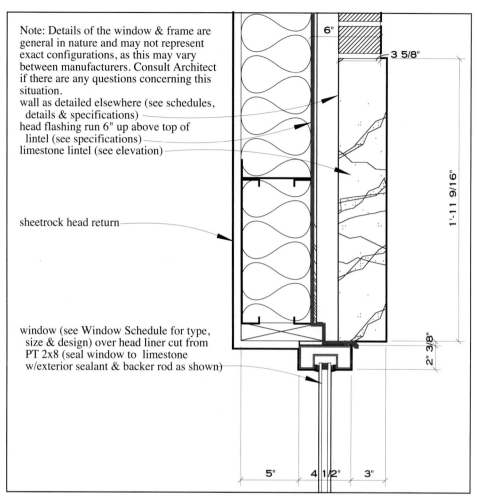

Note: Details of the window & frame are general in nature and may not represent exact configurations, as this may vary between manufacturers. Consult Architect if there are any questions concerning this situation.

wall as detailed elsewhere (see schedules, details & specifications)

head flashing run 6" up above top of lintel (see specifications)

limestone lintel (see elevation)

sheetrock head return

window (see Window Schedule for type, size & design) over head liner cut from PT 2x8 (seal window to limestone w/exterior sealant & backer rod as shown)

6"

3 5/8"

1'-11 9/16"

2" 3/8"

5" 4 1/2" 3"

Window Head Detail w/Stone Lintel

SCALE

1 1/2"
1'-0"

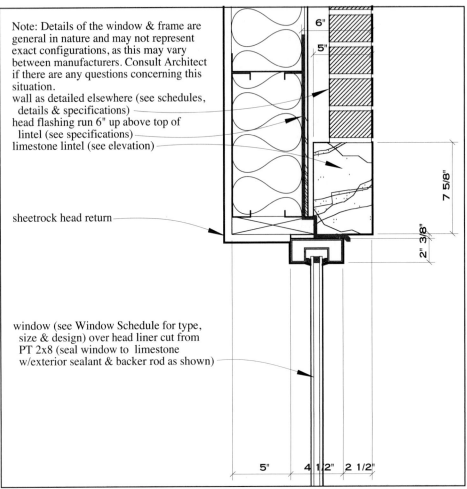

Note: Details of the window & frame are general in nature and may not represent exact configurations, as this may vary between manufacturers. Consult Architect if there are any questions concerning this situation.

wall as detailed elsewhere (see schedules, details & specifications)

head flashing run 6" up above top of lintel (see specifications)

limestone lintel (see elevation)

6"

5"

7 5/8"

2 3/8"

sheetrock head return

window (see Window Schedule for type, size & design) over head liner cut from PT 2x8 (seal window to limestone w/exterior sealant & backer rod as shown)

5"   4 1/2"   2 1/2"

DRAWING #

Window Head Detail w/Stone Lintel

SCALE
1 1/2"
1'-0"

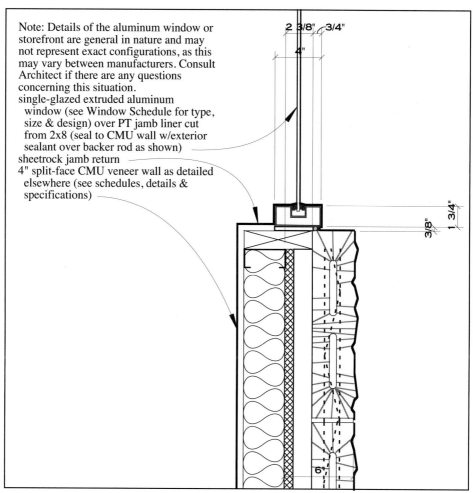

Note: Details of the aluminum window or storefront are general in nature and may not represent exact configurations, as this may vary between manufacturers. Consult Architect if there are any questions concerning this situation.

single-glazed extruded aluminum window (see Window Schedule for type, size & design) over PT jamb liner cut from 2x8 (seal to CMU wall w/exterior sealant over backer rod as shown)

sheetrock jamb return

4" split-face CMU veneer wall as detailed elsewhere (see schedules, details & specifications)

2 3/8" 3/4"

4"

1 3/4"

3/8"

6"

DRAWING #

Aluminum Window Jamb Detail

SCALE
1 1/2"
1'-0"

WAJ001
853

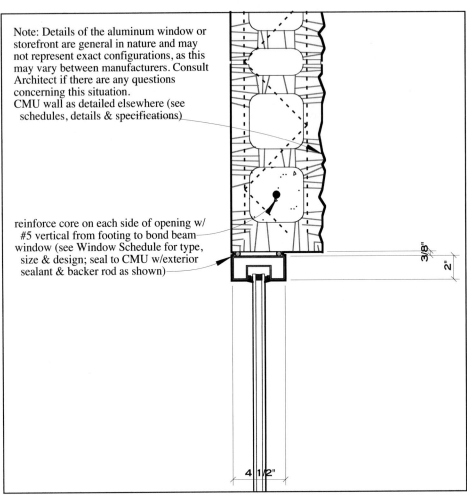

Note: Details of the aluminum window or
storefront are general in nature and may
not represent exact configurations, as this
may vary between manufacturers. Consult
Architect if there are any questions
concerning this situation.
CMU wall as detailed elsewhere (see
  schedules, details & specifications)

reinforce core on each side of opening w/
  #5 vertical from footing to bond beam
window (see Window Schedule for type,
  size & design; seal to CMU w/exterior
  sealant & backer rod as shown)

3/8"

2"

4 1/2"

DRAWING #

Aluminum Window Jamb Detail

SCALE
1 1/2"
1'-0"

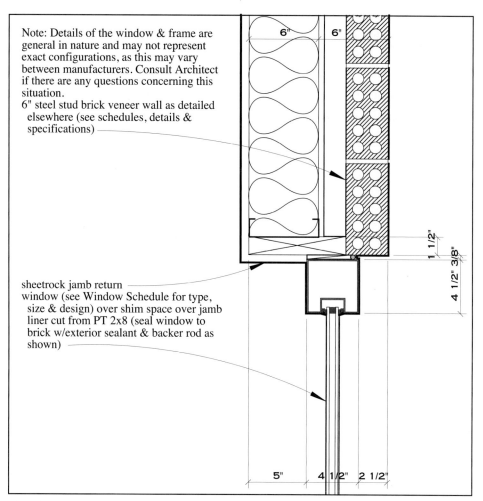

Note: Details of the window & frame are general in nature and may not represent exact configurations, as this may vary between manufacturers. Consult Architect if there are any questions concerning this situation.

6" steel stud brick veneer wall as detailed elsewhere (see schedules, details & specifications)

sheetrock jamb return
window (see Window Schedule for type, size & design) over shim space over jamb liner cut from PT 2x8 (seal window to brick w/exterior sealant & backer rod as shown)

6" 6"

1 1/2"
3/8"
4 1/2"

5" 4 1/2" 2 1/2"

Aluminum Window Jamb Detail

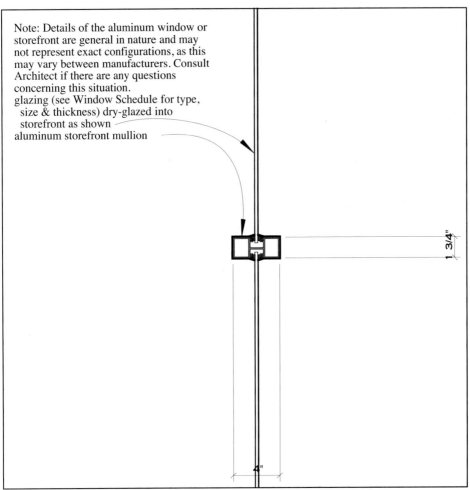

Note: Details of the aluminum window or
storefront are general in nature and may
not represent exact configurations, as this
may vary between manufacturers. Consult
Architect if there are any questions
concerning this situation.
glazing (see Window Schedule for type,
  size & thickness) dry-glazed into
  storefront as shown
aluminum storefront mullion

1 3/4"

4"

Storefront Window Mullion

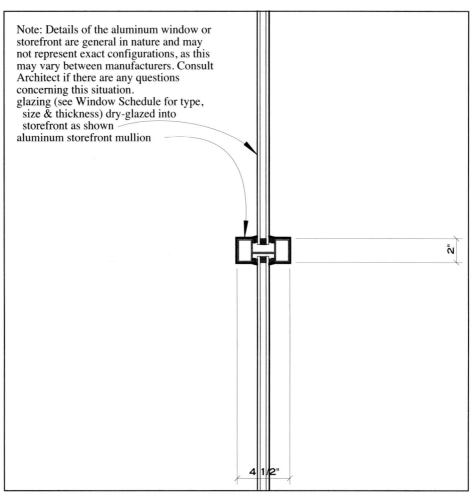

Note: Details of the aluminum window or
storefront are general in nature and may
not represent exact configurations, as this
may vary between manufacturers. Consult
Architect if there are any questions
concerning this situation.
glazing (see Window Schedule for type,
  size & thickness) dry-glazed into
  storefront as shown
aluminum storefront mullion

2"

4 1/2"

Storefront Window Mullion

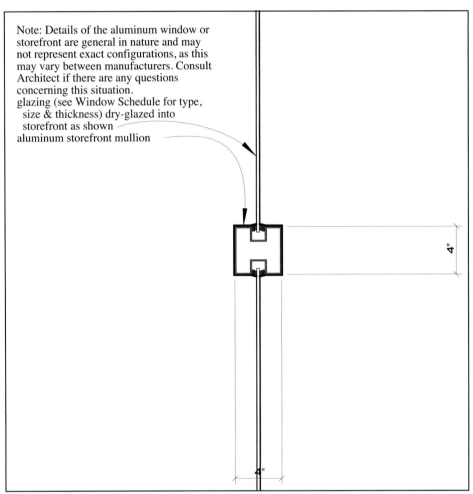

Note: Details of the aluminum window or
storefront are general in nature and may
not represent exact configurations, as this
may vary between manufacturers. Consult
Architect if there are any questions
concerning this situation.
glazing (see Window Schedule for type,
  size & thickness) dry-glazed into
  storefront as shown
aluminum storefront mullion

4"

4"

DRAWING #

Storefront Window Mullion

SCALE

1 1/2"
1'-0"

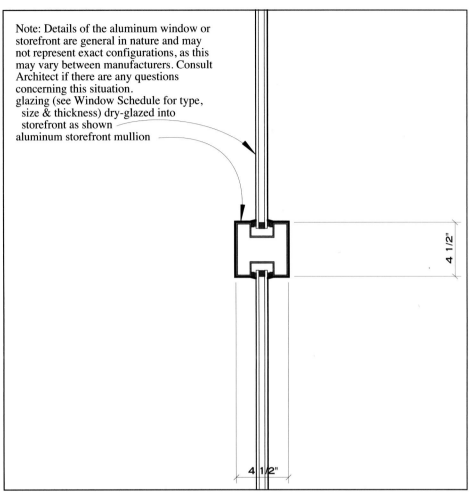

Note: Details of the aluminum window or storefront are general in nature and may not represent exact configurations, as this may vary between manufacturers. Consult Architect if there are any questions concerning this situation.
glazing (see Window Schedule for type, size & thickness) dry-glazed into storefront as shown
aluminum storefront mullion

4 1/2"

4 1/2"

Storefront Window Mullion

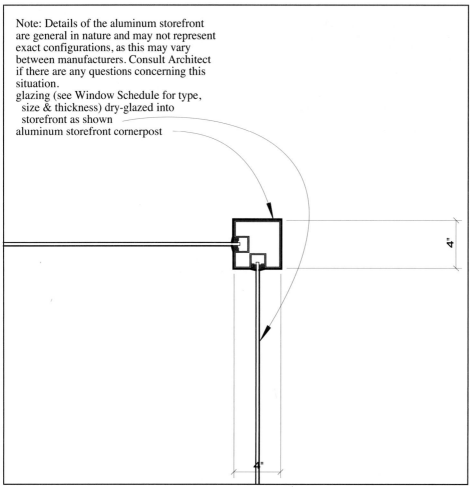

Note: Details of the aluminum storefront
are general in nature and may not represent
exact configurations, as this may vary
between manufacturers. Consult Architect
if there are any questions concerning this
situation.
glazing (see Window Schedule for type,
   size & thickness) dry-glazed into
   storefront as shown
aluminum storefront cornerpost

4"

4"

DRAWING #

Storefront Window Cornerpost Detail

SCALE

1 1/2"
1'-0"

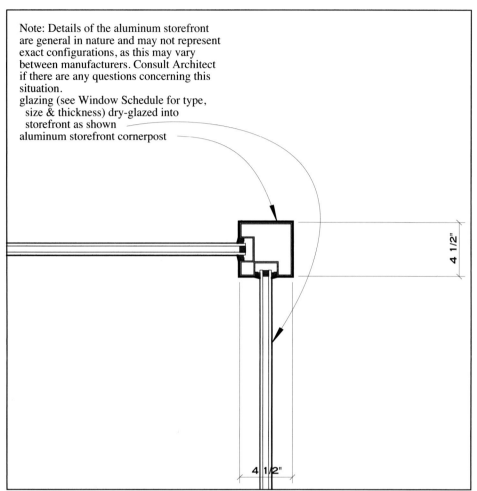

Note: Details of the aluminum storefront
are general in nature and may not represent
exact configurations, as this may vary
between manufacturers. Consult Architect
if there are any questions concerning this
situation.
glazing (see Window Schedule for type,
  size & thickness) dry-glazed into
  storefront as shown
aluminum storefront cornerpost

4 1/2"

4 1/2"

Storefront Window Cornerpost Detail

DRAWING #

SCALE
1 1/2"
1'-0"

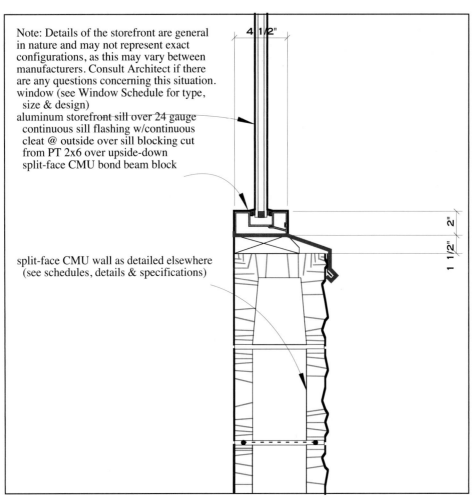

Note: Details of the storefront are general in nature and may not represent exact configurations, as this may vary between manufacturers. Consult Architect if there are any questions concerning this situation.
window (see Window Schedule for type, size & design)
aluminum storefront sill over 24 gauge continuous sill flashing w/continuous cleat @ outside over sill blocking cut from PT 2x6 over upside-down split-face CMU bond beam block

4 1/2"

2"

1 1/2"

split-face CMU wall as detailed elsewhere (see schedules, details & specifications)

DRAWING #

Aluminum Window Sill Detail

SCALE
1 1/2"
1'-0"

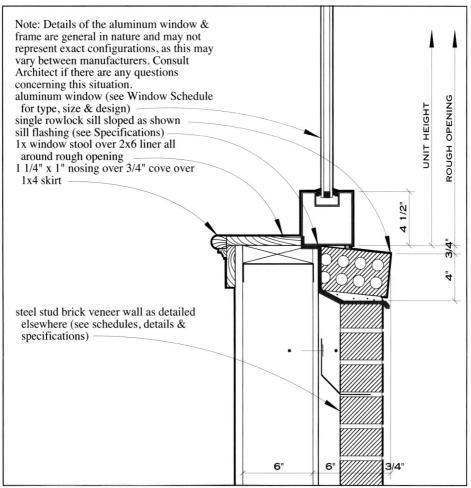

Note: Details of the aluminum window &
frame are general in nature and may not
represent exact configurations, as this may
vary between manufacturers. Consult
Architect if there are any questions
concerning this situation.
aluminum window (see Window Schedule
  for type, size & design)
single rowlock sill sloped as shown
sill flashing (see Specifications)
1x window stool over 2x6 liner all
  around rough opening
1 1/4" x 1" nosing over 3/4" cove over
  1x4 skirt

steel stud brick veneer wall as detailed
  elsewhere (see schedules, details &
  specifications)

UNIT HEIGHT

ROUGH OPENING

4 1/2"

3/4"

4"

6"   6"   3/4"

DRAWING #

Window Sill Detail @ Brick Veneer

SCALE
1 1/2
1'-0"

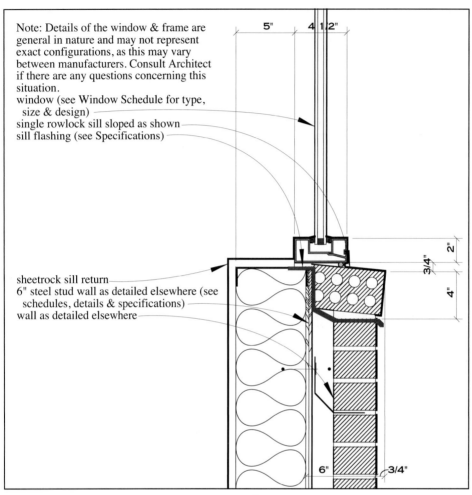

Note: Details of the window & frame are general in nature and may not represent exact configurations, as this may vary between manufacturers. Consult Architect if there are any questions concerning this situation.

window (see Window Schedule for type, size & design)

single rowlock sill sloped as shown

sill flashing (see Specifications)

sheetrock sill return

6" steel stud wall as detailed elsewhere (see schedules, details & specifications)

wall as detailed elsewhere

5"

4 1/2"

2"

3/4"

4"

6"

3/4"

Window Sill Detail @ Brick Veneer

SCALE
1 1/2"
1'-0"

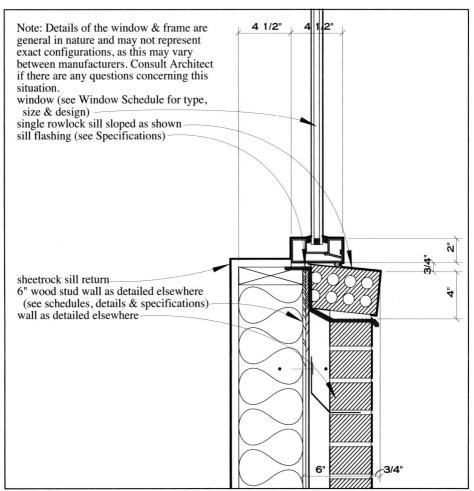

Note: Details of the window & frame are
general in nature and may not represent
exact configurations, as this may vary
between manufacturers. Consult Architect
if there are any questions concerning this
situation.
window (see Window Schedule for type,
  size & design)
single rowlock sill sloped as shown
sill flashing (see Specifications)

4 1/2"   4 1/2"

2"
3/4"
4"

sheetrock sill return
6" wood stud wall as detailed elsewhere
  (see schedules, details & specifications)
wall as detailed elsewhere

6"   3/4"

Window Sill Detail @ Brick Veneer

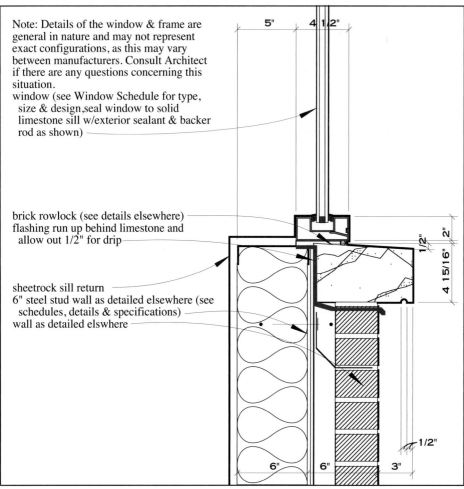

Note: Details of the window & frame are
general in nature and may not represent
exact configurations, as this may vary
between manufacturers. Consult Architect
if there are any questions concerning this
situation.
window (see Window Schedule for type,
  size & design,seal window to solid
  limestone sill w/exterior sealant & backer
  rod as shown)

brick rowlock (see details elsewhere)
flashing run up behind limestone and
  allow out 1/2" for drip

sheetrock sill return
6" steel stud wall as detailed elsewhere (see
  schedules, details & specifications)
wall as detailed elswhere

5"   4 1/2"

1/2"   2"

4 15/16"

1/2"

6"   6"   3"

DRAWING #

Aluminum Metal Window Sill Detail

SCALE

1 1/2"
1'-0"

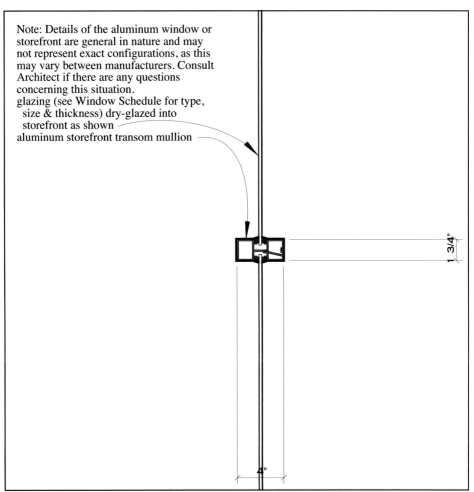

Note: Details of the aluminum window or storefront are general in nature and may not represent exact configurations, as this may vary between manufacturers. Consult Architect if there are any questions concerning this situation.
glazing (see Window Schedule for type, size & thickness) dry-glazed into storefront as shown
aluminum storefront transom mullion

1 3/4"

4"

Storefront Window Transom Mullion

SCALE
1 1/2"
1'-0"

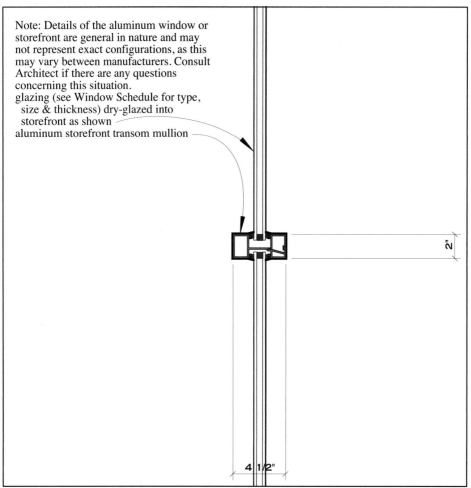

Note: Details of the aluminum window or
storefront are general in nature and may
not represent exact configurations, as this
may vary between manufacturers. Consult
Architect if there are any questions
concerning this situation.
glazing (see Window Schedule for type,
  size & thickness) dry-glazed into
  storefront as shown
aluminum storefront transom mullion

2"

4 1/2"

DRAWING #

Aluminum Transom Window Mullion

SCALE
1 1/2"
1'-0"

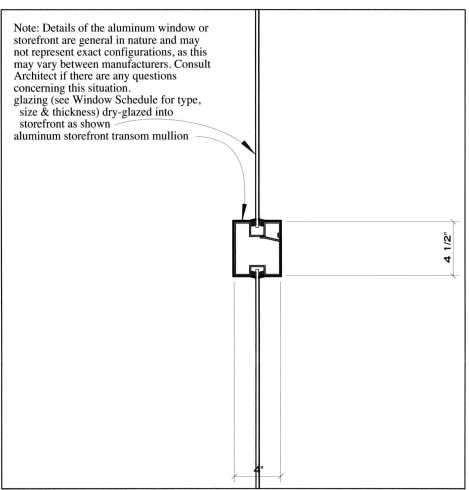

Note: Details of the aluminum window or
storefront are general in nature and may
not represent exact configurations, as this
may vary between manufacturers. Consult
Architect if there are any questions
concerning this situation.
glazing (see Window Schedule for type,
  size & thickness) dry-glazed into
  storefront as shown
aluminum storefront transom mullion

4 1/2"

4"

Storefront Transom Window Mullion

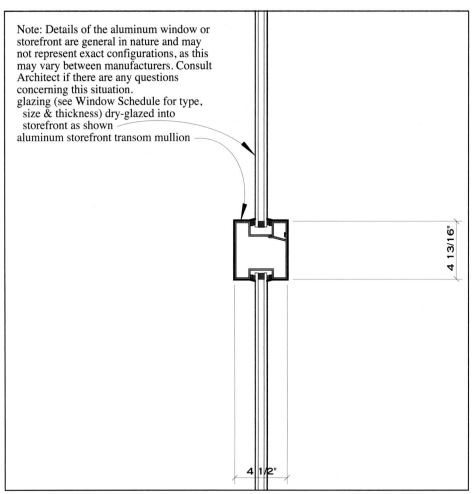

Note: Details of the aluminum window or storefront are general in nature and may not represent exact configurations, as this may vary between manufacturers. Consult Architect if there are any questions concerning this situation.
glazing (see Window Schedule for type, size & thickness) dry-glazed into storefront as shown
aluminum storefront transom mullion

4 13/16"

4 1/2"

DRAWING #
_____

Aluminum Transom Window Mullion

SCALE
1 1/2"
1'-0"

WAT004
870

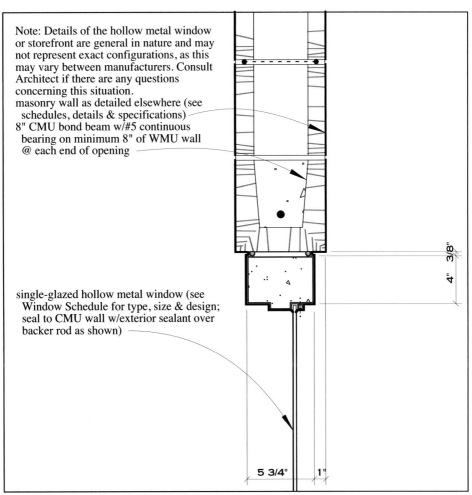

Note: Details of the hollow metal window
or storefront are general in nature and may
not represent exact configurations, as this
may vary between manufacturers. Consult
Architect if there are any questions
concerning this situation.

masonry wall as detailed elsewhere (see
  schedules, details & specifications)
8" CMU bond beam w/#5 continuous
  bearing on minimum 8" of WMU wall
  @ each end of opening

single-glazed hollow metal window (see
  Window Schedule for type, size & design;
  seal to CMU wall w/exterior sealant over
  backer rod as shown)

4" 3/8"

5 3/4" 1"

DRAWING #

Hollow Metal Window Head Detail

SCALE
1 1/2
1'-0"

WHH003
871

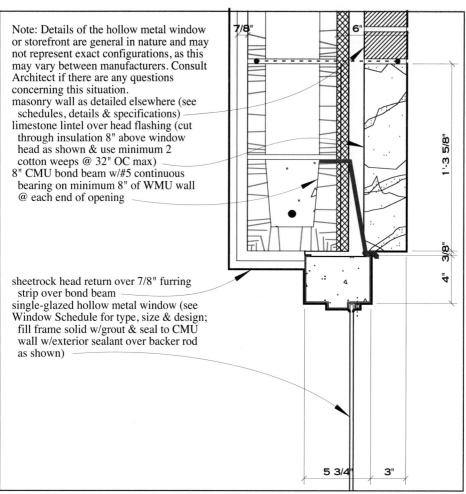

Note: Details of the hollow metal window or storefront are general in nature and may not represent exact configurations, as this may vary between manufacturers. Consult Architect if there are any questions concerning this situation.

masonry wall as detailed elsewhere (see schedules, details & specifications)

limestone lintel over head flashing (cut through insulation 8" above window head as shown & use minimum 2 cotton weeps @ 32" OC max)

8" CMU bond beam w/#5 continuous bearing on minimum 8" of WMU wall @ each end of opening

sheetrock head return over 7/8" furring strip over bond beam

single-glazed hollow metal window (see Window Schedule for type, size & design; fill frame solid w/grout & seal to CMU wall w/exterior sealant over backer rod as shown)

7/8" 6" 1'-3 5/8" 3/8" 4" 5 3/4" 3"

DRAWING #

Hollow Metal Window Head Detail

SCALE 1 1/2 1'-0"

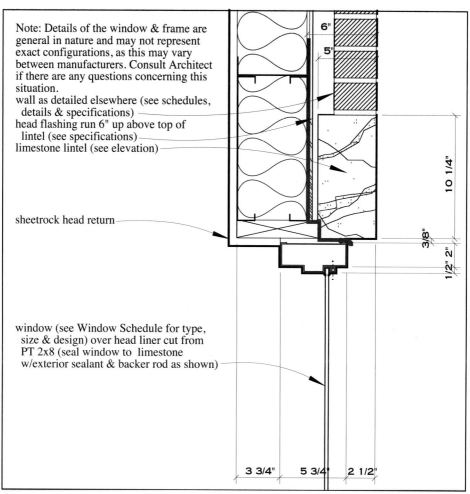

Note: Details of the window & frame are general in nature and may not represent exact configurations, as this may vary between manufacturers. Consult Architect if there are any questions concerning this situation.

wall as detailed elsewhere (see schedules, details & specifications)

head flashing run 6" up above top of lintel (see specifications)

limestone lintel (see elevation)

6"

5"

10 1/4"

3/8"

1/2"

2"

sheetrock head return

window (see Window Schedule for type, size & design) over head liner cut from PT 2x8 (seal window to limestone w/exterior sealant & backer rod as shown)

3 3/4"   5 3/4"   2 1/2"

DRAWING #

Window Head Detail w/Stone Lintel

SCALE
1 1/2"
1'-0"

WHH005
873

Note: Details of the window & frame are
general in nature and may not represent
exact configurations, as this may vary
between manufacturers. Consult Architect
if there are any questions concerning this
situation.
wall as detailed elsewhere (see schedules,
  details & specifications)
head flashing run 6" up above top of
  lintel (see specifications)
limestone lintel (see elevation)

sheetrock head return

window (see Window Schedule for type,
  size & design) over head liner cut from
  PT 2x8 (seal window to limestone
  w/exterior sealant & backer rod as shown)

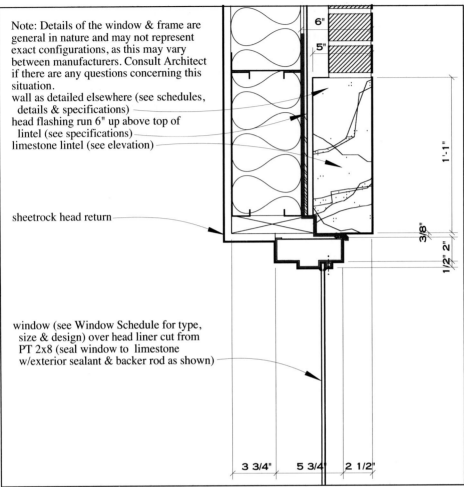

6"

5"

1'-1"

3/8"

1/2" 2"

3 3/4"   5 3/4"   2 1/2"

DRAWING #

Window Head Detail w/Stone Lintel

SCALE

1 1/2"
1'-0"

WHH006
874

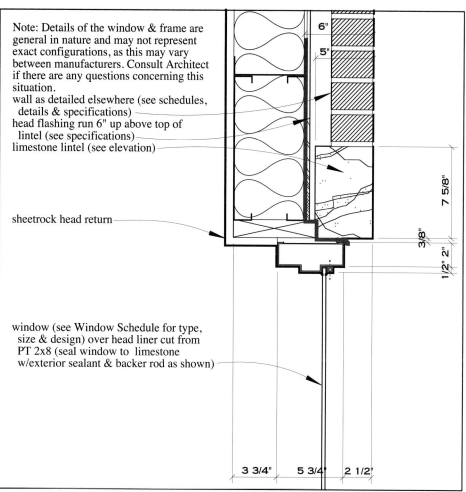

Note: Details of the window & frame are general in nature and may not represent exact configurations, as this may vary between manufacturers. Consult Architect if there are any questions concerning this situation.

wall as detailed elsewhere (see schedules, details & specifications)

head flashing run 6" up above top of lintel (see specifications)

limestone lintel (see elevation)

sheetrock head return

6"

5"

7 5/8"

3/8"

1/2" 2"

window (see Window Schedule for type, size & design) over head liner cut from PT 2x8 (seal window to limestone w/exterior sealant & backer rod as shown)

3 3/4"   5 3/4"   2 1/2"

DRAWING #

Window Head Detail w/Stone Lintel

SCALE

1 1/2"
1'-0"

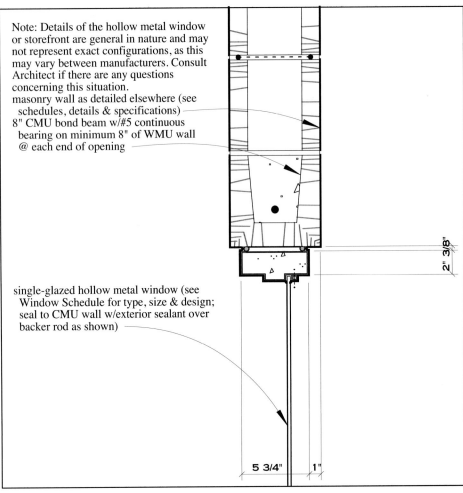

Note: Details of the hollow metal window
or storefront are general in nature and may
not represent exact configurations, as this
may vary between manufacturers. Consult
Architect if there are any questions
concerning this situation.
masonry wall as detailed elsewhere (see
  schedules, details & specifications)
8" CMU bond beam w/#5 continuous
  bearing on minimum 8" of WMU wall
  @ each end of opening

single-glazed hollow metal window (see
  Window Schedule for type, size & design;
  seal to CMU wall w/exterior sealant over
  backer rod as shown)

2" 3/8"

5 3/4"   1"

DRAWING #

Hollow Metal Window Head Detail

SCALE

1 1/2
1'-0"

WHH008
876

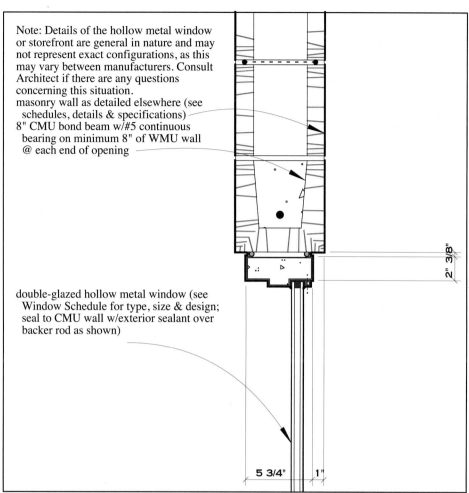

Note: Details of the hollow metal window
or storefront are general in nature and may
not represent exact configurations, as this
may vary between manufacturers. Consult
Architect if there are any questions
concerning this situation.
masonry wall as detailed elsewhere (see
  schedules, details & specifications)
8" CMU bond beam w/#5 continuous
  bearing on minimum 8" of WMU wall
  @ each end of opening

double-glazed hollow metal window (see
  Window Schedule for type, size & design;
  seal to CMU wall w/exterior sealant over
  backer rod as shown)

2" 3/8"

5 3/4"   1"

Hollow Metal Window Head Detail

SCALE
1 1/2
1'-0"

DRAWING #

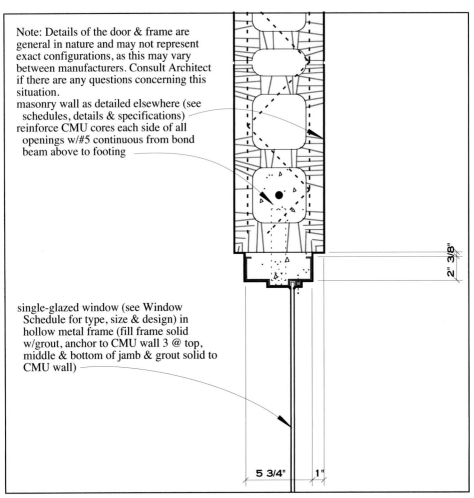

Note: Details of the door & frame are general in nature and may not represent exact configurations, as this may vary between manufacturers. Consult Architect if there are any questions concerning this situation.

masonry wall as detailed elsewhere (see schedules, details & specifications)

reinforce CMU cores each side of all openings w/#5 continuous from bond beam above to footing

single-glazed window (see Window Schedule for type, size & design) in hollow metal frame (fill frame solid w/grout, anchor to CMU wall 3 @ top, middle & bottom of jamb & grout solid to CMU wall)

2" 3/8"

5 3/4"   1"

DRAWING #

Hollow Metal Window Jamb Detail

SCALE
1 1/2
1'-0"

WHJ001
878

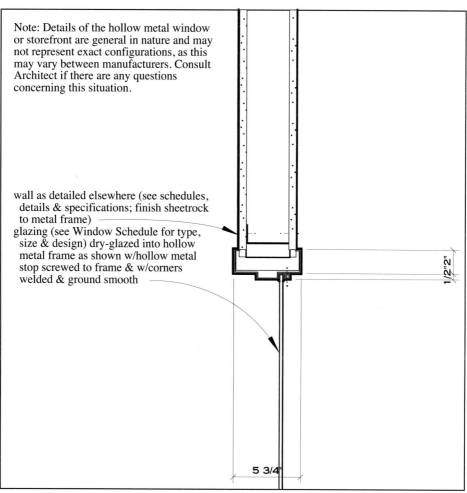

Note: Details of the hollow metal window or storefront are general in nature and may not represent exact configurations, as this may vary between manufacturers. Consult Architect if there are any questions concerning this situation.

wall as detailed elsewhere (see schedules, details & specifications; finish sheetrock to metal frame)
glazing (see Window Schedule for type, size & design) dry-glazed into hollow metal frame as shown w/hollow metal stop screwed to frame & w/corners welded & ground smooth

1/2"2"

5 3/4"

DRAWING #

Hollow Metal Window Jamb Detail

SCALE
1 1/2"
1'-0"

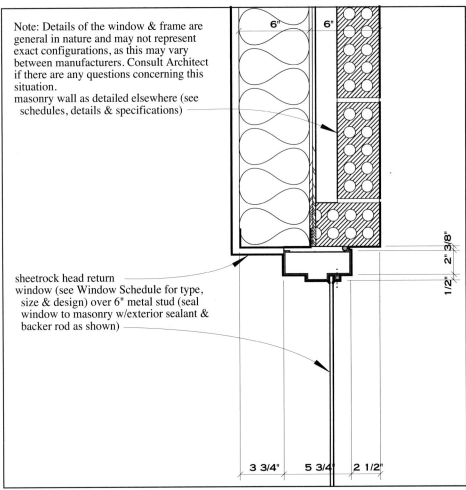

Note: Details of the window & frame are general in nature and may not represent exact configurations, as this may vary between manufacturers. Consult Architect if there are any questions concerning this situation.
masonry wall as detailed elsewhere (see schedules, details & specifications)

6"   6"

2" 3/8"
1/2"

sheetrock head return
window (see Window Schedule for type, size & design) over 6" metal stud (seal window to masonry w/exterior sealant & backer rod as shown)

3 3/4"   5 3/4"   2 1/2"

DRAWING #

Hollow Metal Window Jamb Detail

SCALE
1 1/2"
1'-0"

WHJ003
880

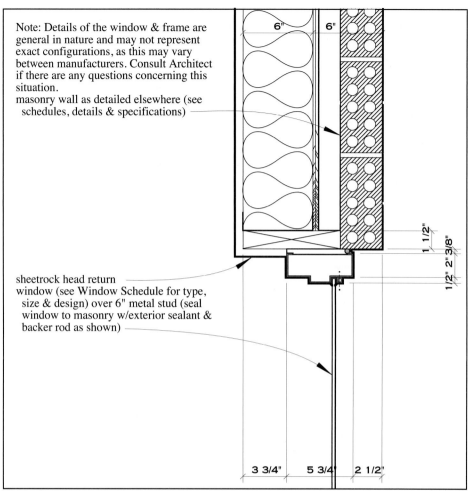

Note: Details of the window & frame are general in nature and may not represent exact configurations, as this may vary between manufacturers. Consult Architect if there are any questions concerning this situation.

masonry wall as detailed elsewhere (see schedules, details & specifications)

6"   6"

1 1/2"

2" 3/8"

1/2"

sheetrock head return

window (see Window Schedule for type, size & design) over 6" metal stud (seal window to masonry w/exterior sealant & backer rod as shown)

3 3/4"   5 3/4"   2 1/2"

DRAWING #

Hollow Metal Window Jamb Detail

SCALE
1 1/2"
1'-0"

WHJ004
881

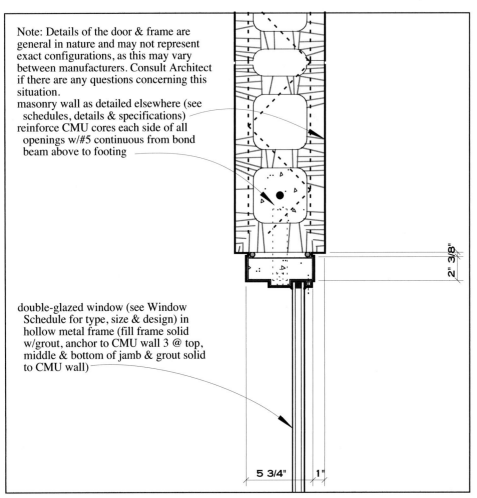

Note: Details of the door & frame are general in nature and may not represent exact configurations, as this may vary between manufacturers. Consult Architect if there are any questions concerning this situation.

masonry wall as detailed elsewhere (see schedules, details & specifications)

reinforce CMU cores each side of all openings w/#5 continuous from bond beam above to footing

2" 3/8"

double-glazed window (see Window Schedule for type, size & design) in hollow metal frame (fill frame solid w/grout, anchor to CMU wall 3 @ top, middle & bottom of jamb & grout solid to CMU wall)

5 3/4"   1"

DRAWING #

Hollow Metal Window Jamb Detail

SCALE

1 1/2
1'-0"

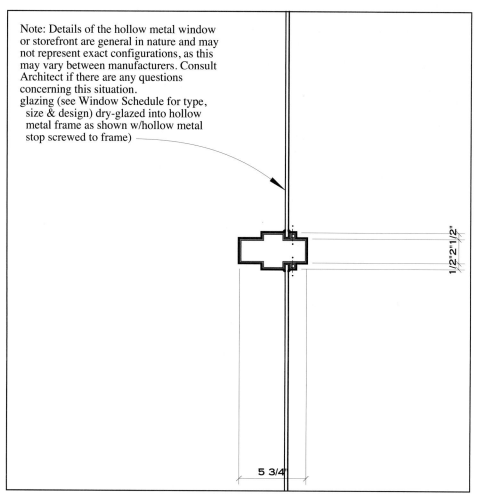

Note: Details of the hollow metal window or storefront are general in nature and may not represent exact configurations, as this may vary between manufacturers. Consult Architect if there are any questions concerning this situation.
glazing (see Window Schedule for type, size & design) dry-glazed into hollow metal frame as shown w/hollow metal stop screwed to frame)

5 3/4"

1/2" 2" 1/2"

DRAWING #

Hollow Metal Mullion Detail

SCALE

1 1/2"
1'-0"

Note: Details of the hollow metal window
or storefront are general in nature and may
not represent exact configurations, as this
may vary between manufacturers. Consult
Architect if there are any questions
concerning this situation.

glazing (see Window Schedule for type,
  size & design) dry-glazed into hollow
  metal frame as shown w/hollow metal
  stop screwed to frame & w/corners
  welded & ground smooth
upside-down bond beam CMU @ sill
CMU wall as detailed elsewhere (see
  schedules, details & specifications)

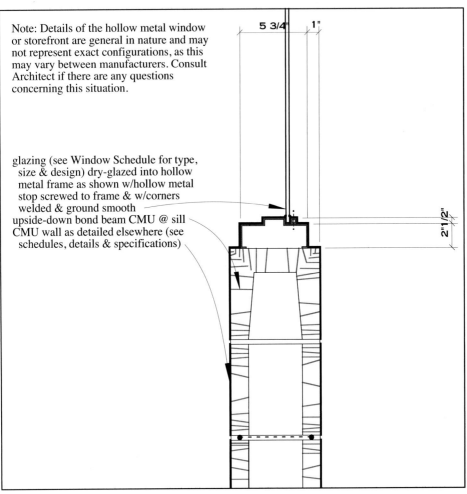

5 3/4"   1"

2"1/2"

DRAWING #

Hollow Metal Window Sill Detail

SCALE
1 1/2"
1'-0"

WHS001
884

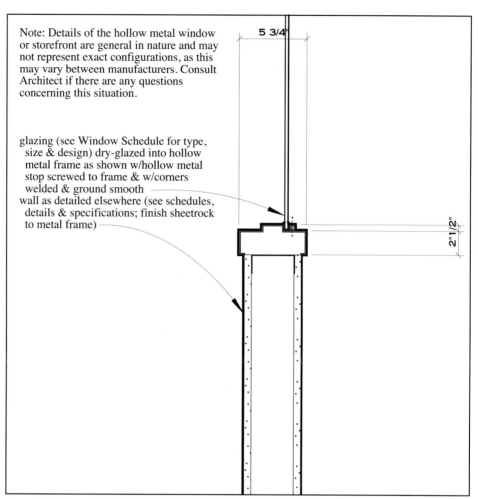

Note: Details of the hollow metal window or storefront are general in nature and may not represent exact configurations, as this may vary between manufacturers. Consult Architect if there are any questions concerning this situation.

glazing (see Window Schedule for type, size & design) dry-glazed into hollow metal frame as shown w/hollow metal stop screwed to frame & w/corners welded & ground smooth
wall as detailed elsewhere (see schedules, details & specifications; finish sheetrock to metal frame)

5 3/4"

2"1/2"

Hollow Metal Window Sill Detail

SCALE
1 1/2"
1'-0"

DRAWING #

WHS002
885

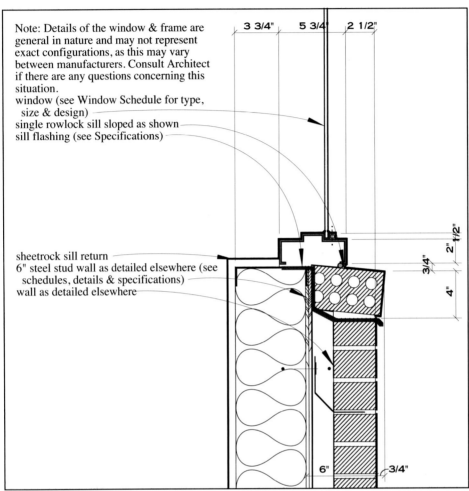

Note: Details of the window & frame are
general in nature and may not represent
exact configurations, as this may vary
between manufacturers. Consult Architect
if there are any questions concerning this
situation.
window (see Window Schedule for type,
 size & design)
single rowlock sill sloped as shown
sill flashing (see Specifications)

3 3/4"   5 3/4"   2 1/2"

1/2"
2"
3/4"
4"

sheetrock sill return
6" steel stud wall as detailed elsewhere (see
 schedules, details & specifications)
wall as detailed elsewhere

6"   3/4"

Window Sill Detail @ Brick Veneer

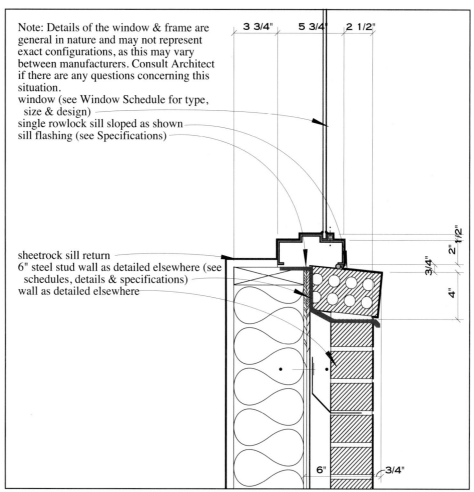

Note: Details of the window & frame are general in nature and may not represent exact configurations, as this may vary between manufacturers. Consult Architect if there are any questions concerning this situation.

window (see Window Schedule for type, size & design)
single rowlock sill sloped as shown
sill flashing (see Specifications)

3 3/4"   5 3/4"   2 1/2"

sheetrock sill return
6" steel stud wall as detailed elsewhere (see schedules, details & specifications)
wall as detailed elsewhere

1/2"   2"   3/4"   4"

6"   3/4"

DRAWING #

Window Sill Detail @ Brick Veneer

SCALE
1 1/2
1'-0"

Note: Details of the hollow metal window
or storefront are general in nature and may
not represent exact configurations, as this
may vary between manufacturers. Consult
Architect if there are any questions
concerning this situation.

5 3/4"   1"

glazing (see Window Schedule for type,
  size & design) dry-glazed into hollow
  metal frame as shown w/hollow metal
  stop screwed to frame & w/corners
  welded & ground smooth
upside-down bond beam CMU @ sill
CMU wall as detailed elsewhere (see
  schedules, details & specifications)

2"1/2"

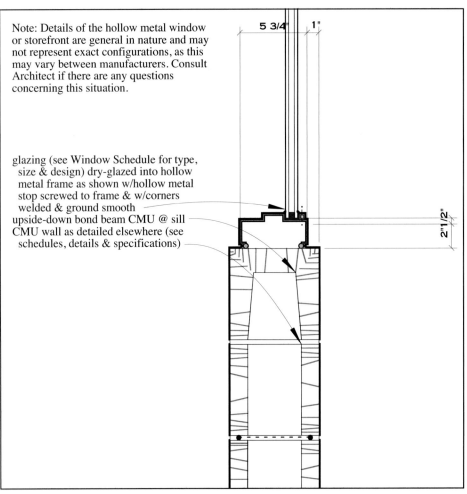

DRAWING #

Hollow Metal Window Sill Detail

SCALE

1 1/2"
1'-0"

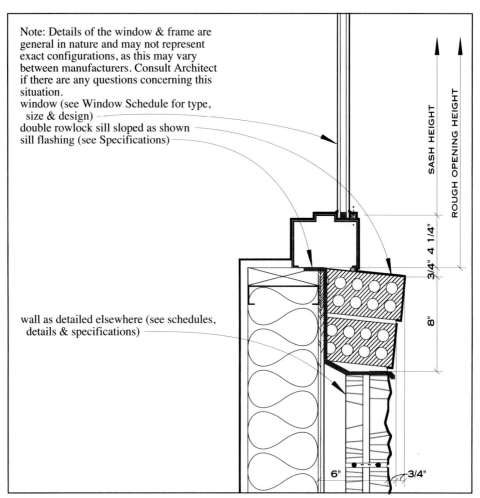

Note: Details of the window & frame are general in nature and may not represent exact configurations, as this may vary between manufacturers. Consult Architect if there are any questions concerning this situation.

window (see Window Schedule for type, size & design)
double rowlock sill sloped as shown
sill flashing (see Specifications)

wall as detailed elsewhere (see schedules, details & specifications)

SASH HEIGHT

ROUGH OPENING HEIGHT

4 1/4"

3/4"

8"

6"

3/4"

DRAWING #

Window Sill Detail @ Brick Veneer

SCALE

1 1/2

1'-0"

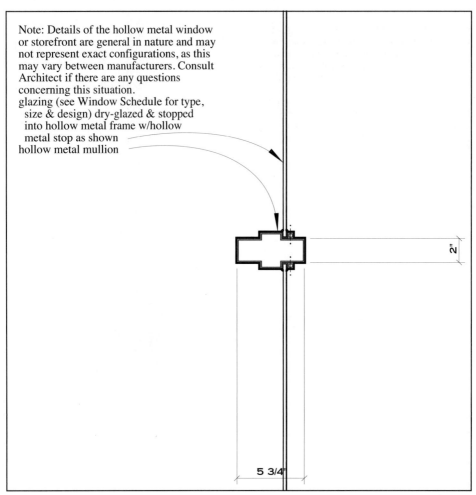

Note: Details of the hollow metal window
or storefront are general in nature and may
not represent exact configurations, as this
may vary between manufacturers. Consult
Architect if there are any questions
concerning this situation.
glazing (see Window Schedule for type,
  size & design) dry-glazed & stopped
  into hollow metal frame w/hollow
  metal stop as shown
hollow metal mullion

2"

5 3/4"

DRAWING #

Window Transom or Mullion Detail

SCALE
1 1/2"
1'-0"

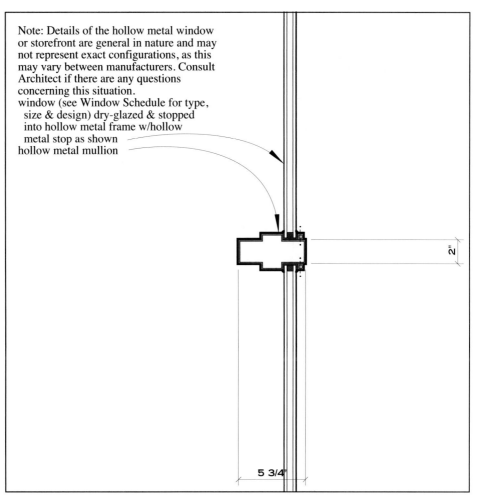

Note: Details of the hollow metal window or storefront are general in nature and may not represent exact configurations, as this may vary between manufacturers. Consult Architect if there are any questions concerning this situation.
window (see Window Schedule for type, size & design) dry-glazed & stopped into hollow metal frame w/hollow metal stop as shown
hollow metal mullion

2"

5 3/4"

Window Transom or Mullion Detail

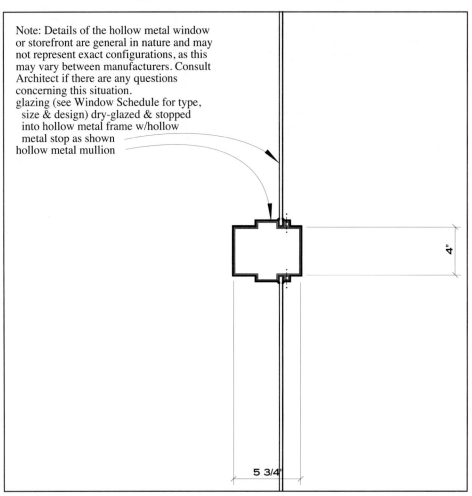

Note: Details of the hollow metal window
or storefront are general in nature and may
not represent exact configurations, as this
may vary between manufacturers. Consult
Architect if there are any questions
concerning this situation.
glazing (see Window Schedule for type,
  size & design) dry-glazed & stopped
  into hollow metal frame w/hollow
  metal stop as shown
hollow metal mullion

4"

5 3/4"

DRAWING #

Window Transom or Mullion Detail

SCALE

1 1/2"
1'-0"

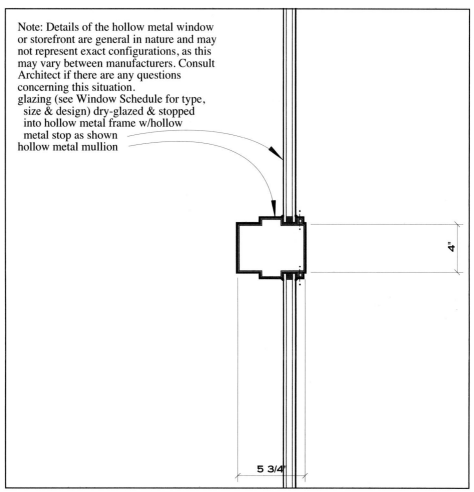

Note: Details of the hollow metal window
or storefront are general in nature and may
not represent exact configurations, as this
may vary between manufacturers. Consult
Architect if there are any questions
concerning this situation.
glazing (see Window Schedule for type,
    size & design) dry-glazed & stopped
    into hollow metal frame w/hollow
    metal stop as shown
hollow metal mullion

4"

5 3/4"

Window Transom or Mullion Detail

SCALE
1 1/2"
1'-0"

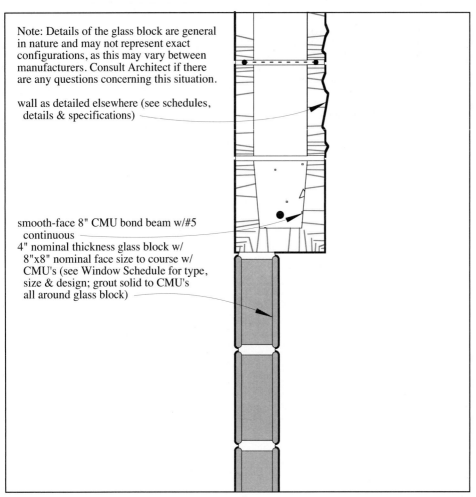

Note: Details of the glass block are general in nature and may not represent exact configurations, as this may vary between manufacturers. Consult Architect if there are any questions concerning this situation.

wall as detailed elsewhere (see schedules, details & specifications)

smooth-face 8" CMU bond beam w/#5 continuous
4" nominal thickness glass block w/ 8"x8" nominal face size to course w/ CMU's (see Window Schedule for type, size & design; grout solid to CMU's all around glass block)

DRAWING #

Glass Block Window Head Detail

SCALE
1 1/2"
1'-0"

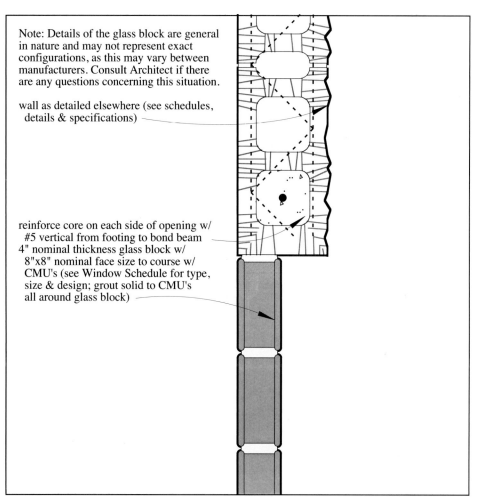

Note: Details of the glass block are general in nature and may not represent exact configurations, as this may vary between manufacturers. Consult Architect if there are any questions concerning this situation.

wall as detailed elsewhere (see schedules, details & specifications)

reinforce core on each side of opening w/ #5 vertical from footing to bond beam
4" nominal thickness glass block w/ 8"x8" nominal face size to course w/ CMU's (see Window Schedule for type, size & design; grout solid to CMU's all around glass block)

DRAWING #

Glass Block Window Jamb Detail

SCALE
1 1/2"
1'-0"

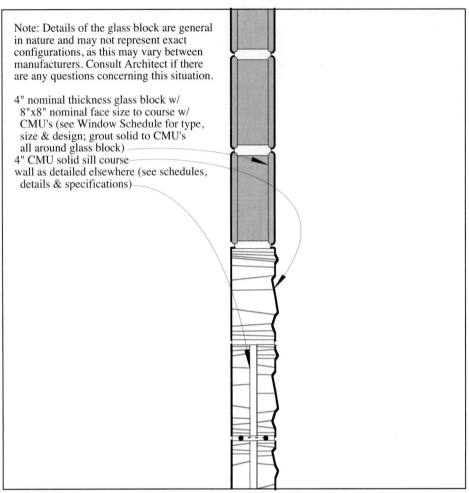

Note: Details of the glass block are general
in nature and may not represent exact
configurations, as this may vary between
manufacturers. Consult Architect if there
are any questions concerning this situation.

4" nominal thickness glass block w/
 8"x8" nominal face size to course w/
 CMU's (see Window Schedule for type,
 size & design; grout solid to CMU's
 all around glass block)
4" CMU solid sill course
wall as detailed elsewhere (see schedules,
 details & specifications)

Glass Block Window Sill Detail

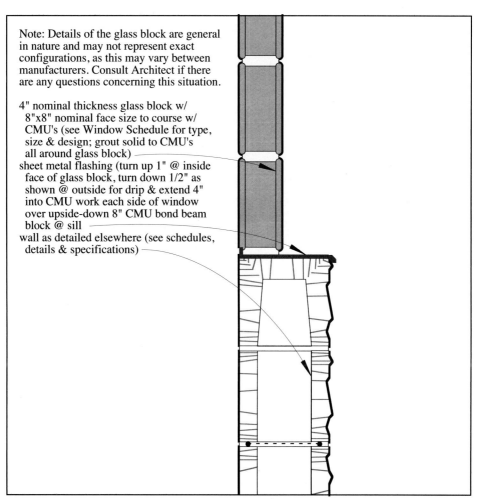

Note: Details of the glass block are general in nature and may not represent exact configurations, as this may vary between manufacturers. Consult Architect if there are any questions concerning this situation.

4" nominal thickness glass block w/ 8"x8" nominal face size to course w/ CMU's (see Window Schedule for type, size & design; grout solid to CMU's all around glass block)

sheet metal flashing (turn up 1" @ inside face of glass block, turn down 1/2" as shown @ outside for drip & extend 4" into CMU work each side of window over upside-down 8" CMU bond beam block @ sill

wall as detailed elsewhere (see schedules, details & specifications)

DRAWING #

Glass Block Window Sill Detail

SCALE
1 1/2"
1'-0"

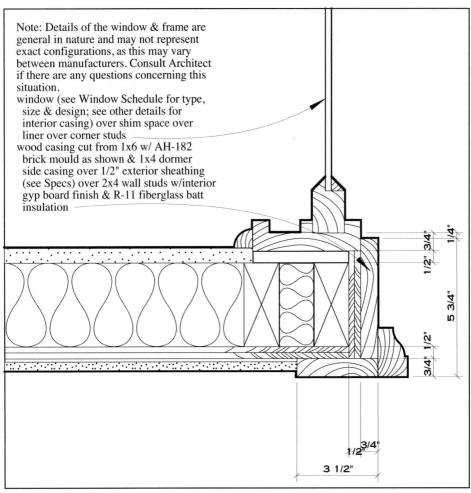

Note: Details of the window & frame are
general in nature and may not represent
exact configurations, as this may vary
between manufacturers. Consult Architect
if there are any questions concerning this
situation.
window (see Window Schedule for type,
  size & design; see other details for
  interior casing) over shim space over
  liner over corner studs
wood casing cut from 1x6 w/ AH-182
  brick mould as shown & 1x4 dormer
  side casing over 1/2" exterior sheathing
  (see Specs) over 2x4 wall studs w/interior
  gyp board finish & R-11 fiberglass batt
  insulation

1/4"

3/4"

1/2"

5 3/4"

1/2"

3/4"

3/4"

1/2"

3 1/2"

DRAWING #

Dormer Framed Window Jamb Detail

SCALE
$\frac{3"}{1'-0"}$

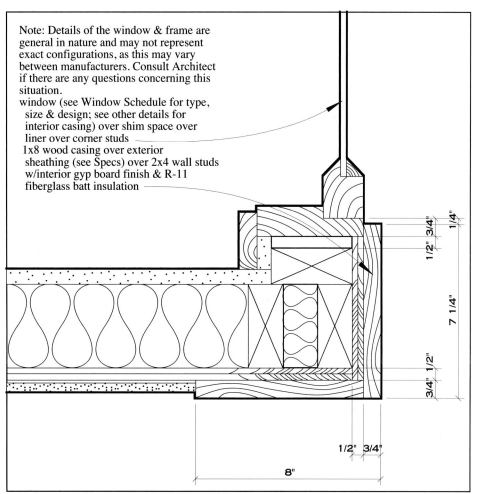

Note: Details of the window & frame are general in nature and may not represent exact configurations, as this may vary between manufacturers. Consult Architect if there are any questions concerning this situation.
window (see Window Schedule for type, size & design; see other details for interior casing) over shim space over liner over corner studs
1x8 wood casing over exterior sheathing (see Specs) over 2x4 wall studs w/interior gyp board finish & R-11 fiberglass batt insulation

1/4"
3/4"
1/2"
7 1/4"
1/2"
3/4"

1/2" 3/4"

8"

DRAWING #

Dormer Window Jamb Detail

SCALE
3"
1'-0"

WWDJ002
899

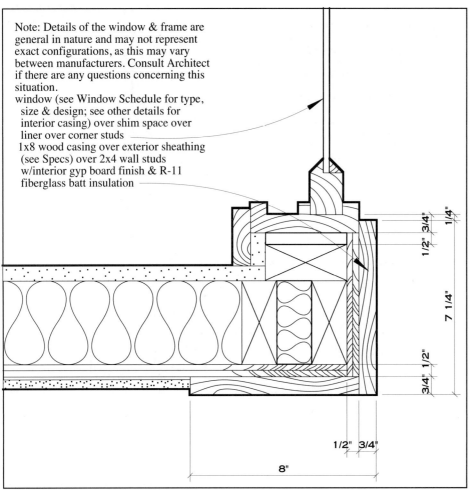

Note: Details of the window & frame are
general in nature and may not represent
exact configurations, as this may vary
between manufacturers. Consult Architect
if there are any questions concerning this
situation.
window (see Window Schedule for type,
 size & design; see other details for
 interior casing) over shim space over
 liner over corner studs
1x8 wood casing over exterior sheathing
 (see Specs) over 2x4 wall studs
 w/interior gyp board finish & R-11
 fiberglass batt insulation

1/4"
3/4"
1/2"
7 1/4"
1/2"
3/4"

1/2" 3/4"

8"

DRAWING #

Dormer Window Jamb Detail

SCALE
3"
1'-0"

WWDJ003
900

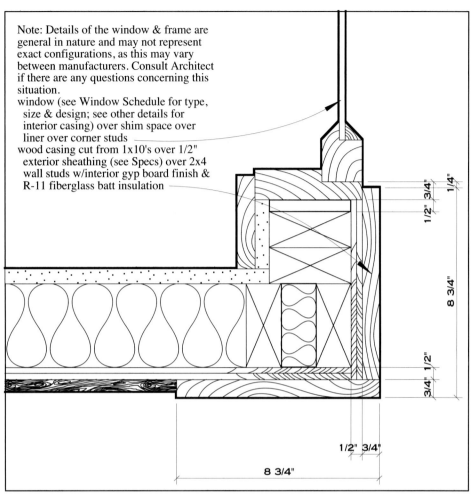

Note: Details of the window & frame are general in nature and may not represent exact configurations, as this may vary between manufacturers. Consult Architect if there are any questions concerning this situation.

window (see Window Schedule for type, size & design; see other details for interior casing) over shim space over liner over corner studs

wood casing cut from 1x10's over 1/2" exterior sheathing (see Specs) over 2x4 wall studs w/interior gyp board finish & R-11 fiberglass batt insulation

1/4"
1/2" 3/4"
8 3/4"
1/2"
3/4"

1/2" 3/4"
8 3/4"

DRAWING #		SCALE
	Dormer Window Jamb Detail	$\frac{3"}{1'\text{-}0"}$

WWDJ004
901

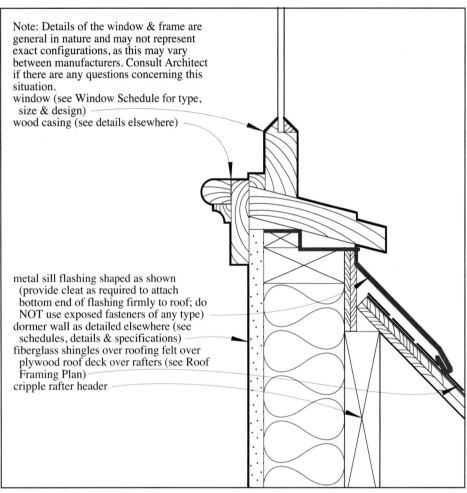

Note: Details of the window & frame are
general in nature and may not represent
exact configurations, as this may vary
between manufacturers. Consult Architect
if there are any questions concerning this
situation.
window (see Window Schedule for type,
  size & design)
wood casing (see details elsewhere)

metal sill flashing shaped as shown
  (provide cleat as required to attach
  bottom end of flashing firmly to roof; do
  NOT use exposed fasteners of any type)
dormer wall as detailed elsewhere (see
  schedules, details & specifications)
fiberglass shingles over roofing felt over
  plywood roof deck over rafters (see Roof
  Framing Plan)
cripple rafter header

DRAWING #

Dormer Window Sill Detail

SCALE
3"
1'-0"

WWDS001
902

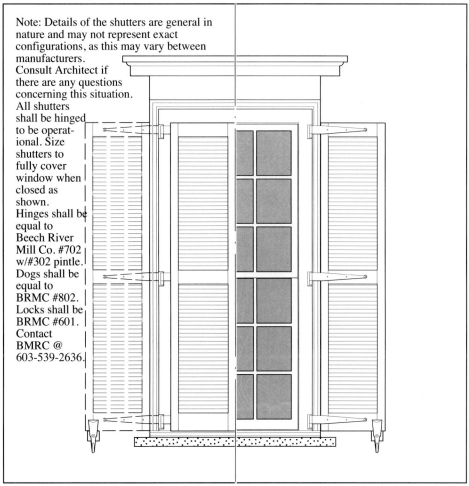

Note: Details of the shutters are general in nature and may not represent exact configurations, as this may vary between manufacturers. Consult Architect if there are any questions concerning this situation. All shutters shall be hinged to be operational. Size shutters to fully cover window when closed as shown. Hinges shall be equal to Beech River Mill Co. #702 w/#302 pintle. Dogs shall be equal to BRMC #802. Locks shall be BRMC #601. Contact BMRC @ 603-539-2636.

| DRAWING # | | | |

Shutter Elevation

SCALE
NO SCALE

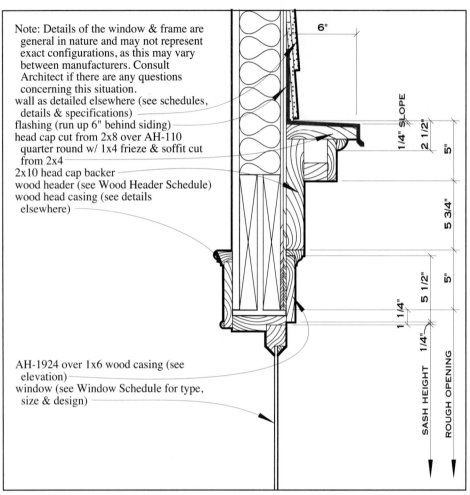

Note: Details of the window & frame are general in nature and may not represent exact configurations, as this may vary between manufacturers. Consult Architect if there are any questions concerning this situation.

wall as detailed elsewhere (see schedules, details & specifications)

flashing (run up 6" behind siding)

head cap cut from 2x8 over AH-110 quarter round w/ 1x4 frieze & soffit cut from 2x4

2x10 head cap backer

wood header (see Wood Header Schedule)

wood head casing (see details elsewhere)

AH-1924 over 1x6 wood casing (see elevation)

window (see Window Schedule for type, size & design)

6"

1/4" SLOPE

2 1/2"

5"

5 3/4"

5"

1 1/4"

5 1/2"

1/4"

SASH HEIGHT

ROUGH OPENING

DRAWING #

Window Head Detail @ Frieze

SCALE
1 1/2"
1'-0"

WWH001
904

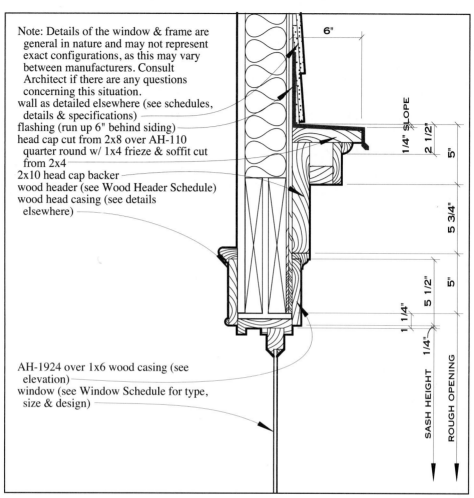

Note: Details of the window & frame are
  general in nature and may not represent
  exact configurations, as this may vary
  between manufacturers. Consult
  Architect if there are any questions
  concerning this situation.
wall as detailed elsewhere (see schedules,
  details & specifications)
flashing (run up 6" behind siding)
head cap cut from 2x8 over AH-110
  quarter round w/ 1x4 frieze & soffit cut
  from 2x4
2x10 head cap backer
wood header (see Wood Header Schedule)
wood head casing (see details
  elsewhere)

AH-1924 over 1x6 wood casing (see
  elevation)
window (see Window Schedule for type,
  size & design)

6"

1/4" SLOPE

2 1/2"

5"

5 3/4"

5 1/2"

5"

1 1/4"

SASH HEIGHT   1/4"

ROUGH OPENING

Window Head Detail

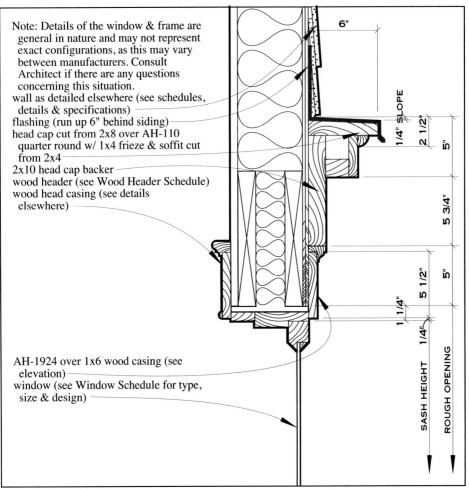

Note: Details of the window & frame are
general in nature and may not represent
exact configurations, as this may vary
between manufacturers. Consult
Architect if there are any questions
concerning this situation.
wall as detailed elsewhere (see schedules,
details & specifications)
flashing (run up 6" behind siding)
head cap cut from 2x8 over AH-110
quarter round w/ 1x4 frieze & soffit cut
from 2x4
2x10 head cap backer
wood header (see Wood Header Schedule)
wood head casing (see details
elsewhere)

AH-1924 over 1x6 wood casing (see
elevation)
window (see Window Schedule for type,
size & design)

6"

1/4" SLOPE

2 1/2"

2"

5"

5 3/4"

5 1/2"

5"

1 1/4"

SASH HEIGHT 1/4"

ROUGH OPENING

DRAWING #

Window Head Detail

SCALE

1 1/2"
1'-0"

WWH003
906

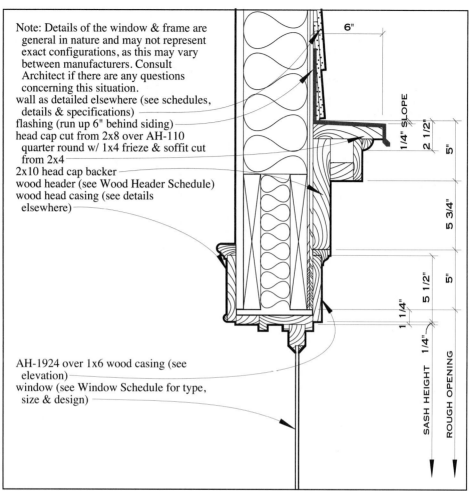

Note: Details of the window & frame are
   general in nature and may not represent
   exact configurations, as this may vary
   between manufacturers. Consult
   Architect if there are any questions
   concerning this situation.
wall as detailed elsewhere (see schedules,
   details & specifications)
flashing (run up 6" behind siding)
head cap cut from 2x8 over AH-110
   quarter round w/ 1x4 frieze & soffit cut
   from 2x4
2x10 head cap backer
wood header (see Wood Header Schedule)
wood head casing (see details
   elsewhere)

AH-1924 over 1x6 wood casing (see
   elevation)
window (see Window Schedule for type,
   size & design)

6"

1/4" SLOPE

2 1/2"

5"

5 3/4"

5"

1 1/4"

5 1/2"

1/4"

SASH HEIGHT

ROUGH OPENING

Window Head Detail

SCALE
1 1/2"
1'-0"

WWH004
907

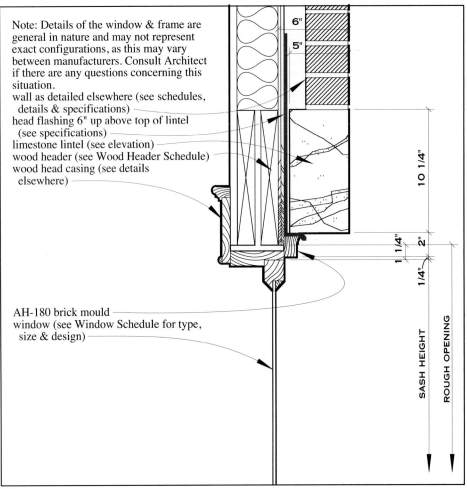

Note: Details of the window & frame are general in nature and may not represent exact configurations, as this may vary between manufacturers. Consult Architect if there are any questions concerning this situation.

wall as detailed elsewhere (see schedules, details & specifications)

head flashing 6" up above top of lintel (see specifications)

limestone lintel (see elevation)

wood header (see Wood Header Schedule)

wood head casing (see details elsewhere)

AH-180 brick mould

window (see Window Schedule for type, size & design)

6"

5"

10 1/4"

1 1/4"

2"

1/4"

SASH HEIGHT

ROUGH OPENING

DRAWING #

Window Head Detail w/Stone Lintel

SCALE

1 1/2"

1'-0"

WWH005

908

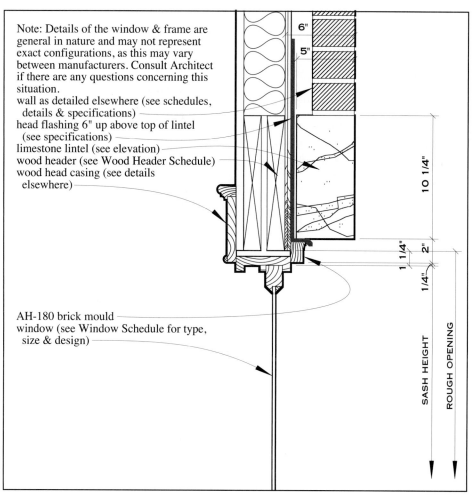

Note: Details of the window & frame are general in nature and may not represent exact configurations, as this may vary between manufacturers. Consult Architect if there are any questions concerning this situation.

wall as detailed elsewhere (see schedules, details & specifications)

head flashing 6" up above top of lintel (see specifications)

limestone lintel (see elevation)

wood header (see Wood Header Schedule)

wood head casing (see details elsewhere)

AH-180 brick mould

window (see Window Schedule for type, size & design)

6"

5"

10 1/4"

1 1/4"

2"

1/4"

SASH HEIGHT

ROUGH OPENING

Window Head Detail w/Stone Lintel

SCALE
1 1/2"
1'-0"

WWH006
909

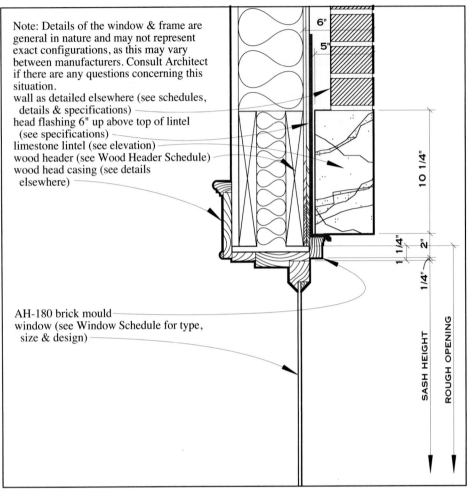

Note: Details of the window & frame are
general in nature and may not represent
exact configurations, as this may vary
between manufacturers. Consult Architect
if there are any questions concerning this
situation.

wall as detailed elsewhere (see schedules,
  details & specifications)
head flashing 6" up above top of lintel
  (see specifications)
limestone lintel (see elevation)
wood header (see Wood Header Schedule)
wood head casing (see details
  elsewhere)

6"

5"

10 1/4"

1 1/4"

2"

1/4"

SASH HEIGHT

ROUGH OPENING

AH-180 brick mould
window (see Window Schedule for type,
  size & design)

| DRAWING # | Window Head Detail w/Stone Lintel | SCALE 1 1/2" 1'-0" |

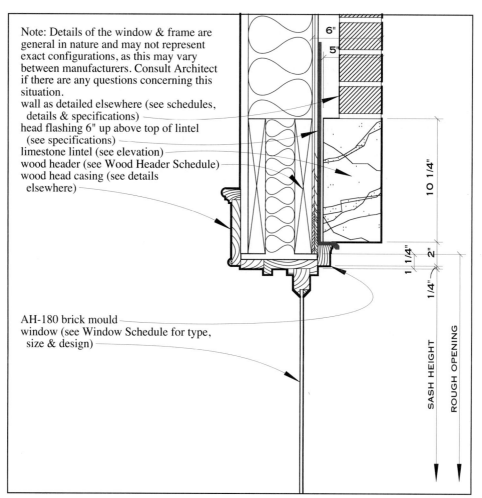

Note: Details of the window & frame are
general in nature and may not represent
exact configurations, as this may vary
between manufacturers. Consult Architect
if there are any questions concerning this
situation.
wall as detailed elsewhere (see schedules,
   details & specifications)
head flashing 6" up above top of lintel
   (see specifications)
limestone lintel (see elevation)
wood header (see Wood Header Schedule)
wood head casing (see details
   elsewhere)

AH-180 brick mould
window (see Window Schedule for type,
   size & design)

6"

5"

10 1/4"

1 1/4"

2"

1/4"

SASH HEIGHT

ROUGH OPENING

Window Head Detail w/Stone Lintel

SCALE
1 1/2"
1'-0"

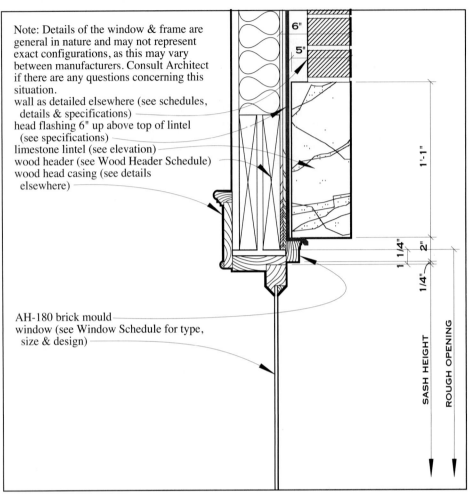

Note: Details of the window & frame are
general in nature and may not represent
exact configurations, as this may vary
between manufacturers. Consult Architect
if there are any questions concerning this
situation.
wall as detailed elsewhere (see schedules,
  details & specifications)
head flashing 6" up above top of lintel
  (see specifications)
limestone lintel (see elevation)
wood header (see Wood Header Schedule)
wood head casing (see details
  elsewhere)

AH-180 brick mould
window (see Window Schedule for type,
  size & design)

6"

5"

1'-1"

1 1/4" 2"

1/4"

SASH HEIGHT

ROUGH OPENING

Window Head Detail w/Stone Lintel

SCALE
1 1/2"
1'-0"

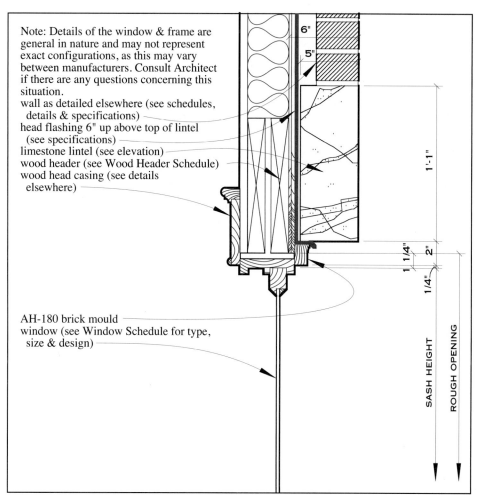

Note: Details of the window & frame are general in nature and may not represent exact configurations, as this may vary between manufacturers. Consult Architect if there are any questions concerning this situation.

wall as detailed elsewhere (see schedules, details & specifications)

head flashing 6" up above top of lintel (see specifications)

limestone lintel (see elevation)

wood header (see Wood Header Schedule)

wood head casing (see details elsewhere)

6"

5"

1'-1"

1 1/4"

2"

1/4"

AH-180 brick mould

window (see Window Schedule for type, size & design)

SASH HEIGHT

ROUGH OPENING

DRAWING #

Window Head Detail w/Stone Lintel

SCALE
1 1/2"
1'-0"

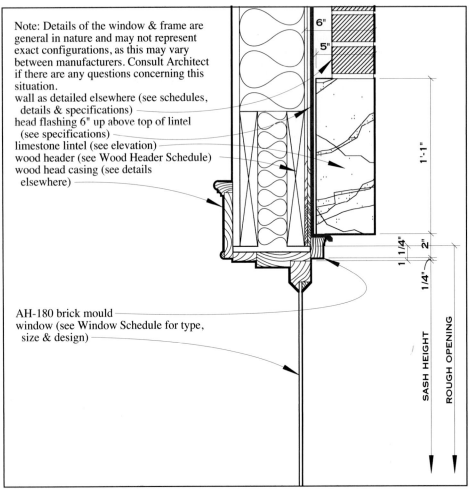

Note: Details of the window & frame are general in nature and may not represent exact configurations, as this may vary between manufacturers. Consult Architect if there are any questions concerning this situation.

wall as detailed elsewhere (see schedules, details & specifications)

head flashing 6" up above top of lintel (see specifications)

limestone lintel (see elevation)

wood header (see Wood Header Schedule)

wood head casing (see details elsewhere)

6"

5"

1'-1"

1 1/4"

2"

1/4"

AH-180 brick mould

window (see Window Schedule for type, size & design)

SASH HEIGHT

ROUGH OPENING

DRAWING #

Window Head Detail w/Stone Lintel

SCALE
1 1/2"
1'-0"

WWH011
914

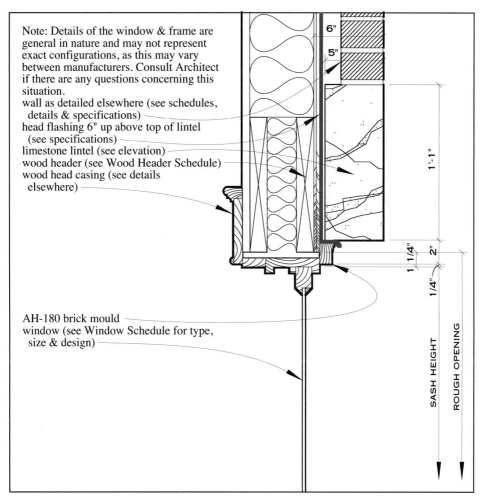

Note: Details of the window & frame are general in nature and may not represent exact configurations, as this may vary between manufacturers. Consult Architect if there are any questions concerning this situation.

wall as detailed elsewhere (see schedules, details & specifications)

head flashing 6" up above top of lintel (see specifications)

limestone lintel (see elevation)

wood header (see Wood Header Schedule)

wood head casing (see details elsewhere)

AH-180 brick mould

window (see Window Schedule for type, size & design)

6"

5"

1'-1"

1 1/4" 2"

1/4"

SASH HEIGHT

ROUGH OPENING

Window Head Detail w/Stone Lintel

SCALE
1 1/2"
1'-0"

WWH012
915

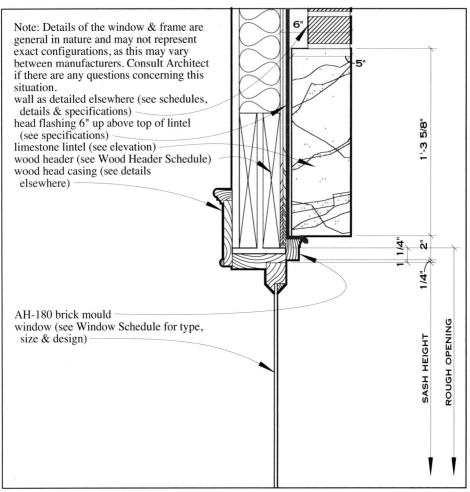

Note: Details of the window & frame are
general in nature and may not represent
exact configurations, as this may vary
between manufacturers. Consult Architect
if there are any questions concerning this
situation.

wall as detailed elsewhere (see schedules,
 details & specifications)

head flashing 6" up above top of lintel
 (see specifications)

limestone lintel (see elevation)

wood header (see Wood Header Schedule)

wood head casing (see details
 elsewhere)

AH-180 brick mould

window (see Window Schedule for type,
 size & design)

6"

5"

1'-3 5/8"

1 1/4"

2"

1/4"

SASH HEIGHT

ROUGH OPENING

Window Head Detail w/Stone Lintel

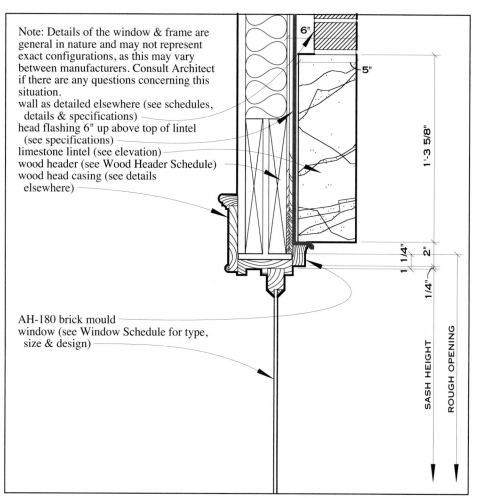

Note: Details of the window & frame are
general in nature and may not represent
exact configurations, as this may vary
between manufacturers. Consult Architect
if there are any questions concerning this
situation.
wall as detailed elsewhere (see schedules,
 details & specifications)
head flashing 6" up above top of lintel
 (see specifications)
limestone lintel (see elevation)
wood header (see Wood Header Schedule)
wood head casing (see details
 elsewhere)

AH-180 brick mould
window (see Window Schedule for type,
 size & design)

6"

5"

1'-3 5/8"

1 1/4"

2"

1/4"

SASH HEIGHT

ROUGH OPENING

DRAWING #

Window Head Detail w/Stone Lintel

SCALE
1 1/2"
1'-0"

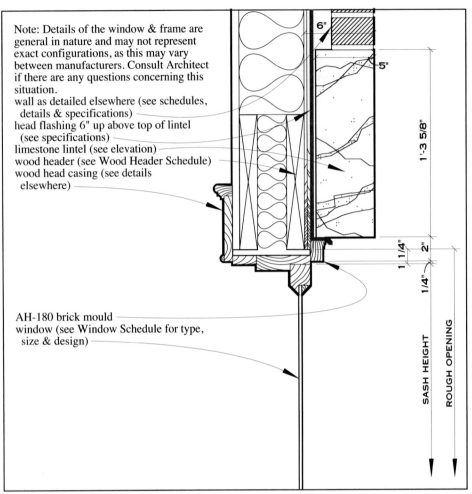

Note: Details of the window & frame are general in nature and may not represent exact configurations, as this may vary between manufacturers. Consult Architect if there are any questions concerning this situation.

wall as detailed elsewhere (see schedules, details & specifications)

head flashing 6" up above top of lintel (see specifications)

limestone lintel (see elevation)

wood header (see Wood Header Schedule)

wood head casing (see details elsewhere)

6"

5"

1'-3 5/8"

1 1/4"

2"

1/4"

SASH HEIGHT

ROUGH OPENING

AH-180 brick mould

window (see Window Schedule for type, size & design)

DRAWING #

Window Head Detail w/Stone Lintel

SCALE
1 1/2"
1'-0"

WWH015
918

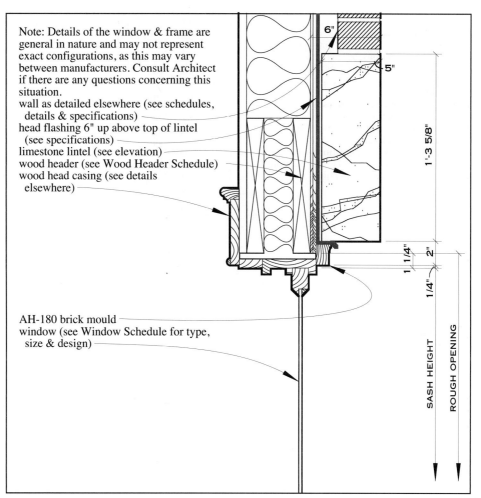

Note: Details of the window & frame are
general in nature and may not represent
exact configurations, as this may vary
between manufacturers. Consult Architect
if there are any questions concerning this
situation.
wall as detailed elsewhere (see schedules,
  details & specifications)
head flashing 6" up above top of lintel
  (see specifications)
limestone lintel (see elevation)
wood header (see Wood Header Schedule)
wood head casing (see details
  elsewhere)

6"

5"

1'-3 5/8"

1 1/4"

2"

1/4"

SASH HEIGHT

ROUGH OPENING

AH-180 brick mould
window (see Window Schedule for type,
  size & design)

DRAWING #

Window Head Detail w/Stone Lintel

SCALE

1 1/2"
——
1'-0"

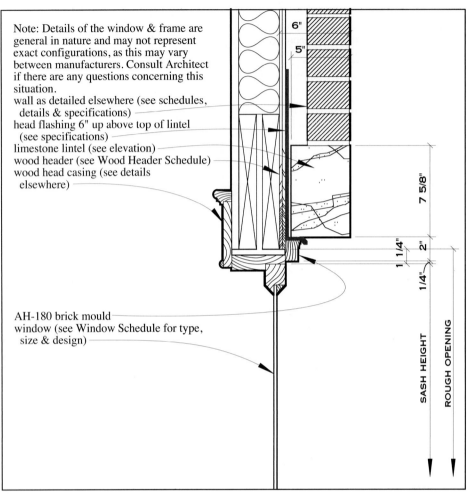

Note: Details of the window & frame are general in nature and may not represent exact configurations, as this may vary between manufacturers. Consult Architect if there are any questions concerning this situation.

wall as detailed elsewhere (see schedules, details & specifications)

head flashing 6" up above top of lintel (see specifications)

limestone lintel (see elevation)

wood header (see Wood Header Schedule)

wood head casing (see details elsewhere)

6"

5"

7 5/8"

1 1/4"

2"

1/4"

SASH HEIGHT

ROUGH OPENING

AH-180 brick mould

window (see Window Schedule for type, size & design)

Window Head Detail w/Stone Lintel

SCALE
1 1/2"
1'-0"

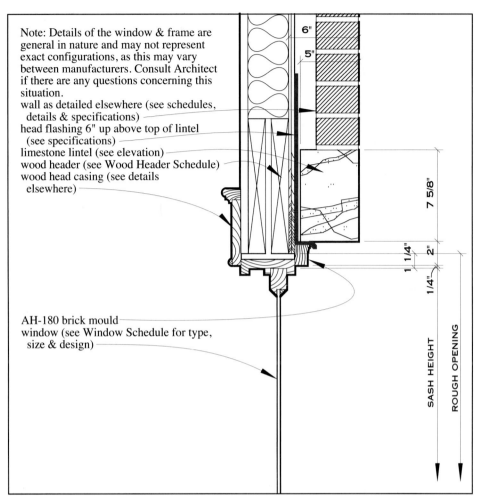

Note: Details of the window & frame are general in nature and may not represent exact configurations, as this may vary between manufacturers. Consult Architect if there are any questions concerning this situation.

wall as detailed elsewhere (see schedules, details & specifications)

head flashing 6" up above top of lintel (see specifications)

limestone lintel (see elevation)

wood header (see Wood Header Schedule)

wood head casing (see details elsewhere)

6"

5"

7 5/8"

1 1/4"

2"

1/4"

AH-180 brick mould

window (see Window Schedule for type, size & design)

SASH HEIGHT

ROUGH OPENING

Window Head Detail w/Stone Lintel

DRAWING #

SCALE
1 1/2"
1'-0"

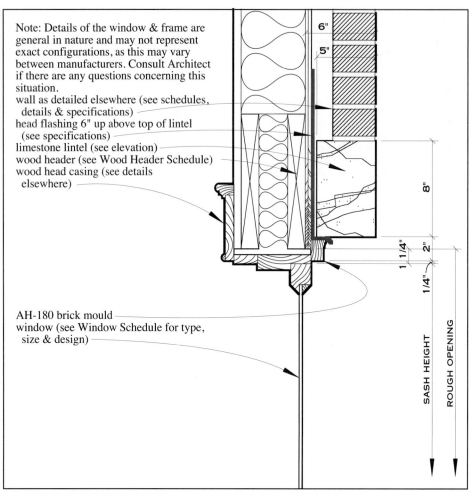

Note: Details of the window & frame are
general in nature and may not represent
exact configurations, as this may vary
between manufacturers. Consult Architect
if there are any questions concerning this
situation.

wall as detailed elsewhere (see schedules,
   details & specifications)

head flashing 6" up above top of lintel
   (see specifications)

limestone lintel (see elevation)

wood header (see Wood Header Schedule)

wood head casing (see details
   elsewhere)

AH-180 brick mould

window (see Window Schedule for type,
   size & design)

6"

5"

8"

1 1/4"

2"

1/4"

SASH HEIGHT

ROUGH OPENING

Window Head Detail w/Stone Lintel

WWH019
922

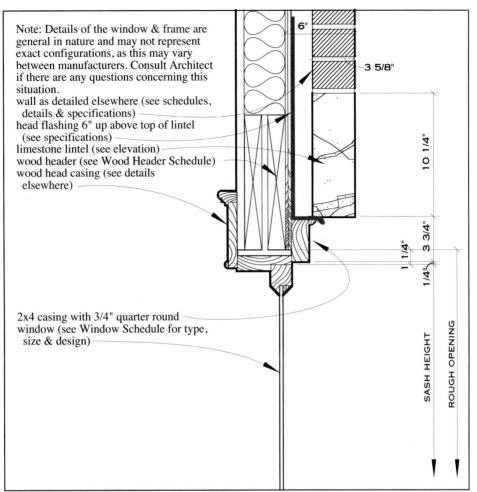

Note: Details of the window & frame are general in nature and may not represent exact configurations, as this may vary between manufacturers. Consult Architect if there are any questions concerning this situation.

wall as detailed elsewhere (see schedules, details & specifications)

head flashing 6" up above top of lintel (see specifications)

limestone lintel (see elevation)

wood header (see Wood Header Schedule)

wood head casing (see details elsewhere)

6"

3 5/8"

10 1/4"

3 3/4"

1 1/4"

1/4"

2x4 casing with 3/4" quarter round

window (see Window Schedule for type, size & design)

SASH HEIGHT

ROUGH OPENING

Window Head Detail w/Stone Lintel

SCALE 1 1/2" / 1'-0"

DRAWING #

WWH021
923

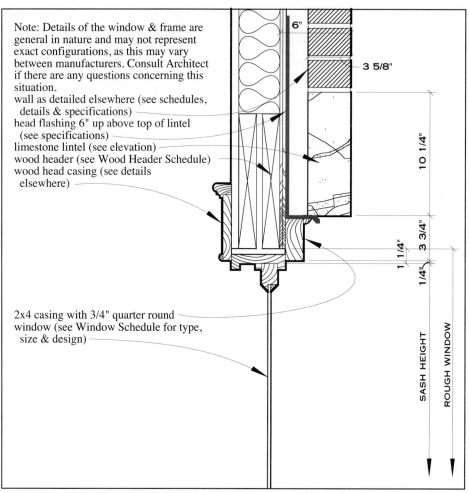

Note: Details of the window & frame are
general in nature and may not represent
exact configurations, as this may vary
between manufacturers. Consult Architect
if there are any questions concerning this
situation.

wall as detailed elsewhere (see schedules,
  details & specifications)

head flashing 6" up above top of lintel
  (see specifications)

limestone lintel (see elevation)

wood header (see Wood Header Schedule)

wood head casing (see details
  elsewhere)

2x4 casing with 3/4" quarter round

window (see Window Schedule for type,
  size & design)

6"

3 5/8"

10 1/4"

3 3/4"

1 1/4"

1/4"

SASH HEIGHT

ROUGH WINDOW

DRAWING #

Window Head Detail w/Stone Lintel

SCALE
1 1/2"
1'-0"

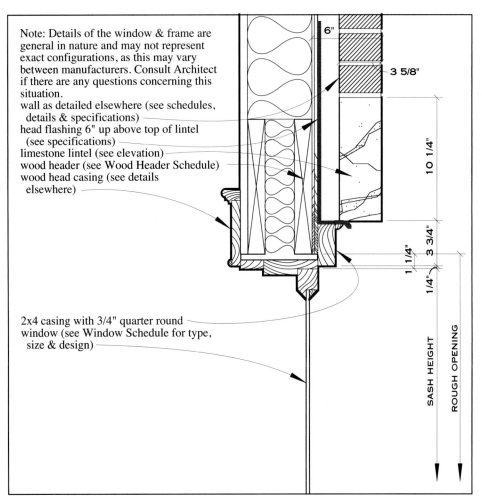

Note: Details of the window & frame are general in nature and may not represent exact configurations, as this may vary between manufacturers. Consult Architect if there are any questions concerning this situation.

wall as detailed elsewhere (see schedules, details & specifications)

head flashing 6" up above top of lintel (see specifications)

limestone lintel (see elevation)

wood header (see Wood Header Schedule)

wood head casing (see details elsewhere)

2x4 casing with 3/4" quarter round

window (see Window Schedule for type, size & design)

6"

3 5/8"

10 1/4"

3 3/4"

1 1/4"

1/4"

SASH HEIGHT

ROUGH OPENING

Window Head Detail w/Stone Lintel

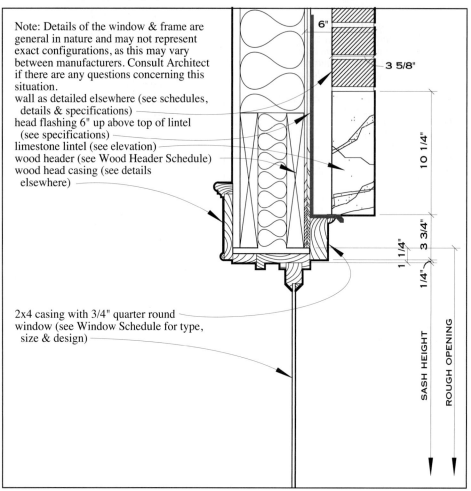

Note: Details of the window & frame are
general in nature and may not represent
exact configurations, as this may vary
between manufacturers. Consult Architect
if there are any questions concerning this
situation.
wall as detailed elsewhere (see schedules,
  details & specifications)
head flashing 6" up above top of lintel
  (see specifications)
limestone lintel (see elevation)
wood header (see Wood Header Schedule)
wood head casing (see details
  elsewhere)

6"

3 5/8"

10 1/4"

3 3/4"

1 1/4"

1/4"

SASH HEIGHT

ROUGH OPENING

2x4 casing with 3/4" quarter round
window (see Window Schedule for type,
  size & design)

Window Head Detail w/Stone Lintel

SCALE
1 1/2"
1'-O"

WWH024
926

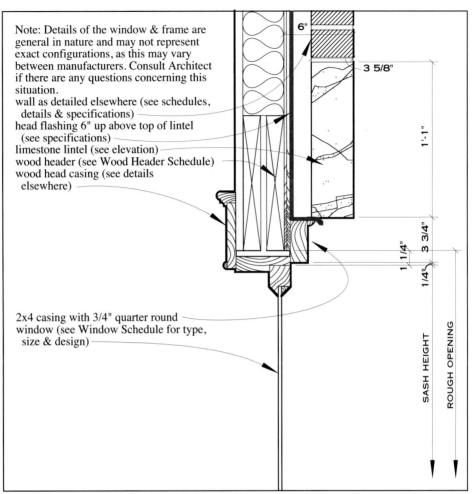

Note: Details of the window & frame are general in nature and may not represent exact configurations, as this may vary between manufacturers. Consult Architect if there are any questions concerning this situation.

wall as detailed elsewhere (see schedules, details & specifications)

head flashing 6" up above top of lintel (see specifications)

limestone lintel (see elevation)

wood header (see Wood Header Schedule)

wood head casing (see details elsewhere)

2x4 casing with 3/4" quarter round window (see Window Schedule for type, size & design)

6"

3 5/8"

1'-1"

3 3/4"

1 1/4"

1/4"

SASH HEIGHT

ROUGH OPENING

DRAWING #

Window Head Detail w/Stone Lintel

SCALE
1 1/2"
1'-0"

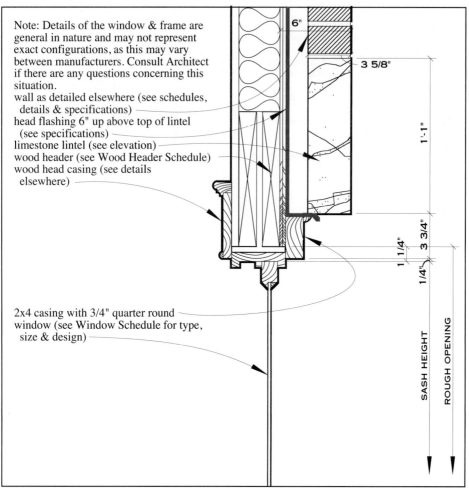

Note: Details of the window & frame are
general in nature and may not represent
exact configurations, as this may vary
between manufacturers. Consult Architect
if there are any questions concerning this
situation.
wall as detailed elsewhere (see schedules,
  details & specifications)
head flashing 6" up above top of lintel
  (see specifications)
limestone lintel (see elevation)
wood header (see Wood Header Schedule)
wood head casing (see details
  elsewhere)

6"

3 5/8"

1'-1"

3 3/4"

1 1/4"

1/4"

SASH HEIGHT

ROUGH OPENING

2x4 casing with 3/4" quarter round
window (see Window Schedule for type,
  size & design)

DRAWING #	Window Head Detail w/Stone Lintel	SCALE
		1 1/2" / 1'-O"

WWH026
928

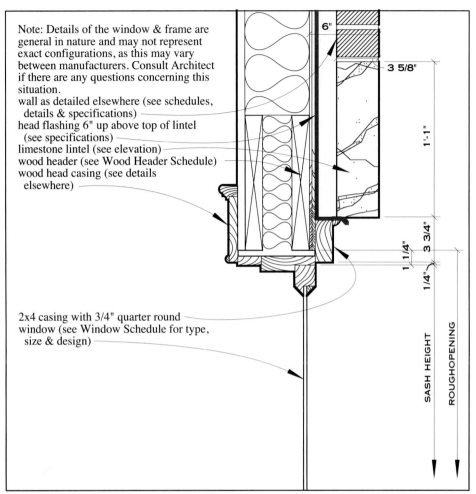

Note: Details of the window & frame are general in nature and may not represent exact configurations, as this may vary between manufacturers. Consult Architect if there are any questions concerning this situation.

wall as detailed elsewhere (see schedules, details & specifications)

head flashing 6" up above top of lintel (see specifications)

limestone lintel (see elevation)

wood header (see Wood Header Schedule)

wood head casing (see details elsewhere)

6"

3 5/8"

1'-1"

3 3/4"

1 1/4"

1/4"

2x4 casing with 3/4" quarter round window (see Window Schedule for type, size & design)

SASH HEIGHT

ROUGHOPENING

Window Head Detail w/Stone Lintel

DRAWING #

SCALE
1 1/2"
1'-0"

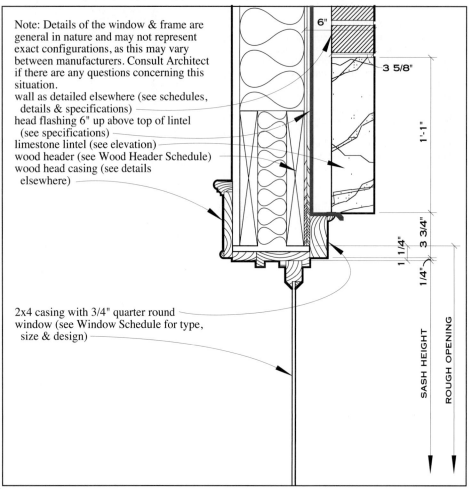

Note: Details of the window & frame are general in nature and may not represent exact configurations, as this may vary between manufacturers. Consult Architect if there are any questions concerning this situation.

wall as detailed elsewhere (see schedules, details & specifications)

head flashing 6" up above top of lintel (see specifications)

limestone lintel (see elevation)

wood header (see Wood Header Schedule)

wood head casing (see details elsewhere)

2x4 casing with 3/4" quarter round

window (see Window Schedule for type, size & design)

6"

3 5/8"

1'-1"

3 3/4"

1 1/4"

1/4"

SASH HEIGHT

ROUGH OPENING

 DRAWING #

Window Head Detail w/Stone Lintel

 SCALE
1 1/2"
1'-0"

WWH028
930

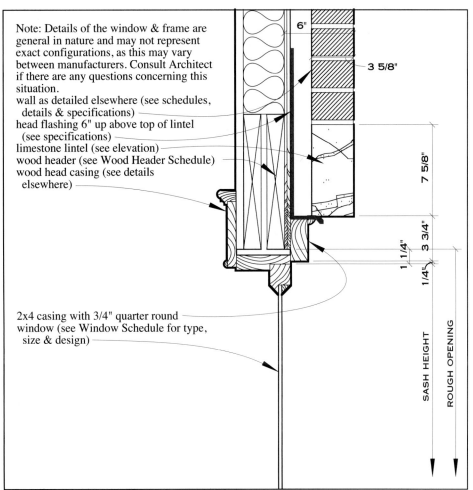

Note: Details of the window & frame are general in nature and may not represent exact configurations, as this may vary between manufacturers. Consult Architect if there are any questions concerning this situation.

wall as detailed elsewhere (see schedules, details & specifications)

head flashing 6" up above top of lintel (see specifications)

limestone lintel (see elevation)

wood header (see Wood Header Schedule)

wood head casing (see details elsewhere)

2x4 casing with 3/4" quarter round window (see Window Schedule for type, size & design)

6"

3 5/8"

7 5/8"

1 1/4"

3 3/4"

1/4"

SASH HEIGHT

ROUGH OPENING

Window Head Detail w/Stone Lintel

DRAWING #

SCALE
1 1/2"
1'-0"

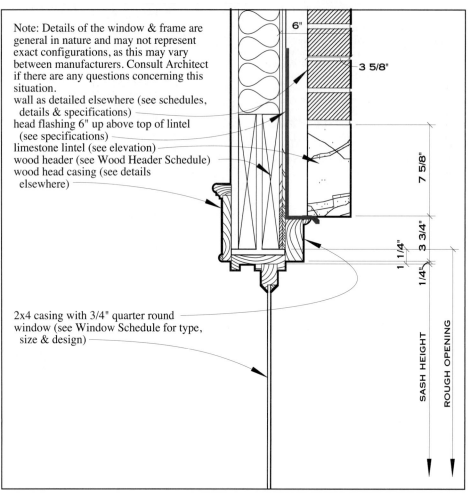

Note: Details of the window & frame are general in nature and may not represent exact configurations, as this may vary between manufacturers. Consult Architect if there are any questions concerning this situation.

wall as detailed elsewhere (see schedules, details & specifications)

head flashing 6" up above top of lintel (see specifications)

limestone lintel (see elevation)

wood header (see Wood Header Schedule)

wood head casing (see details elsewhere)

2x4 casing with 3/4" quarter round

window (see Window Schedule for type, size & design)

6"

3 5/8"

7 5/8"

3 3/4"

1 1/4"

1/4"

SASH HEIGHT

ROUGH OPENING

DRAWING #

Window Head Detail w/Stone Lintel

SCALE

1 1/2"
1'-0"

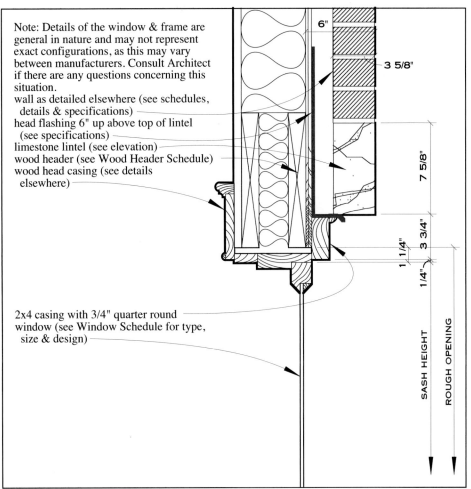

Note: Details of the window & frame are general in nature and may not represent exact configurations, as this may vary between manufacturers. Consult Architect if there are any questions concerning this situation.

wall as detailed elsewhere (see schedules, details & specifications)

head flashing 6" up above top of lintel (see specifications)

limestone lintel (see elevation)

wood header (see Wood Header Schedule)

wood head casing (see details elsewhere)

2x4 casing with 3/4" quarter round window (see Window Schedule for type, size & design)

6"

3 5/8"

7 5/8"

3 3/4"

1 1/4"

1/4"

SASH HEIGHT

ROUGH OPENING

Window Head Detail w/Stone Lintel

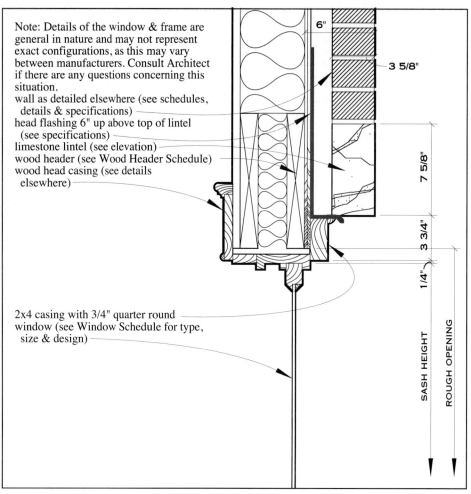

Note: Details of the window & frame are general in nature and may not represent exact configurations, as this may vary between manufacturers. Consult Architect if there are any questions concerning this situation.

wall as detailed elsewhere (see schedules, details & specifications)

head flashing 6" up above top of lintel (see specifications)

limestone lintel (see elevation)

wood header (see Wood Header Schedule)

wood head casing (see details elsewhere)

2x4 casing with 3/4" quarter round

window (see Window Schedule for type, size & design)

6"

3 5/8"

7 5/8"

3 3/4"

1/4"

SASH HEIGHT

ROUGH OPENING

DRAWING #

Window Head Detail w/Stone Lintel

SCALE
1 1/2"
1'-0"

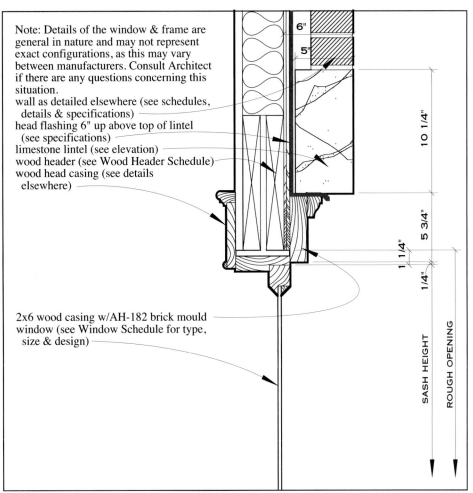

Note: Details of the window & frame are general in nature and may not represent exact configurations, as this may vary between manufacturers. Consult Architect if there are any questions concerning this situation.

wall as detailed elsewhere (see schedules, details & specifications)

head flashing 6" up above top of lintel (see specifications)

limestone lintel (see elevation)

wood header (see Wood Header Schedule)

wood head casing (see details elsewhere)

2x6 wood casing w/AH-182 brick mould window (see Window Schedule for type, size & design)

6"

5"

10 1/4"

5 3/4"

1 1/4"

1/4"

SASH HEIGHT

ROUGH OPENING

DRAWING #

Window Head Detail @ Stone Lintel

SCALE
1 1/2"
1'-0"

WWH033
935

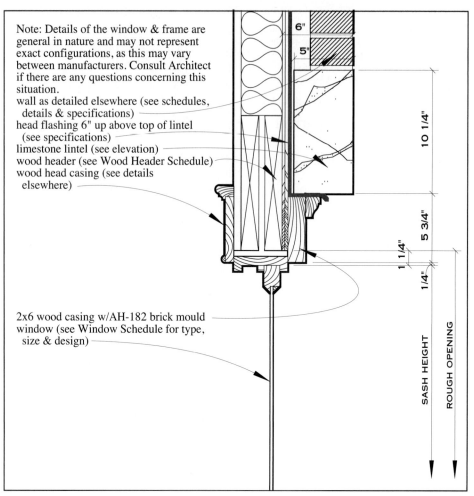

Note: Details of the window & frame are general in nature and may not represent exact configurations, as this may vary between manufacturers. Consult Architect if there are any questions concerning this situation.

wall as detailed elsewhere (see schedules, details & specifications)

head flashing 6" up above top of lintel (see specifications)

limestone lintel (see elevation)

wood header (see Wood Header Schedule)

wood head casing (see details elsewhere)

2x6 wood casing w/AH-182 brick mould window (see Window Schedule for type, size & design)

6"

5"

10 1/4"

5 3/4"

1 1/4"

1/4"

SASH HEIGHT

ROUGH OPENING

Window Head Detail w/Stone Lintel

SCALE
1 1/2"
1'-0"

WWH034
936

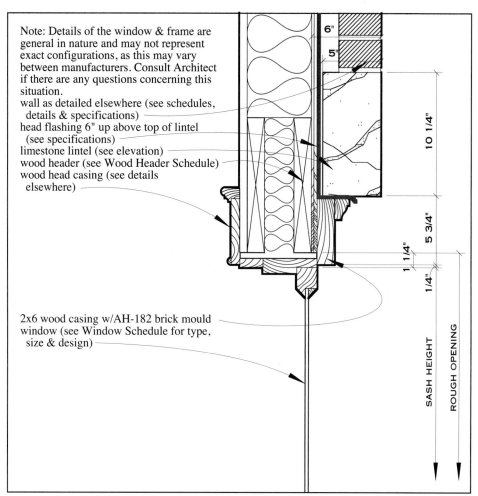

Note: Details of the window & frame are general in nature and may not represent exact configurations, as this may vary between manufacturers. Consult Architect if there are any questions concerning this situation.

wall as detailed elsewhere (see schedules, details & specifications)

head flashing 6" up above top of lintel (see specifications)

limestone lintel (see elevation)

wood header (see Wood Header Schedule)

wood head casing (see details elsewhere)

2x6 wood casing w/AH-182 brick mould window (see Window Schedule for type, size & design)

6"

5"

10 1/4"

5 3/4"

1 1/4"

1/4"

SASH HEIGHT

ROUGH OPENING

Window Head Detail w/Stone Lintel

DRAWING #

SCALE
1 1/2"
1'-0"

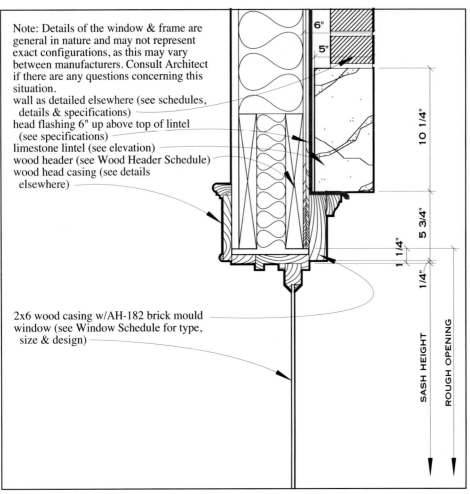

Note: Details of the window & frame are general in nature and may not represent exact configurations, as this may vary between manufacturers. Consult Architect if there are any questions concerning this situation.

wall as detailed elsewhere (see schedules, details & specifications)

head flashing 6" up above top of lintel (see specifications)

limestone lintel (see elevation)

wood header (see Wood Header Schedule)

wood head casing (see details elsewhere)

2x6 wood casing w/AH-182 brick mould window (see Window Schedule for type, size & design)

6"

5"

10 1/4"

5 3/4"

1 1/4"

1/4"

SASH HEIGHT

ROUGH OPENING

DRAWING #

Window Head Detail w/Stone Lintel

SCALE
1 1/2"
1'-0"

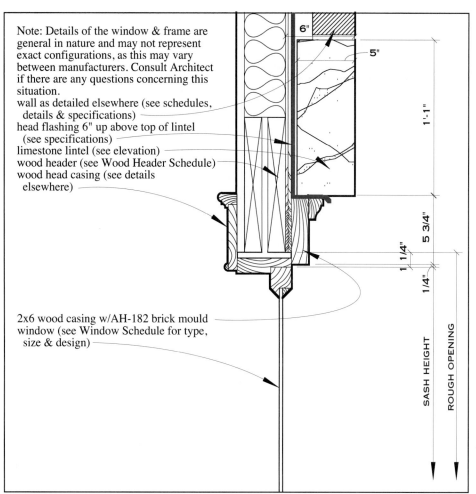

Note: Details of the window & frame are general in nature and may not represent exact configurations, as this may vary between manufacturers. Consult Architect if there are any questions concerning this situation.

wall as detailed elsewhere (see schedules, details & specifications)

head flashing 6" up above top of lintel (see specifications)

limestone lintel (see elevation)

wood header (see Wood Header Schedule)

wood head casing (see details elsewhere)

2x6 wood casing w/AH-182 brick mould window (see Window Schedule for type, size & design)

6"

5"

1'-1"

5 3/4"

1 1/4"

1/4"

SASH HEIGHT

ROUGH OPENING

DRAWING #

Window Head Detail @ Stone Lintel

SCALE
1 1/2"
1'-0"

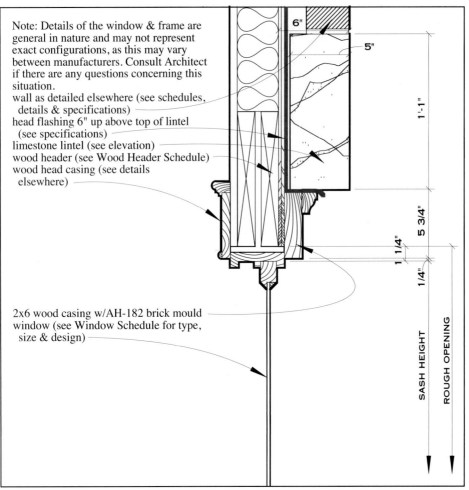

Note: Details of the window & frame are general in nature and may not represent exact configurations, as this may vary between manufacturers. Consult Architect if there are any questions concerning this situation.

wall as detailed elsewhere (see schedules, details & specifications)

head flashing 6" up above top of lintel (see specifications)

limestone lintel (see elevation)

wood header (see Wood Header Schedule)

wood head casing (see details elsewhere)

2x6 wood casing w/AH-182 brick mould

window (see Window Schedule for type, size & design)

6"

5"

1'-1"

5 3/4"

1 1/4"

1/4"

SASH HEIGHT

ROUGH OPENING

Window Head Detail w/Stone Lintel

SCALE

1 1/2"
1'-0"

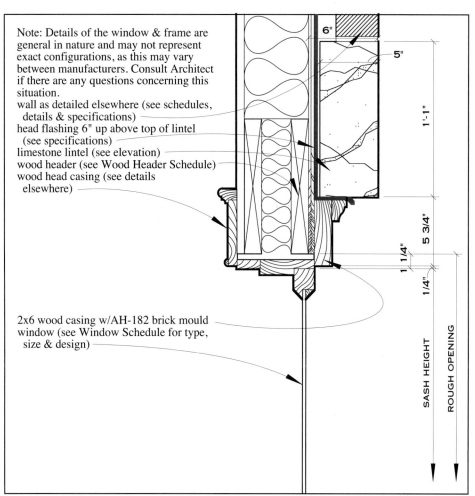

Note: Details of the window & frame are
general in nature and may not represent
exact configurations, as this may vary
between manufacturers. Consult Architect
if there are any questions concerning this
situation.

wall as detailed elsewhere (see schedules,
 details & specifications)

head flashing 6" up above top of lintel
 (see specifications)

limestone lintel (see elevation)

wood header (see Wood Header Schedule)

wood head casing (see details
 elsewhere)

2x6 wood casing w/AH-182 brick mould
window (see Window Schedule for type,
 size & design)

6"

5"

1'-1"

5 3/4"

1 1/4"

1/4"

SASH HEIGHT

ROUGH OPENING

Window Head Detail w/Stone Lintel

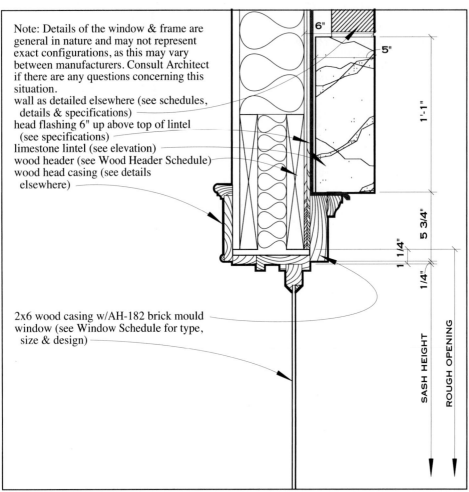

Note: Details of the window & frame are general in nature and may not represent exact configurations, as this may vary between manufacturers. Consult Architect if there are any questions concerning this situation.

wall as detailed elsewhere (see schedules, details & specifications)

head flashing 6" up above top of lintel (see specifications)

limestone lintel (see elevation)

wood header (see Wood Header Schedule)

wood head casing (see details elsewhere)

2x6 wood casing w/AH-182 brick mould

window (see Window Schedule for type, size & design)

6"

5"

1'-1"

5 3/4"

1 1/4"

1/4"

SASH HEIGHT

ROUGH OPENING

DRAWING #

Window Head Detail w/Stone Lintel

SCALE
1 1/2"
1'-0"

WWH040
942

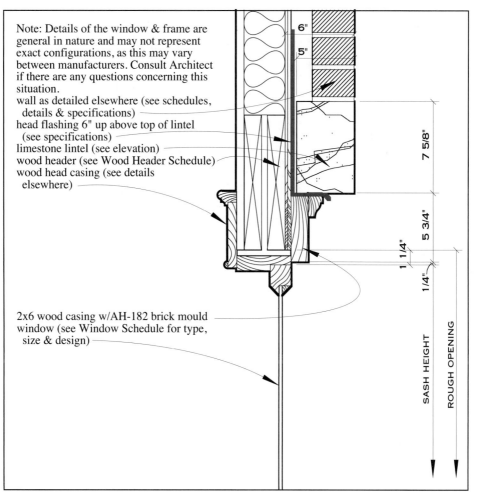

Note: Details of the window & frame are general in nature and may not represent exact configurations, as this may vary between manufacturers. Consult Architect if there are any questions concerning this situation.

wall as detailed elsewhere (see schedules, details & specifications)

head flashing 6" up above top of lintel (see specifications)

limestone lintel (see elevation)

wood header (see Wood Header Schedule)

wood head casing (see details elsewhere)

2x6 wood casing w/AH-182 brick mould window (see Window Schedule for type, size & design)

6"

5"

7 5/8"

5 3/4"

1 1/4"

1/4"

SASH HEIGHT

ROUGH OPENING

Window Head Detail @ Stone Lintel

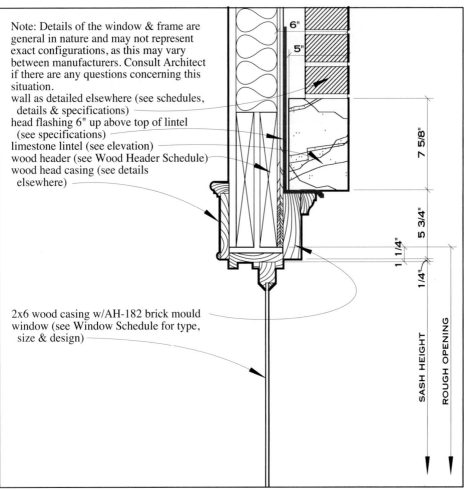

Note: Details of the window & frame are
general in nature and may not represent
exact configurations, as this may vary
between manufacturers. Consult Architect
if there are any questions concerning this
situation.

wall as detailed elsewhere (see schedules,
    details & specifications)

head flashing 6" up above top of lintel
    (see specifications)

limestone lintel (see elevation)

wood header (see Wood Header Schedule)

wood head casing (see details
    elsewhere)

2x6 wood casing w/AH-182 brick mould
window (see Window Schedule for type,
    size & design)

6"

5"

7 5/8"

5 3/4"

1 1/4"

1/4"

SASH HEIGHT

ROUGH OPENING

Window Head Detail w/Stone Lintel

SCALE

1 1/2"
1'-0"

WWH042
944

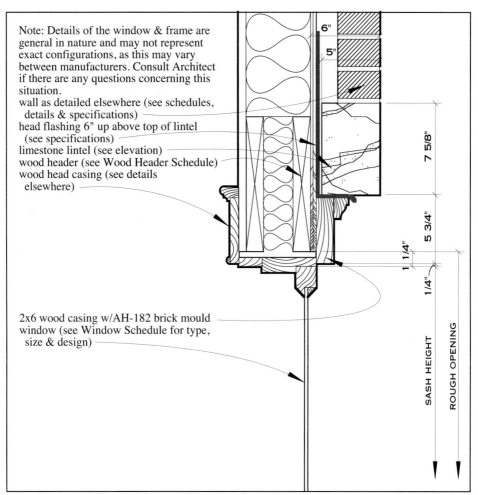

Note: Details of the window & frame are
general in nature and may not represent
exact configurations, as this may vary
between manufacturers. Consult Architect
if there are any questions concerning this
situation.

wall as detailed elsewhere (see schedules,
  details & specifications)

head flashing 6" up above top of lintel
  (see specifications)

limestone lintel (see elevation)

wood header (see Wood Header Schedule)

wood head casing (see details
  elsewhere)

2x6 wood casing w/AH-182 brick mould
window (see Window Schedule for type,
  size & design)

6"

5"

7 5/8"

5 3/4"

1 1/4"

1/4"

SASH HEIGHT

ROUGH OPENING

Window Head Detail w/Stone Lintel

DRAWING #

SCALE
1 1/2"
1'-0"

WWH043
945

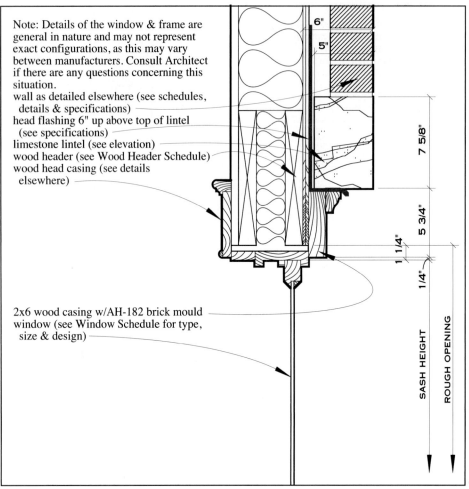

Note: Details of the window & frame are general in nature and may not represent exact configurations, as this may vary between manufacturers. Consult Architect if there are any questions concerning this situation.

wall as detailed elsewhere (see schedules, details & specifications)

head flashing 6" up above top of lintel (see specifications)

limestone lintel (see elevation)

wood header (see Wood Header Schedule)

wood head casing (see details elsewhere)

2x6 wood casing w/AH-182 brick mould

window (see Window Schedule for type, size & design)

6"

5"

7 5/8"

5 3/4"

1 1/4"

1/4"

SASH HEIGHT

ROUGH OPENING

DRAWING #

Window Head Detail w/Stone Lintel

SCALE

1 1/2"
1'-0"

WWH044
946

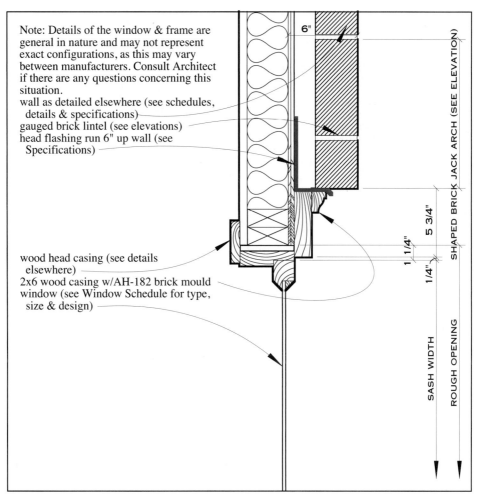

Note: Details of the window & frame are general in nature and may not represent exact configurations, as this may vary between manufacturers. Consult Architect if there are any questions concerning this situation.

wall as detailed elsewhere (see schedules, details & specifications)

gauged brick lintel (see elevations)

head flashing run 6" up wall (see Specifications)

wood head casing (see details elsewhere)

2x6 wood casing w/AH-182 brick mould window (see Window Schedule for type, size & design)

6"

SHAPED BRICK JACK ARCH (SEE ELEVATION)

5 3/4"

1 1/4"

1/4"

SASH WIDTH

ROUGH OPENING

DRAWING #

Window Head Detail @ Brick Veneer

SCALE
1 1/2
1'-0"

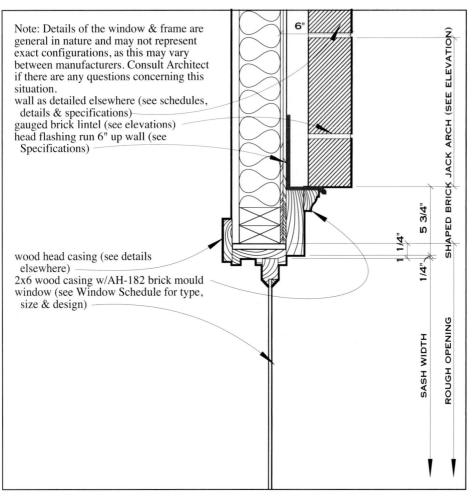

Note: Details of the window & frame are
general in nature and may not represent
exact configurations, as this may vary
between manufacturers. Consult Architect
if there are any questions concerning this
situation.

wall as detailed elsewhere (see schedules,
  details & specifications)

gauged brick lintel (see elevations)

head flashing run 6" up wall (see
  Specifications)

6"

SHAPED BRICK JACK ARCH (SEE ELEVATION)

5 3/4"

1 1/4"

1/4"

wood head casing (see details
  elsewhere)

2x6 wood casing w/AH-182 brick mould
window (see Window Schedule for type,
size & design)

SASH WIDTH

ROUGH OPENING

DRAWING #

Window Head Detail @ Brick Veneer

SCALE
1 1/2
1'-0"

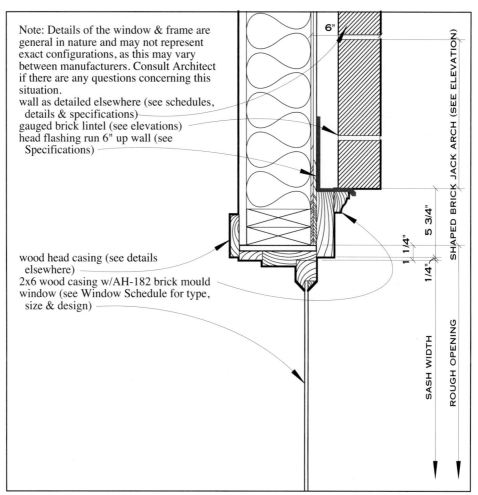

Note: Details of the window & frame are general in nature and may not represent exact configurations, as this may vary between manufacturers. Consult Architect if there are any questions concerning this situation.

wall as detailed elsewhere (see schedules, details & specifications)

gauged brick lintel (see elevations)

head flashing run 6" up wall (see Specifications)

wood head casing (see details elsewhere)

2x6 wood casing w/AH-182 brick mould

window (see Window Schedule for type, size & design)

6"

SHAPED BRICK JACK ARCH (SEE ELEVATION)

5 3/4"

1 1/4"

1/4"

SASH WIDTH

ROUGH OPENING

Window Head Detail @ Brick Veneer

SCALE
1 1/2
1'-0"

DRAWING #

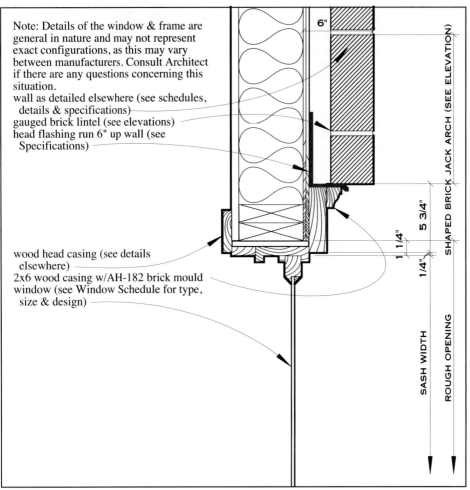

Note: Details of the window & frame are general in nature and may not represent exact configurations, as this may vary between manufacturers. Consult Architect if there are any questions concerning this situation.

wall as detailed elsewhere (see schedules, details & specifications)

gauged brick lintel (see elevations)

head flashing run 6" up wall (see Specifications)

6"

SHAPED BRICK JACK ARCH (SEE ELEVATION)

wood head casing (see details elsewhere)

2x6 wood casing w/AH-182 brick mould window (see Window Schedule for type, size & design)

5 3/4"

1 1/4"

1/4"

SASH WIDTH

ROUGH OPENING

Window Head Detail @ Brick Veneer

SCALE
1 1/2
1'-0"

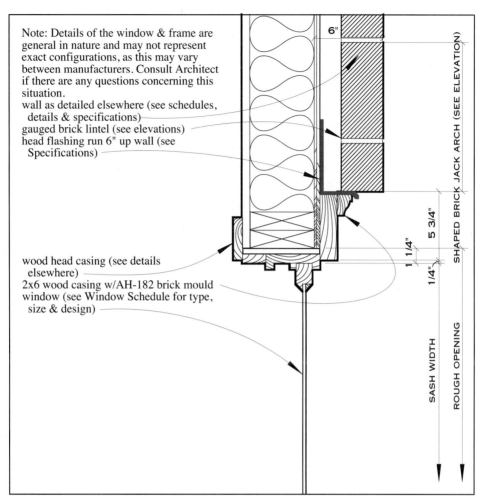

Note: Details of the window & frame are general in nature and may not represent exact configurations, as this may vary between manufacturers. Consult Architect if there are any questions concerning this situation.

wall as detailed elsewhere (see schedules, details & specifications)

gauged brick lintel (see elevations)

head flashing run 6" up wall (see Specifications)

6"

SHAPED BRICK JACK ARCH (SEE ELEVATION)

5 3/4"

1 1/4"

1/4"

wood head casing (see details elsewhere)

2x6 wood casing w/AH-182 brick mould window (see Window Schedule for type, size & design)

SASH WIDTH

ROUGH OPENING

| DRAWING # | Window Head Detail @ Brick Veneer | SCALE 1 1/2" / 1'-0" |

WWH049
951

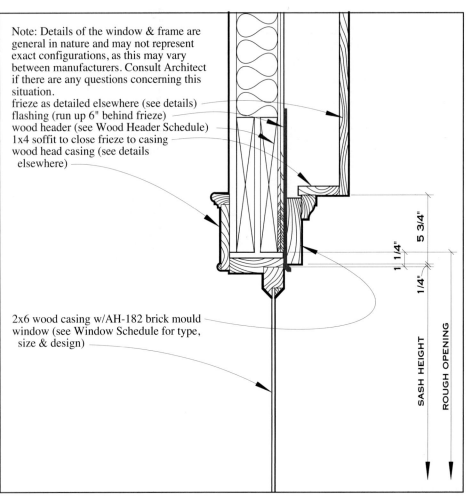

Note: Details of the window & frame are
general in nature and may not represent
exact configurations, as this may vary
between manufacturers. Consult Architect
if there are any questions concerning this
situation.

frieze as detailed elsewhere (see details)
flashing (run up 6" behind frieze)
wood header (see Wood Header Schedule)
1x4 soffit to close frieze to casing
wood head casing (see details
 elsewhere)

2x6 wood casing w/AH-182 brick mould
window (see Window Schedule for type,
 size & design)

5 3/4"

1 1/4"

1/4"

SASH HEIGHT

ROUGH OPENING

DRAWING #

Window Head Detail @ Frieze

SCALE

1 1/2"
1'-0"

WWH050
952

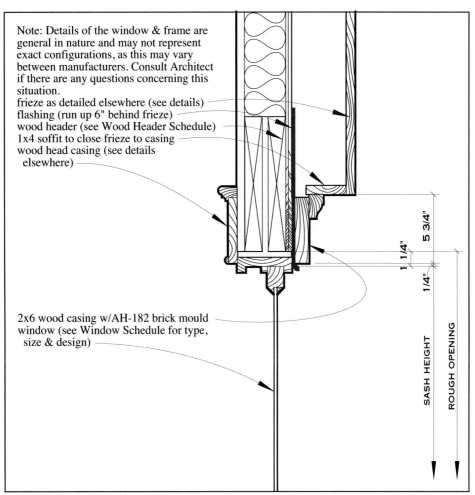

Note: Details of the window & frame are general in nature and may not represent exact configurations, as this may vary between manufacturers. Consult Architect if there are any questions concerning this situation.

frieze as detailed elsewhere (see details)
flashing (run up 6" behind frieze)
wood header (see Wood Header Schedule)
1x4 soffit to close frieze to casing
wood head casing (see details elsewhere)

2x6 wood casing w/AH-182 brick mould
window (see Window Schedule for type, size & design)

5 3/4"

1 1/4"

1/4"

SASH HEIGHT

ROUGH OPENING

Window Head Detail @ Frieze

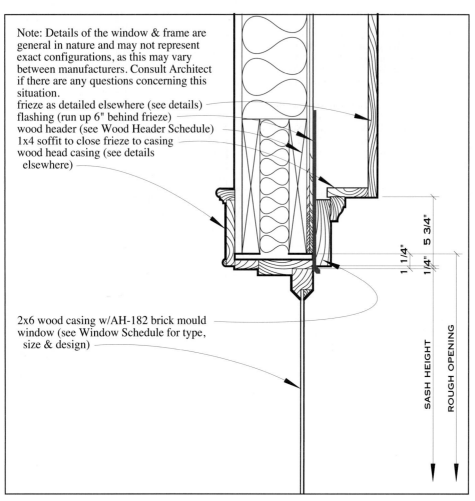

Note: Details of the window & frame are
general in nature and may not represent
exact configurations, as this may vary
between manufacturers. Consult Architect
if there are any questions concerning this
situation.
frieze as detailed elsewhere (see details)
flashing (run up 6" behind frieze)
wood header (see Wood Header Schedule)
1x4 soffit to close frieze to casing
wood head casing (see details
  elsewhere)

2x6 wood casing w/AH-182 brick mould
window (see Window Schedule for type,
  size & design)

1 1/4"

5 3/4"

1/4"

SASH HEIGHT

ROUGH OPENING

Window Head Detail @ Frieze

SCALE
1 1/2"
1'-0"

WWH052
954

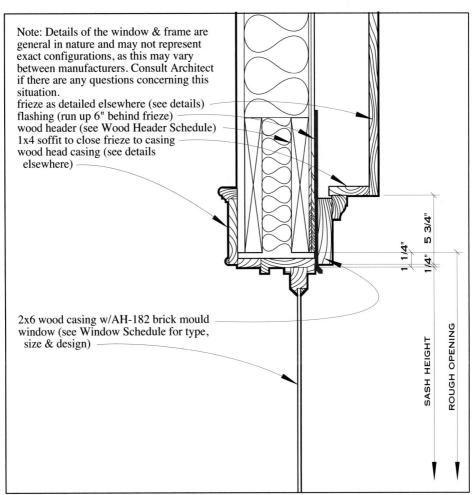

Note: Details of the window & frame are general in nature and may not represent exact configurations, as this may vary between manufacturers. Consult Architect if there are any questions concerning this situation.

frieze as detailed elsewhere (see details)

flashing (run up 6" behind frieze)

wood header (see Wood Header Schedule)

1x4 soffit to close frieze to casing

wood head casing (see details elsewhere)

2x6 wood casing w/AH-182 brick mould

window (see Window Schedule for type, size & design)

1 1/4"

5 3/4"

1/4"

SASH HEIGHT

ROUGH OPENING

Window Head Detail @ Frieze

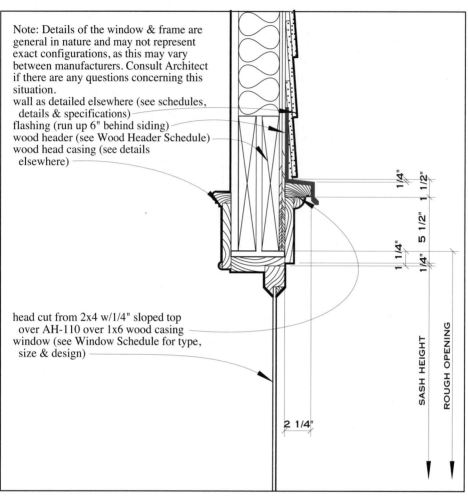

Note: Details of the window & frame are general in nature and may not represent exact configurations, as this may vary between manufacturers. Consult Architect if there are any questions concerning this situation.

wall as detailed elsewhere (see schedules, details & specifications)

flashing (run up 6" behind siding)

wood header (see Wood Header Schedule)

wood head casing (see details elsewhere)

head cut from 2x4 w/1/4" sloped top over AH-110 over 1x6 wood casing

window (see Window Schedule for type, size & design)

1/4"

1 1/2"

1/4"

5 1/2"

1 1/4"

SASH HEIGHT

ROUGH OPENING

2 1/4"

DRAWING #

Window Head Detail

SCALE

1 1/2"
1'-0"

WWH063
956

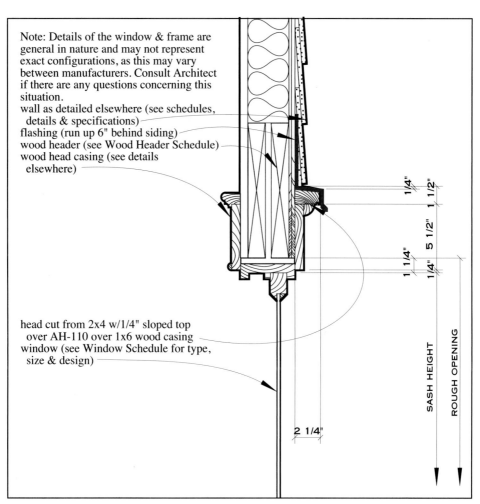

Note: Details of the window & frame are general in nature and may not represent exact configurations, as this may vary between manufacturers. Consult Architect if there are any questions concerning this situation.

wall as detailed elsewhere (see schedules, details & specifications)

flashing (run up 6" behind siding)

wood header (see Wood Header Schedule)

wood head casing (see details elsewhere)

head cut from 2x4 w/1/4" sloped top over AH-110 over 1x6 wood casing

window (see Window Schedule for type, size & design)

1/4" 1/2" 1 1/2"

5 1/2"

1 1/4" 1/4"

2 1/4"

SASH HEIGHT

ROUGH OPENING

Window Head Detail

SCALE
1 1/2"
1'-0"

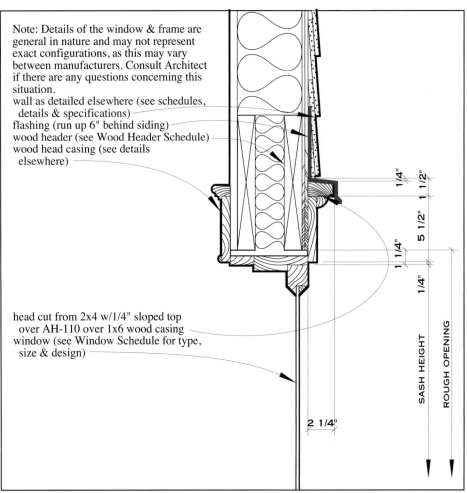

Note: Details of the window & frame are
general in nature and may not represent
exact configurations, as this may vary
between manufacturers. Consult Architect
if there are any questions concerning this
situation.

wall as detailed elsewhere (see schedules,
   details & specifications)

flashing (run up 6" behind siding)

wood header (see Wood Header Schedule)

wood head casing (see details
   elsewhere)

head cut from 2x4 w/1/4" sloped top
   over AH-110 over 1x6 wood casing

window (see Window Schedule for type,
   size & design)

1/4"

1 1/2"

1/4"

5 1/2"

1 1/4"

1/4"

SASH HEIGHT

ROUGH OPENING

2 1/4"

DRAWING #

Window Head Detail

SCALE

1 1/2"
1'-0"

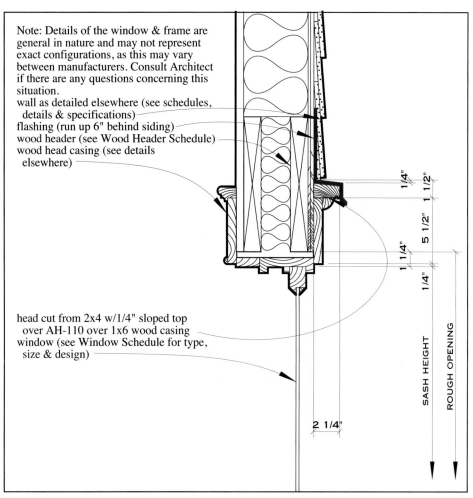

Note: Details of the window & frame are general in nature and may not represent exact configurations, as this may vary between manufacturers. Consult Architect if there are any questions concerning this situation.

wall as detailed elsewhere (see schedules, details & specifications)

flashing (run up 6" behind siding)

wood header (see Wood Header Schedule)

wood head casing (see details elsewhere)

head cut from 2x4 w/1/4" sloped top over AH-110 over 1x6 wood casing

window (see Window Schedule for type, size & design)

1/4"

1 1/2"

5 1/2"

1 1/4"

1/4"

2 1/4"

SASH HEIGHT

ROUGH OPENING

Window Head Detail

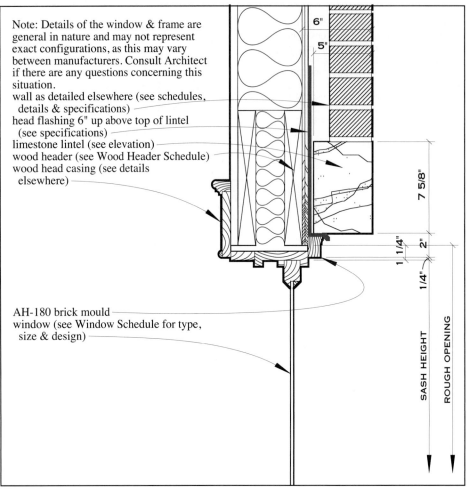

Note: Details of the window & frame are general in nature and may not represent exact configurations, as this may vary between manufacturers. Consult Architect if there are any questions concerning this situation.

wall as detailed elsewhere (see schedules, details & specifications)

head flashing 6" up above top of lintel (see specifications)

limestone lintel (see elevation)

wood header (see Wood Header Schedule)

wood head casing (see details elsewhere)

AH-180 brick mould

window (see Window Schedule for type, size & design)

6"

5"

7 5/8"

1 1/4"

2"

1/4"

SASH HEIGHT

ROUGH OPENING

Window Head Detail w/Stone Lintel

Note: Details of the window & frame are
general in nature and may not represent
exact configurations, as this may vary
between manufacturers. Consult Architect
if there are any questions concerning this
situation
AH-1924 over 1x4 head casing

wall as detailed elsewhere (see schedules,
   details & specifications)

1x4 window casing over head frame cut
   from 1x6

1/4" plate glass stopped to frame w/
   WM937 1 1/4" stops (allow 1/16" air
   space around glass for movement)

3 5/8"

1/4" REVEAL TYPICAL   1 1/4"

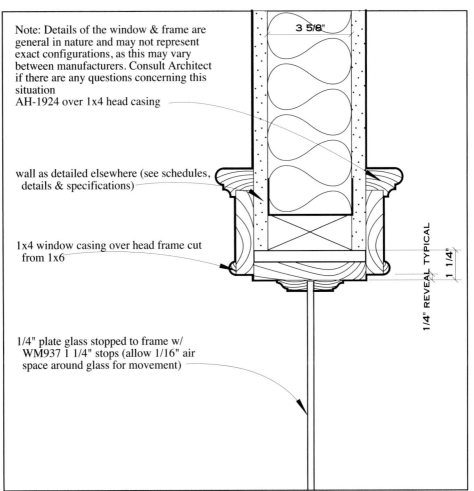

Fixed Window Head Detail

WWH075
961

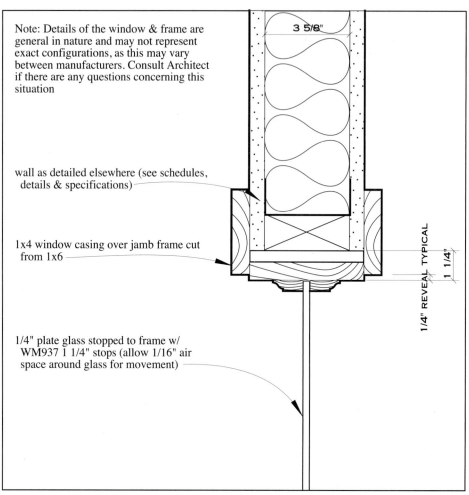

Note: Details of the window & frame are general in nature and may not represent exact configurations, as this may vary between manufacturers. Consult Architect if there are any questions concerning this situation

3 5/8"

wall as detailed elsewhere (see schedules, details & specifications)

1x4 window casing over jamb frame cut from 1x6

1/4" REVEAL TYPICAL

1 1/4"

1/4" plate glass stopped to frame w/ WM937 1 1/4" stops (allow 1/16" air space around glass for movement)

DRAWING #

Fixed Window Head Detail

SCALE
3"
1'-0"

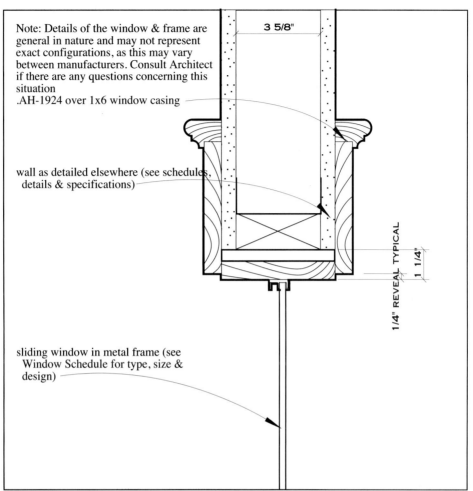

Note: Details of the window & frame are general in nature and may not represent exact configurations, as this may vary between manufacturers. Consult Architect if there are any questions concerning this situation
.AH-1924 over 1x6 window casing

3 5/8"

wall as detailed elsewhere (see schedules, details & specifications)

1/4" REVEAL TYPICAL

1 1/4"

sliding window in metal frame (see Window Schedule for type, size & design)

Window Head Detail w/ Wood Casing

SCALE
3"
1'-O"

WWH077
963

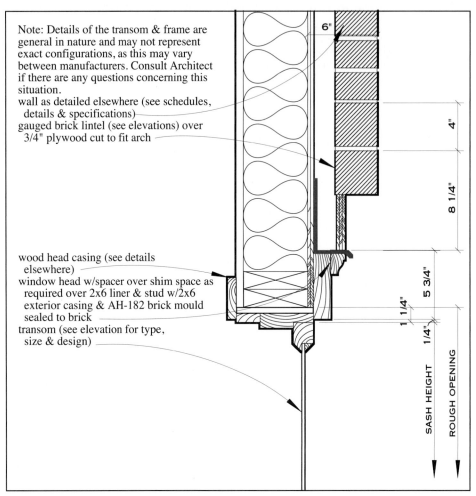

Note: Details of the transom & frame are general in nature and may not represent exact configurations, as this may vary between manufacturers. Consult Architect if there are any questions concerning this situation.

wall as detailed elsewhere (see schedules, details & specifications)

gauged brick lintel (see elevations) over 3/4" plywood cut to fit arch

6"

4"

8 1/4"

wood head casing (see details elsewhere)

window head w/spacer over shim space as required over 2x6 liner & stud w/2x6 exterior casing & AH-182 brick mould sealed to brick

transom (see elevation for type, size & design)

5 3/4"

1 1/4"

1/4"

SASH HEIGHT

ROUGH OPENING

DRAWING #

Transom Detail @ Brick Veneer

SCALE
1 1/2
1'-O"

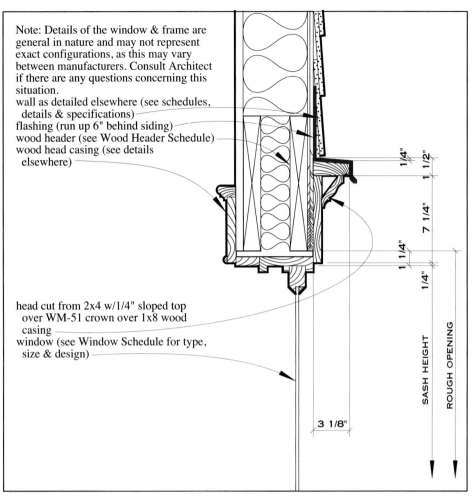

Note: Details of the window & frame are general in nature and may not represent exact configurations, as this may vary between manufacturers. Consult Architect if there are any questions concerning this situation.

wall as detailed elsewhere (see schedules, details & specifications)

flashing (run up 6" behind siding)

wood header (see Wood Header Schedule)

wood head casing (see details elsewhere)

head cut from 2x4 w/1/4" sloped top over WM-51 crown over 1x8 wood casing

window (see Window Schedule for type, size & design)

1/4"

1 1/2"

7 1/4"

1 1/4"

1/4"

SASH HEIGHT

ROUGH OPENING

3 1/8"

Window Head Detail

DRAWING #

SCALE

1 1/2"
1'-0"

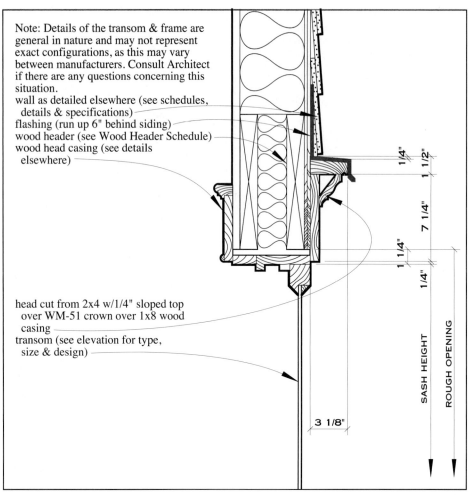

Note: Details of the transom & frame are
general in nature and may not represent
exact configurations, as this may vary
between manufacturers. Consult Architect
if there are any questions concerning this
situation.
wall as detailed elsewhere (see schedules,
　details & specifications)
flashing (run up 6" behind siding)
wood header (see Wood Header Schedule)
wood head casing (see details
　elsewhere)

head cut from 2x4 w/1/4" sloped top
　over WM-51 crown over 1x8 wood
　casing
transom (see elevation for type,
　size & design)

1/4"

1 1/2"

7 1/4"

1 1/4"

1/4"

SASH HEIGHT

ROUGH OPENING

3 1/8"

Transom Head Detail

WWH081
966

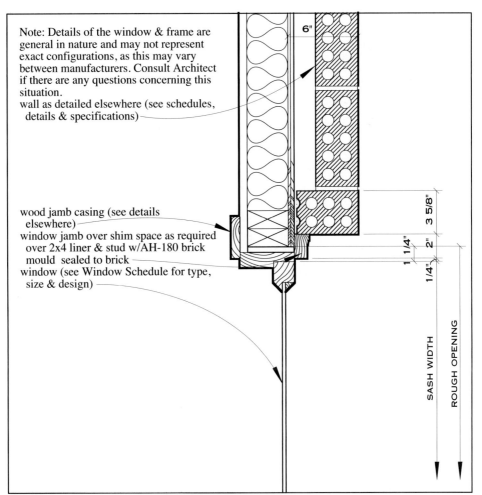

Note: Details of the window & frame are general in nature and may not represent exact configurations, as this may vary between manufacturers. Consult Architect if there are any questions concerning this situation.

wall as detailed elsewhere (see schedules, details & specifications)

6"

wood jamb casing (see details elsewhere)

window jamb over shim space as required over 2x4 liner & stud w/AH-180 brick mould sealed to brick

window (see Window Schedule for type, size & design)

3 5/8"

1 1/4"

2"

1/4"

SASH WIDTH

ROUGH OPENING

DRAWING #

Window Jamb Detail @ Brick Veneer

SCALE

1 1/2
1'-0"

WWJ002
967

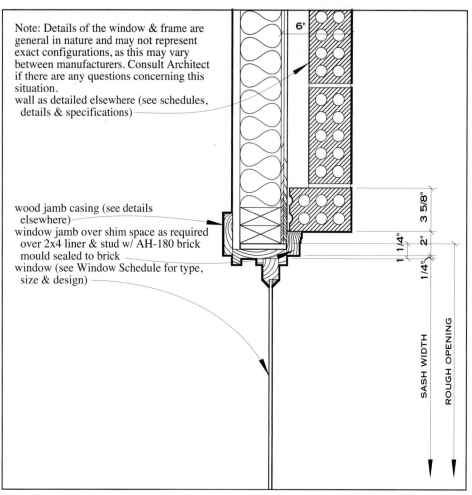

Note: Details of the window & frame are general in nature and may not represent exact configurations, as this may vary between manufacturers. Consult Architect if there are any questions concerning this situation.

wall as detailed elsewhere (see schedules, details & specifications)

6"

wood jamb casing (see details elsewhere)

window jamb over shim space as required over 2x4 liner & stud w/ AH-180 brick mould sealed to brick

window (see Window Schedule for type, size & design)

3 5/8"

1 1/4" 2" 1/4"

SASH WIDTH

ROUGH OPENING

Window Jamb Detail @ Brick Veneer

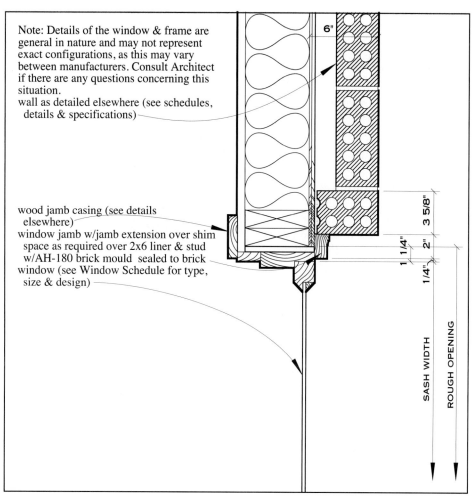

Note: Details of the window & frame are general in nature and may not represent exact configurations, as this may vary between manufacturers. Consult Architect if there are any questions concerning this situation.

wall as detailed elsewhere (see schedules, details & specifications)

6"

3 5/8"

1 1/4"

2"

wood jamb casing (see details elsewhere)

window jamb w/jamb extension over shim space as required over 2x6 liner & stud w/AH-180 brick mould sealed to brick

window (see Window Schedule for type, size & design)

1/4"

SASH WIDTH

ROUGH OPENING

DRAWING #

Window Jamb Detail @ Brick Veneer

SCALE
1 1/2
1'-0"

WWJ004
969

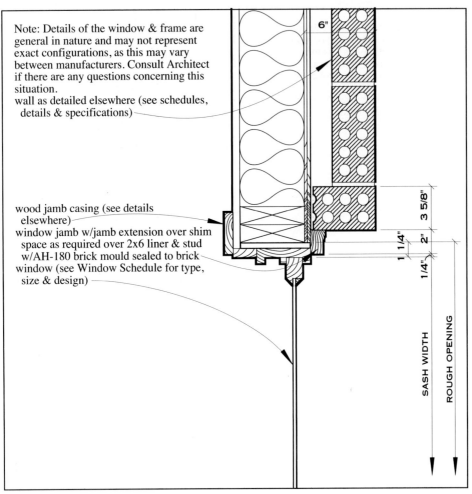

Note: Details of the window & frame are general in nature and may not represent exact configurations, as this may vary between manufacturers. Consult Architect if there are any questions concerning this situation.

wall as detailed elsewhere (see schedules, details & specifications)

6"

3 5/8"

wood jamb casing (see details elsewhere)

window jamb w/jamb extension over shim space as required over 2x6 liner & stud w/AH-180 brick mould sealed to brick

window (see Window Schedule for type, size & design)

1 1/4"

2"

1/4"

SASH WIDTH

ROUGH OPENING

Window Jamb Detail @ Brick Veneer

WWJ005
970

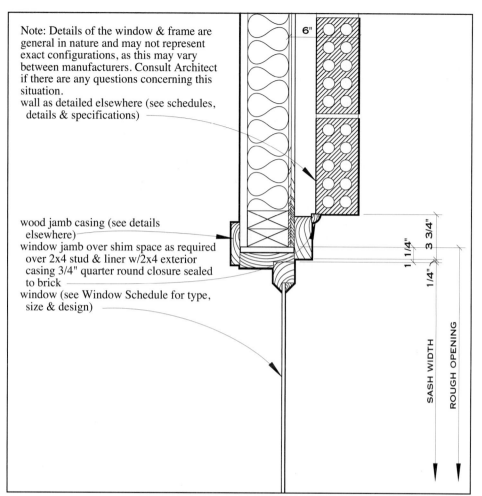

Note: Details of the window & frame are general in nature and may not represent exact configurations, as this may vary between manufacturers. Consult Architect if there are any questions concerning this situation.

wall as detailed elsewhere (see schedules, details & specifications)

6"

wood jamb casing (see details elsewhere)

window jamb over shim space as required over 2x4 stud & liner w/2x4 exterior casing 3/4" quarter round closure sealed to brick

window (see Window Schedule for type, size & design)

1 1/4"

3 3/4"

1/4"

SASH WIDTH

ROUGH OPENING

Window Jamb Detail @ Brick Veneer

SCALE
1 1/2
1'-0"

WWJ008
971

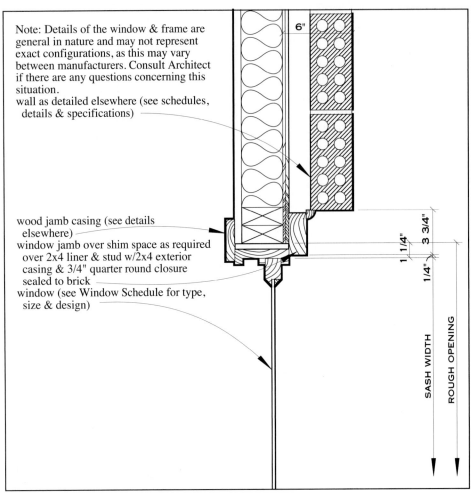

Note: Details of the window & frame are general in nature and may not represent exact configurations, as this may vary between manufacturers. Consult Architect if there are any questions concerning this situation.

wall as detailed elsewhere (see schedules, details & specifications)

6"

wood jamb casing (see details elsewhere)

window jamb over shim space as required over 2x4 liner & stud w/2x4 exterior casing & 3/4" quarter round closure sealed to brick

window (see Window Schedule for type, size & design)

3 3/4"

1 1/4"

1/4"

SASH WIDTH

ROUGH OPENING

Window Jamb Detail @ Brick Veneer

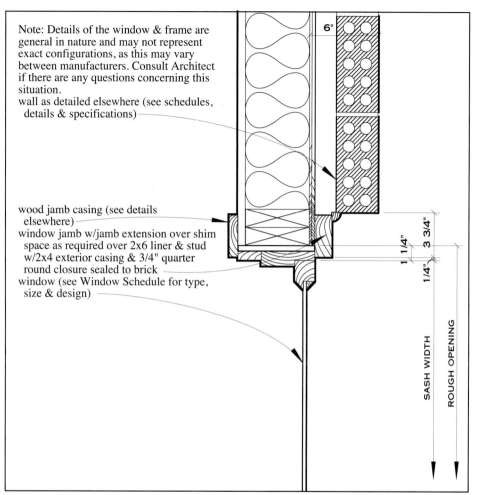

Note: Details of the window & frame are general in nature and may not represent exact configurations, as this may vary between manufacturers. Consult Architect if there are any questions concerning this situation.

wall as detailed elsewhere (see schedules, details & specifications)

6"

wood jamb casing (see details elsewhere)

window jamb w/jamb extension over shim space as required over 2x6 liner & stud w/2x4 exterior casing & 3/4" quarter round closure sealed to brick

window (see Window Schedule for type, size & design)

1 1/4"

3 3/4"

1/4"

SASH WIDTH

ROUGH OPENING

Window Jamb Detail @ Brick Veneer

SCALE
1 1/2
1'-0"

WWJ010

973

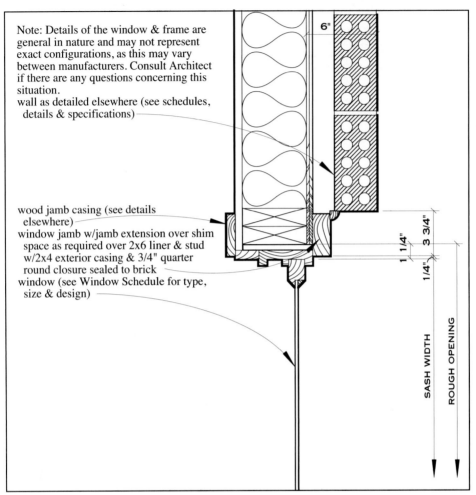

Note: Details of the window & frame are
general in nature and may not represent
exact configurations, as this may vary
between manufacturers. Consult Architect
if there are any questions concerning this
situation.
wall as detailed elsewhere (see schedules,
 details & specifications)

6"

wood jamb casing (see details
 elsewhere)
window jamb w/jamb extension over shim
 space as required over 2x6 liner & stud
 w/2x4 exterior casing & 3/4" quarter
 round closure sealed to brick
window (see Window Schedule for type,
 size & design)

3 3/4"

1 1/4"

1/4"

SASH WIDTH

ROUGH OPENING

DRAWING #

Window Jamb Detail @ Brick Veneer

SCALE
1 1/2
1'-0"

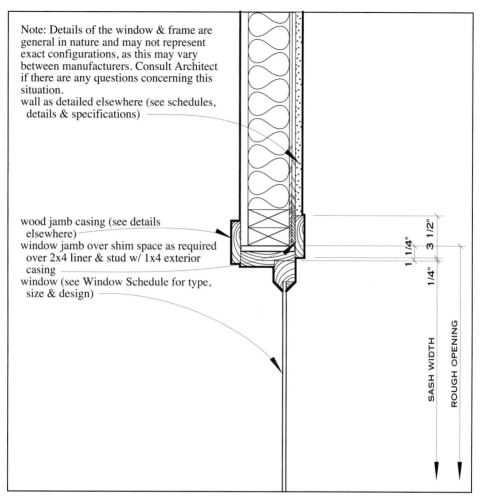

Note: Details of the window & frame are general in nature and may not represent exact configurations, as this may vary between manufacturers. Consult Architect if there are any questions concerning this situation.

wall as detailed elsewhere (see schedules, details & specifications)

wood jamb casing (see details elsewhere)

window jamb over shim space as required over 2x4 liner & stud w/ 1x4 exterior casing

window (see Window Schedule for type, size & design)

1 1/4"

3 1/2"

1/4"

SASH WIDTH

ROUGH OPENING

Window Jamb Detail

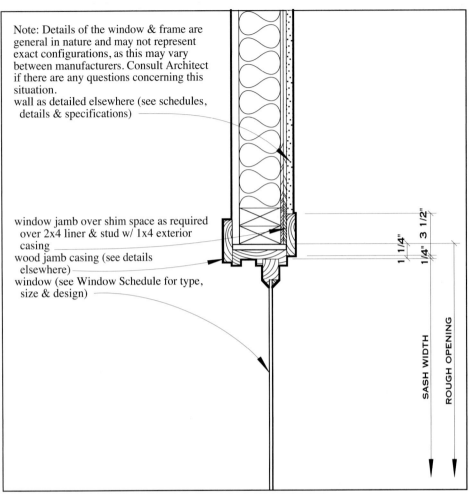

Note: Details of the window & frame are general in nature and may not represent exact configurations, as this may vary between manufacturers. Consult Architect if there are any questions concerning this situation.

wall as detailed elsewhere (see schedules, details & specifications)

window jamb over shim space as required over 2x4 liner & stud w/ 1x4 exterior casing

wood jamb casing (see details elsewhere)

window (see Window Schedule for type, size & design)

1 1/4"

3 1/2"

1/4"

SASH WIDTH

ROUGH OPENING

Window Jamb Detail

DRAWING #

SCALE

1 1/2

1'-0"

WWJ013
976

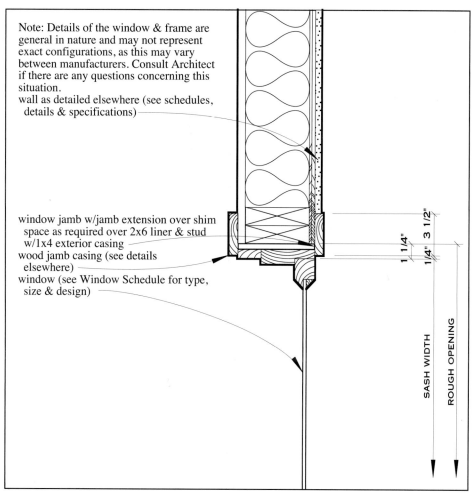

Note: Details of the window & frame are general in nature and may not represent exact configurations, as this may vary between manufacturers. Consult Architect if there are any questions concerning this situation.

wall as detailed elsewhere (see schedules, details & specifications)

window jamb w/jamb extension over shim space as required over 2x6 liner & stud w/1x4 exterior casing

wood jamb casing (see details elsewhere)

window (see Window Schedule for type, size & design)

1 1/4"

1/4"

3 1/2"

SASH WIDTH

ROUGH OPENING

Window Jamb Detail

SCALE
1 1/2
1'-0"

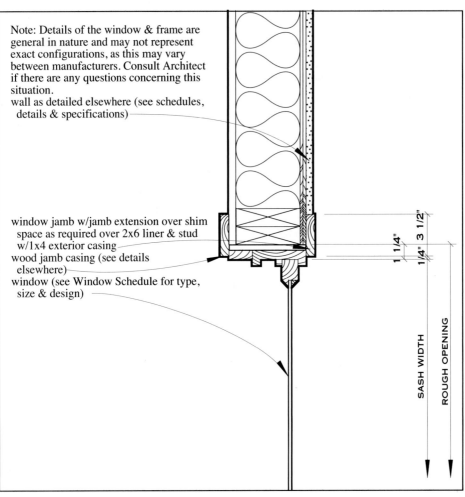

Note: Details of the window & frame are general in nature and may not represent exact configurations, as this may vary between manufacturers. Consult Architect if there are any questions concerning this situation.

wall as detailed elsewhere (see schedules, details & specifications)

window jamb w/jamb extension over shim space as required over 2x6 liner & stud w/1x4 exterior casing

wood jamb casing (see details elsewhere)

window (see Window Schedule for type, size & design)

1 1/4"

3 1/2"

1/4"

SASH WIDTH

ROUGH OPENING

Window Jamb Detail

SCALE
1 1/2"
1'-0"

WWJO15
978

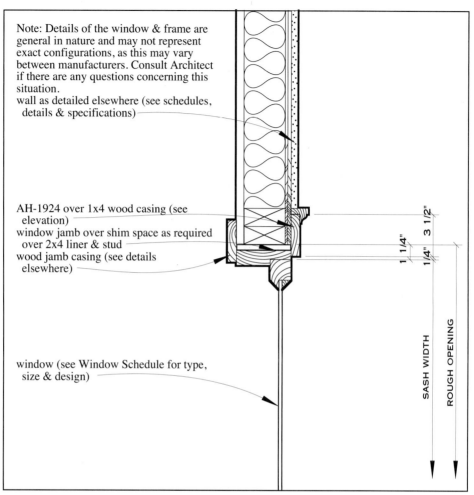

Note: Details of the window & frame are general in nature and may not represent exact configurations, as this may vary between manufacturers. Consult Architect if there are any questions concerning this situation.

wall as detailed elsewhere (see schedules, details & specifications)

AH-1924 over 1x4 wood casing (see elevation)

window jamb over shim space as required over 2x4 liner & stud

wood jamb casing (see details elsewhere)

window (see Window Schedule for type, size & design)

3 1/2"

1 1/4"

1/4"

SASH WIDTH

ROUGH OPENING

DRAWING #

Window Jamb Detail

SCALE
1 1/2
1'-0"

WWJ016
979

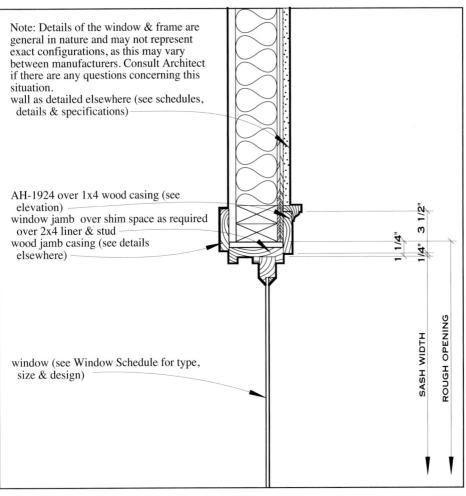

Note: Details of the window & frame are general in nature and may not represent exact configurations, as this may vary between manufacturers. Consult Architect if there are any questions concerning this situation.

wall as detailed elsewhere (see schedules, details & specifications)

AH-1924 over 1x4 wood casing (see elevation)

window jamb over shim space as required over 2x4 liner & stud

wood jamb casing (see details elsewhere)

window (see Window Schedule for type, size & design)

1 1/4"

1/4"

3 1/2"

SASH WIDTH

ROUGH OPENING

Window Jamb Detail

DRAWING #

SCALE

1 1/2
1'-0"

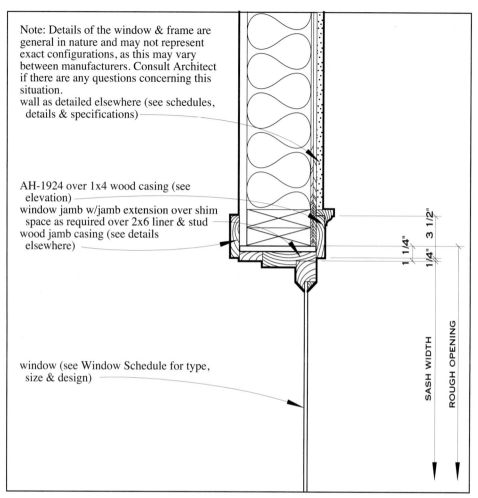

Note: Details of the window & frame are
general in nature and may not represent
exact configurations, as this may vary
between manufacturers. Consult Architect
if there are any questions concerning this
situation.
wall as detailed elsewhere (see schedules,
details & specifications)

AH-1924 over 1x4 wood casing (see
elevation)
window jamb w/jamb extension over shim
space as required over 2x6 liner & stud
wood jamb casing (see details
elsewhere)

window (see Window Schedule for type,
size & design)

3 1/2"

1 1/4"

1/4"

SASH WIDTH

ROUGH OPENING

DRAWING #

Window Jamb Detail

SCALE

1 1/2
1'-0"

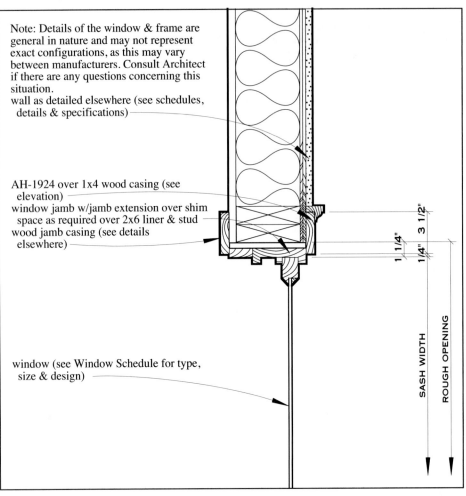

Note: Details of the window & frame are
general in nature and may not represent
exact configurations, as this may vary
between manufacturers. Consult Architect
if there are any questions concerning this
situation.
wall as detailed elsewhere (see schedules,
  details & specifications)

AH-1924 over 1x4 wood casing (see
  elevation)
window jamb w/jamb extension over shim
  space as required over 2x6 liner & stud
wood jamb casing (see details
  elsewhere)

window (see Window Schedule for type,
  size & design)

1 1/4"

1/4"   3 1/2"

SASH WIDTH

ROUGH OPENING

Window Jamb Detail

WWJO19
982

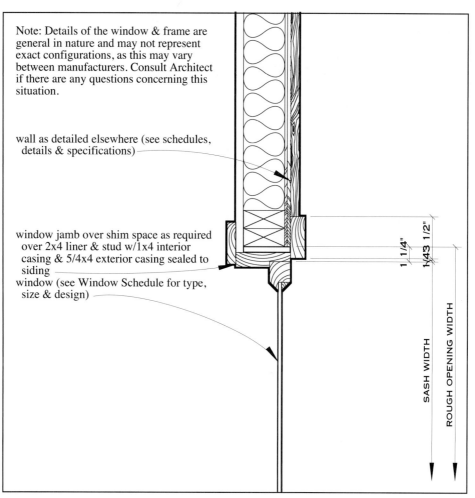

Note: Details of the window & frame are general in nature and may not represent exact configurations, as this may vary between manufacturers. Consult Architect if there are any questions concerning this situation.

wall as detailed elsewhere (see schedules, details & specifications)

window jamb over shim space as required over 2x4 liner & stud w/1x4 interior casing & 5/4x4 exterior casing sealed to siding

window (see Window Schedule for type, size & design)

1 1/4"

43 1/2"

SASH WIDTH

ROUGH OPENING WIDTH

DRAWING #

Window Jamb Detail @ Wood Siding

SCALE

1 1/2 / 1'-0"

WWJ020
983

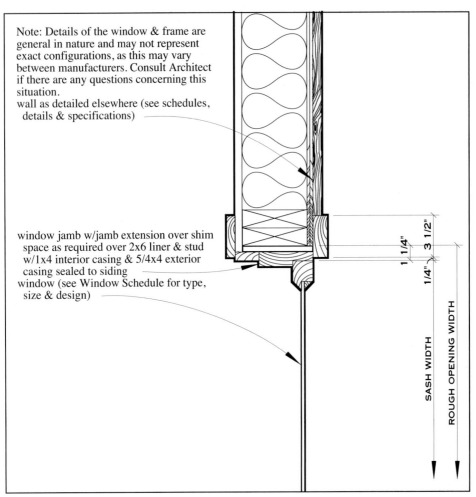

Note: Details of the window & frame are general in nature and may not represent exact configurations, as this may vary between manufacturers. Consult Architect if there are any questions concerning this situation.

wall as detailed elsewhere (see schedules, details & specifications)

window jamb w/jamb extension over shim space as required over 2x6 liner & stud w/1x4 interior casing & 5/4x4 exterior casing sealed to siding

window (see Window Schedule for type, size & design)

3 1/2"

1 1/4"

1/4"

SASH WIDTH

ROUGH OPENING WIDTH

DRAWING #

Window Jamb Detail @ Wood Siding

SCALE

1 1/2 / 1'-0"

WWJ021
984

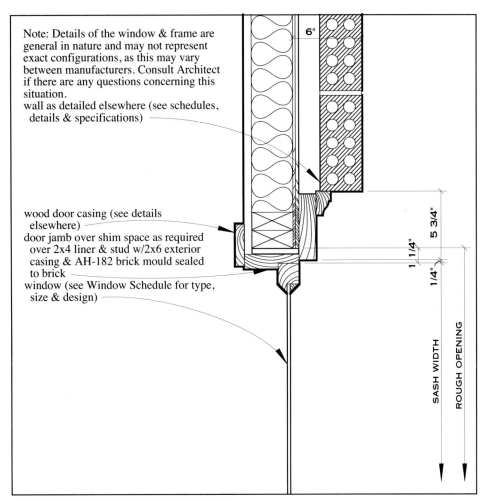

Note: Details of the window & frame are general in nature and may not represent exact configurations, as this may vary between manufacturers. Consult Architect if there are any questions concerning this situation.

wall as detailed elsewhere (see schedules, details & specifications)

6"

wood door casing (see details elsewhere)

door jamb over shim space as required over 2x4 liner & stud w/2x6 exterior casing & AH-182 brick mould sealed to brick

window (see Window Schedule for type, size & design)

5 3/4"

1 1/4"

1/4"

SASH WIDTH

ROUGH OPENING

Window Jamb Detail @ Brick Veneer

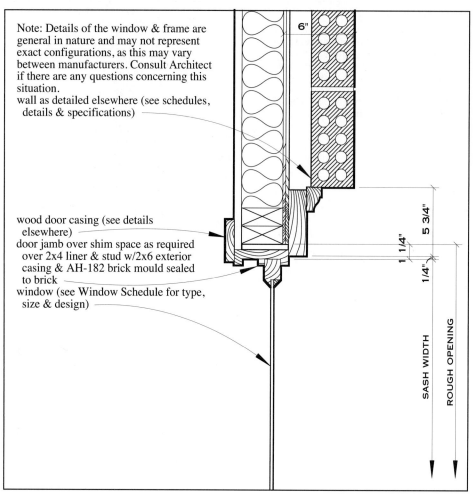

Note: Details of the window & frame are general in nature and may not represent exact configurations, as this may vary between manufacturers. Consult Architect if there are any questions concerning this situation.

wall as detailed elsewhere (see schedules, details & specifications)

wood door casing (see details elsewhere)

door jamb over shim space as required over 2x4 liner & stud w/2x6 exterior casing & AH-182 brick mould sealed to brick

window (see Window Schedule for type, size & design)

6"

5 3/4"

1 1/4"

1/4"

SASH WIDTH

ROUGH OPENING

DRAWING #

Window Jamb Detail @ Brick Veneer

SCALE

1 1/2
1'-0"

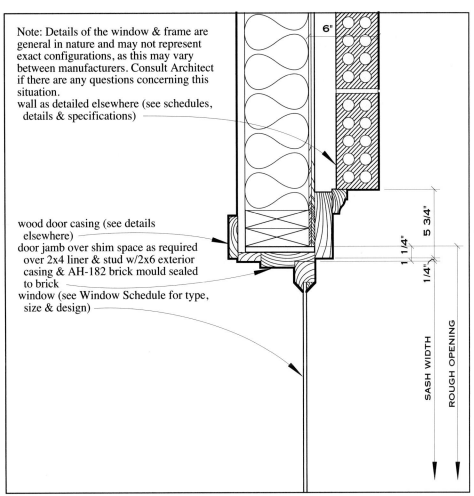

Note: Details of the window & frame are general in nature and may not represent exact configurations, as this may vary between manufacturers. Consult Architect if there are any questions concerning this situation.

wall as detailed elsewhere (see schedules, details & specifications)

6"

wood door casing (see details elsewhere)

door jamb over shim space as required over 2x4 liner & stud w/2x6 exterior casing & AH-182 brick mould sealed to brick

window (see Window Schedule for type, size & design)

5 3/4"

1 1/4"

1/4"

SASH WIDTH

ROUGH OPENING

DRAWING #

Window Jamb Detail @ Brick Veneer

SCALE

1 1/2

1'-0"

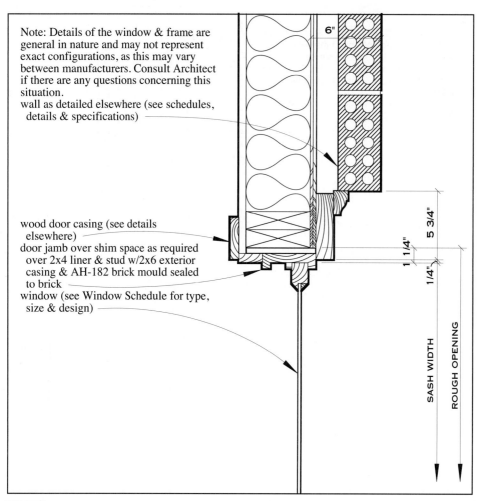

Note: Details of the window & frame are general in nature and may not represent exact configurations, as this may vary between manufacturers. Consult Architect if there are any questions concerning this situation.

wall as detailed elsewhere (see schedules, details & specifications)

6"

wood door casing (see details elsewhere)

door jamb over shim space as required over 2x4 liner & stud w/2x6 exterior casing & AH-182 brick mould sealed to brick

window (see Window Schedule for type, size & design)

5 3/4"

1 1/4"

1/4"

SASH WIDTH

ROUGH OPENING

DRAWING #

Window Jamb Detail @ Brick Veneer

SCALE
1 1/2
1'-0"

WWJ025
988

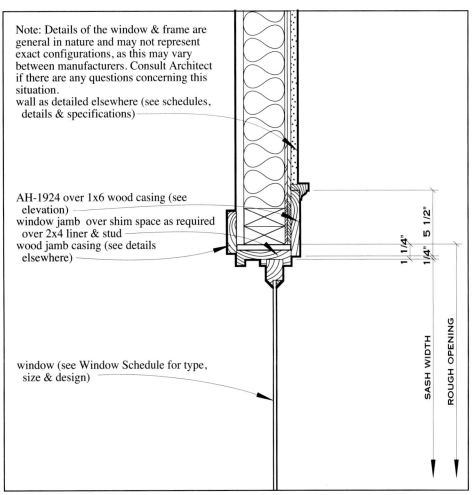

Note: Details of the window & frame are general in nature and may not represent exact configurations, as this may vary between manufacturers. Consult Architect if there are any questions concerning this situation.

wall as detailed elsewhere (see schedules, details & specifications)

AH-1924 over 1x6 wood casing (see elevation)

window jamb over shim space as required over 2x4 liner & stud

wood jamb casing (see details elsewhere)

window (see Window Schedule for type, size & design)

1 1/4"

5 1/2"

1/4"

SASH WIDTH

ROUGH OPENING

Window Jamb Detail

DRAWING #

SCALE
1 1/2
1'-0"

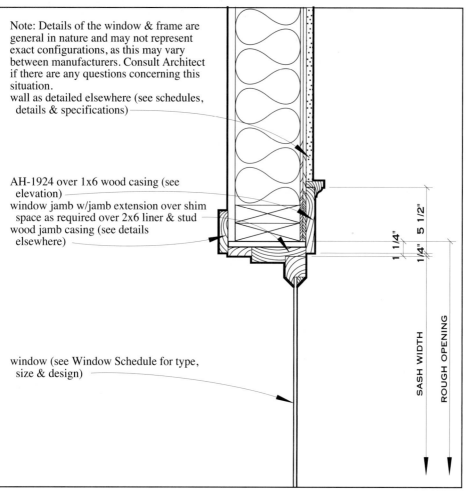

Note: Details of the window & frame are general in nature and may not represent exact configurations, as this may vary between manufacturers. Consult Architect if there are any questions concerning this situation.

wall as detailed elsewhere (see schedules, details & specifications)

AH-1924 over 1x6 wood casing (see elevation)

window jamb w/jamb extension over shim space as required over 2x6 liner & stud

wood jamb casing (see details elsewhere)

window (see Window Schedule for type, size & design)

5 1/2"

1 1/4"

1/4"

SASH WIDTH

ROUGH OPENING

DRAWING #

Window Jamb Detail

SCALE
1 1/2"
1'-0"

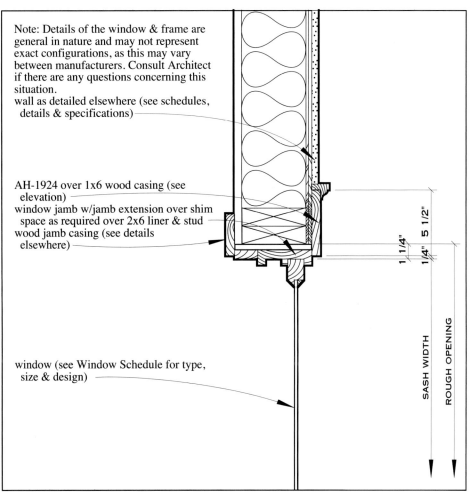

Note: Details of the window & frame are general in nature and may not represent exact configurations, as this may vary between manufacturers. Consult Architect if there are any questions concerning this situation.
wall as detailed elsewhere (see schedules, details & specifications)

AH-1924 over 1x6 wood casing (see elevation)
window jamb w/jamb extension over shim space as required over 2x6 liner & stud
wood jamb casing (see details elsewhere)

window (see Window Schedule for type, size & design)

1 1/4"

1/4"

5 1/2"

SASH WIDTH

ROUGH OPENING

DRAWING #

Window Jamb Detail

SCALE
1 1/2"
1'-0"

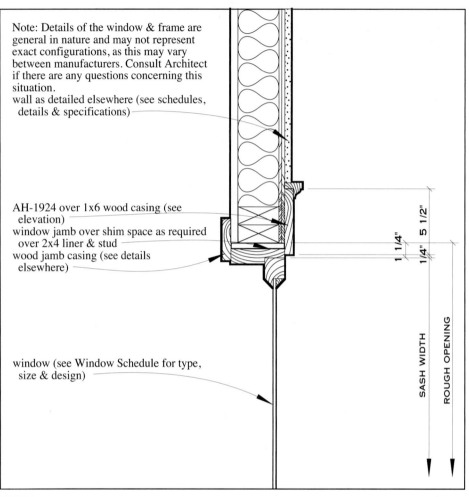

Note: Details of the window & frame are general in nature and may not represent exact configurations, as this may vary between manufacturers. Consult Architect if there are any questions concerning this situation.

wall as detailed elsewhere (see schedules, details & specifications)

AH-1924 over 1x6 wood casing (see elevation)

window jamb over shim space as required over 2x4 liner & stud

wood jamb casing (see details elsewhere)

window (see Window Schedule for type, size & design)

1 1/4"

1/4"

5 1/2"

SASH WIDTH

ROUGH OPENING

Window Jamb Detail

DRAWING #

SCALE
1 1/2
1'-0"

WWJ031
992

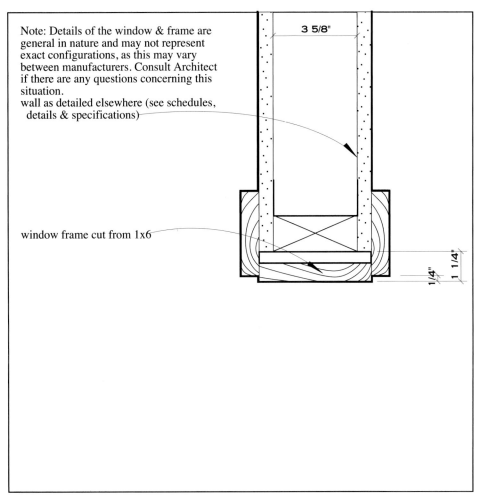

Note: Details of the window & frame are general in nature and may not represent exact configurations, as this may vary between manufacturers. Consult Architect if there are any questions concerning this situation.
wall as detailed elsewhere (see schedules, details & specifications)

3 5/8"

window frame cut from 1x6

1 1/4"

1/4"

Window Jamb Detail w/ Wood Casing

SCALE
3"
1'-0"

WWJ033
993

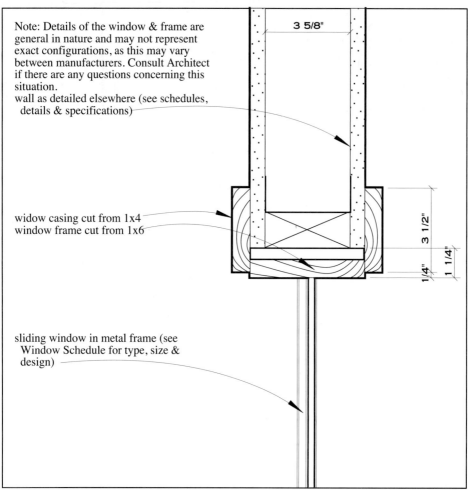

Note: Details of the window & frame are general in nature and may not represent exact configurations, as this may vary between manufacturers. Consult Architect if there are any questions concerning this situation.

wall as detailed elsewhere (see schedules, details & specifications)

3 5/8"

widow casing cut from 1x4
window frame cut from 1x6

3 1/2"

1/4" 1 1/4"

sliding window in metal frame (see Window Schedule for type, size & design)

Window Jamb Detail w/ Wood Casing

SCALE
3"
1'-0"

DRAWING #

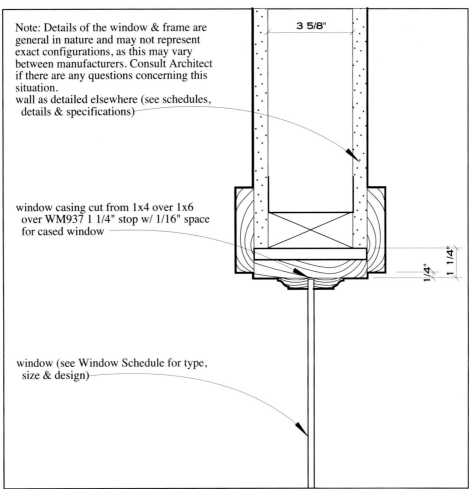

Note: Details of the window & frame are general in nature and may not represent exact configurations, as this may vary between manufacturers. Consult Architect if there are any questions concerning this situation.
wall as detailed elsewhere (see schedules, details & specifications)

3 5/8"

window casing cut from 1x4 over 1x6 over WM937 1 1/4" stop w/ 1/16" space for cased window

1 1/4"

1/4"

window (see Window Schedule for type, size & design)

 DRAWING #

Window Jamb Detail w/ Wood Casing

 SCALE
3"
1'-0"

WWJ035
995

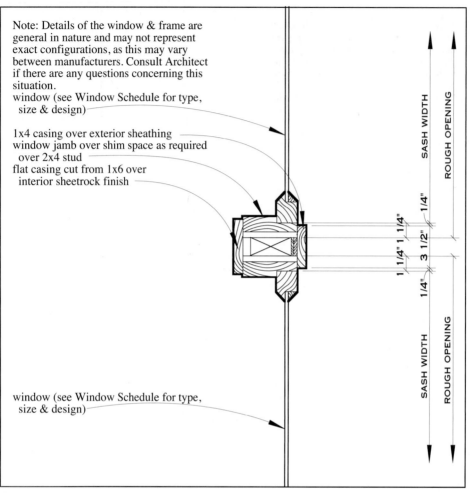

Note: Details of the window & frame are general in nature and may not represent exact configurations, as this may vary between manufacturers. Consult Architect if there are any questions concerning this situation.

window (see Window Schedule for type, size & design)

1x4 casing over exterior sheathing
window jamb over shim space as required over 2x4 stud
flat casing cut from 1x6 over interior sheetrock finish

window (see Window Schedule for type, size & design)

SASH WIDTH

ROUGH OPENING

1/4"

1 1/4" 1 1/4"

3 1/2"

1/4"

SASH WIDTH

ROUGH OPENING

Window Mullion Detail

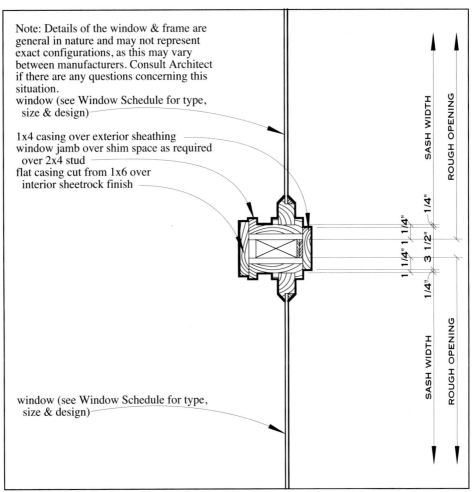

Note: Details of the window & frame are
general in nature and may not represent
exact configurations, as this may vary
between manufacturers. Consult Architect
if there are any questions concerning this
situation.
window (see Window Schedule for type,
  size & design)

1x4 casing over exterior sheathing
window jamb over shim space as required
  over 2x4 stud
flat casing cut from 1x6 over
  interior sheetrock finish

window (see Window Schedule for type,
  size & design)

SASH WIDTH

ROUGH OPENING

1/4"

1 1/4" 1 1/4"

3 1/2"

1/4"

SASH WIDTH

ROUGH OPENING

Window Mullion Detail

SCALE
1 1/2
1'-O"

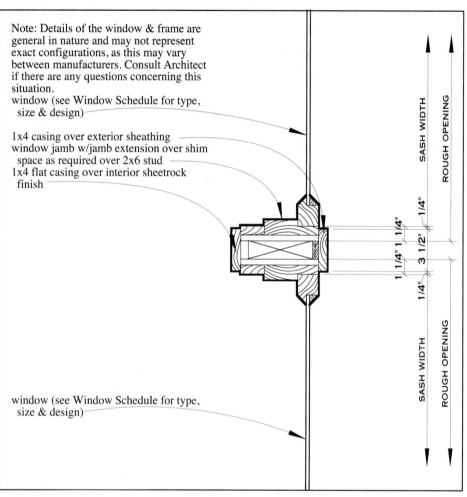

Note: Details of the window & frame are
general in nature and may not represent
exact configurations, as this may vary
between manufacturers. Consult Architect
if there are any questions concerning this
situation.

window (see Window Schedule for type,
  size & design)

1x4 casing over exterior sheathing
window jamb w/jamb extension over shim
  space as required over 2x6 stud
1x4 flat casing over interior sheetrock
  finish

window (see Window Schedule for type,
  size & design)

SASH WIDTH

ROUGH OPENING

1/4"

1/4" 1 1/4"

1 1/4" 3 1/2"

1/4"

SASH WIDTH

ROUGH OPENING

Window Mullion Detail

DRAWING #

SCALE
1 1/2
1'-0"

WWM003
998

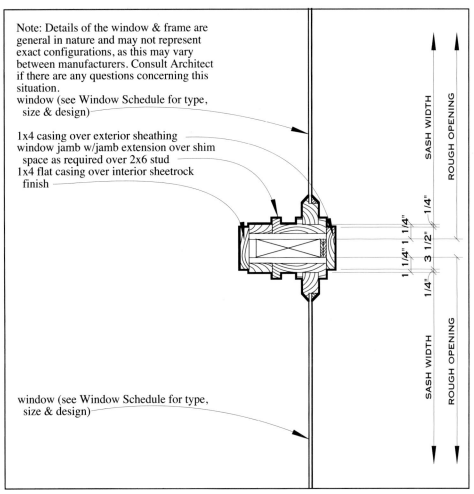

Note: Details of the window & frame are general in nature and may not represent exact configurations, as this may vary between manufacturers. Consult Architect if there are any questions concerning this situation.
window (see Window Schedule for type, size & design)

1x4 casing over exterior sheathing
window jamb w/jamb extension over shim space as required over 2x6 stud
1x4 flat casing over interior sheetrock finish

window (see Window Schedule for type, size & design)

SASH WIDTH

ROUGH OPENING

1 1/4" 1 1/4"

1/4"

3 1/2"

1/4"

SASH WIDTH

ROUGH OPENING

DRAWING #

Window Mullion Detail

SCALE
1 1/2
1'-0"

WWM004
999

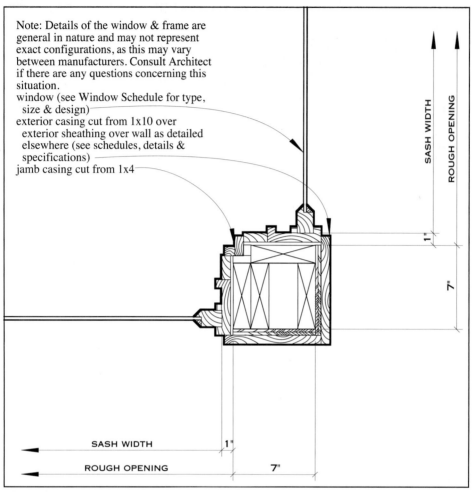

Note: Details of the window & frame are general in nature and may not represent exact configurations, as this may vary between manufacturers. Consult Architect if there are any questions concerning this situation.

window (see Window Schedule for type, size & design)

exterior casing cut from 1x10 over exterior sheathing over wall as detailed elsewhere (see schedules, details & specifications)

jamb casing cut from 1x4

SASH WIDTH

ROUGH OPENING

1"

7"

SASH WIDTH

ROUGH OPENING

1"

7"

Wood Window Mull @ Corner

WWM009
1000

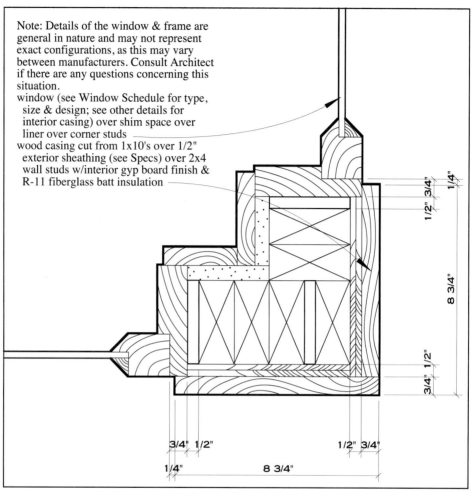

Note: Details of the window & frame are
general in nature and may not represent
exact configurations, as this may vary
between manufacturers. Consult Architect
if there are any questions concerning this
situation.
window (see Window Schedule for type,
   size & design; see other details for
   interior casing) over shim space over
   liner over corner studs
wood casing cut from 1x10's over 1/2"
   exterior sheathing (see Specs) over 2x4
   wall studs w/interior gyp board finish &
   R-11 fiberglass batt insulation

1/4"   3/4"   1/2"   8 3/4"

3/4"   1/2"   1/2"   3/4"

1/2"   3/4"   1/4"   8 3/4"   3/4"   1/2"

Corner Window Jamb

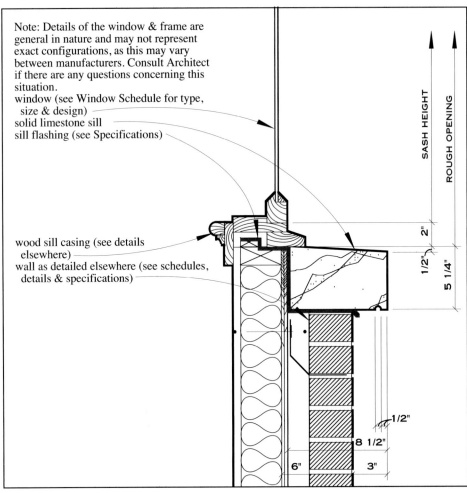

Note: Details of the window & frame are general in nature and may not represent exact configurations, as this may vary between manufacturers. Consult Architect if there are any questions concerning this situation.

window (see Window Schedule for type, size & design)
solid limestone sill
sill flashing (see Specifications)

wood sill casing (see details elsewhere)
wall as detailed elsewhere (see schedules, details & specifications)

SASH HEIGHT
ROUGH OPENING

2"
1/2"
5 1/4"

1/2"
8 1/2"
6"   3"

DRAWING #

Stone Sill Detail @ Brick Veneer

SCALE
1 1/2"
1'-0"

WWS001
1002

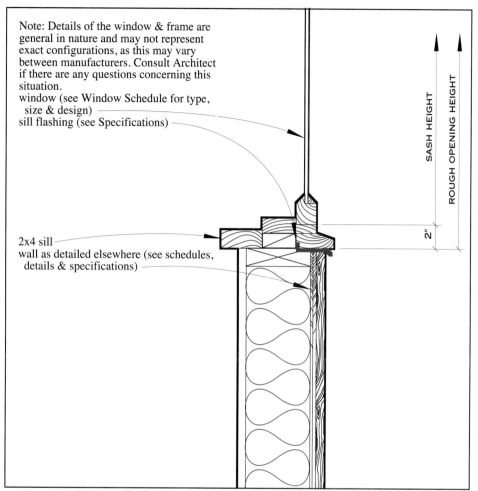

Note: Details of the window & frame are general in nature and may not represent exact configurations, as this may vary between manufacturers. Consult Architect if there are any questions concerning this situation.

window (see Window Schedule for type, size & design) —

sill flashing (see Specifications) —

2x4 sill —

wall as detailed elsewhere (see schedules, details & specifications) —

SASH HEIGHT

ROUGH OPENING HEIGHT

2"

DRAWING #

Window Sill Detail @ Vertical Siding

SCALE

1 1/2"
1'-0"

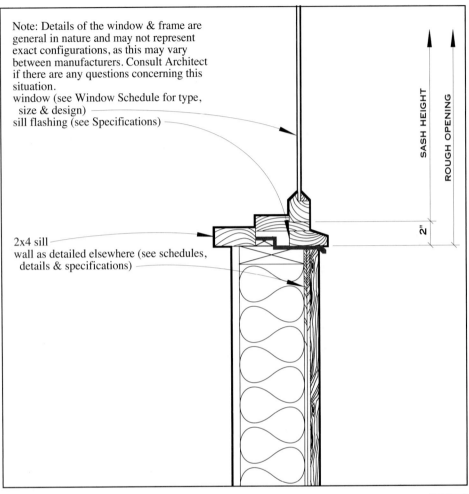

Note: Details of the window & frame are general in nature and may not represent exact configurations, as this may vary between manufacturers. Consult Architect if there are any questions concerning this situation.

window (see Window Schedule for type, size & design)

sill flashing (see Specifications)

2x4 sill

wall as detailed elsewhere (see schedules, details & specifications)

SASH HEIGHT

ROUGH OPENING

2"

Window Sill Detail @ Vertical Siding

SCALE
1 1/2"
1'-0"

WWS004
1004

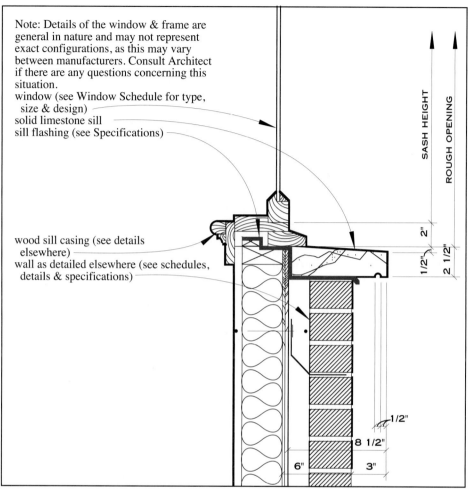

Note: Details of the window & frame are general in nature and may not represent exact configurations, as this may vary between manufacturers. Consult Architect if there are any questions concerning this situation.

window (see Window Schedule for type, size & design)
solid limestone sill
sill flashing (see Specifications)

wood sill casing (see details elsewhere)
wall as detailed elsewhere (see schedules, details & specifications)

SASH HEIGHT

ROUGH OPENING

2"

1/2"

2 1/2"

1/2"

8 1/2"

6"   3"

DRAWING #

Stone Sill Detail @ Brick Veneer

SCALE
1 1/2"
1'-0"

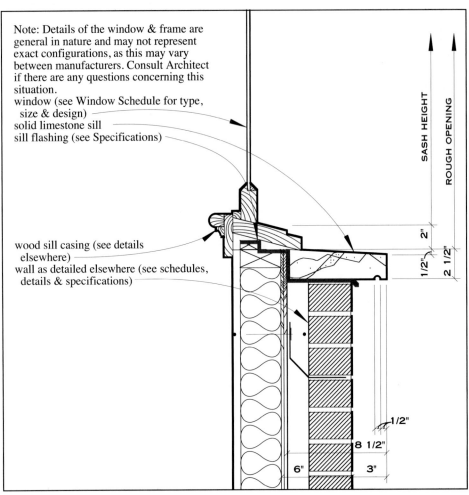

Note: Details of the window & frame are
general in nature and may not represent
exact configurations, as this may vary
between manufacturers. Consult Architect
if there are any questions concerning this
situation.
window (see Window Schedule for type,
    size & design)
solid limestone sill
sill flashing (see Specifications)

SASH HEIGHT

ROUGH OPENING

2"

1/2"

2 1/2"

wood sill casing (see details
    elsewhere)
wall as detailed elsewhere (see schedules,
    details & specifications)

1/2"

8 1/2"

6"   3"

Stone Sill Detail @ Brick Veneer

SCALE
1 1/2"
1'-0"

WWS007
1006

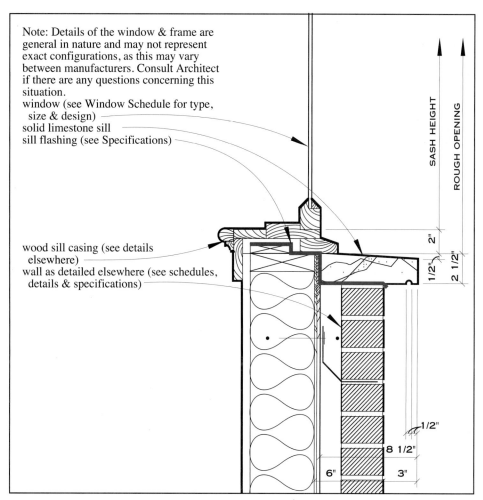

Note: Details of the window & frame are general in nature and may not represent exact configurations, as this may vary between manufacturers. Consult Architect if there are any questions concerning this situation.

window (see Window Schedule for type, size & design)

solid limestone sill

sill flashing (see Specifications)

wood sill casing (see details elsewhere)

wall as detailed elsewhere (see schedules, details & specifications)

SASH HEIGHT

ROUGH OPENING

2"

1/2"

2 1/2"

1/2"

8 1/2"

6"

3"

DRAWING #

Stone Sill Detail @ Brick Veneer

SCALE

1 1/2"
———
1'-0"

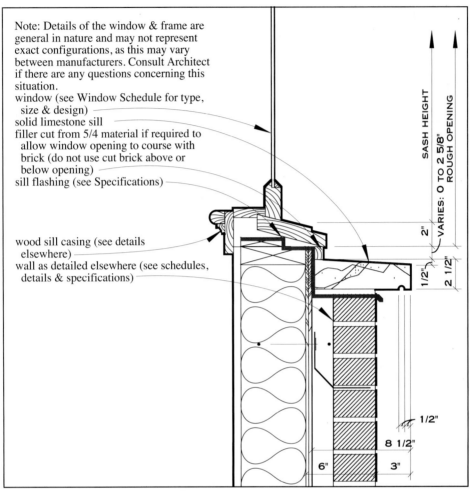

Note: Details of the window & frame are
general in nature and may not represent
exact configurations, as this may vary
between manufacturers. Consult Architect
if there are any questions concerning this
situation.

window (see Window Schedule for type,
  size & design)

solid limestone sill

filler cut from 5/4 material if required to
  allow window opening to course with
  brick (do not use cut brick above or
  below opening)

sill flashing (see Specifications)

wood sill casing (see details
  elsewhere)

wall as detailed elsewhere (see schedules,
  details & specifications)

SASH HEIGHT

VARIES: 0 TO 2 5/8"
ROUGH OPENING

2"

1/2"

2 1/2"

1/2"

8 1/2"

6"

3"

DRAWING #

Stone Sill Detail @ Brick Veneer

SCALE

1 1/2"
1'-0"

WWS009
1008

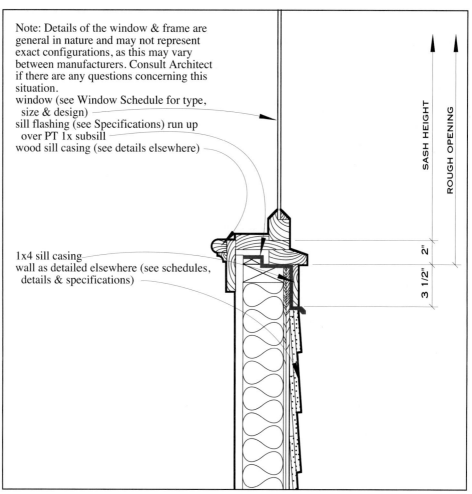

Note: Details of the window & frame are general in nature and may not represent exact configurations, as this may vary between manufacturers. Consult Architect if there are any questions concerning this situation.

window (see Window Schedule for type, size & design)

sill flashing (see Specifications) run up over PT 1x subsill

wood sill casing (see details elsewhere)

1x4 sill casing

wall as detailed elsewhere (see schedules, details & specifications)

SASH HEIGHT

ROUGH OPENING

2"

3 1/2"

DRAWING #

Window Sill Detail

SCALE
1 1/2
1'-0"

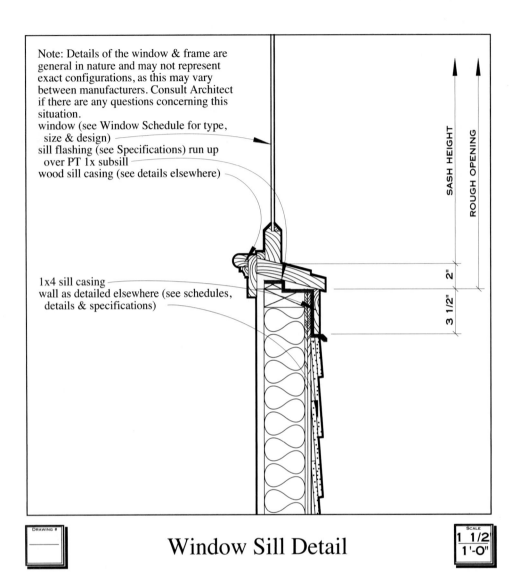

Note: Details of the window & frame are general in nature and may not represent exact configurations, as this may vary between manufacturers. Consult Architect if there are any questions concerning this situation.

window (see Window Schedule for type, size & design)

sill flashing (see Specifications) run up over PT 1x subsill

wood sill casing (see details elsewhere)

1x4 sill casing

wall as detailed elsewhere (see schedules, details & specifications)

SASH HEIGHT

ROUGH OPENING

2"

3 1/2"

DRAWING #

Window Sill Detail

SCALE
1 1/2
1'-0"

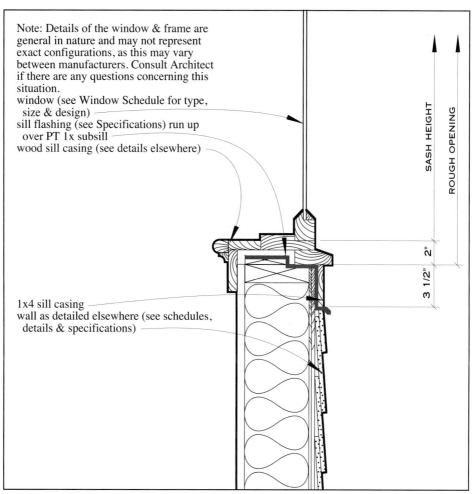

Note: Details of the window & frame are general in nature and may not represent exact configurations, as this may vary between manufacturers. Consult Architect if there are any questions concerning this situation.

window (see Window Schedule for type, size & design)

sill flashing (see Specifications) run up over PT 1x subsill

wood sill casing (see details elsewhere)

1x4 sill casing

wall as detailed elsewhere (see schedules, details & specifications)

SASH HEIGHT

ROUGH OPENING

2"

3 1/2"

DRAWING #

Window Sill Detail

SCALE
1 1/2
1'-0"

WWS012
1011

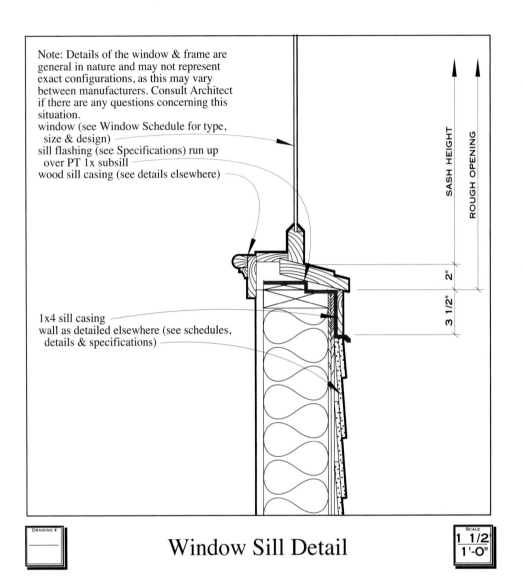

Note: Details of the window & frame are
general in nature and may not represent
exact configurations, as this may vary
between manufacturers. Consult Architect
if there are any questions concerning this
situation.
window (see Window Schedule for type,
  size & design)
sill flashing (see Specifications) run up
  over PT 1x subsill
wood sill casing (see details elsewhere)

1x4 sill casing
wall as detailed elsewhere (see schedules,
  details & specifications)

SASH HEIGHT

ROUGH OPENING

2"

3 1/2"

DRAWING #

SCALE

1 1/2
1'-0"

Window Sill Detail

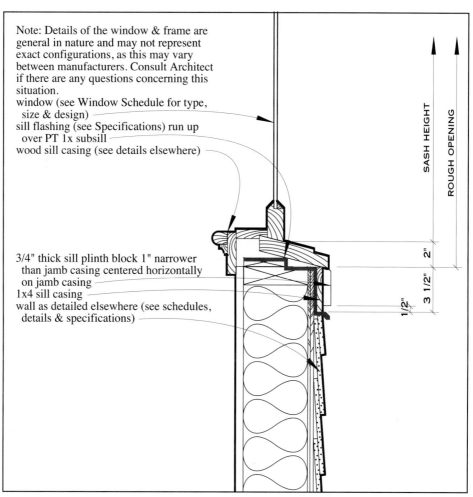

Note: Details of the window & frame are general in nature and may not represent exact configurations, as this may vary between manufacturers. Consult Architect if there are any questions concerning this situation.

window (see Window Schedule for type, size & design)

sill flashing (see Specifications) run up over PT 1x subsill

wood sill casing (see details elsewhere)

3/4" thick sill plinth block 1" narrower than jamb casing centered horizontally on jamb casing

1x4 sill casing

wall as detailed elsewhere (see schedules, details & specifications)

SASH HEIGHT

ROUGH OPENING

2"

3 1/2"

1/2"

Window Sill Detail

SCALE
1 1/2
1'-0"

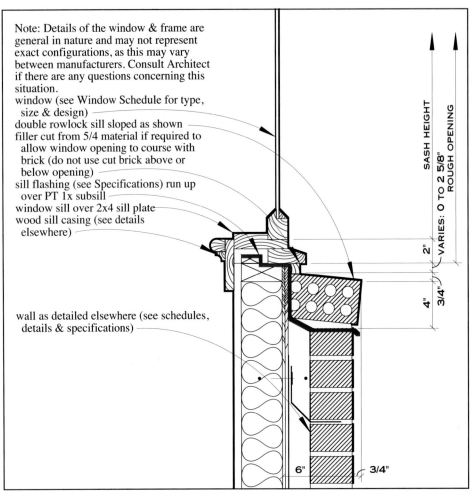

Note: Details of the window & frame are general in nature and may not represent exact configurations, as this may vary between manufacturers. Consult Architect if there are any questions concerning this situation.

window (see Window Schedule for type, size & design)

double rowlock sill sloped as shown

filler cut from 5/4 material if required to allow window opening to course with brick (do not use cut brick above or below opening)

sill flashing (see Specifications) run up over PT 1x subsill

window sill over 2x4 sill plate

wood sill casing (see details elsewhere)

wall as detailed elsewhere (see schedules, details & specifications)

SASH HEIGHT

VARIES: 0 TO 2 5/8" ROUGH OPENING

2"

4"

3/4"

6"

3/4"

DRAWING #

Window Sill Detail @ Brick Veneer

SCALE

1 1/2
1'-0"

WWS015
1014

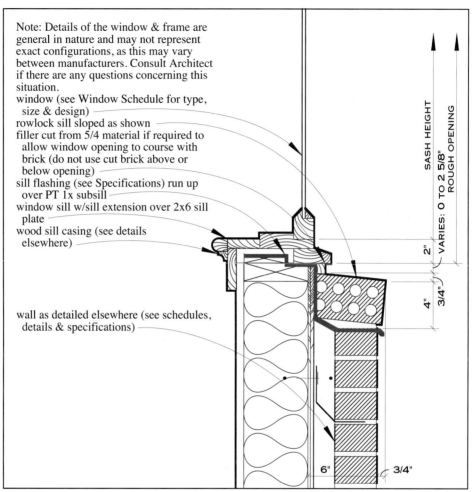

Note: Details of the window & frame are general in nature and may not represent exact configurations, as this may vary between manufacturers. Consult Architect if there are any questions concerning this situation.

window (see Window Schedule for type, size & design)

rowlock sill sloped as shown

filler cut from 5/4 material if required to allow window opening to course with brick (do not use cut brick above or below opening)

sill flashing (see Specifications) run up over PT 1x subsill

window sill w/sill extension over 2x6 sill plate

wood sill casing (see details elsewhere)

wall as detailed elsewhere (see schedules, details & specifications)

SASH HEIGHT

VARIES: 0 TO 2 5/8" ROUGH OPENING

2"

4"

3/4"

6"   3/4"

Window Sill Detail @ Brick Veneer

SCALE
1 1/2"
1'-0"

WWS016
1015

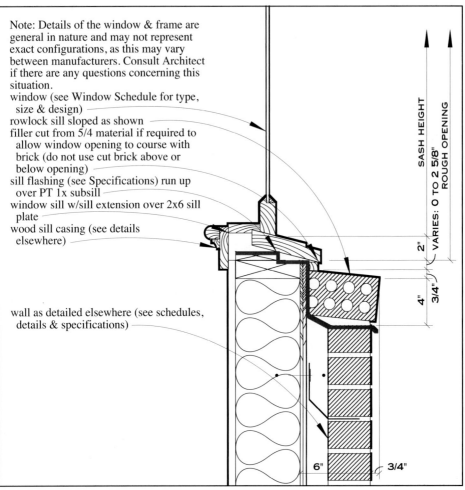

Note: Details of the window & frame are
general in nature and may not represent
exact configurations, as this may vary
between manufacturers. Consult Architect
if there are any questions concerning this
situation.
window (see Window Schedule for type,
    size & design)
rowlock sill sloped as shown
filler cut from 5/4 material if required to
    allow window opening to course with
    brick (do not use cut brick above or
    below opening)
sill flashing (see Specifications) run up
    over PT 1x subsill
window sill w/sill extension over 2x6 sill
    plate
wood sill casing (see details
    elsewhere)

wall as detailed elsewhere (see schedules,
    details & specifications)

SASH HEIGHT

VARIES: 0 TO 2 5/8"
ROUGH OPENING

2"

4"

3/4"

6"

3/4"

DRAWING #

Window Sill Detail @ Brick Veneer

SCALE

1 1/2
1'-0"

WWS017
1016

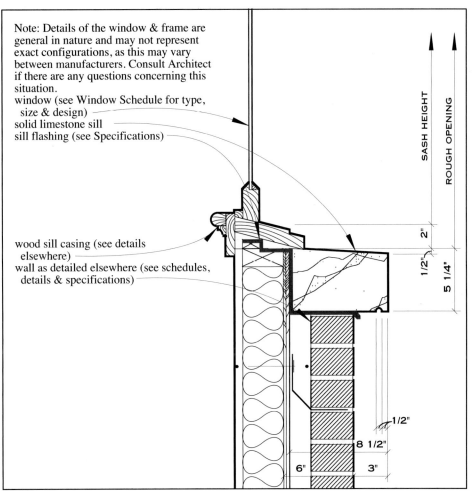

Note: Details of the window & frame are
general in nature and may not represent
exact configurations, as this may vary
between manufacturers. Consult Architect
if there are any questions concerning this
situation.

window (see Window Schedule for type,
    size & design)
solid limestone sill
sill flashing (see Specifications)

wood sill casing (see details
    elsewhere)
wall as detailed elsewhere (see schedules,
    details & specifications)

SASH HEIGHT

ROUGH OPENING

2"

1/2"

5 1/4"

1/2"

8 1/2"

6"   3"

DRAWING #

Stone Sill Detail @ Brick Veneer

SCALE

$\dfrac{1\ 1/2"}{1'\text{-}0"}$

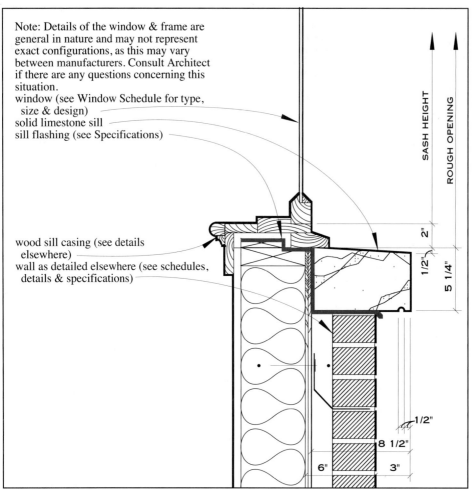

Note: Details of the window & frame are general in nature and may not represent exact configurations, as this may vary between manufacturers. Consult Architect if there are any questions concerning this situation.

window (see Window Schedule for type, size & design)

solid limestone sill

sill flashing (see Specifications)

wood sill casing (see details elsewhere)

wall as detailed elsewhere (see schedules, details & specifications)

SASH HEIGHT

ROUGH OPENING

2"

1/2"

5 1/4"

1/2"

8 1/2"

6"   3"

Stone Sill Detail @ Brick Veneer

SCALE
1 1/2"
1'-0"

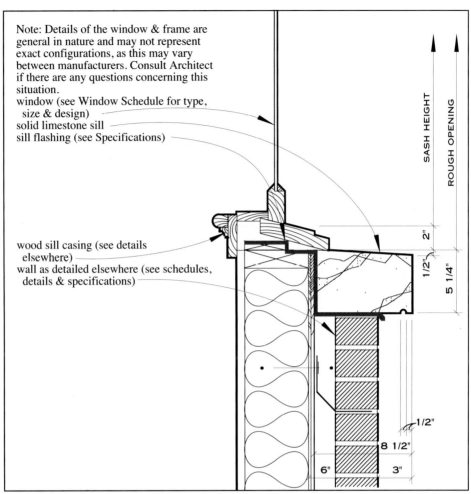

Note: Details of the window & frame are general in nature and may not represent exact configurations, as this may vary between manufacturers. Consult Architect if there are any questions concerning this situation.

window (see Window Schedule for type, size & design)
solid limestone sill
sill flashing (see Specifications)

wood sill casing (see details elsewhere)
wall as detailed elsewhere (see schedules, details & specifications)

SASH HEIGHT

ROUGH OPENING

2"

1/2"

5 1/4"

1/2"

8 1/2"

6"   3"

Stone Sill Detail @ Brick Veneer

SCALE
1 1/2"
———
1'-0"

WWS020
1019

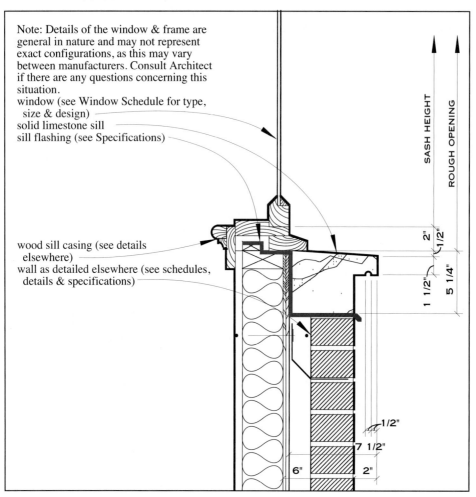

Note: Details of the window & frame are
general in nature and may not represent
exact configurations, as this may vary
between manufacturers. Consult Architect
if there are any questions concerning this
situation.
window (see Window Schedule for type,
  size & design)
solid limestone sill
sill flashing (see Specifications)

wood sill casing (see details
  elsewhere)
wall as detailed elsewhere (see schedules,
  details & specifications)

SASH HEIGHT

ROUGH OPENING

2"

1/2"

1 1/2"

5 1/4"

1/2"

7 1/2"

6"

2"

DRAWING #

Stone Sill Detail @ Brick Veneer

SCALE

1 1/2"
1'-0"

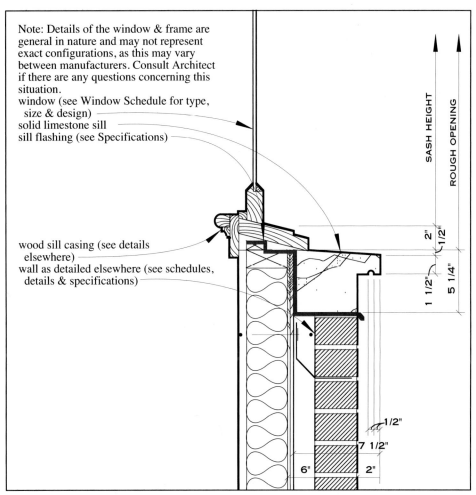

Note: Details of the window & frame are general in nature and may not represent exact configurations, as this may vary between manufacturers. Consult Architect if there are any questions concerning this situation.
window (see Window Schedule for type, size & design)
solid limestone sill
sill flashing (see Specifications)

wood sill casing (see details elsewhere)
wall as detailed elsewhere (see schedules, details & specifications)

SASH HEIGHT
ROUGH OPENING

2"
1/2"
1 1/2"
5 1/4"

1/2"
7 1/2"
6" 2"

Stone Sill Detail @ Brick Veneer

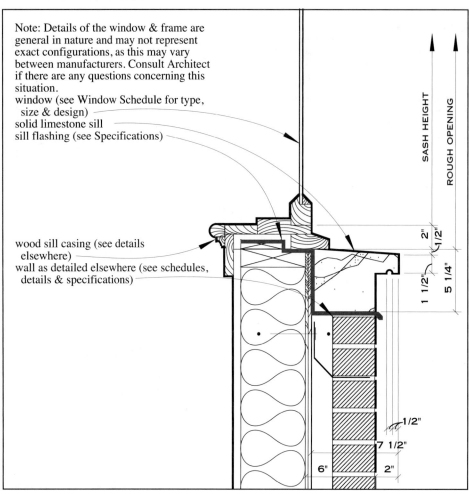

Note: Details of the window & frame are general in nature and may not represent exact configurations, as this may vary between manufacturers. Consult Architect if there are any questions concerning this situation.

window (see Window Schedule for type, size & design)

solid limestone sill

sill flashing (see Specifications)

wood sill casing (see details elsewhere)

wall as detailed elsewhere (see schedules, details & specifications)

SASH HEIGHT

ROUGH OPENING

2"

1/2"

1 1/2"

5 1/4"

1/2"

7 1/2"

6"

2"

DRAWING #

Stone Sill Detail @ Brick Veneer

SCALE
1 1/2"
1'-0"

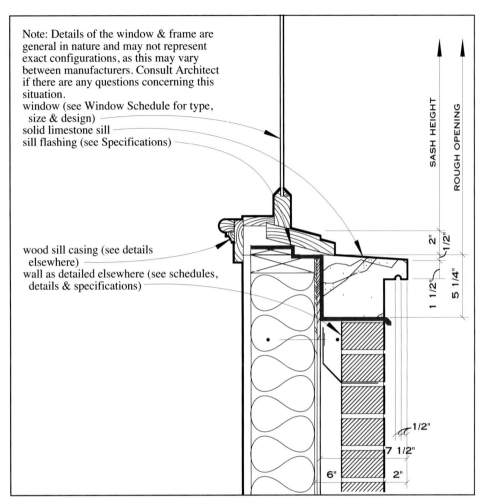

Note: Details of the window & frame are general in nature and may not represent exact configurations, as this may vary between manufacturers. Consult Architect if there are any questions concerning this situation.
window (see Window Schedule for type, size & design)
solid limestone sill
sill flashing (see Specifications)

wood sill casing (see details elsewhere)
wall as detailed elsewhere (see schedules, details & specifications)

SASH HEIGHT

ROUGH OPENING

2"

1/2"

1 1/2"

5 1/4"

1/2"

7 1/2"

6" 2"

Stone Sill Detail @ Brick Veneer

DRAWING #

SCALE
1 1/2"
1'-0"

WWS024
1023

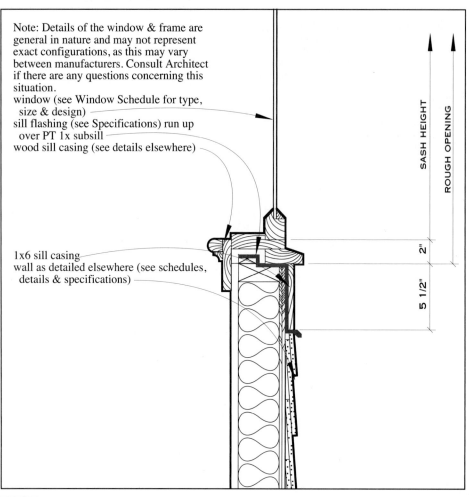

Note: Details of the window & frame are
general in nature and may not represent
exact configurations, as this may vary
between manufacturers. Consult Architect
if there are any questions concerning this
situation.
window (see Window Schedule for type,
 size & design)
sill flashing (see Specifications) run up
 over PT 1x subsill
wood sill casing (see details elsewhere)

1x6 sill casing
wall as detailed elsewhere (see schedules,
 details & specifications)

SASH HEIGHT

ROUGH OPENING

2"

5 1/2"

Window Sill Detail

SCALE
1 1/2
1'-0"

DRAWING #

WWS025
1024

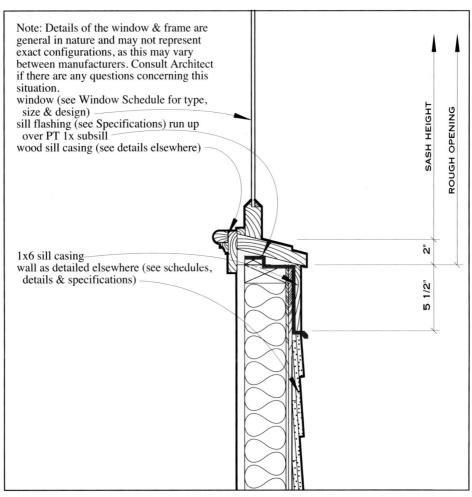

Note: Details of the window & frame are
general in nature and may not represent
exact configurations, as this may vary
between manufacturers. Consult Architect
if there are any questions concerning this
situation.
window (see Window Schedule for type,
 size & design)
sill flashing (see Specifications) run up
 over PT 1x subsill
wood sill casing (see details elsewhere)

1x6 sill casing
wall as detailed elsewhere (see schedules,
 details & specifications)

SASH HEIGHT

ROUGH OPENING

2"

5 1/2"

Window Sill Detail

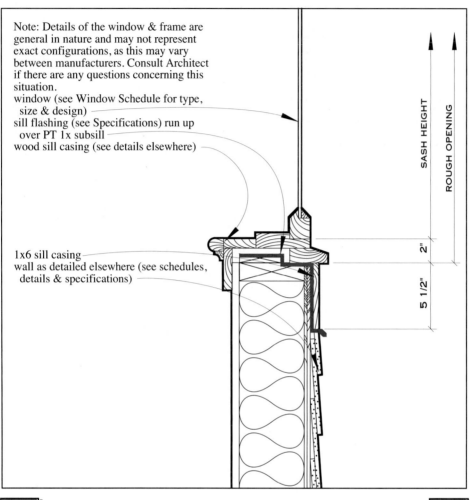

Note: Details of the window & frame are
general in nature and may not represent
exact configurations, as this may vary
between manufacturers. Consult Architect
if there are any questions concerning this
situation.
window (see Window Schedule for type,
  size & design)
sill flashing (see Specifications) run up
  over PT 1x subsill
wood sill casing (see details elsewhere)

1x6 sill casing
wall as detailed elsewhere (see schedules,
  details & specifications)

SASH HEIGHT

ROUGH OPENING

2"

5 1/2"

DRAWING #

Window Sill Detail

SCALE

$\dfrac{1\ 1/2}{1'\text{-}0''}$

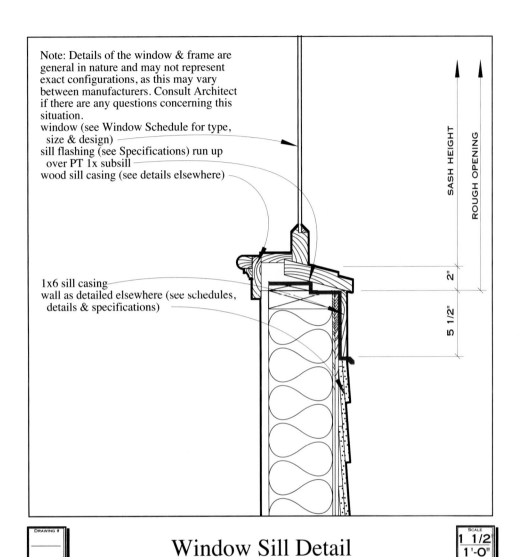

Note: Details of the window & frame are general in nature and may not represent exact configurations, as this may vary between manufacturers. Consult Architect if there are any questions concerning this situation.

window (see Window Schedule for type, size & design)

sill flashing (see Specifications) run up over PT 1x subsill

wood sill casing (see details elsewhere)

1x6 sill casing

wall as detailed elsewhere (see schedules, details & specifications)

SASH HEIGHT

ROUGH OPENING

2"

5 1/2"

DRAWING #

Window Sill Detail

SCALE
1 1/2
1'-0"

WWS028
1027

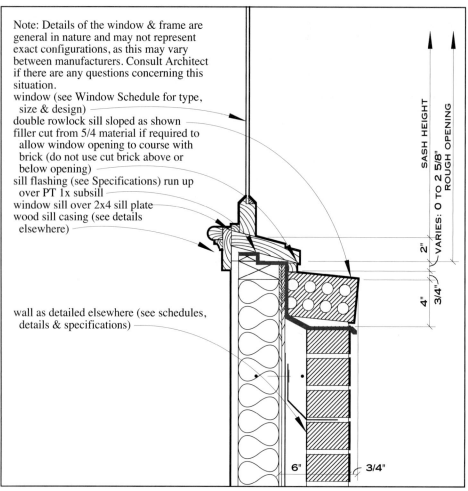

Note: Details of the window & frame are general in nature and may not represent exact configurations, as this may vary between manufacturers. Consult Architect if there are any questions concerning this situation.

window (see Window Schedule for type, size & design)

double rowlock sill sloped as shown

filler cut from 5/4 material if required to allow window opening to course with brick (do not use cut brick above or below opening)

sill flashing (see Specifications) run up over PT 1x subsill

window sill over 2x4 sill plate

wood sill casing (see details elsewhere)

wall as detailed elsewhere (see schedules, details & specifications)

SASH HEIGHT

VARIES: 0 TO 2 5/8" ROUGH OPENING

2"

4"

3/4"

6"

3/4"

DRAWING #

Window Sill Detail @ Brick Veneer

SCALE

1 1/2
1'-0"

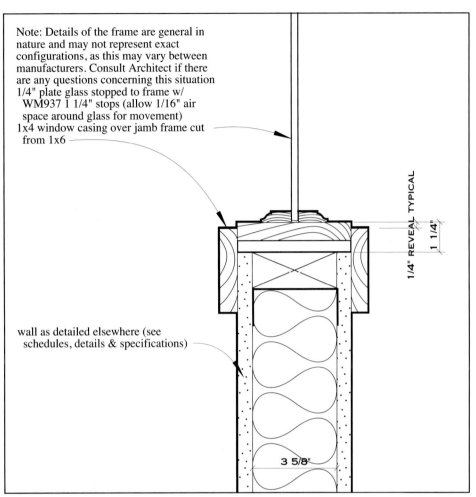

Note: Details of the frame are general in
nature and may not represent exact
configurations, as this may vary between
manufacturers. Consult Architect if there
are any questions concerning this situation
1/4" plate glass stopped to frame w/
 WM937 1 1/4" stops (allow 1/16" air
 space around glass for movement)
1x4 window casing over jamb frame cut
 from 1x6

1/4" REVEAL TYPICAL

1 1/4"

wall as detailed elsewhere (see
 schedules, details & specifications)

3 5/8"

DRAWING #

Fixed Window Sill Detail

SCALE
3"
1'-0"

WWS036
1029

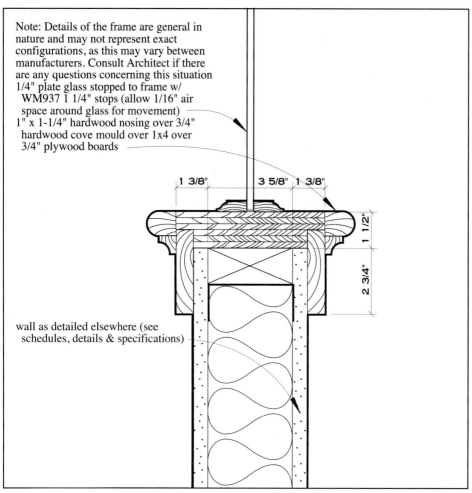

Note: Details of the frame are general in
nature and may not represent exact
configurations, as this may vary between
manufacturers. Consult Architect if there
are any questions concerning this situation

1/4" plate glass stopped to frame w/
WM937 1 1/4" stops (allow 1/16" air
space around glass for movement)

1" x 1-1/4" hardwood nosing over 3/4"
hardwood cove mould over 1x4 over
3/4" plywood boards

1 3/8"   3 5/8"   1 3/8"

1 1/2"

2 3/4"

wall as detailed elsewhere (see
schedules, details & specifications)

DRAWING #

Fixed Window Sill Detail

SCALE
$\frac{3"}{1'-0"}$

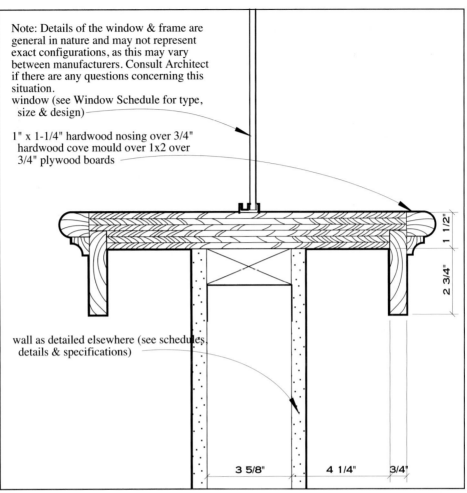

Note: Details of the window & frame are general in nature and may not represent exact configurations, as this may vary between manufacturers. Consult Architect if there are any questions concerning this situation.
window (see Window Schedule for type, size & design)

1" x 1-1/4" hardwood nosing over 3/4" hardwood cove mould over 1x2 over 3/4" plywood boards

wall as detailed elsewhere (see schedules, details & specifications)

1 1/2"

2 3/4"

3 5/8"   4 1/4"   3/4"

DRAWING #

Window Sill Detail w/ Wood Casing

SCALE
3"
1'-0"

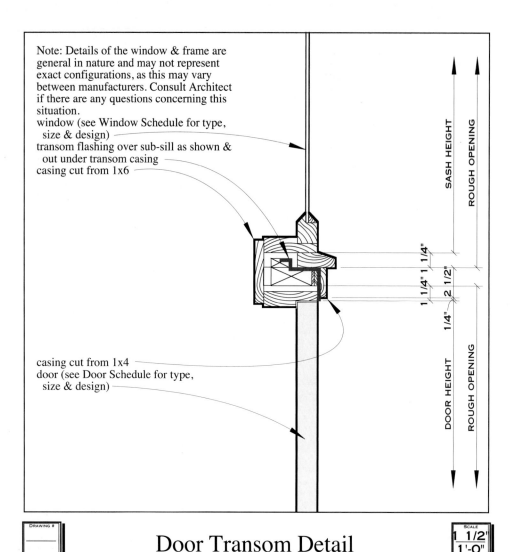

Note: Details of the window & frame are
general in nature and may not represent
exact configurations, as this may vary
between manufacturers. Consult Architect
if there are any questions concerning this
situation.
window (see Window Schedule for type,
  size & design)
transom flashing over sub-sill as shown &
  out under transom casing
casing cut from 1x6

casing cut from 1x4
door (see Door Schedule for type,
  size & design)

SASH HEIGHT

ROUGH OPENING

1 1/4" 1 1/4"

1 1/4" 1" 2 1/2"

1/4"

DOOR HEIGHT

ROUGH OPENING

DRAWING #

Door Transom Detail

SCALE
1 1/2"
1'-0"

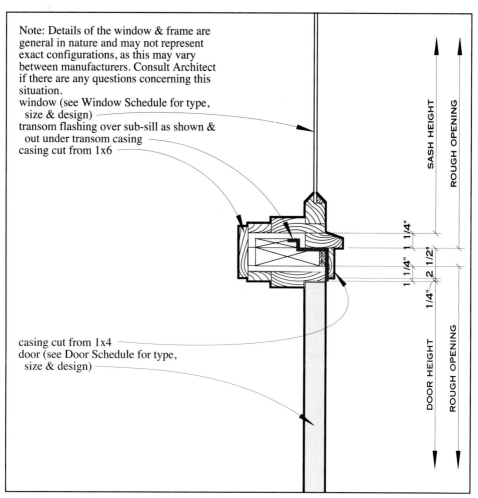

Note: Details of the window & frame are general in nature and may not represent exact configurations, as this may vary between manufacturers. Consult Architect if there are any questions concerning this situation.

window (see Window Schedule for type, size & design)

transom flashing over sub-sill as shown & out under transom casing

casing cut from 1x6

casing cut from 1x4

door (see Door Schedule for type, size & design)

Door Transom Detail

SCALE
1 1/2"
1'-0"

WWT002
1033

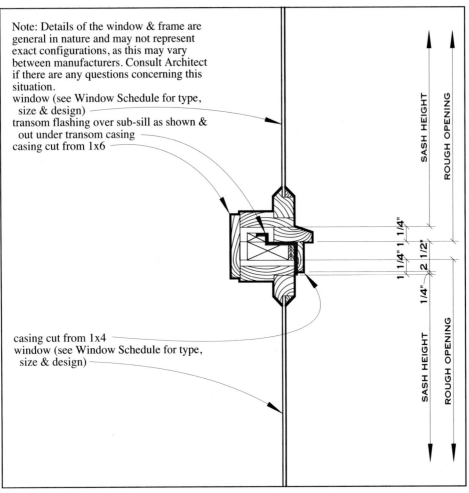

Note: Details of the window & frame are general in nature and may not represent exact configurations, as this may vary between manufacturers. Consult Architect if there are any questions concerning this situation.

window (see Window Schedule for type, size & design)

transom flashing over sub-sill as shown & out under transom casing

casing cut from 1x6

casing cut from 1x4

window (see Window Schedule for type, size & design)

SASH HEIGHT

ROUGH OPENING

1 1/4"

1 1/4"

2 1/2"

1/4"

SASH HEIGHT

ROUGH OPENING

DRAWING #

Window Transom Detail

SCALE
1 1/2"
1'-0"

WWT005
1034

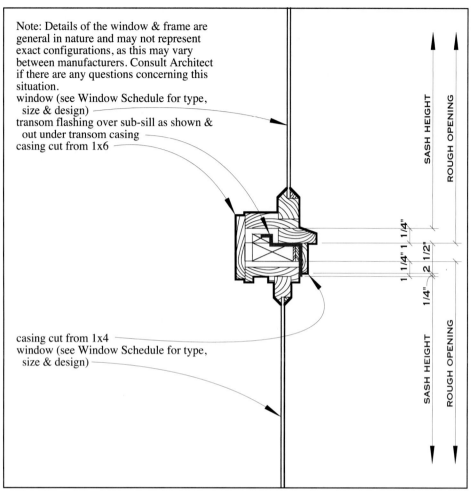

Note: Details of the window & frame are general in nature and may not represent exact configurations, as this may vary between manufacturers. Consult Architect if there are any questions concerning this situation.

window (see Window Schedule for type, size & design)

transom flashing over sub-sill as shown & out under transom casing

casing cut from 1x6

casing cut from 1x4

window (see Window Schedule for type, size & design)

SASH HEIGHT

ROUGH OPENING

1 1/4"

1 1/4" 1

1/4"

2 1/2"

SASH HEIGHT

ROUGH OPENING

Window Transom Detail

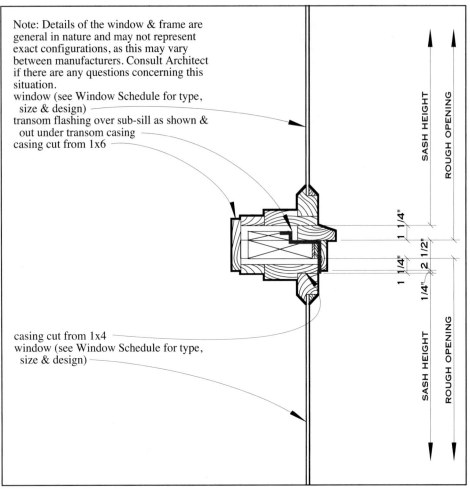

Note: Details of the window & frame are
general in nature and may not represent
exact configurations, as this may vary
between manufacturers. Consult Architect
if there are any questions concerning this
situation.
window (see Window Schedule for type,
  size & design)
transom flashing over sub-sill as shown &
  out under transom casing
casing cut from 1x6

casing cut from 1x4
window (see Window Schedule for type,
  size & design)

SASH HEIGHT

ROUGH OPENING

1 1/4"

1/2"

1/4"

2 1/2"

1/4"

SASH HEIGHT

ROUGH OPENING

Window Transom Detail

DRAWING #

SCALE
1 1/2"
1'-0"

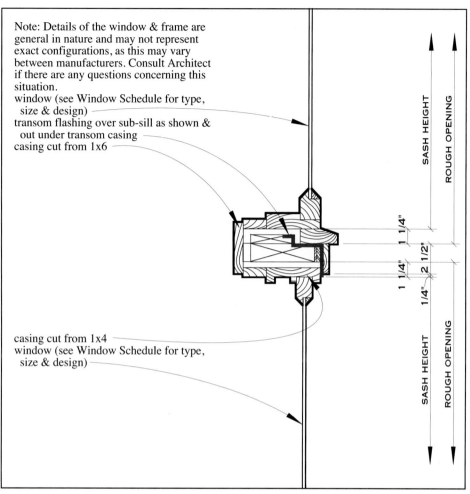

Note: Details of the window & frame are
general in nature and may not represent
exact configurations, as this may vary
between manufacturers. Consult Architect
if there are any questions concerning this
situation.
window (see Window Schedule for type,
  size & design)
transom flashing over sub-sill as shown &
  out under transom casing
casing cut from 1x6

casing cut from 1x4
window (see Window Schedule for type,
  size & design)

SASH HEIGHT

ROUGH OPENING

1 1/4"

2 1/2"

1 1/4"

1/4"

SASH HEIGHT

ROUGH OPENING

DRAWING #

Window Transom Detail

SCALE

1 1/2"

1'-0"